The New and Complete

BUSINESS

OF

LICENSING

THE ESSENTIAL GUIDE FOR
MONETIZING INTELLECTUAL PROPERTIES

Greg Battersby   Danny Simon

Endorsed by

Kent Press
▪ **Westport, CT** ▪

This publication is designed to provide accurate and authoritative information regarding the subject matter covered. It is sold with the understanding that the publisher is not engaged in rendering legal, accounting or other professional services. If legal or other professional assistance is required, the services of a competent professional person should be sought.

From a *Declaration of Principles* jointly adopted by a Committee of the American Bar Association and a Committee of Publishers and Associations

Printed in the United States of America

ISBN: 13: 978-1-888206-11-1

To Susan – 48 years of marriage and now over 40 books. I don't know how you withstood either, but I couldn't imagine life without you.

-Greg

To the things that mean the most – wife Carey for her friendship and love, daughter Jane and her Boone who lights up my life, The Wellington – all new and delicious, and my faithful stuffed champions Dorothy and Doggie Arf Arf for their steadfast support.

-Danny

ABOUT THE AUTHORS

Greg Battersby is managing member of the intellectual property law firm of The Battersby Law Group, LLC in Westport, CT. He has more than 45 years of experience in patents, trademarks and licensing law. Before founding Battersby Law Group, he had been a founding partner in Grimes & Battersby and had previously been associated with two major New York City IP law firms and was senior counsel at Gulf & Western Industries (now Viacom) which was the owner of Paramount Pictures.

Greg has an A.B. degree from Seton Hall University a law degree from Fordham Law School where he was an editor of Fordham's *Urban Law Journal*. He is admitted to practice in both New York and Connecticut and as a patent attorney before the U.S. Patent & Trademark Office.

For the past 25 years, he has served as General Counsel for the International Licensing Industry Merchandisers' Association ("LIMA") and is a member of its Executive Committee. He is also a member of LIMA's Licensing Hall of Fame—the only practicing attorney ever so inducted. He and Danny Simon are Co-Deans of LIMA's CLS Program. He has also been an officer and member of the Board of Directors of the New York Intellectual Property Law Association ("NYIPLA").

Greg is a prolific author, having written more than 40 books on various licensing and IP topics, including the two-volume, seminal book on the law of merchandising entitled *The Law of Merchandise & Character Licensing* published by Thomson Reuters/West. It was originally published in 1985 and is updated annually. He also writes two annual books each year for Wolters Kluwer entitled *Licensing Royalty Rates* and *Licensing Update*. He's also the author of Kluwer's *License Agreements: Forms and Checklists*.

He is a founder and executive editor of *The Licensing Journal* and the *IP Litigator*, both published by Wolters Kluwer Publishing and is the legal columnist for *Total Licensing*. He has written more than 50 articles on various licensing and IP topics and given more than 200 talks on the subject before a wide range of audiences, including the INTA, LES, AIPLA, LIMA and other organizations.

He has been qualified as an expert in more than thirty actions on licensing related matters.

Greg turned a passion for baseball into a business, having invented a computerized video baseball/softball pitching and cricket bowling simulator for which he has received 13 U.S. patents and numerous international ones. In his spare time, he founded and runs a company called ProBatter Sports (www.probatter.com) which manufactures and sells these simulators to a wide range of customers including a dozen Major League teams and more than 300 colleges and commercial training facilities.

Danny Simon is a thirty-five plus year veteran of the licensing industry with expertise in all phases of the merchandising and licensing process. Having built the licensing divisions for Lorimar Productions, 20th Century Fox and Carolco Pictures, he opened his own licensing agency in 1992 in Los Angeles, CA, called The Licensing Group, Ltd.

Danny has been a pioneer in entertainment licensing with a focus on material geared to the teen plus market. Beginning with the television program DALLAS, he was among the first to license adult, prime-time television entertainment and, with DYNASTY, he was the first to apply branding techniques to television shows. He also developed successful licensing programs for M*A*S*H, Fall Guy, Alf, Rambo, Terminator 2: Judgment Day, Mortal Kombat, Baywatch, U.S. Secret Service, Arnold Schwarzenegger and David Hasselhoff.

He has also succeeded in feature film development. With MORTAL KOMBAT, he produced the first-ever film adaptation of a video game. He's a partner in an entertainment development company that sold the rights to the MATT HELM book series to DreamWorks and Paramount, where it is currently in development as a motion picture.

For 18 years, Danny taught a continuing college level course on entertainment licensing at UCLA. He's a founding member of LIMA and has been its president and a two-time member of its Board and is a member of LIMA's Licensing Hall of Fame. With Greg Battersby, he developed and serves as Co-Dean of LIMA's Certificate of Licensing Studies ('CLS") program.

Danny also is a regular lecturer on a variety of licensing topics around the world and serves as an international licensing consultant, providing consulting services to the Hong Kong Trade Development Council and other international groups.

He has been qualified as an expert witness on licensing issues in over 25 different litigations.

Over the years Danny has written many articles on licensing for various industry publications. He is a regular contributor to the *Licensing Update* book published annually by Wolters Kluwer and writes a monthly column on entertainment licensing for *The Licensing Journal*.

Preface

The licensing of brands, characters, sports team names, college logos and artwork, often called "merchandising," has become a global business. While it may have begun as a fad, it has exploded into a $250+ billion worldwide industry at retail and generates more than $7 billion in annual royalty income for those property owners who are savvy enough to license their properties for a wide variety of consumer products.

About 8 years ago, we introduced the first *Basics of Licensing* book which was intended to be an abbreviated handbook for licensors. Endorsed by the Licensing Industry Merchandisers' Association (LIMA), the book was well received by the licensing industry and was followed by a revised version a couple of years later. We followed it with a "Licensee" edition and then finally an "International" edition. Each edition was popular among licensing professionals and supported by LIMA.

Recognizing that there was a degree of commonality between these editions, coupled with the fact that the industry has expanded by leaps and bounds since the first series, we concluded that it was time for the definitive work on licensing, hence, *The Business of Licensing* which combines and updates the best of all three prior editions and takes the subject to the next level.

This book has certainly stretched the limits of our imagination. While we believe that it remains written in an easy-to-read format that takes the reader through the nuts and bolts of how to conduct a licensing program and handle many of the problems that one might face, we have included a substantial amount of reference material to make it a definitive and useful reference guide for the industry.

We have included an expanded history of merchandising, including the properties that have made the industry famous, some of the more imaginative examples of licensed products and recognizing many of those people who made the industry what it is today.

Finally, we have assembled an extensive collection of the forms that any licensing professional may need, which we intend to provide the purchasers with electronic access to the forms via Dropbox.

The preparation of any book of this type requires the assistance of several people and a preface is the ideal place to give recognition to their contributions and express our appreciation and thanks for their efforts. First and foremost is our editor, Michelle Houle, who worked tirelessly on helping us compile much of the material and keep us on track all along the way. Most importantly, Michelle helped us refine the work into something that can be readily understood by both the novice and experienced licensing professional.

We were also fortunate to have the cooperation of many licensing pros who provided some excellent overviews of their areas, particularly on the international front. These Contributors are identified in the prefatory section of this work.

It is also important for us to note that this book has been developed with the endorsement of the International Licensing Industry Merchandisers' Association ("LIMA"), the central trade organization for this industry and who participates financially from its sales. As such, the folks at LIMA deserve special mention, particularly Charles Riotto, LIMA's recent past President. Charles provided us with great support and guidance at every step of the way Maura Regan, who succeeded Charles as President, came to LIMA from Sesame Workshop where she headed the licensing program. Maura has also been extremely supportive of this project.

Finally, a word of special thanks to an individual who we consider to be one of five nicest people in the entire world, LIMA's Senior Vice-President of Member Relations and resident historian, who has been there since the beginning, Louise Caron. Her help in developing the chapter on the history of licensing is greatly appreciated.

We hope you find this book to be both an informative and useful guide to the business of licensing. Enjoy the read.

Greg Battersby & Danny Simon

About the Contributors

Francesca Ash became involved in the licensing industry in 1978 when she co-organized the first-ever character merchandising conference and exhibition. In the 1980s she became the first non-American officer of LIMA — a position she held for two years. Acknowledged as an expert in licensing on a worldwide basis, in 2003 she co-founded Total Licensing and currently is responsible for publishing Total Licensing magazine, a worldwide publication with readers in over 100 countries. In addition, she publishes Total Art Licensing, Total Licensing Australia, Total Licensing UK and co-publishes The Total Licensing Report. In 2014, she launched Total Licensing's latest magazine, Total Brand Licensing. Francesca regularly addresses seminars and conferences around the world. She can be contacted at francesca@totallicensing.com

Eric Belloso is a specialist in generating revenues throughout all the value chain of the global rights management and entertainment business. With a professional experience of over 20 years developing and exploiting IPs internationally, Eric has developed his carrier working, amongst others, with companies such as BRB Internacional, Paramount Pictures, Sony Pictures Home Entertainment, Sony Computer Entertainment, Zinkia, DreamWorks and currently with Viacom & Nickelodeon as Senior Director, Consumer Products, Iberia and France. This experience allowed him to represent brands as diverse as the Spanish national football (Soccer) team, Star Trek, Pokémon, PlayStation, Pocoyó, the DreamWorks portfolio and most recently Paw Patrol, SpongeBob or the Teenage Mutant Ninja Turtles and to be able to manage project within practically all the facets of the IP business (TV rights (FTA, Pay TV, SVOD....), toys, licensing strategy, licensing agents, live shows, videogames and cinema exploitation, internet and virtual worlds). Based in Madrid (Spain) since 2000, Eric speaks fluently in Spanish, French and English and holds an Executive MBA from el Instituto de Empresa (IE) since 2007.

Dalia Benbassat, VP of Corporate Relations and Executive Associate at Tycoon Enterprises is a graphic artist by profession and has developed a long-standing career in licensing beginning in 1996 when she joined the Tycoon Group. She started in Equity Promotions (then partners of the group), in charge of the development and sale of promotional premiums, then progressively engaged in licensing by becoming head of Promotions for Tycoon Enterprises in 2001, and Director of Licensing a few years after. Dalia has been directly involved in the success of landmark brands such as Pokémon, Star Wars or Yugioh! from all business angles including Promotions, Marketing and Retail. She amasses great experience working via Tycoon for major studios including 20th Century Fox, Turner, Sesame Workshop, Marvel Entertainment, Rovio Mobile, Sanrio or Universal Pictures, among significant others. Since 2006, she has overseen corporate relations and in-bound licensing at Tycoon and has greatly contributed to the shaping of Tycoon Group into the pan-regional network it is today. She participates regularly in local and International Licensing forums and seminars and is currently a member of the Board at LIMA-PROMARCA (LIMA MEXICO). Dalia can be reached at dalia@tycoon.mx

Roger Berman, President of ZenWorks, has been active in Japanese, East Asian and global licensing for over 30 years. His creative content management and brand development experience is wide-ranging across property categories such as characters and entertainment, sports, lifestyle and fashion brands, designers and illustrators, and corporate logos. From 2008 to 2010, he managed the Japan branch of LIMA, the global licensing industry trade body, and is currently its Operations Advisor and a past-director. Berman has lived in Japan since 1984 and is fluent in Japanese. Berman's company, Tokyo-based ZenWorks Co., Ltd., delivers specialized license consulting, agency and media services to content creators and IP owners entering Japan and East Asian markets as well as facilitates international market expansion for Japanese content producers and licensors. ZenWorks focuses on helping clients attain sustainable and lasting business models for their creative content through a highly focused, hands-on approach curated to clients' goals, needs, and circumstances. Agency representations focus on design, sports and lifestyle brands such the Victoria & Albert Museum, Slazenger, No Fear and Aspen; consulting clients include Kikkoman, Benesse Corporation and TV Tokyo; ZenWorks also has sales partnerships with Total Licensing (media), Kilogrammedia (PR), Character Databank (market research) and UBM (licensing trade shows). Website: www.zenworks.jp. Enquiries: info@zenworks.jp

Lanning G. Bryer is a Partner in the New York office of Ladas & Parry LLP, Angela Lam is an associate in the New York office of Ladas & Parry LLP, and Lorena Mersan, is a recent L.L.M. graduate of Columbia University School of Law and Visiting Lawyer in the New York office of Ladas & Parry LLP. He can be reached at LBryer@ladas.com

Tony Bugg is the Managing Director of LIMA-Australia. He held senior Sales and Marketing roles for over 20 years. He was the founder of the local licensing on-line and magazine publication, The Bugg Report which he rebranded at Bugg Toys and Licensing. He is a director of the Australian Toy Association. He can be reached at tbugg@licensing.org

Pete Canalichio is the author of Expand, Grow, Thrive, a brand expansion and licensing expert, expert witness and TEDx speaker. An instructor at Mercer, Pete founded the LASSO Academy, which is dedicated to building the competency of organizations in the field of brand expansion and extension. He can be contacted at pete.canalichio@brand-licensingexpert.com

Hubert Co is President of Empire Multimedia Corporation, one of the largest and most established licensing agencies in Asia. Based in the Philippines, Empire Multimedia also has several offices in Southeast Asia and Greater China. For more than 30 years, Empire has represented a diverse portfolio of intellectual properties from character, lifestyle to entertainment brands targeting all ages across all markets in Asia, China and now Korea. Being in the licensing business for three decades, Empire has achieved several firsts in the Philippines: first to license direct to retailer in the early '80s, first to license attraction walks, multilevel marketing and wireless licensing. With Hubert's leadership and vast licensing experience, Empire Multimedia has become one of the most trusted licensing agents in Asia. Website: www.empiremultimedia.com. Enquiries: licensing@empiremultimedia.com

Marilu Corpus is President and Chief Executive Officer of Click! Licensing Asia, Inc. Founded in 1988, Click! Licensing has grown to be one of the leading brand management companies in Asia managing 9 countries in Greater China, Southeast Asia, with Korea as the latest addition, representing world class brands from pre-school brands as well as entertainment, fashion and lifestyle brands. CLICK's work begins from creating strategies to implementation of licensing programs for the long-term benefit of the brands. Marilu started her career in Licensing in 1984 with United Media Licensing International Division in New York working on the PEANUTS and GARFIELD for 7 years and later as Vice President of

MGM (Metro Goldwyn Mayer) as Vice President of International Licensing and Merchandising. Marilu is currently on the Board of Directors of the Licensing Industry Merchandisers' Association (LIMA) and the LIMA Foundation. She can be reached at mariluc@clicklicensingasia.com

Elias Fasja is Founding Partner and President at Tycoon Enterprises, one of the largest and most influential licensing and merchandising agencies in Latin America. Tycoon has consistently introduced to the market the hottest contemporary entertainment brands, as well as big "classics" and a careful selection of premium properties derived from the film, television, interactive, sports and lifestyle fields, including Angry Birds, Hello Kitty, The Simpsons, Plaza Sésamo, Real Madrid and Universal Pictures, among others. Tycoon has recently expanded its scope of services and geographical coverage, raising the bar for industry standards across Latin America, from Mexico to Brazil. Previously, Mr. Fasja was the President of PROMARCA from 2008 to 2012, and CEO at Grupo Carel S.A. de C.V. from 1977 to 1992. He can be reached at efasja@tycoon.mx

Marici Ferreira is currently Executive Director of EP Grupo and Chairman of Barzilian Licensing Association (ABRAL). Marici has over 20 years of exeperience and publises business magazines and hold events for the trademarket of Toy, Toddlers and Licensing sectors. Ahead ABRAL, Marici work to develop and promote the licensing Market at Brazil.

Hussein Ftouni is the Founder & CEO of Copyright Licensing Agency, Dubai, United Arab Emirates. Mr. Ftouni is an entrepreneur with over fifteen years of experience in the licensed consumer products industry, with expertise gained first in distributing licensed products for other licensees, then acquiring licensing rights, developing and manufacturing, marketing and distributing various ranges of licensed products, then into developing strategies for brand building, launching licensing programs for various international brands and properties. He can be reached at hftouni@licensing.org He

Kelvyn Gardner has been involved in the international licensing business for over thirty years. A graduate of King's College, London, his early business career led him into marketing and licensing with Italian children's collectables company, *Panini*. After a successful period, Kelvyn and three colleagues started *Merlin Publishing* in 1989 to market licensed stickers and trading cards. The company grew throughout Europe and in just five years annual sales reached US $80 million. *Merlin* was the UK's fastest-growing private company in 1995. Since 1998 Kelvyn has worked as a consultant in the licensing industry through his company, *Asgard Media*. Clients include *Yoplait, The Topps Company* and *Finsbury Food Group*. At the 2013 *Licensing Awards* in London, Kelvyn was presented with the *Honorary Achievement Award* for his work in licensing. Kelvyn has spoken at conferences in London, Manchester, Frankfurt, Milan, Paris, New York, Dubai, Hong Kong, Delhi, Berlin, Seoul and Tokyo. He speaks good Italian, competent French and Spanish, and basic conversational Japanese. In 2017 Kelvyn featured prominently in the ITV documentary 'Stuck on You' recounting the history of football stickers. Since 2006 he has held the mantle of Managing Director of the UK division of LIMA, the Licensing Industry Merchandisers Association. Kelvyn is also a trustee of the Light Fund, the licensing industry's independent charity. He can be reached at kgardner@licensing.org

Elias Hofman is President of EXIM Licensing USA, Inc., a marketing organization which explores all opportunities involving licensing, promotions, merchandising, entertainment, TV and stage shows productions and which covers the entire Latin America region. As a regional player with 30 years of experience, the group has 15 offices across the region with + 300 local executives and employees with great knowledge and expertise in the different markets. Mr. Hofman can be reached at ehofman@eximlicensing.com.

Fuad Khan is an accomplished licensing and marketing executive and founder of Word of Web, a Brand Management Firm, where he is helping brand owners and licensees to find a solid revenue stream through brand extension and licensing. Prior to going independent, Fuad served as a Senior Sales Executive at Alicom Licensing, where he has done deals in the Nordic across all categories for more than six years for FOX Consumer Products, CBS Consumer Products, Paramount Licensing, Jim Henson Company and American Greetings. Fuad holds a M.Sc. in International Business Administration from the LiU School of Management (Linköping University). He is fluent in 4 languages and lives happily married with three young children in Stockholm, Sweden. He can be reached at fuad@wordofweb.se

Kyeongwon Kwak is the LIMA Representative for Korea. Kyeongwon can be reached at kkwak @licensing.org.

Sir Michael Ah-Yue Lou is President of V.I.P. Entertainment & Merchandising AG, Hamburg. Sir Michael, originally an investment banker who mainly advised governments in developing countries on loan syndication, became by coincidence the licensee for the DALLAS board game. Because of the success of his first venture into licensing, in 1981 he founded V.I.P. Promotions, which soon became one of the leading independent licensing agents in the German speaking area and was converted in 1999 into the present stock corporation. Over the years, VIP has represented numerous proprietors of renowned brands, including IBM, Pepsi Cola, General Motors, Fabergé, Pierre Cardin; characters and celebrities including, Star Wars, Indiana Jones, James Bond, Tarzan, Terminator, James Dean, Elvis Presley, Marilyn Monroe, Michael Jackson, Madonna, Britney Spears and The Beatles; sport properties like the NFL National Football League, UCLA, NCAA, the International Tennis Federation; charities like the Princess Diana Memorial Fund, the Vatican Library or the Non-Violence Project and other popular properties. Sir Michael (M.B.A.) is the author of numerous articles on licensing and merchandising and a frequent speaker at various seminars, business schools and universities. He was also a consultant to the Club of Rome (Germany) and the founding President of the European License Marketing & Merchandising Association (ELMA) and its CEO through 2008. www.vip-ag.com. He can be reached at m.lou@vip-ag.com

Marty Malysz is President of Dependable Solutions, Inc. providing brand licensing operations automation to financial licensing processes and creative procedures. He manages a 25-person team with offices through the US and the UK providing royalty systems, product approvals content management and trademark licensing automation to clients in the US, Australia, Spain, Sweden, Italy, France, Denmark, Germany, United Kingdom, Netherlands and China. He has 30 years of experience automating 500 entertainment, sports, corporate brand and apparel licensing companies around the world and is a former LIMA Board member. mmalysz@dependablerights.com.

Gianfranco Mari is the co-founder and Chairman of DIC2, the first Italian independent licensing agency he founded with his brother Loris. The firm represents hundreds of licensors, including LCA, Twenty Century Fox, Larry Harmon, Carolco, CBS, Marvel Comics, Hanna & Barbera, MGM, Universal Studios, Edgar Rice Burroughs, Zorro Productions,

Mattel, Les Editions Albert Rene, Minikim, Hallmark, Nintendo, LCI, The Pokémon Company, Viacom, NFL, General Motors, John Sands, Penthouse and many others. He can be reached at gianfranco@dic2.com

Gaurav Marya is Chairman, Franchise India Holdings Limited and the LIMA Representative in India. Gaurav can be reached at gmarya@licensing.org

Maria del Carmen Rotter, better known as Maca Rotter in the industry, founded the business in Mexico for Televisa Consumer Products successfully managed for over 16 years and restarted by founding LA PANADERIA LICENSING & MARKETING along with a team of more than 30 people who has been together for over 12 years. Kept the leadership and transitioned all representations to the new Company. Manage the Kids strategy of Televisa, productions and co-productions as well as programming for the main slot for Preschool in the Country. Maca has been 7 times awarded in the Top 100 Mexican women in business by Expansion. In 2015 awarded among the 14th executives in the first edition of Women to Watch Mexico from Ad Age. Recently founded a Company along the team that have built this dream together for many years creating *La Panaderia Licensing & Marketing* (The Bakery) to "bake brands", starting 2017 as an entrepreneur being able to keep all support from Televisa and the Studios that have also been represented in the past decade to be part of this a new adventure, finding a purpose to work meaningfully. Maca is the author of the first book ever published in Spanish about Licensing and Merchandising, (2014). Second edition was published in 2017. Awarded as one of the TOP Global "Influentials" 2017 by LICENSE Magazine. After many years created the first diploma for Licensing along Universidad Panamericana and LIMA in 2017-2018. She can be reached at macarotter@panaderia.xyz

Luis Salazar is President of Compañía Panamericana de Licencias (CPL), one of the largest promotional and licensing agencies in Latin America. The company has more than 30 years of experience working with the marketing departments of local and multinational companies to improve their marketing performances. This is achieved through promotions and/or the successful use of licensed characters, movies, artists, singers and other properties. The Peruvian-based company handles many popular properties from the entertainment industry. These include cartoons, animated series, movies, live TV series, artists, singers, etc., and representation covers most of South and Central America. Companies represented include Cartoon Network, DHX Media, Grupo Chespirito, IMPS, Televisa, Saban, Sega of America, Viz Media, Warner Bros. Consumer Products, among others. As a result of strategic commercial expansion, the company now has operations in Argentina, Brazil, Bolivia, Chile, Colombia, Ecuador, Mexico, Paraguay, Peru, Uruguay, Venezuela, Honduras, Panama, El Salvador, Guatemala, Costa Rica, and Dominican Republic. Compañia Panamericana de Licencias (CPL) handles licensing and promotions throughout Latin America, that range from local and pan-regional to those conducted globally. Visit CPL's web site at www.cpl.com.pe.

Rohit Sobti is the CEO & Co-Founder - Brand Monk Licensing (www.brandmonk.co). He is a business leader in entertainment and licensing industry with 21 years of experience in developing new businesses, exploiting the intellectual property and Brand extension in India and International Markets. Sobti has worked closely with a variety of music publishers, record labels, Film Theatre, Retailers and Television channels both in India and Overseas. Prior to setting up Brand Monk Licensing, he was Vice President - Licensing and Merchandising at Yash Raj Films (YRF). Sobti can be reached at rohit@brandmonk.co

Cyril Speijer is one of the co-founders of BN Licensing B.V., an independent and experienced licensing agency in the Benelux. Founded in 2011, BN Licensing represents a broad collection of some of the world's most well-known character properties, design properties, entertainment and sports brands. The company handles all sales and marketing related business as well as the monitoring and protection of all brands represented. Before founding BN Licensing, Cyril was the founder of Wavery Productions B.V. in 1967 and has over 46 years of experience as a licensing agent. For 22 years, Cyril was director of NFL Properties B.V. and for NHL Enterprises B.V., which was the international office based in Holland for trademarks, licensing and overseeing the international agent network for these "Americana" brands. Cyril is an active participant in LIMA, where he served twice as a board member and in 1994 was awarded the "LIMA International Licensing Agent of The Year" award and is a member of LIMA's Licensing Hall of Fame.

Hakan Tungaç is the Turkish representative of the International Licensing Industry Merchandisers' Association (LIMA) and is currently a doctorate student of History at Istanbul University. Mr. Tungaç is a Board Member and International Relations Director of the Turkish Press & Publishers Copyrights & Licensing Union. He is currently the managing director of Sentries Licensing Company. Besides his professional work career, he is an actor and has appeared on 3 TV series and a motion picture.

Peter Van Raalte is a partner in Infinity Licensing and a former LIMA Chairman. He started his career at the Saturday Evening Post, followed by leadership positions at Turner Home Entertainment, Scholastic Entertainment, Joester-Loria Group, Madison Square Garden before forming Infinity Licensing. He has represented such properties as the HANNA-BARBERA ANIMATION LIBRARY, MGM, CARTOON NETWORK, CLIFFORD THE BIG RED DOG, MAGIC SCHOOL BUS. JEEP, CHRYSLER and PEPPA PIG. He can be contacted at peter@infinitylicensing.com

Tani Wong has over 20 years in licensing business and has gained extensive experience in the industry. She has in-depth knowledge about licensors, licensees, merchandising, publishing, marketing, promotions and events. To recognize her dedication and service to the licensing industry, she was awarded the "20 Most Outstanding Licensing Practitioners" at the 8th China Beijing International Cultural & Creative Industry Expo in 2013. Apart from running her own consultancy, she is the Managing Director of LIMA China office since 2009. She manages the Hong Kong offices to promote licensing to companies in Greater China and Southeast Asia. Tani had served as Sales Director for Greater China, Southeast Asia & India at Warner Bros. She managed a wide portfolio from animation, movie to sports team and events with local agents in the region. Prior to that, Tani joined Disney Consumer Products where she cultivated her enthusiasm in licensing. She can be reached at twong@licensing.org

Christian Zeidler is Owner and Managing Director of 20too – The Premium Licensing Specialist. 20too – The Premium Licensing Specialist is a leading licensing company located in Dubai, United Arab Emirates. The company specializes in representing global entertainment brands and portfolios of IP owners such as Hasbro, Paws, IMPS, CreaCon and others. In his role as Managing Director, Christian Zeidler manages one of the leading licensing agencies in the region of the Middle East and North Africa. Together with his team they represent some of the world's most popular entertainment and character brands, such as

Transformers, My Little Pony, The Smurfs, City of Friends, Garfield, Nerf or Monopoly. In addition, 20too also specializes in teens/adult brands and are currently managing the IP portfolio of India's leading film studio called Yash Raj Films. Besides this, Christian Zeidler has successfully introduced additional servicing components to his clients and 20too also offers excellent product design and premiums sourcing services to the local industry.

Table of Contents

ABOUT THE AUTHORS V

ABOUT THE CONTRIBUTORS IX

CHAPTER 1 DEFINING THE WORLD OF LICENSING... 1

   1.1 DEFINITIONS AND TERMINOLOGY 1
      1.1.1 Forms of Licensing 1
      1.1.2 Contractual Terms 2
   1.2 TYPES OF PROPERTIES 4
      1.2.1 Art.. 4
      1.2.2 Celebrity 5
      1.2.3 Collegiate.. 6
      1.2.4 Corporate 7
      1.2.5 Entertainment 8
      1.2.6 Fashion 9
      1.2.7 Music 10
      1.2.8 Non-Profits 11
      1.2.9 Publishing 11
      1.2.10 Sports 12
   1.3 TYPES OF LICENSED PRODUCTS 13
   1.4 ADVANTAGES OFFERED BY LICENSING AND REASONS FOR ITS POPULARITY 14

CHAPTER 2 HISTORY OF LICENSING... 17

   2.1 THE PROPERTIES 17
   2.1.1 THE BEGINNING 17
      2.1.2 The 1940's 21
      2.1.3 The 1950's 22
      2.1.4 The 1960's 24
      2.1.5 The 1970's 26
      2.1.6 The 1980's 28
      2.1.7 The 1990's 32
      2.1.8 The 21st Century 34
   2.2 UNIQUE LICENSED PRODUCTS 37
      2.3.1 The Pioneers 52
      2.3.2 The Legendary Creators.. 54
         2.3.2.1 Motion Pictures and Television 54
         2.3.2.2 Print Media... 54
   2.3.3 THE LEGENDARY AGENTS, CONSULTANTS AND SUPPORT PROVIDERS............................... 55
         2.3.3.1 Entertainment 55
         2.3.3.2 Corporate 58
         2.3.3.3 Celebrity and Music 60
         2.3.3.4 Art 61
         2.3.3.5 Consultants/Manufacturer's Reps 62
         2.3.3.6 The Manufacturers/Licensees.. 62
         2.3.3.7 Colleges 64
         2.3.3.8 Sports.. 65
         2.3.3.9 The Press... 65
         2.3.3.10 The Lawyers and Accountants 66

2.3.3.11 Retailers 67
2.3.3.12 The Trade Associations and Trade Shows 68
2.3.3.13 International 69

CHAPTER 3 THE LICENSING INDUSTRY TODAY 73

3.1 SIZE AND SCOPE OF THE INDUSTRY 73
3.2 THE MAJOR LICENSORS 76
3.3 MOST POPULAR LICENSED PROPERTIES 77
3.4 LIMA LICENSE OF THE YEAR AWARD WINNERS 79
3.5 THE MAJOR LICENSEES 80
3.6 LIMA LICENSEE OF THE YEAR AWARD WINNERS 85
3.7 THE MAJOR LICENSING AGENCIES 89
3.8 INTERNATIONAL SCOPE OF THE INDUSTRY 89
    3.8.1 Introduction 89

CHAPTER 4 THE LICENSE AGREEMENT 95

4.1 INTRODUCTION 95
4.2 THE LICENSE AGREEMENT 95
    4.2.1 Definitions 95
    4.2.2 Grant of Rights 97
    4.2.3 Term of the Agreement 98
    4.2.4 Compensation Provisions 99
    4.2.5 Sub-Licensing 99
    4.2.6 Accounting Provisions 100
    4.2.7 Quality Control Provisions 102
    4.2.8 Representations and Warranties 103
    4.2.9 Indemnification and Insurance 104
    4.2.10 Termination Provision 105
    4.2.11 Boilerplate Provisions 106

CHAPTER 5 COMPENSATION AND ROYALTY RATES 109

5.1 INTRODUCTION 109
5.2 SETTING ROYALTY RATES 109
5.3 TYPES OF ROYALTY RATES 112
    5.3.1 Royalty Rates on Domestic Sales 112
    5.3.2 Royalty Rates on F.O.B. Sales 113
    5.3.3 Royalty Rates on Direct Sales 114
    5.3.4 Royalty Rates for Services 114
    5.3.5 Sub-licensing Royalties 115
    5.3.6 Split Royalty Rates 115
    5.3.7 Royalty Rates on Closeout Sales 115
    5.3.8 Royalty Rates For Digital Products 116
5.4 AVERAGE ROYALTY RATES 116
5.6 MARKETING CONTRIBUTIONS 119

CHAPTER 6 IDENTIFYING AND CLEARING LICENSING PROPERTIES ... 121

6.1 EVALUATING PROPERTIES FOR LICENSING 121
6.2 HOW WELL KNOWN IS THE PROPERTY? 122
6.3 OWNERSHIP CONSIDERATIONS 124
6.4 CLEARING PROPERTIES 127

CHAPTER 7 SELECTING THE RIGHT LICENSE FOR YOUR PRODUCTS ... 131

7.1 Introduction 131
7.2 Understanding Your Own Product 131
7.3 Developing Reasonable Expectations and Goals 132
7.4 Finding and Evaluating the Right Properties 132
    7.4.1 Prospecting for the Right Property *132*
    7.4.2 Objective *133*
    7.4.3 Fit *133*
    7.4.4 Timing *134*
    7.4.5 Cost *135*
7.5 Conducting Proper Due Diligence 136
    7.5.1 How Well Known Is The Property? *137*
    7.5.2 Know Who Owns the Property *138*
7.6 Status of the Property's Protection 139
7.7 Consider the Licensor's Track Record 140
7.8 Support from The Licensor 140

CHAPTER 8 THE LICENSOR–LICENSEE RELATIONSHIP **141**

8.1 Introduction 141
8.2 The License Application 141
8.3 The Negotiations 142
8.4 Term Sheets/Deal Memos 149

CHAPTER 9 LICENSING AGENTS AND CONSULTANTS **151**

9.1 Introduction 151
9.2 The Role and Compensation of a Licensing Agent 152
9.3 Licensing Agent Agreement 155
9.4 Sub-Agents and International Licensing Agents 160
9.5 Manufacturer's Consultants/Representatives 162
9.6 Making the Relationship Work 163

CHAPTER 10 THE RETAILER'S ROLE IN LICENSING **165**

10.1 Introduction 165
10.2 The Retailers Role in the Licensing Equation 166
10.3 What Are Retailers Looking For? 167
10.4 How to Get Retail Placement 168
10.5 Think Smaller—Limited Distribution 169
10.6 Retailer Strategies beyond the Top Ten 169
10.7 Direct to Retail Licenses 171
10.8 Transition to On-Line Retail 173

CHAPTER 11 BEST PRACTICES FOR LICENSORS **175**

11.1 Introduction 175
11.2 The Licensing Department 175
    11.2.1 The Marketing Group *176*
    11.2.2 The Sales Group *179*
    11.2.3 The Contract Administration and Legal Group *182*
    11.2.4 The Finance Group *184*
    11.2.5 The Retail Group *184*
    11.2.6 The Creative Group *185*
11.3 International Licensing 187
11.4 Using Technology to Better Manage a Licensing Program 188
11.5 Building a Compelling Licensing Plan 195

11.6 CREATING A COMPELLING BRAND GUIDE..197
11.7 FORECASTING IN TODAY'S LICENSING WORLD 198

CHAPTER 12 BEST PRACTICES FOR LICENSEES **199**

12.1 INTRODUCTION...199
12.2 PROSPECTING FOR THE RIGHT PROPERTY 199
   12.2.1 The Internet 199
   12.2.2 Licensing Directories and Trade Publications 199
   12.2.3 Domestic and International Licensing Trade Shows 199
   12.2.4 Other Vehicles 200
12.3 MATCHING THE PRODUCT TO THE LICENSE...200
12.4 THE LICENSING TEAM 201
12.5 PRODUCT DEVELOPMENT 202
   12.5.1 Brand Style Guide 202
   12.5.2 Manufacturing Agreement...203
   12.5.3 Trade Shows 203
   12.5.3 Social Compliance...204
   12.5.4 Product Approvals...204
12.6 MARKETING AND SALES 204
12.7 ADMINISTRATION OF THE LICENSING PROGRAM...205
   12.7.1 Legal Administration 205
   12.7.2 Licensee Application Form..205
   12.7.3 Deal Memo 206
   12.7.4 License Agreement 206
   12.7.5 Approval Forms 206
   12.7.6 Royalty Report Form..207
12.8 FINANCIAL ADMINISTRATION...207

CHAPTER 13 MARKETING AND PROMOTING LICENSING PROPERTIES AND LICENSED PRODUCTS . **209**

13.1 INTRODUCTION...209
13.2 ADVERTISING PROGRAMS...209
13.3 EFFECTIVE PUBLIC RELATIONS 210
13.4 INNOVATIVE PROMOTIONS 213
13.5 USING SOCIAL MEDIA TO GROW YOUR BRAND AND PRODUCT 215
13.6 MARKETING FUNDS...220

CHAPTER 14 PROTECTING LICENSING PROPERTIES **221**

14.1 INTRODUCTION...221
14.2 DEVELOPING A PROTECTION PLAN 221
14.3 TRADEMARK PROTECTION 222
14.4 COPYRIGHT PROTECTION 225

CHAPTER 15 INTERNATIONAL LICENSING **229**

15.1 GREATER EUROPE 229
   15.1.1 Introduction 229
15.1.2 BENELUX...230
   15.1.3 Germany...237
   15.1.4 Italy 246
   15.1.5 Spain..253
   15.1.6 United Kingdom..259
   15.1.7 The Nordic Region 263

15.1.8 Turkey...267
15.1.9 Russia 274
15.2 MIDDLE EAST AND NORTH AFRICA (MENA)...283
15.2.1 MENA 286
15.3 SOUTH ASIA...291
15.3.1 India 291
15.4 ASIA 298
15.4.1 Japan 300
15.4.2 China 310
15.4.3 Korea 316
15.5 SOUTHEAST ASIA 321
15.6 AUSTRALIA 327
15.7 LATIN AMERICA 332
15.7.1 Brazil...334
15.7.2 Colombia, Chile, Ecuador, Peru, Venezuela and Central America 337
15.7.3 Mexico...341

CHAPTER 16 INTERNATIONAL INTELLECTUAL PROPERTY PROTECTION 357

16.1 INTRODUCTION...357
16.2 INTERNATIONAL PROTECTION OF TRADEMARKS, COPYRIGHTS AND RELATED RIGHTS 358
16.2.1 Harmonization of IP Laws...358
16.2.2 International Intellectual Property Treaties 359
16.3 TRADEMARKS...362
16.3.1 Trademark Clearance and Adoption 363
16.3.2 Basis of Registrability of Trademarks...363
16.3.3 Reasons for Registering Your Trademark 365
16.3.4 Deciding Where to Register your Trademark 366
16.3.5 Maintaining your Trademark Rights 370
16.4 COPYRIGHT AND RELATED RIGHTS...370
16.4.1 Copyrights 370
16.4.2 Related Rights 373
16.4.3 Collective Management of Copyrights and Related Rights 374
16.5 LICENSE AGREEMENT TERMS AND REGISTRATION REQUIREMENTS...................374
16.5.1 License Agreement Terms. 374
16.5.2 Registration Requirements..375
16.6 CONCLUSION 376

CHAPTER 17 BATTERSBY'S RULES ON LICENSING.. 379

CHAPTER 18 SIMON SAYS ABOUT LICENSING 381

CHAPTER 19 ETHICS AND SOCIAL COMPLIANCE... 383

19.1 ETHICS IN LICENSING 383
19.2 ENSURING SOCIAL COMPLIANCE 385
19.3 THE BSR REPORT 386

CHAPTER 20 MOST COMMON MISTAKES IN LICENSING.. 387

CHAPTER 21 SPECIAL CONSIDERATIONS FOR DIFFERENT TYPES OF PROPERTIES/PRODUCTS 391

21.1 INTRODUCTION...391
21.2 DIFFERENT TYPES OF PROPERTIES..391
21.2.1 Entertainment Properties 391
21.2 2 Celebrity Properties 392
21.2.3 Corporate or Brand Properties 393

21.2.4 Art and Designer Properties *393*
21.2.5 Collegiate Properties *394*
21.2.6 Sports Properties *395*
21.2.7 Event Properties *395*
21.3 DIFFERENT TYPES OF PRODUCTS 396
21.3.1 Food and Beverage Licensed Products *396*

CHAPTER 22 ACCOUNTING, AUDITING AND TAX CONSIDERATIONS 397

22.1 INTRODUCTION 397
22.2 AUDIT PROVISIONS IN THE LICENSE AGREEMENT 397
22.2.1 Right to Audit *398*
22.2.2 Record Keeping *398*
22.2.3 Interest on Findings *399*
22.2.4 Extrapolation *399*
22.2.5 Recovery of Audit Fees *399*
22.3 WHEN SHOULD AN AUDIT BE PERFORMED? 400
22.4 SELECTING THE ROYALTY AUDITOR 401
22.5 PREPARING FOR THE ROYALTY AUDIT 401
22.6 INFORMATION REQUIRED FROM THE LICENSEE 402
22.6.1 Sales Journals, Invoices, Cash Receipts, and Banking Records *402*
22.6.2 Manufacturing and Purchasing Records *403*
22.6.3 Inventory Records *403*
22.6.4 Credit Memo Journals *403*
22.6.5 General Ledgers, Tax Returns and Financial Statements *403*
22.6.6 Product Catalogs *404*
22.6.7 Price Lists *404*
22.7 ROYALTY AUDIT PROCEDURES 404
22.8 THE ROYALTY AUDIT REPORT 405
22.8.1 Common Monetary Findings *405*
22.8.2 Common Non-Monetary Findings *406*
22.9 ACCOUNTING PROVISIONS IN LICENSE AGREEMENTS 406
22.9.1 Definition of Terms *406*

CHAPTER 23 DEALING WITH INFRINGERS AND COUNTERFEITERS 411

23.1 INTRODUCTION 411
23.2 WHY INFRINGEMENT SHOULD NEVER BE UNDERESTIMATED 412
23.3 THE COUNTERFEITING INDUSTRY—A GROWING MARKET 416
23.4 IDENTIFYING COUNTERFEIT PRODUCTS 422
23.5 ANTICOUNTERFEITING TECHNOLOGY 422
23.6 STEPS TO TAKE AGAINST INFRINGERS 423
23.6.1 Cease and Desist Letters *424*
23.6.2 Keeping a Perspective on Litigation *424*
23.6.3 Theories of Litigation *425*
23.6.4 Litigation Strategies *428*
23.7 INTERNATIONAL ENFORCEMENT OF TRADEMARKS, COPYRIGHTS, AND RELATED RIGHTS 430
23.7.1 Issues an International Enforcement Program Should Address *430*
23.7.2 When and Where to Set Up an Enforcement Program *432*
23.7.3 Resources for an Enforcement Program *434*

APPENDICES **439**

APPENDIX-1 LIMA CODE OF BUSINESS PRACTICES **441**

APPENDIX-2 LICENSEE PROPOSAL 443

APPENDIX-3 DEAL MEMO 445

APPENDIX-4 LICENSE AGREEMENT 448

APPENDIX-5 PRODUCT CATEGORIES 467

APPENDIX-6 STYLE GUIDE 476

APPENDIX-7 APPROVAL FORM GUIDE & FORM 483

APPENDIX-8 MARKETING PLAN OUTLINE 487

TIMELINE .... ERROR! BOOKMARK NOT DEFINED.

APPENDIX-9 CHANNELS OF DISTRIBUTION CHECKLIST 489

APPENDIX-10 SAMPLE ROYALTY REPORT 492

APPENDIX-11 LICENSING AGENT AGREEMENT 493

APPENDIX-12 SUB-AGENT AGREEMENT 499

APPENDIX-13 CONSULTING AGREEMENT 507

APPENDIX-14 NON-DISCLOSURE AGREEMENT 511

APPENDIX-15 MANUFACTURER'S REPRESENTATIVE AGREEMENT 513

APPENDIX-16 TRADEMARK CLASSES 519

APPENDIX-17 FORM VA COPYRIGHT APPLICATION 523

APPENDIX-18 FORM TX COPYRIGHT APPLICATION 527

APPENDIX-19 FORM PA COPYRIGHT APPLICATION 531

APPENDIX-20 FORM SR COPYRIGHT APPLICATION 535

Chapter 1
Defining the World of Licensing

1.1 Definitions and Terminology

Over the years, the licensing industry has developed a set of terms that need to become understood if one is to function effectively in the industry.

1.1.1 Forms of Licensing

The term **"licensing"** typically means any transaction in which the owner of intellectual property grants another party the right to use such intellectual property, typically in exchange for some form of consideration or payment. Absent the grant of such a right or license, the other party's use of the intellectual property would be considered an infringing use. Thus, the license constitutes a defense to infringement. Licensing is, therefore, the monetization of an existing asset.

> **Licensing:**
>
> **The grant of the right to use another party's intellectual property on their products or services in exchange for financial consideration, typically a royalty.**

"Intellectual property" can take many forms including, for example, musical works, literary works, artwork, drawings, inventions, discoveries, designs, patents, trademarks, names, logos, legends, industrial designs, trade dress, celebrity rights, etc. Regardless of the type, the one constant is that it must be protectable under some form of intellectual property protection, e.g., as a patent, trademark, copyright, right of publicity or trade secret. Intellectual property is frequently referred to simply as **"IP."**

There are many types of licensing, virtually all of which will depend, in large measure, on the type of intellectual property involved. For example, when the intellectual property being licensed is technology or is covered by a patent, the licensing of such technology or patent is typically called **"technology licensing"** or **"patent licensing."** Similarly, when the property being licensed is computer software, the licensing of the software is normally called **"software licensing."** When a trademark is being licensed, it is typically referred to as **"trademark licensing."**

When a character from a book or motion picture is the property being licensed, such licensing is commonly called **"character licensing."** Similarly, when a corporate brand is the subject matter, it is typically called **"brand licensing."**

When one licenses a highly recognizable brand or character for goods or services in categories different from the one where the brand or character had originally been popularized, such licensing is frequently called **"brand extension licensing"** or simply **"merchandising."**

This book will focus primarily on merchandising, although at times the terms "merchandising" and "licensing" may be used interchangeably throughout the work. It should be appreciated that the term merchandising may have other meanings, particularly in the retail

1

or marketing fields. In the retailing field, merchandising means something other than licensing, e.g. some form of "a sales promotion as a comprehensive function, including market research, development of new products, coordination of manufacture and marketing, and effective advertising and selling."

1.1.2 Contractual Terms

The grant of a license to a manufacturer is typically done pursuant to a written **"license agreement"** or **"license agreement."** While oral licenses may occur, the clear majority are granted under formal, written license agreements.

In the context of licensing, the owner of the IP that is granting the license is commonly called a **"property owner"** or **"licensor"** while the party receiving the license to use the intellectual property on their product is typically called a **"licensee."**

The intellectual property being licensed is normally called the **"property"** or, more accurately, the **"licensed property,"** while the products for which the license is being granted are typically called the **"licensed products or licensed articles."** If the intellectual property is being licensed for use in conjunction with a service, e.g., restaurant services, those services would be called the **"licensed services."**

It is quite common to include **"schedules"** in a license agreement to more accurately and completely define both the licensed property and the licensed products or licensed services.

There are different types of license grants. An **"exclusive license"** is one in which the licensee is the only party receiving the right to use the licensed property for the licensed products to the exclusion of everyone, including the licensor. There may be some instances, however, in an exclusive license where the licensor reserves the right to use the licensed property itself for such products, but that would have to be specifically stated.

A **"non-exclusive license"** is one in which the licensee is granted the right to use the licensed property for the licensed products on a non-exclusive basis so that the licensor may make similar grants to other parties. In merchandising, most licenses are non-exclusive, even where the licensor may have no intention of granting a similar right to anyone else. This is done primarily to protect the licensor should the licensee underperform or even declare bankruptcy. In such event, the licensor might be able to find others to step into the shoes of the bankrupt licensee during the pendency of the bankruptcy proceeding.

> Most merchandising license agreements are non-exclusive even where the licensor may not intend to grant other similar licenses.

Virtually all licenses are granted for fixed periods of time, e.g., three (3) years. Products that require a long development period or a large capital investment are often longer, or, alternatively, for so long as the licensee continues to sell licensed products (called **"Life of Product"** license). The length of a license grant is typically called its **"term."** In many cases, a licensee is given an **"option"** to renew the license for additional terms upon meeting certain conditions. In such cases, the initial period may be called the **"initial term"** and the renewal period may be called the **"renewal term."**

Most licenses will restrict the licensee's use of the property to a geographical area, e.g., North America or the European Union, and this is typically called the **"licensed territory."**

Similarly, a licensor may want to restrict the licensee's sales of the licensed products to a specific market or channel of trade, e.g., "mass market" or "Internet" and possibly even specific retail outlets within that market or channel. Such distribution limitations are commonly referred to as the **"channels of distribution."**

Licensors may want to exclude certain rights from the license grant, either to give it the freedom to exploit those rights itself or to be able to grant such rights to others. Many licensors will exclude the right to use the property as a **"premium"** or in conjunction with a **"promotion."** The exclusion of premium is very common in licensing agreements for movie and television properties. The reason is that premiums and promotional products are not typically sold as merchandise through the normal channels of distribution but, instead, are given away to the public to promote the licensed property and/or the company offering the premium, e.g., McDonald's BAKUGAN Happy Meal Program, in which BAKUGAN toys were given away by McDonald's to help promote BAKUGAN property and drive sales of McDonald's products.

The most common form of compensation for the right to use a licensed property on a licensed product is the payment of a **"royalty"** to the licensor, which is a percentage of the licensee's **"net sales"** of the licensed products. "Net sales" is always a defined term in any license agreement and will vary from license agreement to license agreement. It is often defined as the licensee's gross sales of licensed products, less certain agreed-upon deductions, usually **"discounts and allowances"** and any **"returns"** by the retailer or consumer.

> Merchandising licensors will usually require the licensee pay a Minimum Guaranteed Royalty and an Advance.

At the time a licensee enters into a license agreement, the licensee is typically required to pay the licensor an **"advance"** against its future earned royalty obligations—think of it as a prepayment of royalties. In most instances, the advance is creditable against the licensee's future earned royalty obligations. Thus, if the licensee paid a $100,000 advance, it would not need to pay any additional earned royalties until such earned royalty obligation exceeded the amount of the advance, i.e., $100,000.

Most licensors require that the licensee pay a **"guaranteed minimum royalty,"** often referred to as simply the **"minimum"** or **"guarantee."** Guarantees are intended to protect the licensor if the licensee's net sales prove to be lower than anticipated. As the name implies, the licensee is guaranteeing that it will pay the licensor a certain minimum amount of royalties over a given period during the term of the license regardless of what the earned royalties may be.

Although there are several ways to apply this guaranteed minimum royalty obligation, in most instances it only applies when the licensee's earned royalties fall below the minimum for that period. In such case, the licensee is obligated to supplement its earned royalty payments to meet the guarantee for that period.

In addition to the payment of a royalty, many licensors require their licensees to also contribute to a **"common marketing fund"** or **"CMF"** which the licensor collects from all its licensees and uses to support and promote the property and the licensing program. These payments are occasionally called a **"marketing royalty"** because they are frequently calculated as a percentage of the licensee's net sales of licensed products in much the same manner that the royalty is calculated.

Many licensees use third parties to manufacture the licensed products for them and/or sell or distribute them. These third parties are called **"manufacturers"** or **"distributors."** This practice is not **"sub-licensing,"** which is almost always prohibited. In sub-licensing, the licensee grants a third party the same rights that it had received from the original property owner or licensor, not simply the right to manufacture or distribute products for it.

1.2 Types of Properties

There are a variety of different types of properties that can be merchandised or licensed, although most constitute words, names, titles, symbols, designs, character or personality images or likenesses that have acquired a wide degree of public recognition through mass media exposure. Licensing properties typically fall into different categories, including:

- Art
- Celebrity
- Collegiate
- Corporate
- Entertainment
- Fashion
- Music
- Non-Profit
- Publishing
- Sports

1.2.1 Art

Art properties can be virtually any image or work of art. In the case of prominent artists such as THOMAS KINKADE, WARREN KIMBLE or DENA FISHBEIN, the artist's name can also be included as part of the licensed property.

It's been said that in art licensing, "it's all about the image." Consumers are purchasing the licensee's products primarily because of the artwork or image that appears on the products and licensees are licensing the artwork for the same reason. There are two principle reasons for licensing the artwork of an outside artist: it provides the licensee with unique artwork, and/or lowers the licensee's development costs which makes the licensing of artwork very attractive. While artwork is licensed for a host of different types of licensed products, including apparel and printed matter, it is also extensively licensed for use in advertising and on packaging.

While publishers and manufacturers have been using other people's artwork and images for decades, the practice of licensing such artwork has been a more recent trend. In the "early days," artwork was typically purchased by a manufacturer for a nominal sum of money, rather than licensed on a royalty-bearing basis.

As the licensing business grew, however, artists (and their agents) recognized that they could potentially earn far more money by licensing such works to the licensee rather than selling it outright as they would then be sharing in the revenues earned by the licensee using the artwork. Consequently, many artists stopped trying to sell their artwork outright and, instead, turned to licensing to potentially share in the sales that the artwork generated.

As art licensing grew in popularity, so too did the sizes of the advances and guarantees that a publisher or manufacturer was willing to pay for the right to use the artwork. In many instances, these advances and guarantees were significant and, frequently, were never earned off by the licensee.

As a result, the business model changed... again. While most artwork is still licensed rather than simply sold or assigned, the current trend is towards smaller advances and guarantees. Though the artist may still be able to ride the crest of a very successful licensed product, these smaller advances and guarantees protect the licensee if the licensed products do not sell up to the expectations of the parties when the agreement was negotiated. In short, business sanity has set in.

According to the 2018 LIMA Survey of the Licensing Industry, the three largest categories of licensed products for art properties were gifts & novelties, housewares and paper products.

1.2.2 Celebrity

Undeniably, we live in a world in which people are fascinated by celebrities. Magazines such as *People* and *In Touch* have generated subscriber bases in the millions and huge web followings simply because people want to closely follow the lives of their favorite celebrities. The United States has even elected celebrities as its president. It should not, therefore, come as any surprise that when a celebrity elects to put his or her name on a product or otherwise associate themselves with that product, more people will want to buy that product. The celebrity licensing category functions because of this basic premise.

In a nutshell, celebrity licensing is the licensing of a celebrity's name, image or likeness for use on a licensed product or in association with the advertising or promotional material for that product, to enhance the sales of such product. The value of the license is tied directly to the popularity and "fame" of the celebrity which, unfortunately, can change over time, in some cases, very abruptly.

In the early days, the celebrity might be required to act as a spokesperson for the licensed product, e.g., appearing in an infomercial on television or in print ads extolling the virtues or benefits of the licensed product and telling consumers why they should buy it. It has, however, evolved into one where the celebrity often simply licenses the right to use their name or image on the licensed product in a more classic licensing style.

In some instances, the celebrity might be required to make a promotional appearance or two with selected retailers, appear on the Home Shopping Network or to wear the licensed product on the "Red Carpet" before a Hollywood event, but the promotional support required is usually minimal, and has been replaced in many agreements by requiring the celebrity to support the product through the use of some form of social media, e.g., Facebook or Twitter.

 Ironically, the celebrity doesn't even have to be alive to be licensable. The licensing of deceased celebrities has become big business and, as a result, there are licensing agencies that specialize in this niche area. For example, it has been reported that the estates of such deceased celebrities as ELVIS PRESLEY and MICHAEL JACKSON continue to derive significant revenue from licensing the names and likeness of these individuals despite their passing.

A manufacturer needs, however, to be careful when taking a celebrity license for a living celebrity since their fame and public image can be fleeting. If the celebrity's personal life doesn't go the way everyone expected, not only will the celebrity's career suffer, but so will the sales of their licensed products. For example, after evidence of Tiger Woods' marital infidelity hit the media, not only did his golf game suffer but so did the sales of TIGER WOODS licensed products. The insertion of a "Morals" clause affords the licensee some protection in such cases where the behavior of the celebrity generates negative publicity.

According to the 2018 LIMA Survey of the Licensing Industry, the three largest categories of licensed products for celebrity properties were apparel, gifts & novelties, and health & beauty.

1.2.3 Collegiate

Over the past few decades, collegiate licensing has become a very important part of the licensing industry, as colleges and universities now regularly grant licenses to third parties to use their names, logos or mascots for a host of different types of licensed products. The royalty income generated by such licensing programs is used by these schools to support a wide variety of their athletic, academic and other quality of life programs.

While sales of collegiate licensed products were initially confined to college bookstores and alumni catalogs, distribution channels for such products have greatly expanded as collegiate brands have grown in popularity. Today, a significant amount of collegiate licensed products is carried by most major retailers on a national basis.

As one might expect, the success of a college licensing program is frequently tied to the success of its athletic teams. If a college wins a national football championship or makes an appearance in the NCAA's Final Four basketball tournament, the college will almost certainly see a meteoric rise in the sale of its licensed merchandise with a corresponding jump in the royalty revenue that it receives—a double win. It was reported that the 2018 Final Four in which Villanova ultimately prevailed, produced between $20-35 million in sales of licensed products.

An example of how athletic fame and fortune can translate into increased royalty revenue is BOISE STATE's experience. When it decided to change its logo and take its football program onto a national stage, the college experienced a ten-fold jump in its royalty revenues over a six-year period. More significantly, the sale of its licensed products expanded from local stores to national retailers.

The viability of a college brand is not just limited to success on the athletic field. Schools such as OXFORD, HARVARD and PRINCETON have developed strong licensing programs on the strength of their academic reputations.

Interestingly, even colleges with unique or "catchy" names or from popular geographical regions have found success in the marketplace, e.g., SLIPPERY ROCK UNIVERSITY or the UNIVERSITY OF HAWAII. For many years, UCLA sold a significant number of licensed products in Japan, finding that Japanese consumers were seeking an association with the California lifestyle.

Not to be outdone by its member schools, the NCAA has even jumped into the licensing arena, developing licensing programs based on the names of its various tournaments, e.g., the FINAL FOUR. Similarly, the various football bowl games, e.g. the ROSE BOWL, have licensed such names for a variety of different products.

The collegiate licensing marketplace is an interesting one because more than half of the colleges and universities use the same agent, i.e., IMG College Licensing, formerly The Collegiate Licensing Company ("CLC"). Another significant portion of the schools use Learfield Licensing Partners, while a handful of the remaining schools are either represented by Fermata (owned by Fanatics) or are independent and conduct their own licensing programs. IMG College and Learfield reached an agreement to merge in 2017 and, as of this writing,  were still working out the details of such merger. The combined company would include media marketing rights and licensing representation services for a majority of the colleges and universities in the U.S.

According to the 2018 LIMA Survey of the Licensing Industry, the three largest categories of collegiate licensed products were apparel (by a large margin) accessories, video games and sports.

1.2.4 Corporate

In the early years of licensing, the corporate world watched with great interest as the entertainment industry jumped in and found it to be an excellent way of promoting their brand names and underlying products, while generating additional revenue at the same time.

It is, therefore, no surprise that corporations eventually followed suit and used licensing as a means of both increasing their bottom lines and further enhancing their brands' identities. Today, more and more major corporations with highly recognizable brands and trademarks have turned to licensing.

While the prospect of generating additional revenue is always important to most corporations, many have developed licensing programs for other reasons. For example, some have found it to be a cost-effective vehicle for diversifying their product lines and entering product categories that they had not previously explored.

For example, in the early 1980's Winnebago Industries was mired in a depressed recreational vehicle market. While sales of RV's were down dramatically due to the gas crisis, the Winnebago mark was still a widely known and respected brand. Capitalizing on the public awareness of its name, Winnebago decided to diversify into the exploding camping market by licensing the WINNEBAGO mark for a line of sleeping bags, tents and other outdoor products. It was a classic example of how licensing can permit a company to leverage the power of its brand into other markets for little or no capital investment or risk.

Other corporations have entered the licensing arena to help strengthen their underlying trademark rights. For example, the Coca-Cola Company decided to pursue licensing opportunities at the suggestion of its trademark attorneys who were concerned about the company's ability to enforce their valuable trademark rights against individuals who were selling a variety of COKE products in categories and on goods that were totally unrelated to soft drinks.

Coca-Cola proceeded by setting up what has become one of the largest corporate licensing programs in the world, with more than 300 different licensees manufacturing thousands of such diverse licensed COCA-COLA products as beach towels, boxer shorts, baby clothing, jewelry and even fishing lures. The company opened several COCA-COLA stores around the world carrying a wide array of licensed products, many of which express a nostalgia theme based on early COKE advertising campaigns.

More significantly, the Coca-Cola licensing program has been financially successful beyond anyone's wildest imagination and the revenue that it generates adds directly to the bottom line. At one point, it was reported that the program netted at least $70 million in annual profits or about 0.3% of its total net operating revenues—all while strengthening the company's trademarks in the process. It also does not hurt, of course, that the wide spread sale and distribution of licensed COCA-COLA merchandise continues to help promote (and some may say advertise) the primary COKE soft drink products.

Some companies, particularly those in the alcohol and tobacco industries, have relied on licensing for promotional purposes since governmental regulations significantly restrict their ability to advertise through conventional media channels. Licensing permits these companies to still convey their marketing messages through the sale of licensed products which bear their marks, while also serving as a lucrative revenue producer.

According to the 2018 LIMA Survey of the Licensing Industry, the three largest categories of licensed products for corporate brands were food & beverage, apparel and housewares.

1.2.5 Entertainment

Entertainment and character properties are, of course, the most visible of all types of licensing properties and always produce the largest revenues in the industry worldwide.

Entertainment properties come from virtually all segments of the entertainment industry, although the largest source of such properties is Hollywood through its motion pictures and television shows.

For example, the SPONGEBOB character featured in Nickelodeon's hit television show *SPONGE BOB SquarePants*, has become a major force in children's licensing as well as the subject of dozens of promotional programs for almost all the major retailers and fast food chains.

Similarly, the *Sesame Street* characters, ELMO, BIG BIRD and OSCAR THE GROUCH, have become licensing legends due, in large measure, to the constant exposure that these properties receive every day on television. Such children's characters as MICKEY MOUSE, WINNIE THE POOH, BUGS BUNNY and PETER RABBIT found their origins in various media formats in the early 20th century and remain popular today because of their continued media exposure.

Blockbuster Hollywood motion pictures have produced some of the most successful licensing programs in the industry, the best example being the Star War films. In recent years there has been a string of motion pictures based on superheroes, e.g., SPIDERMAN, HULK, BATMAN, and SUPERMAN, that have spawned successful licensing programs. The tremendous licensing success of such characters has resulted in the studios creating their own "Consumer Products Divisions", a/k/a licensing departments, responsible for the licensing of their properties.

Highly popular toys and video games have also been successful incubators for entertainment properties. BARBIE started out as a popular fashion doll for Mattel and, through licensing, has become a franchise. Similarly, the GI JOE action figure by Hasbro has been extensively merchandised for a wide array of products. MARIO, a featured character in an early Nintendo video game called Donkey Kong, has not only been extensively licensed, but has morphed into Nintendo's official "mascot."

Interestingly, this category has expanded with the growth of technology. Software, video games and mobile phones have made significant use of entertainment properties as the basis for games, wallpaper and even accessories such as game controllers, mobile phone cases and even licensed earbuds.

According to the 2018 LIMA Survey of the Licensing Industry, the three largest categories of licensed products for entertainment properties were toys & games, software and video games and apparel.

1.2.6 Fashion

Fashion or designer properties have been a staple of the licensing industry for years due, in large measure, to the wide variety of different properties available and the vast number of products for which they are licensed. One need only walk through the clothing section of any department store or, for that matter, look at the different fashion brands in his or her own closet to see the impact that these properties have had. The reason for their success is very simple and one that retailers readily understand: the presence of a fashion brand on a product *sells*.

Consumers have come to expect seeing a fashion brand—any fashion brand—on an article of apparel since it conveys the impression that the underlying product is better designed and of a higher quality than the generic version. Irrespective of whether that proposition is true or not, in fashion licensing, perception becomes reality and, as a result, a vast number of clothing products and related accessories today carry some fashion brand—either that of a real designer or a "house" brand to convey the same impression.

Designers brands such as PIERRE CARDIN, ANNE KLEIN, BILL BLASS, OSCAR DE LA RENTA, and CALVIN KLEIN clearly started the trend and have paved the way for the next generation of designers, including TOMMY HILFIGER, DONNA KARAN and VERA WANG and now TORY BURCH and KATE SPADE. Spin-offs or extensions of these properties, such as TOMMY or POLO, have enjoyed enormous popularity.

Fashion brands don't always have to be a designer's name. They can, instead, convey a certain lifestyle image, e.g., NAUTICA, FUBU, TOMMY BAHAMA, GUESS? and HANG TEN. Many retailers have developed their own fashion brands, e.g., the ROUTE 66 apparel line at K-Mart, or Walmart's ATHLETIC WORKS brand.

The names of some of the famous design houses are also licensable, as demonstrated by the success of the CHANEL and LOUIS VUITTON lines of licensed products where good design prevails.

Some of the top catalogs have not only branded their own products but licensed out their names for ancillary products such as the EDDIE BAUER line of SUV's by Ford. That said, some fashion designers are uncomfortable with the idea of licensing, since they would like the public to believe that all products bearing their brands are produced by their company, not by a third-party licensee.

At the end of the day, however, fashion licensing is all about design and quality. Fashion properties that feature good design and offer quality and value will ultimately prevail and bring the consumer back, year after year.

According to the 2018 LIMA Survey of the Licensing Industry, the three largest categories of licensed products for fashion properties were apparel, accessories, and health and beauty products.

1.2.7 Music

The music industry rocks when it comes to producing hot licensing properties. Such bands and performers (alive or dead) as the BEATLES, ROLLING STONES, TAYLOR SWIFT, KATY PERRY, LADY GAGA, BEYONCE, ELVIS PRESLEY, MICHAEL JACKSON, PINK, JUSTIN TIMBERLAKE AND FLEETWOOD MACK have not only sold a vast amount of merchandise at their concerts and while on tour (called "venue sales"), their licensed products have also found their way into traditional channels of retail distribution.

The JESSICA SIMPSON brand has proven to be enormously successful at retail, most notably through the sale of licensed shoes, handbags and accessories, selling over a billion dollars in licensed products over its first ten years. USHER has licensed his name (and persona) for a wide range of products, including cologne and aftershave lotion. Similarly, the total concert merchandise sales of BRITANY SPEARS' licensed products have been in the tens of millions of dollars, the BRITTANY SPEARS' line of cosmetics for Elizabeth Arden and JENNIFER LOPEZ's line of toiletries have all sold well.

Rock bands have likewise come to recognize the power of their brand. At their height, the all-female British group ATOMIC KITTEN even created its own branded line of clothing called AK BRANDS. The use of music videos has proven to be an excellent way to sell branded merchandise for rock stars, as Australian pop star KYLIE MINOGUE proved when she appeared in a music video that successfully promoted her licensed line of lingerie for Agent Provocateur. Licensing has also penetrated the growing electronic dance music market, as popular DJ's such as DJ DEADMAU5 now have their own lines products including apparel and headphones.

According to the 2018 LIMA Survey of the Licensing Industry, the three largest categories of licensed products for music properties were apparel, health and beauty products and gaming.

1.2.8 Non-Profits

Foundations, organizations, charities and associations regularly use licensing to both convey their message to the public as well as a source of fund raising. Non-profit organizations, such as the American Society for the Prevention of Cruelty to Animals ("ASPCA"), have embraced licensing for these purposes. Revenue generated from the ASPCA's licensing program helps fund its national humane initiatives while promoting brand recognition in the minds of consumers.

Similarly, the World Wildlife Fund ("WWF") works closely with companies and individuals in marketing partnerships, where licensees are permitted to use its PANDA logo and WWF name. Again, such programs serve the important dual function of not only generating royalty income for the WWF but also of building awareness for its activities. In addition, the WWF engages in cause-related marketing promotions and sponsorship programs.

Some associations even set up their own related entities to directly engage in licensing. For example, the American Association of Retired People ("AARP") created AARP Financial Inc. to license and endorse credit cards, insurance products and financial services. The AARP name appears on mutual funds, IRAs, CD's, and a group that provides financial advice to its members. New York Life sells AARP Life Insurance policies and annuities; The Hartford sells AARP-branded auto and home insurance to AARP members; and other "partners" sell AARP motorcycle and mobile-home insurance. An AARP Visa credit card is offered by Chase Bank.

According to the 2018 LIMA Survey the three largest product categories carrying Non-Profit Properties were apparel, food & beverage and gifts & novelties.

1.2.9 Publishing

Many of the most popular entertainment properties trace their roots back to the publishing industry, particularly the children's book market.

HARRY POTTER HARDBACKS

There is, of course, a fine line between pure publishing properties and entertainment properties since many entertainment properties came from the publishing industry and vice-versa. For example, the PEANUTS and GARFIELD characters grew out of syndicated comic strips of the same name and the popular characters

PETER RABBIT and WINNIE THE POOH first appeared in children's books. Many of the superhero characters that became enormously popular because of blockbuster motion pictures originated in comic books, including SUPERMAN, BATMAN, and SPIDERMAN. The HARRY POTTER franchise is the current leading example of successful publishing to licensing property.

According to LIMA's 2017 Survey of the Licensing Industry, the three largest categories of licensed products bearing publishing properties were home décor, gifts and lawn and garden products.

1.2.10 Sports

For decades, sports properties have consistently been among the most popular licensing properties due, no doubt, to the worldwide passion for athletics. Sports licensing is a global business and, with few exceptions, appeals to a very wide group of potential consumers. While the popularity of certain sports such as soccer, basketball, cricket and hockey transcend geographical boundaries, others such as baseball and football are enormously popular, mainly in the United States.

The major professional sports leagues in the United States, i.e., Major League Baseball, the National Football League, the National Basketball Association and the National Hockey League, all have strong licensing programs that are run by the "Properties" divisions of their respective league offices. These entities control the licensing rights for all their team logos and properties. Thus, if a company wants to take a license to use, for example, the NEW YORK GIANTS logo, on its product, it would need to coordinate this through NFL Properties. The same is true for each of the other professional sports leagues.

Team names and logos are not the only type of licensable sports properties, certain individual players are themselves equally popular. Professional athletes, such as LEBRON JAMES, STEPHEN CURRY, TOM BRADY and CLAYTON KERSHAW, are all featured in very prominent and successful licensing programs.

In professional sports, the licensing rights for individual players are typically handled by the player or their agent, while "group licensing rights" are typically handled through the respective players association for that sport, e.g., the NFL Players Association.

Since sports licensing will frequently involve the licensing of both teams and players, it can get complicated. For example, if someone wanted to run a promotion featuring all members of the Los Angeles Dodgers that also included the DODGERS mark, they would need to apply for a group license from the MLB Players Association for the names and likenesses of these players *and* MLB Properties for the right to use the DODGERS mark.

Professional sports leagues and players are not the only sources of sports properties. The United States Olympic Committee ("USOC") has long relied on its licensing and sponsorship programs to generate revenue to help underwrite its costs. Licensees regularly pay royalties to the USOC to use the OLYMPICS LOGO, while sponsors pay sponsorship fees and provide goods and services for the right to be called an "Official Sponsor" of the program. Some of

these fees are substantial because of the esteem that a sponsor gains through its ability to associate itself with one of the strongest and most recognized marks in the world.

The International Federation of Association Football ("FIFA"), which is the international governing body for soccer and who oversees the FIFA World Cup tournaments, also relies extensively on licensing to support its efforts.

Tennis and golf stars such as MARIA SHARAPOVA and TIGER WOODS, and soccer stars such as LIONEL MESSI and CHRISTIANO RINALDO look to licensing as a major source of their income. Not to be outdone, the governing bodies for these sports, e.g., the PGA, LPGA, and USTA, all regularly license out the use of their names and logos to raise money thereby help to support the growth of their respective sports.

According to the 2018 LIMA Survey of the Licensing Industry, the three largest categories of licensed products for sports properties were apparel, gifts & novelties and software and video games.

1.3 Types of Licensed Products

In the early years of licensing, most licensed products were low end, consumer products, typically called "buttons, badges, and posters." That has changed dramatically as the industry has grown and become more established. Today, licensing has expanded into almost every imaginable product and service category, including those that feature high-end luxury goods and services.

If one simply reviewed the Classification List published by the United States Patent & Trademark Office, they would find that there is at least some licensing activity in more than 30 of the 42 different classes. See Appendix-16 for a list of the trademark classes.

According to LIMA's 2018 Annual Survey of the Licensing Industry, the following categories of licensed products generate most of the licensing revenue in the industry:
- Apparel: (Adult, Kids)
- Accessories: (Head Wear, Jewelry & Watches, Etc.)
- Food/Beverage: (Beverage, Candy, Etc.)
- Footwear: (Adult, Kids)
- Home Decor: (Furniture, Home Furnishings)
- Gifts/Novelties: (Collectibles, Gift, Etc.)
- Health/Beauty: (Health, Cosmetics, Etc.)
- Housewares: (Kitchenware, other Houseware Products)
- Music/Video
- Infant Products (Apparel, Furniture, Accessories, Etc.)
- Publishing (Novels, Story Books, Calendars, Etc.)
- Sporting Goods (Apparel, Equipment, Etc.)
- Paper Products/School Supplies (Art, Greeting Cards, Lunch Boxes, Bags/Totes, Etc.)
- Toys/Games: (Dolls/Action Figures, Games, Pre-School, Etc.)
- Software/Videogames: (Handheld, Software, Accessories, Etc.)

Of these possible categories, the three categories that recorded the most sales were apparel, toys & games and software and video games. A chart illustrating estimated revenues by product category for 2017 is as follows:

Global Retail Sales of Licensed Merchandise, By Product Category, 2017

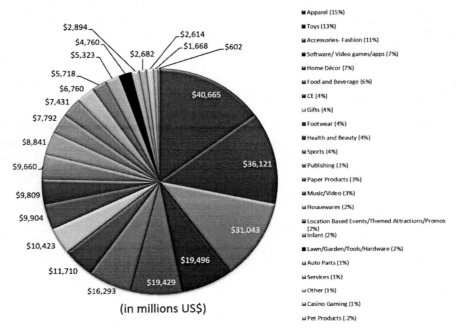

(in millions US$)

Legend:
- Apparel (15%)
- Toys (13%)
- Accessories- Fashion (11%)
- Software/ Video games/apps (7%)
- Home Décor (7%)
- Food and Beverage (6%)
- CE (4%)
- Gifts (4%)
- Footwear (4%)
- Health and Beauty (4%)
- Sports (4%)
- Publishing (3%)
- Paper Products (3%)
- Music/Video (3%)
- Housewares (2%)
- Location Based Events/Themed Attractions/Promos (2%)
- Infant (2%)
- Lawn/Garden/Tools/Hardware (2%)
- Auto Parts (1%)
- Services (1%)
- Other (1%)
- Casino Gaming (1%)
- Pet Products (.2%)

Values shown on chart: $40,665, $36,121, $31,043, $19,496, $19,429, $16,293, $11,710, $10,423, $9,904, $9,809, $9,660, $8,841, $7,792, $7,431, $6,760, $5,718, $5,323, $4,760, $2,894, $2,682, $2,614, $1,668, $602

While the industry has come to expect licensed toys and t-shirts, there have been some "non-traditional" licenses granted over the years that one prominent licensing agent categorized as, "What Were You Thinking???" Examples of these "non-traditional" licenses include an INDIANAPOLIS COLTS bird bath, NORMAN ROCKWELL boxer shorts, a WIZARD OF OZ Menorah, MICKEY MOUSE full sized toilet seats, a KISS casket and WWE talking soap. *Time* magazine published an article on the "Top Ten Oddball Celebrity Branded Products," which included: HULK HOGAN's Pastamania, SHAQUILLE O'NEAL's Shaq-Fu video game, STEVEN SEAGAL's Lightning Bolt energy drink and DANNY DEVITO's Limoncello.

1.4 Advantages Offered by Licensing and Reasons for Its Popularity

What makes licensing so popular? The obvious answer is that *it sells products*. From a property owner's perspective, there is little doubt that the opportunity to generate additional royalty income is the primary motivating factor behind setting up a licensing program. Licensing also provides many secondary benefits, including:

- Providing additional exposure for the licensor's underlying products or services;
- Allowing the licensor to better leverage its advertising expenditures;
- Providing a hedge against the normal fluctuations of a licensor's basic business model;

- Allowing the licensor to achieve a high return on a minimal investment;
- Permitting the licensor to expand into new markets and test different new product areas;
- Providing a terrific merchandising advantage for a brand in a different context;
- Permitting the licensor to test for possible future expansion into other countries;
- Allowing the licensor to expand into other levels and areas of retail;
- Allowing the licensor to further promote products of a type where there are governmental restrictions on what can be said;
- Allowing a property owner to re-launch a brand or product line;
- Controlling how a brand is positioned and appears; and
- Strengthening the licensor's underlying trademark rights by expanding the breadth of the goods or services on which the brand is used.

For the manufacturer, or licensee, licensing provides the following advantages:

- Reducing the cost of product development;
- Offering a cost-efficient way to expand into other product categories;
- Creating instant consumer awareness and credibility using a well-known, trusted brand or property;
- Enhancing manufacturer's products with positive attributes;
- Providing a shortcut to the marketplace without the time and cost of building a brand from scratch;
- Providing marketing clout which can help sell other non-licensed products;
- Allowing the manufacturer to create a product line that will generate recognition and appeal to retail buyers;
- Allowing manufacturers to limit the size of their art and design staffs; and
- Giving the manufacturer the ability to compete against larger, more established, companies.

While the benefits of licensing to a licensor far outweigh any potential risks, there are risks, to wit:

- Losing control of a property through shoddy manufacturing, poor quality, use on inappropriate products and negative publicity;
- Dilution of the core brand image or value;
- Shortened lifespan by oversaturation of the market; and
- If the licensor fails to live up to its responsibilities, it may jeopardize its ability to attract good licensees in the future.

The Licensing Industry Merchandiser's Association ("LIMA"), on its website,[1] identified the following advantages that merchandising offers to licensees:

- **Gaining the consumer awareness and marketing benefit of a well-known brand, character, logo, design, etc.** The most obvious benefit to a manufacturer or service provider that licenses a brand, character, design or other piece

---

[1] LIMA Website, 2018 at http://www.licensing.org/education/intro-to-licensing/why-license/

of intellectual property is the marketing power it brings to the product. It can take hundreds of thousands or millions of dollars to build a brand from scratch, and licensing represents a way for a manufacturer to take advantage of all the brand building and image building that has gone on before. A child in a toy store doesn't seek "an action figure." He's generally looking for a character he's fond of. Faced with a choice among several cleaning implements, a shopper might be drawn by one that bears the brand of a well- known cleaning fluid, rather than a more generic label. In making the decision about whether to take on a license, a manufacturer often weighs the potential royalty payments against the cost of building a brand on its own.

- **Moving into new distribution channels.** Taking on a license might help a manufacturer whose brand has been marketed in, for example, mass merchandise outlets, to market a more upscale, high quality line in specialty stores or department stores that wouldn't carry the lower end products.

- **Reducing in-house costs.** A manufacturer who licenses artwork or designs to be applied to home textiles, wall coverings, housewares, or on apparel has less reliance on in-house art staffs that would otherwise need to be maintained.

- **Enhancing authenticity and credibility.** The publisher of a car-racing videogame might license a host of well-known automotive brands and car models to lend legitimacy and authenticity to the game. Similarly, a maker of automotive parts or accessories will license the car brand to establish it in the consumer's mind that its products will work seamlessly with the cars of the parent brand.

Chapter 2
History of Licensing

2.1 The Properties

2.1.1 The Beginning

Although there is little historical documentation establishing exactly when the licensing of famous brands or characters began, rumor has it that its origin traces back to the Middle Ages when Roman Catholic Popes granted licenses to local tax collectors for the right to be associated with the Church in exchange for the payment of "royalties" to the Vatican. It is believed that this practice continued for several years and formed the basis for what would eventually become modern day licensing.

The practice of paying royalties for the right to use another's name or likeness is believed to have begun in the 18th Century when two British ladies of nobility were reported to have permitted (or licensed) a cosmetics manufacturer to use their name on its products and, in exchange, would receive a percentage of the revenues generated from the sale of such products.

Licensing, as we know it today, began in earnest in the 1870's when it is believed that Adolphus Busch allowed manufacturers to use the name BUSCH on a wine key that included a small blade, foil cutter and a basic cork screw to enhance sales of the key.

One of the most famous licensing characters of all time, PETER RABBIT, traces its origins back to 1901 when Beatrix Potter designed and patented a soft toy based on the PETER RABBIT character that had appeared in a book she wrote and self-published in 1901. In 1902, Ms. Potter entered into an agreement with the British publisher, Frederick Warne & Co., who then published a color version that same year. It is believed that PETER RABBIT was the first licensed character.

In 1902, New York Herald cartoonist, Richard Outcault, created the BUSTER BROWN character as part of a comic strip and, two years later, began licensing the rights to the character to more than 20 licensees. One of the licensees used the character on a shoe that was introduced in the 1904 World's Fair. That same year, the Brown Shoe Company purchased the licensing rights to the BUSTER BROWN property, reportedly for $200.

Former President, Theodore "Teddy" Roosevelt, is associated with the creation of the name TEDDY BEAR, which started out as a licensing property before becoming the generic

name for a toy product. It was reported that after his presidency, Roosevelt had gone on a bear hunt in Mississippi but, despite spending three days in the woods, never saw a single bear. Roosevelt then came upon an old, injured bear, which he could not bring himself to shoot. Instead, he ordered it to be put down to end its suffering. Political cartoonist, Clifford Berrymore, published a political cartoon about the episode in various newspapers. A shopkeeper, Morris Michtom, saw the cartoon, contacted the former President and asked for permission to call a pair of stuffed bears that he had in his store window, TEDDY BEARS. The store would ultimately become the Ideal Novelty and Toy Company and the name TEDDY BEAR was eventually licensed to toy companies with the royalties used to establish the National Parks.

The GIRL SCOUTS (originally named Girls Guides of America) organization was founded in 1912 and soon, thereafter, began licensing its name for a line of "Official" GIRL SCOUTS products. It is believed that over the years, the mark has appeared on more than 1800 different products, including the famous GIRL SCOUTS cookies.

The RAGGEDY ANN character was created in 1915 by Johnny Gruelle as a soft doll and, three years later, was introduced as part of a book entitled *Raggedy Ann Stories*. In 1920, her brother RAGGEDY ANDY, who dressed in a sailor suit and hat, was introduced as a sequel to that work. RAGGEDY ANN was inducted into the National Toy Hall of Fame in 2002 and her brother joined her in 2007.

LITTLE ORPHAN ANNIE was created by Harold Gray in 1924 and first appeared as a comic strip in the *Chicago Tribune*. The comic strip was published for more than 80 years by Tribune Media Services until the final installment appeared on June 13, 2010. In 1924, a LITLLE ORPHAN ANNIE radio show was launched with Ovaltine as its sponsor.

In 1926, A.A. Milne published in England the first of what would become a series of books on the adventures of WINNIE THE POOH. The books met with moderate success but when a U.S. based licensing agent, Stephen Slesinger, acquired the U.S. and Canadian licensing, television and recording rights to the character in the early 1930's, a licensing legend was born. Slesinger, a licensing pioneer, immediately launched an aggressive licensing program around the character that would reportedly generate more than $50 million in licensing revenues. In the 1940's, POOH became the first Sunday morning television cartoon series. Disney acquired all rights to the character in 1961 and, soon thereafter, entered one of the first direct to retail licenses with Sears for the property. Today, POOH is a global icon and thousands of different POOH licensed products are sold around the world. POOH was the winner of LIMA's License of the Year Award in 1996 and possibly the most famous licensing character of all time.

MICKEY MOUSE was created by Walt Disney and Ub Iwerks on November 28, 1928 as a replacement for another Disney character, OSWALD THE LUCKY RABBIT. The character was based on a cartoon called STEAMBOAT WILLIE that had appeared earlier that year. Disney didn't waste any time in licensing the character for a variety of merchandise, including a license to Waldburger, Tanner in Switzerland for MICKEY & MINNIE handkerchiefs. MICKEY MOUSE would go on to become a corporate icon for Disney and is recognizable in virtually every country in the civilized world.

BUCK ROGERS (originally named Anthony Rogers) first appeared in a comic strip in 1929 and then, later, in a series of motion pictures and television shows. Created by Philip Francis Nowlan, the character was an immediate hit as a licensing property and pioneered character-based, licensed merchandising. One of the most popular BUCK ROGERS toys was the Rocket Pistol that was introduced at the 1934 Toy Fair in New York and which sold out at Macy's in less than three hours after it was introduced.

LOONEY TUNES started out in 1930 as an animated cartoon series produced by Harman-Ising Pictures. In 1944, Warner Bros. purchased the rights and library and continued production through the 1960's. It was the first animated theatrical series and would ultimately serve as the cornerstone of Warner Bros. licensing group, the LICENSING CORPORATION OF AMERICA, headed by JOE GRANT another of the industry's pi-  oneers. The series featured such highly recognizable characters as BUGS BUNNY, DAFFY DUCK, PORKY PIG, ELMER FUDD, SYLVESTER, TWEETY, WILE E. COYOTE, ROAD RUNNER, YOSEMITE SAM, and SPEEDY GONZALES.

BETTY BOOP is an animated cartoon character created by Max Fleischer with help from animators including Grim Natwick. She originally appeared in the *Talkartoon* and *Betty Boop* film series, which were produced by Fleischer Studios and released by Paramount Pictures. She has also been featured in comic strips and mass merchandising.

The child actress, SHIRLEY TEMPLE, began her career in 1932 and it immediately skyrocketed. In 1935, she received a special Academy Award and would go on to star in such blockbusters as *Curly Top* and *Heidi*. Her licensing program quickly followed. She was reported to have made more than $100,000 in royalties before 1935 and her licensing income for 1936 was reportedly more than $200,000. Ideal Toy produced the first SHIRLEY TEMPLE doll in the 1930's and it is believed that more than $41 million of these dolls were sold by 1941.

SUPERMAN, a fictional, super-hero created by Jerry Siegel and Joe Shuster, was created in 1932 and the rights were eventually acquired by Detective Comics, Inc. (now DC Comics) in 1938. With the distinctive costume having a large "S" on his chest and cape, SUPERMAN was perhaps the first super-hero character and would eventually be licensed for a host of different products, from comic books to licensed capes. The earliest reported licensed SUPERMAN product was a 1939 button signifying membership in the SUPERMAN Club of America. By 1942, sales of SUPERMAN comic books surpassed 1.5 million copies and the Navy Department even provided copies of the comic books as part of standard supplies for U.S. Marines. The SUPERMAN property remains popular today, fueled by the release of blockbuster motion pictures by Warner Bros.

One of the major licensors, DC COMICS, was created in 1934 as National Allied Publications. It would ultimately become one of the largest and most successful comic book publishers, developing and popularizing such characters as SUPERMAN, BATMAN, WONDER WOMAN, GREEN LANTERN, CAPTAIN MARVEL, and CATWOMAN. DC Comics is now the publishing division of DC Entertainment Inc., a Warner Bros. subsidiary.

HOPALONG CASSIDY, played by William Boyd, first appeared on the big screen in 1935 and achieved immediate success. The character was originally created in 1904 by Clarence E. Mulford as part of a series of books, but it was Boyd's film version in 1935 that would popularize it. Boyd appeared on the covers of *Look*, *Life*, and *Time* and, reportedly, earned millions of dollars from licensing and endorsement deals. It is believed that HOPALONG CASSIDY was the first character ever licensed for a child's lunch box and more than 600,000 licensed lunch boxes were reportedly sold in the first year of sales. By 1950, there were more than 100 HOPALONG CASSIDY licensees selling more than $70 million in licensed products.

In 1938, Stephen Slesinger and Fred Harman introduced the western comic strip, RED RYDER, and it was immediately syndicated by Newspaper Enterprise Association. Slesinger, of POOH fame, developed a successful licensing program based on the property, with licenses for comic books, novels, rodeos and various products. RED RYDER BB guns were first produced in 1938 under license by Daisy Outdoor Products and are still in production today, making it the longest continuous licenses in the history of licensing.

MARVEL COMICS, which would ultimately become a major force in licensing, was formed in 1939 by Martin Goodman. Its first publication, entitled *MARVEL Comics #1*, appeared in October 1939 and introduced several new superheroes, including, the HUMAN TORCH. MARVEL would go on to develop some of the most famous superhero characters in the industry, many of which were extensively licensed and adapted for motion pictures and television. Some of its most famous superhero characters include SPIDER-MAN, IRON MAN, X-MEN, WOLVERINE, the HULK, FANTASTIC FOUR, CAPTAIN AMERICA, and GHOST RIDER.

The BATMAN character, created by Bob Kane and Bill Finger, also debuted in 1939, when it first appeared in a DC Comics publication. BATMAN's secret identity was Bruce Wayne, a successful American playboy who would put on a bat costume and working with his partner, Robin, fight crime in Gotham City. It spawned such memorable characters as the JOKER, PENGUIN and BATGIRL and the character's popularity increased in 1989 after the release of the *BATMAN* motion picture. *Forbes* magazine estimated the BATMAN character to be the 9th "richest" fictional character in history, with revenues of at least $5.8 billion.

2.1.2 The 1940's

The 1940's represented not only the end of the Great Depression but the creation of some of today's most popular properties.

The ARCHIE property, created by John Goldwater, Vic Bloom and Bob Montana, made its first appearance in December 1941 in *PEP Comics* #22 and, the following year, would become the basis of its own publication. Archie Comics has developed some of the most recognizable characters in the industry, including JUGHEAD, BETTY & VERONICA, JOSIE & THE PUSSYCATS and SABRINA THE TEENAGE WITCH. These

characters have all translated into motion pictures and television shows and have been heavily licensed along the way.

THOMAS THE TANK ENGINE, a fictional locomotive, first appeared in 1946 in a series of books by Rev. W. Awdry and his son, Christopher. The property would lay somewhat dormant, however, until 1979 when a British producer named Britt Allcroft discovered it and invested all her life savings to turn the character into a television series called *Thomas the Tank Engine and Friends* (later, *Thomas and Friends*, with Ringo Starr as the narrator). The television series and resultant licensing program were immediate hits and THOMAS has been licensed for a wide range of products ranging from toy trains to videos, books, apparel and toys. It was LIMA's License of the Year for 1993.

The HOWDY DOODY show was one of the most popular children's television shows from 1947 until 1960. Created by Bob Smith, Martin Stone, Allan Stone and Roger Muir, it featured a red-headed, freckled face puppet named HOWDY DOODY who was an outgrowth of puppeteer Frank Paris and host Buffalo Bob Smith. Rhoda Mann built the puppet and was its operator. It was one of the first shows to be broadcast in color and, because of its enormous popularity, was heavily merchandised by Allan Stone. In

1955, for example, its producers published a 24-page catalog that featured such licensed products as puppets, various food products including apples and kale, toys and clothing, comic books and other publications. Howdy Doody even ran for president in 1948 supported by "Howdy Doody for President" buttons.

In 1947, Bill France, Sr. created the National Association for Stock Car Auto Racing (NASCAR). It would eventually become the largest sanctioning body of stock car racing in the world and the sponsor of the three largest racing series. NASCAR currently sanctions over 1500 races in more than 100 race tracks throughout the United States, Canada, Japan, Mexico and Australia. Its 75 million fans purchase over $1 billion of licensed NASCAR products every year, most notably apparel and die-cast autos.

2.1.3 The 1950's

The decade commenced with the creation of PEANUTS, which would become one of the most popular licensing properties of all time. Based on a syndicated comic strip created by Charles M. Schulz, it featured CHARLIE BROWN, SNOOPY and LUCY. The strip ran for almost 50 years until Schultz's death in 2000, with 17,897 strips published during that period. At its peak, the comic strip had a readership of 355 million in 75 different countries in 21 languages. It was reported that the strip and the related licensing earned Schulz more than $1 billion. PEANUTS characters have been  licensed for virtually every product imaginable on earth....and beyond. NASA's Apollo 10 lunar module was named SNOOPY and the command module was named CHARLIE BROWN.

In 1952, we saw the first musician get into the licensing arena, when jazz guitarist, LES PAUL joined forces with Gibson Guitar to produce a LES PAUL branded guitar. The product, which was a collaboration between the two, debuted to much fanfare and, over the years, has acquired somewhat iconic status as the instrument of choice for many leading guitarists, including Slash, formerly of Guns 'N Roses, and Trey Anastasio the front man for Phish. Versions of the guitar are still produced today.

The first PLAYBOY magazine was published in 1953 by Hugh Heffner with Marilyn Monroe on the cover and as its centerfold. Not only did the magazine set the world on its heels, but it spawned a host of licensed PLAYBOY products, the first being a pair of PLAYBOY cufflinks that was introduced in 1959 and worn by all the Playboy Bunnies at its clubs. It has been reported that the company currently derives about 10% of its revenues from its licensing division, Playboy Enterprises, which licenses the PLAYBOY name, the RABBIT HEAD design and a host of images. One of its more interesting licensed products is a case of wine featuring images of classic Playmates. More than $1.5 billion of licensed products are sold annually on a worldwide basis.

In the 1950's, ABC Television popularized the American frontiersman, DAVY CROCKETT, in a series of television shows and a motion picture starring Fess Parker. While the show and movie were moderately successful, the sales of licensed DAVY CROCKETT products sold extraordinarily well. At its peak, it was reported that DAVY CROCKETT coonskin caps were selling at the rate of 5,000 per day. More than $300 million of

licensed products were sold by 1955 and, by 2001, licensed sales topped $2 billion.

The public's fascination with western sagas continued in 1954, when a television series, staring Gail Davis, debuted about western legend ANNIE OAKLEY. She was a female sharpshooter who regularly performed in exhibitions such as *Buffalo Bill's Wild West* show. The ANNIE OAKLEY character was licensed for a wide range of children's products, including toys, trading cards and apparel.

The JAMES BOND 007 character was created by writer Ian Fleming in 1953 and was later featured in twelve novels and 22 motion pictures, the longest running of which was the 1962 feature *Dr. No*. The licensing program started at LCA with "Goldfinger" and LCA represented it for many years. The JAMES BOND 007 character was heavily licensed, particularly for toys, comic books, men's cologne and video games. The first video game was released in 1983 by Parker Brothers for the Atari, Commodore and Colecovision platforms. Other JAMES BOND video games have been produced by Electronic Arts and Activision based on *Goldeneye 007*.

Without question, one of the most extensively licensed properties of all time is ELVIS PRESLEY who hit the world stage in 1954 and would go on to redefine the meaning of success for a celebrity license—both before and after the singer's death.

Called the "King of Rock and Roll," ELVIS PRESLEY became a pop icon and is the best-selling solo artist of all time. His licensing program has been equally successful. Elvis Presley Enterprises licenses all ELVIS related properties, including his name, image and voice, song titles such as *Blue Suede Shoes*, *Jailhouse Rock* and *Hound Dog* and words and phrases that have become associated with ELVIS, including GRACELAND, TCB and KING OF ROCK AND ROLL. It's been reported that Elvis Presley Enterprises' licensing revenues in 2009 (more than 30 years after his death) were $24.3 million.

Jim Henson's KERMIT THE FROG was first introduced in 1955 as a five-minute spot for WRC-TV's *Sam and Friends*. KERMIT would ultimately become the host of his own show, *The Muppet Show*, as well as appear regularly on *Sesame Street*. In 1970, KERMIT would star in *The Muppet Movie* and his single, The Rainbow Connection, would reach 25th on the Billboard Hot 100. The character has been used extensively in advertising programs and KERMIT is recognizable throughout the world. Not surprisingly, sales of licensed KERMIT merchandise have remained strong over the years.

Sports licensing really began to take hold in the 1960's due, in large part, to the efforts of

Pete Rozelle who, in 1956, became General Manager of the then Los Angeles Rams. Rozelle recognized the licensing potential of the LOS ANGELES RAMS name and logo and aggressively sought licensees for a variety of different licensed products—to both help promote the team and to raise additional revenue. Rozelle's genius was quickly recognized and, in 1959, he would become Commissioner of the National Football League. Rozelle oversaw the development of one of the most successful professional sports leagues in the world, with a licensing program that quickly emerged as a model for all other sports to follow.

HANNA-BARBERA Productions was formed in 1957 by animation directors William Hanna and Joseph Barbera, in  partnership with Columbia Pictures and would go on to dominate American television animation for fifty years, producing such successful cartoon shows as the FLINTSTONES, SCOOBY-DOO, YOGI BEAR SHOW, JETSONS and the HUCKLEBERRY HOUND show.

The SMURFS property was first introduced in 1958 as a comic strip in a Belgian magazine, *Spirou*, by cartoonist Peyo and would soon grow to become a comic and television franchise. The comic strip was translated into English and later became a television series produced by Hanna-Barbera Productions. Licensing of SMURF figurines commenced in 1959 by Dupuis Animation Studios. Schleich, a German toy company, became the largest producer of SMURF figurines, many of which were given away as promotional items. It has been reported that since their introduction, more than 300 million SMURF figures have been sold.

PADDINGTON BEAR, that polite fictional bear with a hat and suitcase who loves marmalade sandwiches, made his first appearance in 1958 in the first of a series of books written by Michael Bond and illustrated by Peggy Fortnum. The books would eventually be published in more than 30 languages and sell more than 30 million copies. Over the years, it is reported that more than 265 licenses were granted for PADDINGTON products in virtually every civilized country in the world. The character was so popular in England that the character was featured on a coin and postage stamp.

The 1950's closed out with the launch by Mattel of the first BARBIE doll at New York Toy Fair in March 1959. BARBIE was designed by Ruth Handler and was marketed as a "Teenage Fashion Model." The reception was extraordinary, as product literally flew off retailers' shelves. Mattel sold more than 350,000 units in the first year after introduction. BARBIE would go on to become a cultural icon—a section of Times Square in New York City was named Barbie Boulevard for a week and Andy Warhol created a painting of the character. It has also become a licensing franchise and the BARBIE property has been licensed for virtually every conceivable type of licensed product. There are even pop-up BARBIE stores in cities around the world.

2.1.4 The 1960's

The 1960's opened with the debut of the FLINTSTONES, an animated television sitcom produced by Hanna-Barbera which ran from September 1960 until April 1966. It portrayed a working class, stone-age family headed by Fred Flintstone, his wife Wilma, and their neighbors, Barney and Betty Rubble. Many believe that it was an animated satire of the Honeymooners and was one of the first television shows ever to be broadcast in color. The FLINTSTONES licensing program pursued new and different types of licensed products. For example, Miles Laboratories developed

a line of children's FLINTSTONE vitamins in the shape of the show's characters and Post Foods sold a line of PEBBLES cereals that are still being sold today.

1960 was also the year that John Lennon, Paul McCartney, George Harrison and Ringo Starr joined forces in Liverpool, England to form the what would become the most successful rock group of all time—the BEATLES. Almost immediately, the group was a household name, both musically and in licensing. Their opening song, *I Want to Hold Your Hand*, sold more than 2.6 million copies in the United States during a two-week period and their initial appearance on *The Ed Sullivan Show* had a 40 percent market share. BEATLES merchandise sold as fast as the group's music. It was estimated that Americans spent $50 million in 1964 for licensed BEATLES merchandise. Remco Toys ramped up to manufacture 100,000 BEATLES dolls but received orders for an additional 500,000, while Lowell Toy sold BEATLES wigs at the rate of 35,000 per day. Some considered BEATLES licensing as the biggest marketing opportunity since Disney created MICKEY MOUSE.

In 1963, the National Football League formed a wholly owned subsidiary called NFL Properties and charged it with the responsibility for licensing the name and logos of its teams and related properties, including the soon to be created SUPER BOWL. It was the first licensing division of any professional sports league. In time, NFL Properties would become one of the most dominating sports licensing groups in the world, with retail sales of licensed NFL products believed to top $3 billion. The other sports leagues soon followed suit—MLB Properties was formed in 1966 and NBA Properties was formed in 1967.

Scholastic Books published the first of what would become the CLIFFORD THE BIG RED DOG book series in 1963. Written by William Bridwell, the series was at least partially responsible for launching Scholastic as a major publisher. The featured character, CLIFFORD, entered life as the runt of the litter but would grow to over 25 feet long because of his owner's love. CLIFFORD would be featured in videos, as a television series and on a host of different licensed products.

The popularity of American folk heroes continued throughout the decade. In 1964, the television series *Daniel Boone* debuted, featuring Fess Parker as the main character, DANIEL BOONE. The show also starred country western singer Jimmy Dean and former football star, Roosevelt Grier and would remain on the air through 1970. Like the other shows involving folk heroes, it was heavily licensed.

G.I. JOE was introduced by Hasbro in 1964, originally as the *Adventures of G.I. Joe*, but later as simply G.I. JOE to downplay its war theme. The toy would go on to create the "action  figure" category of toys. While G.I. JOE characters are not superheroes, *per se*, they all have special skills in martial arts, weapons and explosives. The character has been used and licensed extensively by Hasbro and has evolved into comic books, motion pictures and video games.

ANPANMAN, a fictional character created by Takashi Yanase, was introduced in Japan as a series of books in 1968. The character would ultimately become one of Japan's most popular animated children's cartoon series of all time. By 2006, more than 50 million ANPANMAN books have been sold in Japan and it was made into a television series. It is Japan's most popular fictional character and has been licensed for a variety of products, including apparel, video games, toys and snack foods.

One of the longest running children's television shows of all time, SESAME STREET, premiered in 1969. Produced by Sesame Workshop (originally Children's Television Workshop), it has been a pioneer of contemporary educational television and was the first pre-school educational television program to base its content on laboratory and formative research. The show has developed and licensed such characters as OSCAR THE GROUCH, BIG BIRD, BERT, ERNIE and, of course, ELMO, all of which have become household names. SESAME STREET's first licensee was Western Publishing which, in 1971, published the first of what would become more than 600 individual titles based on the characters. SESAME STREET's biggest impact on licensing has been in the toy area, initially with Tyco Toys and subsequently with Mattel and Hasbro. SESAME STREET remains one of the strongest licensing brands of all time, reportedly with licensed product sales of more than $1.3 billion annually.

2.1.5 The 1970's

The decade started off in a big way when New York fashion designer, RALPH LAUREN created his soon to be famous, POLO brand, as part of a line of women's suits that he designed. In 1972, he introduced a short sleeved, mesh shirt with the POLO logo on it and a fashion industry fad was born. The shirt gained fame when it appeared in the motion picture, *The Great Gatsby*. By 2009, the RALPH LAUREN empire grew to more than $5 billion and it paved the way for other fashion designers such as PIERRE CARDIN, CALVIN KLEIN, GLORIA VANDERBILT and TOMMY HILFIGER.

In 1972, American Greetings introduced the HOLLY HOBBIE character which had been created by writer and illustrator of the same name who lived in New England and who had previously written a series of children's books called *Toot and Puddle.* American Greetings bought her artwork that depicted a cat-loving, rag dress-wearing, little girl in a giant bonnet and a licensing legend was born. HOLLY HOBBIE was featured by American Greetings in a line of greeting cards and, in 1974, Knickerbocker Toys marketed the first licensed HOLLY HOBBY product—a rag doll.

The animated series Science Ninja Team Gatchaman, or simply GATCHAMAN, was first produced in Japan in 1972 by Tatsunoko Productions. It involved a group of teens who helped protect the planet from an alien invasion. The property was adapted into several English language versions, including one by Sandy Frank Entertainment named the *Battle of the Planets*. The series would become a worldwide television hit and is rumored to have had an influence on George Lucas' development of the STAR WARS property.

HELLO KITTY, a fictional character designed by Yuko Shimizu, was first introduced in Japan by Sanrio in 1975 as a vinyl coin purse and, a year later, found its way into the United States. HELLO KITTY proved to be an immensely popular licensing property and more than $4 billion of licensed products are sold annually, ranging from dolls to stickers, greeting cards, apparel, accessories, school supplies, dishes and home appliances. There are currently two HELLO KITTY theme parks in Harmonyland and Sanrio Puroland, Japan.

By the mid-1970's, Hollywood studios had discovered the power of licensing to generate additional revenue while helping to promote a motion picture or television show. Paramount Pictures was a leader in this area, having developed licensing programs for virtually all of their television series, including HAPPY DAYS, LAVERNE & SHIRLEY and MORK & MINDY, as well as such motion pictures as STAR TREK and John Travolta's first three motion pictures, SATURDAY NIGHT FEVER, GREASE and URBAN COWBOY. These programs all generated significant amounts of revenue for Paramount and created a model for other studios to follow.

The 1970's also saw the emergence of MARY ENGELBREIT who would pioneer the art licensing category. Engelbreit started out as a greeting card designer and illustrator working for an advertising agency in St. Louis. Her first success was a greeting card featuring a girl looking at a chair piled high with bows with the saying, "Life Is Just a Chair of Bowlies." She granted her first art license later in the decade and has endured as a licensing success ever since, winning LIMA's Art License of the Year in both 2001 and 2003.

STRAWBERRY SHORTCAKE was created in 1977 by Muriel Fahrion while working as a greeting cards illustrator for American Greetings. Each of the characters had strawberry scented hair and lived in a world called Strawberryland. When American Greetings presented the concept to Bernie Loomis at Kenner Toys, a licensing phenomenon emerged. The success of the property led American Greetings to create its own licensing group, called Those Characters from Cleveland. Throughout the 1980's, the character was licensed extensively and was the basis of several television specials. It was re-introduced with a different look in 2002 and, once again, became quite popular, particularly on toys, DVD's and video games.

When the first STAR WARS motion picture was released on May 25, 1977 by Twentieth Century Fox, it set the licensing industry on its ear. Created by George Lucas, the STAR WARS film franchise would ultimately total ten in number as of April 2018 with at least two more planned. Each one of which was a blockbuster. Total box office revenues for the motion pictures were almost $9 billion, which made the series the highest revenue producer of all time. While the movies were hits, the licensing success was unmatched by any property, either before or after. Bernie Loomis and Kenner Products were, once again, at the center

of the licensing program, as the STAR WARS licensee for toys and action figures. When first introduced, Kenner could not manufacture product fast enough to meet consumer demand and it resorted to giving coupons to consumers for later redemption. From 1977 to 1985, Kenner sold more than 300 million STAR WARS action figures and its success paved the way for other studios and toy companies to produce their own line of license action figures. In an industry where the word "franchise" is overused, the STAR WARS property is truly a franchise.

The GARFIELD character was born out of a comic strip of the same name that was first published by Jim Davis in 1978. It featured a quirky, but lovable, cat named after Davis' grandfather as well as a dog called ODIE. By 2007, GARFIELD was syndicated in more than 2500 newspapers and journals and is considered the most widely syndicated comic strip of all time. GARFIELD has been featured on television shows, in motion pictures and adapted for host of licensed products, most notably toys, plush and apparel products.

The CABBAGE PATCH KIDS were created by Debbie Morehead and Xavier Roberts in 1978. The dolls were originally sold at local craft shows in Cleveland, Georgia until Roger Schlaifer of Schlaifer Nance & Company stepped in. He re-named them the CABBAGE PATCH KIDS, licensed the rights to Coleco Toys, and watched them become the the hit of the 1982 holiday season. Stores could not keep sufficient inventory to meet demand. Lines formed outside of many stores that announced that they had received a shipment. After Coleco's bankruptcy, Mattel, Hasbro and Play Along each marketed their own versions with modest success. It was reported that at its peak, there were over 150 CABBAGE PATCH licensees for products ranging from diapers to cereal to apparel. In 1984 alone, it was reported that more than $2 billion of CABBAGE PATCH products were sold at retail and, over its lifespan, retail sales were at least $4.5 billion.

The DALLAS television series was first aired in the fall of 1978 and would run through 1991. Produced by Lorimar Productions (and licensed by the co-author of this book) and starring Larry Hagman as J.R. Ewing, it was a primetime soap opera about an affluent Texas family in the oil and cattle ranching business. DALLAS was one of the first adult properties ever to be licensed and demonstrated that entertainment licensing was not all about children's themes. The show paved the way for other adult merchandisable properties such as KNOTS LANDING, FALCON CREST and DYNASTY.

2.1.6 The 1980's

The CARE BEARS property was created by Elena Kucharik in 1981, originally for use on a line of greeting cards by American Greetings. Two years later, Bernie Loomis and Kenner Toys developed and began selling a line of plush products based on the characters and the

licensing program was off to the races. A television series based on the characters ran from 1985 until 1988 and it was also featured in three motion pictures. The characters were re-introduced as toys in 2002 by Play Along Toys with modest success. The CARE BEARS property ushered in a new era in licensing—the birth of the half-hour, animated, syndicated television series which was distributed to local television channels across the United States and abroad. Previously, the dominant platform for children's programming was Saturday morning television that only aired weekly. Syndication of half-hour animated shows aired five times a week in after school time slots and provided greater exposure for their properties. The gamble with syndication paid off for a number of properties, including MASTERS OF THE UNIVERSE and MY LITTLE PONY and fueled the licensing industry for most of the 1980's. The bubble would, however eventually burst, unfortunately at great cost to the producers.

In a bizarre twist, a 1982 court decision finding that Champion Products' production of non-licensed UNIVERSITY OF PITTSBURGH clothing did **not** constitute trademark infringement, produced the exact opposite result. At the time of the decision, Champion was selling more than $100 million of  apparel bearing the logos of as many as 10,000 different schools and colleges. Instead of destroying any hope for the colleges to license out their names and logos, reasonable minds prevailed, and a business solution was reached. Champion fell in line, recognized that these schools and colleges had valid rights, and began to take licenses to use their marks on its products. Thus, the collegiate licensing industry was born.

Shortly before the *Pitt* decision, a former football coach from Alabama, Bill Battle, formed the COLLEGIATE LICENSING COMPANY ("CLC"), that would go on to represent almost half the colleges in the emerging collegiate licensing industry. It was reported that in 2017, CLC, now a part of IMG, generated more than $4.5 billion in worldwide sales of collegiate licensed products.

E.T. was the blockbuster movie of 1982. Produced and directed by Steven Spielberg and written by Melissa Mathison, it was about a lonely boy who befriended an extraterrestrial called E.T. Box office sales skyrocketed, and, for a period, E.T. was the most financially successful motion picture of its time. While the E.T. character was heavily merchandised, it is perhaps best known for creating a concept called product placement, where a product is featured in the movie for the express purpose of promoting it. In E.T.'s case, that product was Hershey's Reese's Pieces which was portrayed as E.T.'s favorite candy.

In 1982, Crown Publishers published the first MARTHA STEWART book entitled *Entertaining*, and an empire began. Ms. Stewart then collaborated with Time Publishing in 1990 to develop a magazine called *Martha Stewart Living* which would eventually enjoy a circulation of 2 million readers. That led to a series of successful television shows and specials and, ultimately, the creation of the company, Martha Stewart Living Omnimedia, which would go public in 1999. Kmart has carried her licensed line of home furnishing products for decades and a licensed MARTHA STEWART line of paint is sold through Sears. It is now part of Sequential Brands.

POUND PUPPIES was created in 1983 by Mike Bowling, a former Ford factory worker who, when he saw the look of love on the face of his young daughter for one of her dolls, remembered that same feeling from his own childhood after going to the pound to pick out a pet. The first POUND PUPPIES doll was marketed in Canada in 1984 by Irwin Toys and, a year later, Tonka began marketing it in the United States. It would eventually generate more than $300 million in sales in 35 different countries and spawn a wide range of licensed products.

The TEENAGE MUTANT NINJA TURTLES was a collaboration between Kevin Eastman and Peter Laird. Using money from a tax return, they formed Mirage Studios in 1984 and published a comic book that featured these characters as a parody of MARVEL's superheroes. It became enormously popular, principally because of the efforts of their licensing agent, Mark Freedman, who developed a licensing program with Playmates Toys. Throughout the 1980's and 1990's, TURTLE's li-

censees produced a wide range of licensed products and it was LIMA's License of the Year in 1991.

By the mid-1980's, licensing properties were coming from every imaginable source. A 1986 commercial for the California Raisin Advisory Board spawned a property that would receive LIMA's award for the Most Impactful Property of the year in 1988—the CALIFORNIA RAISINS. These characters were featured in the commercial dancing to the Marvin Gaye song, "I Heard It Through the Grapevine." With Applause as its primary toy licensee, sales of licensed products exploded. It was the first time that a commercial formed the basis for a licensing program.

Not to be outdone, Arby's restaurants launched a licensing program based on the catchy phrase WHERE'S THE BEEF. The phrase was licensed for a line of apparel and even found its way into the 1984 Vice-Presidential debate. The trend of licensing out catchy advertising slogans or characters has continued to this day, as evidenced by the licens-

ing program conducted by former LIMA chairman Brian Hakan, for the TACO BELL CHIHUAHUA, who had been featured in advertisements for the restaurant. Similarly, the Mars Corporation regularly licenses the M&M's characters that are featured in Mars' television and print ads for its line of M&M's candy products.

In 1986, Scholastic published the first of what would become a series of children's books called the MAGIC SCHOOL BUS. These books were written by Joanna Cole and illustrated by Bruce Degan and featured an elementary school teacher, Mrs. Frizzle, who would take their readers on field trips to interesting places aboard a magical school bus. The books would eventually lead to a television series, a series of traveling museums and a very successful licensing program.

In 1987, Sheryl Leach of Dallas, Texas created the character **BARNEY** while overseeing pro-

duction of a series of home videos entitled *Barney and the Backyard Gang* starring Sandy Duncan. While the DVD's were modestly successful, the character would ultimately be changed and became the basis for a PBS series that debuted in 1992 called *Barney & Friends*. The show was popular; however, its related licensing program was a real hit, particularly in the plush and toy areas. BARNEY won LIMA's License of the Year award in 1994.

It was during the 1980's that major corporations began testing the waters, having recognized the advantages that licensing offered. Licensing assisted some companies in expanding the breadth of their trademark protection, while helping others promote the sale of their underlying products. Regardless of the reason for getting involved in licensing, all welcomed the additional revenue that it brought to their bottom line. Corporations with well-known brands such as COCA-COLA, HARLEY DAVIDSON, PEPSI, COORS

and JOHN DEERE all began to explore licensing activities with a significant amount of success. It was estimated, for example, that the COCA-COLA licensing program generated more than $70 million in net royalty income during its peak.

THE SIMPSONS, an animated television series created by Matt Groening, debuted on Fox

in 1989 and is still on the air, which makes it the longest running, scripted prime time television show of all time. Featuring the characters HOMER, MARGE, BART, LISA and MAGGIE, it is a spoof on American family life. *THE SIMPSONS Movie* was released in 2007 and grossed more than $525 million. Its enormous popularity has made it a licensing and media franchise, with the characters appearing on virtually every conceivable type of licensed product. By 2003, it was reported that there were more than 500 SIMPSONS' licensees worldwide. In the first 14 months after release of the motion picture, it is believed that more than $2 billion of licensed merchandise were sold. A Fox executive called the SIMPSONS, "without a doubt, the biggest licensing entity that Fox has had, full stop, I would say from either TV or film."

2.1.7 The 1990's

GOOSEBUMPS featured a group of characters that grew out of a children's horror books series written by R. L. Stine and published by Scholastic. Over 62 GOOSEBUMPS books were authored between 1992 and 1997, the first being *Welcome to Dead House*. A series of additional spin-off titles followed as well as various licensed products, including at least three board games by Milton Bradley and video games by DreamWorks Interactive. GOOSEBUMPS won LIMA's License of the Year award for 1993.

TERMINATOR 2: JUDGMENT DAY or simply T2, a science fiction motion picture directed by

James Cameron and starring Arnold Schwarzenegger, was released in 1991 as a sequel to the original Terminator movie from 1984. It was one of the first "R" rated motion pictures to ever spawn a licensing program and has become the most successful licensed "R" rated film of all time. The licensing program, conducted by former LIMA President and co-author, Danny Simon, was led by Kenner Toys and Acclaim Entertainment. Universal Theme Parks also developed a licensed T2-3D attraction.

The MIGHTY MORPHIN POWER RANGERS, which was based on a popular Japanese property called Kyōryū Sentai Zyuranger about four teenagers who were selected to fight evil, hit the television screens in 1993 as a live-action television series. It was produced by Haim Saban and immediately became an overnight hit—both as a TV show and licensing property. The series ran for three years and "morphed" into a feature motion picture called *Mighty Morphin Power Rangers: The Movie*.

The POKÉMON property was created by Satoshi Tajiri in 1996 and launched by Nintendo that same year as a role-playing video game. It would become the second most successful video game-based franchise of all time, behind Mario Bros., selling more than 200 million copies. Under the watchful eye of LIMA Hall of Fame member Al Kahn at 4Kids Entertainment, it would also grow into a strong licensing property, with licenses for trading cards, apparel, books, and other media forms. POKÉMON was LIMA's licensed entertainment character of the year in 2000.

Comedy Central first broadcast its animated sitcom called **SOUTH PARK** in 1997 and, since

its introduction, it has consistently earned the highest rating of any basic cable program. Created by Trey Parker and Matt Stone for an adult audience with satirical humor, it focuses on four children and their adventures in a Colorado town. It is reported to generate several million dollars a year in royalties and licensed products include a pinball machine by Sega and games and puzzles by Fun 4 All. In 1998, SOUTH PARK T-shirts were the largest selling specialty T-shirts in the United States.

Another true legend of licensing, HARRY POTTER, was introduced in June 1997 when J.K. Rowling's first novel (of what would become a series) entitled *HARRY POTTER and the Philosopher's Stone* was published. It described the exploits of a young wizard, HARRY POTTER, and his friends at the Hogwarts School of Witchcraft and Wizardry. Over 400 million copies of these books would be sold in 67 different languages making Rowling perhaps the only billionaire author. The Warner Bros. motion pictures have each achieved blockbuster status and are among the highest grossing films of all time. As one would expect, licensing has been extensive, particularly in the toy, game, video and costume areas and a *Wizarding World of HARRY POTTER* theme park was opened in Orlando, FL.

1997 also saw the TELETUBBIES property emerge. Created by Anne Woode and produced by Ragdoll Productions, it debuted in a BBC children's television series of the same name. The program was aimed at pre-school viewers, although it drew adult viewers because of its humor. A total of 365 episodes were run in both the UK and the United States. The show received several broadcasting awards and the property won LIMA's Best Overall License of the Year award in 1999.

DORA THE EXPLORER, an animated television series featuring Dora Marquez, first aired in September 1999 on Nickelodeon. The show, which was created by Chris Gifford, Valerie Walsh, and Eric Weiner, would continue until 2006 and be heavily merchandised along the way with DORA action figures, play sets, DVDs, cosmetics, hygiene products, ride-on toys, books, board games, plush dolls, apparel, handbags, play tents and play kitchens.

The animated CGI character, BOB THE BUILDER, was created by Keith Chapman and first appeared on the BBC in 1999. BOB is a building contractor who takes on various building projects, including renovations, construction and repairs. The show's theme song, *Can We Fix It*, sold more than a million copies in the UK. The show has been extraordinarily popular and is aired in virtually every television market around the world and its licensing program, managed by HIT Entertainment, has been equally successful. The property was named as LIMA's Entertainment/Character License of the Year in 2002.

Another potentially classic property was introduced in 1999, when Nickelodeon launched the animated television series, *SPONGE BOB SquarePants*, created by Stephen Hillenburg.

SPONGEBOB lives in an underwater city called Bikini Bottom. The show would become Nickelodeon's top-rated show and a feature film based on the character was released in 2004. Sales of licensed SPONGEBOB merchandise have been very strong. It was reported that in 2002, sales of SPONGEBOB dolls sold at the rate of 75,000 per week. Other licensed products include cereal, video games, clothing and electronics. The character has also been used extensively in promotional programs for virtually every fast food and convenience store chain and by almost all major retailers.

2.1.8 The 21st Century

Licensing in the New Millennium has tended to focus more on Hollywood's "blockbuster" motion pictures, many of which were based on characters developed in the prior century. For example, two HULK motion pictures, based on the MARVEL superhero, were released, the first in 2003 and the sequel in 2008. The 2003 release earned $62.1 million in its opening weekend and would go on to gross almost $250 million worldwide. The sequel, *The Incredible Hulk*, out-grossed the original, with worldwide box office receipts of more than $263 million, and another $60 million in DVD sales. As would be expected, the sales of licensed products based on both motion pictures were strong.

Sony Pictures released three different SPIDERMAN motion pictures in the decade, all based on the original MARVEL characters. The original SPIDERMAN motion picture was released in 2002, SPIDERMAN 2 was released in 2004 and SPIDERMAN 3 in 2007. The trilogy grossed almost $2.5 billion at the box office and won multiple awards. All three motion pictures were heavily merchandised by Sony and SPIDERMAN and SPIDERMAN 2 received LIMA's Best Overall License of the Year award for 2003 and 2005.

LIMA's award for the Best Overall License of the Year for 2006 went to STAR WARS: Episode III Revenge of the Sith which was released in 2005 and would be the latest episode of the STAR WARS movies. All were written and directed by George Lucas and produced by Lucasfilm Ltd. The film broke a number of box office records and would ultimately gross almost $850 million, placing it behind only the highest grossing film of 2005, Warner Bros.' blockbuster, HARRY POTTER and the Goblet of Fire. Both motion pictures continued their history of strong licensing programs.

Disney's blockbuster motion pictures, PIXAR CARS and HIGH SCHOOL MUSICAL, won LIMA's Entertainment License of the Year awards for 2007 and 2008, respectively. PIXAR

CARS was directed by John Lasseter and Joe Ranft and featured the voices of prominent Hollywood actors, including Paul Newman and Michael Keaton. PIXAR CARS premiered in May 2006 at Lowe's Motor Speedway in North Carolina and the related licensing program was nothing short of sensational. It was reported that retail sales of licensed merchandise, including scale models of its cars, broke records for a Disney-Pixar film with more than $5 billion of licensed products sold. The *New York Daily News* reported that sales of its licensed merchandise were $600 million just two weeks after its release.

HIGH SCHOOL MUSICAL 2, which was the sequel to the Disney Channel Original Movie, HIGH SCHOOL MUSICAL, debuted on the Disney Channel in 2007 to 17.3 million viewers-- about 10 million more than for the original movie. That made it the most highly viewed Disney Channel movie to date. Ultimately, HIGH SCHOOL MUSICAL 3: SENIOR YEAR was released the following year in theatrical distribution.

The Hollywood Blockbuster formula of superhero movies continued throughout the dec-

ade. In 2008, Warner Bros. released a sequel to its 2005 BAT-MAN *Begins* motion picture, entitled the DARK KNIGHT, which was written and directed by Christopher Nolan. It set box office records everywhere and would become the seventh largest grossing movie of all time which, no doubt, contributed to its success as a licensing property.

The trend of licensing blockbuster movies continued into 2009, first with the release of Paramount's TRANSFORMERS: REVENGE OF THE FALLEN which brought in more than $400 million at the domestic box office followed by Fox's release of AVATAR in 2009 which produced more than $750 million at the box office. Both motion pictures have generated strong licensing programs. It was reported that Hasbro, which owned the rights to TRANSFORMERS, had over 220 licensees for products across virtually all categories while Fox had over 125 licensees for the AVATAR property across at least four major categories, including video games, toys, apparel and publishing.

The decade was not, however, all about movie licensing. The BRATZ doll, introduced by MGA Entertainment in 2001, proved to be not only a very successful doll but also a strong licensing property. Trendy and cutting edge, it was reported that more than 125 million BRATZ dolls were sold in its first five years and, by 2005, global sales of all BRATZ products topped $2 billion. From 2001 through 2010, it is believed that MGA had produced or licensed more than 550 different BRATZ dolls and products. BRATZ was the winner of LIMA's License of the Year award for 2004.

In 2002 artist Jim Benton came on the licensing scene in a big way with a smiling bunny called HAPPY BUNNY. Complete with catchy sayings, Carole Postal and COP Corp. developed a strong licensing program for the property covering a broad array of products, including key chains, computer mouse pads, energy drinks, school supplies, clothing, etc. HAPPY BUNNY was named LIMA's Art Licensing Property of the Year in 2006.

BAKUGAN, a Japanese animated television series produced by TMS Entertainment and Japan Vistec, debuted in 2007 in Japan and soon became popular in the United States and Canada. Not surprisingly, it spawned a line of licensed games led by Spin Master as its major toy licensee. Other licensed products included branded digital cameras, alarm clocks and other electronic products. BAKUGAN was selected by LIMA in 2009 as the Best Overall Licensed Program of the Year.

Disney has dominated the New motion pictures including PIXAR MUSICAL, TOY STORY, FROZEN Lucasfilm, the current including STAR WARS: THE Millennium with a host of CARS, HIGH SCHOOL and, after its acquisition of generation of STAR WARS, FORCE AWAKENS and

ROGUE ONE: A STARWARS STORY properties which dominated the merchandising stage in rapid fire succession.

ANGRY BIRDS is a video game franchise created by a Finnish company, Rovio Entertainment. By 2015, more than 3 billion copies of the game had been downloaded. It expanded to motion pictures and, ultimately, licensing, becoming the hottest licensing property in 2012. Activision's SKY-LANDERS, which was introduced in 2011, enjoyed similar success. By 2016, over 300 million toys had been sold and the franchise has become the 11th biggest console franchise of all time.

One of the more unusual properties that captured the public's attention, albeit for a relatively short period of time, was DUCK DYNASTY which emanated from a reality television show in the A&E Channel of the same name where it broke several ratings records. Sales of mostly adult licensed products topped $400 million by 2014, primarily in Walmart.

The British animated pre-school animated television series PEPPA PIG took a while to capture the attention of the licensing industry but by 2010 more than £200M of licensed products had been sold in the UK. As of 2018, the property had been licensed to more than 60 licensees on a worldwide basis.

Spin Master Entertainment's CGI animation series, PAW PATROL came on the scene in 2013 with Nickelodeon's support. The series focuses on a boy named Ryder who led a pack of search and rescue dogs known as the PAW Patrol. The property accounted for more than 40% of Spin Master's revenues in 2016 and the toy line, introduced by Spin Master, quickly climbed to the top of the charts in the US, UK and France. Toys "R" Us listed the PAW Patroller vehicle as the "hottest" selling toy in 2015.

The New Millennium also saw the emergence of a host of celebrities who licensed their names, images and likenesses for a wide variety of licensed products, some with extraordinary success. One of the most successful celebrity programs of the decade was the JESSICA SIMPSON brand program which, through the efforts of her master licensee, the Camuto Group (headed by Vince Camuto of NINE WEST fame), become a billion-dollar brand at retail before being acquired by Sequential Brands which also owned and controlled the licensing of MARTHA STEWART, ELLEN TRACY and EMERIL LAGASSE, among other.

The OLSEN TWINS, Mary Kate & Ashley, joined Simpson on the billion-dollar level mostly through their line of classic licensed apparel and accessory products, initially through Walmart. While in their 20's, Forbes estimated that their net worth in 2007 was more than $300 million due, principally, to the licensing empire that they have helped establish through the efforts of The Beanstalk Group.

Other celebrities, including JACKIE SMITH, JENNIFER LOPEZ, BRITANY SPEARS, DAVID BECKHAM, CINDY CRAWFORD, LADY GAGA, have all entered the licensing arena with varying degrees of success, mostly good.

Perhaps the two best known celebrity licensors of all time are former basketball player MICHAEL JORDAN and golfer TIGER WOODS. While MICHAEL JORDAN continues to remain a licensing heavyweight, principally because of his relationship with Nike, the TIGER WOODS experience demonstrates the risks of celebrity licensing. WOODS, who reportedly earned almost $100 million in endorsement and licensing deals in 2009 and 2010, saw his golf score rise sharply while his licensing income fell precipitously after charges of his marital infidelity were made public. Other prominent sports stars who earn significant sums through licensing and endorsements include fellow golfer, PHIL MICKELSON, basketball superstar LEBRON JAMES, baseball stars ANTHONY RIZZO and CLAYTON KERSHAW, football players TOM BRADY and ODELL BECKHAM, JR., tennis player ROGER FEDERER and soccer star LIONEL MESSI.

The property PLEASANT GOAT AND BIG BIG WOLF, a Chinese animated television series, was launched in China in 2005. Created by Huang Weiming, Lin Yuting and Luo Yinggeng, it is broadcast on more than 40 local television stations and almost 1000 episodes have been aired. The first motion picture based on the television series was released in 2009 and set a box office record in China for a Chinese animated film, earning more than $8 million during the opening weekend. A second movie was released in 2010. It is one of the most popular licensed characters in China.

2.2 Unique Licensed Products

When people think of merchandising licensed products, they think of such traditional licensed products like T-Shirts, posters, caps, badges and toys. While those types of products represent a significant amount of all licensed products, particularly for entertainment and sports properties, the world of licensing has expanded to include a host of unique licensed products as shown in the following pages.

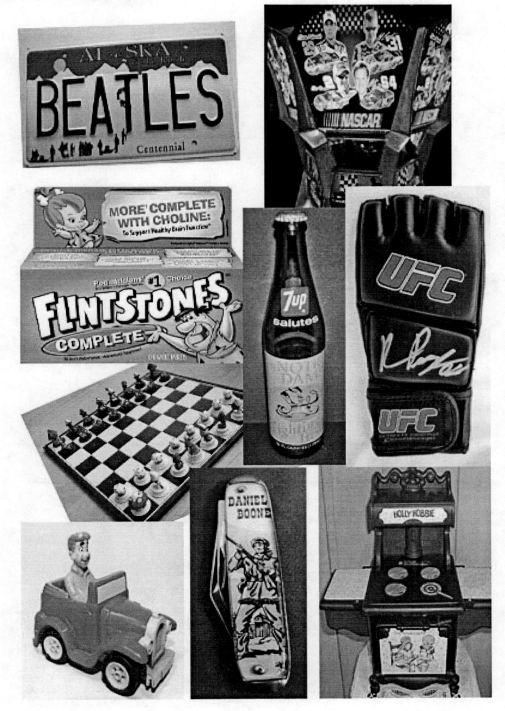

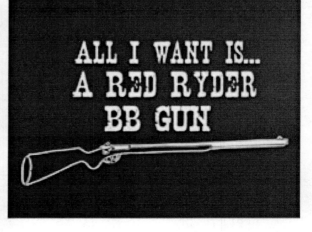

100% ALL ALUMINUM
BICYCLE LICENSE PLATE

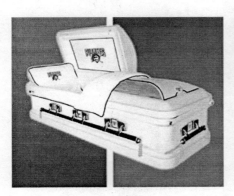

2.3 The People Who Made Licensing Great[2]

2.3.1 The Pioneers

Murray Altchuler* will be remembered for his role in forming and growing LIMA, but many forget that he was a moving force in the early years of licensing. He was hired in the 1960's by Allan Stone and Jay Emmet at Licensing Corporation of America ("LCA"), originally to handle premiums and promotions. LCA was the licensing powerhouse of the time with such properties as MLB, NBA, JAMES BOND, BATMAN, SUPERMAN and others.

Connie Boucher* founded Determined Productions in 1961 to develop products based on licensing characters, the first being a calendar featuring PEANUTS characters. That led to a book series and licensing program involving the PEANUTS characters. She would later get involved with licensing for the World Wildlife Federation.

Walt Disney*, began his career in 1920 when he founded the Walt Disney Company and, eight years later, when he created the most popular cartoon character of all-time, MICKEY MOUSE and later provided a voice for the character. He subsequently created such classic characters as SNOW WHITE AND THE SEVEN DWARFS, FANTASIA, PINOCCHIO, DUMBO, BAMBI, CINDERELLA and MARY POPPINS.

"Friz" Freleng was the creator of the Warner Bros. cartoon series LOONEY TUNES and MERRIE MELODIES, introducing such characters as BUGS BUNNY, PORKY PIG, TWEETY BIRD, SYLVESTER THE CAT, YOSEMITE SAM and SPEEDY GONZALEZ. He won 5 Academy Awards and 3 Emmy Awards. After leaving Warner Bros., he produced *The Pink Panther Show*.

Joe Grant* was president and eventually Chairman of the Board of LCA, the licensing arm for Warner Bros., and ran Time Warner Sports. In addition to representing the studio's properties, he oversaw licensing for the major sports leagues, e.g., MLB, NHL, etc., before they created their own Properties divisions. He was instrumental in the formation of the Licensing Industry Association (a precursor to LIMA), personally financing their early years.

Irv Handelsman was one of old-time marketing guys in licensing who claims to have created the MICKEY MOUSE Club and, among other properties, WOODY WOODPECKER as well as Jay Ward Production's popular characters including ROCKY THE FLYING SQUIRREL, BULLWINKLE THE MOOSE, BORIS AND NATASHA, DUDLEY DO-RIGHT, and several others.

---

[2] This does not portend to be a complete collection of those individuals who are responsible for "making licensing great." The list was compiled based on recommendations from a panel of licensing professionals. Honestly, there were hundreds, if not thousands, more who could have been mentioned. The authors apologize to anyone who may feel that they were omitted and welcome submissions for future inclusion in updated versions of this book. Also, note that they individuals are listed in alphabetical order since it would have been impossible to rank their order of importance.

* Designates a member of the LIMA Licensing Hall of Fame

William Hanna* and **Joseph Barbera*** met when they worked together at MGM and collaborated to create TOM AND JERRY. In 1957, the co-founded the most successful animation studio in the business, Hanna-Barbera Productions, which produced shows featuring such characters as THE FLINTSTONE, THE HUCKLEBERRY HOUND SHOW, THE JETSONS, SCOOBY-DOO, THE SMURFS and YOGI BEAR which reached more than 300 million viewers in the 1960's.

Larry Harmon purchased the licensing rights to the BOZO THE CLOWN character in 1956 and began aggressively marketing it in nearly every major U.S. market and other countries. He also produced Popeye The Sailorman cartoons in 1960 and he subsequently promoted a Laurel and Hardy TC Cartoon series.

The colorful ~~Honest~~ **Ed Justin** handled most of Paramount's licensing business in the 1970's, including the Robert Stigwood movies, including *Grease*, *Urban Cowboy* and *Saturday Night Fever*. He had previously overseen licensing at Columbia Pictures and NBC. His entre' into licensing was fortuitous, having met the head of NBC while running a girl's summer camp for overprivileged girls which led to his working with Martin and Allan Stone on the HOWDY DOODY show.

Kay Kamen*, a/k/a/ the "Father of Modern Licensing," approached Walt Disney in 1932 seeking a MICKEY MOUSE license for hats and wound up overseeing a licensing program that produced almost a thousand different types of MICKEY MOUSE Products. At the height of the Depression, he got General Foods to pay $1 million for the right to put MICKEY MOUSE cut-outs on the back of its cereal boxes.

Hank Saperstein was a producer who specialized in licensing television characters such WYATT EARP, THE LONE RANGER, LASSIE and ROY ROGERS and served as the licensing agent for ELVIS PRESLEY. He produced the *Mr. Magoo* television series and licensed such celebrities as DEBBIE REYNOLDS, ROSEMARY CLOONEY, CHUBBY CHECKER and the THREE STOOGES.

Stephen Slesinger was one of the true fathers of the licensing industry, acquiring and commercializing the North American merchandising and entertainment rights for WINNIE-THE-POOH from A. A. Milne in the 1930s. He developed and licensed RED RYDER and KING OF THE ROYAL MOUNTED. His widow, Shirley Slesinger Lasswell, took over his licensing efforts in the 1950's, including licensing Pooh to Disney.

In 1948, Martin Stone, the producer of *The Howdy Doody Show*, asked his brother, **Allan Stone**, to take over the merchandising of the property. It marked the first time that a licensing program was developed based on a television show and it would ultimately generate a host of licensed products. Stone Associates went on to represent The HONEYMOONERS and LASSIE. With Jay Emmett, he formed LCA, the first agency devoted exclusively to licensing. LCA developed the licensing programs for BATMAN, SUPERMAN and JAMES BOND as well as the NBA and MLB. Stone left LCA in 1970 to form Hamilton Projects where he consulted with McDonald's, Sesame Street and the Smithsonian Institution. His son, Michael, and Seth Siegel joined him in 1982.

Walter Wormser* was the founder of Wormser Company in the 1940's which manufactured and marketed women's and men's apparel, underwear and sleepwear and children's pajamas which included licensed cartoons from Warner Bros., Universal Pictures, and Sony Pictures. He is a charter member of the LIMA Hall of Fame.

2.3.2 The Legendary Creators

2.3.2.1 Motion Pictures and Television

Jim Henson* was a puppeteer and cartoonist who created the MUPPETS and founded Muppets, Inc. (later the Jim Henson Company) in 1958. He became famous in 1969 when he joined the children's educational television program Sesame Street and helped develop characters for the series, including KERMIT THE FROG, ROWLF THE DOG, and BERT AND ERNIE.

Sheryl Leach created the children's show, *Barney & Friends*, featuring a dinosaur. She started with a series of home videos called *Barney and the Backyard Gang* which were sold direct to the public. In April 1992, the first episode of *Barney & Friends,* aired on PBS. HIT Entertainment would later acquire the rights and control the merchandising.

George Lucas* is a filmmaker best known as the creator of the *STAR WARS* and *Indiana Jones* franchise motion picture series. He created and served as CEO of Lucasfilm which was eventually sold to Disney. The STAR WARS movies are the highest grossing films of all time and spawned a new era of merchandising

Haim Saban is a producer who produced and distributed such children's television programs as *Power Rangers* which was built around a live action, superhero television show. He also developed and produced INSPECTOR GADGET, M.A.S.K., DRAGON QUEST, HE-MAN and MASTERS OF THE UNIVERSE as well as Western adaptations of Japanese tokusatsu shows.

Steven Spielberg is one of the most successful all-time filmmakers, having produced dozens of motion pictures of all genres. The one movie that produced the most successful licensing program was E.T. THE EXTRA-TERRESTRIAL, about a young boy and the alien that he befriends. It was the largest grossing film of all time launched an enormously successful licensing program. He co-founded DreamWorks Studios.

2.3.2.2 Print Media

Jim Davis* is a cartoonist best known as the creator of the comic strips *GARFIELD* which has been published since 1979. It is currently syndicated in over 2500 newspapers read by more than 300 million people every day. He also wrote or co-wrote all the *GARFIELD* television specials and produced *GARFIELD & Friends*, a Saturday morning series and oversaw the related merchandising programs.

Charles Schulz* created the comic strip *Peanuts* which featured, among other characters, SNOOPY and CHARLIE BROWN. At its peak, *Peanuts* was published daily in 2600 papers in 75 countries in 21 languages. Revenue from the comic strip and associated licensing which was handled by United Media exceeded $1 billion per year.

2.3.3 The Legendary Agents, Consultants and Support Providers

2.3.3.1 Entertainment

Lester Borden oversaw the licensing department at Columbia Pictures during the 1980's and 1990's and was responsible for developing the GHOST-BUSTERS licensing program based on the movie of the same name with Dan Aykroyd.

Leigh Anne Brodsky* heads the licensing group at Discovery Communications which licenses brands such as the DISCOVERY CHANNEL, TLC, ANIMAL PLANET and DISCOVERY KIDS. She was previously MD of Peanuts Worldwide/Iconix and, prior to that, was President of Nickelodeon Consumer Products overseeing such brands as SPONGE BOB SQUAREPANTS, DORA THE EXPLORER, BLUE'S CLUES, and SOUTH PARK. She is a former LIMA Board member.

Bev Cannady* made her name in licensing at Mattel as the individual who would respond to the letters addressed to "Dear Barbie." She has been called by some as the "Godmother of Licensing" and served on the LIMA Board of Directors.

Jack Chojnacki* was the co-president of Those Characters from Cleveland, a division of American Greetings in the 1980s. He assisted in the creation of several AGC franchises, including STRAWBERRY SHORTCAKE and the CARE BEARS and served as executive producer of *The Care Bears Movie*. He helped out with two other AGC properties, MADBALLS and POPPLES.

Mark Freedman was one of the most successful independent licensing agents and producers in the industry, most notably for his discovery and launch of the TEENAGE MUTANT NINJA TURTLES property which he developed into a $3 billion entertainment and consumer products licensing business, culminating in its sale to the Nickelodeon network in 2009.

Mike Georgopolis was the EVP at United Media in charge of the licensing of PEANUTS and GARFIELD and was largely responsible for their success in the 1980's. He was ahead of his time in terms of developing a licensing program and systems that were efficient and are still being used today.

Brad Globe* was the President of Warner Bros. Consumer Products, succeeding Dan Romanelli in 2005. He developed a themed entertainment business led by THE WIZARDING WORLD OF HARRY POTTER and the state-of-the-art touring exhibition, *HARRY POTTER: The Exhibition* as well as championing the creation of innovative retail programs such as "Walmart Premiere Night" with "Man of Steel."

Steve Herman has always been a professional's professional, having overseen some of the most visible licensing programs in the industry. He began with Taft Merchandising and Hanna-Barbara and ultimately headed up the licensing departments for Marvel Comics, King Features Syndicate/Hearst Entertainment and GOOSEBUMPS, retiring as the head of Archie Comics Entertainment.

Jerry Houle is CEO and founder of Bliss House and was an adjunct professor at Babson's Graduate Business School where he taught a course in licensing. He was a former corporate VP for Milton-Bradley Company and Jim Henson's MUPPETS as well as advertising manager for Fisher-Price Toys and was a moving force in the creation of the Licensing Industry Association.

Al Kahn* entered the licensing  arena as head of licensing at Coleco Toys, overseeing the CABBAGE PATCH program. From 1991 until 2011, he was CEO of Leisure Concepts and 4Kids Entertainment which he turned into a global powerhouse, producing the POKÉMON series that aired on Kids' WB! in the United States and the Yu-Gi-Oh! Japanese animated franchise.

 **Tim Kilpin** has worked on virtually all sides of the licensing equation. Currently CEO of the Consumer Products Division at Activision Blizzard, he had previously been Mattel's President, having worked his way up on the consumer products side which included a successful launch of Mattel's MONSTER HIGH which produced several billion dollars in global retail sales. He had been an EVP at Disney and is a former LIMA board member.

Danny Kletzky is a licensing veteran beginning at Warner Bros which led him to his own company, Entertainment Licensing Associates. He entered into a joint venture with Tokyo based Kaliya K.K. to seek and develop Japanese intellectual property. He was one of the first agents to get behind video game-based licensing with *Capcom* and the *Street Fighter* movie and the Hasbro toy line.

 Mark Matheny is a founder of Licensing Matters Global, a full-service, worldwide licensing agency. He was formerly President of Global Brands Group in Singapore that handled the rights to FIFA WORLD CUP and the PGA TOUR and, before that, was an EVP of Warner Bros Consumer Products Group in charge of international licensing. He is a former LIMA Chairman.

Al Ovadia was VP of Licensing at Twentieth Century Fox where he launched THE SIMPSONS licensing program which has become one of the longest running programs in the industry. He also headed the licensing program at Sony where he co-managed SPIDERMAN's film-based licensing program with Marvel and headed licensing for Turner Network's wrestling program.

Maura Regan, LIMA's newly designated President, joined LIMA after a career as head of licensing at Sesame Workshop where she oversaw the licensing of such characters as BIG BIRD, GROVER and ELMO. She had previously worked at Jim Henson Company, MTV Networks and Scholastic Entertainment. She's a formed LIMA Chairman and was named as a "Game Changer" by *License Global.*

Howard Roffman* has, for the past 30 years, led the licensing team at Lucasfilm, managing such properties as STAR WARS and INDIANA JONES which have exceeded $20 billion in worldwide consumer sales under his leadership. He helped launch a publishing program that included more than 80 *New York Times* best-sellers which helped bolster an ongoing licensing and merchandising effort.

Dan Romanelli* was the President of Warner Bros. Worldwide Consumer Products division for 23 years since its inception, taking a sleepy licensing arm to a $50 billion worldwide business. His 500-man department handled such properties as LOONEY TUNES, HARRY POTTER, BATMAN, SUPERMAN, SCOOBY-DOO, Hanna-Barbera, and others. He helped establish the Warner Bros. Studio Store.

Roger Schlaifer is a designer and licensing agent, best known for his licensing of the CABBAGE PATCH KIDS and ANDY WARHOL as part of his company, Schlaifer Nance. Working under a master license agreement with Xavier Roberts' company, Original Appalachian Artworks in 1981, he turned the CABBAGE PATCH KIDS property into a household word, generating over $4 billion in retail sales of licensed merchandise.

Lois Sloane* was credited for being potential for classic film licensing. VP of Licensing for MGM/UA, and global licensing division managing all before starting SloaneVision. She's a one of the first to recognize the She began her career at IMG, was a launched Turner Broadcasting's of Turner's film and animation library former President of LIMA.

Danny Simon* is a 30+ year industry veteran having built the licensing divisions for Lorimar Productions, 20th Century Fox and Carolco Pictures and now operating The Licensing Group. With DALLAS and DYNASTY, he was among the first to license adult TV entertainment, following it with M*A*S*H, FALL GUY, ALF, RAMBO, TERMINATOR 2: JUDGMENT DAY, MORTAL KOMBAT, BAYWATCH, ARNOLD SCHWARZENEGGER and DAVID HASSELHOFF. He is a former LIMA Chairman and co-dean of LIMA's CLS program.

Peter Van Raalte started at the Saturday Evening Post, followed by leadership positions at Turner Home Entertainment, Scholastic Entertainment, Joester-Loria Group, Madison Square Garden and Infinity Licensing. He has represented such properties as the HANNA-BARBERA ANIMATION LIBRARY, MGM, CARTOON NETWORK, CLIFFORD THE BIG RED DOG, MAGIC SCHOOL BUS. JEEP, CHRYSLER and PEPPA PIG. He is a former LIMA Chairman.

Stanley Weston* was an inventor and licensing agent. He started out as a dress salesman who would later join Allan Stone and Jay Emmett at LCA. He was instrumental in creating the G.I. JOE toy line in 1963, as well as the concept of the action figure which he sold to Hasbro. He formed Leisure Concepts which licensed products based on the likeness of FARRAH FAWCETT, STAR WARS and NINTENDO. During the 1980s, he oversaw the creation of the THUNDERCATS animated series.

Maggie Young made her name in licensing while at Lucasfilm licensing the STAR WARS property and characters. She would eventually leave to take over licensing for Paramount Pictures before starting her own very successful agency, Maggie Young & Associates. She is a former LIMA Board member.

2.3.3.2 Corporate

Allison Ames is CEO of The Beanstalk Group, succeeding its founder, Michael Stone. She has been with Beanstalk for more than 20 years, overseeing the licensing initiatives for such diverse brands as HGTV, STANLEY BLACK & DECKER, PURINA, AIRHEADS, the U.S. ARMY, MARY-KATE and ASHLEY, SALMA HAYEK and DANSKIN. She also created Beanstalk's Manufacturer Rep division, leading projects for clients such as ConAgra.

Wes Anson, Chairman of CONSOR, was one of the first licensing professionals to focus on the corporate or brand side of the business, particularly from a valuation point of view. A Harvard MBA, he has been with Booz-Allen & Hamilton, Playboy Enterprises and Hang Ten International. He has published over 150 articles on licensing, IP and valuation issues.

Nancy Bailey* and her Florida based company, Nancy Bailey & Associates, were at the forefront of trademark and brand extension licensing, developing and managing licensing programs for several Fortune 100 companies including BURGER KING. Her company was eventually acquired by Beanstalk.

Scott Bannell recently retired from Stanley Black & Decker where he was VP Brand Management & Licensing, responsible for brand management, positioning and licensing of such brands as BLACK & DECKER, STANLEY, DEWALT. Over his 20+ year career, he oversaw the first comprehensive program in the home improvement category, overseeing sponsorship opportunities with DISNEY, NASCAR and PROFESSIONAL BULL RIDERS.

Elise Contarsy is the VP of Brand Licensing for Meredith Corporation and has lead successful brand building programs for MARTHA STEWART. Her work on the BETTER HOMES & GARDENS program at Walmart and in the real estate sector are particularly noteworthy and are largely responsible for Meredith being ranked as the second largest licensor by *License Global*.

Ciaran Coyle is VP and head of Global Brand Licensing for Electrolux whose licensing portfolio includes more than 50 brands, including AEG, ZANUSSI and FRIGIDAIRE. He had previously been President of Europe and Asia Pacific for Beanstalk where he worked on brands such as HARLEY-DAVIDSON, JACK DANIEL'S, STANLEY, BLACK & DECKER, PROCTER & GAMBLE, JAGUAR, LAND ROVER and VOLVO. He is a Chairman of LIMA.

Kate Dwyer is Group Director of Coca-Cola's Global Licensing Division where she is responsible for developing brand extensions for the world's most recognized brand, COCA-COLA, and 20 other billion dollar brands. She is recognized as a transformational leader who leverages innovative business solutions to drive sustainable results and was named "Game Changer" by *License Global* Magazine. Under her leadership, the Coca-Cola licensing business has tripled and maintained growth for nine of the last ten years

Allan Feldman,* who began brand licensing in the mid-1970's, was one of the first to bring trademark licensing into industrial products and to utilize direct-to-retail licensees (via a $5 billion deal between Kmart and White-Westinghouse). His clients include AT&T, CRAFTSMAN, DEL MONTE, FRIGIDAIRE, HP, INGERSOLL RAND, MOBIL CORPORATION, UNITED AIRLINES, WESTINGHOUSE, AMERICAN DIABETES ASSOCIATION, and the SAN DIEGO ZOO.

Carole Francesca of Broad Street Licensing Group, has experience on both the client and agency side, creating and implementing unique licensing programs for brands such as UNILEVER, BURGER KING, CULINARY INSTITUTE OF AMERICA, CHESEBROUGH POND'S, DISNEY, MGM/UNITED ARTISTS, and ABC-TV, both domestically and worldwide. She is an expert in licensing food and beverage brands and is a former LIMA Chairman.

Brian Hakan is another LIMA Chairman, who has worked on both sides of the licensing equation—as a licensee developing licensed products for the NCAA and professional sports leagues including the NBA, ABC's Wide World of Sports and the IVY LEAGUE Conference. Perhaps his greatest success was in developing a licensing program for Taco Bell's YO QUIERO CHIHUAHUA character.

Gayle Jones recently retired as Head of Licensing for Proctor & Gamble where she oversaw licensing for more than 20 years, managing the global licensing of brands such as TIDE, FEBREZE, MR. CLEAN, VICKS and BRAUN. P&G has been active in licensing since the mid-1980's when it acquired VIDAL SASSOON. She was active and a moving force in SPLICE.

Debra Joester* and **Joanne Loria*** founded the Joester-Loria Group in 1999 and are known for producing innovative, such well-known brands such CORONA beer. Their re- multi-billion-dollar success exceptional, enjoying

brand extension programs for as PEPSI, MOUNTAIN DEW and launch of CARE BEARS was a story and their work on JEEP was success in China and South Africa.

They took ERIC CARLE, a literary property without entertainment, into a global licensing success.

Glen Konkle and **Blair McCaw** formed Equity Management in the early 1980's and has provided corporate trademark licensing services with one of the largest full-time, in house sales force in the licensing industry. While concentrating on automotive brands such as GENERAL MOTORS, CHEVROLET, CADILLAC, AC DELCO, GOODYEAR and SAAB, he also developed programs for KAWASAKI, DR. PEPPER, SIKORSKY and PUREX.

Len Reiter left General Mills in 1986 and formed Bradford Licensing. With brands such as PEPSI, KAWASAKI and FORD, he was able to build a stable and profitable business that specialized in corporate licensing. He would build licensing programs around FRITO LAY and KFC as well as PEZ candy. He passed away in 2007.

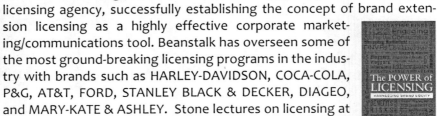

When **Michael Stone** and **Seth Siegel** formed Beanstalk in 1991, they created a "super" licensing agency, successfully establishing the concept of brand extension licensing as a highly effective corporate marketing/communications tool. Beanstalk has overseen some of the most ground-breaking licensing programs in the industry with brands such as HARLEY-DAVIDSON, COCA-COLA, P&G, AT&T, FORD, STANLEY BLACK & DECKER, DIAGEO, and MARY-KATE & ASHLEY. Stone lectures on licensing at Baruch, LIU Post, Boston Univ., Babson Univ., Wharton School of Business and F.I.T and is the author of *The Power of Licensing: Harnessing Brand Equity* to be published in 2018. Siegel, who also frequently lectured on licensing and was a regular columnist for *Brandweek*, departed Beanstalk in 2005 while Stone remained as its CEO and is now its Chairman.

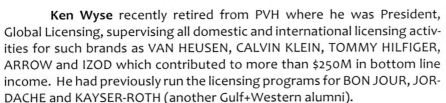

Ken Wyse recently retired from PVH where he was President, Global Licensing, supervising all domestic and international licensing activities for such brands as VAN HEUSEN, CALVIN KLEIN, TOMMY HILFIGER, ARROW and IZOD which contributed to more than $250M in bottom line income. He had previously run the licensing programs for BON JOUR, JORDACHE and KAYSER-ROTH (another Gulf+Western alumni).

2.3.3.3 Celebrity and Music

Del Furano* of Live Nation is considered a "true legend" in music licensing and merchandising, having overseen the licensing for such top groups as THE BEATLES, KISS, MADONNA, U2, AC/DC and JUSTIN TIMBERLAKE. He launched major retail branding programs for artists such as BRITNEY SPEARS, RUN DMC, JESSICA SIMPSON, CELINE DION and OZZY OSBOURNE. He had previously founded and ran Sony Signatures.

Mark McCormack* founded the International Management Group ("IMG") which represented such sports figures and celebrities as golfers ARNOLD PALMER, JACK NICKLAUS and GARY PLAYER. His clients were a top 10 list of famous athletes. He also handled special projects for MARGARET THATCHER, MIKHAIL GORBACHEV, POPE JOHN PAUL II, and TIGER WOODS. IMG subsequently acquired Collegiate Licensing Company.

Roger Richman was another leader in the representation of deceased celebrities including the estates of ALBERT EINSTEIN, MARILYN MONROE, SIGMUND FREUD, THE WRIGHT BROTHERS and BELA LUGOSI. He was a framer of the California Celebrity Rights Act which gave the heirs of such celebrities control over how a celebrity's image, voice or name is used posthumously.

Mark Roesler is chairman of CMG Worldwide, the exclusive representative for over 300 famous celebrities, including JAMES DEAN, JACKIE ROBINSON and ELLA FITZGERALD. Representing the estates of many deceased celebrities such as MARILYN MONROE, he was the driving force behind Indiana's Right of Publicity statute which is the model for other states. He has been the keynote speaker for many trade organizations, including the INTA.

2.3.3.4 Art

Paul Cohen of the Creatif Licensing Division of the Brand Liaison Agency has represented designers and classic artists for more than 30 years. He achieved notoriety from his successful worldwide licensing program for the MOPPETS and was responsible for the establishment and growth of the MARY ENGELBREIT enterprise.

Shirley Henschel, a/k/a Alaska Momma, started her career by licensing major auto racing drivers, including STIRLING MOSS. She has also represented comic strip characters including LITTLE ORPHAN ANNIE, BRENDA STARR, GASOLINE ALLEY and others before starting Alaska Momma in 1979 whose licenses included the NORFIN TROLLS, the NERDS characters and Mel Odum's GENE Doll.

Susan Meek has been more of an industry generalist, starting her career at Hallmark Cards where she worked her way into licensing. Since then, she has worked as VP of International Licensing for Elvis Presley and John Wayne as well as VP of Licensing for licensees such as Hedstrom Corporation, Imperial Wall Décor, Precious Moments and Dan River Inc.

Joanne Olds of The Buffalo Works has represented brands and, artists on all three sides of the business—retail, manufacturing and licensing representation. Her artists have included THOMAS KINKADE, MARJOLEIN BASTININ, UK ARTISTS STEVEN BROWN, TIFFANI TAYLOR and she will be working with KATHY IRELAND on a collection of branded art and wall décor for the home.

Carole Postal of COP Corp is an industry veteran with extensive experience in all categories, having started in licensing at Turner Broadcasting and Sesame Workshop and has represented Harvey Comics, Britt Allcroft and Paramount Pictures. She became well known in the art category for her work involving Jim Benton's HAPPY BUNNY property and other non-media brands including PINK COOKIE DESIGN and BARCODE KITTIES. She has been a member of Board of Directors of both LIMA and K.I.D.S.

2.3.3.5 Consultants/Manufacturer's Reps

Woody Browne of Building Q (which he established in 1992), started in licensing by managing the lunch-box business at Thermos and subsequently at Tonka Toys and Tyco Toys. Since then, he has represented some of the most well-known manufacturers in diverse categories, including apparel and accessories, collectibles, food, publishing and toys. He is a Past LIMA Chairman.

Gary Caplan*, of Gary Caplan, Inc., has been in the forefront of the licensing industry since the 1970's and is often called "the Godfather of Licensing." After working at Stuart Hall as VP Sales and Marketing, he formed his own consulting company representing manufacturers seeking licenses which essentially created the "Manufacturer's Consultant" category. He is a founding member of LIMA and a member of the Warner Bros. Consumer Products Hall of Fame.

Cheryl Stoebenau* started at Hallmark Cards and Coleco Toys where she worked on such successful licensing programs as SHIRT TALES and RAINBOW BRITE at Hallmark and CABBAGE PATCH KIDS while at Coleco working with Al Kahn. She formed CAS Marketing to focus on representing manufacturers and help them build strong licensing portfolios. She is a former LIMA Board member.

2.3.3.6 The Manufacturers/Licensees

Marty Abrams of Mego Toys has been called the "Father of Action Figures," having produced highly collectible action figures based on DC and MARVEL Comics characters. Mego's product lines have included MAGNA DOODLE, SKYDANCERS, MICRONAUTS and EARLY NINTENDO which it launched in the U.S. There are now over 750,000 websites mentioning products by Mego.

Ray Butman* was an executive at Western Publishing which published a line of Golden Books which were based on a myriad of licensed characters. An early license deal with Disney led to many Disney-Golden Books collaborations. In 1971 Western entered into an agreement with Children's Television Workshop to publish a line of Golden Books featuring the MUPPETS.

Stan Clutton,* most recently of Mattel and Fisher-Price, was responsible for the development of such iconic toys such as TICKLE ME ELMO AND ROCK and ROLL ELMO. He played a key role in the success of Fisher-Price's licensed products and continually maintained strong relationships with licensors and inventors from around the world.

Ben Cooper established Ben immediately began marketing DONALD DUCK and SNOW SUPERMAN and ZORRO and BATMAN. By the late 1940's it costume manufacturers in the retailers.

Cooper, Inc. in 1937 and almost costumes based on Disney characters WHITE and LATER DAVY CROCKETT, ULTIMATELY SPIDERMAN and was one of the largest Halloween US, selling costumes to the major

Neil Friedman, *currently CEO of Alex Brands, has been at the forefront of the toy industry since the early 1970's, leading Lionel Leisure, Just Toys, Gerber Products, Hasbro, MCA, Tyco Toys, Fisher-Price and Mattel as well as Toys "R" Us before joining Alex Brands. The TICKLE ME ELMO launch in 1999 based on the Sesame Street character was one of the industry's greatest success stories. He is a former LIMA Chairman and a member of the TIA Hall of Fame.

John Gildea is retired senior executive at Hasbro, is credited with creating Hasbro's licensing group. the licensing division at Hasbro. He developed strategic relationships with such licensors as Disney, Warner Bros., Lyrick Studios, Sesame Workshop, Scholastic Publications and Nickelodeon. He also served as Sr. VP of Consumer Products as Cookie Jar Entertainment.

Steve Harris joined Franco Manufacturing in 1980 and was its Director of Licensing for 11 years. During that period, he brought licensing to the beach towel industry. He networked with virtually all major licensors and was a charter member of LIMA. He has spoken frequently at industry seminars and was elected twice to the LIMA Board of Directors.

Stephen* **and Alan Hassenfeld*** each served as Chairman and CEO of Hasbro, succeeding their father Merrill. During Stephen's tenure, he increased Hasbro's profitability by 85% annually based on the phenomenal success of its G.I Joe and Transformers line of products. During his reign, Hasbro acquired Milton Bradley, Knickerbocker, Playskool, Child Guidance and Coleco Industries, the bankrupt manufacturer of Cabbage Patch dolls. Upon Stephen's untimely death, Alan assumed control and continued Hasbro's growth and turned it into an entertainment company. Both brothers are members of the TIA Hall of Fame.

Bernie Leifer* who started out in banking, joined SG Footwear about 30 years ago and transformed the small, privately owned slipper manufacturer into a fashion licensing powerhouse with entertainment and lifestyle brands, including Sesame Street, Power Rangers, Pokémon, Perry Ellis, Chinese Laundry, Dockers and Harley-Davidson. He is a former LIMA Chairman.

Bernie Loomis was a toy developer and marketer who introduced some of the world's most notable brands including Chatty Cathy, Barbie, Hot Wheels, Baby Alive and Strawberry Shortcake. His biggest marketing success was bringing a then-unknown film property called STAR WARS to the toy shelves in 1977 while at Kenner/General Mills. Every toy company he worked for became "the world's largest toy company" during his tenure.

Bob Lorberbaum, of Springs Industries, was the first manufacturer to license characters and properties for children's licensed bedding products and helped create the concept of a whole children's room, complete with bedding. While at Lawtex Industries in 1979, prior to its acquisition by Springs Industries, he was largely responsible for bringing into the United States one of the earliest and most popular of all novelty licenses, the Smurfs.

Harry Nizamian was the CEO of Dakin Toys in San Francisco who worked on developing unique licensed products throughout the 1980's. His most successful one was the GARFIELD "Stuck on You" plush product for car windows that was extremely popular through the country.

Jerrold Robinson* was President and CEO of Pilgrim Industries which manufactured various stationary products bearing character licenses. He was also a director of Reflexite Corporation. He was a Founder of the Licensed Merchandisers' Association ("LMA") in approximately 1980 which was formed because the other trade association, the Licensing Industry Association ("LIA") was restricted to for Licensors and Agents only.

Jack Weissman* was the originator of character licensing in footwear when he obtained the licensing rights for the PEANUTS characters. He later licensed E.T, NFL footwear, PAC-MAN slippers and BUDWEISER athletic footwear. He was also a principal in a licensed school supply company, Plymouth Inc. and went on to create Marketing Licensing Associates.

2.3.3.7 Colleges

Bill Battle* is a former college football player and athletic director of the University of Alabama who, in the early 1980's, created and then ran the Collegiate Licensing Company (now IMG-CLC). He built CLC into a national leader representing more than 200 colleges, universities, bowls and conferences and producing more than $4 billion of sales of collegiate licensed merchandise. He is a member of the ICLA Hall of Fame.

Anne Chasser established the licensing program at OHIO STATE University in the late 1970's. While at OSU, she became president of the INTA and helped found and lead the ACLA (now "ICLA"). She also served as the Assistant Commissioner of Trademarks for the US Patent & Trademark Office and is a member of ICLA Hall of Fame.

Steve Crossland created the licensing program as the University of Southern California in 1975 and, after recognizing the potential of collegiate licensing, created International Creative Enterprises ("ICE") which represented other colleges. In July 1993, he joined forces with Bill Battle and CLC and focus his attention on the international markets.

Dick Rademaker, a former executive at Champion Products, formed the Licensing Resource Group ("LRG") in May 1991 which went on to represent a host of college licensing programs and eventually rival CLC. He created industry-leading technology and blazed trails in brand development, online enforcement and license management. He was one of the most respected people in the industry. LRG would later be acquired by Learfield Licensing in 2014.

Jack Revoyr is the retired Director of Licensing for UCLA and was one of the founders of the ACLA formed in 1986. He helped develop the first international collegiate licensing program in Japan. He wrote the first book on collegiate licensing entitled, *The Complete Guide to Collegiate Licensing* and a general licensing book, the *Primer on Licensing*. He is a member of ICLA's Hall of Fame.

Rick Van Brimmer succeeded Anne Chasser at Ohio State University and oversees the licensing program, athletic merchandising and sponsorship and affinity contracts. He grew revenues from less than $1 million to more than $14 million. He is a past Chairman of ICLA and LIMA, a member of the ICLA Hall of Fame and teaches a licensing course at Oho State.

2.3.3.8 Sports

John Bello joined NFL Properties ("NFLP") in 1979 as one of its first employees and quickly became its president. He grew it from $30 million to $3 billion by the time he left in 1993. He created the model by which every major sports league operates. He then formed South Beach Beverage Company that marketed a "New Age" beverage product called SOBE that he sold to Pepsi for a reported $370 million.

Ralph Irizarry was a member of the sports marketing group at Licensing Corporation of America where he helped develop the licensing programs for the major sports leagues before they assumed control. After leaving LCA, he formed ROI Marketing where he was the North American licensing agent for the FIFA Women's World Cup and the Women's United Soccer Association.

Rick Isaacson first joined IMG in Licensing which grew into the licensing company in the world. company's longest-term programs for IMG's most PALMER and TIGER WOODS; its CHAMPIONSHIPS; and for various brands like STEINWAY. 1968 and went on to found IMG largest celebrity, trademark, and event When he left IMG in 2006, Rick was the employee. He created licensing renowned athletes, including ARNOLD biggest properties, like the WIMBLEDON

Sal LaRocca heads the licensing group at the National Basketball Association where he is responsible for all aspects of the NBA, WNBA and NBA Development League merchandising business. He was responsible for the completion of the NBA's global merchandising and marketing partnerships with ADIDAS and SPALDING. He has been a member of LIMA Board of Directors.

Rick White was the former CEO of Major League Baseball Properties ("MLBP") and oversaw its expansion from 1988 to 1994. He shaped it into the most dominant licensing, marketing and publishing organization in professional sports, growing annual retail sales of baseball licensed merchandise from $200 million to over $6 billion in six years.

2.3.3.9 The Press

Francesca Ash, publisher of London-based Total Licensing Group, is one of the most recognized names in licensing and was one of the first to promote the globalization of the industry. She started A4 Publications with Christopher Sykes which published *The Worldwide Licensing Directory* and now also publishes *Total Brand Licensing, Total Art Licensing, Total*

Licensing UK and *Total Licensing Australia*.

Arnold Bolka* founded The Licensing Letter in 1977. After introducing the newsletter, he helped organize the Licensed Merchandisers' Association ("LMA") for manufacturers and licensees and served as its Executive Director. He played a role in merging LMA with the Licensing Industry Association ("LIA") to form LIMA in 1985.

  In 1983, when many thought licensing was a fad marketing trend that would fade, **Harvey Stern, Judy Basis** and **Jim Silver** saw licensing as a nascent industry and formed Adventure Publishing and launched the first magazine directed to the new industry, the *Licensing Book*.

 Steven Ekstract is the Group Publisher of *License Global*, which he helped launch in 1998 and which has become a leading source of news and trends for the global consumer products and licensing industry. A publishing industry veteran, he had previously been associated with *The Hollywood Reporter, Premier Magazine* and *VideoPro*.

Ira Mayer is a journalist who had succeeded Arnold Bolka in 1988 as publisher of *The Licensing Letter* and other associated publications. He continued publishing this newsletter until its sale in 2012. He's been an active speaker on licensing topics and developed conference programs on entertainment marketing and licensing under the *Licensing Letter* banner.

2.3.3.10 The Lawyers and Accountants

 **Greg Battersby*** became LIMA's counsel in 1995 and spent the next 23 years overseeing its legal affairs, serving on its Executive Committee and chairing its education committee. Because of his legal representation of a wide array of licensing clients; his more than 200 talks on the subject; and his publication of more than 40 books on licensing and related IP issues, including the seminal treatise entitled *The Law of Merchandise & Character Licensing* he was instrumental in creating the law of merchandising.

Tom Harrison is a former Disney auditor who formed Royalty Management Associates in 1983 to exclusively conduct on-site licensee royalty reviews. He has provided licensors with a cost-effective way to develop an audit plan, so they can visit all Licensees, making the on-site visits an integral and on-going part of their operation.

Bruce Hosmer was LIMA's first counsel. His work in licensing traces back to his days at Gulf + Western where he did the Paramount Pictures licensing and related IP work. He played a major role in structuring LIMA's relationship with Expocon for the Licensing Show.

Jim Kipling is a veteran toy industry attorney who was General Counsel for Kenner-Parker/Tonka Toys and eventually VP Law at Hasbro. He negotiated the first two rounds of the STAR WARS licenses on behalf of Kenner as well as the rights to BATMAN, JURASSIC PARK and TERMINATOR movie series as well as licenses with the NFL, NBA, MLB and NHL.

David Rosenbaum is a former Paramount Pictures attorney who has enjoyed a great career in licensing before his untimely passing. He has represented many players in licensing and was an expert in legal issues involving video and computer games and related technology and the licensing of brands, character, comic book, entertainment and sports properties.

Charles Schnaid is a retired partner of the accounting firm, Miller Kaplan, Arase & Co. with over 5 decades of experience as an accountant. He developed a specialty in royalty accounting and, in addition to working for a myriad of different licensing clients, has been an accounting referee in high profile licensing cases. He's a former LIMA Board member.

Bruce Siegal is Senior Counsel at Learfield Licensing, after having spent 30+ years serving as CLC's VP and General Counsel. He was a member of CLC's senior management team, active in working with the NCAA and law enforcement in pursuing infringers and counterfeiters. He is a founding member of CAPS – Coalition to Advance the Protection of Sports logos, the IP protection and enforcement alliance that includes the pro leagues and collegiate institutions. He is a member of the ICLA Hall of Fame.

Judy Willis was a staff attorney for both Parker Bros. and Mattel and eventually became Mattel's Sr. VP of Business Affairs where she was negotiating license agreements around the world for Mattel's properties, including BARBIE and HOT WHEELS. She enjoyed one of the best reputations of any attorney in licensing.

2.3.3.11 Retailers

Cindy Levitt is VP General Merchandise Manager at Hot Topic. She is a veteran of the retail industry and has been involved in licensing for decades and its impact on retail. She started as a buyer with May Department Stores before joining Hot Topic as its first buyer. She then became VP Music and Licensing before eventually assuming her current position. She is a frequent speaker on licensing issues and is LIMA's Vice-Chairman.

Beth Schlansky is president of Beth Schlansky, Inc which provides licensing agent and consulting services for licensors, manufacturers and retailers. For many years, she had been VP Licensing for the retailer Spencer Gifts and was a LIMA Board member where she shed light on many retailer issues.

Sy Ziv served Toys "R" Us for 26 years in a variety of positions, including EVP. He helped develop and frame the Toys "R" Us concept and made contributions to nearly every facet of the promotional toy business. He was the first retailer to feature licensed characters and is a member of the TIA Hall of Fame as well as serving on the LIMA Board of Directors.

2.3.3.12 The Trade Associations and Trade Shows

LIMA Founder Murray Altchuler

In the late 1970's, a group of property owners and licensors formed what they called The Licensing Industry Association and chose **Vicki Jones** as its Executive Director. On April 1983, a group of manufacturers and licensees formed the Licensed Merchandisers' Association under the direction of **Arnold Bolka** of the Licensing Letter and **Jerry Robinson** of Pilgrim Industries.

These two organizations merged in 1985 and formed The Licensing Industry Merchandisers Association ("LIMA") under the direction of ex-Licensing Corporation of America executive, **Murray Altchuler**. Altchuler continued as the head of LIMA until his retirement in 1997 when he was succeeded by **Charles Riotto**.

Today, under the guidance of Mr. Riotto, LIMA is now the leading trade organization for the global licensing industry. Its membership includes over 1,300 companies and individuals engaged in the marketing of licensed properties, both as agents and as property owners, manufacturers, consultants, publications, lawyers, accountants, and retailers, etc. in the licensing business. Mr. Riotto will retire effective June 30, 2018 and **Maura Regan**, formerly Licensing Director at Sesame Workshop, will succeed him effective July 1, 2018.

LIMA's mission is to foster the growth and expansion of licensing around the world, raise the level of professionalism for licensing practitioners, and create greater awareness of the benefits of licensing to the business community at large. LIMA maintains offices in the United States (headquarters), Australia, Brazil (ABRAL), China, Germany, Japan, Mexico and the United Kingdom, with representatives in Canada, France, India, Italy, Korea, Russia and the Middle East. Members in over 40 countries enjoy access to an array of benefits, including extensive educational programming and worldwide networking events. LIMA is the exclusive sponsor of events organized by UBM's Global Licensing Group: Licensing Expo, Brand Licensing Europe, Licensing Expo Japan, Licensing Expo China, and the NYC Summit. Visit licensing.org for more information and to utilize licensing's definitive online resource.

Alfred (Fred) Favata* was president of Expocon Mgt. Assoc., a major producer of trade shows worldwide. Twenty-three years ago, he realized that licensing was an emerging and viable industry that would benefit from a professional trade show.... The Licensing Show. His vision was to create an environment in which all individuals involved in the business of licensing would come together to establish relationships, educate, and discuss emerging trends. This included character, sports, corporate, fashion and entertainment. He saw the future of licensing not only as a marketing tool, but eventually developing into an industry that would have a major influence on culture. He proved prophetic.

2.3.3.13 International

The Creators

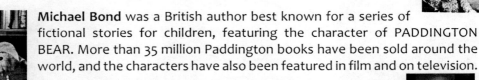

A.A. Milne was an English author, best known for his books from the 1920's about the teddy bear called WINNIE-THE-POOH and his friends PIGLET, EEYORE and others. The Pooh characters were licensed by his agent, Stephen Slesinger, to Disney and are some of the most successful properties of all time.

Michael Bond was a British author best known for a series of fictional stories for children, featuring the character of PADDINGTON BEAR. More than 35 million Paddington books have been sold around the world, and the characters have also been featured in film and on television.

Pierre Culliford, a/k/a/ Peyo, was a Belgian cartoonist best known for his work on the comic strips THE SMURFS and JOHAN AND PEE-WIT, in which the Smurfs first appeared. THE SMURFS centered on a group of small blue, fictional creatures that live in mushrooms. Peyo began producing comic strips for daily newspapers shortly after World War II.

Joanne Rowling a/k/a **J. K. Rowling**, is a British novelist, best known for her HARRY POTTER fantasy series. Her books have won multiple awards and sold more than 400 million copies, becoming the best-selling book series in history. They are the basis for one of the largest and most successful licensing programs in history.

The Agents and Representatives

Africa

Michael Eve was the Managing Director of Trigger Licensing and was one of the first licensing agents in South Africa. He was on the initial Advisory Board of *The Merchandising Reporter.*

Asia

Marilu Corpus is CEO of Click Licensing Asia which she formed in 1998. She had previous been the International Licensing Director for United Media Licensing and MGM. Under her direction, Click grew to become a leading Asian Brand Management Company, operating in 8 different countries with a corporate headquarters in the Philippines. She is the first Asian representative to sit on LIMA's Board.

Hubert Co is president of Empire Multimedia Corporation in the Philippines which he has developed into a premier licensing firm that has expended into 8 different countries over a 30-year period.

Australia and New Zealand

Fred Gaffney was one of the first licensing agents in Australia, representing properties such as STAR WARS, BARBIE, DISNEY and SESAME STREET as well as developing programs for home-bred Australian children's shows, such as BANANAS IN PAJAMAS, to be exported abroad. He is known around Australia as "Mr. Licensing" and is widely considered one of the pioneers of the licensing industry.

Tom Punch founded Haven Licensing in New South Wales in 1994 which has won multiple worldwide licensing agency of the year awards representing properties from 20th Century Fox, Sesame Workshop, HIT Entertainment, and MGA Entertainment.

Benelux

Cyril Speijer* of Wavery Productions has been a "go-to agent" for character and brand licensing for more than 50 years in his native Netherlands. He has managed the rights to the characters ASTERIX & OBELIX as well as LUCKY LUCKE and represented Lucasfilm, Universal, EON Productions, United Media, and others. He is a former LIMA Board member.

Canada

Sandie Hatch is the CEO of Voo Doo Entertainment and one of the first licensing agents in Canada. She has been a supporter of the licensing industry for decades and has overseen some of the early international expansion of LIMA as its VP International.

France

Jean-Michel Biard of JMB Consulting first entered the licensing business in 1964 and has represented such properties in France as BATMAN, SUPERMAN, CHARLIE CHAPLIN, LAUREL & HARDY, BUGS BUNNY, DAFFY DUCK, THE MUPPETS, BARBIE, THE FLINTSTONES, PEANUTS, ZORRO, NINTENDO and THE NINJA TURTLES, to name but a few. He was LIMA's first non-American member.

Pierre Gaucher formed RMP Licensing in France in the 1980's representing properties such as BETTY BOOP and other King Feature properties. RMP was eventually acquired by Biplano SAS.

Germany

Gunter Vetter is the Managing Director of Euro Lizenzen, a licensing agency in Munich which he founded in 1980 and which specializes in the development of licensing programs for character, art, publishing, entertainment, properties and corporate brands in the European markets. He is the winner of a LIMA Lifetime Achievement Award.

Michael Lou is the CEO at V.I.P. Entertainment and Merchandising in Hamburg Germany which he founded in 1980. He is President, European License Marketing & Merchandising Association and regularly represents and consults with major property owners. He is the author of numerous articles and publications in the field including the Germany section of this work.

Japan

Hidehiko Kanda of the International Merchandising Company in Tokyo was among the first to seek out possible licensees for US sports brands, first with Mark McCormack of IMG and later as an independent consultant. He was key in finding major licensees for UCLA which resulted in a surprisingly successful licensing program.

Douglas Kenrick, the founder of Douglas Kenrick (Far East) Limited, was a pioneer in licensing in Japan representing the only true port-of-call for overseas licensors entering the Japanese market in the 1960's. During that period, he represented most of the major brands and celebrities including THE BEATLES, TWIGGY, 007, DC COMICS, WARNER BROS. etc.

Shintaro Tsuji* is the founder of the Tokyo-based character-branded merchandise company Sanrio with its HELLO KITTY property. He has served as the producer for the animated movies Sanrio made from 1977 to 1985 and is a storywriter.

Mexico

Elias Fasja-Cohen* started in licensing in 1977 as a fashion licensee for the French brand Cacharel and later with Perry Ellis. In 1990, he co-founded Tycoon Enterprises which soon became the agent for brands such as Cartoon Network, Mattel, FIFA, the NFL and many others.

Maca Rotter is currently President & CEO of La Panaderia Licensing & Merchandising, a company she formed after heading the licensing business for Televisa where she acquired experience in wholesale and retail distribution strategies working with brands. She is the author of the only Hispanic published book about Licensing.

South America

Elias Hoffman was the founder and president of the Exim Licensing Group in Argentina and grew it into the largest licensing agency in South America. He was a LIMA Board member.

Sweden

Peder Tamm founded Sweden's Plus Licens Plus in 1977 which is Europe's largest independent licensing company. With 30+ years of licensing know-how, he oversees related offices in Russia, Eastern Europe, Paris and Tokyo. He specializes in movie and TV-driven Entertainment Properties and fashion-driven Design Rights.

United Kingdom

David Cardwell & Richard Culley formed what is now known as CPLG in 1974 which is now the largest agency in Europe. It was the first licensing agency to open multiple branches in other countries when it entered into a joint venture with Merchandising Munchen headquartered in Amsterdam, making it the first Pan-European Agency. He received the UK Honorary Achievement Award.

Richard Culley

Nicholas Durbridge founded the Copyrights Group in 1984 which became one of the leading licensing agents in England, representing such classic properties as PETER RABBIT, PADDINGTON BEAR, FATHER CHRISTMAS and the GREENWICH POLO CLUB. He was a pioneer of pre-school licensing.

Kelvyn Gardner has been LIMA-UK's MD for the past decade. He began in licensing in 1979 by marketing Disney products for an Italian publishing company. He later founded Merlin Publishing which became the fastest growing private company in the UK based on his ability to get key licenses. He is a recipient of the UK Honorary Achievement Award.

Andrew Maconie of LMI was one of the early executives of IMG under Mark McCormack. He founded LMI with initial representation rights from Lucasfilm for STAR WARS and INDIANA JONES. He also successfully launched NFL licensing in the UK in the 1980s.

John Sinfield founded PSL Licensing with Chris Patrick which was one of the first independent licensing agencies in England. The business endured for almost 40 years before his untimely death. He received the UK Honorary Achievement Award.

Robert Sutherland, now of the Redan Company, had previously managed MARVEL's licensing business for a decade before embarking out on his own in the 1980's. He pioneered comic books for preschoolers.

Walter Tuckwell of Walter Tuckwell and Associates was one of the early pioneers in licensing in the UK. He is most famous for creating and licensing the mascot for the 1966 FIFA World Cup in England, i.e., the WORLD CUP WILLIE.

Chapter 3
The Licensing Industry Today

3.1 Size and Scope of the Industry

It's unlikely that any of the exhibitors and attendees who gathered in the basement of a New York City hotel for the first Licensing Show in 1981 would have ever have imagined that they were witnessing the birth of an industry. That first show, which was produced by Expocon Management Associates and its president, Fred Favata, had a couple of dozen tabletop exhibits and less than a thousand attendees.

Danny Simon at Early Licensing Show

Thirty-six years later, that same show, now called Licensing Expo, has moved to and become a Las Vegas extravaganza with over 5,000 brands and properties being exhibited to over 20,000 attendees from over 65 countries.

Licensing Expo 2017

The current owner of the Expo is UBM, LLC who purchased the show rights from Advanstar Communications who had bought out Expocon years before. UBM recently announced plans to merge with London-based Informa PLC which, after the merger, will become one the largest exhibition countries in the world, with assets more than £6 billion.

It is also unlikely that any of the attendees in 1981 would have ever believed that it would spawn almost a dozen licensing shows outside the United States, many of which are significantly larger than the original New York Show. The Hong Kong Licensing Show held in early January, and

BLE Show in London

China Licensing Expo

now in its 16th year, is the second largest licensing show. The 2018 event drew a record attendance of 22,000, from over 100 countries and regions. Brand Licensing Europe, held every fall in London, is perhaps the third largest of these international shows with 280+ brands and more than 7,500 attendees and exhibitors in 2017.

Other international licensing shows include the Brand Licensing & Merchandising Show in India, the China Licensing Expo, the Licensing Mart and the Day of Licensing in Germany, the Dubai Character and Licensing Fair, and the Licensing Expo Japan in Tokyo.

In addition, there are licensing events or pavilions taking place at other industry-specific trade shows such as the Bologna Book Fair in Italy and MIPCOM in France, as well as several other trade events that feature licensed products such as New York Toy Fair, Magic and CES.

Likewise, few of the attendees at that first licensing show could have envisioned that the licensing industry would grow to a size that supports more than half a dozen trade publications devoted exclusively to licensing, including *The Licensing Letter*, *Total Licensing* which includes editions for at least three other countries), *License Global*, *The Licensing Book*, *Royalties* and *The Licensing Journal* as well as publications in Spain (*Licencias Actualidad*, based in Barcelona), Germany (the *Licensing Press*, based in Rodermark), France (*Kazachok*, based in Paris) and India (*License India*, based in New Delhi). In addition, licensing topics are regularly covered in industry-specific publications, including *KidScreen*, *Brand Week*, *Billboard*, *Variety* and *Women's Wear Daily*.

Similarly, it is difficult to imagine that those who attended the 1981 Licensing Show would ever believe that the "licensing industry" could actually support a trade association with more than 1,300 corporate members—the International Licensing Industry Merchandisers Association "("LIMA"). LIMA was formed in 1985 through the merger of two separate organizations: The Licensing Industry Association ("LIA"), which had only licensor members, and the Licensed Merchandisers Association ("LMA"), whose members were primarily licensees.

The "licensing industry" also supports another trade association directed exclusively to collegiate licensing, the International Collegiate Licensing Association, which has almost 500 members.

Since 2000, LIMA has sponsored and published an annual Licensing Survey, initially conducted by the Graduate Business School at Yale University that reported on licensing revenues received by licensors through the sale of licensed products in North America. The Survey broke down the revenues by property type and product category. In 2015, LIMA expanded this survey to a worldwide study by working with Brandar Consulting Group, LLC. These Licensing Surveys not only report on the industry for the present year, but also compare the results with prior years to identify trends.

Global retail sales of licensed merchandise grew to $271.6B in 2017, a 3.3% increase over the $262.9B reported for the prior year. Most of the growth in 2017 was entertainment-centric, driven by the content-rich entertainment/character, celebrity, art and music categories. These results are very much in line with the record year at the movie box office worldwide, where ticket sales were driven by blockbusters like Star Wars: The Last Jedi, Wonder Woman and Guardians of the Galaxy 2.

LIMA's Worldwide Survey of the Licensing Industry is published annually & available at www.licensing.org. It is free to LIMA members and at a nominal cost to non-members.

Royalties generated by licensing revenues in 2017 rose 2.6% from last year to $14.5B. The slightly lower increase in royalty revenues is the by-product of a 1.2% decrease in the weighted average industry royalty rate from 8.2% to 8.1%.

The 2018 LIMA Survey reported yearly licensing revenues broken down by each property type and product category, as follows:

Global Retail Sales of Licensed Merchandise, By Property Type, 2017

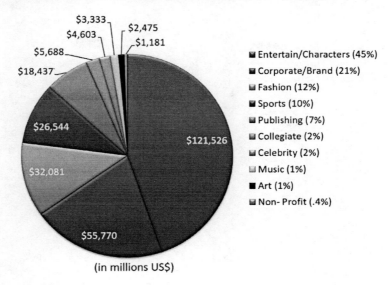

$3,333 $2,475
$4,603 $1,181
$5,688
$18,437
$26,544
$32,081
$121,526
$55,770

- Entertain/Characters (45%)
- Corporate/Brand (21%)
- Fashion (12%)
- Sports (10%)
- Publishing (7%)
- Collegiate (2%)
- Celebrity (2%)
- Music (1%)
- Art (1%)
- Non- Profit (.4%)

(in millions US$)

Global Retail Sales of Licensed Merchandise, By Product Category, 2017

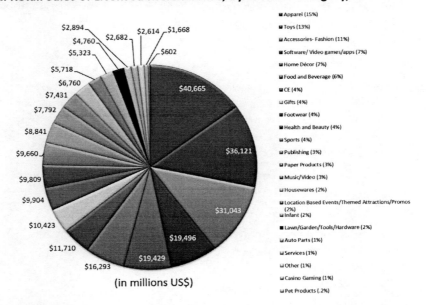

$2,894 $2,614 $1,668
$4,760 $2,682
$5,323 $602
$5,718
$6,760 $40,665
$7,431
$7,792
$8,841
$9,660 $36,121
$9,809
$9,904 $31,043
$10,423
$19,496
$11,710
$19,429
$16,293

- Apparel (15%)
- Toys (13%)
- Accessories- Fashion (11%)
- Software/ Video games/apps (7%)
- Home Décor (7%)
- Food and Beverage (6%)
- CE (4%)
- Gifts (4%)
- Footwear (4%)
- Health and Beauty (4%)
- Sports (4%)
- Publishing (3%)
- Paper Products (3%)
- Music/Video (3%)
- Housewares (2%)
- Location Based Events/Themed Attractions/Promos (2%)
- Infant (2%)
- Lawn/Garden/Tools/Hardware (2%)
- Auto Parts (1%)
- Services (1%)
- Other (1%)
- Casino Gaming (1%)
- Pet Products (.2%)

(in millions US$)

The Survey also addresses and considers which countries or territories sold the most licensed products. The following is a geographic distribution of sales by region:

Global Retail Sales of Licensed Merchandise, By Region, 2017

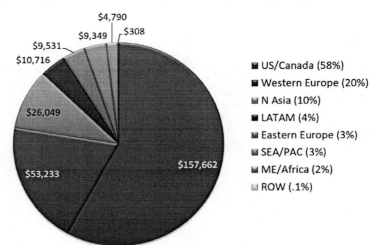

$4,790
$9,349 $308
$9,531
$10,716

$26,049

$53,233

$157,662

- US/Canada (58%)
- Western Europe (20%)
- N Asia (10%)
- LATAM (4%)
- Eastern Europe (3%)
- SEA/PAC (3%)
- ME/Africa (2%)
- ROW (.1%)

(in millions US$)   Chart C

It should be appreciated that a full copy of the 77 page "LIMA 2018 Licensing Industry Survey" is available free to LIMA members as a direct download at https://www.licensing.org/research/licensing-survey/ Information is provided at that webpage for non-members who would like to purchase the survey. This Survey is published annually about the time of each year's Licensing Expo so one should check back annually for the then current Survey.

3.2 The Major Licensors

There is no question that Disney is now by far the largest and most powerful licensor, particularly after its acquisition of Marvel and Lucasfilm. It's virtually impossible, however, to determine with any degree of accuracy the ranking of the next nine property owners since many licensors consider their actual licensing revenues a closely guarded secret. Thus, any attempt to create such a list is nothing more than pure speculation.

License! Global published a list of Top 150 Licensors in 2018 based on what they estimated to be total sales at retail of their licensed products. The top ten in that list based on total worldwide retail sales in billions were:

1. Walt Disney Company$53.3 B
2. Meredith Corp. $23.2B
3. PVH $18B
4. Universal Brand Development $7.3B
5. Hasbro $7.1 B
6. Iconix Brand Group $7B
7. Warner Bros. Consumer Product Group $7B
8. Major League Baseball $5.5B Estimated
9. Nickelodeon $5.5B
10. Authentic Brands Group $5.3B

3.3 Most Popular Licensed Properties

The 10 most popular licenses in 2017 for kids in the United States according to a LIMA research report conducted by Brand Arts entitled *Awareness and Popularity of Brands and Properties Among Children* in October 2017 were: BATMAN, LEGO, NIKE, SPIDERMAN, SPONGEBOB SQUAREPANTS, PAW PATROL, MICKEY MOUSE, BARBIE, HARRY POTTER and DISNEY.[3] The most popular sports properties were BARCELONA FC, REAL MADRID, NEW YORK YANKEES, NBA, and LOS ANGELES LAKERS.

In 2017, LIMA commissioned a research program identifying the most popular licenses for children 0-14. The program identified the following properties as most popular for this age demographic:

- BATMAN
- NIKE
- LEGO
- SPONGEBOB SQUAREPANTS
- BARBIE
- DISNEY
- ADIDAS
- TOM & JERRY
- HARRY POTER
- MICKEY MOUSE

Popularity varied by age group. For example, for ages zero-two, MICKEY MOUSE was the leading property; for ages three-six, it was PEPPA PIG; and for ages seven-nine and 10-14, it was NIKE.

The study also considered which properties were the most mentioned as a function of their origin and reported as follows:

Cartoons
- SPONGEBOB SQUAREPANTS
- PAW PATROL
- MICKEY MOUSE
- TOM & JERRY
- PEPPA PIG
- BTEEN TITANS GO
- MY LITTLE PONY
- SCOOBY DOO
- PJ MASKS
- ADVENTURE TIME

Movies
- FROZEN
- MOANA

- TROLLS
- CARS THE MOVIE
- MINIONS
- HARRY POTTER
- STAR WARS
- SPIDER MAN
- AVENGERS
- TOY STORY

Books
- HARRY POTTER
- MICKEY MOUSE
- WINNIE THE POOH
- DIARY OF A WHIMPY KID
- CURIOUS GEORGE
- BATMAN
- CURI THE CAT IN THE HAT
- SPIDERMAN
- FROZEN
- ELMO

TV Shows
- RAW PATROL
- SPONGEBOB SQUAREPANTS
- SESAME STREET
- MICKEY MOUSE
- IJESSIE
- PEPPA PIG
- MICKEY MOUSE
- THE WALKING DEAD
- MY LITTLE PONY
- DORA THE EXPLORER

Comics
- BATMAN
- SPIDER-MAN
- SUPERMAN
- WONDER WOMAN
- IRON MAN
- THE INCREDIBLE HULK
- THOR
- HARLEY QUINN
- CAPTAIN AMERICA
- SUPER GIRL

The top celebrities, according to the study, were JUSTIN BIEBER, SELENA GOMEZ, JOJO SIWATAYLOR SWIFT, KATY PERRY, THE ROCK, VIN DIESEL, MILEY CYRUS, BEYONCE and KIM KARDASHIAN, while the top sports celebrities were LIONEL MESSI, CHRISTIANI

MINALDO, LEBRON JAMES, MICHAEL JORDAN and STE-
PHEN CURRY.

A complete copy of the LIMA's Study entitled "Awareness
and Popularity of Brands and Properties Among Children"
dated October 2017 is available on LIMA's website at
www.licensing.org free to its members. Non-members
should contact LIMA at 212-244-1944 for copies at a nominal charge.

> LIMA's Study entitled
> "Awareness and Popu-
> larity of Brands and
> Properties Among Chil-
> dren" dated October
> 2017 is available on
> LIMA's website at
> www.licensing.org. It is
> free to members and at
> a nominal cost to non-
> members.

The NPD Group reported that in 2018 the top licenses
across all ages were: PAW PATROL, MICKEY MOUSE, FRO-
ZEN, NFL and DISNEY PRINCESS. They had reported in
2017 that licensed books made up 12 percent of all book
sales, as well as 28 percent of all children's book sales. It
found that DR. SEUSS was the leading book license in
2017, followed by James Patterson, HARRY POTTER, DIARY OF A WIMPY KID AND STAR
WARS. However, when it comes to top licensor, Disney was the leader due to its vast assortment of characters. The remaining top license owners include Penguin Random House,
Scholastic, Abrams and Nickelodeon/Viacom. The top publishers in 2017 were Penguin Random House, The Walt Disney Company, Scholastic, The Hachette Book Group and Harper
Collins.

3.4 LIMA License of the Year Award Winners

The following Properties were named LIMA's "Licenses of The Year" since 1989:

> 1989: CALIFORNIA RAISINS
> 1990: BATMAN
> 1991: TEENAGE MUTANT NINJA TURTLES
> 1992: THE LITTLE MERMAID
> 1993: THOMAS THE TANK
> 1994: BARNEY & FRIENDS
> 1995: LION KING
> 1996: WINNIE-THE-POOH
> 1997: GOOSEBUMPS
> 1998: RUGRATS
> 1999: TELETUBBIES
> 2000: POKEMAN
> 2001: POWERPUFF GIRLS
> 2002: BOB THE BUILDER
> 2003: SPIDERMAN
> 2004: BRATZ
> 2005: SPIDERMAN 2
> 2006: STAR WARS
> 2007: PIXAR CARS
> 2008: HIGH SCHOOL MUSICAL
> 2009: BAKUGAN
> 2010: THE TWILIGHT SAGA: NEW MOON
> 2011: TOY STORY 3

2012: ANGRY BIRDS
2013: SKYLANDERS
2014: DUCK DYNASTY
2015: FROZEN
2016*[4] STAR WARS: THE FORCE AWAKENS, PEPPA PIG, GIRL SCOUTS
2017*ROGUE ONE: A STARWARS STORY, PAW PATROL, GIRL SCOUTS
2018* JOJO SIWA

3.5 The Major Licensees

In its August 2017 issue, *License! Global* [5]identified the top licensees in their respective products categories as follows:

ACCESSORIES

- Accessory Innovations (www.accessories-innovatons.com)
- Alfilo Brands (www.afilo.com)
- Essential Brands (www.essentialbrands.com)
- Fantasia Accessories (www.fantasia.com)
- Fast Forward (www.fastforwardny.com)
- Fifth Sun (www.fifthsun.com)
- FAB Starpoint (www.fabny.com)
- High IntenCity (www.highintencity.com)
- Majesty Brands (www.majestybrands.com)
- Nouveau Eyewear (www.nouveaueyewear.com)
- MAD Engine (www.madengine.com)
- Safilo (www.safilogroup.com)
- SHR Jewelry Group (www.shrjewelrygroup.com)
- Spray Ground (www.sprayground.com)
- VMC Associates (www.vmcaccessories.co.uk)

APPAREL
- ABG Accessories (www.abgnyc.com)
- Adjmi Apparel Group (www.adjmi.com)
- Alfilo Brands (www.afilo.com)
- Bentex Group (www.bentex.com)
- Berkshire Fashions (www.berkshireinc.om)
- Bioworld (www.bioworldcorp.com)
- Blues Clothing (www.blues-clothing.com)
- Changes (www.changesonline.com)
- Children's Apparel Network (www.childrensapparelnetwork.com)
- Cooneen by Design (www.cooneenbydesign.com)
- Cudlie Accessories (www.cudlieny.com)
- Elope (www.elope.com)
- Essential Brands (www.essentialbrands.com)

---

[4] After 2015, LIMA replaced their "License of the Year" category with separate awards for different property categories.

[5] Note that License Global updates this list annually in its August edition. Copies are available online at www.licenseglobal.com

- Freeze (www.freeze-showroom.com)
- Her Universe (www.heruniverse.com)
- High Point Design (www.moret.com)
- Hybrid (www.hybridapparel.com)
- Isaac Morris Limited (www.isaacmorris.com)
- Jellifish Kids (www.jellifishkids.com)
- Jinx (www.jinx.com)
- MAD Engine (www.madengine.com)
- Millennium Apparel Group (www.magbrands.com)
- Misirili (www.misirili.co.uk)
- Miworld Accessories (www.miworldaccessories.com)
- MJC International (www.gomjc.com)
- Neon Tuesday (www.neontuesday.com)
- New Era Cap (www.neweracap.com)
- New York Accessory Group (www.nyagroup.com)
- NYD Apparel (www.ntdapparel.com)
- Oleas Enterprises (www.odmart.com)
- Paul Dennicci (www.dennici.co.uk)
- Planet Sox (www.planetsox.com)
- Ripple Junction (www.ripplejunction.com)
- Roy Lowe & Sons (www.roylowe.co.uk)
- Sahinler (www.sahanier.fr)
- Time 100 (www.time100.cn)
- Trevco (www.trevcoinc.com)
- Trau & Loevener (www.trau-loevener.com)
- Ty (www.ty.com)

AUTOMOBILE ACCESSORIES
- Kaufman Exports (www.kaufman-neuheiten.de)

COSTUMES
- Disguise (www.disguise.com)
- Rubie's Costume Co. (www.rubies.com)

ELECTRONICS
- Bentex Group (www.bentex.com)
- Sakar (www.sakar.com)

FINANCIAL SERVICES
- Card.com (www.card.com)

FOOD
- Candyrific (www.candyrific.com)
- DecoPac (www.decopac.com)
- Golden West Food Group (www.gwfg.com)
- Jelsert (www.jelsert.com)
- Kinnerton Confectionary (www.kinnerton.com)
- Ping Solutions (www.pingsolutions.com)
- White Coffee (www.whitecoffee.com)

FOOTWEAR
- ACI International (www.aciint.com)

- Alfilo Brands (www.afilo.com)
- BBC International (www.bbcint.com)
- Caleres (www.caleres.com)
- Crocs (www.crocs.com)
- Leomil Group (www.leomilgroup.com)
- SG Companies (www.thesgcompanies.com)

FURNITURE
- Delta Children's Products (www.deltachildren.com)

HEALTH & BEAUTY AIDES
- Corsair International (www.corsair.co.uk)
- Coty (www.coty.com)
- Grosvenor Consumer Products (www.grosvenor.eu.com)
- Keep Me Group (www.keepmegroup.com)

HOLIDAY DÉCOR
- Kurt S. Adler (www.kurtadler.com)

HOME & HOUSEWARES
- Avec UK (www.avekus.com)
- Bentex Group (www.bentex.com)
- Betesh Group (www.beteshgroup.com)
- Character World (www.characterworld.uk.com)
- Essential Brands (www.essentialbrands.com
- Jay Franco and Sons (www.jfranco.com)
- Just Funky (www.justfunky.com)
- The Northwest Company (www.thenorthwest.com)
- Stor (www.storeline.es)
- Thermos (www.thermos.com)
- Silver Buffalo (www.silver-buffalo.com)
- Vandor (www.vandorproducts.com)

JEWELRY
- The Carat Shop (www.the caratshop.co.uk)

LUGGAGE

- Fast Forward (www.fastforwardny.com)
- FAB Starpoint (www.fabny.com)

PARTY/EVENTS
- American Greetings Properties, (www.americangreetings.com)
- Amscan (www.amscan.co.uk)
- Unique Enterprises (www.favors.com)

PET PRODUCTS
- Bentex Group (www.bentex.com)
- Sentiments (www.sentimentsinc.us)

PUBLISHING
- Bendon Publishing (www.bendonpub.com)
- Centum Books (www.centumbooksltd.co.uk)
- Darkhorse Publishing (www.darkhorse.com)
- Egmont UK (www.egmont.co.uk)
- Hallmark (www.halmark.com)
- IDW Publishing (www.idwpublishing.com)

- Parragon (www.parragon.com)
- Penguin Random House (www.penguinrandomhouse.com)
- Scholastic (www.scholastic.com)
- Titan Books (www.titanbooks.com)

SLEEPWARE

- AGE Group (www.agegroup.com)
- Alfilo Brands (www.afilo.com)

STATIONERY

- American Greetings Properties, (www.americangreetings.com)
- Blueprint Collection (www.blueprintcollections.co. uk)
- Danilo Promotions (www.danilo.com)
- GB Eye (www.gbeye.com)
- Hallmark (www.halmark.com)
- Innovative Design (www.innovativenyc.com)
- Pyramid International (www.pyramidinternational.com)
- Savvi (www.savvistuff.com)
- The Topps Company (www.topps.com)

TOYS/NOVELTIES

- Bandai America (www.bandai.com)
- Candyrific (www.candyrific.com)
- Caratmundi (www.cartimundi.com)
- Caeco (www.caeco.com)
- Character Options (www.character-online.com)
- Cryptozoic Entertainment (www.cryptozoic.com)
- Fisher-Price (www.fisher-price.com)
- Forever Collectibles (www.forevercollectibles.com)
- Funko (www.funko.com)
- Giochi Preziosi Group (www.giochipreziosi.it)
- Golden Bear Products (www.goldenbeartoys.com)
- Hasbro (www.hasbro.com)
- Hot Toys (www.hottoys.com.hk)
- Huffy (www.huffybikes.com)
- Jakks Pacific (www.jakks.com)
- Jazzwares (www.jazzwares.com)
- Jellifish Kids (www.jellifishkids.com)
- Kids II (www.kidsii.com)
- Kidz Toys Tech (www.kidztech.net)
- LEGO Company (www.lego.com)
- Mattel (www.play.mattel.com)
- Merlin Entertainment (www.merlinentertainment.biz)
- Mezco (www.mezcotoys.com)
- McFarlane Toys (www.mcfarlane.com)
- Monogram International (www.monogramdirect.com)
- NECA (www.necaonline.com)
- Playmates Toys (www.playmatestoys.com)
- Pro and Pacific Co (www.propacific-toys.com.hk)

- Provaliant (www.provaliantgroup.com)
- Ravensburger (www.ravensburger.com)
- Sideshow Collectibles (www.sideshowtoy.com)
- TCG Toys (www.tcgtoys.com)
- Tomy Corp (www.tomy-usa.com)
- Wicked Cool Toys (www.wickedcooltoys.com)

VIDEO GAMES/ELECTRONICS
- Activision (www.activision.com)
- Electronic Arts (www.ea.com)

WATCHES
- Accutime Watch Corp. (www.accutimewatch.com)

IMG/Collegiate Licensing Company ("CLC") makes their licensee lists available on-line, searchable by school and type of licensed products. Click https://www.clc.com/Licensing-Info/Client-License-List.aspx. They had previously published a list of their top collegiate licensees in 2015 which included:

COLLEGIATE NON-APPAREL LICENSEES
1. EA Sports
2. Wilson Sporting Goods
3. Rawlings Sporting Goods
4. Tervis Tumbler Company
5. Commemorative Brands dba Balfour
6. Northwest Company
7. Team Beans
8. Logo Chair
9. Wincraft
10. Herff Jones

COLLEGIATE APPAREL LICENSEES
1. NIKE USA
2. Knights Apparel
3. Gear for Sports
4. Sports Licensed Div. of the adidas Group
5. Top of the World
6. Colosseum Athletics Corporation
7. Twins Enterprise
8. VF Imagewear (Section 101 by Majestic)
9. College Concepts
10. Outerstuff Ltd.

COLLEGIATE TOP LOCAL LICENSEES
1. Southern Collegiate Apparel
2. My Profile
3. Holy Shirt
4. University Co-Operative Society
5. A-Game Apparel
6. Kentucky Wholesale

7. J & W Interest
8. Anton Sport
9. JCS Enterprises
10. Bear Basics

3.6 LIMA Licensee of the Year Award Winners

The following licensees were named LIMA's "Licensees of The Year" in their respective categories, going back to 2005:

2017

- Apparel/Footwear/Accessories: Coach – Mickey & Minnie Mouse/Disney Coach Collection
- Appliances/Automotive/Electronics/Hardware/Housewares/Paint
  Select Brands: Disney/Pixar – Pixar Collection Slow Cooker
- Digital: NextGames – AMC's The Walking Dead: No Man's Land
- Mobile Game: Food/Beverage *(Tie) and* Finsbury Foods – Shopkins Cupcake Queen Cake & The J.M. Smucker Company – Pillsbury™ Girl Scout Cookie™ Inspired Baking Mixes
- Health & Beauty Aids: Clinique – Crayola Limited Edition Chubby Stick Lip Balm
- Home Décor: Jay Franco & Sons, LLC – STAR WARS Back-to-College & Adult Bedding
- Publishing/Social Expression/Back-to-School: Scholastic Five Nights at Freddy's: The Silver Eyes – Novel from Scholastic
- Toys/Games/Novelties/Role-Play: Mattel – DC Super Hero Girls Action Figures

2016

- Apparel/Footwear/Accessories: Peter Alexander for Sesame Street (sleepwear, outwear and accessories)
- Appliances/Automotive/Electronics/Hardware/Housewares/Paint:
  The Sherwin-Williams Company for HGTV HOME paint
- Digital Apps, Software: VideoStory Toys for The World of Eric Carle/The Very Hungry Caterpillar (apps)
- Food/Beverage: The Republic of Tea for Downton Abbey
- Health & Beauty Aids: Lovehoney for Motörhead Official Pleasure Collection
- Home Décor, domestics, furniture, giftware, textiles: Pottery Barn for STAR WARS Millennium Falcon Bed
- Publishing/Social Expression/Back-to-School: Moleskine for BATMAN Limited Edition Collection
- Toys/Games/Novelties/Role-Play: Sphero for STAR WARS BB-8 app-enabled Droid

2015

- Best Character or Toy Brand Licensee: Hard Goods: LAFOOD, Sesame Street healthy food
- Best Character or Toy Brand Licensee, Soft Goods: Under Armour, Captain America collection

- Best Corporate Brand Licensee: Reynolds Consumer Products/Hefty Brand, Arm & Hammer – Hefty Ultimate waste bags
- Best Digital Licensee: Jazwares, LLC, Minecraft Overworld Series #2 Toys
- Best Film, Television, or Entertainment (Animated) Licensee: Hard Goods – (tie) JAKKS Pacific, Disney's FROZEN/Snow Glow Elsa doll; Playmates Toys, Teenage Mutant NINJA TURTLES product line
- Best Film, Television, or Entertainment (Animated) Licensee Soft Goods: Havaianas, Despicable Me flip flops
- Best Film, Television, or Entertainment (Live Action) Licensee Hard Goods: Lovehoney, Fifty Shades of Grey: Official Pleasure Collection
- Best Film, Television, or Entertainment (Live Action) Licensee Soft Goods: Accessory Innovations, STAR WARS R2D2 light-up & voice-activated backpack
- Best Lifestyle Art, Design or Fashion Licensee: Samick Musical Instrument Co. Ltd., Paul Frank musical instruments line
- Retailer of the Year: Kohl's Department Stores, Disney's FROZEN
- Best Sports or Sports-Themed Entertainment Licensee: ISC Sports Pty Ltd., National Rugby League and MARVEL Heroes jerseys

2014

- Best Art or Design Licensee of the Year: Junk Food Clothing Co. for Jean-Michel Basquiat
- Best Celebrity Licensee of the Year: Thomas Pink Limited for The Beatles
- Best Character or Toy Brand Licensee of the Year – Hard Goods: LEGO for LEGO STAR WARS
- Best Character or Toy Brand Licensee of the Year – Soft Goods: Junk Food Clothing Co. for DC Comics
- Best Corporate Brand Licensee of the Year: Bassett Furniture for HGTV HOME Design Studio Only at Bassett
- Best Digital/New Media Licensee of the Year: Jazwares for Minecraft
- Best Film, Television, or Entertainment Licensee of the Year – Hard Goods: Playmates Toys, Inc. for Teenage Mutant NINJA TURTLES
- Best Film, Television, or Entertainment Licensee of the Year - Soft Goods: Accessory Innovations for Teenage Mutant NINJA TURTLES
- Best Sports Licensee of the Year: Junk Food Clothing Co. for Vintage NFL
- Best Retailer of the Year: Hot Topic for Doctor Who

2013

- Best Art or Design Licensee of the Year: Kids Preferred for The Very Hungry Caterpillar/The World of Eric Carle)
- Best Character or Toy Brand Licensee of the Year – Hard Goods: LEGO (for MARVEL Super Heroes)
- Best Character or Toy Brand Licensee of the Year – Soft Goods: Alfred Angelo (for Disney Fairy Tale Weddings)
- Best Corporate Brand Licensee of the Year: Sherwin-Williams (for HGTV HOME)
- Best Film, Television, Celebrity, or Entertainment Licensee of the Year – Hard Goods: CVS/Pharmacy (for NUANCE Salma Hayek)

- Best Film, Television, Celebrity, or Entertainment Licensee of the Year – Soft Goods: Vans (for Yo Gabba Gabba!)
- Best Sports Licensee of the Year: Junk Food Clothing Co. (for Vintage NFL)
- Best Retailer of the Year: Hot Topic (for The Hunger Games)

2012

- Best Art or Design Licensee of the Year: Navigate Ltd. (for Very Hungry Caterpillar/children's gardening products)
- Best Character or Toy Brand Licensee of the Year – Hard Goods: Commonwealth Toy & Novelty Co. (for Angry Birds toy & novelty products)
- Best Character or Toy Brand Licensee of the Year – Soft Goods: SG Footwear (for Pillow Pets/slipper collection)
- Best Character or Toy Brand Licensee, Soft Goods: Loungefly for Hello Kitty
- Best Corporate Brand Licensee: Shabby Chic for Simply Shabby Chic at Target
- Best Corporate Brand Licensee of the Year – Hard Goods: Thermos L.L.C. (for Under Armour/hydration bottles)
- Best Corporate Brand Licensee of the Year – Soft Goods: SGI Apparel (for Harley-Davidson/children's apparel & accessories)
- Best Film, Television, Celebrity, or Entertainment Licensee of the Year – Hard Goods: Redan Publishing Ltd. (for Peppa Pig/Fun to Learn and Bag-O-Fun magazines)
- Best Film, Television, Celebrity, or Entertainment Licensee of the Year – Soft Goods: Jay Franco and Sons, Inc. (for STAR WARS/home collection)
- Best Sports Licensee of the Year – Hard Goods: Topps International (for Indian Premier League Cricket Attax/trading card game)
- Best Sports Licensee of the Year – Soft Goods: Junk Food Clothing (for NFL/Junk Food Vintage NFL)

2011

- Best Character or Toy Brand Licensee, Hard Goods: smart USA for Hello Kitty
- Best Art or Design Licensee: Dom Pérignon for Andy Warhol
- Best Film, Television, Celebrity, or Entertainment Licensee, Hard Goods: LEGO for HARRY POTTER
- Best Film, Television, Celebrity, or Entertainment Licensee, Soft Goods: Awake, Inc. for Glee
- Best Sports Licensee: JAKKS Pacific, Inc. for Ultimate Fighting Championship

2010

- Art Licensee of the Year: LF USA's Kids Headquarters Investments Division for Paul Frank
- Character/Toy Brand Licensee, Hard Goods: Digital Blue for LEGO
- Character/Toy Brand Licensee, Soft Goods: Mighty Fine for Peanuts
- Corporate Brand Licensee, Hard Goods: Creative Designs International, a division of JAKKS Pacific, Inc. for Black & Decker
- Corporate Brand Licensee, Soft Goods: adidas Originals for Vespa
- Film, Television, Celebrity, or Entertainment Licensee of the Year, Hard Goods: Cardinal Industries, Inc. for The Twilight Saga: New Moon

- Film, Television, Celebrity, or Entertainment Licensee, Soft Goods: National Entertainment Collectibles Association, Inc. for The Twilight Saga: New Moon
- Sports & Sports-Themed Entertainment Licensee: Electronic Arts for FIFA

2009

- Art Brand Licensee: Toynami for Skelanimals
- Character Brand Licensee, Hard Goods: Kodak Gallery for Hello Kitty
- Character Brand Licensee, Soft Goods: Briefly Stated, Inc. for Disney Characters
- Corporate Brand Licensee: Sakar for Crayola
- Film, Television & Entertainment Brand Licensee, Hard Goods: Spin Master Ltd. For Bakugan
- Film, Television & Entertainment Brand Licensee, Soft Goods: National Entertainment Collectibles Association, Inc. for Twilight
- Sports & Sports-Themed Entertainment Brand Licensee, Hard Goods: Electronic Arts for Madden NFL 08
- Sports & Sports-Themed Entertainment Brand Licensee, Soft Goods: The Northwest Company, LLC for Collegiate Sports Program

2008

- Art Brand Licensee: FTD, Inc. for Vera Wang
- Character Brand Licensee, Hard Goods: Creative Designs International, a Div. of JAKKS Pacific, Inc. for Disney Princess
- Character Brand Licensee, Soft Goods: Mighty Fine for Disney Couture
- Corporate Brand Licensee: JAKKS Pets, a Div. of JAKKS Pacific, Inc. for American Kennel Club and Unilever for Life Savers Popsicle
- Film, Television & Entertainment Brand Licensee, Hard Goods: JAKKS Pacific, Inc. for Hannah Montana
- Film, Television & Entertainment Brand Licensee, Soft Goods: Millennium Apparel Group, Inc. for Hannah Montana
- Sports & Sports-Themed Entertainment Brand Licensee: Hallmark for ESPN

2007

- Art Brand Licensee: Levi Strauss & Co. for Andy Warhol
- Character Brand Licensee, Hard Goods: Scholastic Inc. for Its Happy Bunny
- Character Brand Licensee, Soft Goods: Steve & Barry's for MARVEL
- Corporate Brand Licensee, Hard Goods: Fisher-Price, Inc. for Power Wheels Jeep Hurricane
- Corporate Brand Licensee, Soft Goods: Mighty Fine for McDonald's
- Film, Television & Entertainment Brand Licensee, Hard Goods: Fisher-Price, Inc. for T.M.X. Elmo
- Film, Television & Entertainment Brand Licensee, Soft Goods: Disguise, Inc. for Pirates of the Caribbean
- Sports Brand Licensee: Steve & Barry's for Starbury

2006

- Character Brand Licensee, Hard Goods: CSS Industries, Inc. for Mr. & Mrs. Potato Head
- Character Brand Licensee, Soft Goods: Jerry Leigh Apparel for Its Happy Bunny
- Corporate Brand Licensee, Hard Goods: Fisher-Price, Inc. for Cadillac Escalade
- Corporate Brand Licensee, Soft Goods: Mighty Fine for Ford, Mustang, Pinto
- Film, Television & Entertainment Brand Licensee, Hard Goods: Hasbro, Inc. for STAR WARS
- Film, Television & Entertainment Brand Licensee, Soft Goods: Kids Headquarters for DORA THE EXPLORER
- Sports Brand Licensee: Digital Blue for Tony Hawk

2005

- Character Brand Licensee, Hard Goods: Modern Publishing for Care Bears
- Character Brand Licensee, Soft Goods: Disguise, Inc. for Care Bears
- Corporate Brand Licensee: Mead for Scholastic Brands
- Film & Television Brand Licensee, Hard Goods: Fisher-Price for Dora The Explorer
- Film & Television Brand Licensee, Soft Goods: Disguise, Inc. for Spider-Man 2
- Sports Brand Licensee: United States Playing Card Co. for World Poker Tour

3.7 The Major Licensing Agencies

In its April 2018 issue of *License Globa*[6]*l*, that publication listed what it believed to be the top 10 global licensing agencies by way of sales of licensed products in 2017. That list included:

1. CAA-GBG $12.8 B
2. IMG $12.1 B
3. LMCA $6.85 B
4. Beanstalk $6.5 B
5. Equity Management $6.1 B
6. Global Icons $5.6 B
7. Brand Central $2.7 B
8. CPLG $2.2 B
9. Joester-Loria Group $1.9 B
10. Striker Entertainment $1.5 B

A complete list of all licensing agents is available on LIMANET, LIMA's on-line directory, at http://www.licensing.org/limanet/directory/agents/ While LIMANET is restricted to LIMA members for certain searching, the list of licensing agents is open to both LIMA members and non-members alike.

3.8 International Scope of the Industry

3.8.1 Introduction[7]

---

[6] License Global updates this list annually. Reference can be had at www.licenseglobal.com

[7] Written by Gisela Abrams, LIMA's Sr. VP, Global Partnerships

While merchandising may have started out as an American phenomenon, it has since become truly international in scope. Properties are being developed and promoted in virtually every country in the world and products bearing those properties are similarly being sold worldwide. The global reach of merchandising is reflected in the makeup and structure of LIMA, which now has offices in the United Kingdom, Germany, China, Hong Kong, Australia and Tokyo as well as regional groups in Italy, Spain & Portugal, New Europe, India, Dubai and Brazil.

LIMA's membership is further reflective of the international scope of the industry, with approximately half of its membership coming from countries outside the United States. Most significantly, it is clear to anyone working in this industry that future growth of licensing activity will occur primarily in emerging markets and on a global scale.

The LIMA 2018 Survey illustrated, geographically, the impact of licensing abroad as shown in the following figure:

Licensing is a global business. While the U.S. remains the largest market for licensed goods and services, 42% of licensed retail sales happen elsewhere. So as the world keeps getting smaller and running faster, properties and brands are well-served to develop their international strategies early on.

Before anything else, it's vital to make sure that you've registered your trademarks in the countries and for the product classifications you intend to use. It's a financial, legal and strategic decision for the brand owner. Registration for multiple categories in multiple countries can quickly become expensive, so part of creating your strategic roadmap will be to identify the priority markets and priority product categories. Obviously, as the brand grows into new geographic areas and categories, you'll have to file for those, too.

Depending on whether a brand is based in entertainment, corporate, sports, fashion, publishing or celebrity, there will be different market-entry strategies to consider. But many of the same basic questions apply in determining whether a brand is ready for international expansion:

- Is there awareness in the new territories?
    - Are there enough assets or other means of engagement to sustain awareness until and after the ancillary product is brought to market?
- Is the brand the same in the new territory as it is in its original market?
    - What, if any, are the differences in how consumers perceive the brand?
    - How will this affect your target demographics and product categories?
- What's your strategy for entering new territories?

Regardless of a brand's category, it is crucial that it have visibility in the new territory. After all, if the license is totally unknown, it will lack the emotional draw and connection among a targeted consumer base that is necessary to launch a licensing effort. An entertainment brand must have a media platform, whether TV, movies, locally relevant on-demand platforms or publishing. For other categories consider such drivers as local digital and social media engagement, on-shelf presence and/or robust marketing and advertising campaigns in another product classification (CPG, automotive, corporate), or celebrity connections (fashion, music).

You've also got to understand the local competitive landscape, especially as it pertains to local/regional brands that may not be familiar globally, but will have significant share, presence and loyalty among local consumers and retailers. For example, preschoolers (and, importantly, their parents) often are attracted to the local characters and TV shows that the parent grew up with. As kids get older, they're more likely to transition to global characters and brands.

It's also extremely important to be cognizant of the local retail structure. Who are the major mass merchants? Are there any big local department stores? Are specialty retailers important? What about mom-and-pops? Where do consumers most often go to buy the kind of product that you're thinking of licensing out? What are the big online marketplaces?

If you're ready to explore taking a brand into international markets, there a few possible models to consider:

- Multi-territory/Global licensee
- Local Office
- International Agent
- Master licensee

Multi-Territory/Global Licensee

Arguably the easiest way to enter a new market is to grant an existing licensee rights in the new territories. It is important that the territory and product categories covered by the agreement be precisely defined. For example, listing the territory as "Southeast Asia" leaves open possible questions of specifically which countries are included. Despite this being a lower-risk entry, the brand-owner should still have considered the questions spelled out earlier: is there enough awareness, and does the brand resonate in the same way in the new market as it does in the existing one? (That's important especially if your licensee is taking the exact same product it already makes for one country into another.)

You want your licensee, and local retailers, to have a positive first experience with the brand and product. Using this approach, the licensee will work with a local distributor unless they have the relationship with local retailers to distribute product directly. Note that this is a more opportunistic approach and doesn't lead to a full-fledged or long-term licensing program. It can be helpful though, as a bell-weather to see if your property and merchandise resonates and help determine future opportunities.

Local Office

Another option for a brand owner is to open a local office in the new territory that's being targeted. Arguably, setting up your own local offices will give you the most control over how the brand is positioned, distributed and portrayed to consumers. But it's also the most expensive option, at least initially, since it requires an investment in personnel, office space, administrative and legal costs and other aspects related to setting up a business. While it allows for higher margins in the long run, as the brand owner, you'll have to ask yourself whether there would be enough revenue/ return on investment to justify the time and cost.

International Agent/Representative

Perhaps the most common method that brand owners use for handling business outside their home market it to hire an agent or representative. Using a local agent not only helps with language barriers, it is a relatively quick way to gain intimate knowledge of the marketplace, the retail landscape, consumer preferences, and cultural nuances. A good agent also will have established connections to retailers and to the best-in-class local licensees.

The agent's role is to represent the licensor's property and help build the brand and ancillary business based on an agreed upon strategic roadmap. While the licensor should drive the strategy, a successful partnership will result from collaborating on local implementation - and at points deviating from that plan due to take advantage of unique opportunities and local differences.

Some of the roles and obligations of an International Agent are to:

- Identify, recommend and negotiate deals with the licensees
- Facilitate execution of the contract on the licensee's side (and sometimes the licensor needs some nudging, too)
- Support product development and approvals, i.e., filter product submissions to the licensor to ensure compliance with the style guides
- Present the brand/property to potential partners, be they licensees, retailers or promotional partners
- Seek opportunities and activations for the brand such as promotions, events, marketing or publicity
- Collect advances, royalties and minimum guarantee payments from licensees
- Administer royalty reports
- Review the competitive and retail landscape and update licensor on a regular basis
- Identify trends – at times very local – that the brand could exploit or should be aware of
- Some agents go further, with capabilities such as:
  - In-house/agency art-directors to design products for the licensees which helps consistency and give the sense of a coherent program across multiple licensees
  - In-house/agency product approval for greater speed to market (if the brand owner allows)
  - Sell-in support for licensees to the retailers, as the agent tends to know the property better than the licensees
  - Support in localizing the brand's social-media efforts and platforms, and/or recommending vendors to do this
  - Identifying local celebrities, tastemakers and supplying them with product; in our world of social-media influencers and celebrities, your brand

worn/used and more importantly photographed on a celebrity can move the needle and keep/make the brand more relevant

Master Licensee

A master licensee can fulfill the same function as an agent. Additionally, it has the right to sublicense the brand, and the obligation to handle all the financial and legal back-end based on agreed-upon templates (such as royalty collection/reporting and sublicense agreements). A master licensee will aggregate the sublicensee's financials and is responsible and liable for the proper conduct of the sublicensees. Unlike an international agent, the master licensee typically pays the brand owner a yearly minimum guarantee. Given the added obligations that master licensees have, their commission is typically higher than an agent's, e.g., at around 40%-50%. The advantage for the licensor is less back-end work tracking contracts, reports and collections. Such an arrangement can sometimes be found in smaller territories, with generally smaller licensees and royalty revenues.

Finding the Right Agent

If you've decided that hiring an agent is the best model for you, you're faced with the challenge of finding the best one to help you meet your goals.

LIMA members can access and search LIMA's online directory at LIMANET to search for agents, and you can always contact your local LIMA office or representative, or the NY Headquarters, if you need additional help. Trade publications and trade shows are another great way to find out who's who, and what properties and brands they represent. Depending on your brand you may prefer a boutique agency, or an agency with offices in multiple territories.

While you want an agency with experience with the type of brand/property you want to launch internationally, it should also be weighed against their overall portfolio. If an agent represents too many of the same type of properties, you may not get the attention you want and need. Meet with several possible agents and think about whether you can envision working with them (their business practices, personalities, presentations, etc.) on an ongoing basis. Do not be afraid to trust your instincts when choosing a representative. After all, they will be the ones who will be taking care of your brand in the new market daily.

Compensation

Agents generally work on commission -- a percentage based on the royalties that are earned within the territory. The commissions can vary based on the product category that is licensed (publishing vs. products vs. promotions vs digital, etc.), but generally tend to run between 20-35%. In some instances, brand-owners have global agents that in turn will hire local/regional sub-agents. Sub-agent commissions will be slightly lower, between 15-25% depending on categories and the agreements with the master agents.

Territory

It is generally a good idea to give your agents exclusivity for the territories they were appointed for. Having more than one agent representing you creates confusion and inconsistencies which, in the end, is bad for the brand. As mentioned earlier, make sure that the territory covered by the agreement is well defined and that the agent has the capability and knowledge to do business in all the countries specified in the contract.

Style Guides

A well thought-out and comprehensive style guide is an essential tool for the brand owner to maintain brand consistency – an important factor in scaling a multi-territory licensing program. It sets out the look and feel of the brand – approved colors and logos, portrayals of characters, packaging requirements and other aspects of maintaining a unified look. In an age in which style guides commonly live online on password-protected sites, they also can be easily updated to allow brand owners to refresh looks and adapt to fashion and consumer trends, or to incorporate local seasonal themes and art treatments, e.g., Chinese New Year in China, Cherry Blossom in Japan or Diwali in India.

Logos and phrases can be adapted and translated for local territories. If that's done, however, be sure to involve your brand-marketing and legal teams, since as any new variations may need to be trademarked again.

Once you have a more established licensing program in a market, it may make sense to collaborate with locally relevant (and recognizable) artists. Visiting the international market(s) not just with the business people but also with the designers is a great way to infuse local relevancy, engage is some trend-spotting, and allows your art directors, designers and product development team to understand the market better, which in turn will positively inform their work when creating style guides and reviewing submissions.

Communication

Regular communication between the brand-owner and the international agent is critically important. You should start out any big partnership or when engaging a new agent with a brand-immersion day or days across the various departments. This should include marketing, designers, finance, legal and any other relevant vertical depending on the brand/property. Ensure that you and your team visit the international market regularly. Visit the retailers, and not just the ones that carry your brand. Meet with the licensees. Most importantly, plan summits involving all the licensees and possibly key retailers to update them about the brand, the activities. Share and learn from successes and best practices both locally and from other territories. Listen, be clear, and be curious!

Chapter 4
The License Agreement

4.1 Introduction

The cornerstone of any licensing program is the license agreement that is entered between the licensor and a licensee, as it will govern the eventual relationship between the parties. A good license agreement can make the program run smoothly, while a bad one can cause more problems than either party needs. It is often the case that once the license agreement is signed the parties never find need to refer to the document again, but should the need arise its contents and structure become crucial.

License agreements can take many shapes and forms and it is the rare case that one licensor will use the same form agreement as another licensor. Moreover, while the property owner/licensor typically starts off with a "standard" agreement, negotiations between the parties will ultimately result in a few changes. Consequently, the final signed agreements may vary significantly from one licensee to another. In an ideal situation, however, the core provisions of the licensor's standard agreement will remain consistent.

4.2 The License Agreement

When the parties conclude their negotiations, regardless of whether a term sheet or deal memo is signed, it is time to memorialize their agreement into a formal, written license agreement. The first question that immediately comes to mind is which party should prepare the agreement?

The answer may depend on whether the license agreement is part of a larger licensing program conducted by the licensor or is a one-shot agreement. It is usually incumbent on the licensor to prepare the first draft of the agreement, since it owns the intellectual property rights and has a vested interest in preserving those property rights. This is particularly true if the transaction is part of a larger licensing program. The licensor will want to have a certain degree of uniformity among all its licensees since it will not typically want to have different licensees operating under very different license agreements. Indeed, maintaining some degree of uniformity for a licensing program is important.

4.2.1 Definitions

The terminology used in most license agreements varies often and is almost always a reflection of the attorney drafting the agreement. For a better understanding of the terms most frequently used, Chapter 1 offers a useful reference point.

Different licensors call different things by different names. At the end of the day, however, it doesn't matter what something is called, it only matters what it means. What is important is that the parties expressly define what the key terms mean, and these definitions are typically contained in the first part of every license agreement.

4.2.2 Grant of Rights

The one essential provision in any license agreement is the "Grant of Rights" provision, since this is where the licensor formally grants to the licensee the right to use its intellectual property. It typically identifies the specific elements of the property that are being licensed and for what purpose(s). If the property includes multiple components or elements of artwork, it may be advisable to physically attach the artwork or define the components separately in an attached schedule or exhibit. In some cases, this provision may also identify any specific elements that are not being licensed since the inclusion of both helps to avoid future misunderstandings.

Also expressed in the grant of rights is the type of license being granted, e.g., exclusive versus non-exclusive. To review, an exclusive license agreement is one in which the licensee is the only party that can use the licensed property on the licensed products in the licensed territory for sale in a specific channel of distribution. Note that the grant is restricted by these four parameters: the licensed property; the licensed product; the licensed territory and the channel(s) of distribution. This means that the licensor can grant other exclusive (or non-exclusive) agreements to third parties for items other than the licensed property, or for products other than the licensed product, or for sale outside the licensed territory or in different channels of distribution.

Some licensors, although reluctant to grant any exclusive license, may be amenable to include a provision in the license grant which prohibits them from granting any competitive licenses for the same property for the same product in the same territory, provided that the licensee is not in breach of any provision of the agreement. This is frequently referred to as "backdoor exclusivity" since it protects both parties. The reason why a licensor may be reluctant to grant an exclusive license is the fear that the licensee may not perform or go bankrupt, in which case they could grant other licenses to competitors to fully commercialize the property. Backdoor exclusivity gives the licensee exclusivity while it is performing under the agreement but allows the licensor to seek other licensees should the licensee cease performing.

Care should be taken when granting an exclusive license because it may impede the licensor's ability to negotiate with other potential licensees at the end of the then current term and certainly will prevent the new licensee from commencing the marketing and sale of new product until the end of the current exclusive license. There should at least be a specific provision in the license grant to allow the licensor to engage in negotiations with new licensees during the last few months of the term of the current agreement and possibly even allow a new licensee to introduce products subject to commencement of sales after termination of the current agreement.

Channels of distribution have become more specific in recent years. Licensors will not only restrict the licensee's sales to a specific channel, e.g., mass market, but name specific retailers or stores to which the licensee can only sell. If the licensee wants to sell to stores not on the approved list, they will need to obtain the licensor's approval before commencing sales. It is imperative that any such approval by the licensor be fully documented since that is one thing that the licensor's auditors will focus on when audit times comes and the failure to properly document such approval can result in, at best a penalty, and at worst a notice of termination of the agreement. This is increasing important for licensees.

A checklist for possible Channels of Distribution is found in Appendix-9.

In a non-exclusive grant, the licensee may be one of potentially several licensees permitted to use the licensed property for the licensed product in the licensed territory and within the channels of distribution. As noted previously, the trend in licensing is toward non-exclusive licenses, which are far less risky for licensors.

> Sublicensing is generally not permitted in the merchandising area although a licensee can have products manufactured for it.

The license agreement should also recite whether the licensee has the right to grant sub-licenses to third parties. If the licensee is permitted to grant a sub-license, it is advisable for the licensor reserve the right of pre-approval, be a named party in the sub-license agreement or, at the very least, be notified of such grant. If sub-licensing is allowed, the agreement needs to clearly establish how the sub-licensing revenues will be handled.

Finally, the agreement should provide that the licensee will operate within the licensed territory and not knowingly ship the licensed products to entities outside the licensed territory or sell the licensed products to parties that it knows will ship the licensed products outside the licensed territory. Obviously, this provision is intended to address the issue of gray market goods where goods authorized for distribution in one country are shipped into another country that has not been authorized by the licensor.

The licensor may attempt to specifically reserve rights to certain future technologies. This has been a hotly contested issue over the years, particularly involving entertainment and motion picture rights and whether film grants included videocassette and eventually digital rights. As such, many licensors now specifically reserve all non-granted rights including, rights in any future developed technologies that incorporate the licensed property.

There may be cases where the licensee has pre-existing materials that it owns and wants to continue to own after conclusion of the license agreement, e.g., video game engines, etc. The agreement should specifically identify such materials and provide that they will remain the property of the licensee after termination or expiration of the agreement although all elements of the licensed property must be removed.

Care needs to be taken when attempting to impose control over where the licensee may sell the licensed products or the way they may sell and distribute such items, since certain restrictions could conflict with relevant antitrust laws. It is preferable to simply identify those territories or channels where the licensee can sell and distribute licensed products rather than identify those territories or channels where they cannot sell or distribute. As previously noted, sometimes, inclusion of the official language(s) that can be used when referencing the licensed product will tend to limit the markets in which the product can be distributed. Specification of language rights is often provided for in publishing agreements.

4.2.3 Term of the Agreement

The term of any license agreement will define the relevant period during which the license agreement shall remain in effect. The term may vary depending upon the licensor's pre-established criteria, or the product category. Many licensors will only grant licenses for a term of two or three years although, as mentioned, licenses for certain product categories, e.g., video games, are commonly granted for longer terms due to the time and/or cost required to develop such products. The terms of agreements that relate to copyrighted materials, e.g., in publishing agreements, are typically tied to the length of copyright protection afforded such properties. A survey by the *Licensing Letter* in 2018 reported that the most common terms of license agreements were between two (27%) and three (40) years.

In those instances where the term is established for a fixed period, a licensee will frequently request one or more options to renew the license agreement for extended terms. Options are intended to protect a successful licensee from a licensor who wishes to leverage the licensee's success and seek out a new licensee on better terms after expiration of the initial agreement. An option gives the licensee some contractual assurance that, if it has been successful, it will be able to continue the license.

The exercise of an option, however, is generally dependent upon the licensee meeting certain threshold performance-related criteria. For example, a licensor may grant a license for a fixed term of two years with the option to renew the agreement for an "extended" or "renewal" term of an additional two years *provided* that the licensee has submitted $[X] in royalty payments, was not in breach of any material provision of the agreement and notified the licensor in writing of its intention to renew the agreement at least 30 days prior to the expiration of the term then in effect.

4.2.4 Compensation Provisions

The way the licensor is compensated for the use of the licensed property by the licensee and any sub-licensees can vary widely. Possible options include:

- A one-time lump sum payment to the licensor;
- Ongoing royalty payments to the licensor, based solely on sales of licensed products by the licensee, with no advance or guaranteed minimum payment;
- Either of the above, except that the licensor is paid an advance and/or a guaranteed minimum royalty payment, which is usually recoupable against future royalty earnings.

As explained in Chapters 1 and 9, the most common form of compensation is a royalty calculated as a percentage of the licensee's net sales of the licensed products. To reiterate, "Net Sales" is almost always a term specifically defined in every license agreement. Though the actual definition varies, it will always be based on the licensee's gross sales of licensed products less certain enumerated deductions. These details of will change from agreement to agreement. For the reasons explored previously, a licensee should pay very particular attention to how net sales is defined as this can have an enormous impact on its royalty obligation.

> Net sales definition is critically important—it's at least gross sales less discounts, allowance and returns.

Again, it should also be appreciated that various types of royalties are frequently charged. Each is a function of how the licensed products are distributed, such as when the licensed products are manufactured offshore, or in such cases where the licensee may also sell the licensed products directly to consumers. F.O.B. (sometimes called an L.C. or Letter of Credit) rates are typically between two and four percentage points higher than domestic rates due, principally, to the fact that F.O.B. sales are made at a lower price point. In those instances where the licensee has both the right and the ability to sell the licensed products directly to the consumer, the royalty rate may also fluctuate. Direct sales, as this is usually referred to, provides the manufacturer the ability to sell products at the retail price. Therefore, many licensors will require that the royalty be paid on the higher retail price rather than on the wholesale price.

Most licensors require licensees to pay an advance against royalties upon execution of the license agreement, as well as some form of minimum royalty obligation. The advance against royalties is just that—an advance against the licensee's actual earned royalty obligations. It is therefore creditable against the licensee's future earned royalty payments due the licensor. In most instances, it is treated as non-refundable.

The need for an advance is quite important in the licensing industry, as it accelerates the licensor's cash flow. In most instances, the licensee will not commence the sale of licensed products for months, if not years, after entering into the agreement. Without an advance, some licensors could go more than eighteen months before they begin to see any actual royalties from a licensee. The other reason for an advance is that it serves as a further incentive to ensure that the licensee will not simply take a license and then sit idle with the property. By paying an advance, the licensee has made a definitive financial commitment to the program.

There may be some instances where a licensor requires the licensee to pay a non-refundable, non-creditable licensee fee at the time the license agreement is executed for the right to take the license. This is not very common but does occur in some categories.

Many license agreements also include a minimum royalty provision that can be either guaranteed or non-guaranteed. A guaranteed minimum royalty, as the name implies, means that the licensee is committed to paying a certain minimum amount in royalties to the licensor over either the term of the license or for a specific period. That way, if the licensed products are a failure, the licensor knows it will receive at least some minimum amount in royalties. In certain categories, e.g., art licensing, licensees will not agree to any minimum guarantee, although they may be willing to agree to a "non-guaranteed" minimum royalty which, if not met, will give the licensor the right to terminate the agreement.

4.2.5 Sub-Licensing

Few, if any, merchandising licensors allow their licensees to engage in sub-licensing since they want to control the ultimate use of their properties. While there are certainly ways to control how and what a sub-licensee does with the property, in practice, controlling a sub-licensee is inherently more difficult for a property owner than controlling a licensee.

It should be noted that—*as a matter of law*—a licensee has the right to sub-license its rights in the absence of a specific prohibition in the agreement, which is why most merchandising license agreements expressly prohibit sub-licensing.

There are, however, instances in which sub-licensing is permitted, typically with respect to international rights where sub-licensing can be a valuable substitute for a distribution arrangement. In those instances, the terms of any sub-license grant should be addressed. An alternative to sub-licensing international distributors is a sub-distribution agreement. Under this type of agreement, the licensee would continue to remain obligated to pay the licensor a royalty on product sales on the same royalty basis as for all other sales.

Where sub-licensing is permitted, the license agreement should further address how the licensor will be paid for sales made by the sub-licensee. In many cases, the licensor and licensee simply agree to share the sub-licensing revenues on some mutually agreeable basis. Again, a 50-50 split between the licensor and the licensee of net sub-licensing income (gross sub-licensing income less the cost of conducting the program, or an agent's commission if an outside agent is used) is quite common. Such a formula gives the licensee the ability to deduct its operational costs against such income prior to an equitable sharing of the profits with the licensor.

Another approach to allocating sub-licensing revenue is where the licensor receives the same royalty on the sub-licensee's sale of products as it would from the original licensee for its own sales. In such a situation, the licensee may elect to charge the sub-licensee a higher royalty than it is paying to the licensor and retain the difference.

4.2.6 Accounting Provisions

As mentioned above, one of the most important considerations in any license agreement is the definition of net sales, since this is the basis for calculating the licensee's royalty obligation to the licensor. In most any license agreement, "Net Sales" refers to the licensee's gross sales of the licensed products less whatever deductions the parties agree to permit, e.g., shipping costs, taxes, credits and discounts, and returns. It should be appreciated that the actual definition of net sales will vary from licensor to licensor and, for some, even from one product category to another.

A licensee should make certain that it has the right to deduct non-recoupable "government fees" from its gross sales. Similarly, licensors should not permit a licensee to deduct the cost of manufacturing and/or promoting the licensed product, or the cost of the royalty paid to the licensor.

Some licensors may limit the right of the licensee to deduct all returns—it may limit the deduction only to certain types of returns, e.g., defective products.

A common practice in structuring licenses for publishing properties and in certain other industries where unsold goods are returnable is that the licensee will have the right to deduct a "Reserve for Returns" from the royalties due on a per quarter basis. A fixed percentage of royalties, often 20% to 30%, is deducted from the total royalty payment to compensate for the return of the product. Most agreements will require that any reserve deducted must be accounted for in next royalty report. Therefore, if the licensee deducts a reserve of 20% in the preceding quarter when actual returns equal only 10% of the reserve deducted, the remaining 10% that is outstanding will be added to the current royalties due.

Some companies prefer to negotiate a flat percentage for all deductions rather than attempt to individually itemize each one. Such percentages normally range from between 5 % and 10% of gross sales. The inclusion of returns in this flat fee deduction can, however, cause problems for some licensees, particularly in industries where returns are commonplace. Similarly, many licensors impose a cap on the amount of such deductions.

Royalty accounting for most licensees is typically provided on a quarterly calendar basis with statements and payments due within 30 (sometimes 45) days after the conclusion of the previous quarter. Thus, licensees will normally report and pay royalties by January 30th, April 30th, July 30th and October 30th of each year. In certain industries, such as publishing, royalty accounting is provided less frequently, e.g., semi-annually or annually. Alternatively, in situations where a licensed property is particularly hot or when the reliability of the licensee comes into question, royalty accounting may be required monthly.

The agreement should clearly spell out what form the licensee's royalty statement should take and the degree of specificity required in the accounting. Many licensors require electronic reporting, in addition to hard copy. A good practice is to append a copy of a sample royalty statement to the agreement. Many licensors also require that the royalty statement be certified by an officer of the licensee to underscore the need for accurate and truthful reporting.

Questions frequently arise as to when a royalty obligation accrues, e.g., upon the sale or payment of the item. Many license agreements specifically address this question and typically require that the royalty obligation will accrue at the earliest date possible, e.g., when an order is placed rather than when payment is received.

Another question frequently presented involves the issue of inter-company sales at a discount. Most agreements provide that in such a situation, the transfer will be deemed a sale and the price can be no lower than the typical selling price for the licensed product to a third party. The failure to provide language dealing with this issue can allow the licensee to be able to distribute the licensed products at a lower effective royalty cost. There have been occasions where licensees established a bogus entity to purchases the licensed products, which then became the paper entity that distributed them to retail.

The payment question is always an issue, particularly if the licensee is in a different country. Most licensors require that all payments be made in the licensor's national currency, typically by check or wire transfer drawn on a bank in the licensor's country. This is done to avoid incurring bank collection fees. Currency fluctuations could, however, be a reason for requiring that royalties are paid in the licensee's currency.

A "blocked currency" provision is frequently requested by a licensee, particularly when it is selling product in countries where it might be difficult to get currency out of that country. Many licensors refuse to agree to such a provision, particularly if the licensee knowingly sells into a market where there is the possibility that currency will be blocked.

The agreement should also provide that the licensee will pay interest on any late payments made to the licensor. It is a good idea to establish how interest will be calculated, e.g., 0.5% per month from the date the payment was originally due. Some licensors fix the interest rate at the current cost of money, e.g., prime interest rate, or cite a specific interest index as the basis used to calculate interest due. If underpayments of royalties have occurred over a prolonged period, computing interest charges can be complicated because interest rates tend to fluctuate.

Many licensors include an acceleration provision in the agreement which provides that, upon termination of the agreement for cause, all outstanding guaranteed monies will become immediately due and payable. This avoids the unpleasant situation of having to wait (or worse yet, chase) a terminated licensee for outstanding monies.

The licensor should have the right to audit the licensee's books and verify the accuracy of the licensee's accounting. Reasonable notice is normally required, and the inspection should be at the licensee's place of business during reasonable business hours. The licensor should have the right to make copies of what it is shown during the audit, and the licensee should be required to cooperate with the audit. It might be wise to specify that the audit provision survives termination of the license agreement to avoid conflicts where a licensor elects to audit a terminated licensee.

> **Licensors need to include an audit provision giving them the right both during and after the Term of the agreement to inspect the licensee's books.**

The license agreement should further provide that in the event the audit reveals an underpayment above a threshold amount, the licensee will not only be required to pay the underpayment with interest but will also have to pay the licensor's audit costs and any attorneys' fees required to collect same. The actual threshold amount will vary from license to license, but it is common to set it as a percentage of the amount paid for the period, e.g., 3% to 5%. Some agreements provide that if the underpayment reaches a second, but higher, threshold amount, e.g., 25%, the licensor may also terminate the agreement.

The agreement should further include a provision that requires the licensee to maintain all its books and records for inspection over a period and at a location where they can be easily inspected. A typical period for retaining records is three years from the date to which they pertain. See Chapter 20 for a more thorough treatment of accounting issues.

4.2.7 Quality Control Provisions

Every merchandising agreement gives the licensor the right to exert some degree of quality control over the licensed products produced by the licensee. There are many reasons for such a provision, although the most important one is that the licensing of a trademark without monitoring the quality of the licensed products is considered "naked licensing" and can result in a loss of the property owner's underlying trademark rights.

Most licensors prefer to monitor the quality of the licensed products even if the property being licensed is not a trademark. They will frequently require the licensee to submit samples of the licensed products for review and approval at various stages of the development and manufacturing process. Such submissions are for the purpose of reviewing the actual licensed products to ensure that they meet certain minimal quality levels, as well as to confirm that the licensed property is being properly used and that all appropriate legal notices are included.

In the merchandising area, at a minimum, licensors will typically require a licensee to submit samples of the licensed products at the following stages:
- Preliminary artwork depicting the licensed property;
- Final artwork depicting the licensed property;
- Initial prototypes of the licensed products;
- Final prototypes of the licensed products; and
- Production run samples of the licensed products.

While the above may appear to be "overkill," it is important to ensure that the licensee is on the right track to manufacturing licensed products of a type and style that will be eventually approved by the licensor. Such a policy is beneficial for the licensee, since it helps identify any potential problems at an early stage and allows the licensee to make the necessary changes and corrections before starting its production run. Making changes at the earliest stages of product development will very often save the licensee both money and time.

A WORD OF CAUTION: most licensees are more than capable of producing the products without any help from the licensor. Ideally, the professional licensor is supportive of the licensee and does not use the approval process to assert artistic control over the licensed product. Reviewing products for quality and to ensure that they comply with trademark and marking requirements is far different from using the process to insist that a certain color is of the proper hue, for instance; unless, of course, such details are necessary to comply with the property's style-guide.

In addition to the licensed products, most licensors will require the right to approve a licensee's proposed packaging as well as the placement of any intended advertising. This measure helps to assure that the selected media outlets are of a type and style consistent with the image that the licensor wants to portray, that they properly depict the licensed property and that they contain all appropriate legal notices.

One primary concern of every licensee is that the licensor will unreasonably delay consideration of its sample product submissions. As noted earlier, most licensees are working on very tight production schedules, usually dictated by a retailer. If a licensor fails to act promptly in the review and approval process, it can have a significant negative impact on the success of the licensed product.

Professional licensors are rarely, if ever, dilatory in their review of sample submissions, although the actual process does take time. One way to approach this issue in the agreement is to establish a set timeframe for conducting the review and a provision for what happens if the licensor does not respond within such a timeframe. Most licensees want a failure to respond within the set period to constitute approval, while most licensors will insist that such a failure to respond be deemed disapproval. This, of course, is a matter of negotiation and compromise is always possible.

4.2.8 Representations and Warranties

Every licensor will be asked to make certain representations and warranties to the licensee, including:
- Licensor has the right to enter into the subject agreement and there are no other agreements in place that conflict with it;
- Licensor is the sole and exclusive owner of the property; and
- Property does not infringe upon the rights of any third party.

The first two warranties are relatively straightforward. The last one, however, can be problematic. This warranty is tantamount to a guarantee that the licensee's use of the property will not infringe upon anyone else's intellectual property rights. That is a very serious warranty and one that most licensors do not take lightly—particularly with respect to relatively new properties. Such a warranty requires the licensor to conduct extensive trademark and copyright searches to ensure that the use by the licensee of the licensed property will not result in the infringement of the rights of another party. For a more in-depth discussion of this issue, see Chapter 20.

Most licensors require a licensee to warrant that it will use its best efforts or, at least, reasonable commercial efforts, in advertising, promoting, and marketing the product. It is also common for a licensor to require that the licensee commence actual distribution of the licensed product by a specific date to maintain its rights under the agreement. For example, a toy licensee may be required to introduce the licensed product by New York Toy Fair 2018 (the "Product Introduction Date") and commence shipment of licensed products by another certain date, e.g., April 30, 2018 (the "Initial Shipment Date" or "Distribution Date"). The licensee's failure to meet either of these dates would give the licensor the right to terminate the agreement.

If the agreement is a worldwide agreement, consideration must be given to the distribution of the licensed product outside the United States. Frequently, the licensee is given one year from the introduction in the United States to introduce and begin selling the product abroad. Consideration may also be given to approaching this on a country-by-country basis. For example, if the licensee has not begun selling product in a country by a date, the licensor has the right to delete (or "recapture") that country from the license grant.

4.2.9 Indemnification and Insurance

Indemnification means that in the event a third party should make a claim against or sue one party to the license based on the actions (or inactions) of the other, the other party will be responsible for defending such claim and paying any costs or judgments arising from a lawsuit.

In most license agreements, the following cross indemnities are typically provided:

- Licensor will indemnify the licensee against claims based on any breach of the licensor's warranties, including claims for infringement; and

- Licensee will indemnify the licensor against claims based on any breach of licensee's warranties, including claims for product liability.

The first is simple; if the licensee gets sued because its use of the licensor's property infringes the rights of another party, the licensor is responsible and should defend and bear all costs associated with any subsequent lawsuit. This is one of the reasons why it is so important to first clear a property before commencing a licensing program, since the licensor will typically be responsible for any such claim. As stated earlier, there is no faster way to derail a licensing program than to find out that the property being licensed infringes the rights of an outside third party. The cost of even defending an infringement lawsuit can easily run into the millions of dollars and the potential liability is even larger.

The second situation is also very straight forward. If the licensee's products are defective or cause injury or death to a third party, it is the licensee's responsibility and it should be prepared to defend and indemnify the licensor because of any such claims.

Most licensors require that a licensee carry product liability insurance to fund its indemnity obligation and, further, that the licensor and its licensing agent be added as a named insured to the insurance policy. In this manner, both parties are clearly covered. There is typically no cost or fee for adding an additional party to such a policy. By extension, most licensors will require that they be notified should the licensee fail to maintain such coverage or, alternatively, change the limits of their coverage. In many agreements failure to maintain the required product liability coverage gives the licensor the right to terminate the agreement.

The licensor should take special care in reviewing these policies, paying attention to the licensee's selection of the carrier as well as the limits of product liability insurance. The minimum product liability limits will vary according to the type of licensed product. Obviously, any licensed product that can be considered reasonably dangerous, including knives or lighters or any products that can be ingested, including food products, candy, and drinks, should justify a higher limit of insurance than the standard level of $2 to $5 million per occurrence.

Some licensors will require that the licensee also carry "advertiser's insurance" which covers actions for trademark and copyright infringement and, at times, even patent infringement. Care should be taken with such type of insurance if the licensee is a publisher because some policies specifically carve out publishing activities which can be a problem if the licensee does engage in publishing activities.

4.2.10 Termination Provision

> The termination provision is, perhaps, the most important provision in any license agreement, since it will be the first provision reviewed should a problem develop between the parties.

The termination provision is, perhaps, the most important provision in any license agreement, since it will be the first provision reviewed should a problem develop between the parties. If the relationship between the parties proceeds in the manner both expected at the time they entered into the agreement, there may never be an occasion to review the written document in any significant detail. However, if a problem develops in the underlying relationship between the parties and one party wants to end the relationship, the termination provision will become critically important.

A well-drafted termination provision should give the licensor the right to terminate the agreement upon the occurrence of certain events, including:

- Licensee's failure to obtain the licensor's product approvals prior to the distribution of the licensed goods.
- Licensee's failure to introduce product prior to the product introduction date;
- Licensee's failure to meet the initial shipment date;
- Licensee's failure to maintain product liability insurance;
- Licensee's failure to make the minimum royalty payments;
- Licensee's failure to continuously sell or market products;
- Recall of the product by the Consumer Product Safety Commission;
- Licensee's protracted inability to conduct business; or
- Licensee's repeated failure to pay royalties when they come due.

In addition to the above, both parties should have the right to terminate the agreement on notice (normally thirty days) in the event of a breach of a material provision of the agreement by the other party and the party's failure to cure that breach within the notice period.

It may also be advisable for the licensor to have the option to terminate a portion of the license agreement and reclaim some of the rights being granted without terminating the entire agreement. For example, a licensor might want to reclaim a country where sales did not commence by the distribution date or even a particular type of licensed product that was simply not introduced or sold.

The termination provision should similarly address the issue of what the licensee can (and cannot) do after termination or expiration of the agreement. In most cases, the licensee will be required to cease all manufacture of the licensed products, return all the licensor's materials and provide the licensor with an accounting of all inventory on hand. Most terminated licensees will be permitted to dispose of any existing inventory for a limited "sell-off" period, provided that the termination was not the result of inferior quality products or improper use of the property. The length of such a sell-off period will vary from agreement to agreement.

4.2.11 Boilerplate Provisions

The use of the term "boilerplate" can be misleading because it implies that these provisions are blindly included in every agreement without thought or consideration. Nothing could be further from the truth. These provisions are very much intended to govern the conduct of the parties and to control how certain events will be treated. That alone makes them practically as important as the provisions discussed above.

Some of the more important "boilerplate" provisions establish:
- Who is responsible for obtaining and maintaining intellectual property protection, both domestically and internationally;
- Who is responsible for pursuing infringers and how any recovered assets are to be divided;
- Way notices are to be given under the agreement;
- Way disputes are to be resolved and what law will control;
- Conditions under which the parties may assign the agreement along with its rights and obligations; and
- Integration of the agreement and amendments.

Intellectual Property Protection

It is typically the licensor's responsibility to obtain and maintain intellectual property protection for the property. This is understandable since it is the actual owner of such property rights and the licensee is paying for the right to use the property. A property owner should think seriously before allowing another party, particularly a licensee, to assume responsibility for protecting its intellectual property.

The question of who should pay for international trademark protection is not always as clear-cut, however, principally because of the expense associated with obtaining and maintaining such protection. As explained earlier, international trademark protection must be acquired on a country-by-country basis and, as such, can get very costly. Some property owners (particularly smaller ones) are simply not in a financial position to undertake an international filing program without some assistance from its licensees. In such instances, it is not uncommon for the licensee to advance the costs associated with an international filing program with the understanding that it will be able to take a credit against its royalty obligations in the amount of such expenses. Clearly, this approach benefits both parties.

In this regard, the agreement should specifically address how much cooperation between the parties is expected and obligate the licensee to cooperate with and assist the licensor in refining the intellectual property rights protection. This will, of course, help to avoid subsequent disputes involving a refusal by the licensee to execute any necessary documents to perfect such rights.

A "licensee estoppel" provision is frequently contained in license agreements that do not involve patents. This provision prevents the licensee from challenging the validity of the licensor's underlying intellectual property rights. While courts have consistently held that licensee estoppel provisions relating to patent rights violate the antitrust laws, they are allowed in trademark and merchandising agreements.

Third Party Infringements

The right to sue infringers typically rests with the licensor. While most intellectual property statutes provide that actions can only be brought by the owner of the intellectual property rights, some courts have held that an exclusive licensee can bring an action for infringement. To address this, many license agreements expressly provide that the licensor is the only party that can initiate an action against an infringer. Some licensors do allow a licensee to bring an action of its own, however, either with the licensor's consent or if the licensor does not act in a timely manner.

In any event, the agreement should not require the licensor to pursue all infringements. Enforcement litigation is extremely expensive and there is always a law of diminishing returns. That is not meant to imply that property owners should not take reasonable steps to stop the infringement of its intellectual property rights, but the rule of reason needs to apply. It might simply not be worth spending $100,000 in legal fees to shut down a company that is selling $350 worth of infringing product. This issue is explored in fuller detail in Chapter 20.

Notices

Every license agreement needs to specifically provide how notices are to be given under the agreement and how payments are to be made, including notices for breach. There are instances where a party might want to include its counsel and its licensing agent in the notice provision to ensure that an actual copy of the notice is immediately received and acted upon.

Disputes and Forum

Most agreements address the question of disputes, specifically, what law is to apply and how and where disputes are to be handled. In domestic licensing situations, the governing law is of lesser importance since federal law will typically apply, although questions of contract interpretation can vary significantly from state to state. What is important for a licensor, however, is to make sure that all its license agreements consistently provide for interpretation under the same state law to avoid a situation where a court sitting in one state interprets a provision differently than a court sitting in another state. In international licensing, the choice of law provision becomes particularly important and requires thorough review by qualified legal counsel.

How and where disputes will be resolved is also an important consideration. The choice is typically between litigation versus arbitration and where any such proceeding will be held.

Mediation is a very effective tool for dispute resolution and a few licensors regularly require mediation as an initial step in the dispute resolution process.

Assignability and Transfer

Courts typically consider license agreements to be personal and, as such, they may not be assigned as a matter of law without the consent of the other party. Most licensors reaffirm this in the body of their agreement.

An issue that has been of prominence in recent years involves the "transfer" of a license agreement, where it moves along with a corporation that was acquired by another corporation. In such event, no assignment of the agreement is typically required. This provision can have serious consequences on a licensee who is seeking to be sold or go public. To avoid this outcome (or at least assert some authority over it), many licensors expressly prohibit the "transfer" of the license agreement if control of the licensee changes hands.

There is a trend among licensors, particularly the studios and sports leagues, to impose a "transfer fee" on the licensee as a condition for their approval. This is aimed at licensees that are going public or are being acquired. Their rationale is that the value of these licensees has increased on the strength of their licenses and, as such, the licensors should realize a share of such increase. It is not uncommon to see transfer fees in the six and seven figures. If a licensee knows that they will possibly be in play during the term of their license agreement, they should look long and hard at this provision and try to have it eliminated or at least minimized.

> **LICENSEES** beware the transfer fee—a fee the licensor may impose if the licensee is sold or goes public

Force Majeure

"Force Majeure" is a doctrine intended to protect the licensee in the event of excusable non-performance caused by an act of God, the government, war, terrorism, fire, flood, or labor troubles. Such a provision will typically excuse such non-performance during the period of trouble and then for a fixed period thereafter.

No Joint Venture

While many licensors commonly refer to their licensees as "partners," they are not so as a matter of law. In fact, most license agreements expressly state that the parties are not partners or joint venturers.

Integration

Every agreement typically includes and should end with an integration clause, which provides that the license agreement is the final and entire understanding between the parties, incorporates all prior written or oral agreements between the parties and may not be changed or modified except by written agreement signed by all parties.

Chapter 5
Compensation and Royalty Rates

5.1 Introduction

While there are a host of different ways to "value" a license, most merchandising license agreements require that the licensee pay a royalty to the licensor for the right to use the licensed property. A royalty is a percentage of the licensee's net sales of licensed products paid to the licensor.

The reason why the royalty model is so commonly used is that it permits the licensor to be able to share in the licensee's success in selling its licensed products. As the licensee's sales (and attendant revenues) increase, the amount of royalties paid to the licensor increase proportionately. Thus, the licensor can share in the licensee's "upside."

The licensor's "downside" is protected by the requirement that a licensee pay a guaranteed minimum royalty, or simply a "minimum guarantee." That way, the licensor is assured of receiving a certain minimum amount if the licensee's sales (and corresponding royalty payments) prove to be less than robust.

5.2 Setting Royalty Rates

In the overall licensing world, there are four different methodologies used by economists to establish or set an appropriate royalty rate for a transaction:

- Cost Approach
- 25% Rule
- Income Approach
- Market Approach

The first three valuation techniques are primarily used for setting royalty rates in transactions that involve patent and/or technology transfer licensing. In these areas, there can be a vast difference between the types of properties being licensed, e.g., software, computer hardware, biotech, chemical processing methods, etc., as well as the way the licensee uses the licensed property. As such, there are aspects of virtually every technology licensing transaction that make comparing them almost impractical.

The "cost approach" measures how much the licensee would have to invest if it were to develop the property itself. It then arrives at a royalty rate that would compensate the licensor for the approximate amount of such a hypothetical investment. This is clearly the least relevant method for arriving at a reasonable royalty for the licensing of any type of intellectual property, particularly a merchandising property, since it ignores the market value of the property or its income potential.

The "25% rule" assumes that the royalty rate should equal approximately 25% of the licensee's gross profits from the sale of licensed products on a pre-tax basis. This method ignores the fact that every licensed property is different and that there are marketing costs associated with the sale of such products and an inherent risk. The 25% rule also fails to consider what the impact of a 25% royalty rate would be on the retail price of the licensed item.

The "income approach" measures how much the property can generate over its lifetime, considering such factors as: (i) the amount of income that can be generated by the property; (ii) the duration of the projected income stream; and (iii) the risk associated with the use of the property. It is, perhaps, the fairest means of establishing royalty rates.

Finally, there is the "market approach" which is the approach frequently used in the merchandising area for setting royalty rates, particularly for "average" properties that are being licensed for commodity type products, e.g., T-shirts, board games, etc. This approach is, by far, the easiest to understand and to calculate. The "market approach" considers the rates charged in the market for similar types of properties and then compares the property to the overall market. It requires both an active public market, and an abundance of comparable properties. When considering average properties and commodity products for merchandising, both factors are widely present, and the resulting royalty charged will most likely allow the licensed item to be marketed at an attractive price point.

The "market approach" is used every day by real estate brokers in attempting to arrive at an asking price for a piece of real estate, i.e., by comparing the property in question to comparable properties in the neighborhood during the relevant period. The method is also commonly used for determining the value of franchises, computer hardware, vehicles, and the like. This is not meant to imply that a licensing property is the same as a house, but the analogy is being made simply as an example of how the valuation process typically works.

Economists who rely on the market approach frequently build databases of royalty rates charged for comparable licensing transactions in related areas. From that, they can develop a matrix for arriving at an appropriate royalty rate for a property when it is being licensed for a product.

The challenge, of course, is to find truly comparable properties to compare or, for that matter, comparable products. For example, both STAR WARS and MEN IN BLACK are properties based on popular motion pictures, yet one commanded royalty rates significantly higher than the other. The reasons for this difference are attributable to several factors, including:

- The strength of the property in the industry;
- Whether the property is dominant in its industry;
- The existence of an identifiable customer base;
- The demographics of the audience;
- The strength of the licensees that were brought onboard; and
- The commercial history of the property.

So, how does one arrive at the "right" royalty rate for a property when licensing it for a specific product?

For the experienced licensor with a long track record, the inquiry typically starts with looking at the last deal the property owner did for a comparable property and a similar product. In most cases, the licensor then will "adjust" that rate depending upon a number of factors unique to the specific deal, e.g., the licensee's anticipated profit margin, the extent of the competition, the popularity of the particular property, the manner in which it is going to be sold, whether there are significant development costs in creating the products, whether the licensee will need to invest significant sums in advertising and promoting the product, whether the property is protectable, etc. In some instances, the desired retail price point may also be a factor in establishing the royalty rate.

Licensors need to be fully conscious of the potential problems that its licensees will face in the marketplace and the economics of their industry. If a licensor insists on charging a very high royalty for a low margin item, the licensee runs the risk of having to set the price too high relative to its competition, thereby potentially pricing the product above a competitive price point.

The food industry is a prime example of one that typically commands lower rates, since most food producers operate on very small margins. Most licensors charge substantially lower royalty rates for these types of products, e.g., perhaps half of the royalty rate charged for a higher margin item such as apparel. This differentiation is also one reason why some of the larger licensing departments organize their sales staff by industry. By enabling each group to develop an understanding of the dynamics at play in a given industry, they are better positioned to work intelligently with their licensees on arriving at a compensation package that makes financial sense for everyone.

> **Royalty rates vary, which is most often due to a product's margin of profit, and the reason royalties for food products are typically lower than for apparel.**

Setting a royalty rate for a new property that is controlled by an unproven owner can, however, be more challenging and especially so if the licensed product being considered is unique. It would be advisable for a new property owner to consult with agents and other licensors in its category and to review industry surveys and reference materials.[8]

Royalty rate negotiations are ultimately the same; the licensor will seek the highest rate possible while the licensee will want to pay a much lower rate. In most negotiations, the parties tend to meet somewhere in the middle and arrive at a compromise rate. That said, a licensee needs to provide the licensor with justified reasons for lowering the rate—something more than simply, "I can't pay that much." Reasonable licensors will usually listen to such arguments and, if valid, may well adjust the rate accordingly.

Negotiations for hot properties can be the most difficult, particularly where there is competition for a license, or a licensee needs to appease the licensor to achieve a goal and maintain its relationship. In such a situation, a licensor may be less willing to compromise on the royalty rate.

There are different theories concerning how to open royalty rate negotiations with licensees. Some licensors prefer to avoid setting a figure directly and ask that the licensee simply "make them an offer." The number of problems with this approach could fill up a book of its own, since it implies that the property owner is truly receptive to considering

---

[8] Such references include the annual series published by Wolters Kluwer in its annual publication, *Licensing Royalty Rates 2018* by Battersby and Grimes; EPM's *The Licensing Letter's Royalty Trends Report*; ABA Press' *Fundamentals of Intellectual Property Valuation* by Anson; and Wiley's *Royalty Rates for Licensing Intellectual Property* by Parr.

"offers," which is rarely the case... unless, of course, the offer is higher than what they had originally contemplated. Such an approach creates an "auction" environment, which might well work on eBay, but is generally not preferable for the rest of the world.

Most licensors follow a more traditional approach, in which they advise a licensee of what their average royalty rate is for the property and see where that takes them. Such an approach certainly places each prospective licensee on an equal footing and avoids surprises for both parties. Even those licensors, however, are typically prepared to negotiate lower royalty rates for products that command lower margins.

Whichever approach a property owner takes, the most important thing is that it needs to carefully consider its property, including its strengths and weaknesses, fully investigate the market, take the licensee's perspective into consideration and, ultimately, agree to a royalty rate that will make the license workable for all parties. The property owner needs to remain flexible regarding the establishment of the actual royalty charged since, at the end of the day, it is the licensee who will determine the "right" royalty rate for a deal.

For example, a licensor may truly believe that its property is the next WINNIE THE POOH and establish a royalty rate of 14% because that is what he thinks Disney gets for POOH. When the licensing program gets launched, however, and the licensor finds no licensees interested in paying that rate, the licensor will need to "rethink" its strategy if it is truly interested in actually having a licensing program.

Reality is the name of the game. Many a licensing program has failed simply because the property owner arbitrarily sets a standard royalty rate that was simply not appropriate for the particular property.

5.3 Types of Royalty Rates

The licensing industry has changed dramatically over the past twenty years and, in response to these changes, most licensors have different average royalty rates to accommodate the various ways that licensed products are sold in the marketplace. These specific rates include:

- Domestic Royalty Rate
- FOB Royalty Rate
- Royalty Rate on Direct Sales
- Royalty Rate for Services
- Sublicensing Royalty Rate
- Split Royalty Rate
- Digital Sales

5.3.1 Royalty Rates on Domestic Sales

When a licensor refers to its average royalty rate, it is usually referring to the royalty rate that is applied to licensed products sold on a domestic, landed, wholesale basis through normal or conventional channels of distribution, i.e., typically from domestic warehouses to a distributor or directly to a retailer. This is also the royalty rate typically reported in most of the studies on

> Published royalty rates are typically domestic wholesale rates based on the wholesale price for the licensed products.

royalty rates and other types are normally adjusted off of this rate.

It should be appreciated that in the domestic market, royalty rates are rarely, if ever, applied to the retail selling price of a licensed product. There are, of course, exceptions, e.g., publishing, video games, etc., but, as a rule, it is the licensee's wholesale selling price that will typically serve as a starting point for determining the royalty base.

The domestic, landed royalty rate can apply to virtually all types of licensed products, irrespective of where they are manufactured, provided that they are actually sold to the retailer (or wholesaler) on a domestic landed basis with the manufacturer bearing the cost of shipping the product from its point of manufacture.

The price to the retailer or distributor is a "loaded" price and typically includes the licensee's cost of manufacturing the product, advertising or promotional costs, shipping expenses from the point of manufacture, insurance, possibly an agent's or sales representative's commission, taxes, and a profit. The combination of all these costs and expenses is what determines the manufacturer's wholesale price.

5.3.2 Royalty Rates on F.O.B. Sales

With many licensed products being manufactured off-shore, it has become common for retailers to take delivery of these products on an "F.O.B." (free-on-board) basis at their point of manufacture, which is typically in the Far East. The retailer then assumes the responsibility and cost for the transportation of these products to their eventual point of sale.

By taking possession at the point of manufacture and bearing the transportation costs, the retailer is frequently able to negotiate a significant reduction in the selling price of the product, often by as much as 30-40% from the domestic landed price. Retailers have found that they may be able to obtain lower shipping costs than a licensee, because they are often able to consolidate products from a number of manufacturers and may also avail themselves of larger volume discounts that might be unavailable to a manufacturer.

From the licensor's perspective, this practice can have a dramatic impact on the royalty revenue that it actually receives from a licensee. If the licensor applied the same royalty rate used for domestic sales to F.O.B. sales (which can be sold for as much as 40% below the domestic landed price), the licensor would receive significantly lower royalty revenue due to the product's reduced sales price.

For example, if a 10% royalty rate was applied to a $10 product sold on a landed basis, the licensor would receive $1 in actual royalty revenue for every item sold on a landed basis. If that same $10 product was sold on an F.O.B. basis to the retailer at $6, the licensor would only receive $0.60 in royalty revenue for every item sold on a FOB basis. Thus, maintaining the same royalty rate for both types of sales could effectively reduce the licensor's actual earned royalty income by as much as 40%.

As a result, most licensors will provide for an "F.O.B. Royalty Rate" on goods sold in such manner. Frequently, the differential is at least one percentage point and, more commonly, between 2 and 4 percentage points higher than the standard royalty. Thus, if the royalty rate for products sold on a domestic or landed basis is 10%, the F.O.B. royalty rate is typically set at between 12% and 14%.

5.3.3 Royalty Rates on Direct Sales

Many licensees not only sell their licensed products to retailers and wholesalers, but also sell the licensed products direct to consumers through their own mail order catalogs, factory stores and on their websites. Since the retail selling price for such direct sales is typically higher than the wholesale price, a royalty rate adjustment may also be necessary. For example, if the same royalty rate that was used for these wholesale sales was applied to its direct sales, the licensee could be paying a significantly higher royalty amount to the licensor. Thus, for example, if a toy company sold a plush product to a retailer for $10, it would pay the licensor $1 in royalties at a 10% royalty rate. If, however, the same product was sold direct to consumers on its website at $20, i.e., the price at which its retailers would be selling the product, its actual royalty to the licensor would be $2 if the same royalty rate applied.

It should be appreciated that most licensees who engage in direct sales are reluctant to sell their licensed product on a direct basis at a price much lower than that being charged by their retailers, lest they undercut their retailers' sales and possibly damage their relationship.

To compensate for the growing popularity of direct sales, a licensor may want to negotiate a different (and probably lower) royalty rate for such direct sales where the royalty is applied to retail and not the wholesale price. This will allow both parties to benefit from the increased profits generated through such sales.

The counter argument to retaining the royalty at the same percentage, or close to it, on direct sales, is the simple fact that the licensee generates significantly more profit from direct sales than from wholesale sales. This is due to the fact the licensee is selling product at a (higher) retail price point not a (lower) wholesale price. Logic dictates that if the licensee is receiving a greater profit from direct, so too should the licensor. What should be subtracted from direct sales before calculating royalties are the costs for shipping, handling and taxes, as there is often little to no profit generated from these charges.

Although the above information presents two divergent points of view, both should be taken into consideration when negotiating the royalty rate paid on direct sales. If the licensee is the entity conducting the direct sale of the licensed products, meaning there is no third party also profiting from the sale, attempt to keep the royalty percentage consistent on both the product sold at a wholesale price point and that sold by the licensee at a retail price. If the licensee balks at this, ask the licensee to provide what (if any) costs the licensee incurs on direct sales. If there are (actual) incurred costs, adjust the royalty accordingly.

5.3.4 Royalty Rates for Services

A few licensed properties, particularly characters and celebrities, are used by licensees for advertising and promotional purposes. For example, SNOOPY has become the corporate "spokes dog" for Metropolitan Life Insurance Company and GARFIELD has been used to promote Embassy Suites.

Calculating a royalty rate for using a property in conjunction with the sale of such services can be difficult and there is hardly a standard method or model used by all licensors. One method that has been used is to negotiate an appropriate royalty rate and then apply it to the amount of advertising media purchased by the licensee. Setting the royalty rate at a point between 2% and 15% of the actual media buy has been done in several instances with the understanding, of course, that more popular properties would command higher rates.

That said, the value of having SNOOPY appear on the Met Life blimp that flies over dozens of NFL and college football games a year is incalculable using this formula. In such situations, another approach is to simply charge an annual fee for the licensee's right to the use the property, that reflects how extensively the property will be used in its media buys and promotional activities.

5.3.5 Sub-licensing Royalties

While most licensors will not permit their licensees to sub-license their rights to a third party, in those rare instances where sub-licensing is allowed, the question always arises as to how the licensor should be compensated.

There are different methods for allocating sublicensing income, which include applying the licensee's own royalty obligation to the sale of sub-licensed products. Another commonly used method is to simply divide up the sub-licensing revenues between the licensee and the licensor pursuant to some equitable formula. A 50-50 split between the two is not uncommon, although circumstances and will dictate whether the licensor's share is higher or lower.

In any event, one factor to consider is the cost associated with locating and administering the sub-licensee, e.g., where the licensee is acting in more of an agent capacity. Such costs are frequently borne by the licensee out of its share of the sub-licensing revenue.

5.3.6 Split Royalty Rates

As the popularity of licensing has grown, so have the number of situations where a licensee takes multiple licenses for combined use on the same licensed products, e.g., a MICKEY MOUSE and UNIVERSITY OF MICHIGAN branded baseball cap; or where multiple sports licenses are taken, e.g., a license from MLB Properties to use a team name in combination with the name and image of one or more players. It is also quite common for a manufacturer to add licensed music and/or graphics to the product and, in other cases, may have to pay a designer or inventor for the right to use licensed technology or patents.

As one can readily appreciate, a licensee that finds itself in the unenviable position of having to pay royalties to two, three or even four different property owners for the same product may conclude that it simply cannot afford to absorb multiple royalty obligations and still offer competitively priced product.

In such instances, it is not uncommon for one or more of the licensors to agree to a reduced royalty rate to permit the product to remain economically viable in the marketplace. The question, of course, becomes which of the property owners will agree to reduce their otherwise "standard" royalty rate to allow the deal to occur. The answer is simple: the one with the least leverage.

5.3.7 Royalty Rates on Closeout Sales

Most licensors are reluctant to provide for lower royalty rates for closeout sales, believing that since the selling prices of the licensed products will be lower in closeout, their effective earned royalties will be similarly lower. Since the margins on closeout sales are lower than on traditional sales, some licensors may agree to reduce the royalty rates as well on such sales.

5.3.8 Royalty Rates For Digital Products

Attempting to establish appropriate royalty rates for a digital product, e.g., music, content, apps, simulcasting, webisodes, etc. is challenging at best, impossible at worst. In almost all cases, the rates are negotiated depending upon the specific deal and frequently instead of trying to price the license under a royalty rate model, the parties simply agree upon a flat fee to use the entirety of the property.

5.4 Average Royalty Rates

The following average merchandising royalty rates by property type were reported in a 2017 study by Wolters Kluwer in its book *Licensing Royalty Rate 2017*:

Average Royalty Rates, North America 2016

Product Category	Art		Celebrity		Entertainment		Collegiate		Corporate		Fashion		Events		Sports	
	Avg.	Range	Avg.	Range	Avg.	Range	Avg.	Range	Avg.	Range	Avg.	Range	Avg.	Range	Avg.	Range
Cosmetics, Perfume	N/A	N/A	10.0%	5-12%	8.0%	5-10%	8.0%	7-12%	7.0%	5-8%	7.0%	5-10%	8.0%	5-9%	7.0%	4-7%
Pharmaceuticals	N/A	NA	9.0%	5-10%	6.0%	5-9%	N/A	N/A	5.0%	4-8%	N/A	N/A	N/A	N/A	8.0%	5-10%
Metal Goods	5.0%	3-6%	10.0%	7-14%	11.0%	7-16%	10.0%	7-12%	9.0%	5-12%	6.5%	4-10%	10.0%	8-12%	10.0%	9-12%
Electronics, Software	4.8%	3-6%	10.0%	1-12%	9.0%	2-16%	10.0%	7-12%	8.0%	3-10%	5.0%	4-8%	10.0%	8-12%	10.0%	9-16%
Jewelry	5.0%	3-9%	10.0%	5-14%	11.0%	7-16%	10.0%	6-12%	10.0%	5-12%	7.0%	5-10%	12.0%	10-14%	10.0%	9-12%
Gifts	6.5%	4 - 9%	10.0%	6-12%	11.0%	7-16%	10.0%	6-12%	8.0%	6-12%	7.0%	4 - 9%	12.0%	8-12%	10.0%	9-12%
Stationery & Publishing	6.0%	3-12%	10.0%	5-10%	11.0%	7-16%	10.0%	7-12%	9.0%	10.0%	9.0%	5-15%	12.0%	10-14%	10.5%	9-12%
Leather Goods	5.0%	3-5.5%	10.0%	6-12%	11.0%	7-16%	10.0%	7-12%	8.0%	6.5-9.5%	7.0%	5-10%	11.0%	10-14%	10.0%	9-12%
Housewares, Bedding	6.0%	3-12%	9.0%	4-10%	11.0%	7-16%	10.0%	7-12%	8.0%	5-9.5%	8.0%	4-11%	12.0%	10-14%	11.0%	9-12%
Apparel	6.0%	3-12%	10.0%	7-15%	12.0%	7-16%	10.0%	8-18%	11.0%	6.5-12%	8.5%	4-12%	12.0%	10-14%	11.0%	9-12%
Toys, Sporting Goods	5.0%	3-6%	9.5%	5-10%	11.0%	8-16%	10.0%	7-12%	10.0%	5-12%	7.0%	4-10%	12.0%	10-14%	10.0%	9-12%
Foods	2.5%	1-4%	3.0%	2-4%	4.0%	3 - 8%	2.5%	3-10%	4.0%	3.5-8%	N/A	N/A	3.0%	3-8%	3.0%	3-8%
Non-Alcoholic Beverages	N/A	NA	4.0%	1-9%	3.5%	2-5%	N/A	N/A	4.0%	3-7%	N/A	N/A	5.0%	3-7%	5.0%	3-6.5%
Alcoholic Beverages	N/A	N/A	5.0%	1-10%	5.0%	1-4%	N/A	N/A	5.0%	3-8%	N/A	N/A	N/A	N/A	6.0%	5-9%

It should be appreciated that these rates are the average royalty rates charged for domestic, landed "net sales" of licensing properties and are in the mid-range for each property type, i.e., in the 25-75% percentile. Thus, blockbuster properties will command higher rates while lesser known or non-promoted properties will fall below the range. Obviously, the actual royalty rate chosen will vary as a function of the property and, more importantly, the type or category of product on which the property is used.

Literally, whole books are written on what merchandising royalties are appropriate for different properties used in combination with various types of licensed products. One such reference, Battersby & Grimes', *Licensing Royalty Rates*, is published by Aspen Publishers and revised annually. The work features an extensive chart that provides detailed information covering eight different categories of licensing properties and their corresponding royalty ranges for more than 1500 types of licensed products. Further information about this book is available at www.aspenpublishers.com.

5.5 Net Sales, Advances and Guarantees

While the actual royalty rate that a licensor charges a licensee for the right to use its property is important, it is but one of several compensation issues on which the parties must come to agreement. As one can imagine, there is a tremendous degree of interplay between each of these different negotiation points.

In some cases, particularly with respect to new, emerging properties that have little or no track record, a licensee may be prepared to pay a higher royalty rate in exchange for a reduction in the advance and/or guarantee sought by the licensor. Understandably, if the licensee does not have total confidence that the licensed products will sell through, it will want to avoid facing a high guarantee obligation at the end of the license for products that ultimately did not perform well. An increased royalty rate could be more palatable though, on the rationale that if the licensed products are a success then the licensee can afford to pay the higher royalty. Alternatively, if the licensor insists on requiring the licensee to commit to a high guarantee, it may have to make a concession on the royalty rate charged.

Similarly, it should be appreciated that the royalty rate is usually applied to a licensee's net sales of the licensed products, which is represented by the gross sales figure less certain defined discounts, allowances, deductions and credits. Licensees will usually want to take as many deductions and allowances as possible to reduce the ultimate net sales figure, while a licensor will want to limit them as much as possible since the greater the number of deductions permitted, the lower the royalty income will be that it receives. One of the most closely scrutinized details in any royalty investigation is always the issue of the discounts and allowances that a licensee may take versus what it is permitted to take under the license agreement.

Some licensors have simply required that royalties be calculated on a licensee's gross sales, with no credits allowed for any discounts, allowances or deductions. The theory behind such approach is that it avoids arguments over whether a deduction was permissible or not. In such a situation, it might be necessary to account for this by lowering the royalty rate because the gross sales number will always be higher than any net sales number. For further information on how "Net Sales," "Advances" and "Minimum Guarantees" are defined and calculated, reference should be made to the discussion of these topics in Chapters 10 and 20.

5.6 Marketing Contributions

Depending upon the category of licensed property, many licensors will require a contribution from most, if not all, of its licensees to a common marketing fund ("CMF"). The amount of such contribution is typically based on a percentage of the licensee's net sales of licensed products, often with a minimum payment required every quarter and/or year. Many view it simply as an additional royalty obligation. While less than 50% of licensors impose the payment of a CMF, virtually all the studios and sports league impose such a requirement. The range for these CMF contributions varies greatly, although most fall between 1% and 3% and, depending on how successfully a licensed product sells, can become substantial.

Always an issue is exactly what the licensor is required to do with the revenue that it receives from these marketing contributions. Typically, the fund is used to purchase media and advertising space for the collective benefit of all licensees involved with the program. While the licensor's actual obligation may be stated in the license agreement, it is generally assumed that the funds will not be used to underwrite the licensor's operating costs.

Chapter 6
Identifying and Clearing Licensing Properties

6.1 Evaluating Properties for Licensing

Now that you've gone through the history of licensing and seen some of the success stories, it's time to start looking at your own property to see whether it may be possible to duplicate the success of others.

What must be understood from the very start is that licensing is a financial venture. Therefore, the opening task for the licensor is to determine why anyone would invest in licensing its property. Alternatively, from the licensee's point of view, the task is to determine whether a property is worth the investment. Both questions sound simple, but they are not always easy to answer. Regardless of which side of the license equation you are on—licensor or licensee—success in licensing requires the ability to judge accurately if a property has legitimate potential for licensing. At this stage, it is also very important to make sure that use of the property in question will not conflict with or infringe the rights of any other party. These are big hurdles, but they must be cleared before embarking on the development of any licensing program.

This first step in the process requires that the property owner remain strictly objective although, admittedly, this can be difficult. Nobody believes that their baby is ugly and, similarly, everybody thinks that their property is the best thing since sliced bread. The property owner needs to accurately assess its property, whether it's a cartoon character, a house brand or a piece of artwork, and realistically determine whether it is something that, if used by another party, could help that party sell its products or services and justify the payment of a royalty.

Since objectivity is important, it is frequently helpful to bring in an independent licensing consultant to provide conduct an evaluation. Simply because a house brand works for one's own product, or a comic strip character may be enjoyed by local readers, that doesn't necessarily mean that it will have universal appeal on other types of products or in other regions. Thus, an independent evaluation of the licensing potential of the property is generally worthwhile.

In evaluating licensing properties, consultants will typically consider such factors as:

- How well known is the property?
- If the property is not well known, does it have the potential to generate licensees on the strength or appeal of its images, e.g., art properties?
- Is the property legally protected for at least the key product categories?
- Does the owner really "own" or at least "control" licensing rights for the property?
- Has the property been extensively promoted and, if not, can it be better promoted in the future?
- If it is used on a wider range of products, will it appeal to a broader class of consumers?
- What's the competition from other properties?
- If used by others, will it create legal problems?

Objectively evaluating a potential licensing property at the beginning will save everyone a great deal of time and expense in the long run.

6.2 How Well Known is the Property?

Potential licensees will want to know the answer to this question before they even consider taking a license. After all, the right to commercially exploit the recognition and popularity of the property is typically the main reason that a manufacturer is willing to take a license and pay a royalty for using it. Hence, the property owner will need to know just how popular and widely recognized its property is before proceeding with any licensing program, as it will need to convey this information to prospective licensees.

There are certain instances where licensees will take a license before a property becomes well known, e.g., a new motion picture. In those cases, the property owner will need to explain in detail what it intends to do to promote the property and make it a household word by the time the licensee's sales of licensed products actually commence. Taking a chance on a motion picture from an established studio with a big name cast and a director with a great track record may justify taking such a risk.

Taking a license for a corporate brand isn't much different—if the corporation is well established with good name recognition in a field that will answer many questions. The difference might be, however, where a licensee wants to take a license for a brand extension into an area which is unrelated to the goods where the corporation has established its name. For example, taking a license for a brand such as PLAYTEX may be relatively seamless where the licensee is looking to extend the brand from undergarments to outer garments. Taking that same license for a brand extension into jewelry boxes, however, may prove problematic since the consumer would not normally relate PLAYTEX to jewelry boxes.

The licensing of artwork is, of course, different, since in most cases promotion is not very important—licensees are usually only interested in the uniqueness or appeal of the artwork. The prospective licensee might even prefer if the artwork was not extensively exposed, to avoid having a competitor see it and quickly develop its own version.

There are many objective ways to determine how well known a property has become. For starters, most licensing consultants will ask:

- How long has the property been used for its primary products or services?
- What were the sales and the breadth of distribution of products or services bearing this property?
- Have sales of these products or services been local, national or international and what was the breakout between these three areas?
- Has the property been regularly featured in advertising or promotions and, if so, for how long, where; and how much was spent on media buys during the period?
- Has the property received media attention and, if so, how much and why?
- Has the property owner ever been approached about potentially licensing the property and, if so, what were the details?

It might also be helpful to research the property on the Internet using various search engines to see how often the property comes up and what people are saying about it. That is an easy and very inexpensive way to measure the public recognition of a potential licensing property. It is also quite helpful in determining whether there are other parties using the same or similar properties that could potentially pose problems for a licensing program.

For established characters and brands, there are services that will measure the extent of a property's public recognition and popularity and even compare it against like properties. One such service, the "Q Score" provided by Marketing Evaluations, Inc., is a measurement of the familiarity and appeal of a brand, company, celebrity or television show in the United States. A higher Q Scores means that the property is better regarded by the public. This service is used extensively by marketing, advertising and PR firms and, if the resultant Q Score is sufficiently high, it might be an important point to make in the eventual "pitch" to a prospective licensee.

For example, *The Wrap* reported that the most "liked" television actors in Fall 2017 television shows according to their Q Scores were:

- Michael Weatherly +37
- Mark Harmon +35
- Taylor Kinney +35
- Jim Parson +34
- Johnny Galecki +32
- Terrence Howard +32
- Shemar Moore +32
- Joe Montegna +31
- Jussie Smolett +31
- Tom Ellis +31
- Guillermo Diaz +31

Licensing consultants might also want to run their own market studies or surveys to determine the merchandising potential of a property. These are done in much the same way that toy companies will play or test market a new toy product, using mockups of potential licensed products and gauging the reaction of consumers to such products. There are several independent market research and survey companies who will conduct such research and even run surveys to gauge consumer reaction to products that might bear a property.

These surveys can also be helpful in determining the best way to use a property on products. Such surveys may not only help the property owner with its subsequent licensing program but may even give the property owner some insight on how to best present the property on its own primary products. This type of data can be invaluable for future licensees and may help convince an otherwise reluctant licensee to take a license.

The American Marketing Association (www.ama.org) publishes an annual list of what they consider to be the top 50 market research firms. Reference should be made to the firms identified in that list.

Any or all these steps will help the property owner make that all-important determination—is my property the type of property that, if licensed, will help a licensee sell its products or services? If, after such an evaluation, the answer to that question is in the affirmative, the property owner is ready to proceed to the next step in the process.

6.3 Ownership Considerations

Once it has been determined that the property has a potential value for use as a licensing property, the actual work begins. The property owner must confirm that it in fact owns the property to be licensed or, at the very least, controls the licensing rights to that property.

While these considerations may appear rather straight forward, this is not always the case and, if overlooked at an early stage, may have enormous consequences. One such example is the battle that developed between MGA Entertainment and Mattel over the rights to the BRATZ property. Clearly, MGA Entertainment developed and extensively marketed BRATZ dolls, but Mattel claimed that since the original designer of the property had been working for Mattel at the time of its creation, Mattel owned their underlying rights. This dispute led to years of expensive litigation and, during the pendency of the dispute, cast a giant shadow over the viability of the property in the marketplace. MGA ultimately prevails but the combined legal fees in that case were in the eight figures.

> Confirming that the property owner does, in fact, own the property, is essential before proceeding into a licensing program. If there is any doubt, Google Mattel v. MGA.

Confirming that the property owner does own or control the rights to the property being licensed is essential before proceeding further. In virtually every license agreement, the licensor is required to warrant to potential licensees that it owns or controls rights to the property and can grant the license. Should another party claim ownership in the property (even a related entity), the licensor may find itself in a breach situation that could potentially place the entire program in jeopardy. Under companion indemnity obligations in many license agreements, a licensor may be potentially liable for any damages that its licensee might suffer should it turn out that another party was the rightful owner of the property.

This inquiry is usually not necessary in connection with the licensing of a corporate brand that has been used for decades, if not centuries. For example, when the Coca-Cola Company decided to develop a licensing program for a trademark that it has owned and used for more than a hundred years, there may not have been the need to consider this issue beyond simply looking at the face of its federal trademark registration(s). Unfortunately, for many property owners, their trademark rights may not go back as far as Coca-Cola's.

That said, the fact that a property owner may own a trademark for use on one category of products does not necessarily mean that it owns it for other categories. For reasons that will be described more fully in this chapter and the next, trademark rights are typically specific to product categories. The property owner must make certain that it not only has rights to use the trademark on its own products, but that it is or will be the owner of such rights on its licensee's products and services.

For example, the Yale trademark is a very strong mark for educational services because of its use by Yale University. Nevertheless, that same mark has been used for decades by the manufacturer of locks and such use would potentially block Yale University from entering related security fields.

A problem developed years ago with respect to the OLYMPICS trademark following the 1932 Olympic Games in Los Angeles. After the Games, several businesses sprung up using the OLYMPICS name as a mark and business trade name. When the USOC came to clear potentially conflicts in conjunction with the 1984 Olympic Games, again in Los Angeles, they needed to deal with these established businesses who had decades of legitimate use of the mark.

The question of international rights is another important consideration, particularly if a worldwide licensing program is contemplated. Trademark rights are territorial, i.e., you acquire rights only in those countries where you have used the trademark and/or registered it. If, for example, the property owner is a U.S. corporation that has never conducted business outside the United States or registered its brand in other countries, a good time to find that out is before signing on as an international licensee.

Care should be taken when the property is a corporate brand, since some companies set up trademark holding companies that own the corporate trademarks and then license the rights to the individual subsidiaries. This is typically done for tax reasons. In such a situation, the property owner must make certain that the entity that owns the trademarks is the entity that will conduct the licensing program or, if not, that there is a license agreement in place that gives that entity the right to conduct the program and grant licenses or sub-licenses.

It should be appreciated that these inquiries and considerations typically only relate to situations where the property is protected as a trademark. When a property is protected under the copyright laws, the considerations concerning product categories and countries are far less important since copyrights are not product specific and, under international conventions, they provide greater protection internationally.

The licensing of potentially copyrighted artwork does, however, present different problems, since the issues involving creation and ownership can be complex. Some of the questions that need to be asked in such situations are:

- If the creators of the property were not employees of the property owner, did they perform tasks under a "work for hire" agreement or did they otherwise validly assign their rights to the property owner?
- Were the creators of the property under any obligation or agreement with another party that might prevent them from validly conveying their rights to the property, e.g., BRATZ?
- Does the property include any components that were licensed (not assigned) to the property owner, and, if so, are these rights conveyable to licensees?
- If there are multiple layers in a corporate structure, does the entity that will be conducting the licensing program own or have a right to use the property?
- In the case of studio licensing, are there conflicting agreements with producers, directors, talent, etc. that might impact the studio's ability to conduct a licensing program, or provide rights to essential elements such as actors' likenesses?
- Are there any conflicting agreements involving the property that may limit what the property owner can do with the property, e.g., rights of first refusals, options or security agreements?

Of the above questions, the one that can be of greatest concern is where the property is created by an independent contractor rather than an employee. By law, if an employee creates such a copyrightable work, the employer is generally deemed the owner of that work by virtue of the employer/employee relationship. However, when the property is created by an independent contractor, the contractor may retain ownership of the copyright to the property if there was no written "work for hire" agreement in place with the property owner, or if the rights to it were not otherwise assigned.

> If a company uses an independent contractor to develop artwork, it MUST have a written agreement with that contractor stating that such work was done on a "work for hire" basis.

The meaning of this is simple: if a company uses an independent contractor to develop artwork, etc., then it **MUST** have a written agreement with that contractor stating that such work was done on a "work for hire" basis or an agreement providing that the contractor assigns its copyright rights to the company, lest the contractor may be found to retain the copyright rights to the work.

Since many companies regularly use outside designers and independent contractors rather than employees to create new designs, this issue is a very important one and demands thorough consideration. There is no faster way to derail a licensing program than to discover that the licensor is not the owner of the property but, instead, it is owned by the outside designer who did the design work and retained the copyright rights.

As noted above, studio licensing presents some unique issues because the rights that they may wish to license are often multifaceted, with different elements derived from and potentially owned by different entities. Consider, for example, the STAR WARS property which consists of different elements, including:

- STAR WARS logo;
- Character names, e.g., LUKE SKYWALKER;
- Representations of the actors playing the role of LUKE SKYWALKER;
- Images of the vehicles used in the motion picture;
- Images of weapons used in the motion picture;
- The musical score played during the motion picture or voices of the actors; and
- Selected sets used in the motion picture.

To confirm ownership of each of these elements, it may be necessary to review literally dozens of agreements between all the parties involved with the motion picture.

Under normal circumstances, the studio owns the licensing rights but there are instances where a producer, writer, actor, vendor, supplier or even the creator of the property may have some residual rights that could potentially impact ownership of the licensed property and must be sorted out before a licensing program gets underway.

Similarly, when one is dealing with a television show that features a popular actor or actress, the line between what the studio may own versus what the actor playing the lead role may own can be blurry. For example, the television series "Everybody Loves Raymond" was based on the comedy of its star, Ray Romano. If, for example, a manufacturer wanted to produce a line of bobble head "Ray" dolls, would it need a license from the television studio or from the actor, or from both? Again, a careful review of all the agreements is necessary to confirm that the eventual licensor owns the rights being licensed.

A property owner needs to address and satisfactorily resolve all these issues before embarking on a licensing program. Since virtually every issue is different, it is recommended that a property owner discuss its specific issues with their intellectual property counsel to avoid any surprises during the eventual licensing program.

6.4 Clearing Properties

The purpose of clearing a property for use in a licensing program is to make sure that when a licensee uses the property, such use will not infringe the rights of a third party. Licensees are typically not willing to take a license for a property that could potentially expose them to liability. As such, prudent property owners will want to first "clear" a property for all contemplated uses before proceeding further.

As noted before, trademark rights are category specific. That means that when one adopts and acquires rights in a trademark for a category of good, its rights are typically limited to use of that property for that category (and, in some instances, to closely related categories) since unfettered use may potentially confuse consumers as to the source or origin of the related products.

It is not uncommon for two different owners to use the same mark for two different categories of goods. This happens quite often and is perfectly acceptable, provided that there is no "likelihood of confusion" between both uses. This is the reason why Paramount Pictures can own and use the mark PARAMOUNT for entertainment services while Paramount Chicken can own and use the identical PARAMOUNT mark for food products—the goods are sufficiently diverse that consumers would not be confused into believing that a Hollywood studio was producing chicken, or vice versa. As noted above, it can prevent a university such as Yale University from licensing the YALE mark for locks, keys and other related security products.

It should be appreciated that licensing has had a very significant impact on the way a court or the U.S. Patent & Trademark Office views the breadth of trademark protection. Prior to the advent of licensing, these finders of fact would view a trademark and the goods or services on which they were being used in a somewhat parochial manner, e.g., NYU was the name of a prestigious university, not the name of a key chain or on the front of a sweatshirt. These finders of fact have now come to understand that trademark owners now regularly grant third parties the right, under license, to use their trademarks on what would otherwise been seemingly unrelated goods. As such, they afford such trademark owners much wider latitude in determining the scope of protection afforded such marks.

Again, trademarks are also territorial in nature. Simply because a party acquires rights for a trademark in the United States, doesn't necessarily mean that it has rights in other countries in the world unless it has taken appropriate steps to protect the mark in those countries.

How does one clear a trademark for use in a licensing program? The simple answer is to search, search, and then search some more. Trademark searches are conducted on a few different levels. A good starting point for property owners is the website maintained by the United States Patent and Trademark Office ("PTO") at www.uspto.gov, which is available at no charge to the public and includes existing United States trademark registrations as well as pending applications. The PTO database is relatively current and is an excellent starting point for any search.

Additionally, it may be wise to run an Internet search using any of the major search engines to see if anyone is using the proposed property or mark for the same or similar types of products.

Unless a worldwide licensing program is absolutely ruled out, it is advisable to also search on the various international databases. The WIPO database is one place where international trademark searching can be done and is accessible at www.wipo.int/ipdl/en/madrid.

At the end of this initial round of searching, the property owner should have an excellent idea whether there are other parties who may have acquired rights in the property that could potentially conflict with their licensee's use of the property.

A WORD OF WARNING—it is the rare trademark that is cleared for use in all classes in all countries. Some conflicts will almost always be found, and it is, therefore, prudent for a property owner to consult with its intellectual property counsel to consider all the references found and obtain an opinion that use of the property for the contemplated licensed products will not infringe the rights of a third party.

An intellectual property attorney may want to expand the search, using more extensive databases that include state trademark office records and, if warranted, expand the international portion of the search.

Similarly, it may well be advisable to request that an outside search firm conduct an extensive common law search to determine whether another party might be using the mark but never got around to registering it since use of a trademark is sufficient to create rights in the mark. One of the more prominent trademark search firms is CompuMark at www.compumark.com.

It should also be appreciated that the line between whether use of a mark on a certain product is likely to cause confusion with a slightly different mark on a different product is a complex one. If there is any doubt, the advice of the property owner's intellectual property counsel should be sought.

Clearing artwork or material that is otherwise covered by a copyright is much more difficult and time consuming. This is due, in large measure, to the vast number of copyrights that have been registered with the U.S. Copyright Office as well as the difficulty in being able to quickly and easily search them. For example, there may be thousands of copyright registrations for "superhero characters" but without manually reviewing each of these images, it is difficult to determine whether a new superhero character is substantially similar to a prior copyrighted one. As such, despite conducting a copyright search, one never truly knows whether they have found the most relevant references.

A word of caution here—copyright protection is a function of the "deposits" which are attached to the copyright registration. The mere presence of a copyright registration is only step one in attempting to determine the scope of protection. It is essential to review the deposits that go along with the registration certificate since without looking at these deposits, it is impossible to answer the question whether the works are substantially similar.

Another inherent problem with copyright searching stems from the fact that copyright owners do not always register their copyright claims immediately, if at all. They may choose to wait to file an application only if an infringement problem surfaces.

Actual copyright searching may not always be necessary, however, since the basis for any claim of copyright infringement is actual copying. If the creator of the property is *certain* that its work is original and was not copied from another's work, there may not be a need to perform any copyright search since, under such a scenario, there could be no copyright infringement. Reliance on the creator's assurance that the work was not copied, however, is very thin reed since memories fade and what one may consider inspiration for a new work, others might consider slavish copying.

The courts do recognize that proving actual copying is difficult, if not impossible and, as a result, permit a copyright owner to establish infringement by showing that the alleged infringer had access to the copyrighted work and that the two works are "substantially similar."

There is the issue of "public domain" material. Material that was never protected, or material whose protection expired, is in the public domain and can be freely adopted by all. Attempting to determine whether something has entered the public domain is not an easy analysis, particularly if the work goes back decades. The Copyright Law has changed at least three times over the past 75 years and each change impacted what rights the owner had, if any. Attempting to determine whether a work is in the public domain needs to be made by experienced intellectual property counsel familiar with the applicable law.

Some properties, by their very nature, are in the public domain. One example of a public domain property that was successfully licensed is the Statute of Liberty in New York City. The fact that it was in the public domain did not, however, prevent the Statute of Liberty Foundation from developing and conducting a very lucrative licensing program to commemorate its 100th anniversary in 1976. The Foundation created an "official" artist's rendering of the famous structure, obtained appropriate trademark and copyright protection for the rendering, and then proceeded to license the rights to it. The program would go on to generate millions of dollars for the Foundation.

While non-licensed manufacturers could certainly produce their own representations of the famous lady based on their own designs, they could not use any of the IP that had been protected by the Foundation. As it turned out, the public flocked to the "official" products over the unlicensed imitations.

When considering public domain material, a property owner must be creative, attempt to develop some form of IP protection and use that IP protection as the basis of its program.

Chapter 7
Selecting the Right License for Your Products

7.1 Introduction

For the licensee, the single biggest factor determining success or failure in licensing is selection of the right property. Although it sounds easy enough, licensees very often get it wrong, which invariably leads to disappointing results. This chapter provides tips and guidelines for analyzing property choice that will help to avoid selecting the wrong property. Such important factors to consider include: product fit, understanding of expectations and goals, property evaluation and conducting proper due diligence.

7.2 Understanding Your Own Product

Having a complete understanding of your product is essential to achieving success in licensing. This goes well beyond the actual product itself; it extends to knowing the product's core consumer base, which products directly compete with it, the price point boundaries and the effects likely to result from the application of the license to the product.

When asked, who does the product appeal to, licensees are renowned for responding with statements such as "almost everyone," or "all little girls" (or boys), or some other vague definition of the prospective consumer. Most likely, this definition is not accurate, as products by and large tend to appeal to a more specific consumer base. True, sales to consumers outside of this core consumer group are frequently achievable and perhaps even likely. However, a wise policy is to compute sales forecasts based *only* on projected sales to the core consumer demographic. By basing sales estimates solely on core consumer estimates, sales that involve non-core consumers will provide some buffer against forecasting errors.

> To be successful, you need to have a complete understanding of your own product and intended consumer.

Two pieces of information can be of significant help in developing reasonable product offerings. The first is having sound knowledge of those products that are directly competitive. This information allows the licensee to better judge what the likely effects will be of producing a licensed version of the item. The other is to analyze what sales appeal the prospective license will afford to your product.

By virtue of the fact that use of a license will require paying a royalty on each unit sold, the cost per unit escalates. The royalty, like any other cost incurred in producing a product, is a factor in determining the cost price, and therefore, will impact both the wholesale and retail price points.

Thus, the key question becomes, will this additional cost sufficiently affect product sales to the retailer and/or the consumer? In order to keep products priced competitively, is the licensee forced to absorb some or all of royalty, which will lower profit margins? Alternatively, is the strength of the license such that the consumer will be receptive to an increase in price? Knowledge of the retail price range of competitive products places the licensee in a better position to understand just how elastic retail prices are, and therefore, more capable of determining what the impact will be from the addition of the royalty.

7.3 Developing Reasonable Expectations and Goals

Before making a commitment to secure a property, the licensee should have a clear understanding of what the reasonable expectations and goals to be achieved from the license are. Yes, the primary objective is of course to increase sales, but this is not the only consideration; the key question is, *how* will the license help achieve that goal. Taking the time to examine how the license will potentially help achieve greater sales provides an understanding of more underlying factors, which also will prove very valuable. For example, will the license help achieve greater shelf space, aid in the development of additional product SKU's, support efforts to acquire additional retail distribution, and/or aid in selling additional products within the broader product line?

It is also important to set reasonable sales expectations which then must be assessed in relationship to the projected costs that will be incurred because of acquiring the license. Such costs are not simply the Advance and Guarantee commitments to the licensor, but must include those related to product development, packaging and marketing expenditures. For some products, particularly in the toy and electronic areas where molds and software development are necessary, the development costs can far exceed the costs of any advance or guarantee.

If, for example, recouping these costs requires an additional 15% increase of sales, then a license that projects only a 10% sales increase will mean a potential loss of 5%. It is obvious that no licensee would proceed if the results were likely to generate a loss, but without analyzing what the increase in costs will be from committing to the license, the licensee may not be able to anticipate this.

7.4 Finding and Evaluating the Right Properties

On the floor of the annual Las Vegas Licensing Expo trade show it is estimated that something like 5,000 properties are offered for licensing. While that number may seem a bit overwhelming, relying on impulse is not a particularly wise or effective approach to selecting the right property to license.

Choosing the right property, one that is best suited to both product and need, is *the* most critical decision for any licensee and, without some form of a checklist, the task is that much harder. Defining the criteria that a license must meet from the outset can simplify the process immensely. By way of an analogy, selecting the right property is like purchasing a pair of shoes: The first step is to focus only on those shoes that meet the intended need (objective); then determine whether they are comfortable (fit); are they in stock (timing); and are they affordable (cost)?

7.4.1 Prospecting for the Right Property

As discussed earlier, there are a plethora of ways to find potential properties to license, most notably:

- The Internet
- Licensing Directories
- Licensing Trade Publications
- Attending Trade Shows

- Employing consultants or manufacturer representatives

7.4.2 Objective

As used here, *objective* means the intended benefits derived from the selection of a property. Before venturing out, it is imperative that the licensee has a clear understanding of those goals that acquisition of a property should accomplish (and no, *"to sell more stuff"* does not constitute a complete list of goals). Without such knowledge, it is almost impossible (luck notwithstanding) to make the right selection.

Creating a list of objectives is simply identifying those (hoped for) results that a license can generate. Whether the goal is to reach a new consumer demographic, extend the appeal of a product line to a broader age range, or to achieve distribution into a new segment of the retail market, without comprehension of purpose, the process is primed for failure.

At the end of the day, however, when considering possible licensing properties, a manufacturer needs to ask one question, "How will this help me sell my product?"

7.4.3 Fit

The simplicity of the word *fit* is misleading. Unlike shoe shopping, determining the right fit between property and product may not be as simple or obvious. In licensing, the term *fit* refers to the selection of a property that will complement the intended product. Fit also applies to the potential for the property to assist in meeting pre-established objectives, such as increasing sales or opening new lines of distribution.

The relationship between property and product should be symbiotic, meaning that the license will prove helpful in developing a better or more appealing product, and the property will be well served by its application to the product. The term 'symbiotic' is ideal for describing what the licensee and licensor should strive for in their relationship, as both entities should be mutually enhanced through their collaboration. Achieving this requires that both entities are secure in the alliance, and that the relationship meets the criteria of being logical and/or natural.

> If the property you are considering has already been licensed, research how other licensees are using the property to insure it's consistent with your own plans.

Typically, it is easy to spot those combinations that are ill conceived or the result of a "forced fit" between the license and product. Licensed items for which this disconnect is apparent do not coalesce into a unified product and are not only likely to be unsuccessful at retail, they may indeed have a resounding negative impact on the property. Conversely, combinations of product and property that are in harmony and perceived as line extensions rather than licensed merchandise, are more likely to not only enjoy good sales, but to also reinforce the appeal of the licensed property.

In addition to ensuring that the combination of the two elements produces a good product, *fit* should also be measured by the property's capacity to support the licensee's objectives. As an example, if the objective is to create a licensed product that will generate considerable appeal to 4-6-year-old girls, then the selected property should provide evidence that it has appeal to this specific demographic.

One approach to establishing whether the selected property is compatible with the product's core consumer is to request from the licensor any market data which supports that this is in fact true; the more credible the proof, the greater the assurance of its fit.

If that property has been licensed for products that are already available at retail, a trip to the stores to inspect those items is a wise investment of time and effort. When there, speak with the retailer to determine their impression and that of their customers.

Also, request a list of the property's current licensees. Simply reviewing the names of companies already committed to the program may reveal useful information. There is, of course, an obvious resource, the Internet. Spending some time online might also deliver valuable information and insights about the property that perhaps are not so readily shared by the licensor.

The last point under the fit column is consideration of what the wholesale and retail price points are likely to be. As the creation of any product requires an investment, the licensee must ascertain whether selecting a license will require a capital investment above the level of the traditional development budget. It is also important to consider what impact the per unit royalty fee will have on price points.

Finally, does the license demand compliance with a marketing program that entails certain financial obligations? Any or all these factors are likely to affect product price points and, as such, financial considerations should be included on the checklist when judging fitness.

7.4.4 Timing

This point is best presented by example. For a manufacturer of school supplies, there is a reasonably narrow retail window in which to market this sort of merchandise. Although products such as notebooks, rulers or paste can be found at retail year-round, the bulk of such goods are generally only sold from mid-July through mid-September. For a manufacturer in search of a new property for the next season, timing as it relates to the introduction date of a property into the consumer market is a very crucial factor. A feature film with a Christmas release date, even if it has the support of a huge marketing and promotion budget, is likely to be either forgotten or old news by mid-summer. Of course, there are exceptions, but Las Vegas probably offers better odds.

"Seasonal" goods, e.g., products such as holiday-related merchandise, calendars, various forms of apparel and of course school supplies, to name a few, operate with fixed limits as to the dates when such goods must hit the retailer shelf and the date by which such merchandise is usually removed. With a limited retail window, it is important to carefully consider not only the timing from a seasonal perspective (as referenced above), but timing as it relates to consumer tastes or interests as well.

As a further example using school supplies again, we know that late Summer to early Fall is when most of such merchandise is sold. At the same time, using the category of sports to illustrate the point, the baseball season is heading toward its playoffs and, therefore, is likely to receive increased media exposure. As such, for the manufacturer of school supplies interested in taking a sports license, is baseball a comparatively better property to bet on than hockey, whose season typically starts in early October – well after the school supply retail window? In most instances, yes. This isn't to suggest that hockey is not a product fit for school supplies; it is simply a matter of considering the effect of timing and using such information to make an informed decision.

There are of course a few properties (usually referred to as evergreens) where timing is of little or no concern. MICKEY MOUSE, for example, is not going away any time soon.

There are, however, several licensing categories where timing is a significant worry. As noted above, motion pictures are one example, and television programs are another. For instance, a new television show that is highly promoted prior to its debut could, in fact, not even last through the first season. This means that licensees could find themselves in the unenviable position of having product ready to market based on a cancelled show.

Perhaps the most time-sensitive properties are those based on fads, or properties that are unlikely to sustain any significant base of consumer support. Likely candidates to fall into this group are properties that lack any meaningful base of exposure. For example, from time to time a marketing campaign can generate substantial exposure and create considerable consumer interest. However, as marketing campaigns are most often fleeting, consumer interest can dissipate as quickly as it is generated.

Seen a WHERE'S THE BEEF T-shirt lately? How about any retailers offering a TACO BELL CHIHUAHUA for sale? Reaching way back, what are the chances of scoring a stuffed SPIKE, THE BUDWEISER BEER bull dog? At one time all three supported popular licensing programs and, about as quickly as they sprung up, they went into extinction.

That is not to say that fads or "short-term" properties should be avoided at all costs, since significant income can be generated by these types of programs. But, usually, they will endure for a reasonably short time period. Success in this type of licensing program comes to those licensees who meticulously manage their production levels, forecast profits based on a one-time sell in of merchandise–as going back to the well to replenish inventory can lead to financially disastrous consequences and deliver product in a timely manner–as delays in getting product onto the retail shelf may result in missing the window of opportunity to achieve a product sell-through.

7.4.5 Cost

Cost as it is used here refers to resources directly allocated to the acquisition of the property, or development of the product, and that most likely will affect the product's wholesale and retail price points. Returning to the shoe analogy, if the price is not a concern, there is likely to be a larger selection. However, price is usually an issue and therefore the budgetary constraints for these expenditures will probably have an impact on the number of different shoes available.

Looking at property acquisition costs, the usual rule of thumb dictates that the *"hotter"* the property the more expensive the rights. Like many things that are in short supply, the greater the competition the higher the price tag. If the property rights are secured under an exclusive basis, it is likely that such rights will be more expensive than rights obtained on a non-exclusive basis.

> If cost is a concern, beware of "hot" properties, particularly if you want exclusive rights.

Also impacting the price is the level of consumer exposure and/or the perceived value of the property. Rights to use a better-known corporate brand or designer label will generally be more expensive than those that are less conspicuous. However, general perception of the property can be an intervening factor. Although a designer label might be well-known, if the label is perceived as waning or outdated, whether true or not, it is likely to affect the financial terms the property owner can obtain from licensees.

What does not necessarily correlate is the price range of a property's core product lines and the cost to obtain a license. Many corporate brands produce inexpensive core products but due to such factors as the popularity of the brand, can command significant financial terms, similar to what a luxury brand can achieve for a license.

In addition to financial obligations to the licensor, important considerations are the anticipated costs likely to be incurred in developing the product line. If creation of the licensed product will not require additional (or significant) costs, this may not be of much concern. However, if committing to a license will necessitate investing in building new product molds, or incorporating new technology, such costs, which are likely to be reflected in the product's price point, must be analyzed in terms of not only profit, but what affect an increased price point might have on sales.

It is important to consider price point, both wholesale and retail, in comparison to generic or other similar licensed products. As similar products are likely to be available in proximity to your product, if the price point of your product is not competitive with other comparable products, then the licensed property must possess the necessary appeal to overcome any possible price resistance the consumer may experience.

Estimated price points of the licensed product may also be useful as a tool in negotiating licensing terms. As an example, if the license is not the strongest or most desirable property in its category (entertainment, corporate brand, or designer label), the licensee might employ the strategy of pricing the item below that of more popular brands, since a lower price may lead to its selection over stronger properties or brands that cost more. With knowledge of production costs, the licensee is in a better position to propose licensing terms that will allow the licensee to achieve the desired retail price.

The Kenner Toy Company (now a division of Hasbro) used such an approach to acquire the toy rights for the film T2. As the property TEENAGE MUTANT NINJA TURTLES was the number one boys' property at the time, Kenner designed a marketing strategy around retailing T2 action figures at one dollar below what was being charged for TEENAGE MUTANT NINJA TURTLE figures. Kenner's offer for T2 toy rights was predicated on payment of a royalty rate that would make this possible. The marketing philosophy made sense, and the offer was accepted.

7.5 Conducting Proper Due Diligence

Warren Buffet's quote, *"In the business world, the rear-view mirror is always clearer than the windshield,"* is one worth remembering. If a licensee knew before committing to a property what the ultimate results would be, then selection of the wrong or inappropriate license would never occur. However, no company can know what results will be achieved at the time it commits to a license. Nonetheless, there are steps that can be taken to minimize risk.

The idiom "*the devil is in the details*" expresses the idea that whatever one does should be done thoroughly and choosing a property to license is no exception. Among the *details* as it applies to property selection is to ensure that proper *due diligence* is conducted. Failure to perform this can be very costly.

One thing that both the licensor and licensee are certain to agree on is that licensing comes with inherent risks. As neither side has a crystal ball that can forecast the future, the licensor cannot guarantee that the property in question will be successful or will remain viable. On the other side, a licensee does not have the luxury of knowing if the selected property will achieve the desired results.

To compensate for the lack of such forecasting skills, conducting a thorough due diligence process *before* committing to a new license is the best alternative. The remainder of this chapter is devoted to providing licensees with a due diligence checklist that should be used prior to signing on the dotted line.

7.5.1 How Well Known Is The Property?

A vast percentage of successful properties share a common value: they enjoy, at the very least, a sufficient level of exposure in the market to influence consumer purchase. Many times, evaluating a property's popularity, whether to the public in general or to a specific segment of the market, will be an easy question to address.

If the property under consideration is an established brand name, a *hot* television show, a top-notch designer label or an artist of world renown, the answer can be obvious. However, this is not always the case. The property being considered may be a young brand, a new television show, an up-and-coming designer or an artist just beginning to achieve notice. If notoriety of the property and, therefore, the potential that it has to stimulate sales, is in question then it requires further consideration on two levels.

First, does the property have enough exposure today to warrant consideration? While the property under review may be new to the market, ideally it should have achieved some level of awareness. If the property has not been exposed to the whole consumer market, then at the very least it should enjoy enough notoriety with a core segment of the market to warrant the licensee's investment. While this may or not be the case at the time the commitment is made to obtain the rights, this should be the status of the property by the time product is launched into the market.

Regardless of the category, a vast percentage of products undergo a development cycle of nine months to one year. Some products, such as "A" title video games or food or beverage products, will experience a longer development period that can extend two or more years.

Therefore, it is important to analyze what state of exposure and level of desirability the property will be experiencing at the time licensed goods are due to reach the retail market. These things can make a critical difference in evaluating the property. Knowing that a film under consideration for licensing will have the support of a $50 million advertising campaign, or that a brand will be launching a new product line likely to generate significant consumer interest, may be the determining factor in proceeding with a license.

Second, in addition to evaluating the exposure component, it is equally important to understand what demographic constitutes the property's core audience. As previously referenced under *Fit,* it is essential that the demographic which the licensed product is intended to reach is consistent with the property's base of support. The closer the compatibility between the two, the better chance for success.

7.5.2 Know Who Owns the Property

Knowing who the actual property owner is may appear simple enough – the party offering the rights – but even this may prove to be a risky assumption. Most of the time the licensor offering the property has the rights, but it is a wise practice to always make certain this is true. Many times, it will require little or no effort – if the Disney Studio is offering rights to MICKEY MOUSE it is a safe assumption the licensor owns such rights. However, if the property is unknown or is presented by a third party, it is prudent to conduct a little due diligence as to who owns the property and what legal protections the property has – particularly as it relates to the potential licensee's product category.

> Find out how the licensor will support its property and try to get it written into the agreement. There is no such thing as too much information.

Researching property ownership does not necessarily require incurring legal fees, nor does it take significant time or effort. It may be as simple as comparing the party named in the copyright and/or trademark notice with the party offering the licensing rights. If these do not match find out why.

The Internet has made it very easy to perform a simple trademark search and find out whether the party presenting rights is in fact the owner. A simple search of the property can be performed by going to *www.uspto.gov*, clicking on "Trademark Search (TESS)" and following the instructions provided. It is important to remember that this method of searching a trademark is not 100 percent reliable, but it may provide sufficient information to verify the ownership of the trademark. If the results are less than satisfying, then it may be appropriate to contact a lawyer and invest in the cost of running a more thorough search.

If another party such as a licensing agent is representing the property, simply asking to see proof of representation of those rights will confirm that information. Since most licensing agents will have a representation agreement with the licensor that grants them those rights, the Grant of Rights segment of that agreement will furnish the necessary proof. If this material cannot be supplied, contacting the property's owner directly to confirm the agent's rights may be a sensible course of action.

If the simple steps outlined above do not generate satisfactory results, it is highly recommended that the next step is to enlist the services of a lawyer to investigate the question of ownership.

Committing to license a property places the licensee in the position of relying on a third party (the licensor) to perform certain functions that can directly affect the company's profitability. As the licensor is usually the source of the core materials necessary to develop the licensed products, retains the right to approve such products and has the right to rescind the rights granted if the licensee fails to perform certain functions, the relationship established between the parties is of great importance. Therefore, it is advisable that the licensee has some knowledge about the licensor, and some insights on how to manage both the business and interpersonal aspects of that relationship.

If the property being considered has current licensees, contacting one or more of them may yield some important information. Questions about the quality of materials provided by a licensor for product development, responsiveness to submission of product for approval and some understanding as to how easy or difficult the licensor is to work with, may influence the decision to proceed with negotiations of a license.

Because undertaking a license requires the investment of both dollars and time, it is advisable that the licensee always adopt a proactive posture in its relationship with the licensor, as assumptions may lead to costly mistakes. For example, instead of assuming that the licensing materials needed to commence product development are "on their way" from the licensor, make certain that they are. The loss of time in commencing product development can greatly affect the ability to meet marketing and distribution deadlines. If a reasonable amount of time has lapsed since the date a product was submitted for approval, check on its status. While being a "squeaky wheel" in tracking such progress may be a nuisance to the licensor, such proactive behavior is likely to ensure that the submitted materials are not simply languishing in someone's In-box. See Chapter 12, for additional commentary on the approvals process.

Although contractually the licensor and licensee are not "partners" (most all license agreements contain language stating that such a relationship has not been established, nor implied), embracing the notion that the relationship between the parties should be conducted like one may prove helpful in fostering a collaborative, collegial association. Asking the licensor for guidance or input may help eliminate unnecessary costs and wasted time. To illustrate, submitting product concepts to the licensor in the early development stage can significantly reduce costs if alterations are necessary. A wise mantra for licensees: *If in doubt, ask.*

7.6 Status of the Property's Protection

Licensing is predicated on acquiring the right to use protected intellectual property; the word *protected* being key. At the very core of licensing is the concept that the available intellectual property rights are under the control and management of the property owner. Therefore, use of such material is accessible only through the owner.

> Understand that taking a license means that it may well be reliant on the licensor to perform certain functions that can affect profitability.

By regulating access and use, the property owner can control not only those parties that can exploit the property, but also the type and quantity of goods produced and the level of retail exposure, where products bearing the property can be sold. Without the benefit of legal protection, such as copyrights or trademarks, a property is simply not viable for licensing purposes.

It is likely that a licensor willing to undertake the time, money and effort to develop a licensing program for their property has made the investment in securing the necessary legal protections. Because trademark protection is usually obtained on a per-category or class basis, before committing to a license, it is prudent to confirm the status of the trademark in the category(s) that correspond to the rights being acquired.

This information can be ascertained by simply asking the licensor for a list of its trademark registrations and/or applications. If they don't include coverage for your products, ask for it.

You may want to take this one step further and run your own confirmatory trademark search to ensure that the licensor is providing you with accurate information. In 99% of all cases with experienced licensors, that will be the case. It may not, however, be the case with B and C-level licensors and should give the potential licensee some pause for concern.

In addition, it is also advisable to know if and how the licensor will protect the property from infringement. A property that achieves a reasonable level of exposure and/or licensing success is prone to becoming a target for trademark piracy – unlawful use of protected marks. With the potential for piracy, it is also beneficial to understand what actions the licensor is likely to take when or if this should occur. For more on this topic, see Chapter 21 on infringement and counterfeiting.

It is important to appreciate the fact that most licensors simply cannot afford to prosecute every case of infringement. However, knowledge of what actions a licensor is prepared to take against infringers may also be a factor in determining which property a licensee will choose.

7.7 Consider the Licensor's Track Record

In the fine print of most ads promoting investments in mutual funds or stocks are often the words, *"past performance is not a guarantee of future performance."* This is also true in licensing, as a licensor's prior success does not necessarily mean that the next property will fare as well.

Nevertheless, if the licensor has indeed managed successful licensing programs in the past, prospective licensees can be at least somewhat reassured that the licensor has the ability to conduct and manage a successful licensing program. The opportunity to work with an experienced licensor versus a new, *untested* one, should also factor in deciding whether to move forward.

If a licensor has conducted previous licensing programs, there are also former licensees who may be willing to provide feedback on their own experience with the licensor. In weighing such impressions, though, it is important to remember that opinions are just that and should not necessarily be taken as facts. That said, such first-hand information about the licensor may prove to be beneficial.

7.8 Support from The Licensor

Before ending this section on conducting due diligence, one last thing to consider is: How will the licensor support the license? Understanding what support the licensing program will receive from the licensor is important and knowledge *always* trumps assumption. The potential licensee needs to find out what the marketing plans are for both the short and long term. Will it involve the use of media, if so what form and how often? Are there any plans to create any promotions for the property? If that is a possibility, asking whom the licensor is likely to collaborate with is certainly a fair question.

Some licensors require payment of a common marketing fund ("CMF") payment, which is often an additional royalty of between one and three percent. If this is required, ask how such funds will be used, who will be of disbursing them and for what forms of media.

Chapter 8
The Licensor–Licensee Relationship

8.1 Introduction

Licensing is a process that is fundamentally based on two separate parties cooperating to generate a product, service or promotion. The property owner/licensor and the licensee, who will manufacture or produce the licensed products, enter into a license agreement that will define the terms of their business relationship. The respective roles and obligations of each party are the focus of this chapter.

The age-old question, "which came first, the chicken or the egg?" applies when assessing the roles that each party plays in licensing, as well as their relative importance. The fact is that it really doesn't matter which is more important or influential, since both the egg and the chicken perform a vital function in this relationship. Similarly, the willing participation and cooperation of both parties to a license agreement are also necessary if the collaboration is to succeed. Like the chicken vs. the egg question, there is little purpose served in assigning greater significance to one party over the other, as each plays a distinctive and integral role.

8.2 The License Application

The process leading up to the negotiation and finalization of a license agreement can start in several different ways, although the most common are:
- The licensee initiates the contact, either directly or using a manufacturer's representative or consultant; or
- The licensor reaches out and contacts the licensor directly. Licensors will typically reach out to manufacturers with whom they may have had a prior relationship or others who have a positive reputation in the industry for manufacturing the type of product that they are seeking with the requisite levels of quality.

In either event, the next step is typically for the licensee to complete and submit a License Application Form or License Proposal to the licensor which will provide the licensor with all relevant information concerning the licensee's business, finances, their experience and references, and what they propose by way of a licensing relationship. A sample of such a License Application Form is found in Appendix-2. This is a good practice that should be followed by all licensors.

When the licensor receives the completed application, it should do more than simply read and file it. If the prospective licensee looks good "on paper," the licensor should use it as a starting point. The licensor would be well advised to fully check the references which are requested in most applications and contact those references to learn how the licensee performed. While past performance is no guarantee of future success, such information can provide insights about the prospective licensee, and influence the decision to pursue a licensing relationship.

Vetting a prospective licensee should be done thoroughly, not simply by looking at a Dun & Bradstreet report. References should be checked, particularly with other licensors in the industry to see whether the licensee was able to produce the types of products that the licensor is seeking from the new licensee. It might also be advisable to check with retailers to understand how they perceive the manufacturer and their ability to meet the retailer's demands. Bottom line is that this is the time for the licensor to make sure that the licensee is the right fit for the program....not after the deal is signed and deadlines are quickly approaching.

> Licensors need to thoroughly vet a prospective licensee, not simply check their D&B. Contact references and other licensors.

In a recent article in *License Global*, Jeff Lotman, Global Icons' CEO, identified what he considered to be the four biggest warning signs that you might not have found the right licensee. These were:

- **They have no patience**. Licensing is not a get rich scheme. Good programs take time to develop and licensees who don't understand that could potentially be problematic.
- **They don't respect the process**. If they're not willing to fill out a 10-page business plan, they're probably not serious about doing all the work required to make the program a success.
- **They want the world**. While all licensees potentially want global rights, a very small percentage of them actually operate on a global basis. The smartest licensors think globally but act regionally.
- **They focus on the short term**. The smartest licensors don't chase short term payouts, they think decades, not quarters.

His advice to licensor clients is to never accept the first deal you're offered, and the biggest company isn't always the best. Instead, the longest-lasting and most lucrative deals spring from deep research. Who's the best manufacturer? Who has the best distribution network? Who provides the best royalty rate?

8.3 The Negotiations

After vetting the prospective licensee, the parties are then ready to begin the negotiation process. These early negotiations are preliminary. While it is the rare negotiation that covers all the points that will ultimately be included in the final license agreement, most negotiators will start with the essential elements of the business transaction. If the parties cannot reach agreement on the fundamental business terms, it may not be worthwhile to proceed any further.

The following items will typically be discussed during most licensing negotiations:
- What licensed properties will be included in the agreement, i.e., the licensed property?
- Are there any elements of the property that will not be included in the license, e.g., the likeness of an actor?
- What are the specific products or services that will be included in the license, i.e., the licensed product(s)?

- In which territory will the licensee be able to sell licensed products, i.e., the licensed territory?
- In what retail channels will the licensee be permitted to sell the licensed products, i.e., the channels of distribution?
- How long will the licensee be able to produce and sell licensed products, i.e., the term?
- Can the licensor grant similar licensing rights to other parties, i.e., exclusive or non-exclusive rights?
- When does the licensee have to begin marketing and selling licensed products, i.e., the product introduction and distribution dates?
- How much does the licensee have to pay for the right to sell licensed products, i.e., the royalty, advance and guarantee?

These early negotiations are typically handled by the relevant business executives charged with responsibility for negotiating the license. While there are occasions where one or both parties may be accompanied by their attorneys during these negotiations, the presence of counsel is usually reserved for larger or more complex transactions. Where the licensing executives are experienced, and the issues are relatively straightforward, there is no need to involve counsel at this point. The purpose of these negotiations is to arrive at some consensus relative to the business terms of the eventual license agreement and there is normally sufficient time later in the process for the attorneys to get involved and conclude the agreement.

The negotiations leading up to a license agreement are like most other business negotiations, i.e., typically, one party is in a stronger bargaining position than the other. Similarly, one party may have a stronger incentive to enter into the license than the other, which can shift the bargaining leverage to the other party.

In negotiation, leverage is not always about size and power but, more commonly, about a party's need to enter into the agreement, which can be the result of a variety of different circumstances. For example, one party might have a desire to enter a particular market and the license is their means of accomplishing it, while another party might desperately need to incorporate a licensed property in its product line to stay competitive. Whatever the motivations, it is rare that both parties have equal leverage in licensing negotiations.

The objective of these negotiations is to narrow the issues and conclude an agreement. In successful negotiations, both sides must be prepared to compromise and ultimately reach a workable agreement. It should never be win-win for one side and lose-lose for the other side.

The following cartoon is an example of how these negotiations should **not** proceed:

The object of this cartoon is that the sole purpose of negotiation is never to drive a stake through your opponent's heart but, rather, to arrive at a workable deal.

There are many schools of thought with respect to negotiation and there are many courses offered on the subject, including those from some of the major universities. For example, Harvard Business School offers a program on Negotiation for Executives. Taking such courses for licensing executives might be very useful.

The most effective negotiators are the ones who do their homework before negotiations commence. They know exactly who they're dealing with. They thoroughly understand the property and the products; the market; they understand the retail landscape and know the property and how the product fits, and they are familiar with how similar deals are structured and the payment terms for such deals. The best negotiators are the one who recognize that if the ultimate deal doesn't work for both parties, there will be problems down the road and some of these problems can be catastrophic to one or both parties.

A technique employed by some negotiators is the "Take it or Leave it" approach, typically when there is a larger disparity in the bargaining leverage between the parties and one side is assuming a more aloof position—some may call it condescending. Many an attorney or executive has heard the dreaded statement, "This issue is non-negotiable. If your client won't accept it, we're done." Translated, that means "Take it or leave it."

A licensee or licensor should NEVER be intimidated by such a threat since it could simply be a negotiating ploy. Unfortunately, there is no accurate way to know for sure what is in the mind of the other negotiator and whether he is serious or simply bluffing. One needs to follow their own instincts and determine whether they have really reached the end of the negotiations or whether there is more room, while at the same time giving consideration as to how important it is to conclude the license. The best way to test a take it or leave it response is to simply make an offer and see how it is received.

It should never be forgotten that the licensing industry is a small industry and there are not all that many players. People who you negotiate with today may well be the same people who you negotiate with next year or five years from now. One should never burn bridges in any negotiation and should always remain calm and professional. There is no place in these negotiations for temper or ego.

While many of the specific terms of the license agreement will be deferred to negotiation of the actual formal agreement, this is the time to negotiate the business terms and memorialize them in a deal memo or term sheet. A sample Deal Memo is attached as Appendix-3.

The following are key issues that should be addressed in a deal memo or term sheet.

Definition of Licensed Products

In this regard, it is important that the parties discuss and agree upon the specific licensed property that will be included in the license agreement as well as the licensed products for which the property is being licensed. In defining the property, it's important to define it specifically, e.g., does the licensed property include simply the PEANUTS name, or does it include the right to use the characters CHARLIE BROWN and SNOOPY?

When defining the licensed products, it is similarly important to be as specific as possible and rights should be limited to only those products that the licensee is capable of manufacturing and selling. Broad definitions should be avoided wherever possible.

For example, if the licensee intends to use the licensed property on T-shirts, the licensor would be well advised to define the licensed products more specifically, e.g., "100% cotton men's T-shirts without a collar from sizes S-XL."

A list of possible product categories for licensed products is contained in Appendix-5.

Exclusivity

This, of course, leads us to the question of exclusivity. Will the license be exclusive to the licensee, exclusive to the licensee with the licensor reserving the right to produce the licensed products itself, or simply non-exclusive? It is also possible to negotiate partial exclusivity. This refers to a situation in which the licensee obtains exclusivity for a specific segment of a product category only, and not the entire category. As an example, a licensee will be able to produce a product that sells within a limited price range or is produced in only one format or manufactured in only one type of material. If the category in question is broader than a single price range, or includes similar products produced from a variety of materials, the licensee might be able to negotiate exclusivity by price or materials. In recent years, the trend has been toward non-exclusive licenses since they pose far fewer problems if the licensee does not perform as expected or, worse yet, goes into bankruptcy. Additionally, some entities, such as state-funded universities, have a policy of only granting non-exclusive licenses.

Term of the License

The parties need to discuss and agree upon the length or "term" of the agreement. The term of the agreement is always a difficult negotiation since the licensee will want the agreement to extend for as long as possible, while the licensor will want to limit it to a relatively short period of time. The licensee's position is that it will be investing substantial sums in developing and marketing the licensed products and will therefore require time to recoup its initial investment. Conversely, the licensor is concerned that it will be tying up its valuable property right for a prolonged period with no guarantee that the licensee will fully exploit the property.

> Licensees should seek options to renew the agreement if they achieve certain milestones. That permits the licensee to potentially develop a long-term relationship with the licensor and property.

The typical compromise is to set the term for a reasonable period, e.g., two to three years, with the licensee having the option to renew for additional periods upon meeting certain performance criteria. For example, the term might be for two years with two separately exercisable options to renew the agreement for additional extended terms of two years each. There are notable exceptions where longer terms of, perhaps, five to seven and maybe even ten years are the accepted standard. Use of such longer terms, however, are usually reserved for product categories that require the licensee to make a sizeable investment in the development of the product, and/or when the product requires a more extensive development period, e.g., video games.

If the licensee has the right to renew the license for one or more extension terms (licensing term(s) that follow the original term), frequently the licensee is compelled to deliver notice to the licensor of the intent to renew the license agreement, sometime before the renewal date. The required period as to when the licensee must provide such notice will be addressed in the original license agreement. The average time frame for delivery of such notice is usually 30 to 90 days prior to the end date of the license agreement.

The licensee's right to renew the license is (usually) subject to the licensee meeting some pre-determined financial threshold, which is often expressed as a minimum amount of royalty income paid during the term of the license agreement. Like so many other points in the license agreement, the terms that a licensee must meet to have the right to renew the agreement are subject to negotiation. If the license agreement provides for the right to renew, licensees are well advised to calendar the date that notice to the licensor is due. Failure to provide such notice may provide the licensor with the right to disallow the grant of an extended term.

Territory and Channels of Distribution

Similarly, there is a basic difference between what the licensor and licensee each wants with respect to the licensed territory. Most licensors prefer to limit the territory to only those countries where the licensee can demonstrate its ability to distribute licensed products. Most licensees, on the other hand, will want to extend the territory as broadly as possible, usually on the chance that they may expand into those countries in the future. Caution should be exercised when granting broad territorial rights to a licensee, without reasonable assurances at the start of the agreement that it is capable of distributing the licensed product in each of the desired markets.

Where a licensee requests the rights to a broad territory, but the licensor is uncertain that it can fully exploit them, one possible compromise is to consent to the proposed licensed territory for a limited period and impose specific performance requirements on the licensee. For example, if the licensee does not commence the sale of licensed products in Australia within 18 months from the date of execution of the agreement or generate at least US $100,000 in royalties from sales in Australia within 24 months from such date of execution, the licensor shall have the right to delete Australia from the licensed territory.

Channels of distribution are different from the geographical licensed territory. Channels will be directed to how and where the licensee will sell the licensed products, e.g., mass market, specialty market, Internet, direct, etc. A list of the possible choices for channels of distribution is included in Appendix-9.

Introduction and First Sale Dates

The negotiation of product introduction dates and first sale or retail distribution dates are also important to ensure that the licensee will commit to getting product into the retail market. If such dates are not met, the licensor would have the right to terminate the agreement. Some licensors may tend to minimize this requirement with licensees who commit to paying a sizeable advance and a large guarantee, but that should never be a reason to totally ignore these performance requirements.

If the license is for an entertainment property that is tied to the release of a motion picture or the airing of a television show, the licensor may require a holdback on product introduction to make sure that product is not available at retail until the motion picture is released, or within close proximity to the film's release.

Compensation

The issue of compensation has been left to last in this discussion because to many licensing executives it is the most important provision and, theoretically, consumes the most negotiating time. In actuality, however, the financial terms of many license agreements typically generate the least amount of negotiation. Many licensors have fixed in their minds what they are looking for in terms of financial requirements, taking the normal variances between product categories into consideration. For example, if someone wanted to take a license for a Disney character, the royalty rate will almost never be negotiated—it will probably be the same as the other 150 license agreements that Disney has granted for that property.

There may, however, be some give and take on the advances and minimum guarantees, particularly in tougher economic times. Still, these numbers are heavily based on the licensee's sales projections. For example, if the agreed upon royalty rate was 12% and the licensee has projected a million dollars in total net sales for the licensed product, the licensor will typically apply that royalty rate to the projected sales figure and arrive at an appropriate guarantee and advance based on such projections. Some licensors will require that the guarantee be equal to at least half of the projected royalties for a royalty period and then pay half of the guarantee as an advance.

It should be appreciated, however, that these percentages are simply a starting point for negotiation and licensees will (and should) always seek to negotiate a lower percentage for the guarantee, e.g., 25-40% and the corresponding advance. Since the licensor is relying on the licensee's own projections, a licensee would be well advised to be conservative in its sales projections to provide a "comfort zone" in negotiating the guarantee and advance.

Where there often is significant room to negotiate compensation, is when there is little or no history for that property type and/or product and, as such, no established royalty rate exists. In these situations, the parties may spend significant amounts of time negotiating the royalty rate and any advances or guarantees. The standards used to determine an appropriate compensation package will be discussed in much greater detail later in this book.

The guarantee is an essential part of the financial compensation contained in most license agreements. Although the licensor is entitled to earn a royalty on each licensed product sold, the rationale for including a guarantee is based on the fact that there is no assurance the product will succeed in the retail market *or* that the licensee will maximize the opportunity to use the licensed property during the term of the agreement. Whether or not the licensee successfully exploits the rights granted by the licensor, the licensor has provided the licensee with certain rights to the property. Therefore, the guarantee assures that, regardless of whether the licensee can successfully or fully exploit the licensing rights held, the licensor will receive a certain minimum amount of money for the rights that were granted.

The real question is, as it has always been, how do the parties establish a fair guarantee for those rights that the licensee is acquiring? Be assured, a reasonable advance or guarantee is not some budget number that the licensor needs to achieve for his quarterly or yearly balance sheet, or some "ideal" dollar amount that would satisfy a producer or superior. Advances and guarantees must reflect realistic sales projections which, in some measure, are representative of the popularity of the property, the sales appeal of the product in question and, certainly, the current economic conditions of the marketplace.

One rule of thumb in arriving at a reasonable guarantee is for the parties to first agree upon a royalty rate and then, taking that royalty rate, apply it to the licensee's projected sales, arriving at a projected royalty payment. Setting the guarantee at 50% of that projected royalty payment with 50% of the guarantee for the first year to be paid as an advance is an approach that many licensors use and is hard to argue with since it relies on the licensee's own projected numbers.

> Setting the guarantee at 50% of the licensee's projected sales is an accepted way to establish a guarantee, with 50% of the guarantee to be paid as an advance.

If you are negotiating for the right to license a popular property, but in a product category that has only limited appeal, the financial terms should reflect both factors. The same is true if the general economic conditions of the market are soft and overall retail sales are down. These considerations must be considered to arrive at a financial compensation package that is both equitable and realistic for both parties. To proceed otherwise, creates a lopsided deal that will prove difficult to enforce, is likely to be re-negotiated down the road or, worse, may strain future relations between the licensor and licensee.

Too often, license agreements are negotiated in the *heat of the moment*, with little thought given to the fact that there will be other properties and opportunities to consider in the future. It is this same mentality that can lead licensors to push for unreasonable and excessively high advances and guarantees; terms that might meet their own current budgetary demands, but which are otherwise impractical in the context of realistic sales projections or current market trends.

Likewise, throngs of unwitting licensees frequently overlook, or plainly ignore, glaring pitfalls when driven by impulse or blinded by unbridled optimism. Too many simply lock onto an attractive, potentially lucrative licensing opportunity although the up-front obligations involved may be unwarranted.

For any property to attract interest from licensees, it must exhibit a certain level of originality and appeal to convince them that, if used on licensed products, it can generate significant consumer sales.

When negotiating the terms of a license, it is reasonable to assume that the property owner has already made a considerable investment of time and money to create the property. This is the licensor's contribution to the licensing process. It cannot be overlooked and, as such, any fair licensing transaction should include some form of advance payment made up-front by the interested licensee for the right to use the property. Typically, the advance is payable upon signing of the license agreement. As its name implies, the advance (usually) represents a pre-payment of royalties that the licensee can credit towards future royalties due the licensor. The amount of the advance is frequently a percentage of the negotiated guarantee. Whether the advance is payable as a single payment upon signing the license agreement or made as a series of payments within a certain time frame, is always negotiable.

8.4 Term Sheets/Deal Memos

One of the most effective ways to ensure that these oral negotiations between a licensor and a prospective licensee ultimately result in a formal license agreement is using a basic term sheet or deal memo, which is entered into between the parties at the end of their negotiations. The term sheet is normally a one or two-page document outlining the salient business provisions that were negotiated, but usually leaves out most of the legal points. When the term sheet is initially prepared, specific business terms, such as the royalty rate, advance, territory, etc., are usually left blank and it serves as a checklist for the negotiations between the parties. At the end of the negotiations, the parties can then insert the appropriate numbers agreed upon during the negotiations.

The term sheet is intended to serve as a preliminary document that memorializes what the parties have negotiated, subject to entering into a formal agreement within a stated period of time. The term sheet should state that the failure to conclude a formal agreement by a predetermined date will result in its expiration. This insures that the term sheet does not become a binding agreement if the parties fail to conclude a formal license agreement.

Term sheets are particularly useful when the initial negotiations are conducted by the licensing executives with the understanding that the matter will then be turned over to their respective attorneys for finalization of the formal agreement. Absent a term sheet, it is often difficult to "conclude" negotiations, as there is no formal documentation of the terms that have been agreed to by the parties.

Despite the existence of a completed term sheet, one party may occasionally decide to reopen the negotiations. The existence of a signed term sheet, however, makes it more difficult for one side to try to renegotiate points that have been previously agreed-upon.

Ideally, the term sheet should address the following essential elements of the arrangement:

- Nature of the grant (exclusive versus non-exclusive);
- Clear and specific identification of the property and product(s) to be covered by the license;
- Licensed territory;
- Term or period of the agreement, usually including specific dates for both;
- Renewal options, including any requirements that must be met;
- Royalty rate, advances and guaranteed minimum royalties, and any specific dates by which such payments must be made;
- Dates when marketing and distribution will commence;
- Amount of product liability insurance required; and
- Time period within which a definitive formal agreement will be worked out.

A sample term sheet/deal memo is included here as Appendix-3.

Chapter 9
Licensing Agents and Consultants

9.1 Introduction

Every new licensor asks the same question when it faces the task of conducting a licensing program—should I do this myself or should I retain an independent licensing agent and let them run the program?

Licensing programs succeed because of the efforts of quality, hard-working people with experience in the area. Thus, the answer is simple: if the property owner is satisfied that it possesses such personnel with sufficient expertise, it should proceed on its own. If not, the property owner should consider retaining a licensing agent and letting them assume responsibility for the entire program.

There are many licensing agents and consultants readily available to assist the property owner in guiding them through the licensing maze. Most are former in-house licensing professionals from the studios, sports leagues and corporations who have formed their own firms or joined existing agencies. As such, they typically bring with them contacts and relationships with other licensors and licensees. While their clients include several first-time licensors, many well-known and established licensors simply prefer to outsource their entire licensing programs to such professionals and are content to sit back and let them work their magic.

It should be appreciated that while these individuals are called "licensing agents," they are not "agents" *per se* in a legal sense, since they typically do not have the power to bind or sign agreements on behalf of the property owner. Instead, their role is to find the most qualified licensees for the property, negotiate the best (and hopefully reasonable) licensing terms and present those licensing opportunities to the property owner for consideration, approval and eventually, signature of a licensing agreement. In addition to the sales and marketing functions, licensing agents also have responsibility for administering the licensing program, which most often includes the following: routing product approvals to and from the licensor, tracking licensees for adherence to any performance obligations provided for in the licensing agreement, collecting royalties, creating quarterly licensing reports for submission to the licensor and paying royalties due the licensor.

Irrespective of the type of property that they handle, almost all licensing agents are compensated in the same way, i.e., they receive a commission or percentage of the licensing revenue that they generate for the property owner. Some may also receive a monthly fee or retainer on top of their commission which may (or may not) be creditable against the commission.

When some property owners look at these percentages, they frequently ask whether the agent is worth it. Most property owners realize that it's often necessary to spend money to make money and an incentivized agent will typically work harder for the property owner and maximize licensing revenues. Many understand that receiving 65% of a larger pie is far better than keeping 100% of a smaller pie or, worse yet, no pie. Moreover, it must be appreciated that the licensing agent will typically bear many of the costs and expenses associated with running the program, thus saving the property owner significant sums in the process.

Licensing agents bring with them credibility in their field and an ability to open doors that the property owner may not otherwise be able to enter. Also, based on their experience in the industry, they are frequently able to negotiate the best deal possible for the property owner. Thus, over the long run, most good agents earn their commission.

There is also a middle ground, where some property owners bring licensing consultants on board to help jump-start the program which they will eventually internalize. There are many available licensing professionals who will work on a consulting basis. Rather than assume responsibility for conducting the entire licensing program, these individuals will consult with and assist the property owner in creating and running their own licensing department. Licensing consultants are typically paid on a fee or retainer basis although, in some situations, they may also receive a small commission or bonus based on the number of licenses that they help create or develop and/or the amount of royalties generated.

Licensing consultants are particularly effective at conducting an independent review or audit of a licensing program, or when a licensor wants to expand its program into different types of licensed products. For example, a property owner who might want to add an apparel line to its licensing program might retain the services of a licensing agent or consultant with experience in the apparel category to find the right licensee(s) for the property.

9.2 The Role and Compensation of a Licensing Agent

The reasons property owners elect to retain the services of a licensing agent vary. Some decide to engage an agent because they lack the requisite expertise, while others bring an agent on board because they don't have the time or in-house resources. Still others decide to use an agent because they believe the agent will help them penetrate markets at a much faster rate than if they tried to do it themselves.

Whatever the reason, the first step is to find the right licensing agent for both the property owner and the property, which begins by identifying possible agents who are knowledgeable in the type of property in question. This can be done by asking friends and colleagues for recommendations or by thoroughly researching the names of agents who possess compatible skills.

The LIMA database at www.licensing.org is an excellent way to initiate this process. One of the search fields is labeled "licensing agents" and they are further indexed by property type. It is relatively easy to identify qualified licensing agents with the right skill set, as often an agent's listing (or website) will list their areas of licensing expertise and/or include the specific properties that each represents.

Selecting a licensing agent is very different from buying a house where brokers repeatedly advise that it's all about, "location, location, location." While the location of the agent and their proximity to the property owner is convenient, it should not be the determining factor. In today's sophisticated telecommunications environment, and with the convenience of overnight delivery services, geographic location of an office has become almost irrelevant. Selection of an agent should be based solely on the agent's ability to provide the best representation of the property. Most property owners quickly learn that with the selection of the right agent, face-to-face meetings are seldom required.

After identifying potential agents or brokers, it is important to meet with them to discuss representing the property. The agent will obviously want to see the property before agreeing to represent it and a property owner should not be reluctant to show it to them. Some property owners may want the prospective agent to sign a confidential disclosure agreement, although such an agreement is probably unnecessary except in cases where truly confidential information is to be shared with the agent, e.g., business plans, marketing information, etc.

The property owner should ask the agent for a description of its background and capabilities as well as a list of references, particularly similar properties that it has represented in the category. We live in an age of specialization and most agents specialize in representing particular types of properties, e.g., corporate, art, entertainment, etc. Simply because an agent has successfully represented a property in one category, e.g., a sports property, does not mean that the same agent will be equally successful with a different type of property, e.g., an art property.

Licensing is a relationships business. The agent's role is to deal with and develop relationships with potential licensees. At the same time, manufacturers are similarly specialized. As such, an agent who works primarily with manufacturers that have only taken sports licenses in the past may not have sufficient contacts or relationships with manufacturers who specialize in licensing art properties. The objective is to take full advantage of the agent's relationships with manufacturers and retailers. The best way for that to happen is to retain an agent with strong contacts among the best potential licensees for that category of property.

During these meetings and interviews, the question of compensation should be discussed. This is an essential element of the relationship and should not be avoided. As stated above, most agents are paid on a commission basis, i.e., they receive a percentage of the gross revenues generated by any licensees that use the property. Gross revenues include *all* monies, paid by both licensees and sub-licensees, as well as any entertainment revenues. Commission rates vary widely and are typically negotiable, although they tend to range between 25% and 40% with most in the 30%-35% range.

Some agents will seek an ongoing fee or retainer in addition to the commission. This may be paid on a monthly or quarterly basis and is frequently paid only during the first year or so of the relationship. Agreeing to pay a retainer may result in the agent agreeing to lower its commission rate. For example, an agent who typically charges a 35% commission may agree to work for a 25% commission if the property owner also paid a $10,000 per month retainer.

When some property owners look at these percentages, they frequently ask whether the agent is worth it. Most property owners realize that it is often necessary to spend money to make money, and an incentivized agent will typically work harder for the property owner and maximize licensing revenues. Many understand that receiving 65% of a larger pie is far better than keeping 100% of a smaller pie or, worse yet, having no pie at all. Moreover, it must be appreciated that the licensing agent will typically bear many of the "usual" costs and expenses associated with operating the licensing program, thus saving the property owner the expenditure of those costs.

Licensing agents bring with them credibility in their field and an ability to open doors that the property owner may not otherwise be able to enter as quickly or at all. Also, based on their experience in the industry, they are frequently better skilled in the negotiation of licensing agreements, and thus often generate better terms than the property owner might achieve. In the long run, most good agents will "earn" their commission and will either save the property owner both time and money and/or increase royalty income.

When a retainer is paid, the parties need to agree on whether that retainer will be treated as a non-creditable fee or whether it is creditable against any commission due the licensing agent, in much the same way as an advance against royalties by a licensee is handled. Both are acceptable and common although this should be discussed and established upon up front so that there are no surprises. In almost all instances, retainers are non-refundable, except in the event of a material breach of the agreement by the agent.

Similarly, the parties need to agree who will be responsible for the costs and expenses that the agent will incur in connection with its duties. Normally, the agent is responsible for all its own operating costs and expenses. Property owners are, however, typically required to bear the costs associated with protecting the property; any required legal or auditing support; artwork; marketing materials; developing a style guide and sales materials; any materials necessary to commence product development and exhibition costs at the various licensing shows and other trade shows.

In selecting an agent, the property owner should make sure that there is the right "chemistry" with the agent. The agent will not only be representing the property but the property owner as well. It is, therefore, important that the agent fit the right mold. Much of what an agent will be required to do is based on trust. Therefore, the property owner should have a good feeling that the agent not only can, but will, represent the property owner's best interests.

As a matter of basic due diligence, the property owner should check the agent's references, speaking with other property owners that they represent. Ask them how it worked out and whether they were satisfied with the agent's performance. While the agent will probably only provide the names of satisfied clients, what these satisfied clients have to say (or not say) can be revealing.

Perhaps the most important question to ask each of their clients is, "did the agent actually do everything that they said they would do for you before you retained them?" If the answer is yes, the property owner has probably found the right agent. If the answer is no, don't simply dismiss the agent—dig further. The fact that an agent may not have been able to develop a successful licensing program for a property does not mean that the agent didn't do a good job; some properties are simply not merchandisable no matter how hard the agent may have tried.

Most agents will only work on an exclusive basis, which means that the property owner will be contractually tied to that agent for the term of the agent agreement. During that period, any licenses that are entered into within the agent's territory, whether developed by the agent or others, will be subject to the payment of a commission to the agent.

The reason for this is that the agent does not want the property owner or any third party working behind its back and potentially negotiating for the same rights with a different potential licensee. If this should happen, it can damage the credibility of the property and even expose the property owner to potential liability. If nothing else, it can and often will lead to confusion in the marketplace as to who has the rights to represent the licensor. Potential licensees want to know that they are dealing with *the* entity that has the rights to represent the property.

Similarly, agents will often want to have representation rights that extend as for long as possible—typically for a minimum of two years and, frequently, longer if the selling cycle is abnormally long.

9.3 Licensing Agent Agreement

It is imperative that the agent agreement be in writing to avoid any possible misunder-standing. Nothing should be left to chance. While some agent agreements may take the form of a letter agreement, a formal written agreement is preferable. For reference, a sam-ple Licensing Agent agreement is included at Appendix-11.

Many agents have what they may call a "standard" agreement. The property owner should recognize that an agent's "standard" agreement is typically anything but that—it is probably one of several "standard" agreements that they have and use to fit a particular circumstance. Moreover, the property owner must appreciate that this "standard" agree-ment was undoubtedly drafted by the agent's attorney and will resolve most, if not all, issues in the agent's favor.

Thus, the property owner should be prepared to carefully review and negotiate the agent's proposed agreement. If in doubt, the property owner should consult with counsel to re-view the agreement and provide appropriate suggestions or revisions.

At the very least, a well-drafted agent agreement should address the following issues:
- Whether the agent is to represent *all* of the property owner's properties for all markets, or merely a particular property for a particular market;
- Whether the relationship is exclusive or non-exclusive;
- The territory, or territories, where the agent will operate;
- The term (length) of the relationship, and whether the agent has the right to renew the agreement for additional terms;
- The specific duties and responsibilities of the agent;
- Who will be responsible for reviewing licensee submissions and making ap-provals;
- Who will receive revenues from the licensees and how the revenue will be dis-bursed;
- How the agent will be compensated for its services;
- How and when the agreement may be terminated; and
- Whether the agent will continue to receive a commission after termination of the agreement and, if so, for how long and what the commission will be.

The scope of the agent's representation should be clearly defined to avoid future prob-lems. Will the agent be representing all of the property owner's properties or just one? If the agent is representing all the properties, does that include just the properties currently in existence or will it include future developed properties? Whatever the parties decide, it should be clearly defined in the agreement.

If the agent is being engaged to only handle a specific property, the agreement should make that clear. In such a case, the property owner would be free to use another agent to license its other properties or, alternatively, directly license them on its own.

There are situations where an agent is retained solely to develop a specific licensee or product category. For example, an agent may have a special relationship in the toy industry with a particular toy company that the property owner would like to have as a licensee. In this situation, the property owner might be willing to engage the agent solely to work out a license with that entity while reserving all other rights for itself.

The agent agreement should also define the geographical territory in which the agent may act on behalf of the property owner. The territory of the agent grant is similar to the licensed territory of the eventual license agreement—United States, North America, Japan, worldwide, etc. Before granting worldwide representation rights, however, the property owner should be satisfied that the agent has adequate contacts in all countries in the territory.

The term of the agent relationship also needs to be defined, i.e., the period during which the agent will be representing the property or the property owner. Most property owners prefer to keep the agent's term relatively short, e.g., between six months and a year, which may not be sufficient time for the agent to establish a viable licensing program. Agents usually prefer significantly longer terms, e.g., three or four years. While the "standard" term of representation will depend on the property, what the agreed upon goals are, the type of licensed product(s) the agent is attempting to license and the agent's reputation, the typical term is most often at least two years. The reason for this is simply that licensing programs take time to get established. If the agent is responsible for assisting the property owner in the initial preparation of all requisite materials, this task alone may consume the first six months of the term. If the term was only a year, there would be precious little time for the agent to work the licensing program.

Irrespective of the length of the actual term, the property owner should build into the agreement some mechanism to be able to terminate a non-performing agent, particularly if the agreement is exclusive. This is generally accomplished by including performance milestones that must be met by the agent for it to continue to retain the right to represent the property. Typical milestones include a requirement that the agent generate a certain minimum amount of licensing revenues or conclude a minimum number of license agreements during a particular period. These milestones are negotiable and will depend on the type of property and the territory involved.

Performance is the name of the game in any relationship with an agent. If the agent is performing and meeting its milestones, the agent should be able to retain the rights for a longer period. If, however, the agent is not doing the job and is falling short of reaching these milestones, the property owner should be able to terminate the relationship.

An alternative approach is to provide for a shorter term and build in a series of options for the agent to automatically renew the agreement upon reaching the same or similar milestones. Both approaches are commonly used and equally effective.

As noted above, most licensing agents are not "agents" in the classic sense, since they generally lack the ability to bind the property owner to a license agreement. In actuality, they are more like a sales representative for the property owner.

There are, however, rare situations in which an agent has the power to bind the property owner and may even be a named party to the license agreement. Such a situation should be avoided, if possible, since the resultant relationship can create potential problems, particularly if the property owner ever decides to terminate the agent. Untangling and removing the agent from a host of license agreements can be difficult and is almost always contentious. Thus, the agent should never be given the authority to enter into a license agreement on the property owner's behalf unless necessary.

Agent agreements should clearly spell out the agent's duties and responsibilities in connection with the licensing program. Unfortunately, however, they rarely do—perhaps because many such agreements are drafted by agents. During the discussions leading up to the finalization of the agent agreement, an agent will typically identify, in detail, what it intends to do on behalf of the property owner. This is an excellent road map by which to measure the agent's future performance and the property owner should insist that this list be incorporated into the agent agreement.

The following is a list of certain duties that are commonly expected of the agent:
- Assist the property owner in refining and developing the property into a licensable property;
- Help in determining which product categories the property owner must file in for trademark protection;
- Developing marketing and presentation materials for use in presenting the property to prospective licensees;
- Identifying prospective licensees likely to be interested in taking a license for the property;
- Presenting the property to those prospective licensees most likely to be interested in the property;
- Negotiating the terms of all agreements between the property owner and the licensees;
- Administering the licensing program, including periodically reviewing all licensee submissions of licensed products and associated advertising, packaging and promotional materials to ensure that the quality control provisions of the agreement are met;
- Wherever necessary, personally inspecting the licensee's manufacturing facilities to ensure that the quality control provisions are being complied with; and
- Collecting all advances, guaranteed minimum royalty payments and actual royalty payments from licensees.

In short, the licensing agent should be tasked with doing everything that a vigilant property owner would do if it was running its own licensing program.

The mechanics of how the licensing agent actually gets paid, and by whom, always leads to interesting discussions. Most agents will want to directly receive the revenues from the licensees, have the ability to deduct its commissions and any approved expenses, and then remit the balance (within a specified period) to the property owner.

This is quite typical since the agent normally has the best understanding of what a licensee's expected royalties should be from quarter to quarter. Since this is the agent's principal means of income, they are frequently more diligent than a property owner in ensuring that royalties are promptly paid.

Permitting a well-established licensing agent to collect royalty income directly from a licensee, deduct what it is owed, and then distribute the balance to the property owner, should not pose a problem for most property owners. In fact, that puts the onus on the agent to do the necessary accounting. If such an approach is followed, a property owner may request that the agent deposit these licensee revenues into a dedicated account so as not to co-mingle it with the agent's other assets.

Some property owners may further require that their agent maintain a special bank account in the name of the property owner for receipt and deposit of such royalty payments. The agent would be given access to such special account during the term of the agreement and may deduct its commission and remit the balance to the property owner.

A property owner may not, however, have the same comfort level with an agent that is relatively new to the business. In such instances, the property owner might prefer that licensees remit their royalty payments directly to the property owner who will then assume responsibility for accounting and compensating the agent.

If there is an impasse over this point, one possible compromise is to have the licensees pay their royalties, etc. into an escrow account maintained by a third-party escrow agent, e.g., a bank, an accounting firm, etc. The escrow agent would be empowered to collect such revenues and distribute them to both the agent and property owner in accordance with the terms of an escrow agreement. It should be noted, however, that use of an escrow account usually creates additional expenses that will reduce the amount of income the licensing program will generate.

The "post-termination compensation" provision is, undoubtedly, the most hotly negotiated provision in any agent agreement. This provision governs what, if anything, the agent will receive after expiration or termination of the agent agreement and for how long.

It should be appreciated that since most agents work on a commission basis, their income is back-ended. This means that the agent is paid in the future for the work that is done today. Accordingly, agents want to protect themselves from a situation in which they may have worked tirelessly to develop a successful licensing program for their client, only to be terminated before the future royalty stream commences. Accordingly, most agents will want to continue to receive their commissions after termination or expiration of their agent agreement based on royalty revenues paid by those licenses that they had developed while operating under the agreement.

Property owners are, of course, reluctant, to agree to such an open-ended, post-termination commission stream and will attempt to limit the scope and time of such commission payments. Their concern is that once the agent is terminated, they will have to assume responsibility for managing the program themselves or must pay another agent to assume such responsibility. In either event, they will incur administration costs and the prospect of having to pay a double commission is not terribly attractive to many property owners.

This is a very real issue that undoubtedly generates more disputes than any other provision in an agent agreement. As such, this issue needs to be resolved at the outset of the relationship, NOT after the fact. There are several possible compromises, including:

- The agent will continue to receive its full commission on all revenues paid under all license agreements that were in place as of the date that the agent agreement expired or was terminated for the balance of the term of such license agreements, plus any renewals, modifications, substitutions, or extensions of such license agreements;
- The agent will continue to receive its full commission on all revenues paid under all license agreements that were in place as of the date that the agent agreement expired or was terminated but only through the original term of such license agreements;
- The agent will continue to receive its full commissions on all revenues paid under all license agreements that were in place as of the date that the agent agreement expired or was terminated but only for a fixed period, e.g., three years;
- The agent will receive a reduced commission on all revenues paid under all license agreements that were in place as of the date that the agent agreement expired or was terminated for a fixed period on a declining scale, e.g., 100% commission in year one, 50% in year two, 25% in year three, etc.; or
- any combination of the above.

It should also be noted that if the agent is to continue to receive compensation for licenses the agent generated during the term of representation, the agent may be required to continue the administration of those licenses. In such cases, the owner may want to replace the expired representation agreement with an agreement under which the agent is obligated to perform only administrative duties for those specific license agreements.

Another issue that needs to be addressed when negotiating post-termination compensation for the agent is how to handle those agreements that the agent may have been negotiating as of the date the agent agreement expired or terminated. This is a very common situation because of the amount of time that normally passes between when an agent finds and makes a sales presentation to a potential licensee and the time that the final license agreement is executed. If an agent finds and secures a potential licensee during the term of the agent agreement but the property owner doesn't finalize and sign the license agreement until after the agent agreement terminates or expires, the agent will want to be compensated for its work in finding and securing that licensee.

To protect themselves in such a situation, agents will typically seek to include what is called a "tail" provision in the agent agreement. This usually states that the agent will be entitled to receive its commissions for all license agreements that the property owner entered into during the term of the agent agreement, as well as any agreement that the property owner entered into within six (6) months after termination or expiration of the agent agreement that was based on a presentation made by the agent during the term of the agent agreement. Such a "tail" protects the agent from a property owner who may decide to delay execution of the agreement with the thought that by doing so they could avoid having to pay the agent its commission.

Another provision that some agents require in their agreements with property owners is a representation and warranty that the property owner owns or controls rights to the property and has the right to license the property to third parties. By extension, agents will also typically require that the property owner indemnify them against any claims made by third parties in connection with such warranties. Furthermore, as mentioned in Chapter 10, agents are also likely to insist that the agent and the agency be named as insured parties by the licensee in the product liability policy that the licensee is required to provide during the term of the license. These provisions are fundamental and generally non-negotiable from the agent's perspective.

There may be instances where a property owner or even a licensee wishes to retain the services of a pure consultant to assist it in some manner in conjunction with the licensing program. Such consultants are normally paid on a project or even hourly or daily basis rather than receiving a percentage or commission. A sample Consulting Agreement is provided in Appendix-13.

9.4 Sub-Agents and International Licensing Agents

While location should not be a major consideration in choosing a licensing agent, there are exceptions when it comes to international licensing. A property owner located in California may easily be able to work with a New York based licensing agent for most matters, but it is an entirely different matter when it comes to working with agents in different countries, in different time zones, speaking different languages.

Many licensing agents who oversee worldwide licensing programs (and even property owners running their own licensing programs) regularly employ international agents, in other regions or countries. These international agents may work directly for a property owner that is conducting its own licensing program as an "international agent" or, alternatively, as a "sub-agent" when working for the licensing agent. Irrespective of what they are called, they are responsible for developing the licensing program in a specific country or region.

The advantages of working with international agents are numerous, including more direct contact with local licensees, assistance with administration of the program in such countries, interpretation of local languages and customs, and even transfer of royalties from those countries where there may be currency restrictions, e.g., China, Brazil or India. It should be noted that typically international agents will be the party to whom the royalties are paid, deducting their fees and remitting the balance to the party (agent or owner) who engaged their services.

International sub-agents are generally paid in the same way that a licensing agent is paid, i.e., they receive a commission based on the revenue generated by licensees they secure within their country or region. If they are retained directly by the licensing agent, a sub-agent may share the licensing agent's commissions on that portion of licensing revenues from their country or region. For example, if the licensing agent had negotiated an overall 35% commission with the property owner, the licensing agent and sub-agent might agree that the sub-agent would receive 25% of the total licensing revenues from that country or region while the original licensing agent would receive 10% of the licensing revenues.

In many cases, a licensing agent will negotiate a higher commission rate with the property owner in regions where it is anticipated that sub-agents may be employed to allow for greater flexibility in negotiating such splits, e.g., the licensing agent would receive a 35%

commission where no sub-agent was necessary and a 45% commission where a sub-agent was employed.

If the property owner directly retains the international agent, the property owner would be responsible for payment of the international agent's commission in much the same way that it pays the licensing agent.

How does one find the right international agent? There are licensing agents in virtually all countries throughout the world and most, if not all, are listed in the LIMA database at www.licensing.org which can be searched by country. When a property owner is working with a licensing agent, the selection of the sub-agent is often best left to the licensing agent.

As is the case with most domestic licensing agents, international agents typically have a specialty, e.g., entertainment, sports or celebrity properties. Most have their own individual "styles" and the property owner or licensing agent must be assured that such style meshes with their own. It should be noted that the formation of the European Union has created its own share of issues with respect to licensing and it can impact the way licensing agents operate within the Union. Economically, the European Union is essentially one nation with individual states. Under European Union regulations, if a licensee acquires a license for one country within the Union, e.g., France, it can sell its products in other countries within the Union irrespective of what the license agreement may provide or restrict.

The EU has strictly enforced this requirement and will impose substantial fines if a party attempts to limit such territorial freedom. There are reports of manufacturers being fined as much as €1 million for violating these regulations.

There are, of course, ways to mitigate the impact of these restrictions. For example, publishing licensors may simply grant licenses for language-specific rights, e.g., an English language version, rather than countries *per se*. This may help to limit the sales of products into non-English speaking countries. That said, this regulation has had an enormous impact on licensing and, more particularly, the work of agents and sub-agents within the various EU countries.

Another issue facing many of the international licensing agents is the problem created by gray market or parallel imports, i.e., where a licensee in a certain territory, for example, the United Kingdom, improperly exports otherwise genuine products into another country, e.g., the United States, such that the U.S. licensee is now faced with competition from an unexpected source.

Gray market sales have been an on-going problem in many industries, most notably the photography market in the United States, where New York City camera retailers regularly import and sell genuine products that had been manufactured for sale in other territories. Licensees and licensing agents in a territory face this problem on a regular basis because it can result in reduced sales and, accordingly, lower commissions.

Some highly successful property owners and licensors believe that international agents should be required to pay them for the right to represent their property in a country or territory or, alternatively, should guarantee that they will receive a minimum amount of royalties because of the agent's efforts. While that may occasionally happen, most international agents are reluctant to pay for such a right or consent to performance guarantees.

International agents may, however, agree that if they have not generated a minimum amount of royalty revenues during a certain period, the property owner may terminate their services. A sample sub-agent agreement is included as Appendix-12.

9.5 Manufacturer's Consultants/Representatives

While licensing agents typically work for the property owner or licensor, "consultants" or "manufacturer's representatives" work for the licensee to assist them in selecting the right property or properties for their client. They also assist in making introductions to various licensors and licensing agents, and in consulting with the manufacturer during the program on the marketing side of the business to maximize the sale of the licensed products. As is often the case with licensing agents, most of these manufacturer's representatives are seasoned licensing professionals with decades of licensing experience.

While licensing agents typically hone their expertise by working with major property owners and licensing companies, manufacturer's representatives frequently come from the licensee community, working for some of the major licensees where they would have been able to establish contacts with the major property owners and licensing agents.

Manufacturer's representatives are particularly helpful for manufacturers who are new to licensing and can help initiate them to the process. Many of the most successful licensees recognize the value that these manufacturer's representatives bring and continue their relationships well beyond the early stages.

Initially, they will study the manufacturer's operations and help them determine whether licensing would be profitable for their business and, if so, what category of licensed properties should be considered. They will then make recommendations to the manufacturer on specific properties that may best fit with their product line and how they could be incorporated into their product mix.

Working with the manufacturer, the manufacturer's representative will then reach out to the various property owners and licensing agents to explore whether there is any interest on their part in granting licenses to their clients and, if so, under what terms. If there is interest on the part of both the property owner and their client, the manufacturer's representative will then work on behalf of the manufacturer to negotiate the terms of a license agreement for the property.

Since manufacturer's representatives are intimately familiar with the licensing industry, they understand the norms and standards of licensing deals in these and other categories. As such, they can regularly counsel and advise their clients on the state of the industry, what their competitors are doing, and whether one deal is better than another.

Good manufacturer's representatives will not stop there—they will continue to work with their clients during the licensing program, collaborating with them on product development, marketing strategies and potentially seeking other properties that would fit into their product mix.

Much like a licensing agent, the manufacturer's representative is typically compensated on a commission basis relative to the amount of royalty income that their client pays to the property owner under license agreements for which they are responsible for bringing in. While the range of compensation for a manufacturer's representative depends upon the role they are expected to fill, it is quite common for them to receive about 2% of their client's net sales of licensed products. For example, if their client paid the licensor a 10% royalty on its net sales of licensed products, the client would pay the manufacturer's representative an additional 2% of its net sales as compensation.

It is not uncommon for a manufacturer to pay its manufacturer's representative a monthly retainer for its services which may (or may not) be creditable against the commission. Like most things in licensing, that is the subject of negotiation between the parties. Similarly, there are instances where a manufacturer will simply pay the manufacturer's representative a consulting fee with no commission.

The issue of exclusivity is always an issue with respect to manufacturer representatives since it may dictate when a commission is owed. In the case of an exclusive relationship, the manufacturer's representative is typically paid its commission irrespective of whether they were responsible for acquiring the license or not. In non-exclusive arrangements, however, the manufacturer is only paid a commission on licenses which they were responsible for acquiring. A sample manufacturer's representative or consulting agreement is included at Appendix-15.

9.6 Making the Relationship Work

The secret of working with any outside professional is the same—communication, communication, communication. The more that the property owner or the licensee communicates with its agent or representative, the more helpful these professionals can be.

When working with outside licensing professionals, it is advisable to refrain from adopting the "mushroom theory of management" i.e., keep them in the dark and feed them manure. While this admonition holds true with respect to virtually any outside professional, it is particularly true when working with a licensing professional.

While a licensing professional may possess substantial expertise in the licensing industry and even the category in which they may be working, they probably do not understand all the intricacies of their client's business and rarely know the personalities of its management.

It is advisable to think of the agent as an extension of the entity it is representing. The more information that a property owner or licensee can provide the agent, the more they will likely accomplish. That, alone, should be sufficient incentive to both parties.

Chapter 10
The Retailer's Role in Licensing

10.1 Introduction

A "retailer" is any business that sells goods to the consumer, versus wholesalers or suppliers which typically sell their goods to other businesses or to retailers for re-sale to the consumers. The retail industry is the second largest industry in the United States and employs approximately 12% of its total workforce. Total sales of all retail products in the United States are more than $4.2 trillion.

Mention the word retailer and most people immediately think of Walmart—the world's largest big box store. However, in fact, retailers fall into a few different categories, starting with independently owned, "mom & pop" shops that make up about 90% of the total market. While these small stores constitute most of the total, they account for less than half of all retail sales which shows that consumers like to shop at the big box stores.

The retail market is divided into different categories or sectors, including:

- High-End Department Stores, e.g., Saks Fifth Avenue, Neiman Marcus, Bloomingdales, etc.;
- Mid-Tier Department Stores, e.g., Macy's, Kohl's, J.C. Penney, etc.;
- Big Box or Mass Market Stores, e.g., Walmart, Target, etc.;
- Off-Price Retailers, e.g., TJ Maxx, Marshall's, Ross, etc.;
- E-commerce or on-line retailers, including Amazon.com and eBay.com.
- Specialty Stores, broken down by type of merchandise:
    - Apparel, e.g., The Gap, Abercrombie & Fitch, Ann Taylor, J. Crew, Old Navy, etc.;
    - Cosmetics & Pharmaceuticals, e.g., CVS, Walgreens, Rite Aid, etc.;
    - Electronics, e.g., Best Buy, Radio Shack, etc.;
    - Footwear, e.g., Foot Locker, The Athlete's Foot, etc.;
    - Home Improvement, e.g., Home Depot, Lowes, etc.; Home Products, e.g., Bed Bath & Beyond, Pier 1 Imports, etc.;
    - Jewelry, e.g., Tiffany, Cartier, Zale's, etc.;
    - Office Supplies, e.g., Staples, Office Depot, etc.;
    - Sporting Goods, e.g., Modell's, Dick's Sporting Goods, Sports Authority, etc.;
    - Toys, e.g., Toys "R" Us; FAO Schwartz, etc.; and
    - Grocery Stores, e.g., Kroger's, Safeway, etc.

According to *Deloitte's 2018 Global Power of Retailing* report, the ten largest global retailers by total sales in 2016 were:

1. Walmart (United States) discount stores with $485.9 billion in sales;
2. Costco Wholesale Club (United States), warehouse club with $118.9 billion in sales;
3. Kroger (United States), supermarkets with $115.3 billion in sales;
4. Schwarz Unternehmens Treuhand (Germany), discount stores with $99.3 billion in sales;

5. Walgreens-Boots Alliance (United States), drug, discount store with $97 billion in sales;
6. Amazon.com (United States), online retailer with $94.7 billion in sales;
7. Home Depot (United States), home improvement stores with $94.63 billion in sales;
8. Aldi Group (Germany), discount stores with $84.9 billion in sales; and
9. Carrefour (France), hypermarket/superstores with $84.1 billion in sales;
10. CVS Health Corp. (United States), drug, discount stores with $81.1 billion in sales.

Licensing is all about selling licensed products and retailers sell products. As such, they are critical to the success of a licensing program and, at times, responsible for its failure. For this reason, retailers have a special place in the hearts of both licensors and licensees.

Over the years, retailers have wielded enormous power over licensors and their licensees since they control the shelf space, and, without shelf space, a product is doomed. Retailers, thus, have become accustomed to setting the terms of any relationship with property owners and their licensees, particularly when it involves lesser known properties. While the owners of hot properties and their licensees may be able to set some, or all, of the terms of the relationship, the owners of lesser known properties and their licensees will have a much harder time with retailers.

Licensing Global identified the following retailers as the Retailers to Watch in 2017:

- PetSmart
- Primark
- Staples
- Five Below
- GameStop
- Wayfair
- Spencer's
- JC Penney
- QVC
- Box Lunch
- Lidl
- Colette
- Fanatics
- Alibaba

10.2 The Retailers Role in the Licensing Equation[9]

In 2016, the licensing industry accounted for approximately $262.9 billion in sales of licensed products on a worldwide basis and generated more than $14.1 billion in licensing royalties paid to licensors with the United States and Canada accounting for approximately $152.3 billion in such sales.

There are quite several retail categories, including:

- Mass merchants (Walmart, Target)
- Mid-Tier department stores (Sears, Kohl's, Meijer)

---

[9] Based on a CLS presentation by Carole Postal entitled "The Role of the Retailer in the Licensing Equation," Nov. 21, 2017.

- Grocery (Kroger, Safeway, Publix)
- Convenience (7-Eleven, Supervalu)
- Pharmacy (CVS, Walgreens)
- Home (Home Depot, Lowes, True Value, Bed Bath & Beyond)
- On-Line (Amazon, Zuilily)
- Off-Price (Costco, BJ'S Wholesale Club)
- Value (Dollar General, Family Dollar, Dollar Tree)
- Home Shopping (HSN, QVC)
- Specialty (Teen/Tween, Book, Music, Electronic)
- Independent Mom & Pop
- Catalogs

Of the above categories, mass merchants account for about 32.2% of retail sales followed by specialty stores at 19.2% and department stores at 12%.

Since the top ten largest property owners account for at least 53% of the total retail sales, to secure retail space, the other property owners and their licensees need to understand the retail market to secure what's left of the remaining retail space.

On-line shopping is an increasingly large category, particularly for Gen X and Millennials. According to NPD 2017 Holiday Purchase Intentions Survey, 75% of 2017 holiday shoppers planned on purchasing products on-line with the average shopper spending approximately $793 vs. $467 for brick and mortar purchases.

On-line shopping will probably never replace an in-store experience, but it is changing the marketplace and creating opportunities that do not require shelf space.

10.3 What Are Retailers Looking For?

The answer to this question is straight forward. Retailers want to pay the lowest possible price for the highest quality product that has the most appeal to their customers and, therefore, the greatest potential to generate strong sales. The goal of most retailers is to stock their shelves with targeted merchandise that meets the needs of their customers— at the right price. It's that simple.

Every retailer prefers, if possible, to be the exclusive supplier of a product, because exclusivity gives them an advantage over the competition. It is a way that smaller retailers can compete with the big box stores who have historically outsold them. If the smaller retailer has exclusivity, a big box store cannot beat them on price, simply because they cannot carry the product. Even limited windows of exclusivity are good, since this allows a retailer to promote the products as only being available at their store, which gives them a marketing advantage. While any retailer would obviously prefer exclusivity, they recognize that in most cases that is simply not possible. Nevertheless, there is no harm in asking and most retailers will.

Since lead times for the delivery of products are important to every retailer, having an established track record for reliability can be invaluable, particularly if the manufacturer had previously helped the retailer fill an order on short notice. Thus, property owners and licensees who maintain such relationships hold a significant advantage over competitors that have never worked with the retailer in the past or, worse yet, at one point may have dropped the ball.

Licensors need to be highly conscious of this dynamic. As discussed in previous chapters, most licensees work on a tight schedule to meet deadlines established by retailers. The fastest way to derail that schedule is for the licensor to delay in acting on the licensee's product submissions. If the licensee is unable to meet the retailer's schedule, it can have an enormously detrimental impact on the licensee's ability to effect the sale of those licensed products. Moreover, it can damage the licensee's relationship with the retailer and, potentially, even cast a shadow on the overall program since the retailer may be reluctant to deal with any of the property owner's other licensees.

Retailers are also concerned about the quality of the products that they carry and don't want to sully their reputation by carrying inferior products. More specifically, they don't want to have to deal with handling excessive numbers of returns, a factor that can also have a damaging impact on the property's whole licensing program. Again, this is where a good track record or, at the very least, a great set of references who will attest to the great quality of your products is important.

At the end of the day, however, retailers do not want to take on products that won't sell or where the turnover will be slow. That is why most will expect that the property owner and its licensees provide some form of marketing or promotional assistance with respect to their products, typically in the form of promotions that will get the attention of potential purchasers.

When it comes to promotions, the key is "cool" and the cooler the better. Interactive promotions that offer prizes or rewards are very popular because they involve the potential customer and make them more inclined to spend money to buy the products. Over the years, on-line sweepstakes have also proven very successful.

Hosting celebrity appearances at a retailer's flagships stores is another successful type of promotion, particularly if the products are licensed by that celebrity. Everyone wants to get to meet their favorite sports hero or pop singer. If they also happen to give away autographed baseballs or sing the National Anthem to open the store for the shoppers, it just adds more excitement—which retailers love because it brings in traffic and, therefore, helps sell more products.

10.4 How to Get Retail Placement

When considering the question of how to get retail placement, the manufacturer must ask themselves the questions, "if I was the retail buyer, why would I buy it? Why is my product different and more attractive than a competitive product?" While these appear to be relatively simple questions, the answers may prove to be more challenging than one might like.

Bottom line is to make your product stand out and make the buyer want to buy your product—it's that simple.

Another factor is the ability of the manufacturer to work with a retailer. Retailers are normally on very tight timelines. If the manufacturer is "flexible" and "reliable," they cause less problems for the retailer who will reward them for their cooperativeness and reliability. Missing a promised delivery date to a retailer can be viewed as a Cardinal sin which may take a long time for the buyer to forget the experience.

According to on major retailer, the top 10 ways to build a strong retail partnership are:

- Exclusivity—exclusive product and exclusive content
- Don't over-license the same category
- Keep the channels of retail different—retailers want to be different from each other
- Transparency—retailers don't need details, but they don't want to be blind-sided particularly with competitive products
- Strong Assets and Style Guides—provide them with images and clear verbiage
- Marketing social media—licensors should try to push traffic to their retailers
- Broader merchandise categories—add accessories to apparel, etc.
- Elevated products—there is a void for moderately priced, affordable products
- Be open-minded—work with your retailer on unique promotional programs
- Shop the retailer's stores—licensors need to see how their products are being merchandised and sold

10.5 Think Smaller—Limited Distribution

Since it is critical for a property owner and its licensees to get a retailer to carry its licensed products, the process starts by first getting in the retailer's door and, thereafter, communicating effectively with its decision makers towards ultimately closing the deal. In many instances, that is easier said than done.

In the "old days," property owners and their licensees thought "big." They wanted to see their licensed products sold at all stores in national chains and were frequently unhappy with anything else. The recent recession changed that. Retailers have become more conservative and are reluctant to roll out a line of products on a store-wide basis without first knowing that customers will buy them. Obviously, they do not want to build up large inventories of products that simply don't sell.

The current trend among retailers is limited distribution rather than all-store buys. In today's market, retailers are more willing to take on new products on a test program, or special project basis, because these approaches are far less risky. A further trend in retail is the opening of smaller stores, i.e., stores with smaller footprints. The advantages of these smaller stores are that they serve as testing "labs" for the retailer, who can use them to determine whether a product will sell and whether it's worth rolling out on a larger scale.

Retailer-conscious manufacturers have recognized these developments and have begun working with retailers to accommodate their more conservative tendencies. Manufacturers who are willing to accept limited distribution, versus all-store distribution are looked upon more favorably by retailers. A manufacturer's willingness to play ball with the retailer on more limited distribution can ultimately lead to larger distribution, should the product perform well.

10.6 Retailer Strategies beyond the Top Ten[10]

There is a world beyond the Top Ten global retailers identified at the beginning of this chapter. This is particularly true as the retail landscape continues to change and as the

---

[10] Based on 2009, 2010 & 2011 LIMA CLS presentation entitled Retailer Strategies Beyond the Top 10 by Sean Heitkemper and Todd Donaldson, IMC, 200 York Street Louisville, KY 40203 and Michael Slusar, Brandar Consulting, LLC, 27 Southgate Drive, Annandale, NJ 08801.

number of retailers shrinks almost daily, with many going into bankruptcy never to be heard from again. Between 2008 and 2010 alone, more than seventy-eight retail chains declared bankruptcy while another twenty-six announced major store closings. All told, more than 16,500 brick and mortar retail stores in the U.S closed their doors during this period. Strip malls regularly display "For Rent" signs.

This shrinking landscape has impacted property owners and their licensees because of the fear of partnering with a retailer who is suddenly no longer in business by the time the program is expected to take hold.

The larger concern, for some, is that these bankruptcies are indicative of a trend signaling major shifts in the entire retail marketplace. While the brick and mortar retail model worked well in the twentieth century, it remains to be seen whether it will be as viable in the current one. Many retail experts believe that the time has passed for this model, an outlook being shaped by very real changes in the buying habits of consumers that they expect will only continue. Some, in fact, believe that this last recession ushered in the biggest transformation in consumer behavior to have occurred over the past seventy years.

One also must wonder about whether the explosion of the large chains at the expense of the smaller retailers is healthy….for anyone. If the "too big to fail" concept didn't work for investment banking firms such as Lehman Brothers, how will it work with retailers? The concern is that if one of the mega-chains should fail, it will not only impact its investors and employees, but could well have a dramatic impact on its suppliers and vendors.

If sales of a licensed product to a single retailer represent a significant part of a manufacturer's selling season and that retailer should go bankrupt, it will not only kill that selling season, but it could even shutter the manufacturer as well. Licensors and licensees also face a similar fate if they fall victim to SKU rationalization. This outlook is not intended to stir anxiety, but rather to show that property owners and licensees would be well advised to look beyond the Top Ten as a way of hedging their future security and building momentum for their programs.

The good news is that there is a life outside the Top Ten and it can, in fact, be a good life. While it's far easier to make one sale to a major retailer than 10 sales to different smaller retailers or a thousand sales on a direct basis, spreading sales around to a broader group of customers can offer significantly more security in tough times. Brand and license exclusives at retailers such as Kohl's, Hot Topic and the TJX companies are proof that successful programs outside of the big box setting abound for retailers, licensors and licensees alike. Even regional retailers like Meijer and Belk have found continued success in licensing exclusives.

More importantly, property owners and licensees need to understand that brick and mortar retail may never return to pre-recession levels. Business always tends to gravitate toward efficiency, while consumers tend to gravitate toward convenience. When looking through this lens, it is easy to see that brick and mortar stores are not the most efficient or most convenient way to buy goods.

The most efficient and convenient way for consumers to buy goods is through e-commerce. Some economists believe that there will be a further decline in brick and mortar store sales as the economy picks up, but a rapid acceleration of share gain in e-commerce sales. New malls are not being opened and existing malls are experiencing their highest vacancy rates in decades. In the last few years, Government statistics all show across-the-board declines in the volume of sales by brick and mortar stores, but an increase in the number of e-commerce sales. Property owners and their licensees should recognize this and prepare for the likely shift in marketing channels that is taking place. Observe the emergence of companies like Amazon and Zappos. Watch the major retailers continue to develop their online presence. See DRTV giants QVC and HSN continue to launch new channels. Success for retailers and marketers alike will rely on multi-channel strategies.

If, in fact, the future of retailing is through e-commerce rather than conventional brick and mortar retail channels, the possibilities are endless for property owners and licensees. Some may begin to consider the formerly unheard of, i.e., becoming their own retailer by creating their own e-commerce sites and selling direct to consumers.

While property owners can, of course, allow their licensees to open their own e-commerce site, an alternative approach might be for the property owner to simply create its own site and offer distribution through that site to its licensees as a benefit. Some property owners who have already done this actually charge their licensees to use the infrastructure of their e-commerce site. The creation of such sites is not difficult and if a property owner lacks the resources or expertise to do so, it is something that can easily be outsourced.

Due to the efficiency of both warehousing and mass distribution of products from a single location, licensed products can be sold directly to the consumer at much lower prices than by a brick and mortar store, which must be leased, staffed, heated and powered. That price advantage can and should be passed on to the consumer. One retail consultant, when asked how direct e-commerce sales should be priced, counseled, "Cut the price in half and then lower it."

There are other advantages of selling licensed products through e-commerce. For starters, such sales are typically more profitable for the property owner and its licensees because they absorb both the wholesale and retail margins.

Another advantage of e-commerce selling is that because of the reduced selling costs and the lower resultant retail price, licensed products can favorably compete with private label brands even though they are typically sold by brick and mortar stores at prices below that of licensed products. It may be possible to even undersell a private label brand because of the reduced distribution costs.

It is also possible to use e-commerce to test a new product that may never make it to a retailer's shelf, or as a viable alternative distribution method for products that have had difficulty meeting (often rigid) brick and mortar retail requirements. E-commerce has provided the high-end collectibles category with the means of providing their customers with considerable information about the product, and a significant amount of product exposure. These are factors that make it much easier to sell such merchandise, and which traditional retailers cannot normally provide due to limitations on shelf space.

10.7 Direct to Retail Licenses[11]

There has been a growing trend in licensing of "direct to retail" ("DTR") licenses, where the property owner by-passes the manufacturer and grants a license directly to a retailer

---

[11] Based on LIMA's panel on *Retail Exclusive Licensing,* conducted at the 2010 Licensing University.

for distribution of a line of licensed products. Typically, these licenses are "exclusive," hence the phrase "retail exclusive" licenses. In virtually all cases, they are intended to be sold throughout the entire chain of stores for the retailer.

In such a relationship, the retailer is responsible for sourcing out the manufacture and supply of the licensed products, typically through factories that it has previously worked with in the Far East. The design and actual manufacture of these licensed products are subject to the same quality control reviews and approvals requirements as would be the case in a conventional licensor-licensee relationship.

When one thinks of direct to retail licensing, they generally think of entertainment and celebrity licenses. Early examples of direct to retail licenses include the WINNIE THE POOH program between Disney and Sears that goes back to the 1970's and the JACQUELINE SMITH line of apparel with K-Mart, which started in the 1980's. Direct to retail licenses are not, however, limited to entertainment properties. This approach has also been used, for example, with corporate properties such as Staples, which carries a line of co-branded OXO office products.

It should be appreciated that direct to retail exclusive licenses don't necessarily have to be for the whole property—it can simply be for a version or treatment of the property. For example, Nickelodeon partnered with K-Mart to do an exclusive line of DORA LOVES PUP-PIES products. The property looked like DORA, but with a "slight twist." One fear was that if K-Mart carried this version, it would cannibalize its basic DORA sales. Not only did that not happen, but it enhanced the sales of the original DORA products. Nickelodeon worked collaboratively with K-Mart on its promotion, which included running a series of television commercials, while K-Mart featured it in a series of flyers and other promotions were also done with Shutter-Fly. What made it work were the in-store activations that were viewed by the millions of people walking through K-Mart every day, as well as online activation generated through its web site.

Of the major retailers, Kohl's is one of the leaders in direct to retailer licenses, having exclusive DTR deals with VERA WANG for a line of SIMPLY VERA products as well as DTR licenses for a wide variety of products bearing some of the Iconix brands like MUDD and CANDIE'S. Quick to follow the lead was J.C. Penney's, with brands such as ONE KISS BY CINDY CRAWFORD for jewelry and CONCEPTS BY CLAIBORNE for more than 30 different products. They also incorporated a store-within-a-store concept for the branded line of SEPHORA cosmetics.

DTR licenses offer many advantages to the parties. For the property owner, it virtually guarantees distribution of the licensed products in a specific market with the assurance that the retailer will make a commitment to help support marketing and promotion. Since they have a financial interest in the property, the retailer has a strong incentive to do whatever it takes to help move the products. Retailers will frequently make a "statement" for the product line and dedicate significantly more floor space for such products than they might otherwise have done if they were simply selling another licensee's products.

Direct to retail licenses offer several advantages to the retailer as well. By eliminating the traditional licensee and their profit incentive and going directly to the factory, they can obtain the licensed products at a lower cost than if they had purchased them from a traditional licensee. Similarly, by dealing directly with the factories, they are usually in a better position to control the design and manufacture of the products. Finally, most DTR licenses are retailer-exclusive deals. This gives the retailer a clear competitive advantage over their competition, since such products are only available through that retailer.

No licensing arrangement is perfect, however, and even DTR exclusives can be risky. By granting exclusive distribution to a single retailer, the property owner is prevented from seeing its property widely commercialized by multiple retailers throughout that channel of distribution. Depending on the arrangement, the property owner may even be prevented from entering other channels of distribution since exclusive retailers will not want to see similarly branded products at other stores. Another potential problem for a property owner with exclusive DTR licenses is that their fate is solely in the hands of one retailer. Should the retailer undergo tough times or, worse yet, be forced to close its doors, the property owner would be directly impacted.

DTR licenses also present a few potential problems for retailers as well. Apart from the financial commitments that a retailer must make under the DTR license agreement, e.g., advances, guarantee, etc., it is the retailer who is responsible for financing the design and manufacture of the products in addition to creating sufficient inventory to meet potential demand. Should the products not sell as well as expected, the retailer is faced with the challenge of disposing of any existing inventory.

10.8 Transition to On-Line Retail

The traditional brick and mortar stores has begun to be replace with on-line sales, both by the on-line division of the store itself as well as by on-line retailers such as Amazon. This shift has moved ahead with literally blinding speed. Retailers are closing more and more stores, and this will undoubtedly continue.

These changes are particularly helpful for licensors and licensees, alike. Rather than trying to hit the thousands of brick and mortar stores, they can quickly get nationwide, if not worldwide, exposure through on-line retail. A property owner can use their customer base to drive even better customer sales.

Selling on-line doesn't necessarily have to be about pricing. A product that bears a strong brand can easily sell at full price on-line because of consumer confidence in that brand and related products. This shift to on-line actually requires brands—it makes it more and more important to have a strong brand recognition which benefits the licensing model. With on-line shopping, brands mean more than ever. Strong brands will dominate this model.

The "wake-up" test is where brand owners should be focusing their attention. A consumer wakes up in the morning and decides that they want to buy an item, say a golf shirt. They go on-line and find the shirt they want. While there is competition between the different brands, what drives the purchase is the stronger brand, more so than price.

Chapter 11
Best Practices for Licensors

11.1 Introduction[12]

Once all the preliminary steps have been completed, it's time to start the process of developing a licensing group or department. While the procedures outlined in this chapter are aimed primarily at property owners who are seeking to establish their own licensing departments, many of the steps and procedures are equally applicable to licensing agents who are managing licensing programs for their clients.

The first step in the development of any licensing department is the appointment of a leader to oversee and direct its operations. This individual is typically called a "licensing director" although other titles, such as "licensing manager" or "licensing administrator" are frequently used. Obviously, it is important for the licensing director to have some experience in licensing, preferably on a managerial level. While the actual running of such a department is something that an otherwise sound business manager should be able to easily handle, having experience in the industry will certainly accelerate the learning process and will reduce the chance of errors along the way.

If the person selected to run the licensing department lacks actual licensing experience, it might be a good idea for the property owner to bring in a licensing consultant for a period to assist with establishing the procedures that will be required to run the program. In the licensing industry, experience is important and there really is no substitute for it.

11.2 The Licensing Department

To begin making the critical decisions concerning the structuring and staffing of the department, the property owner should revisit the reasons why it decided to go into licensing in the first place and what its original objectives were. The three most common reasons for embarking on a licensing program are:

- Increasing brand awareness through extensions into other product categories and through the associated PR and advertising;
- Strengthening the property owner's trademark and copyright protection through use of the property on ancillary products; and
- Generating additional revenue through royalty payments.

Not surprisingly, most licensing departments are structured in such a way that they address each of these objectives.

While there are many ways to organize and staff a licensing department, perhaps the most effective way is to divide the group by responsibility with everyone reporting to the licensing director. Typically, this would include the following groups:

- Marketing Group, with responsibility for handling marketing, advertising and public relations;

---

[12] Based on a CLS presentation on *The Fundamentals of Creating and Administering a Licensing Program* by Peter Van Raalte of INFINITY LICENSING, LLC., 229 Midland Avenue, Montclair, NJ 07042

- Sales Group, with responsibility for soliciting and developing retail products licensees; This group often also includes staff for securing promotional and premium opportunities (fast food and consumer products promotions).
- Legal & Contract Administration Group, with responsibility for overseeing legal matters, reviewing and administering all license agreements and supporting the other groups; Most important, they file and/or coordinate trademark protection for the licensed brands domestically and international.
- Finance Group, with responsibility for tracking and collecting royalties, overseeing independent audits and providing reports to the licensing director; and
- Creative Group, with responsibility for developing brand identity, translating brands into images and handling product approvals.
- Retail Group; sometimes part of the sales group but often a stand-alone division, this group is responsible for presenting and building the Property directly with retailers. Working with the highest-level management at retailers they coordinate licensee's products for exclusive launches and for dedicated retail space across the various product categories.

This does not mean that every licensing department requires a minimum of six groups or, for that matter, even requires six different individuals to accomplish these objectives. Many excellent licensing departments are composed of only one or two individuals, each wearing different hats and sharing these different responsibilities. At the same time, other larger departments have more than a hundred people (and possibly more) broken down by groups and sub-groups.

11.2.1 The Marketing Group

The marketing group is responsible for pulling together the marketing material that the sales group will use in seeking out licensees as well as overseeing all marketing, advertising and public relations activities.

Licensing is all about lead times. If a licensor wants to accomplish something in 18 months, steps must be taken today to set the wheels in motion. As such, the marketing group must work with the licensing director to initially develop a merchandising or marketing plan that will serve as a roadmap for the entire licensing program. When and where possible, the inclusion of key imagery for the property should be used. Focusing on a specific core image for promoting the property can often be an effective means of marketing – think of the bat image to represent Batman. An outline of such a plan is found in Appendix-8.

Perhaps the easiest way to create such a merchandising plan is by developing a time line schedule using, for example, the Gantt chart features that are included in such Microsoft Office products as Excel, Visio or Project. Such a schedule should be broken down by product category and, for each category, should identify when: (a) presentations need be made to potential licensees; (b) license agreements must be entered into with licensees; (c) presentations should be made to potential retail partners; (d) products must actually be introduced by licensees; and (e) sales of licensed products should commence. The timeline should also note the dates of all relevant industry trade shows.

In developing the plan, the property owner needs to consider the appropriate lead times that its licensees will need to manufacture, ship and introduce the licensed products, taking into consideration potential delays caused by local customs and holidays, e.g., Chinese

New Year, etc. It should also identify where and when new products in a category are typically introduced.

The marketing group also has responsibility for planning and overseeing the group's attendance and participation at various licensing trade shows, e.g., the licensing shows in Las Vegas, London, Tokyo, Germany, Shanghai and Hong Kong as well as category-specific trade shows such as Toy Fair, MAGIC and the Bologna Book Fair. Since attendance at such trade shows is an essential part of the marketing process and occurs throughout the year at various locales around the world, this can be a time-consuming task, if done thoroughly.

Attending tradeshows is one of the best ways to learn about a specific industry and become knowledgeable about the current trends, styles and new developments in that industry. It is also a good place make or renew contacts with potential licensees and agents. As such, property owners will always want to attend and, ideally, exhibit at these shows.

When attending a trade show, it is important to have a plan. Most trade shows are large but are frequently organized into various sections by category. A great deal of time can be lost by not using the trade show directory, a printed booklet listing all of the exhibitors that most shows also make available as a cellphone app, to see what companies and sections of the show are worth visiting. Trade show directories are also a valuable resource for use after a show, as they often provide excellent information about those companies who exhibited at the show.

Finally, the plan should include other relevant milestones for the program, including the commencement of any advertising programs and where and when such advertisements would be placed. It should further include planned PR programs, as well as consumer and retail promotions. Also, it is important to time trade advertising and PR programs to coordinate with the applicable trade shows that its licensees will attend.

Is advertising worthwhile? It can be expensive and should only be undertaken if the property owner can afford it. More importantly, placement is critical. A great ad in the wrong place will not produce results. The message delivered must be clear, compelling, and provide enough information to connect with the desired audience. Selection of the right advertising vehicles is equally important. If the intent is to reach companies and decision makers in a specific industry, then ads promoting the availability of the property need to appear in the specific trade publications most often read by these individuals.

The best places to advertise for a property owner launching a new licensing program are the leading licensing trade magazines. These magazines are read by a wide variety of manufacturers and retailers and provide the best and most focused exposure to reach the market that is looking to buy licenses.

One of the added benefits of selecting appropriate licensing partners is that licensees can bring to the licensor added value. They can be contractually bound to advertise (at their sole expense) the licensor's branded product to the licensee's specific industry. Toy ads placed by toy licensees are paid for by the licensee and build awareness not only for the specific toy product but also for the brand in general---at no cost to the licensor.

With larger properties/brands, licensors often build in a "marketing fund" – royalties are raised by 1% -2% and the paid-in additional royalties are used to support the licensed merchandise program in general. Sometimes it is used for dedicated in-store signage, brand

THE NEW AND COMPLETE BUSINESS OF LICENSING

advertising listing all licensees, or a promotional event. The entire list of licensed partners helps support the brand for larger impact, benefitting all.

The PR program is also an important element of a property owner's marketing effort since it can create a "buzz" without the expenditure of a tremendous amount of money. It is a particularly good way to build brand awareness. Industry magazines and newsletters (both print and e-mail) thrive on industry news and the marketing group should plan to release a steady stream of communications to stay out in front of potential customers.

If the property lends itself to promotional activities, e.g., parties, branded product giveaways at trade shows, etc., these activities should be planned and built into the merchandising strategy as well.

The marketing group will also create a "licensee summit" event where all licensee and promotional partners will get together to hear the latest plans for the property and to share possible retail opportunities once placement has been made by certain key licensees.

The marketing group is also typically tasked with responsibility for working with both the sales group and the creative group to produce a sales kit that will be used by the sales group in soliciting and closing deals with licenses. A good sales kit will typically include the following components:

- Description of the property to be licensed and the inclusion of any relevant statistics or facts about the property's appeal and/or notoriety;
- Style guide illustrating how the property should be used as well as all the available artwork for the property, which should only be distributed to companies who have signed a licensing agreement;
- Overall merchandising plan to allow a prospective licensee to see how their products fit in with the broader program;
- Demographics of potential purchasers of licensed products and the target audience;
- Broadcast partners and initiatives, identifying air dates, frequency, audience statistics, etc., including the partners' marketing and support plans;
- Comprehensive retail plans identifying potential retail partners and product rollout schedules;
- Licensor's independent advertising and marketing plans to show how the licensing program interacts with the overall business development agenda;
- Advertising and publicity plan identifying planned trade advertising, public relations, mall tours, costume character program, etc.;
- Sizzle video plus PowerPoint sales presentations; and
- Boards and sample product concepts illustrating how the property will potentially look when applied to products.

Finally, the Internet cannot be forgotten. We live in an on-line world and virtually all property owners will create a website featuring its property and licensing program or use a social network such as Facebook to promote the availability of the property. Most go live early in the process and responsibility for the development and maintenance of the site typically falls under the marketing group.

11.2.2 The Sales Group

The sales group is tasked with the responsibility of implementing the merchandising plan by identifying a list of all potential licensed products, a list of possible licensees for each product, and then actually "selling" a license to potential licensees using the sales kit discussed above.

The sales groups of larger licensing departments are typically broken down by property, market segment and then by product category, e.g., MICKEY MOUSE licensed merchandise toy products. The theory behind this is that the relevant sales executive becomes an expert in one industry, capable of not just understanding its key players and spotting trends and dynamics, but of working with the licensee to help develop better product. Selling a license for merchandise sales can be quite different than selling one for promotional sales or directly to retailers.

Finally, the group will include support personnel to assist in making and scheduling appointments and closing deals.

The first order of business for the sales group is to identify those product categories where licensing would be most appropriate and then to develop a list of possible licensed products within those categories. Once done, the group needs to assemble a list of potential licensees for each of these possible licensed products.

This is typically done by researching the category and identifying those manufacturers who would be in the best position to manufacture product of the type and quality required by the licensor, but who also have the resources and distribution channels to maximize sales. While every category typically includes a host of choices, many experienced licensing salesmen find themselves going back to the same manufacturers who they have worked with in the past and did a good job.

This is one area where manufacturer's representatives play a major role because they will approach the sales group on behalf of their clients and sell their clients to the property owner.

Potential licensees can also be identified using the LIMA database of licensees at www.licensing.org. The database is broken down by product categories and types of products within each category. There are also a few industry directories published by the various trade publications.

Finally, potential licensees can also be identified by simply walking the various industry specific trade shows, where virtually all manufacturers in a potential category are present, irrespective of whether they carry or have ever carried licensed products.

Once the sales group creates a list of potential licensees, it must then contact and potentially meet with the most promising manufacturers to discuss licensing opportunities. This is where the sales group must "sell" the license to a potential manufacturer, stressing the benefits that taking a license for the property can offer the licensee. The dynamics of such meetings will largely depend on the property, i.e., whether it's a "hot" property or one that has never been licensed before. Obviously, selling a license for a hot property takes far less effort than trying to convince an otherwise reluctant manufacturer to take a chance with a new, untried property. It's no different than a car salesman trying to sell *Road & Track*'s Car of the Year, versus one that has just recently been introduced.

The basic tools of selling a license[13] are straight forward:

- **Know Your Property.** Do your homework and know all that you can about the property. To the prospective licensee, you *are* the expert on the property you are selling.
- **Know Something About the Category You Are Trying to License.** You cannot successfully sell a manufacturer without knowing some basic information about the product category.
- **Familiarize Yourself with The Potential Licensee.** The more you know about the company you are trying to sell to, the better your chances of success.
- **Know Your Competition.** Be prepared to respond to questions concerning competitive properties. Be able to clearly delineate your property's point-of-difference for why it is a better property for potential licensees to consider.
- **Build Your Case.** Know the strengths and weaknesses of your property—no property is perfect, so acknowledge its shortcomings while accentuating the positives. It's important to have the facts and figures relating to your property at your fingertips. Know what you are trying to accomplish *before* you start your presentation and remember, you are leading the meeting, so know where you are heading! Be able to positively respond to any reasons the potential partner may want to say "no".
- **Good Presentation Tools are Essential.** In today's techno-marketplace, good presentation tools are expected and essential. The better the visual, the easier it is for the prospective licensee to picture the application of your property to his product. Your marketing and sales materials need to be both informative *and* attractive.
- **Believe in and Get Excited About Your Property.** Enthusiasm is infectious. The more excited you are about the property you are selling, the better it will be received. Of course, enthusiasm will not replace or cover up a lack of knowledge about the property, product category or your ability to sell a license!

The salesman should also emphasize the benefits that may be derived from taking a license, including increased sales, the ability to sell other products in their line, building exposure and awareness of the manufacturer's own brand and product line and opening distribution into different channels.

Once the list is narrowed down and there is an expression of interest by one or more potential licensees, they are typically asked to fill out and submit a "licensee Application" in which the prospective licensee provides important information about its company, financial strength, licensing history and manufacturing and distribution capabilities. A sample licensee Proposal or Application is included at Appendix-2.

The Sales group then reviews and evaluates all these completed licensee applications and ultimately selects the one that appears the best fit for the property and the merchandise plan. The evaluation process varies from licensor to licensor, but some of the more important elements considered by most include:

---

[13] Based on a CLS presentation *How to Sell a License* by Danny Simon, President of The Licensing Group, Ltd. 6363 Wilshire Blvd., Los Angeles, CA 90048.

- What type of products they are proposing and whether they will be a good fit for the property;
- What is their quality history, e.g., have they manufactured high quality products in the past;
- Size and structure of the company, e.g., is it a major player in the field or a start-up business;
- Strength of design and manufacturing capabilities, e.g., who will design the products and where and by whom will they be manufactured;
- Capitalization and financial strength, e.g., are they sufficiently capitalized to meet the financial conditions of the license and to put resources behind the license, or are they on the verge of bankruptcy;
- Distribution capabilities, e.g., how and in what markets will they distribute the product;
- How the license will fit in the manufacturer's product mix;
- How the license will fit into the manufacturer's licensed property mix; if they already have a hotter property will your property get the attention it deserves?
- Sales history, e.g., what are their sales revenues and what percentage of their total revenues will the licensed products represent;
- Licensing history, e.g., have they had prior licenses and how have they done with them; and
- What financial terms are they offering.

It should be noted that financial terms were specifically identified as the last consideration because, for a license to be successful, it needs to be more than just about who is willing to pay the highest royalty rate or the largest advance or guarantee. If the licensee is not capable of manufacturing quality product or does not have sufficient market penetration, the selection of such a licensee can cause serious problems for the entire program. Also, if the licensee does not have adequate retail distribution, your licensed products will never be available to the full consumer marketplace.

Most licensors do not simply rely on the potential licensee's answers in the licensee Application but will do their own due diligence to confirm various facts. It is quite common for licensors to run Dun & Bradstreet reports to confirm a potential licensee's financial information and whether they are paying their obligations when they become due. Similarly, licensors will also ask for and check the licensee's references, including bank and credit references, as well as their experience with other licensors.

Once a potential licensee has been vetted and is selected, the final step for the sales group is to "close the deal" on the best terms possible for the licensor. Typically, this process starts with the preparation of a term sheet or deal memo which identifies the relevant terms of the transaction. A sample term sheet or deal memo is included here at Appendix-3.

It is important to keep the entire licensing group aware of how these discussions progress as well as the terms being discussed. In many instances, it might even be necessary for other sections of the property owner's organization be involved or, at the very least, kept advised. The use of a sign-off sheet is a good idea to ensure that the sales group doesn't offer terms or conditions that the property owner is simply unable or unwilling to offer. Getting as many people involved in this process as necessary is important to avoiding an embarrassing situation or, worse yet, one that must be unwound. Frequently, the sales group will work with the contract administration and legal group in this regard.

11.2.3 The Contract Administration and Legal Group

The contract administration and legal functions are typically intertwined as they cover both the legal protection that is required to support a licensing program, as well as the contract administration function. Frequently the same individual or individuals handle both functions

[A] Trademark Clearance and Protection

The necessity for clearing and protecting a licensing property is covered at length in Chapter 6. Trademark clearance is typically the responsibility of the property owner, even if an agent is used.

Prior to launching the licensing program, global trademark searches should be conducted to ensure that the use of the property by potential licensees will not infringe the rights of anyone else. In performing such searches, special attention should be given to third party uses in those classes with the most licensing activity, i.e., apparel, publishing, toys and video games.

If the property is cleared for these classes, appropriate trademark applications should be filed to commence the protection process. For a more thorough discussion of this process, see Chapter 6.

[B] Licensing Forms

Creating a set of standard forms that will be used for the licensing program is very important and should be done at the very outset to insure uniformity throughout the program. Some of the forms that need to be developed are:

- Licensee application form
- Term sheet or Deal Memo
- Standard license agreement
- Approval forms
- Royalty Report form
- Product Approval form

Of all these forms, perhaps the most important is the "standard" license agreement that the property owner will use during the licensing program. Special care should be taken in the development of this standard agreement because it will serve as the operative document that will ultimately define the relationship between the parties. Chapter 10 details what should be contained in a license agreement and a form License Agreement is also included as Appendix-4.

It should be appreciated that license agreements are "evolving" documents, meaning that as issues develop, and lessons are learned from both good and bad experiences, most licensors will adapt their standard license agreements for future deals to address such issues. Unfortunately, it is usually not possible to change an agreement that has already been signed with a licensee, so if the form is properly prepared in the first place, fewer changes will be required going forward.

This is not to suggest or imply that every licensee will accept the property owner's standard form—most will want some changes and that is to be expected. The goal, however, is to keep the changes to a minimum so that there is a degree of uniformity from agreement to agreement within a program.

[C] Contract Administration

As the name would imply, the group's primary function is to ensure that all licensees comply with their obligations under the respective license agreements. The group will have day to day management responsibility for the licensing program and, in this regard, will frequently work in combination with the finance and creative groups.

It is advisable to establish strong, workable internal systems from the very beginning to make sure that the program proceeds smoothly and without any problems. The group should control the paper flow of the licensing process, typically commencing when the initial licensee proposal is accepted, through termination of the licensee. In most cases, the group is responsible for the following activities:

- **Preparation and Completion of the Deal Memo.** It is important that the deal memo be routed through the appropriate groups for review and approval.
- **Licensee Review and Evaluation.** This entails conducting financial and risk management reviews for all potential licensees and ultimately selecting the final licensee. An important consideration is recognizing any potential product liability issues.
- **License Agreement.** This includes the preparation, negotiation and execution of the license agreement and any amendments. It is good practice for summaries of the license agreements to be prepared and circulated to the various departments and kept readily accessible.
- **Licensee Administration.** This requires the development of a docketing system and "punch list" of all relevant due dates by licensees which should be circulated to other relevant departments, e.g., product approval dates to creative, royalties due for finance, etc. Additionally, and perhaps most importantly, it facilitates constant communication with licensees to insure compliance with the terms of the license agreement.

Established licensing programs may quickly find themselves in a position where they must track literally hundreds of licensees on a worldwide basis for multiple licensed properties and licensed products. While some have and continue to do this manually, the better practice is to computerize the operation using a comprehensive contract administration software package that also features a royalty tracking/accounting module. Selecting and implementing the right package at the beginning of the program will avoid having to change procedures and systems in mid-stream, which only complicates the issue since it necessitates data conversion, etc. An effective contract administration software package should be able to:

- Assemble license agreements by the selection of individual clauses;
- Generate summaries of the license agreements and sort these by property, licensee, territory, term and product(s);
- Generate form letters or e-mails to licensees for reminders and failures to comply with due dates;
- Track all licensees, licensed products, submission dates and approval dates;

- Generate monthly reports, invoices and reminders;
- Monitor licensees' royalty and guarantee payment status;
- Manage all other aspects of the licensees' financial requirements and obligations;
- Track third party participation revenues for disbursements; and
- Produce management, sales, marketing and product approval reports as well as other relevant information anytime, anywhere.

While some property owners prefer to develop their own, proprietary, contract administration systems, there are several excellent third-party packages available that will meet the needs of most licensors. Most of these packages are designed to run on PC's and Macintosh platforms and are surprisingly reasonable in price, compared to the cost of developing one's own program. A few of the more commonly used packages as of this writing include the System 7 Universal Rights Management system by Jaguar Consulting; Dependable Rights Manager (DRM) by Dependable Solutions; and the Pelican ProFiles suite by Counterpoint Systems, Inc.

Companies that market off-the-shelf licensing packages can be found in the "support services" section on LIMA's licensing database at www.licensing.org. Most of the companies listed in this section will provide potential customers with evaluation copies of their products as well as detailed sample reports that the program can generate.

11.2.4 The Finance Group

The finance group typically gets involved once the license agreement is signed and licensing revenue starts flowing, i.e., when the advance gets paid. However, the finance group may be used earlier to conduct financial research on prospective licensees. This group is tasked with the responsibility of tracking payments due from both licensees as well as sub-agents in various countries. It will work closely with the contract administration group, utilizing their software to track all payments due and revenues received from licensees. This group also compiles the reports that will enable the property owner to quickly and easily evaluate the success of the overall licensing program, including the status of individual licensed properties, the licensees and the licensed products.

11.2.5 The Retail Group

In the early days of licensing, licensors would sit back and rely on their licensees to interact with the retail community. Times have changed. Successful property owners now understand the key role that the retailers play in the success or failure of a licensing program and actively seek to engage them during the entire process to help licensees maximize the market presence of their licensed products. Consolidation at retail has given major retailers enormous power and the penetration into one or two of the major chains can be the difference between boom or bust for a program.

Many licensors begin presenting their licensed properties and licensing programs to retailers more than a year before licensed products are scheduled to reach the retail shelves, to generate excitement for their properties and pave the way for its licensee's products. Retail presentations should clearly convey:

- Property uniqueness, including identification of writers, production quality and possible storylines;
- Identification of broadcast partners and broadcast plans;

- Identification of key licensing partners, including master toy, apparel, publishing and video game licensees, since retailers want to know who has signed on to the licensing program as a critical part of their evaluation;
- Identification of promotional partners, the amount of advertising support for the property and planned in-store cross promotions;
- Property owner's plan to leverage its own assets and any relationship(s) it may have that could help promote the property, e.g., in-theater and DVD trailers, etc.; and
- Advertising and publicity plans for the property to help create consumer awareness.

Some tips for making retail presentations[14] include:

- **Don't Be Vague.** Make sure your presentation has direction and a point of view specifically tailored for the retailer you are presenting to.
- **Allow the Retailer to Take It In.** Once you make your case, allow the retailer to absorb and interpret it for themselves. They understand their venues best and may know details of which you are unaware.
- **Identify Only Your Actual Licensees.** If you are giving out a licensee list, make sure that the licensees are on board since the retailer may call them.
- **Don't Mention Other Retailers Who Have Passed.** If other retailers have passed on the property, keep it to yourself.
- **Think Out of the Box.** Don't limit yourself to the tried and true. Explore the host of new channels of distribution currently available. They may not be the biggest, but they could ultimately become the most successful and lead to bigger opportunities down the road.
- **Be concise.** Time is precious, so make sure to convey your message in an efficient and concise manner.
- **Be passionate!** Your approach should not be, "I wanted to see what you thought of this property", but rather "I have a new property that is right for you and let me tell you why."

In recent years, many retailers have not been content to simply sell licensed products that were manufactured by conventional licensees but, instead, have gone directly to the property owner and taken "direct to retail" licenses for products, which they then have manufactured in their own factories or by another third party. By eliminating the conventional licensee and their profit from the equation, the retailers are conceivably able to offer the licensed products to the consumer at lower prices. See Chapter 19, for a more thorough discussion of the retailer's role in licensing.

11.2.6 The Creative Group

The creative group is tasked with the responsibility of controlling how the property appears and will be used on the licensed products. It is also responsible for the review and approval of all licensee submissions to ensure that the quality standards are being met and the licensee is using the property correctly on its products.

---

[14] Based on the LIMA webinar entitled *Presenting to Retail: The Good, The Bad and the Ugly,* by David Niggli, former Chief Marketing Officer for FAO Schwartz.

Most property owners provide their licensees with a "style guide" that illustrates how the property should be depicted and used, as detailed in Chapter 13. It is a "road map" for the licensing property and should be closely followed by all licensees. Today, most style guides are delivered in digital format rather than in hard copy and many are maintained on-line for ease of reference by a licensee.

Again, the primary purpose of a style guide is to inform a licensee as to how it may present the property on the licensed products and thereby enable them to create the best licensed products possible. It will also assure that there is uniformity between all licensees regarding how they will each present the property on their products as well as on packaging and in advertising.

A typical style guide will include:

- How the property is to be depicted and displayed, what characters or brands are included, etc.;
- Rules for use of the property, e.g. "Character X should never…"
- If a character is included, what poses can (and cannot) be used;
- Vehicles and environment art guidelines;
- Size ratios of characters, backgrounds, color charts, quotations, logos as well as a color palette and suggested designs that may or may not include key elements such as characters, environments and logos;
- Packaging and hangtags;
- Product concepts;
- Product approval requirements that outline when and how a product must be submitted to the licensor for approval; and
- Legal Notices.

Many property owners prepare their own style guides while others outsource the project to companies that specialize in their preparation. There are several such entities and they can be found in the "support services" section on LIMA's licensing database at www.licensing.org.

As licensees are brought on board, the creative group monitors how the property is incorporated with the licensed products. As spelled out in their license agreements, licensees will be required to submit proposed product, packaging and advertising to the licensor for approval at various stages of the production cycle and it is the responsibility of the creative group to review and approve such submissions. Also, as noted earlier, licensees are typically not permitted to proceed to the next step of any process unless they first obtain written approval of their submissions and, in many instances, the failure of a licensor to expressly approve a submission will be deemed disapproval of the submission.

Many licensors involve the creative group in the licensing process as early as possible so that both parties are on the same page when it comes to product development. By reviewing early renderings of product and packaging, potentially devastating problems can be avoided, e.g., where the licensee has produced and shipped 500,000 products only to find that they are not acceptable to the licensor. When the creative group is involved at an early stage, small problems can often be corrected before they become large and expensive ones or cause delays in the product production cycle.

Keeping track of licensee submissions, let alone the approval and disapproval of such submission is a vital function. The review and approval or disapproval of submitted products demands immediate attention and prompt responses from the licensor. The ability of licensees to meet distribution dates can be greatly impacted by delays in receiving responses from the licensor to materials submitted for approval. Keep in mind that although a licensing agreement may allow the licensor to respond to submissions within X number of days, a prompt response will help to insure timely distribution of licensed products, which can often lead to larger royalty payments.

To ensure the growth and success of the licensing program, it is advisable for the creative group to work with the contract administration group and its computer systems to docket when such submissions are due and when responses are required. A program with 50 licensees, for example, may have to track more than 5,000 required submissions every year—no easy feat to do manually.

11.3 International Licensing

Licensing is a global business, and one cannot simply focus on the country where the property is created and initially merchandised. This is particularly true for entertainment licensing.

If the property is represented by a licensing agent, based on the international distribution of the property, the agent should prepare a compatible international licensing plan and submit it to the property owner before the commencement of any international sales effort. Such a plan should, ideally, include the countries and the products that the agent believes would be appropriate for the property, recommendations for the choice of a sub-agent in a country or region and any further steps that might be necessary to protect the property in these countries.

As is the case with most licensing matters, successful licensors work backwards from the date when they expect licensed products to first hit their respective markets. The following steps should be taken in the development of an international program:

- Immediately after the decision is made to proceed with an international licensing program, seek trademark protection in key categories in each country where licensing is contemplated as well as those countries where licensed products will likely be manufactured, e.g., China, Thailand, Vietnam, Malaysia, etc.;
- Immediately after a broadcast commitment has been obtained:
  - Set up a network of sub-agents in countries where licensing is contemplated;
  - Develop territory-specific tools, e.g., dubbed sizzle reels, translated one-sheet brochures with relevant territory information, broadcast information, global key category partners, etc.; and
  - Identify territory-specific opportunities and work with the appropriate agent(s) to secure them.
- At least one year before the projected launch of licensed products in a country:
  - Create sub-agent representation agreements with those sub-agents who will represent the property in their market;
  - Manage the sub-agents through systems that reinforce deal execution, product development, retail commitments and product roll-out schedules;

- Develop a system that allows for timely receipt and response to product approval submissions; and
- Provide support to toy licensee(s) at international toy fairs in Hong Kong, London and Nuremburg including the creation of sizzle video, posters, costume characters, handouts, etc.

11.4 Using Technology to Better Manage a Licensing Program[15]

So, you are in brand licensing as either a brand owner (Licensor), licensing agency (representing brand owners or licensees) or using an established brand on your product (Licensee) and you want to know if it is time for an automation tool. In context to this paper, an automation tool refers to using computers to improve your brand licensing process, preferably over the web. This chapter is written to help you decide when and why to seek automation and the business advantages you will receive.

Per John Wooden, revered UCLA basketball coach ""Failure is not fatal, but failure to change might be." The key to understanding when to shop for and install a licensing automation tool can be found in the benefits they bring to solve the pains you are currently experiencing. Licensing automation changes and improves your brand knowledge by relieving your team from performing manual and inconsistent business processes and moving into structured routines. To become a successful tool, automation must solve your current problems first and then help you with future problems related to growth, especially as your licensing operations expand.

The benefits of automation commonly address issues associated with higher production volume, increase worker productivity, more efficient use of materials, producing better product quality, improving safety, shortening labor workweeks, and responding to trends in the market. In the licensing industry, the good news is that there are solutions for each of these areas. In this chapter, we will review what benefits automation brings and the common problems solved by it.

Higher Production Volume

You need a significant volume of licensing activity to see any benefits from licensing automation. If you have royalty statements that have hundreds of lines or royalties or complex forecasts running each quarter, you need a database system to help you. With statements of 10,000 lines or more, you need an electronic eye to match all the data back to each contract. Automation is key. Details available from licensees continue to grow even down to sales reported at the SKU, sales type, channel and territory. According to one of the largest licensees in the world, "Without automation, one could not process up to a million lines of data each month and produce royalties in days."

Let's say, you are just starting out in licensing and tearing up the market with a myriad of new deals! This event creates confusion with management, brand owners, agents, subagents and licensees just trying to keep up with demand for products incorporating a hot brand. The quicker pace of licensing requires immediate feedback to move deals along and the more deals you do in a short timeframe has its own complexities. An example of

---

[15] Written by Marty Malysz, president of Dependable Solutions, Inc. www.dependablerights.com

accelerated growth can be evidenced with the **"Miraculous(tm)"**- Tales of Ladybug & Cat Noir TV series, an action comedy super hero animated show that amassed hundreds of licensing contracts all over the world in the first two years. Miraculous is produced by the award-winning studio ZAG/Zagtoon and Method Animation. The CGI series originally premiered on Nickelodeon in the US, currently streams on Netflix USA and is predominantly on Disney Channel in EMEA and LATAM. "As an independent production company, licensing is a critical source for funding our productions and serving our fans." mentions Andre' Lake Mayer, President, Global Brand Strategy & Consumer Products, ZAG Animation Studios. "We quickly implemented automation to fuel our growth, so we could efficiently manage the demands of licensees worldwide."

The product lifecycle of licensing from initial concept to finished SKU sold at retail has many different stages, each of which requires you to capture information from various parties. Everyone begins day one trying to just get by with emails with attachments, excel spreadsheets and a shared Dropbox account, only to find out each process is dependent on many future events. Very soon, your email inbox is cluttered with huge attachments and you are losing track of which products are semi-approved and with whom you are dealing with. Automation helps reduce the network traffic in your email and messaging since all the information is securely held in one location and the complete history is available without having to dig through past emails. "Automation takes away all the tedious tasks of following up at each stage of the product approval lifecycle." Wendy Reid, Hamilton Beach Brands, Inc.

Increased Productivity

A new automated licensing solution must allow you to grow and reduce your need to add resources just to handle administrative tasks. This is commonly referred to as scaling your business without the need of adding more bodies into your department. You may be tempted to assign activities to your existing team which will usually meet with resistance . . . except from the interns. The cost of putting in an automated solution which works 24 hours per day and seldom complains offsets just a single worker's additional salary and overhead. "Each category manager processes their clients' royalty reports directly, so we have full control and transparency" Jess Hatz, Australian Football League licensing manager. "We have already picked up a number of errors in licensees' reporting, due to our systems structure allowing us to identify significant discrepancies on reported royalties." Jeff Coriell | Director of Accounting, Live Nation Merchandise.

One of the key benefits for automation is that it brings together licensees, agents and brand owners along with manufactures, graphic artists and retailers onto a shared platform. Activity must be captured at each step of the way along with any comments or directions in the approval process. This occurs for products, packaging and any other marketing materials along with where the samples are stored. The information is stored through keystrokes, voice commands or commonly used responses which alleviates the need for tedious data entry by one department. Each person working on the product enters in enough information to move it to the next stage thereby limiting the work by you. "When we opened our brand licensing agency "Evolution" we were using spreadsheets to track all our license agreements along with a standalone solution for product development which worked fine until the volume of reporting and SKUs increased." reports Evolution's CFO & COO, "It then became increasingly difficult to comprehensively check that sales for SKUs reported were approved or sold in approved territories. An automated and integrated contract management and PD solution was required to keep track of everything and improve operational efficiencies whilst having a robust system to check contract compliance."

It is tough to run three shifts in any company so leave it up to automation. Automation does not demand overtime and shows up seven days a week, 24 hours a day. Since many companies do business across multiple continents and time zones, a licensing automation tool helps move your licensed products using predefined rules at all hours of the day. You can process hundreds of approvals each day or dozens of royalty statements each day since the matching mechanisms in the database know how to find and flag items you need to follow up on. "We were able to organize our team quickly while managing hundreds of licenses across Italy and Poland using centralized automation." Maurizio Distefano, Founder of Maurizio Distefano Licensing.

Your existing staff becomes much more productive because they spend less time compiling information and more time analyzing your business trends. Licensees can be required to report information about sales made to each retailer, allowing you to see where your products are selling. Even missing information is good to have so you find out where products were approved and not selling or licensed but never produced. You can then take rights from the company not exploiting them to another company who can produce, market and sell your products to their full potential. "The information being reported (or not being reported) is extremely valuable to any licensing business holistically." Michael Cisneros, Licensing Specialist at SEGA of America. "It's imperative that we understand which retailers and markets are supporting our brand, what types of products they are buying, and more importantly - which ones are not."

More Efficient Use of Materials

Having readily available, camera ready and approved artwork helps any brand speed up the approval process. New photos, logos, or designs need to be approved and compared to the style guide ensuring they conform to brand guidelines. Historically, brand owners sent out physical style guides to each licensee with indexed artwork and explicit instructions. Today, brands put all this information online, shortening the approval process. New artwork is available immediately to each person needing it quickly. Pre-approved artwork is securely stored in one central location allowing controlled and monitored access to files.

Automation also helps organize samples both received and sent during the final stages of approvals. Knowing when the samples are received or where the samples are keys to an efficient sample management process. Samples need to be available for many reasons (historical records, trademark registration, marketing, publicity, safety regulations, etc.) so tracking the receipt of each shipment, the quantity, the courier and where they are kept can be tricky without licensing automation. Comprehensive digital asset tools reduce cost and give immediate responses when you exchange artwork and files online. Even when samples are required, you want to track the contractual commitment against the actual number of samples sent to put them into inventory.

Case study: Hallmark Cards, Inc. Before we implemented an end-to-tend system that enabled electronic sharing of design assets, we commonly incurred overnight shipping fees and the ability to track asset usage by a licensee was nearly impossible. A comprehensive digital asset tool reduces costs and results in immediate responses when exchanging art-work and files online. The business environment today requires quick actions and imple-menting a new system supported improved (and faster) decisions. "We approve on aver-age of 125 sku approval submissions each week on our system and you can see how quickly you can amass thousands of images over several years." shares Frank Masterson, Licens-ing Business Enablement Manager, Hallmark Cards, Inc. "We're a global business with many employees around the world who participate in our brand licensing business and they depend on automation to perform tasks efficiently, cost effectively and accurately."

Better Product Quality

Automation allows you to manage all approved products anywhere in the world. Your licensed brand history sits in one place allowing access to information on an "as-needed" basis. It is amazing to see what products sell in one territory and not in another. Certain products are "approved with changes" which throws a wrench in your gears when the changes are not made. In this case, your automation tool can remind you to check the final changes before the products are approved and before a final SKU is produced. "Our brand is growing massively year-on-year, and we're getting interest in more countries and more categories. So, it became necessary to automate to better see what our licensees are doing in what territories, especially approvals," Mark Bell, Merchandise Licensing Manager, Chel-sea FC.

Higher quality goods in the market can be attributed to better design, testing and compli-ance processes. With automation, you keep all this information in one place to improve any product. Each person in the quality control process, which may include engineers, at-torneys, graphic artists, and agents, can make comments or move products along. "As a licensee for many major brands, we have found that automation inside our organization is invaluable to help protect us the next time we are audited by a major entertainment client" Colleen Glendening, Idea Nuova, Inc.

You also gain the ability to spot gray market sales where your product is sold outside of the licensed territory. Some of your products are sold by legitimate licensees to resellers, and you can quickly check sales made outside the bounds of your agreements. These sales can be dealt with quickly when royalties are reported and are not usually recouped from contractual guarantees. "The ability to process royalty statements through an automated validation portal allows us to efficiently identify products being sold outside of contractual granted rights, which significantly enhances our licensing business."

To help build healthy sales channels, you can more easily track sales made through certain retailers. Loading this information into your database, you can see across all licensees to recognize where your products have been embraced by retailers or consumers in certain geographical areas. With stronger sales information, you better target your online mar-keting or traditional advertising spent to support your licensees and have the research and data to support bigger buys at retailers where your products are selling well, or to open new markets for licensees, premium product sales or B2C sales. "Automation enables our entire team to have more of a vision and understanding of our business which is definitely a plus when it comes to ongoing negotiations.' According to Miruna Seitan, Licensing Man-ager at Global Merchandising/Real Madrid Adidas Group.

To help thwart infringers bringing low cost, inferior product into the marketplace, you can measure the goods sold against manufacturer runs by simply requiring authentication labels for each licensee. Using automated tools, licensees can order labels, activate them allowing customs officers or even consumers to check to see if they are genuine branded products. Authentication can also help your accounting department see when sales meet or exceed the labels to help you measure the product in the marketplace.

Improve Safety and Operations Efficiency

The most overworked department is usually the royalty person cramming months of work into 45 days after the end of each quarter to produce statements on time. Automation helps reduce data entry in cumbersome spreadsheets with multiple pivot tables. Sales are loaded electronically to avoid time-consuming data entry tasks and mistakes. Automated tools help spread the workload before the end of quarter crunch time, so you are validating sales and royalty obligations each week or month, well before the quarter-end. "Automated processes not only improve cash flow, but they are by far the best way to keep track of how your license is being exploited," Neena Gordon, President N Gordon Company Inc. "The wealth of information at your fingertips gives you immediate insight into any part of the business and understanding of how your intellectual property is being utilized."

With consumers more aware of what products are made of, where and by whom they are made, Fair Labor standards are important to make sure that manufacturers both local and half-the-world away perform ethically and responsibly. Yes, confirming where the products are made through approved manufacturers help you control your sales channels but also build trust with consumers. Millennials and Gen Z consumers are very electronically aware and can look up reviews to quickly see materials used in any product through their phones

A new government requirement is upon us with the May 25, 2018 enforcement of the General Data Protection Regulation (GDPR). These new regulations apply to any European Union citizen tracked electronically in a database whereby you must be accountable to these individuals. This places a large responsibility on any licensing company tracking individuals to improve the safety of personal individual information (PII). Massive fines (10M USD minimum) and poor public awareness (e.g. Facebook with Russian political interference in 2016 US presidential election) apply to any company who does not take online safety seriously. The good news is that there are online systems designed with privacy in mind and allow you to comply with the new GDPR.

Shortened Work Days

A key component of licensing automation is capturing information at the source and not manually recreating data. For instance, sales come directly from the licensing ERP systems directly to brand owners with details not available in consolidated statements. Information such as the exact sale date, SKU (stock keeping unit), description, sales type, channel and retailer and price, give you more specific details on each transaction. This helps everyone from the licensee, agent to brand owner spend less time compiling data and more time analyzing trends. Since all data is loaded into an indexed database, your reports are much quicker with more detail to help you pinpoint information. "As both a Licensee and Licensor, we receive sales from several sales sources and often found ourselves compiling this data into large master files and tracking down missing information. Since moving to a system such as DRM, we have reduced our processing time significantly and allowed ourselves to report royalties to our Licensors in a timely manner and meet the ad hoc requests." David Edwards, Royalties Manager, Hybrid Apparel

As with most licensed activity, all parties are not under one roof, nor even in the same country. Working remotely requires you to use automation as the central communications tool between all parties to move branded products through their lifecycle. A good Internet connection is all you need to setup your remote office with a good automated licensing tool. Systems also help share the workload across your teams, so you can take advantage of more resources. You can have teams in place close to brand owners and have both the agents and the brands share information securely. So, with brand managers travelling, spikes in workload activity, vacations, trade shows and maternity/paternity or general employee leaves of absence, an automated system allows your need to redistribute the work across your internal team, agents and even subagents. "As our licensing activity has become more global and we are working with clients, licensees and sub-agents across multiple time zones, using automated tools is critical to achieving program goals and providing a high-level of licensing service around-the-clock." Andy Topkins, Partner, Brandgenuity

Responding to Market Trends

Generation Z consumers love to shop online and get their products personalized. This requires quick response to consumer demand to satisfy branded product demand. Unfortunately, the instant access to links in Facebook or Amazon can lead consumers also to infringed goods. Automated tools can help rescue brand owners from these perils by removing illegal content quickly. "With automated detection and takedown notices, we can shut down thousands of infringing products found on social media and online retail sites, every month." Jesper Poulsen, SVP Artist & Brand Development, Epic Rights Inc.

Taking advantage of trends in the market requires knowledge and quick response times. Social media creates instant opportunities for brand owners to act and instantly meet consumer demand. Knowing what catch phrases, designs or slogans are available and for each to be quickly registered and licensed is critical. Back in 1959, Indiana University's Swim Team was the first to rock the University's iconic candy-stripes. The Men's Basketball team adopted the candy-striped warm-up pants in 1971. Today, the red & white vertical design on warm up pants and other products has become an Indiana University trade dress and legendary mark for the entire athletic department and campus. "We must monitor 400+ licensees selling unique goods across the globe," Valerie Gill, University Director of Sponsorships, Licensing, & Trademarks, Indiana University, "and rely on automated processes to keep abreast of what is moving." Reviewing where products are sold can help you spot opportunities where other channels or markets are available and avoid oversaturation of products within distribution channels and markets.

Areas of Licensing Automation

Legal – Tracking trademark registrations as they apply to brands, logos, works or symbols must organize all approved products and to help impede infringed products. Trademarks are registered by class (up to 40) in each territory around the world so you protect your intellectual property.

Contract Management - Contracts are the life-blood of all licensing. Details associated with every product must comply with the terms in the agreement such as the royalty rate, product string, licensed brands (IP), territory, channel and retailer, sales date and sales type.

Product Development – Products originate as concepts are matched to the contract information and require many different people inside and outside the licensing organization to approve each step and stage of the development process. Products are matched up with packaging and eventually end up as a SKU for the financial team.

Advertising – Approvals apply to how your brands are marketed. Images, artwork, advertisements and promotional goods associated with your brand must be approved. When you have cooperative or joint marketing commitments, you can track your advertising income too.

Royalties – For licensees, royalty obligations must be accurate to help lower the royalty payments by taking advantage of every allowable deduction. For brand owners, validating the royalties at the detailed line item is critical to reconciling royalties back to payments and minimum guarantee commitments and ensuring all sales are within the terms of the contract.

Forecasting – Estimating sales by licensees and developing reliable forecasts are more critical today with the new contractual licensing revenue requirements (IFRS15 or ASC606) so you can allocate your revenue properly. Once actual royalty statements are received, collecting royalties electronically gives you the detail you need to make the revenue calculations and compare the forecast to actual sales or guarantee commitments.

Asset Management - Having available artwork and images helps licensees create product more quickly knowing that the creative elements are pre-approved. Online style guides help you instruct licensees on how your brands must be utilized to help cut down on unapproved products. Online assets also allow a licensee to directly access the artwork you have granted them, without requiring your time to email or send artwork.

Financials – All calculations end up in the subledger where you track the monies allocated to each brand and profit center from the royalties, advances and guarantees. This information is eventually sent over the corporate ERP systems to post to your financial statements.

Summary: So, when do you jump into licensing automation? To experience the benefits of automated licensing techniques, you need 20 or more deals before you begin drowning in the volume of product approvals, contract renewals, royalty reporting and forecasting. Another reason to wait is that you will have trouble appreciating the benefits of automation until you have some real-world challenges in your business processes. Yes, with some hurt on, you will be able to find the best remedy to help solve your licensing business aches and pains. Alternatively, if you have 500K USD in royalties coming in (brand owners or agents) or being paid out over the next 12 months (licensees), you will also benefit from licensing automation since you will immediately spot inconsistencies in your business processes easily justifying your licensing automation project. As your branded product volume grows, automation helps you do everything faster with less expense and increases your quality of business processes.

Many companies wait too long and pass each of these two milestones. Becoming an informed buyer is important to find which company offers the best tool and is the right partner for you and your team. Fortunately, you have many companies from which to choose how you automate your business processes. LIMA is a great resource for available solutions partners. Visit LIMA at www.licensing.org online directory under support services/category-software. For a more interactive shopping experience, you can arrange meetings at Brand Licensing Europe (brandlicensing.eu) in London each October or Licensing Expo (www.licensingexpo.com/licensing-show/las-vegas) in Las Vegas each May. Here you can shop reputable companies with offices around the world to help you in your journey of selecting and implementing a licensing automation solution.

11.5 Building a Compelling Licensing Plan[16]

Planning is the key to success in any field, particularly licensing. The key elements to any plan, whether it's for a licensor or for a licensee, are providing the answers to certain key questions, i.e.:

- Is your brand/product merchandisable? Provide answers to the following questions:
    - Is it relevant to the marketplace?
    - What is its value proposition?
    - What is its appeal to consumers in terms of demographics, psychographics, geographics?
    - Does your brand connect with end users?
    - How does your brand/product differentiate itself from others?
    - Does your brand stand out from the competition?
    - What is your value proposition?
    - What are you bringing to the market?
    - Why should a retailer carry your product vs. your competitors since it's a battle for existing shelf space?
    - Aesthetics—will consumers choose your brand over the competition
- Who is your audience? Since you can't be everything to everybody, how will your brand/products be sold at retail
    - Who is your ultimate consumer—focus on your "alpha consumer"?
        - What is their demographic?
        - What ages does your product appeal to? Narrow it down to the specific age group.
    - What are the most appropriate licensed categories? Start somewhere and expand outwardly. You need a core competency, i.e., something you can do better than anyone else.
    - All roads lead to retail. Who are the most appropriate retailers?
        - How can you reach these retailers? Every road leads to retail—licensors and licensees are at the mercy of the retailer's buyer who are segmented, e.g., girl's pre-school toys, adult sleepwear, etc.
        - Two questions retailers will ask are: why your product and why now?

---

[16] Based, in part, on presentation made by Woody Brown of Building Q, www.buildingq.com and JJ Ahearn of Licensing Street, www.licensingstreet.com at Licensing University 2016 entitled Building a Compelling Licensing Plan.

- Where do your consumers buy/client sell? Find the right retailer for your brand and build a success story with a smaller retailer. Success translates and can eventually open the door with a larger retailer.
    - Understand the various categories of retailers, e.g., mass, specialty, mid-tier, drug/grocery, on-line, etc.
    - Really understand the retailer. Walk the malls; learn the retailer's plan-o-grams. Understand how they operate, what they're looking for; what they need.
    - Consider the value channel, e.g., the Dollar Store. People make products for these retailers.
- What categories should your focus on, e.g., to character properties, you're looking at media products, toy products, soft goods, etc. Understand the 80/20 rule—80% of your revenues will typically come from 20% of your partners
    - Media, including publishing, interactive/mobile games, DVD, digital downloads, etc.
        - Publishing is a great way to get out your content
        - Soft goods are easier to enter since they're not capital intensive
        - Toys are capital intensive because tooling is expensive. You need to narrow in on what you want to be. Average age for a child playing with a toy is 6.
- Understand your property and learn which part of it has the most consumer appeal. Create a matrix if your property has multiple elements because retailers will want you to focus on the most saleable elements or characters.
    - Test some of your property with smaller retailers, perhaps in test markets, to identify what elements will sell and on what products to create a matrix
- Go into the "cold water room" and ferret out what are the key selling points for the property/product and the biggest challenges that you'll face
- Create a calendar
    - Determine when you want the product to be in the marketplace and work backwards from there
    - Develop at least a 3 years plan. Retail has an extremely long lead time---sometimes 2-3 years.
- Create a competitive set—compare your property/product vs. your competitors
- Why become a licensee?
- Current assortment—what impact will the new product have on your existing product line? Will it constitute simply an incremental sales increase, or will it replace one of your other products?
    - Will it increase your sales? Will licensed products increase your total revenue and not cannibalize your existing business? Best licensees are those who already have a good business.
    - Will it increase your market share? Will it give you an advantage over your competition?
    - Will it permit you to enter new channels or chains? Will licensed products help expand distribution?
- Legal issues—is it protected? Have you registered the trademarks and copyrights?
- Create Style or Brand Guide. Digital or Dropbox.

- Financials—royalties; guarantees; advances
- Marketing—develop a marketing plan
- Communicate your success.
- Why take the risk of licensing if you're a licensee?
  - Market segmentation—the right license can differentiate you from your core business, creating additional sales opportunities. Licensing is a great differentiator
  - Competitive pressure—keeping up with your competition
  - Expand distribution—grow your read customer base
- Corporate brand licensing
  - Much diversity in its scope
    - Product selection more selective than with other segments
    - Only active in a few segments. Do a great job on fewer categories. Don't want the phonebook of licensees for a corporate brand
  - Strategic concerns about brand extension and dilution of equity
  - Main challenge to effectively articulate their role within a retailer's portfolio
  - Most corporate products hold high brand equity but do not necessarily translate to high royalties. Be cognizant of the potential impact that licensing will have on your core brand. With a brand it's more important to talk quality, consumer touch because the purpose is to increase the value of the overall brand. From a negative side, one bad licensee can significantly impact the corporate's brand.

11.6 Creating a Compelling Brand Guide[17]

The brand guide or style guide is more than simply a collection of assets. It's a true marketing tool, providing the overall look and feel of the program. It's more than merely a collection of the design elements that a licensee might need. It is the foundational element for how a licensor will control their brand and how it will be monetized.

Every detail of the guide, i.e., the logos, the package treatment, the graphic treatments, the social media aspects that need to be promoted, etc. all come into play. The more detailed the licensor can be in the guide, the better the program will become. It is a licensor's opportunity to not only control their program, but to market it.

The guide should have a marketing component to it—explaining to the reader not only how the properties are to be displayed but the reasons for it. Brand guides are used to permit the property owner to extend into all areas, not simply licensing. IT can be a good source of protection for the licensor because it demonstrates the way the brands can and need to be used, telling the licensees and partners as to exactly what they can do and how they should do it.

All uses of the brand should have the same look and feel, from how the product licenses use the brands on their product, to how sports teams use the brands on their stadiums to

---

[17] Based, in part, on presentation by Rob Striar of M Style Marketing, for CLS Program entitled Building a Compelling Brand Guide, Nov. 2017.

how advertisers use the brands in the media. Every single aspect of the brand's use is controlled. It insures that there will be an overall consistency of use of the brands.

On the licensing side, the brand guide should mandate that every single licensed product looks and feels like the brand, no matter the demographic or the retail sku. Everything should be the brand. It should provide a holistic look and feel for the brand. It should include the color palates that are to be used, including the applicable color palette.

A good guide will permit the licensee to literally take the designs and elements right out of the guide and place them on the product. They should always include a business strategy and a trend board.

The effective brand guide includes a functional aspect which includes the logos, the patterns, the graphic treatment, the packaging, the messaging, and the copy, all of which are pulled together and integrated.

Brand guides were initially prepared as hard-copy documents, but many are now on-line so that the licensee can easily download and access the correct use of the brand.

An example of a relatively simple brand guide is provided in Appendix-6.

11.7 Forecasting in Today's Licensing World[18]

The importance of forecasting cannot be overlooked and applies to both licensors and licensees. It is essentially "crystal balling" what you believe will happen during the program and how you will respond. Forecasting allows you to plan strategically and be able to make informed decisions as well as allow you to identify market opportunities, better allocate resources and even help with Sarbanes-Oxley compliance.

Licensors and their agents should concentrate on forecasting the following:

- long-term viability of the licensing program
- how resources will be allocated
- how the rights being granted have been used
- what, if any, corrective actions will be needed

Proper forecasting allows licensors the ability to predict variances in earned royalties versus minimum guarantees and improve renewal negotiations.

Forecasting also is helpful for licensees, as it will help predict expenses, provide insight into material requirements and help with planning, production and distribution of licensed products.

Best practices for forecasting include:

- Establish a process and forecasting template
- Establish a schedule, e.g., monthly, quarterly or annual
- Identify key metrics for your business
- Evaluate implemented strategies
- Continual refinement of forecasting process
- Use of technology solutions

[18] Based on a webinar presented on Feb. 28, 2018 by LIMA entitled "Forecasting in Today's Licensing Arena" by Jon Robinson of Vistex (Jon.Robinson@vistex.com) and Emmanuel Fordjour of Beanstalk (Emmanuel.Fordjour@beanstalk.com).

Chapter 12
Best Practices for Licensees

12.1 Introduction

Whether licenses are the cornerstone of the company's product lines or account for only a small percentage, there are some steps the licensee should take that will make the licensing process easier. This chapter provides licensees with information and suggestions regarding the management of a licensing program and development of licensed products.

12.2 Prospecting for the Right Property

Chapter 5 outlined the basis for selecting the right property and the importance of such factors as Objective, Fit, Timing and Cost. Here the question is where does one find properties? There are many ways to learn about and locate properties available for licensing; it is a matter of knowing where to look. What follows are some suggestions.

> If you only attend one show, make it the June Licensing Expo in Las Vegas — everyone and everything is there.

12.2.1 The Internet

The Internet is certainly a logical choice as a search vehicle for potential licensing properties. One approach is to spend time trying word combinations that might land you on the website of an interesting property. The recommended option for locating current information on properties is LIMA's interactive network, LIMANET at *www.limanet.com*. This database provides licensees with a variety of ways to search for properties, including by specific property types. A brief tour is available and is highly recommended to become quickly familiar with the various ways to use this resource tool.

In addition to LIMANET, LIMA maintains an excellent on-line directory of all licensed properties and products with all relevant contact information, which is available to LIMA members on the LIMA website at *www.licensing.org*.

12.2.2 Licensing Directories and Trade Publications

For those of us who still love paper, there are several industry directories published by the various trade publications that list properties and who represents them. An example of this is the Guide to The Licensing World viewable at *www.licensingworld.co.uk*. Broken down by countries, the guide is an excellent resource. The licensing industry has a few trade magazines that cover all aspects of the industry, including *LICENSE Global Magazine*, *Total Licensing* and *The Licensing Book*. These magazines can be valuable sources for learning about new and existing licensing programs, both in the domestic and world markets. In addition to information about new and existing properties, they are also useful as guides to industry events and trade shows.

12.2.3 Domestic and International Licensing Trade Shows

As mentioned in Chapter 5, there is a growing list of successful licensing tradeshows, which offer licensees an efficient and effective means to review a wide array of properties in a single location. The Las Vegas based Licensing Expo, held in early summer is the world's largest licensing three-day event, drawing exhibitors (property owners) and attendees (manufacturers, retailers, service providers and press) from around the globe.

The Hong Kong Licensing Show and seminar forum for the Asian market (information at: *www.hklicensingshow.hktdc.com*) with attendance exceeding 22,000, has taken its place as the largest licensing tradeshow outside of the United States. Held at the beginning of January in conjunction with the Hong Kong Toy Show, this show attracts attendees from over 100 countries and regions and is now the largest licensing event held in the Asian market.

The well-known and popular London-based Brand Licensing Expo (*www.brandlicensing.eu*) is held annually in mid-fall. This licensing show tends to cater to the European market, attracting attendance from throughout Europe in addition to many (licensors and licensees) from other countries.

An increasing number of other region-specific licensing tradeshows have emerged as important licensing trade events. Notable among these are the China International Licensing Show (*www.chinalicensingshow.com*) that takes place in Shanghai in the fall; July's Seoul Character Licensing Fair (*http://characterfair.kr*); the Dubai International Character & Licensing Fair (*www.character.com*) that occurs in late fall; and the March Bologna Licensing Trade Fair (*www.bolognalicensing.com*) that runs concurrent with the Bologna Children's Book Fair. These shows have become increasingly popular and provide an opportunity for those looking to reach new markets outside the U.S. to consider local properties as a means of achieving such distribution.

12.2.4 Other Vehicles

Other ways to find and research possible licenses include:

- Consider the services of an agent that represents manufacturers to locate and secure licenses (the LIMA Website database has such information);
- Network with non-competitive manufacturers;
- Touch base with the buyers are the cutting-edge retailers such as Hot Topics, Spencer Gifts or Urban Outfitters;
- Discuss upcoming licenses with key licensors;
- Talk with and listen to your customers; and
- Check out what properties are being counterfeited since they are an excellent gauge of what's hot.

12.3 Matching the Product to the License[19]

It's one thing to identify the hot properties, it's an entirely different thing to determine whether it will "fit" your products. Specifically, does it enhance your products?

For example, if your product line is a fish tank or aquarium, look for properties with an underwater or marine theme, e.g., NEMO or SPONGEBOB.

---

[19] Based on a CLS presentation by Will Thompson of Changes entitled Matching the Product to the License on December 13, 2017.

Similarly, if you are looking for a license to enhance the sales of your water heater or air conditioner, you would look for properties that resonant as dependable home brands, e.g., Maytag.

Finally, if you are manufacturing home vaporizers, what better brand would there be than one that helps dispense Vicks Vaporizing medicine?

One of the biggest challenges that a manufacturer will face is trying to convince retailers to carry a product when they don't have the room for additional products. These problems tend to be a function of the type of retailer. For example, specialty retailers tend to want only the "trend du jour"—they want to be the first to justify their higher price point. Similarly, mid-tier and mass merchants want products that have proven themselves with the specialty retailers and everyone wants "just in time" inventory. The solution is the on-line retailer since they are generally less selective.

12.4 The Licensing Team

With the decision to engage in licensing, the first step should be the appointment of a person responsible for overseeing licensing for the company. That individual should become the point person for the licensee in working with the licensor and should possess knowledge about the status of development and distribution of the company's licensed products. Many times, that same person will also facilitate the review of new properties, acting as the company's gatekeeper for receipt of information about new properties. Titles such as Director of Licensing, Licensing Manager or Licensing Administrator are frequently used. Having some experience in licensing, preferably on a managerial level, is certainly a plus and reduces the chance of errors.

If the person selected to run the licensing department lacks actual licensing experience, it might be a good idea to consider engaging the services of a licensing consultant for a period of time. From the beginning it is important to establish procedures for things such as tracking product development, product approvals, reporting of royalties, and compliance with the various terms of the license agreement. An investment that insures that the department is set up properly may save the licensee from making costly mistakes later.

There are several critical components to the licensing process that the licensee must address, including: product development, sales, marketing, retail support and administration. Within most companies, the same departments or people responsible for such operations, regardless of whether not there is a license involved, will handle many of these functions. Because certain procedures must be adhered to regarding licensed products that do not apply to unlicensed goods, e.g., the requirement of securing product and packaging approvals, the person heading up licensing should also be the party responsible for insuring all these obligations are performed.

Creating a licensed product is not much different from the development of other products a company manufactures. However, there are additional steps and requirements that must be considered in manufacturing and marketing licensed goods. As products produced under a license must adhere to standards dictated by the licensor, it is helpful that the departments and/or persons involved in creating, building, or marketing the licensed product become familiar with the property, as such knowledge may prevent costly errors from occurring.

12.5 Product Development

Product development is the first and most important step in the production of licensed products. Before the first product designs are put on paper, it is of paramount importance that everyone involved in the licensing process have an excellent understanding of the property. The development of products that are illogical applications of the license often result in the product's failure to achieve sell-through at retail. Without the benefit of a solid working knowledge of the property, it is difficult at best to create products that adequately reflect the property.

12.5.1 Brand Style Guide

Licensee Tip: A good style guide is critical. It is the licensee's roadmap to producing licensed products.

To commence the product development stage, it will be necessary to acquire all the available artwork and marketing materials from the licensor. Usually referred to as a style guide, this material is essentially the roadmap to producing the licensed products. Some style guides are elaborate manuals containing a wide variety of materials for use in development of product and packaging. Others consist of a few property related images and a limited amount of information about the property. Today, most are delivered in digital format rather than in hard copy and many are maintained on a password protected basis on-line for ease of reference by a licensee. The style guide also assures that there is uniformity between all licensees as to how they will each present the property on their products as well as on packaging and in advertising.

The type of materials supplied will often correlate to the property format. For example, if the property is based on an animation series, chances are the style guide will contain a variety of materials that enables the licensee to correctly reproduce each character. It is likely that views of each character will also be supplied, from all angles, front, side and back – usually referred to as turnarounds – and a size ratio chart to insure that the correct size proportions of each character are maintained.

Other materials such as specific Pantone Matching System (PMS) colors that relate to the character and/or style of dress (color call- outs), images of key objects, backgrounds and even type fonts may be included. If the licensor has created packaging standards for use by licensees, this material will also be included. The style guide may also outline product approval requirements. Last but by no means least will be instructions as to the specific legal information that must appear on product and/or packaging, such as trademark and copyright notices.

In some cases, the licensee has some freedom to interrupt the use of these materials; in other cases, the licensee is required to strictly adhere to the design guidelines provided by the licensor. As style guides deliver the relevant materials needed to transform the property into product, most licensors will only provide the licensee with a style guide after the license agreement is signed, or perhaps payment of the advance. A few licensors charge the licensee a fee for their style guide, and if so, payment of an artwork fee will be provided for in the license agreement.

Worth noting, especially as it applies to animated properties, is the fact that some licensors will make design services available to their licensees for which there is usually a charge.

However, a real benefit to using the services of the licensor's artists is the likelihood that such materials will be approved.

12.5.2 Manufacturing Agreement

For those companies that do not own or maintain their own factories, it is important to know if it is necessary to have the licensor approve of the manufacturing facility that will produce the licensed goods. If approval is needed, it usually requires that the manufacturing facility and licensee sign a Manufacturing Agreement. This document contains several provisions that provide the licensor with certain rights, protections and assurances regarding production of the product. The following are a sample of the type of assurances that the sub-manufacturer must agree to:

> **Adopting an "early & often" policy concerning product approvals is important as it will save time and money.**

- Produce the licensed products only for and under the supervision of the licensee
- Comply with the applicable terms and conditions of the license agreement
- Comply with local laws and fair labor practices
- Conduct product safety tests, etc.
- Allow the licensor to inspect the facility
- Discontinue manufacturing upon expiration or termination of the licensee's agreement

While manufacturing agreements are hardly a new requirement, the amount of attention focused on issues such as unacceptable labor practices, and the disclosure of the use of harmful substances in some products, has increased the importance of this document. If licensees do employ the services of a contract manufacturer, they should be certain that their factories are following the applicable regulations.

12.5.3 Trade Shows

Properties can also be found by simply walking the floor at trade shows. Toy Fair, MAGIC, Housewares Show, E3, Comic Con, and other industry specific trade shows often provide insights to new or emerging properties. Furthermore, these settings offer many examples of how other manufacturers use and incorporate properties in their product lines.

Perhaps the best place to go license shopping is *the* licensing industry tradeshow, International Licensing Expo. Held at the beginning of June annually in Las Vegas, this is a tradeshow dedicated to licensing, where the exhibitors are the property owners and representatives. With an estimated 5,000 properties on display and exhibitors that include Hollywood studios, major brand names, animation companies, car companies, various sports associations, record companies, and artists, just about every conceivable property is represented on the show floor. Many licensors will use this show as the vehicle to debut new properties. The other valuable benefit is the ability to meet with property owners; licensing is a relationship driven business and this is an ideal forum in which to meet decision makers.

An additional benefit of the International Licensing Expo is the opportunity to attend the various seminars that are offered in conjunction with this tradeshow. The Licensing University, which is conducted by LIMA, offers several seminars on a variety of licensing topics. Seminars are designed to accommodate every attendee, regardless of their level of licensing expertise.

12.5.3 Social Compliance

Regardless of whether the licensed products are manufactured by the licensee or by a sub-manufacturer, there is much greater emphasis on what is now known as "Social Compliance." This is due, in large measure, to recent negative media attention focused on working conditions in factories, most notably in China. The problem received national attention in the United States in 1996 because of a controversy involving Kathie Lee Gifford.

12.5.4 Product Approvals

As products the licensee develops are subject to the approval of the licensor, adopting an "early and often" policy concerning product approvals is not only a wise course of action, it is likely to save the licensee both time and money. Regardless of whether there is an obligation to do so, seek comments and recommendations from the licensor in the early stages of product development. Changes in direction or designs are far cheaper and faster early in the design stage as opposed to later in the development cycle. This suggestion also applies to the creation of product packaging.

The licensed product and corresponding packaging must be submitted to the licensor for approval prior to manufacturing. Most license agreements provide the licensor with 14 to 30 days to review products and respond to the licensee with either an approval or comments on what must be corrected. It is important to note that failure of the licensor to respond within the period designated in the license agreement does not necessarily mean product is automatically approved. Most agreements read that the licensor's failure to respond within the designated window of time is deemed to be a disapproval of the product.

In practice, many licensors recognize the necessity of providing timely responses to submitted materials and will comply if possible. It is imperative, however, that production schedules consider the time needed to obtain approvals. Even though most licensors take the approval process seriously, the licensor may not be aware of the licensee's production schedule. If timing is a critical factor, make sure the licensor is aware of that fact. Ultimately, most licensors will resist pressure from the licensee to "rush" approvals. Therefore, it is the responsibility of the licensee to build in time for the approval process when determining production schedules.

12.6 Marketing and Sales

Marketing and sales are certainly key ingredients to achieving success with a property and are lumped together due to the symbiotic relationship between them. To achieve strong sales, the development and use of good marketing materials is required. It is likely that the sales effort to place the licensed products at retail will commence long before the product is manufactured. Thus, the initial sales effort will be based on the use of good marketing materials that reflect a reasonably good representation of the product being offered. Development of the initial marketing materials should commence in connection with the design stage.

As the licensed product is subject to approval by the licensor, the sales and marketing materials developed by the licensee must be submitted for approval. It may save time and money to request from the licensor samples of marketing materials that other licensees had created and were already approved by the licensor. Acquiring examples of materials that have met the criteria for approval may be very beneficial in creating materials that contain the right look and feel and that the licensor will accept.

It is important that assumptions made regarding the development of sales and marketing material be based on an adequate foundation of knowledge. As stated above, there is no escaping that those responsible for the creation of these materials need to possess a good working knowledge of the property. If a question arises about some element of the property that is not fully understood, get clarification from the licensor. The odds of making an error are too great a risk and can result in delays that can affect the launch of the sales and marketing effort.

No license is guaranteed to be successful, but the chance of achieving success is greatly enhanced when there is cooperation and coordination between the product development, marketing and sales groups. The goal of any licensee is to integrate these divergent disciplines to create materials that present a unified look, feel and message about the product and property. Within the company, the person most likely to achieve this is the individual charged with the overall responsibilities for the licensing program. This area is covered further and in greater depth in Chapter 12.

12.7 Administration of the Licensing Program

Legal and financial considerations are important aspects of administering any licensing program. The legal area is charged with responsibility for overseeing such matters as reviewing all licensing related documents and providing oversight as to those contractual obligations which the licensee must perform during the term of the agreement. The finance group, tracks sales of the licensed products and on a quarterly basis prepares royalty reports and makes payment to the licensor of royalties generated from sales.

12.7.1 Legal Administration

It is advisable to establish strong, internal legal systems from the very beginning to make sure that the program proceeds smoothly and without any problems. In licensing there is no shortage of paperwork, as the licensor is certain to require the submissions of forms for each element of the licensing process. This results in creating a paper trail that works to everyone's benefit. Whether it is submission of product for approval, payment of royalties or any changes or alterations to terms of the license agreement, each has its own set of forms. While some of the forms listed below will be the responsibility of departments or individuals outside of the legal department, it is always a good idea that copies of all forms – such as product approval forms – be sent to the legal department to ensure that it is kept apprised of all matters relating to the property.

12.7.2 Licensee Application Form

The form that kicks off the parade of paperwork is likely to be a licensee application form. Not all licensors require the use of an application form, but the number that do is growing. The purpose of this form is to provide the property owner with as much information as possible about the company looking to acquire licensing rights. In addition to general information about the company, an application form is likely to request the following:
- Financial information about the company, including past financial history
- The types of products produced by the company

- How or by whom the licensed products will be developed, and where the licensed goods will be manufactured
- The level of retail distribution (department store, specialty, mid-tier, mass), and the names of some of the company's key retail relationships
- What forms of media are used to market the company's product

In addition to questions about the company, the application form will usually be used by the licensor to obtain information about the offer the licensee is willing to make to obtain the license. This will include:

- The financial terms the licensee is willing to offer for the licensing rights
- A complete description of the product rights the licensee is looking to acquire
- The desired length of term
- The territory in which the licensee can sell products
- Information about how the licensee will market the licensed products
- Dates when the product will commence being marketed and sold

For many licensors, the application form is a very important document, and is frequently used to compare competitive offers if more than one company is vying for the same or similar rights. Although payment terms are a very important consideration, licensors want to license companies that have a strong financial foundation. Therefore, the licensee should make every effort to provide the licensor with as complete a picture of the company as possible. A sample of a proposal or application form can be found in Appendix-2.

12.7.3 Deal Memo

With agreement to the business terms of the license, the licensor is likely to fire off a deal memo to the licensee that contains the terms the two parties have agreed to. This form tends to be a one to two-page agreement and is typically devoid of the mysterious legalese. The deal memo will require the signature by both licensee and licensor, and once signed assures the licensee they have secured the license, unless a problem arises over signature of the longer and more complete license agreement. Many licensors will also want payment of the advance (assuming there is one) and, upon receiving this from the licensee, is often then willing to provide a style guide and any other materials needed that will allow the licensee to commence product development. A sample deal memo is included in Appendix-3.

12.7.4 License Agreement

Signing the deal memo will lead to drafting of the license agreement. The pervious chapter covered the license agreement in detail and the reader is encouraged to review the sample form included at Appendix-4.

12.7.5 Approval Forms

As noted earlier, approval forms that must accompany each submission of product, packaging, and marketing materials will most likely be prepared by the product development group and/or marketing folks. Although each licensor has their own version of the approval form, essentially the required information is very much the same and covers:

- Date of submission
- What is being submitted, e.g., product, packaging, labels, advertising materials, etc.

- Full description of the submitted material
- At what stage of development is the submission being made; is the material being submitted as a design concept or a pre-production sample, etc.

Very often, the approval form will provide for the licensor's response to the submitted material. The form may enable the licensor to check off whether the item is approved, approved pending corrections or disapproved. Many licensors will use the approval pending corrections designation if the item requires minor adjustments to meet approval standards. Once the licensee addresses corrections, the product must be re-submitted. If the submitted material is disapproved, is usually means that it contains too many errors, or is seriously flawed.

Providing space for the Licensor to explain why submitted products were not approved will ensure this valuable information is obtained.

If a product sample requires corrections or is disapproved, it is important that the licensee be informed what element(s) need to be corrected. Such information will enable the licensee to make the necessary corrections more expeditiously, which as stressed above, is very important when production schedules are tight. One way to make sure that specific information concerning what corrections are necessary is requiring the licensor to provide such information on the form when returning products that are not approved as submitted. Given how important it is to understand why a product submission has been rejected, the licensee may consider addressing in the license agreement the obligations of the licensor to provide such detailed information.

A sample product approval guide and form are contained in Appendix 7.

12.7.6 Royalty Report Form

Standard under most license agreements is an obligation on behalf of the licensee to pay royalties on a quarterly basis. A royalty report form is typically required that shows how royalties were computed, in addition to a sales report listing the sales of all licensed products that occurred during the reporting period. The failure to provide quarterly royalty reports is usually considered a breach of the license agreement and, unless rectified within the prescribed time period (10-30 days is average), will give the licensor the right to terminate the license agreement. If an advance is paid upon signing of the deal memo or license agreement, the amount of the advance is usually recoupable by the licensee against future royalties due the licensor. Therefore, it is very likely that initial royalty report(s) will show that no royalties are due until the amount of the advance is offset by royalty earnings. The reader is encouraged to reference the sample form provided in Appendix-10.

12.8 Financial Administration

The principle function of the financial administration staff is to track the licensee's sales on which royalties must be paid, and to create the quarterly royalty reports for submission to the licensee. Tracking of such information requires the cooperation of the sales arm and it is strongly advised that the system to track sales be put in place before commencing sales efforts. It is far easier to track the sales as they occur then to attempt to "catch up" later.

Depending on the number of licenses held by the licensee, investment in a royalty software package may be worth considering. Such software can provide the following functions:

- Track licensed products, submission dates and approval dates
- Generate monthly reports
- Monitor royalty and guarantee payment status
- Manage all aspects of the financial requirements and obligations

Produce management, sales and marketing reports as well as other relevant information.

Chapter 13
Marketing and Promoting Licensing Properties and Licensed Products

13.1 Introduction

The name of the game in licensing is marketing and promotion—for both property owners and licensees alike, albeit for different reasons. Licensors are typically more concerned with promoting the property for use on their primary product or service, e.g., their television show or book, etc. While potentially important if they intend to develop a licensing program, the idea of promoting the property *per se*, i.e., independent of their primary product or service, is more of an afterthought for many.

Similarly, licensees typically have a singular purpose when they look at promotion in that they usually are only interested in promoting their line of licensed products to increase sales thereof.

While licensors and licensees may seem to be approaching the issue of promotion from opposite ends of the spectrum, when a licensing program gets up and running, their interests converge. The more popular and well known a property becomes, the greater its value—for the licensor in terms of increased licensing revenues and for the licensee in terms of increased sales of licensed products.

This is what has led many licensors to create marketing funds to help raise the visibility of their properties. These marketing funds are underwritten collectively by the licensees, usually by having them pay an additional royalty or marketing fee. These marketing fees typically run between 1% and 3% of the licensee's net sales and are pooled together to fund a common promotional program on behalf of the property which covers advertising, promotions and public relations. Presumably, such a program should save the individual licensees from having to conduct their own programs or, at the very least, reduce the amount of money that they may otherwise need to spend for such programs.

13.2 Advertising Programs

Traditional advertising remains the cornerstone of any marketing program. The various licensing trade publications, which include *License Global*, *Total Licensing* and *Licensing Book* are all geared toward accommodating a property owner's advertising needs and requirements. Many of these publications also include electronic versions such as, for example, the *License Global* email newsletter.

Some of these publications publish "dailies" during each of the various licensing shows that are distributed to attendees and exhibitors. For example, *License Global* publishes a daily for the Licensing Expo held in Las Vegas, NV in June of each year as well as at Brand Licensing held in London each fall. Each of these dailies offers a unique advertising opportunity to help promote a property.

There are also several directories of licensing properties as well as trade show directories that accept advertising. The advantage of advertising in a directory rather than a periodic publication is that, at least theoretically, the directory is used all year long and, as such, the advertiser's exposure is greater. Again, these are excellent opportunities to convey a message to a targeted group.

When designing an advertising program, consideration should also be given to running ads in industry specific publications where they can be seen and read by potential licensees and retailers. For example, dedicated toy industry publications include *The Toy Book*, *The Toy Report*, *Specialty Toys and Gifts*, *Toy Wishes*, *Toys 'N Playthings* and *TDMonthly*. *KidScreen* is a trade publication that services kids' entertainment professionals while *Gifts & Decorative Accessories* and *Gift Shop* both focus on the gift industry. The fashion industry has a host of industry specific publications that accept advertising, including *Fashion Market* and *Women's Wear Daily*. For the music industry *Billboard* is perhaps the leading publication, while *PCGamer* is a publication directed to the video game market. *Brandweek* and *Advertising Age* are excellent vehicles for reaching the advertising industry and corporate markets, which also regularly publish licensing-focused feature articles.

On-line advertising cannot be overlooked, particularly on industry specific sites. Many of the above-mentioned publications include on-line editions that accept some form of advertising. In addition, there are a few blogs and websites devoted to specific industries that carry advertising and these should be explored as well.

Obviously, advertising is a highly developed industry and there are a number of excellent advertising agencies that have extensive experience in all forms of advertising. These agencies can provide able assistance to property owners in not only developing their advertising strategy, but in creating excellent copy and advising on its placement so as to maximize exposure.

13.3 Effective Public Relations[20]

"Public relations" is the business of inducing the public to have an understanding of and the goodwill for a person, firm or institution.

Some people believe that because the public generally has a short memory, good public relations merely consists of a story or article that spells the company's name correctly and includes a URL to an active website. A bonus, in some cases, would be if the story contained enough detail for the public to know what the company employees actually do for a living. Obviously, that's not enough.

The objective of a good public relations program is *ubiquity*, which means conveying one's message everywhere or at least to as many places as possible, preferably simultaneously. While that is probably an impossible goal, the closer a publicist gets to that goal, the more effective the program.

The basic requirements for a good publicist are to:

- Know your audience
- Know your message
- Know your objective

---

[20] Based on a presentation made by Dean Bender of Bender/Helper Impact at a 2008 CLS Program entitled, *Innovative Promotions and Creative Public Relations*.

Today's media world offers infinitely more opportunities than ever before because of the virtually endless types of media that are available. In addition to traditional media outlets, e.g., newspapers, magazines, television and radio, the online and mobile worlds have opened an almost unlimited number of new possibilities, not only on traditional websites but through blogs, social networks, digital advertising, and smart phones. Moreover, the list is not a static one—it gets broader and more diverse by the minute. Five years ago, who would have thought that Facebook or Twitter would become the promotional vehicle that they have?

At a recent seminar on the subject sponsored by LIMA, Dean Bender provided an example of one effective public relations program involving a licensed game called Karaoke Revolution American Idol ("KRAI") that was operating under an AMERICAN IDOL license. KRAI was a music-themed, rhythm-action game that was based on the *American Idol* phenomenon and Dean Bender's firm, Bender/Helper Impact, created and executed a comprehensive public relations strategy that was designed to maximize awareness for the game by capitalizing on the huge appeal of the television show.

The overriding objective of the program was to generate publicity for the product throughout the entire *American Idol* television season by taking advantage of specific events, including the selection of the final 24 contestants and the final episode. The specific objectives of the program were to:

- Position the KRAI game as a must-own game for the target consumer;
- Establish recognition of the franchise among all media;
- Take advantage of the television phenomenon to generate coverage in non-traditional media outlets; and
- Reach pop culture and features writers about the *American Idol* phenomenon and its influence on various forms of entertainment.
- In executing the program, the publicists faced several challenges, most notably:
  - They did not have any access to talent;
  - There was only limited access to the product;
  - There was only limited synergy with the television show;
  - Other publishers had released AMERICAN IDOL games in the past;
  - The popularity of the *American Idol* television show had reached its maturity; and
  - Paula Abdul was not a part of the game.

The following four-tiered strategy was chosen:

- Time period #1--street date/premiere of the television season;
- Time period #2--final 24 party;
- Time period #3--season finale;
- Time period #4--holiday gift guides.

The campaign surrounding the premiere of the television season included several individual elements, including: the issue of a press release announcing the product; a mailing to a host of individuals and retailers describing the product; the placement of reviews for the game with notable publications; specific mentions of the game in television stories about the new season and broadcast features in segments about the new season.

A Final 24 Party was staged in Los Angeles with kiosks featuring the KRAI games to promote it. "Talent" was invited to and attended the Final 24 Party to try their hands at the game and broadcast crews and photographers were invited to shoot the talent playing the game so that the videos and photographs could be used later. Finally, video game journalists were invited to attend the event to generate enthusiastic coverage.

The season finale for the *American Idol* series is always the most viewed show of the season and frequently results in *American Idol* "withdrawal" on the part of its viewers. To combat this, the PR program pitched both broadcast and weekly entertainment magazines with stories about what to do after the season ended and how to combat this withdrawal symptom, including the idea of playing the KRAI video game while waiting and getting ready for the next season.

Some of the other "pitches" that were used included:

- When the season ends, the fun still goes on;
- Music Games Roundup;
- Roundup of Games Based on Television Shows (*TV Guide*);
- The Business of *American Idol*; and
- *American Idol* Marketing Story.

The PR program was coordinated with Fox Media Synergy for the *American Idol* show and was targeted at all Fox owned media outlets, e.g., Fox News Channel, Fox News Feed, *NY Post*, etc. It included game reviews, piggyback stories on *American Idol* coverage, product roundups and stories and segments on all games, including KRAI. It resulted in about 10 weekly hits on Fox Baltimore as well as mentions on several other Fox stations, including Chicago and Phoenix, who did one-off competitions.

One of the features of the program was the first-ever, virtual video game competition that took place in highly trafficked malls in major markets where each competitor recited a song on KRAI. The top finishers by score in each market had videos posted on the Internet with the public voting who would become the "Virtual American Idol." Publicity was run on a local, national and trade level.

The results of the program were excellent, generating a total consumer reach of approximately 150 million impressions. It achieved top tier placements in *Disney Adventures*, *Business Week*, the Associated Press, Gannett, *USA Today* (3 hits), *New York Times*, *San Francisco Chronicle*, *Dallas Morning News*, *Washington Post*, *LA Times*, *Chicago Tribune*, *Extra*, Fox News Channel, *Morning Show w/Mike & Juliet*, foxnews.com, E! Online, yahoo.com, ew.com, KOL, maxim.com, and ivillage.

Effective PR can be accomplished in a few different non-traditional ways. One particularly effective (although typically accidental) way is to simply not produce sufficient quantities of the product to meet customer demand, i.e., to create a shortage of the products. For example, when Coleco first introduced its original CABBAGE PATCH dolls, it could (or would) not supply the products fast enough to retailers to meet demand for that product. As lines began forming at various retail establishments so consumers could quickly buy up their meager supply of the product, the story hit the newspapers which further fueled the demand for the CABBAGE PATCH dolls.

Apple Computer had a similar experience when they introduced the iPad and then the 4G version of their iPhone. People lined up to snatch up the product, resulting in literally a mountain of media that served to further drive up the demand for and ultimately sales of the products.

Fisher-Price tried a different approach when it introduced its ELMO dolls for the first time.[21] It is reported that they made a conscious decision to keep the design of the dolls a secret, even after they introduced the product at Toy Fair. Mattel even kept its sales force in the dark as to what the product would look like. They chose to use closed boxes so that people couldn't see what the dolls looked like. Speculation as to the appearance of the product ran rampant which generated a score of newspaper and trade journal articles. The actual unveiling of the product on Good Morning, America resulted in yet another media event that further hyped sales of the product.

When the product was first offered for sale at Toys "R" Us in New York, it sold out in three hours which, again, generated further publicity. The fact that it would ultimately become TIA's Toy of the Year should come as no surprise, since the die had been cast more than a year before by the planning of a creative PR program.

13.4 Innovative Promotions[22]

Many property owners regularly rely on the development and staging of creative promotional programs to further enhance the visibility of and demand for their properties. The combination of an effective public relations program with a creative promotions program can be a killer one-two punch.

Fox Sports, which features an on-air robotic "mascot" that is displayed before many of its sports telecasts, conducted an extremely successful "Name the Robot" contest as a promotion for its shows. The contest embraced and empowered their fans and made them "decision makers." The contest was promoted both on-air as well as online and received more than 50,000 entries and attracted individuals to whom Fox could market permission-based initiatives in the future.

The Fox promotions involving *THE SIMPSONS* television show and related licensed products has similarly met with enormous success. The show has run continuously since 1989 and is the longest running prime time show in television history. The winner of 23 Emmy Awards, the show is seen in over 60 different countries and is broadcast in more than 20 languages.

A SIMPSON's ride opened at Universal Studios Parks in both Orlando and Hollywood in May 2008. Guests are placed in the middle of Krustyland that showcases the back story and humor of THE SIMPSONS. Fox developed several promotions surrounding this ride which have helped both promote the television series as well as the licensing program.

---

[21] Based on a presentation made by Bruce Maguire, CEO of Freeman Public Relations, 16 Furler St., Totowa, NJ 07512 during LIMA's 2008 CLS program titled *Promotional Strategies and Buzz Marketing*.

[22] Based on a program by Howard Nelson, Fox's Vice-President of Worldwide Promotions at a 2008 CLS Program entitled, *Innovative Promotions and Creative Public Relations*.

The characters featured in the ride all had the voices of the original actors. It also included a motion simulator called the "Krusty Mobile" where the rider could twist and turn, plummet and soar, without ever moving more than a couple of feet. The cars even simulate 360-degree barrel rolls. Universal made a financial investment in the ride at a cost about $40 million per ride.

Fox also did a promotion involving its show *Family Guy* which has broadcast more than 100 episodes, sold more than 5 million DVD's and attracted millions to its website every day. The campaign coordinated a national FAMILY GUY promotion with the restaurant chain, Subway. Over 22,000 Subway restaurants participated in this promotion, which featured a fully branded 32oz. collector cup and a sweepstakes. The promotion had two unique elements:

- An interactive web experience featuring the characters from *Family Guy*; and
- A unique animated television commercial featuring Peter Griffin.

The promotion certainly aided Subway. Subway restaurants that had been open for more than year increased sales by 11%. The campaign was considered one of the best of 2007 by the Subway Franchise Advertising Fund Trust Board and the licensing revenue generated for Fox made it the highest grossing promotion in the brand's history.

The use of a licensing property to help advertise or promote the sales of an unrelated product, particularly in a television commercial, can be very effective. For example, Coca-Cola used the STEWIE character from *Family Guy* in a television commercial that it ran during the 2008 Super Bowl which turned out to be the most-watched football game in history, capturing an average of 97.5 million viewers. *USA Today* rated the commercials that were run during the game as the top commercials for the year. The Coca-Cola commercial, which cost millions of dollars to create, was perhaps the most popular. The *Wall Street Journal* described it as, "Awesome and exactly what a Super Bowl commercial should be... It's big, epic, funny and beautiful." While it certainly helped advertise and promote the COCA-COLA products, it also generated a significant license fee for Fox.

Tips for a successful promotion include:

- **Consider the Consumer and Retail Needs.** Where is the opening in the market? Consider different character styles, wardrobe, production design, props, etc. Know your competition and point of difference.
- **Think about Niche Marketing**. Navigating the world beyond Walmart is essential. It's OK to start small to measure consumer demand.
- **Walk the Retail Aisles**. Think like a consumer and retail buyer. Ask questions.
- **Collaborate with Licensors and Licensees**. Be open minded **but** pay attention. Provide access to writers and producers.
- **The World is Competitive....So be Competitive**. Promotion is as competitive as the television industry. Licensees and retailers are increasingly taking a wait and see approach before committing, so be bold and challenge the *status quo*.

13.5 Using Social Media to Grow Your Brand and Product[23]

"Social Marketing" is a low cost, but extremely powerful, way to promote a property. Because of the ease of communicating online, it is a grassroots way to make the world aware of your property and help form relationships with the consuming public. Social Media marketing focuses primarily on such social networks as Facebook, Instagram, Twitter, MySpace and LinkedIn as well as blogs and micro blogs, such as Twitter chat rooms and message boards.

Social media marketing refers to the process of gaining traffic or attention through social media sites. The objective of Social Media Marketing is to attract a user base through Social Media and build a relationship with that bas. It takes time and should be scheduled in advance. 51% of the world or 3.81 billion people are now connected to the Internet and 40% of that are using some form of social media.

Successful licensors and licensees view social media to talk with their customers on a personal manner. It creates a connection and generates a dialog with the customer. They have come to understand that fans love to dialog with them over a multitude of issues. It allows them to communicate with their customer and tell them what they're doing.

Far more licensors are familiar with the importance of social media than licensees, particularly the smaller ones. The licensors should share their expertise and experience with their licensees as it is to their mutual benefit.

From a marketing point of view, it offers advantages over other forms because it creates an interaction with other people rather than sterile sales pitches. Today, people don't necessarily want to be sold, a product or service, they want to get recommendations, irrespective of where it comes. Social media helps the consumer make the decision to purchase or use the product on their own, thereby empowering them.

The Social Media world is dominated by the following websites:

- Facebook
- YouTube
- Twitter
- WhatsApp
- Instagram
- Snapchat
- LinkedIn
- SlideShare

And offer the highest chance to generate traffic for your brand or website. If you have a plan for doing it, this approach will result in building and sustaining a following and ultimate success for your brand.

Facebook

While Facebook is primarily a leisure-centered platform, with game and hobby apps and pages, it can still be effectively used as demonstrated by the 2016 election and aftermath.

---

[23] Based, in part, on CLS Presentation by Natali Cupps DiBlasi, LACED Agency, entitled Using Social Media to Build Your Brand, Nov. 14, 2017

By adding interesting facts and humor to your posts and images that make people smile while still conveying your message.

It's best to use it first with your current customers and website visitors before branching out to the world at large. It's important to make sure that your content is optimized to drive traffic back to your website or blog.

The objective is to have as many people as you can "like" you. The best way to get more likes is by sharing more visual content (such as videos, photos, info-graphics) as it creates a lot of interaction. You can re-share page posts on your Facebook profile to get more views and to take advantage of your Newsfeed.

Facebook has more than 2 billion monthly active users as of June 2017.

YouTube

YouTube is the industry standard for posting videos, etc. The higher resolution the video, the better.

What's important is to make sure that the videos are well-scripted and are changed and updated regularly. The more the merrier.

As of February 2017, there are more than 400 hours of content uploaded to YouTube each minute, and one billion hours of content are watched on YouTube every day. YouTube has announced a 40 channel, Internet based TV subscription service plus it now features 280-character messages.

As of August 2017, the website is ranked as the second-most popular site in the world by Alexa Internet, a web traffic analysis company.

Twitter

Anyone who has been following politics over the past couple of years understands the power of Twitter....both pro and con. It is a personable platform, like text messages, which permits you to convey your message in a very short and concise manner.

Since tweets disappear quickly, it's important to re-tweet or forward messages to stay current. This keeps your followers engaged and interested. If your website is set in WordPress, you can automatically re-market old content.

You can grow your Twitter followers by following active people in the licensing industry and by keeping your account current with helpful information and content. People obtain traffic by tweeting out their blog posts during the day as well as those of others. Attaching images works particularly well. Don't forget to copy anyone who is mentioned so they get acknowledged.

As of 2016, Twitter had more than 319 million monthly active users. On the day of the 2016 U.S. presidential election, Twitter proved to be the largest source of breaking news, with 40 million election-related tweets sent by 10 p.m. that day.

WhatsApp Messenger

WhatsApp Messenger is a freeware and cross-platform messaging and Voice over IP (VoIP) service. The application allows the sending of text messages and voice calls, as well as video calls, images and other media, documents, and user location. The application runs from a mobile device though it is also accessible from desktop computers; the service uses standard cellular mobile numbers. Originally users could only communicate with other users individually or in groups of individual users, but in September 2017, WhatsApp announced a forthcoming business platform which will enable companies to provide customer service to users at scale.

It was acquired by Facebook in February 2014 and by February 2018, had a user base of over 1.5 billion users making it the most popular messaging application at the time. WhatsApp has grown in multiple countries, including Brazil, India, and large parts of Europe.

Instagram

Instagram is a photo and video-sharing social networking service owned by Facebook, Inc. It was launched in October 2010 and added apps for Windows in 2016.

The app allows users to upload photos and videos to the service, which can be edited with various filters, and organized with tags and location information. An account's posts can be shared publicly or with pre-approved followers. Users can browse other users' content by tags and locations, and view trending content. Users can "like" photos, and follow other users to add their content to a feed.

Instagram is an excellent way to convey images of a property or product. As of October 2015, over 40 billion photos have been uploaded to the service

Snapchat

Snapchat is a multimedia messaging app popular in North America and Europe.

One of the principal concepts of Snapchat is that pictures and messages are only available for a short time before they become inaccessible. The app has evolved from originally focusing on person-to-person photo sharing to presently featuring "Stories" of 24-hour chronological content, along with "Discover" to let brands show ad-supported short-form entertainment. Snapchat has become notable for representing a new, mobile-first direction for social media, and places significant emphasis on users interacting with virtual stickers and augmented reality objects.

Snapchat continues to court original creators and innovators with incentives such as earned ad dollars while also strengthening many established network content partnerships.

As of February 2018, Snapchat has 187 million daily active users.

LinkedIn

LinkedIn is probably the major social media tool for businesses and is an excellent way to grow professionally and get new leads and clients. It's geared for business and not socializing. Its main objective is to promote your attributes and achievements in a business setting.

Marketing on LinkedIn starts with a good, friendly yet professional, SEO-optimized profile, and continues with message outreach, content creation and knowledge building in niche-specific groups. Well maintained LinkedIn accounts can attract leads, customers and potential partners.

There are niche groups for a host of different subjects and they offer a good way to network within a group or target audience. As such, it's an excellent way to reach that audience.

LinkedIn will allow you to post articles on your subject in their publishing platform called Pulse without restrictions. One can publish and republish posting or even excepts from books. As such, it provides a free pass to content marketing.

As of April 2017, LinkedIn had 500 million members in 200 countries, out of which more than 106 million members were active.

SlideShare

People come to SlideShare to study material in presentation form that will help them walk away with additional knowledge to use in school, work and life. Its purpose is to education so that they can make educated decisions.

SlideShare presentations should be visual and easily "skimmable" with bullet points as in a PowerPoint deck. Adding a link or a promo or free trial to the deck is an effective way of potentially selling your message.

The website gets an estimated 70 million unique visitors a month and has about 38 million registered users.

Other vehicles for Social Media include:
- Diaspora https://diasporafoundation.org
- ExploreB2B https://exploreb2b.com
- Biznik http://biznik.com
- Xing https://www.xing.com
- EFactor http://www.efactor.com
- Mosaic Hub http://www.mosaichub.com
- Ello.co https://ello.co

Forums

Specialized forums are an excellent way of promoting a brand or your product. They are an easy way to engage in a meaningful discussion with your target audiences and help build a "buzz" around your brand or product.

The typical advice given to anyone who engages in a forum is:

- Build a profile that help visitors know who you are and what you're about;
- Be helpful and supportive of the community; and
- Purchase ads on the forum and be a sponsor.

Useful Tools

There several useful tools that will assist you in managing a Social Media program, including:

- Hootsuite is a Social Media dashboard that allows you to manage multiple Social accounts at the same time
- Viral Content Buzz makes it easier to reach social audiences by social sharing
- Clout is a social influencer tool that allows you to post and schedule posts.

One of the first things a licensor or property owner needs to do is to develop a digital marketing plan. In doing so, it's important to first define the goals of the program, e.g., customer service, brand awareness, market research, etc. Without defining the goals, it's virtually impossible to create a strategy or plan to meet them. Similarly, it's also necessary to prioritize your objectives lest you exhaust your resources. It's far better to excel at one of the areas than to do a mediocre job on all of them.

In crafting such a plan, it's necessary to understand the customer/purchase funnel and then define their goals based on different stages in the funnel because the tactics used will vary depending upon where you are in the funnel.

A proper social media strategy should include:

- Business strategy
  - Defining your goals
  - Target market and personas
  - Assets mapping
  - Position in sales cycles
  - Choice of channels
- Unique storytelling
  - Voice and tone
  - Content types
  - Content calendar
  - Community management
  - Hashtag strategy #
  - Video, video, video
- Paid social media
  - Online advertising strategy
  - Influencer marketing strategy
- Proactive planning
  - Posting frequency
  - Posting time
  - Social media policy
  - Crisis management
- Measurement and analysis
  - Monitoring
  - Measurement
  - Analytics and reporting
  - Assessment

The best social media management tools are:

- Small business and/or enterprise
  - Hootsuite
  - Buffer
  - SoHo Social
  - Talk Walker
  - Brand24
- Enterprise Level
  - Synthesio

- o Sysomos
- o Brandwatch Analytics
- o Crimson Hexagon
- Honorable Mentions
  - o SocialReport.com
  - o Cyfe
  - o Sprout Social
  - o Social Bakers

If you have different purchasers, you will presumably need different programs to appeal directly to such purchasers.

Social media marketing is important in licensing because of the importance of "search." 80% of the journeys start with the search—the consumer starts their research on-line which means that key word research is critical. It's not simply Google, YouTube and Facebook have search engines. Thus, it's important to be listed there.

It's advisable to integrate the social media program with one's PR and advertising programs to obtain maximum exposure.

13.6 Marketing Funds

There are two issues here—the first is where the licensor requires the licensee to contribute to a Common Marketing Fund ("CMF") that the licensor will use to promote the overall brand, not just as it relates to the use of the brand on the licensed products but, for all licensed products. Typically, CMF requirements can range from 0.5% to as high a 5% but are typically in the 1-2%. Most licensors do not require the payment of CMF's, although the studios and the sports leagues generally require such payments.

Licensees perceive these CMF payments as another "slush fund" which is added on to the royalty paid to the licensor. From the licensor's perspective, these monies are used to help promote the brand and, theoretically, should be only applied to out of pocket expenses by the licensor in promoting the brand through advertising, PR and the like, not to defer internal marketing costs.

The second issue is the "Marketing Commitment" that the licensor imposes on the licensee to spend to help promote and advertise the licensed products. It can include TV or print advertising costs, trade show expenses, production of animated shorts for digital distribution, marketing products in licensor-controlled venues, etc. It can be a fixed amount per year or a percentage of the licensee Net Sales of licensed products and will be negotiated between the parties and included in the license agreement.

Chapter 14
Protecting Licensing Properties

14.1 Introduction

Once a property owner has identified the property to be licensed, determined that it is the true owner of that property and there are no potentially conflicting rights, and confirmed that a licensee's use will not infringe the rights of any other party, the next step is to take the necessary measures to protect it BEFORE commencing with the licensing program. The process of securing protection for the property at an early stage is vitally important, since most licensees will insist that the licensor have some form of intellectual property protection in place prior to signing a license agreement that will obligate them to pay the licensor for the right to use the property.

Even if the licensee is "trusting," it will still require that the licensor obtain some protection for the property as soon as practical. It is not unreasonable for a licensee to ask the property owner to put such protection plan in place before it actually commences sales of the licensed products since, once the licensee actually starts to sell licensed products and pay a royalty for such right, it is going to want assurance from the licensor that its competitors cannot compete with it on a royalty-free basis, thereby undercutting the value of the license.

14.2 Developing a Protection Plan

While most property owners and licensees agree that licensed properties must be protected against unauthorized use, the specific form of protection applied will be dictated by the type of property, e.g., as a trademark, copyright or under the right of publicity or patent laws. The property owner should work with its intellectual property counsel to determine the most cost-effective way to protect the property.

The three statutory forms of intellectual property protection include patents, copyrights, and trademarks. Additionally, many states in the United States (although few other countries) recognize the "right of publicity," which provides celebrities with a protectable right in their name, image and likeness. Utility patents are used to protect functional devices and inventions and are rarely used in protecting merchandising properties, although some features of a licensed product may be patented. Design patents are used to protect the ornamental appearance of articles of manufacture and, like utility patents, are rarely used to protect merchandising properties.

Most licensing properties in the merchandising area are protected as trademarks and/or copyrights. A trademark may constitute any word, name, design, logo or shape that functions as an indicator of the source, origin or sponsorship of a product or service. Copyrights protect original works of authorship that are fixed in tangible mediums of expression and include, for example, literary works, pictorial or graphic designs, motion pictures and sound recordings.

To illustrate, the design or image of the MICKEY MOUSE character may be copyrighted as a graphic design. When that image is applied to a product such as, for example, a coffee mug, the same image functions in a trademark sense in that it serves as an indicator that the property owner, Disney, "sponsored" or "licensed" the mug.

It should be appreciated that trademarks and copyrights have specific advantages, as well as disadvantages. For example, copyright protection is immediate. Rights are created upon the creation of a work. Moreover, registration of a copyright is easy and inexpensive, and the registration affords the owner some degree of international protection.

Trademark protection is similarly immediate; one acquires trademark rights when the mark is applied to a product and sold or offered for sale in commerce. The registration process is, however, more complicated, more expensive and ultimately will only protect the property owner in the country where registration is sought. To protect the trademark in other countries, additional registrations must be obtained.

Perhaps the most significant difference between the two is the length of protection that each offer. Copyright rights are valid for only a finite period while trademark rights may continue for so long as the mark is being used in commerce by either the property owner or its licensee. That is the reason why owners of some of the classic properties like MICKEY MOUSE and PETER RABBIT rely on both forms of statutory protection. That way, when the copyrights in the graphic designs expire, their property owners can still rely on trademark protection which will last for so long as the marks continue to be used.

Celebrity rights are protected under what's called a "right of publicity" and which is mostly governed by state law. The right of publicity protects a celebrity's name, image, signature, voice, etc., against commercial exploitation by another. In most cases, registration of the right is required. The right of publicity can also extend to deceased celebrities, although many states require that the right be exercised during the celebrity's lifetime for protection to extend after their death.

There is an obvious overlap between trademarks, copyrights and the right of publicity and celebrities typically rely on all three forms of protection to protect their rights. The trademark laws are used to protect their name when it is used on a product; the right of publicity is used to protect their name and image; and the copyright laws are used to protect a specific image or representation of the celebrity that may form the basis of a licensing program.

There are instances where it may be advisable to contractually limit the disclosure of a property using a Non-Disclosure Agreement. A sample of such an NDA is contained in Appendix-14.

14.3 Trademark Protection

Trademark protection extends to any word, name, symbol, or device, or any combination, that is used to identify and distinguish an individual's goods from those of another and to indicate the source or origin of such goods.

Service marks are marks that are used in association with services rather than products. For example, when the mark McDONALD'S® appears on the outside of a McDonald's® restaurant, that mark is functioning as a service mark to identify the restaurant as one owned by the McDonald's Corp. When, however, it appears on a hamburger wrapper, it is being used as a trademark.

A list of the trademark classes is provided in Appendix-16.

While trademark rights are acquired in the United States upon the first use of the mark, this is not the case in some other countries. Registration of the mark is always advisable and, in some countries, essential to obtaining protection. Registration of a mark in the United States provides certain procedural and substantive advantages for the owner, including a right to sue in federal court for trademark infringement and the establishment of constructive notice of the owner's claim in the mark. A trademark registration will also permit the owner to record the registration with the U.S. Customs Service to stop the importation of infringing and counterfeit products at the border.

Most licensees will demand that the licensor register the mark for the goods or services it will be selling under the license or, at the very least, have applied to register the mark since they want as much protection as the property owner can provide against unauthorized competition.

The requirements for obtaining a trademark registration in the United States are straightforward. To be registered, the mark must be distinctive, i.e., it must distinguish or be capable of distinguishing the owner's products or services over that of another.

That means that the mark cannot be merely descriptive of the goods or services for which registration is being sought, nor can it be a generic reference to the product or service. For example, the name WINNIE THE POOH is potentially registrable for a coffee mug since it is neither the name of the product nor does it describe the product. If, however, one sought to register the words BLUE MUG for a blue coffee mug, it would probably be refused registration because it would be considered descriptive of the product, i.e., a blue mug.

A trademark applicant must be the first party to have used that mark for the subject product or service and he cannot be aware of any other uses of the mark that might be confusingly similar to its mark and use. Thus, if XYZ Company applied to register WINNIE THE POOH for a plush bear based on very recent use, that application would undoubtedly be rejected on the grounds of Disney's earlier use and registration(s).

Trademark applications can be filed with the U.S. Patent & Trademark Office ("USPTO") in one of two ways, as: (1) a use-based application, relying on the applicant's actual use of the mark in interstate commerce; or (2) an intent-to-use application, based on the applicant's *bona fide* intention to use the mark in interstate commerce. Acceptable use of a trademark can be established either by the owner or its licensee.

For a use-based application, the applicant must state the date that the mark was first used on the goods, in both intrastate and interstate commerce, and provide specimens showing how the mark was applied to the goods or used in conjunction with the services for which registration is sought.

In each type of application, the applicant must identify the mark to be registered and the goods or services on which the mark has or will be used. The USPTO divides all types of goods and services into 45 different classes and an applicant must select one or more of them for which registration is being sought.

Trademark applications can be filed either by a paper filing or an electronic filing. The USPTO filing fee for a paper trademark application is (as of 2018) $400 per class, or between $225 and $275 per class if filed electronically. Both types of applications are prosecuted by the PTO in the same manner.

Typically, the property owner will determine what classes to include in the application after consultation with its licensing director and will include those classes where licensing activity is expected.

Most trademark applications for merchandising properties are filed on an intent-to-use basis since they are often filed well in advance of the commencement of the licensing program and, thus, before any use has occurred. The mark must ultimately be used on actual products before any registration can issue, although the property owner may have as much as four years to commence use.

Trademark applications can be filed in the U.S. based on actual use or based on an intent-to-use although rights will not accrue until use commences.

A WORD OF CAUTION: the mere filing of an intent-to-use application does not give the owner any enforceable rights in the trademark until use starts. At that time, the property owner receives the benefit of the filing date of the original application, assuming that the application is still pending at the time. That means that the owner cannot sue an infringer for trademark infringement until it (or its licensee) commences use of the mark on the products.

As noted, there are 45 different classes of goods and services in which one can seek to register a mark. For licensing purposes, the most common classes in which registrations are typically sought are:

Class 9—Electrical and Scientific Apparatus (DVD's and video)
Class 14—Jewelry
Class 16—Paper Goods and Printed Matter
Class 18—Leather Goods
Class 20—Furniture and Articles Not Otherwise Classified
Class 21—Housewares and Glass
Class 25—Clothing
Class 28—Toys and Sporting Goods

If the trademark application meets the necessary requirements, it receives a filing date and serial number and is assigned to a Trademark Examining Attorney who will review the material and conduct a search to see if it is confusingly similar to any other mark.

The application will eventually be either allowed or finally rejected. Rejections can be appealed to an appeals board within the PTO. If it is allowed, the mark will be published for opposition and anyone can oppose registration if they believe that they have a basis for doing so.

If no one opposes the registration of the mark, the procedure differs between use-based applications and those filed on an intent-to-use basis. Unopposed use-based applications proceed directly to registration. Intent-to-use applications, however, will not be registered until use commences and the owner submits a Statement of Use.

Trademark registrations are granted for a term of ten years from the date of registration and may be renewed for an unlimited number of additional ten-year terms upon a showing of continued use. Between the fifth and sixth year of the initial term, the owner must file a declaration demonstrating that the mark is still in use. Failure to file such a declaration will result in the cancellation of the registration.

Once a registration is cancelled (and assuming that the original registrant has ceased use of the mark), anyone may adopt the cancelled mark and commence their own use of the mark and even potentially register it.

A WORD OF CAUTION: the fact that a trademark registration was cancelled doesn't necessarily mean that the original registrant lost its rights in that mark. Some registrations are inadvertently cancelled although use of the mark continues. In that situation, the owner still maintains its underlying rights in the mark and can simply apply to re-register that mark with the same date of first use in the original registration.

The ™ designation is used to identify a property that is considered a trademark by the owner but is not federally registered. Similarly, the designation ℠ indicates that the word, symbol, or logo is considered by its owner to be a service mark. There is no legal necessity for including either designation other than to indicate to the public at large that the user considers it to be its trademark or service mark.

The ® symbol is used to designate a federally registered trademark. Some trademark owners prefer to use the designations "Registered in the U.S. Patent and Trademark Office" or "Reg. U.S. Pat. & TM Off." This is a matter of choice, although the ® symbol is often preferable, simply because it's easier to place.

This is probably a good time to discuss good "trademark practice" for both the property owner and its licensees. The following simple guidelines should always be followed:

- Always use the trademark as an adjective to describe the product for which it is being used, e.g., a STAR WARS toy;
- Always capitalize the trademark relative to the type of product for which it is being used, e.g., a HARRY POTTER book;
- Never use the trademark as a noun or a verb or in the plural form, e.g., "I want to Xerox the drawing"; and
- Always follow each usage of the property with an appropriate trademark notice, e.g., BATMAN™ costume.

14.4 Copyright Protection

Copyright protection covers any original works of authorship fixed in a tangible medium of expression and typically includes the following:

- Literary works;
- Musical works, including any accompanying words;
- Dramatic works, including any accompanying music, pantomimes and choreographic works;
- Pictorial, graphic, and sculptural works;
- Motion pictures and other audiovisual works; and
- Sound recordings.

The actual term of a copyright varies, depending upon the type of work, when it was created and whether it was published or not. In most instances, the term is the life of the author plus 70 years. For works of corporate authorship, the term is typically 95 years from publication or 120 years from creation, whichever first occurs. It should be appreciated that these terms were recently extended.

> One no longer needs to include a copyright notice (©) on a work, but it is good practice to do so.

As stated, copyright rights to a potentially copyrightable work arise upon the creation of the original work. Under prio law, it was necessary to apply a copyright notice to the work to obtain such right, but that requirement was eliminated in 1989 when the United States became a signatory to the Berne Convention.

While the application of a copyright notice is no longer required to create rights in the work, the application of such a notice and the registration of the copyright with the Copyright Office is good practice as it gives notice to potential infringers and offers certain procedural and substantive advantages.

The three elements of the copyright notice are:

- The symbol ©, the word "Copyright," or the abbreviation "Copr.";
- The year of first publication of the work; and
- The name of the owner of the copyright (e.g., a complete copyright notice might be: © LIMA 2018).

If the copyrighted goods are sound recordings, a circled P is used rather than the ©. The legend "All Rights Reserved" should follow the standard copyright notice when distribution is contemplated in South America to conform to the requirements of the Buenos Aires Copyright Convention.

The copyright notice should be affixed to the copies in such a manner and location as to give reasonable notice of the claim of copyright. It should also be permanently legible to an ordinary user of the work under normal conditions of use.

It is advisable to file a copyright application to register the copyright claim with the Copyright Office, since copyright registrations provide the owner with several advantages, including the right to bring an action for copyright infringement and, if successful, to obtain statutory damages and an award of attorneys' fees against an infringer.

To be eligible for copyright protection, the material must be the original work of the author and it must fall within one or more of the protectable categories listed above. While the actual amount of originality required for copyright protection is unclear, it is generally acknowledged that the standard of originality is less than the novelty requirement for patent protection.

Registering a copyright with the Copyright Office is relatively simple and inexpensive. The process requires only the submission of the application for copyright registration (obtainable at www.copyright.gov); deposit of the work for which copyright protection is claimed and the payment of the statutory fee (as of 2018) of $35 for a single on-line application for a single author, same claimant, one work and not for hire and $55 for all other types of on-line applications. The filing fee for a paper application is $85.

A copyright registration affords the property owner the exclusive right to:

1. Reproduce the copyrighted work in copies or phonorecords;
2. Prepare derivative works based on the copyrighted work;
3. Distribute copies or phonorecords of the copyrighted work through sale or other transfer of ownership, or by rental, lease, or lending;
4. Publicly perform or display the copyrighted work, including the individual images of a motion picture or other audiovisual work; and
5. Publicly perform the copyrighted work by means of digital audio transmission sound recordings.

One may seek copyright protection as a "derivative work", i.e., deriving from an earlier copyrighted work. The scope of rights that an owner may have in a derivative work is dependent on the amount of creativity that it added to the original work.

A significant limitation on copyright protection is the "fair use" doctrine, which permits one to use a copyrighted work without the owner's consent for certain specific purposes, e.g., criticism, comment, news reporting, teaching, scholarship, or research. Fair use is more liberally applied when the copyrighted work is primarily factual and informational in nature, e.g., a news story rather than a work of mass market fiction. Similarly, the doctrine is also liberally applied when the use of verbatim quotations is required for accurate reporting.

Unfortunately, the standards for the application of the fair use doctrine are anything but clear. There is no judicial definition of what constitutes "fair use," although the Copyright Act does set forth the following factors to consider as to whether the use made of a work in any particular case is fair use:

1. The purpose and character of the use, including whether such use is of a commercial nature or is for nonprofit, educational purposes;
2. The nature of the copyrighted work;
3. The amount and substantiality of the portion used in relation to the copyrighted work as a whole; and
4. The effect of the use upon the potential market for or value of the copyrighted work.

To prove infringement, a copyright holder must establish ownership of a valid copyright and that the alleged infringer had copied the copyrighted work.

Since trying to prove that someone actually copied a work can be difficult, if not impossible, courts will permit a copyright owner to establish copying by circumstantial evidence, i.e., demonstrating that the alleged infringer had access to the copyrighted work and that the allegedly infringing work was "substantially similar" to the copyrighted work.

Attempting to prove copying by circumstantial evidence only establishes a presumption of copying which the alleged infringer may rebut by establishing that it independently created the work in question. It should be appreciated that while independent creation is a valid defense, when the two works are so similar that they are virtually identical, there is an inference that one was copied from the other.

Copyright applications forms are provided in Appendices 17-20.

Chapter 15
International Licensing

15.1 Greater Europe

15.1.1 Introduction[24]

With over 40 different countries of varying sizes and a population now in the region of 740 million, Europe is one of the most complicated and diverse regions of the world. The European Union, with 28 country members plus the additional four of the European Free Trade Association, may be classified as a single body but the cultural and economic differences between the member states are significant.

Europe has suffered, of course, over recent years, from a significant economic downturn which has impacted on the licensing industry as retail undergoes major changes. Countries such as Spain, Italy, Portugal and Ireland, all of whom are tied to the troubled Euro currency, have had problems. Retail sales in Italy last year suffered their worst ever drop, and while there have been some signs of recovery in Spain, consumer spending is still weak.

E-Commerce is the fastest growing retail market in Europe with sales in the UK, Germany, France, Sweden, The Netherlands, Italy, Poland and Spain showing significant growth. In 2013, whilst traditional retail continued to suffer, online retail in Europe grew by around 21%, dominated by the UK, Germany and France who together are responsible for more than 80% of European online sales.

Quite apart from the economic situation, which has to a greater or lesser extent impacted all European countries, and which, in countries such as Germany, the UK and, to some extent France is showing shoots of recovery, the main point of difference in Europe is that while the territory is classified as one, in terms of consumer preferences and, consequently licensing activity, European countries are very much individual territories with individual tastes.

At this point, it is worth looking at some of the key drivers in the leading European markets.

Germany, of course, is the European powerhouse. From a licensing perspective the children's market is more driven by educational values than most other countries, and parents are less inclined to support some of the action properties that do so well in other European countries. As a result, the German market has some home-grown properties that are hugely successful at home but have yet to travel beyond German borders. Retail, too, in Germany is very different from other countries being decentralized and, in many ways, fragmented. In addition, the market moves slowly, and it takes longer than most countries for a property to finally work.

> E-Commerce is the fastest growing retail market in Europe

---

[24] Written by Francesca Ash, publisher of *Total Licensing*. She can be reached at francesca@totallicensing.com.

France is more open to new licenses, but this market can be difficult, particularly in terms of licensed apparel which, although a key product sector in most countries, is very much less so in France. Homegrown properties continue to be popular, such as Babar or Asterix, with properties from neighboring Belgium, such as Tintin and THE SMURFS, continuing to occupy a strong position. However, France also has the global brands and properties that are present in so many territories with US-originated properties leading the way together with several Japanese brands. In terms of retail, France is home to some of the world's largest chains — Carrefour and Auchan — and these continue to be very important in terms of the retailing of licensed products.

Moving further north, the Nordic region (Sweden, Denmark, Finland, Sweden and Iceland) has always, traditionally, favored non-violent properties which has, over the years, meant several brands that have been popular around the world have failed to have any traction in this region. However, this region has carved its own niche in terms of Internet and app-based brands. Angry Birds from Rovio in Finland has been immensely popular around the world, and following this success, other Nordic tech companies are now entering the market.

The UK which, following a period of recession is now finally showing growth. Licensors, licensees and retailers are showing greater confidence in the market. However, the UK in terms of licensing is a mature market, and the number of properties, particularly in the pre-school sector, outweighs demand. Regarding preferences, the UK still very much follows the lead of the US, probably more than mainland Europe, although the country has a long and proud history of producing properties that subsequently become popular around the world. It is worth remembering that the first true licensed product — the Peter Rabbit doll in 1904 came from the UK, and WINNIE THE POOH was originally created by a AA Milne, a British author. More recently, the country has given the world The Teletubbies and Peppa Pig, both of which have enjoyed tremendous success on a global basis, as have personalities such as David Beckham and sports clubs such as MANCHESTER UNITED.

The retail situation in the UK is one of mixed messages. The key supermarket groups such as Tesco, Sainsburys, Morrisons and Asda (Walmart) are increasingly discounting and slugging it out for market share, a battle that has taken on new significance since deep German discounters Aldi and Lidl have recently become major players, whilst smaller chains are finding it increasingly difficult to compete, particularly when you add the explosive growth of online retailing into the mix. While consumers demand quality, they also demand low prices and while this benefits the end user, it also means the demise of retail stores and chains that have been part of the UK landscape for many years.

In summary, whilst Europe is often lumped together as one large trading bloc, doing business in the region successfully really does require an appreciation and understanding that each country within Europe operates very differently and has unique cultural, historic and other factors that make it unique.

15.1.2 Benelux[25]

Benelux is an economic union in Europe comprising the three neighboring countries of Belgium, the Netherlands and Luxembourg. These countries are in northwestern Europe

---

[25] Written by Cyril Speijer, Wavery Productions.

between France and Germany. Nowadays, it is mostly used in a generic way to refer to the cultural, economic, and geographic grouping. Even though Benelux covers three separate countries, the size and population of the region is rather small. Benelux is 1/7th the size of France. Benelux has one-third as many citizens as Germany. Nevertheless, Benelux is an important group of countries in Europe. With a very attractive financial climate in the Netherlands, many key market companies locate themselves in Holland.

Demographics and Geography

Entity	Capital	Population	Area	Population Density
Netherlands	Amsterdam	16.847.007	41.543 km²	403.7/km²
Belgium	Brussels	11.007.020	30.528 km²	354.7/km²
Luxembourg	Luxembourg	511.840	2.586 km²	194.1/km²
Benelux		28.365.937	74.640 km²	380/km²

Languages

In these three countries, four official languages are spoken; Dutch, French, German and Luxembourgian.

- 82% of the population lives in an area in which Dutch is the official language. In total, there are approximately 23 million people: 16.8 million Dutch citizens and 6.3 million Flemish Belgian citizens.
- 14% of the population lives in an area in which French is the official language. In total, there are approximately 4 million people: 3.5 million Walloon Belgians and 0.5 million Luxembourg citizens.
- 4% of the population lives in a bilingual area (Dutch, French), a total of approximately 1.1 million citizens.

Netherlands. Dutch is the official and foremost language of the Kingdom of The Netherlands. The nation consists of 16.8 million inhabitants of which 96 percent speak Dutch as their mother tongue. Within the Netherlands, there are many different dialects; however, these are often overruled by "Standard Dutch".

Belgium. Belgium, the neighboring nation of the Dutch, has a population of 11 million. Belgium has three official languages: Dutch (sometimes referred to as Flemish), French and German. Approximately 59% of all Belgians speak Dutch as their first language, although French is the mother tongue for over 40%. Dutch is the official language of the Flemish region (northern Belgium). In this region, Dutch is the mother tongue for 97% of the population. Belgian Dutch (Flemish), is the national variety of the Dutch language as spoken in Belgium (with dialect). It is used by default within schools, by the government, by the media and during informal occasions. Nevertheless, the use of the word "Flemish", as to refer to the official language in Flanders, is misleading. The only official language in Flanders is Dutch. In the region of Wallonia (South Belgium), French is considered the mother tongue and finally in a small part of Belgium, German is the official language.

Luxembourg. Three languages are officially recognized in Luxembourg: French, German and Luxembourgian. Each of these three languages is used as the primary language on certain occasions. Luxembourgian is the language that Luxembourgers generally use to speak amongst each other; however, it is not often used in writing. Most official (written) business communication is carried out in French. Usually German is the first language taught in school and is the most used language by the media and by the church. In addition to the three official languages, English is taught in compulsory school and most people in Luxembourg master English as a language, at least in Luxembourg City.

Licensing in Benelux

Until the formation of the European Economic Community (EEC) in 1958, product sales to consumers were easy to check and to monitor. This changed when new international players entered the market. In the field of apparel, a couple of examples of those players are Zara, H&M, among others. In the field of supermarkets Carrefour and Lidle left their origination country. On the other hand, retailers such as Blokker, Zeeman and supermarkets like Albert Heijn and Makro relocated to foreign countries.

The Netherlands has its origins in export. In the 17th century it all started with the VOC, discovering other trade areas, and possible countries for production. With Rotterdam still being one of the world largest ports, the export position remains strong to this day. On the other hand, we did lose the status of being a country for production. Companies such as Philips, C&A, and many others mainly from the apparel industry, had to move their production towards low-wage countries, primarily to stay ahead of the competition price-wise.

In 1948, Benelux (Belgium, the Netherlands, Luxembourg) was formed, 9 years before the EEC was formed. The main goal for its formation was creating an open market between the three countries and stimulating each other's import and export. From then on, licensing contracts were always concluded for the entire Benelux area. Belgium was a sole exception, since this area is divided in two parts, 50% is French-speaking (Wallonia), and 50% is Dutch-speaking (the Flanders area). For publishing, the French rights are usually granted to French-speaking publishers. Almost all producers have representation in the whole Benelux area. Luxembourg produces few in the country, but still is included in the contract because it is part of Benelux.

The formation of the EEC changed many aspects of the licensing industry. The open market is now valid for the entire area, meaning each product now has free access across the EEC. The product is only legal, though, when it officially enters the EEC, or is produced in one of the EEC countries. Fortunately, there are EEC rules that apply for protecting licensing contracts per area. Non-exclusive contracts can only be concluded for one or more parts of the EEC. When concluding a licensing contract for the entire EEC, we talk about an exclusive contract. Adding a restriction in every contract by specifying the language of the licensing area helps to protect against exporting the product into other areas but that requires that the parties define in the licensing contract that the product cannot be adjusted or changed after approval.

A grey area remains the issue of actively offering products to areas other than the specified area. This is a difficult case, because it is hard to determine whether the sale has taken place outside of the contractual area because of the open market.

History

Licensing in Benelux really began in the 1960s. In those days it was all about syndication. Benelux publishers were the first to license. In Belgium, examples of such publishers included Lombard and Dupuis, and in the Netherlands, Oberon and Strengholt were key players. The reason they started using licenses was to syndicate their comics into other publications. Opera Mundi, located in Brussels, at that time represented King Features among others, who was the only one who offered material of third parties.

Disney was the first American organization and was represented by an agent, André Vanneste. The first Dutchman working with rights was Mark Spits. Having worked in advertising, he observed licensing practices in the US, and brought them to the Netherlands. His first rights were Calimero and Little Bear Colico. A few years later, he ceased licensing activities, because business wasn't as expected. Besides the use for syndication, licensing rights were being used for promotional campaigns. In 1967, Cyril Speijer founded Wavery Productions B.V., the first company completely focused on licensing in Europe. As was the case with most licensing agents, he started working on promotional campaigns and, as a result, encountered licensors.

At that time, television was still in its infancy. In the Netherlands, NPS had only one channel broadcasting between 8 PM and 10 PM, and on Saturday children's programs aired between 5 PM and 5.30 PM. In the Flemish area of Belgium, VRT was active and in Wallonia, the BRTF aired programming, but both had little broadcasting time. The climate began to change when airtime grew on a couple of channels. The biggest transformation came in 1989 when commercial channels came into being. More broadcasting time was offered, and the merchandising boom started.

Licensing Today

In some instances, Belgium and the Netherlands are very similar markets, while in others the two are very different, which is quite interesting considering they share a language and almost seem to have no borders between them. Even so, very distinct differences do exist. When looking at the major properties within Benelux, we can determine that Disney, Sanrio's HELLO KITTY and Studio 100 are top of mind at retailers, followed by Nickelodeon's DORA THE EXPLORER, which unlike the others, can be found in virtually every store.

> Unique properties from Benelux include A.O., BUMBA, K3, HOUSE OF ANUBIS, MAYA THE BEE, and WICKIE THE VIKING

Unique properties from Benelux include those produced by Studio 100 and originating in Belgium, including properties such as: A.O., BUMBA, K3, HOUSE OF ANUBIS, MAYA THE BEE, and WICKIE THE VIKING as well as other properties and series focused on kids' entertainment from infant to preschool and all the way up to teens.

In only a few years, Studio 100 produced over 10 properties within Benelux and has experienced great local success with properties such as K3, BUMBA, HOUSE OF ANUBIS and more recently with Hotel 13, which is a co-production. While Studio 100 used to reign mainly within the Benelux and German borders, they have begun to co-produce some series with companies such as the BBC on an international level. Currently, they are expanding their territories due to the MAYA THE BEE brand. Studio 100 will be rolling out an extensive licensing program to support this children's property, which is centered around a show based on the popular '70s character. Studio 100 has already sold the MAYA THE BEE series in over 130 countries.

From the Netherlands, MERCIS is the strongest and most well-known property, and NIJNTJE PLUIS (MIFFY) is a very successful international licensor these days, bringing MIFFY to multiple territories and working with international partners such as KLM. The simplicity of NIJNTJE and the series of books has ruled Dutch bookstores for years. Originally a book character drawn by Dick Bruna, MIFFY has grown into a worldwide children's property. MIFFY is a familiar face at Licensing shows over the past few years and is expected to keep growing and expanding in multiple territories.

Also, from the Netherlands is Dromenjager and their property WOEZEL & PIP, two little dogs that go out on daily adventures. This property was created by Guusje Nederhorst, a young Dutch woman who sadly past away, but whose legacy to her children was carried on by her husband and shared with children all over Benelux. The property has taken Benelux by storm in only a few years' time and created a broad and steady licensing program, which counts as its partners the most prominent infant and pre-school brands and the largest Infant food company, Nutricia. Dromenjager conducts most business within Benelux but are expanding steadily into other territories. Products can be found in almost every store, from pacifiers to complete bedrooms, publishing (where the property originated from) and toys, with most categories covered on a national level, making them one of the big favorites, next to MIFFY.

Finally, from the Netherlands is LIEF! LIFESTYLE, a Dutch lifestyle brand that has grown internationally. With Benelux and Europe as their base markets, they are now expanding into the Far East and even into the US. LIEF! LIFESTYLE originally started out with a children's collection in apparel and accessories and now has numerous licensees in many other categories, such as stationery, health and beauty, and home decoration, the brand has even teamed up with a bike company, creating a special edition LIEF! LIFESTYLE typical Dutch bike. The simplicity and brightness of the brand have a great appeal, together with their chosen ambassadors who are Dutch TV personalities and their kids. LIEF! LIFESTYLE is known in almost any household within the Netherlands and is rapidly spreading throughout the rest of the world. Within the Netherlands they partner with mainly high end and some mid segment licensees to produce products for the home with bright colors and innovative design. Other very successful lifestyle brands are BLOND AMSTERDAM & STUDIO PIP, which are also rapidly increasing licenses on an international level.

Although being a relatively small market, Benelux also proudly possesses some major licensees. For example, Bioworld, which has a prominent position within the top 20 licensees worldwide according to a License Global article published in May 2013. Bioworld has a strong apparel partner to focus on fashion and accessories, and has worldwide distribution carrying a variety of licenses.

Companies such as Belltex (bedding), Leomil (apparel and footwear), BIP (candy), Cartamundi (card games), Sanoma (publishing) and several others are also located within

Benelux and do very well in the international arena. Even though the apparel industry is suffering within the region, some of these players are still part of the international market and growing. On top of that, another interesting development is that some smaller companies are managing, in these harder times, to build out their companies by creating smart business strategies regarding retail, but also by producing/ inventing very innovative new products (app-related, etc.).

Retailers are struggling in this region, as in others, creating some obvious changes with respect to the shopping patterns of the consumer. A shift of ranks has taken place, where companies that used to be considered hard discount, no longer have that image, but are slowly growing into mid- (mass) segment retailers, such as A.S. Watson's Kruidvat in the Netherlands and Belgium.

Kruidvat is one of the largest retailers in Benelux with 19 formulas under their flag such as Kruidvat, Trekpleister, Ice Paris and Savers. Kruidvat welcomes over 3 million visitors in store and receives over 650,000 unique hits to their website on a weekly basis. When looking at the total population of the Netherlands, that is a massive number of consumers. Employing over 12,000 people throughout the Netherlands and Belgium, Kruidvat has clearly taken over a larger part of business within this region. Being a drugstore by origin, they now carry all kinds of products in beauty and health, apparel, candy, and home decoration, while also becoming the number three player in toys. Kruidvat is still known for its bargains but is no longer seen as a hard discounter and therefore a fully recognized player within Benelux when it comes to licenses.

In the Netherlands, Kruidvat is joined by other major retailers such as the Blokker Group (Bart Smit, Blokker, Marskramer etc.), which are all household and toy-related retailers. In addition, there are supermarket chains such as Albert Heijn, C1000 and the Emte group (Jumbo & Sligro). In Belgium, retail channels differ quite a bit; within this region it is the larger supermarket chains that attract most consumers.

Chains such as Colruyt, Carrefour and Delhaize offer complete ranges to meet the consumers' needs. Together they are account for 70% of the Belgian market when it comes to food but being total suppliers they all offer a broad range of products reaching far beyond food. Colruyt, also containing Spar & Alvo stores, is the largest of the three, with around 600 stores; with 225 Colruyt-stores, 80 OKay-stores, 7 Bio-Planets, and 46 stores in the nonfood stores of DreamLand and DreamBaby. They also have several wholesale outlets and various smaller outlets, making Colruyt good for a share of 27.7% (2012) of the Belgian market. Carrefour does have more outlets; 700 Carrefour-stores; 45 Carrefour planet stores and Carrefour-hypermarkets, 438 Carrefour market/GB-supermarkets and 222 Carrefour express neighborhood stores. They make up a smaller part of the total market in shares, at 22.6% (2012). Carrefour is followed very closely by Delhaize, who makes up a share of 22.5% (2012) within the Belgian market.

Consumer Behavior

Dutch people visit supermarkets, mainly for daily needs such as food, beauty and health and some dry goods. Next to that, daily shopping also takes place in drugstore chains, smaller privately owned and/ or specialized stores, toy chains, and smaller privately-owned toy stores. Consumers shop in various outlets. Business consumers use wholesale outlets more frequently in comparison to the individual consumer.

Belgians do often visit the larger supermarket chains for most of their needs (one stop), and the wholesale business in Belgium is larger in comparison to the Dutch market for individual consumers as well. This also goes for the toy store chains (Dreamland & Fun BE), which are often situated next to these supermarkets and rule over smaller stores.

Other Differences between the Dutch and Belgian Markets

In the Netherlands, lifestyle brands are increasing their share within the licensing business and are rapidly expanding current programs in various categories. Mostly used in higher segments of retail or as special editions, companies such as The Royal Dutch Airline KLM, and brands such as BLOND AMSTERDAM, STUDIO PIP and LIEF! LIFESTYLE are very popular and can be found in many households. The Dutch designers and the fresh and bright patterns seem to appeal to the consumer. These brands distinguish themselves from the worldwide properties by blending into households in a subtler way. Although Belgium has an eye and sense for haute cuisine, style and design, brands such as these are not yet catching on regarding licensed products, or at least not on a large scale.

In Belgium, there is still a very strong market for superheroes like SPIDERMAN, BATMAN and THE POWER RANGERS, properties which are a very hard sell elsewhere within the Netherlands.

A similarity between the two main territories that seems to be a current trend in all the Benelux's countries is educational collectivity programs. Both Belgium and the Netherlands have been very successful in this area. Driven by several supermarket chains, both territories had similar promotions where, for 10 or 15 euros, the customer receives a collection of ANIMAL KINGDOM cards to collect and, in the Netherlands, archive in a custom-made collection album, containing information and background on these animals in small pockets the card is placed. In Belgium, they gave away a collection of cards with every 10 or 15 euros spent and for a small cost the consumer could buy a small device that would play the actual sound of the animal in question, by swiping it through the device. Both promotions were hugely successful, one of the major reasons being that these were not only accepted on the school playground, but they were used to in classrooms. Special trading events were even created around these collections. Following this success, several similar programs have been initiated, seemingly to prove that if the collectivity program is educationally accepted, you have a hit, as schools embrace them and word spreads like never before.

Challenges

The overall licensing business within Benelux appears to be decreasing now. Many licensees struggle to keep their head above water and are taking fewer risks. The apparel business especially is suffering with many companies forced to close shop. Buyers are on a very tight budget in every category, due to the hard times, and simply go for the lowest prices and best deals. They expect much more form their suppliers, which in turn makes the suppliers' job more expensive.

Unfortunately, many (potential) licensees are first cutting out the license expenses, which does not necessarily fix their problems. Without a license, it will cost a few cents less on the dollar per product to produce but leaves the manufacturer with a little less volume in return. Selling into retail and keeping prices low are a challenge for (potential) licensees, with materials and fabrics getting more expensive and margins rapidly decreasing every day. Therefore, it has become the licensing agent's responsibility to be more of an advisor in the licensing process. A licensing agent must provide advice on properties, design and even the approach at retail, to make the difference and prove, in the longer run, that adding a property still is very valuable to sales of products.

People recognize characters, designs, sport brands and/or celebrities and relate to them. When the design is appealing and conforms to contemporary trends, the additional appeal of this property will make a difference. So, it most definitely has gotten tougher to sell licenses, but it is a challenge that can be overcome.

On the other hand, in some cases, producers do turn to licenses, and are looking for something new, something fresh, something appealing. In some categories there is a slight increase in licensing, like newly-invented products like apps and game-related categories. High-end products that would like to distinguish themselves have also seen a slight increase. It seems there is a shift, and everybody is looking for that new way of earning money. If agents and (potential) licensees put their heads together, many more happy years of licensing will be created. However, creativity and teamwork are essential ingredients to make that work. Within Benelux we see this already, licensees and agents working together. We are also seeing more innovative designs, which are created by studios both for concept as well as presentations.

I would conclude with one last challenge to present-day licensing in Benelux. Due to EU regulations the borders have faded away, causing confusion and creating, so-called, easy cuts to extra income. Discussions on this and keeping the markets clean is becoming harder and harder especially for the smaller companies, who have come to work under great restraints. It is an ongoing issue, which all agents are trying to minimalize for the sake of their licensees. This is a very contemporary issue, costing a lot of time, efforts and business.

15.1.3 Germany[26]

Introduction to "GSA"

The "German speaking markets" are often referred to as "GSA" for Germany, Austria and Switzerland, because, in earlier times, owners of intellectual property rights (IPR's) usually granted licenses by language areas. As a result, they included the two significantly smaller countries of Austria and Switzerland, the latter because most Swiss also speak German.

At one time, almost all packaging, instruction booklets and care labels in these markets were in German only, so the 1957 Treaty of Rome, which facilitated the "free flow of goods within the European Union," had almost no impact. The purpose of the treaty was that once you licensed a company in/for one EU-member country, you could freely sell to buyers from other EU countries, provided there is no "active soliciting", e.g., do not display/market the products outside the licensed territory). Nowadays, almost all packaging and instructions for products in Europe (or at least the 28-member countries of the EU) are in at least the ten most common EU-languages, because most of them aim for an EU-wide distribution.

---

[26] Written by by Michael A. Lou, www.vip-ag.com

Background

Since its re-unification with the German Democratic Republic ("East Germany"), Germany has some 81.8 million people in about 24 million households (of which about 40% are single households). Austria has roughly 8.5 million citizens in 3.65 million households and Switzerland counts for almost another 9 million of which some 5.67 million have German as their native tongue (though many more speak German in this tri-lingual country).

GSA is not only the largest single language market in the 503 million people European Union (EU) but it also houses the wealthiest citizens. Germany has a GNP of US $44.260, Austria is $47.660 and "banking" Switzerland is $89.970 (on Purchase Power Parity basis), according to the World Bank. (USA: $51.749).

> Germany has the largest single language market in the EU and houses the wealthiest citizens.

However, the other key markets in the EU are not far behind. In all 28-member countries of the EU, the average GNP per person is still US $30.494. The average wealth of Germans totals to about 195.200 Euros (France 229.300; Spain 285.300, despite the crises you can read about at this time). Brexit of England should not affect the strength of the EU significantly and the Brits will try hard to still benefit from the commercial and trade benefits.

This demonstrates the great potential the EU markets have and Germany and Austria in particular, having traditionally acted as the gateways for business with Eastern Europe. Many companies already have distribution subsidiaries or co-operations in the key markets in Eastern Europe (Poland, Hungary and Russia) which are now upgraded by local production facilities.

While the average income in the ten German states that formed part of "Western Germany" is relatively equally spread, the approximately 12.5 million people living in the six former Eastern German states reach only about 80% of the income of their western neighbors, with wages are still somewhat behind.

In Austria, of course, people in urban areas gain relatively more money than in rural areas, but the living standards and infrastructure allows countrywide distribution at even levels. And in Switzerland, wealth seems to part of the lifestyle.

Of course, there are also bad facts: A UNICEF study released in April 2013 (the latest available) reveals that one in seven German children between 11 and 14 years is "unhappy with his or her situation. And only about 30% of the children who are born today into a certain social group have a chance to change into a higher one compared to 37% of those born in 1950 as reported by the Scientific Centre for Social Research in Berlin.

Despite the EU economic problems that are reported on almost daily, GSA is indeed a stronghold within the European markets. GSA can be a productive market for licensing if licensors use common sense and do not expect that every licensing program that succeeded overseas will automatically also do well (or even better) in GSA. In fact, the opposing situation is also true: a property that was not successful in other countries may have a chance to succeed in the German speaking markets. That is because, according to the market research organization Nielsen, 56% of Germans are open to trying new brands, when they asked over than 29,000 Internet users.

The History of Licensing in GSA

It is difficult to estimate licensing numbers before World War II, because there was no tracking of significant brand or entertainment licensing activities in the German speaking markets before then. In 1950, right after World War II ended, the German producer of the popular HUMMEL figurines, Franz Goebel, acquired from Walt Disney the rights to produce MICKEY MOUSE, BAMBI and other Disney characters.

Licensing, according to today's standards, began only with the TV market expanding. Leo Kirch, a young and emerging TV program and film dealer was one of the first people to realize the potential of the ancillary rights. (Berlusconi was not even in the business yet and Murdoch & Co. still thought print products were the media of the future.) Kirch's group initially bought the distribution rights from leading US studios like Warner, Paramount and MGM including the merchandising rights. Later Kirch started to produce its own programming like PIPPI LONGSTOCKING, HEIDI, BEE MAJA, etc., that was also suited for licensing.

Guenther Vetter, who was General Manager of Kirch's licensing arm Merchandising Muenchen GmbH from 1972 through 1981, was the real pioneer of licensing at that time and later said he needed "comprehensive negotiation and convincing skills" to sensitize companies in German-speaking markets for this new business opportunity called merchandising.

Some of these early pioneer licensing properties are still in the market today and are nowadays referred to as "classics." When I started in this business in 1980 (as a licensee for the DALLAS TV series) there was almost no one to get expert advice from other than Guenther Vetter and Brigitte Gosda, who marketed at that time MGM, United Artists and Warner Bros. properties before doing most of the business for Sesame Street and later developed the properties of Bibi Blocksberg and Benjamin Bluemchen into the local kids' classics they are today.

Beyond Entertainment Licensing

Brand licensing started, like in most other places, as brand extension (after the owners of core brands had exploited line extensions). Manufacturers of brand name products tried to extend their product lines away from their core products and, if possible, into other distribution channels. The main reason for extending their products, apart from making money, was to reach the consumer in "competitive-free" environments, i.e., where there was no product of their competitors for the core products. These companies hoped to strengthen their brand awareness, and hence their brand value, by being known to a larger consumer group.

Naturally, some brand companies were not set-up for such "brand extension" and soon consultants (later called licensing agents) appeared that helped the brand companies find the right licensees. Early cases of successful brand licensing strategies were the Olympic Games and the FIFA Soccer Championships (through Adidas subsidiary ISL

International Sports Licensing). It is somewhat odd that the professional soccer leagues, (Bundesliga), which are now so popular, did not begin to license in GSA until they saw what I was able to do with the NFL in the late 1980's, even though American football was not very popular at all in the German speaking markets.

Quite certainly, Kirch's TV and film licensing developed the entertainment licensing in German markets; ADIDAS, PUMA and fashion brands like BOSS, JIL SANDER and WOLF-GANG JOOP, along with some local heroes (like HARIBO) and international corporations from abroad (PLAYSKOOL was one of the first) developed the brand side of it; and soccer teams (Bayern Muenchen and Co.), FIFA and the Olympic Games were the properties that developed sports licensing.

I still remember sitting together with Guenter Vetter in the late 80th over a beer or two forecasting that brand licensing would be the (then) future (because the sport brands were not really brand licensing in our understanding.

The TV Market

With respect to television entertainment licensing, one must know that the TV scene in GSA was far behind all other larger European countries. Until 1962 there was only one TV channel ("Deutsches Fernsehen", nationwide and operated by the government). Then a second governmental channel (ZDF Zweites Deutsches Fernsehen) commenced its nationwide broadcasting and each of the 10 Federal States started to launch its own regional channel (that at early times only broadcasted until the evening and was then joined with "Deutsches Fernsehen", today known as "Das Erste" = The First).

Consequently, the programming was limited in variety, and the bulk of foreign TV-series, which were better suited for licensing, started only when private TV stations commenced their business in 1984. So, television licensing, which historically has generated a clear majority of the licensing business in other markets, started late compared to GSA. I believe that this is why there are many more licensed products in the English, Italian, French or Spanish markets compared to GSA, though GSA represents a very strong licensing market and has probably the most merit with respect to its future development.

Recent Changes in Licensing

In recent years, the channels of distribution of licensed product have undergone significant changes, but so too have the ways licenses are marketed and sold, having refined and captured new ground. With respect to licensing itself, the target groups and/or potential licensees have widened. There are more direct-to-retail licenses being granted, which leaves the retail chains more freedom with respect to sourcing. And cross-licensing with other properties (STAR WARS with LEGO or ANGRY BIRDS, HELLO KITTY and ELVIS) has become very popular.

As far as distribution, changes and developments were more significant in the past two decades, but channels continue to grow and diversify. For example, Tilmann Schneider, who in the mid-1980's headed licensing for the private TV-Giant RTL, "discovered" gasoline stations as new POS for his plush replicas of KOMMISSAR REX, the shepherd detective in a popular TV series, and selling them in greater numbers than the other traditional channels combined. Another example of the expanding distribution channels is the sale of animal health insurance using the licensed image of a popular dog character and distributed through pharmacies/drugstores.

While entertainment and sports licensing were well-established, it was not until the late 80's that brand licensing really became serious business. The German Railway Company used it to support the launch of its new high-speed trains (ICE); Unilever, after they bought Fabergé in the US and went back to Europe to start an upscale brand licensing program, to re-launch its mass market body care line FABERGÉ (Brut de Fabergé); PEPSI to leverage its tiny market share of 8% (vs. COKE with over 50%); followed by numerous fashion brands.

Celebrity licensing was strong in the 80's and 90's with legends like HUMPHREY BOGART, JAMES DEAN, ELVIS PRESLEY, BRUCE LEE and MARILYN MONROE. Growth in the area continued into the late 90's with contemporary stars like MICHAEL JACKSON, TINA TURNER, THE BEATLES, ROLLING STONES and others that were popular through their respective music, just like in many other countries.

In the 21st century there were very few property categories introduced apart from charity licensing. The shift went more toward alternative or additional distribution channels and mainly to direct-to-retail licensing (DTR).

Licensing Today

Major Properties. Most certainly, among the top five most successful properties licensed for kids in GSA are STARS WARS, FROZEN and CARS, even though they seem to weaken somewhat lately, according to the latest findings of the research organization Iconkids & Youth. German classics like BENJAMIN BLUEMCHEN, a friendly elephant walking on two legs and primarily aimed at preschoolers. as well as the German classic BIBI BLOCKSBERG (also supported a film sequel) play also a strong part. There has been little change during recent years with respect to the popularity of these properties depending on seasonal promotions, a new film release or TV broadcast.

> Top properties in Germany today are STAR WARS, FROZEN, CARS, BENJAMIN BLUEMCHEN and BIBI BLOCKSBERG

A good source for tracking popularity and success of kid properties is www.iconkids.com.

The spectacular, significant success of Lego's STAR WARS products showed that two properties that at first glance do not fit can be a surprising success. Same for ELVIS and HELLO KITTY, which became another surprise hit, even if not the size of LEGO. When I was the agent for Lucasfilm back in the 80's I could never have thought of offering LEGO a STAR WARS license, simply because LEGO's bricks where square and old-fashioned, and LUKE SKYWALKER & Co. were the state of the art in youth entertainment. So, you see how easily you can be wrong in judging the market potential of your license. Nevertheless, the message left behind this example is: You never have a chance of getting your property noticed if you do not examine EVERY option.

Sports. In sports licensing there is very little apart from soccer. Soccer is the major sport in Western Europe and is also popular with the Germans, Austrians and Swiss. Some fans will buy any merchandise featuring the logos of their favorite clubs, and the world's top leagues generate the bulk of the business, in addition to seasonal merchandise from the UEFA European championships or FIFA World Cup. But only the top clubs and players really sell, with the "local heroes" of the sport generating the most interest. Even though handball and basketball enjoy an increasing fanbase and greater TV coverage, there is hardly any significant licensing for these sports. Quite surprisingly, Formula 1 car racing has had some success even though it has limited media exposure, and cycling is popular as well. Of course, every four years the Olympic Games create some demand, the winter games because GSA countries tend to win more medals than in the summer games.

Brands. The brand licensing sector is dominated by the fashion licensors. In my last update I wrote that "ESPRIT is one of the main players thanks to its dynamic (and even aggressive) licensing program (that in my opinion tends to over-license the brand)". My opinion seemed to be correct looking at ESPRIT´s situation in 2018. Local brands like S. OLIVER, TOM TAILOR, BRUNO BANANI, BUGATTI, MEPHISTO (a shoe brand), and SCOUT (the brand of the leading school bag) have established their niche in the licensing market. A newcomer is the brand CAMP DAVID of three brothers from Berlin, who use Dieter Bohlen, a former singer and now one of our top TV entertainers as a spokesperson and have achieved some years of ongoing success. Of course, you can also see the international luxury brands on some licensed products, including eyewear, watches and fragrance, most notably.

Some "on air" brands are doing well, like Heidi Klum's TV show, Germany's Next Top Model, or DSDS Germany searching for the Super Star. These brands which appeal to the masses are well-equipped for successful licensing programs. On the other hand, there are no guarantees either. Some TV stations acquire licensing rights along with the show but do not really follow up on it (for instance because they simply have too many of them). A good recent example is the popular show *Dancing with the Stars*, where the licensing arm of the station (RTL) only signed two or three deals over three years. Even cooking shows with famous chefs became a good source for licensing, even in the food business, which seems still underdeveloped in GSA.

An emerging licensing segment is (still) the cause-related licensing for charities like WWF, UNICEF, GREENPEACE, WHATEVER IT TAKES, EIN HERZ FUER KINDER (A Heart for Children) by the Axel Springer publishing company or Deutscher Tierschutzbund (Europe's oldest charity for the protection on animals and nature).

Mobile content licensing is –as everywhere- rather new and works to my knowledge in GSA as in most other key markets though it is still too early to make certain specializations.

Local Heroes. Almost all local properties that command notable sales originate from media exposure, mainly TV. From the same source of the elephant Benjamin Bluemchen comes another local character from Kiddinx GmbH: BIBI BLOCKSBERG, a young witch that has been attracting a young audience for about 20 years now. Then there is "Die Sendung mit der Maus", Germany's answer to Sesame Street; WENDY, a young girl with her horse known from year-long comic books and now from its TV series, and the SANDMAENNCHEN, known by small children for 50 years from its little bedtime story on TV. Of course, we also have numerous characters that come and go depending on their TV presence, just like in most other countries, but I cannot see anyone on the horizon with enough potential for a lasting licensing success. There is simply too much competition that looks confusingly similar.

What you can hardly mix-up is the various city logos that have started their regional licensing business, often by co-branding with established brands.

On the brand side, we have the ADIDAS and PUMA brands as leading licensors, RED BULL and SWAROVSKI from Austria, Bally from Switzerland, HARIBO (known for its fruit gummy bears), THOMAS SABO (a brand that solely emerged from fashion jewelry for young girls) and the various fashion brands mentioned before. A unique property is the DEUTSCHER TIERSCHUTZBUND, an animal charity with 800,000 members. In late 2012, it began to license its logo to endorse meat and poultry from animals that have been brought up in strict conformity with the highest legal standards, so becoming a seal of quality. Now, they are also starting a licensing program for products and services that foster the well-being of animals.

Key Players in the Market

GSA is dominated mainly by licensors and agencies located in Germany, which houses four times as many consumers than Austria and Switzerland together. Most of the leading property owners who license their properties use agents, but of course we also have several companies who have their in-house licensing teams like ADIDAS, PUMA, RED BULL, SWATCH, HUGO BOSS, to name but a few.

From the international side we also have the Walt Disney Company, now located in Munich; Fremantle-Media in Potsdam (near Berlin); Nickelodeon/Viacom right in Berlin; subsidiaries of The Licensing Company and CPLG Copyright Promotions Licensing Group, both in Munich but with headquarters in the U.K.; Warner Bros. Consumer Products with offices in Hamburg and Bravado in Berlin (part of Universal Music).

Today, almost all the TV stations have created their own licensing arms, including:
- RTL Interactive (www.RTLinteractive.de)
- WDR MediaGroup (www.wdr-mediagroup.com)
- ZDF Enterprises (www.zdf-enterprises.de)
- ProSiebenSat1 Licensing (www.ProSiebenSat1Licensing.com)
- RTL Disney Fernsehen (www.Superrtl.de)
- RTL 2 Fernsehen GmbH (www.rtl2.com)

Among the various independent agencies are Bavaria Sonor, headed by Dr. Rolf Moser (www.bavaria-sonor.de); Euro-Lizenzen headed by Guenter Vetter (www.eurolizenzen.net), Team Licensing, headed by Katharina Dietrich (www.teamlicensing.de) and my own V.I.P. Entertainment & Merchandising AG (www.vip-ag.com). These are probably the most experienced ones, while there are several other agencies that were mostly founded by former employees of the other ones. A good source for information is the local licensing magazine at www.licensing-online.com.

Unique Challenges

Successful licensing in GSA begins with the understanding of what I stressed before: even if a licensing program is successful elsewhere, that does not mean that it can be carried over to the GSA markets in the same way. There are a few cases where this works, mostly thanks to heavy media exposure like TV, but in most cases, products that can be licensed in GSA need to make advertising and promotion adjustments to account for local preferences and trade exposure, which must meet the individual Point-of-Sale situations. Clearly, the property must be protected by trademark rights in all relevant classes, and you should have a lawyer on the spot that has ample experience with local copyright and trademark law to defend the rights you want to license.

Role of Agents and Consultants

There is always the question of the hen and the egg. Should you first get legal advice on how to best protect your property in GSA and how to make it fit for licensing or find an agent to evaluate the market potential to see if licensing in GSA could generate more money than needed to cover the legal and administration expenses? I recommend looking first for the right agent for your property. The biggest agent might not always be the best choice at a given moment and the TV station that airs your programming may have too many other properties to look after and may not give the property the desired attention. Of course, in most cases the TV station will try to insist on getting the licensing rights when buying the broadcasting rights, but you always must bear in mind the question what property TV station pushes most: Their own shows/properties or yours?

When George Lucas came to me with the STAR WARS II property back in 1981, I was still relatively new in the business with a short track record. He asked me how much I would generate for STAR WARS and how much of it would I possibly guarantee him in minimum royalties. Luckily, I had done my homework and could present him some evaluation on what I believed we could produce, but we signed no guarantee at all.

All licensors want to have such projections from their potential agents before granting the agency the rights, and all promise not to "bind" the agent to his projections. But if an agent has not lived up to projections, the licensor will remember. And if there is no viable reason as to why the agent could not meet expectations (change of exposure, economic crises, unexpected competition etc.), and this happens two or three times, good licensors will not want that agent to represent their properties. So, the most valuable asset that an agent has is its credibility, in addition to ample market experience, objective judgement and innovative creativity as to the market approach for your property.

Outlook, Projections and Conclusions

The negative news reported over the past years on the economic and financial problems in the EU that have also affected Germany and Austria, have ended. GSA now enjoys a continued strength. As I update my last report Germany's political parties have just signed their coalition agreement that let us hope for another few good years. But licensing in GSA has changed dramatically over the past few years. What was formerly the "bread and butter" business in the region (T-shirts, toys, stationery, bags, etc.) does not generate as many sales for many properties. The market has become more fragmented, both on the property side and on the consumer side.

A key reason is also the growing online business as more and more Web shops take licenses directly, thus starting a harsh competition with the traditional retailers.

GSA has experienced an oversaturation of TV programming, all trying to make money at licensing; hence each of the properties has a smaller share of the market. Moreover, the children's market has changed, with kids maturing earlier and attracted to properties aimed at older audiences. This is heavily influenced by the various new social media tools readily available at all age groups. It is not uncommon to see babies in strollers with computer games in front of them while at the same time parents are talking on their cell phones. Another example of licensees trying to catch up with this trend is the recent PC game "LEGO City Undercover", which shows obvious parallels to the "Grand Theft Auto" game. The near future of licensing in GSA is certainly influenced by Age - the chart below is of interest because it demonstrates to an alarming extent the shift of age group in Germany. Very soon the largest portion of consumers will be over 50 years old.

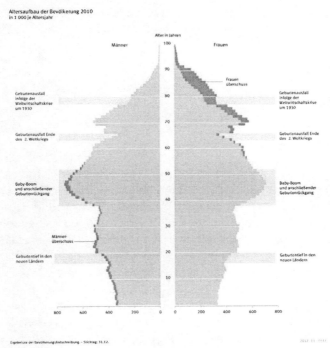

As a conclusion I can say GSA is probably the most fertile ground for licensing in Europe because it is –at least with respect to many categories of licensed products- still far behind France, Italy, Spain and the U.K. if you are not of the mind to "take the money and run" but are seriously interested in building a successful licensing program with longevity and willing to invest adequate funds, you have all that is needed for an attractive ROI.

Brand licensing, in my opinion, has a very promising future. There is a much wider target group (adults vs. kids) and the core product is known because of years of advertising and promotion, hence these properties have an established pre-sold popularity and established positioning/image. Charity (cause-related) licensing is equally promising, yet with smaller target groups as the consumer must decide what charity they favor most.

The new media being offered to consumers brings unpredictability. Licensing involving cell phone technology has not taken hold in this region, while the computer gaming industry has begun to make strides. These games usually have a longer market presence than theatrical releases and hopefully will provide an entry for cell phone games and other properties deriving from the new media scene.

Even licensing virtual properties for PC game players and collectors has already reached a significant market size and seems to still grow, because of the increasing number of people who play on their Smartphones or tablets. And a new playground came around: The licensing of content marketing where you can try to wrap the story of your property nicely (to avoid too much of a pack shot like "advertorial") but can still promote your property on the back of an established brands marketing campaign.

In conclusion, I can say that the German-speaking markets are similar in many ways to other key markets in industrialized countries but offer greater opportunity because of their leading positions within the EU and as gateways to the Eastern European markets. We do not try to reinvent the wheel over here but try constantly to smoothen the ball-bearings.

So, welcome to the "old world"!

15.1.4 Italy[27]

Introduction

It is a somewhat difficult exercise to talk about the forty-year history of licensing in Italy in a few short pages. Born in the second half of 1973—to the best of my knowledge—the licensing industry in Italy is complex and varied. As my company is the oldest independent licensing agency in this industry, I thought I would link my own story to that of licensing in Italy. In the second half of 1973, "Dan Junior Production" was founded, the first independent licensing agency in Italy, which, after a few years, became known as "DIC2 srl" (acronym for "Distribution International Characters"). Before that time, the only company granting licenses for the use of "characters" or "trademarks" was Disney, basically supported by some advertising and marketing agencies that wanted to exploit the launch of new animated films for promotional activities supporting some of their customers' products. As a "merchandising" agency (this is how this new discipline was called at that time before it was more appropriately called "licensing"), we began to seek companies interested in acquiring licenses to characterize their products with the characters we represented or to exploit characters from television programs and animated movies.

History of Licensing

In the first years, talking about "licensing" or "merchandising" was like talking about quantum physics to babies. Customers neither wanted to pay nor calculate royalties for the proposed use of the characters and properties we represented, because no one had, up to this point, felt the need for the characterization of their products. We are extremely grateful to the first licensees, who faced a difficult task given the poor dissemination of audio-visual media at the time (one of Disney's animated movie was distributed every 3-4 years and a couple of TV channels were on air, one of which broadcast children's programs for an hour a day). However, due to the originality of their products and the wide audience that every movie or television series had, many licensees experienced initial success, and

---

[27] Written by Gianfranco Mari, Chairman of DIC2.

the merchandising activity that we were promoting quickly became an important new marketing tool.

Gradually, the licensing business gained more and more acceptance, and many companies began to take an interest in the various characters, well-known brands, editorial and artistic works, sporting marques and events that we represented. Companies saw a valuable strategy that could be used to characterize their products to differentiate them from their competitors or to take advantage of the interest these properties generated among consumers. These early licensees saw the potential in transferring the character/brand awareness to their products which often resulted in considerable savings on marketing investments which many companies would not have been able to afford. Those were the days in which a character that was on television could be counted on to generate several hundred licenses and thousands of products with that character on the market. Easy identification of the right character reduced the risks of manufacturing unsuccessful products that would end up unsold on storeroom and inventory shelves.

Then, in the mid-eighties, a boost to the licensing industry occurred with the emergence of major "private" television networks in Italy. These private networks were born from the merger of several local television channels which eventually became strong enough to compete with RAI, the public television network, for the purchase of important TV series. These TV programs, mainly aimed at children, teenagers and young people, were broadcast in prime-time slots. This led to an exponentially increased number of potential interested licensees. At the same time, the number of specialists proposing licenses also increased. Besides the independent agencies, new representative offices of the major studios, such as Warner, Hanna-Barbera etc., and licensing offices of television networks such as SACIS (RAI) Mediaset etc., were opened in Italy.

What resulted was an excessive number of properties being offered with varied success. After years of introducing the same products and services to consumers, licensing began to experience a slowdown. Now, apart from a few strong properties which collect many of the opportunities, the others gather the crumbs.

Today in Italy, there are two other factors that further hinder the licensing market: first, a severe economic crisis that has slashed the budgets of consumers who do not have enough money to spend on products which are not essential and, second, a strong reduction of companies that survived the economic crisis and tax oppression by the Italian government. The companies who were successful in important licensing areas such as games and toys, back-to-school, clothing and accessories, home products, food, promotions and traditional publishing, at one time numbered in the thousands. But today, it is difficult to determine how many survived the economic downturn and remained in business.

Are we pessimists? I think it is important to be realistic, and to be able, through the creativity that has always characterized the Italian people, to find new opportunities and new properties that will revitalize the licensing business and give back the successes of the past.

Licensing Today

It is clearly impossible to talk about the Italian licensing industry today without first analysing the economic and financial situation in Italy, in the European Union and above all, in new emerging economies around the world. Historically, licensing has had the greatest impact in countries with capitalist economies, where fast-moving consumer goods and even luxury items have found in characters and trademark licensing a useful tool to characterize and impose various products on the market. In these countries, the increase in the price of the licensed products, because of royalties, in comparison to the "unbranded" ones, was not an obstacle, especially in a period when economies were thriving, and those captivating products particularly attracted consumers.

Besides the United States, the strongest growth in licensing has been in Western Europe and in Japan. Today, because of the crisis (which we will highlight below), the new territories which major licensors are looking at are the Far East, with China leading the way as the second largest economy in the world, Russia and the Eastern European countries.

The reasons that led to the establishment of the EU are manifold. We will take into consideration only the economic and distribution aspects that most affect licensing. The EU was formed to ensure the free circulation of goods, more opportunities and financial certainty. Exchanges between the various countries should have become easier thanks to extensive trade networks in all countries. Borders have been opened, and export tax issues have been eliminated, which in theory should have improved economies.

Unfortunately, 10 countries out of 28 have not adopted the Euro currency, and 8 have not adhered to certain Community rules. Each country operates independently regarding VAT rates, taxation, and wages. The rules on the manufacture of goods, services and trade have caused a huge migration of capital, industry and workforces. All the above has led the individual economies to experience a tremendous collapse and created an insecure and unstable climate. Italy along with Greece, Spain, France and several Eastern European countries are facing a serious economic recession. The effect of the recession has been a greater impact on spending by consumers, and consequently, a strong decrease in licenses and royalties generated.

Changes and New Licensing Promotional Media

In Italy, the first and most important change that has occurred with respect to licensing in 2013 is, as said before, the collapse of the licenses and, as a result, the collapse of the revenue due to the economic crisis. In 2013, many licenses – which had been kept alive by licensees because they were somehow able to cover the minimum guarantees, although they didn't generate big revenues – has been abandoned to limit expenditures and investments and refocus resources on more performing properties. A wide proliferation of new thematic channels dedicated to children and teens has occurred following the consolidation of the new digital TV technology. Unfortunately, this has caused the collapse of the audience of individual programs and a great disaffection of young viewers to the characters proposed and, consequently, the collapse of the licensees' interest for those properties.

The traditional media outlets of television, film, books and publishing and console video games, which gave birth to characters and trademarks generating important licensing programs, today are being replaced by computers, iPods, iPads, tablets, phones and

Smartphones, Internet, Facebook, Twitter etc. At the beginning, the Apps developing companies were used to acquire licenses of renowned characters: Superheroes, cartoons characters, sporting events brands, etc.., but soon the Apps themselves generated new characters like ANGRY BIRDS, CUT THE ROPE, etc., turning licensees into licensors.

These new tools are bringing teens back to licensing after they had abandoned the products supported by certain licenses, which were considered "for children". However, a significant share of their financial resources – previously addressed to important areas of licensing such as comics, gadgets, books – are now diverted towards the services offered by phone service providers, dedicated Apps and social networks.

Brands – Characters - Events

In the past, licensing was a tool used by companies to differentiate their products from that of their competitors, but the product was the essential part that had to generate the sales (therefore, the main features were: quality, price, warranty, need and service). Today, brands and characters are used as the main sale instrument, the "must have". Brands and characters are no longer chosen for their meanings or because they create a perfect synergy with the product, but only because they are coveted by consumers. There is an explosion of "phenomenon" brands and characters that are purchased because they sell! Generally, they can exclude any competitor, even if more synergistic with the product.

The explosion of a licensing "phenomenon" often happens very quickly. To reduce risk, companies usually await the "explosion" before deciding to acquire a license without realizing that this is often the most dangerous moment to initiate a license, because as soon as they are ready to place the product on the market, the "phenomenon" could be over. As a result, the risk for the licensee is very high. The quantities manufactured are often very high, as well as the investments. When the "must have" effect ceases, there is an instantaneous death of the product, and everything that remains unsold can only be destroyed.

Today, licensing is mostly used to sell. Licensees chase the characters or brands that are sought after by consumers in that moment. We will list a few as an example of what has been or are at moment a "phenomenon". They are not to be taken as current opportunities, because even the most important ones have an expiration and certainly will not be topical when this book will be published. As with food products, licenses of this kind should bear a "Best before ..." date.

I'll try to give some guidance on how to identify in advance licenses which should give significant results. Take them with care because the identification of a "phenomenon" is something very difficult, particularly for an "old dinosaur" with 40 years of this work on his shoulders.

To better understand what we refer to, the following is a list of the characters and brands that we now call "Phenomenon":

- SMURFS" - Even if their first release is as comics in the early sixties, the phenomenon explodes in 1982 with the appearance of the cartoons on the Fininvest TV network. We don't know how many millions of tiny little blue characters have been sold but, thanks to them, someone bought a real castle. Besides being a great "phenomenon", THE SMURFS may also be defined as a "classic" thanks to everything that has come after then.

- "NINJA TURTLES"- The famous turtles that have rocked the world of licensing in the years 1988-1990. They could also be listed as classic characters since lately they have been relaunched with various films even though the extraordinary success of the late eighties has never been equaled.

- "THE SIMPSONS" - A satiric parody on the American lifestyle. Canale 5 began airing the cartoon in the evenings at the end of 1991, and the outbreak of the Simpsons mania attracted the teen market, a target that until this point was not impressed by products featuring cartoons characters. The success of THE SIMPSONS merchandise continues, thanks to the large amount of TV episodes released (over 500).

- "BEVERLY HILLS 90210" - The first live action series dealing with sensitive issues related to the world of teens, such as drugs, AIDS, homosexuality, alcohol, etc. The series originally aired in 1992 in Italy and became an incredible success following the wave born in the USA and immediately exported throughout Europe and the world. 90201 was a great licensing success in our country that lasted for a few years with hundreds of different products in each category.

- "SAILOR MOON" – Arrived in 1993/1994 on the Mediaset TV, it was a cartoon starring a middle school girl who turns into a warrior with powers that help her fight and save the earth. Four other girls with transforming power will join her to form the team "Sailor Warriors." Great is the success of this series that was supposed to have inspired the creators of THE WINX and the W.I.T.C.H.

- "POKÉMON" – The series arrived in Italy in 2000 and the licensing success was amazing; we could hazard a guess that it was the most important success in the past and present history. Thanks to POKÉMON, some companies have tripled their value on the stock market, and we think that it could become a classic with a constant level of sales of licensed products. Inexplicably, in 2005-2006 the Pokémon Company decided to stop all licenses except for trading cards, Nintendo Video Games and a few other products.

- "SOUTH PARK" – The first satirical series which dealt with issues such as politics, religion, sex, etc., trying to bust the taboo. The first episodes were broadcast on Mediaset in 2000, but thanks to the rumor of great success in the U.S., many products are already in our market. The licensing success is big enough to compete with Pokémon despite its more restricted and adult target.

- "BRATZ"- launched worldwide around 2002-2004 and, unlike most of the other licensing phenomena that have been developed from audiovisual programs (because of publishing successes), BRATZ was born as a toy product. In a short time, the BRATZ dolls, which were "caricatures" of girls at that time, have achieved such success as to exceed sales of the undisputed queen of the industry, the BARBIE doll.

- "WINX" - a group of "flying fairies" (who seem to have been inspired by the predecessor "SAILOR MOON"), were born in 2004-2005 from a successful television series created by the Italian producer Rainbow to contrast the phenomenon BRATZ and especially the classic female character par excellence, BARBIE. The WINX success has exploded in Italy and is expanding throughout the world bringing Italian creativity to the highest levels of success in licensing.

Presently, here are some phenomena that are exploding in Italy and have attracted consumers of licensing products.

- From Disney come the characters from the animated feature film *CARS*, followed by *CARS* 2 and the telenovela, *Violetta*, that is driving all girls from South America, Europe and Africa crazy.
- "PEPPA PIG" - Although the cartoon series was born in the early 2000s in Italy, the great licensing success exploded at the end of 2012 and reached its highest peak in 2013. It is the first time that a "pre-school" character has become a great licensing phenomenon in our country. The success of "EPPA" prevails over the target and involves a good deal of the male and older target.

How to Spot the Next Phenomenon

Regarding the topical brands, it is important, and I am probably stating the obvious, to follow the consumer's taste who is targeted with the product. Usually, this is influenced by major advertising campaigns carried by well-known companies (Fiat 500), or there are companies that set a trend (fashion brand names as GURU, A-STYLE, FIX DESIGN). Young people are very susceptible to "Testimonials", where actresses/actors /music bands star in TV shows (AMICI, ZELIG, BELEN, ONE DIRECTION).

It is more difficult to understand what will become a phenomenon when talking about characters generated from the entertainment industry. It is important to remember the following.

- Constantly monitor foreign markets such as the United States, United Kingdom, Japan, France, and Spain. Analyse the acquisition of a property by leaders in different categories with established history of licensees. In the future, we must certainly keep an eye on China and Russia since their production of entertainment programs and licenses is continuously growing.
- Attend trade fairs (Bologna Licensing Trade Fair, Las Vegas Licensing Expo and Brand Licensing Europe). They are all important sources in finding opportunities. Please note that not all that glitters...
- Attend all presentations of licensors and their agents, especially the most serious, to stay informed about licenses granted, properties' diffusion, promotions, co-marketing activities, style guides and relational difficulties of licensors.
- Try to know the properties that have been acquired by the traditional and most important master licensees both nationally and internationally.
- Keep up with national or international licenses of products related to new technologies and media (Internet, Apps, Social networks)

Proven Classics

In contrast to the phenomena category, characters and brands that have generated and continue to generate excellent revenues for licensees who acquire a license are categorized as "classics". Long-lasting, they keep their value over time with features and performance that are completely different from those of the phenomena characters and brands. Because of their longevity you can acquire their license at any time, they are properties that I think will be topical even when you will have the opportunity to read this publication. Clearly, if at a particular time, the property enjoyed a special event such as new television show or movie release of importance, anniversary or significant new license, which refreshes its relevance, it would be an important opportunity for the licensee, and a chance possibly to renew its product ranges.

Contrary to the phenomenon, where the timing of the acquisition and/or dropping of a license are very important to avoid being left with unsold stock, the licenses for the classics are often renewed for ten-year periods (a good example are the carnival costumes of Zorro) and investments, both for molds and advertising and promotions, are spread over several years of distribution.

Revenues grow more slowly and may stand at lower levels, but in principle, longevity fully compensates this problem. In addition, a license of this kind does not require investments that could throw the company structure into trouble. The product is of fundamental importance for the licensing of classic characters and brands, both for the licensee that, having to keep a product in catalogs for a long time, must ensure quality and durability of the product, and for the licensor that otherwise would see its property damaged permanently by low profile products.

Here are some of the major licensors and their most successful properties, of course from the licensing point of view, particularly in the recent years.

Entertainment Characters:

- Disney with its world-famous Properties: MICKEY MOUSE, DONALD DUCK & CO., WINNIE THE POOH, PRINCESSES.
- LEAR and the invincible GAULS: ASTERIX, OBELIX & CO.
- MARVEL: with SPIDERMAN and the Superheroes
- MATTEL: with the fascinating brand BARBIE and HOT WHEELS
- SANRIO with the sweet kitten HELLO KITTY (now a bit declining)
- CHARLES M. SCHULZ: with evergreen PEANUTS and SNOOPY
- WARNER BROS: with the TWITTY, SYLVESTER THE CAT, SCOOBY DOO

Trademarks and Brands:

- COCA-COLA, FERRARI CARS, FIAT, PLAYBOY, PIRELLI

Fashion Brands:

- ARMANI, DOLCE E GABBANA, FILA, GUCCI, NAVIGARE, ROBE DI KAPPA, VALENTINO

Sporting Brands and Events:

- Football teams: AC MILAN, INTER, JUVENTUS, NAPOLI, ITALIA NATIONAL TEAM
- Formula 1: FERRARI
- Rugby: ITALIA NATIONAL TEAM, ALL BLACKS (more appropriately a small "PHENOMENON")
- World Soccer Championship, GIRO D'ITALIA (bicycle race) (now a bit declining)
- NBA: LAKERS

15.1.5 Spain[28]

Introduction

Spain went through what could be defined as the strongest consumption and economic crisis of its recent history, between 2009 and 2013. After generating more than 40% of the yearly GDP in the construction business during the first decade of this century, this five-year period has seen a drastic change in the business model of the country and the way people are consuming. In 2014, the construction business used to represent only 10.5% of the yearly GDP!

This strong consumption slowdown, that affected all the economic bases of the country, including obviously the retail and the licensing markets, is now part of the history.

As you can see in the chart below, since January 2015, the Spanish economy is recovering at an average level of 3% per year, the consumption is again back to a positive trend and this is impacting the entire economy. Let's analyze the main aspects of this new situation.

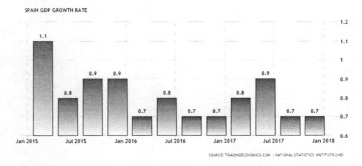

SPAIN GDP GROWTH RATE

SOURCE: TRADINGECONOMICS.COM | NATIONAL STATISTICS INSTITUTE (INE)

With this positive panorama in mind, it is important to also understand the retail landscape of Spain.

The retailer that used to have the most important impact on the entire licensing business, El Corte Inglés (with 84 stores) is still the #1 partner for the entire industry. Nevertheless, this position has been recently threatened by the strong and growing presence of Amazon. Even if the habit of buying online is still quite recent and has experienced one of the slowest introductions in Europe, Spain is now definitely enlisted in the Internet world and more and more customers are buying their products online. Following the latest figures published by NPD, online sales generated 16% of the total toys sold in this country in 2017 vs 36% in countries such as the UK and Germany. This gap implies that the growth margin is still considerable, and all the experts are assuming that Spain will very quickly recover the gap to reach levels equivalent to the rest of the European countries. This new reality is not only affecting El Corte, which, by the way, implemented a very important and aggressive online strategy to match their services to their main competitor.

Carrefour (with 172 centers), the leader, by far, in the hypermarket/supermarket sector is also adapting its strategy and the latest rumors are indicating that not only they will increase their online presence, but they will also focus more and more their effort and energy on the food business.

---

[28] Written by Eric Belloso

Besides those two companies, Toys 'R' Us with 54 stores, that used to be the top toy specialist is, as it is unfortunately happening in the US and in the UK, in a very tricky situation and the very close future will tell whether they will be able to ride out this perfect storm. This new circumstance is obviously affecting the entire licensing business and besides increasing creative model with all the retailers, innovative marketing activities are on the day to day agenda of most local executives to overtake this panorama.

History of Licensing

Like in many countries in the world, Disney and Warner are the precursors of the Spanish licensing business, setting up the rules of the game back in the 70's. Some agencies, such as Promovip and BRB Internacional, began to appear in the 80's either representing third party properties or creating their own IP structure thanks to the creation of local animated series (such as "David the Gnome" or "Dogtanian" in the case of BRB). Since then and most importantly within the last 5 years, the number of agencies evolving in the market has increased dramatically resulting in a situation where, undoubtedly, some of them are having problems to survive.

There are possibly three key recent moments in the history of the Spanish licensing that should be pointed out to understand the current landscape.

The first one is the start-up of the DTT (Digital Terrestrial Television) and the multiplication of TV channels that allowed many more TV-driven products to get into the market. Nowadays, the three FTA kid's channels (Clan TVE, Disney Channel and Boing) are monopolizing the series driven licensing opportunities.

The second one is the elimination of advertisements in the national TV channel TVE. This fact has been fundamental to the introduction of pre-school properties in the market, since previously none of the channels were interested in broadcasting these kinds of products as the audience and rating calculation was only taking into consideration children from 4 years old. With this measure, series such as Caillou, Pocoyó or most recently PEPPA PIG or PAW PATROL, have all enjoyed very successful business stories. If we want to summarize the full FTA context, we could conclude that TVE (Clan) is the specialist in the preschool properties, Disney Channel within 5 – 8 years old girls and Boing into the 5 – 8 years old boys segment.

The third change has been monitored, as everywhere in the world, by the technological revolution with, from one side, the huge penetration of Internet, (YouTube is the fourth most viewed "TV channel" in the country) and, from the other side, the strong presence of Smartphones and tablets that enable the App market to explode. It is estimated that close to 32 million Spaniard (out of a population of 46.5 million people) have some Smartphones, hence the mechanism to reach a very important audience is already in place.

Licensing Today

Spain, like most of European countries, can be defined as an old nation not just through its history but more importantly through its citizens. A look at the population pyramid below shows precisely the demographic problem that the country is and will be facing in the close future.

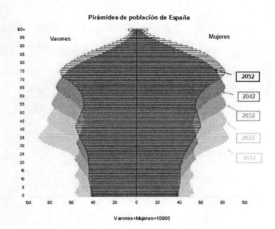

Pirámides de población de España

Varones / Mujeres

2052
2042
2032
2022
2012

Varones+Mujeres=10000

Apart from all the economic and demographical aspects that this pyramid implies, from a licensing standpoint, this chart shows that the young adults are gaining more and more significance with respect to consumer power, hence the importance of sport licensing and fashion brands. This pyramid also assumes that children have a stronger economic power at home. With less and less Spanish families having more than one child, children are considered, in many cases, as the king or queen at home and usually receive more money to spend from their parents. As a result, their power of decision-making inside the family is increasing – a study demonstrated, for instance, that 10% of the cars sold in Spain were bought considering the influence of the children.

This on a licensing perspective means that the number of toys and licensing products that each of them can receive is maintaining the business at reasonable levels. Having said that, the consequences of the above-mentioned fact are also that the market is not increasing at very high level and in 2017, sourcing NPD, the market grew only 0.2%.

Another aspect to take into consideration when analyzing the Spanish reality is the acquisition power of consumers. Below is a chart that shows the salary variation by regions.

SALARIO MEDIO POR COMUNIDAD AUTÓNOMA
Datos en euros para 2016

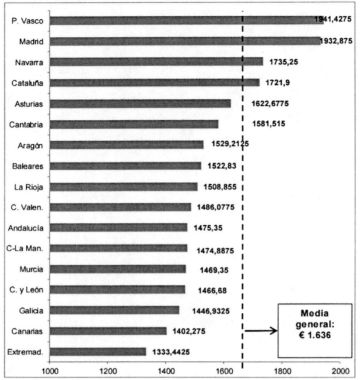

Fuente: Adecco/Barceló & asociados sobre la base de INE

The average monthly gross salary in Spain is estimated at €1,636. However, the latest studies also show that 1 out of 3 Spaniards are what is called "mileurista" (they earn €1,000€ a month). This basically means that to create a licensing mass market phenomenon, the consumer price of any licensed product is another variable to be considered very carefully.

Focusing more precisely on the Spanish licensing market and taking into consideration all the elements mentioned so far, the following trends are evident in the Spanish marketplace in 2018:

- Disney properties are everywhere, and they are still the #1 licensor in the market however the former domination is over and the distance between the mouse company and their competitor is shrinking.

- Preschool properties are growing their presence and the space on shelves is increasing year after year. This situation is favoring companies such as Nickelodeon and E-one with their properties PAW PATROL, BLAZE or SHIMMER & SHINE from one side and PEPPA PIG and PJ MASK from the other.

- Sports licensing, and more concretely football (soccer in the US) with the brands of REAL MADRID and BARCELONA FC are solidifying their dominant positions in the market. As their target audience is young adults, they can afford to position their products with a higher price point in the market.

- Properties based on Internet /App-driven content, such as ANGRY BIRDS, used to be strong a couple of years ago and are currently suffering the multiplication of products available and the lack of a property that outstands.

- Other strong properties include the major fashion brands (ARMANI, RALPH LAUREN, TOMMY HILFIGER) and their licensed products in the high-end area.

- Cinema licensing with properties such as SPIDERMAN, DESPICABLE ME or classics such as STAR WARS can also be bought in many of the shops although as it happened in the rest of the European countries, 2017 has not been a year to be remembered.

- Even if Spain has always been a great incubator of artistic talent, internationally the result has never been significantly recognized. Companies such as Inditex (Zara) or Mango are the only visible tip of the iceberg and this circumstance is also true within the licensing world. The most famous Spanish properties that have seen some licensing success abroad are POCOYÓ (from Zinkia), CHUPA CHUPS (the famous lollipop brand), MOTO GP (worldwide motorbike championship) and obviously the above-mentioned REAL MADRID and BARCELONA FC on the sport licensing side.

Even with strong internal competition, the licensing Spanish market has always been eager to embrace US and UK properties, which are usually very well-perceived by the consumer and seen as aspirational. Introducing a product line in Spain that has been successful in one of those two countries gives any property a competitive advantage in the market in front of buyers (either from TV channels or from the retail).

Spain still has one of the highest European rates of sales from licensed products vs. non-licensed despite facing a complicated 2017 that saw an important decline vs 2016 due to the lack of new properties and the introduction of new generic products based on unicorns or rainbows that are substituting some former licensed dedicated shelves.

> **Spain has one of the highest rates of sales of licensed products versus non-licensed products in all of Europe.**

Another specific characteristic to be taken into consideration when considering operating in the Spanish licensing universe is that brands usually do not last generally forever, and this market is recognized as a good example of brand burner. Very few brands have a long-term support from either retailers or consumers.

Analyzing the market from the beginning of this century, the result is that Pokémon was the top property in the market from 2000 to 2002. Then "Los lunnies", a local pre-school show launched in 2003 by TVE, was the retail reference for another two years. From 2006 SPONGEBOB SQUAREPANTS was the reference in the kid's market, together with POCOYO in the pre-school target. CAILLOU became the reference in this segment from 2008. PAPITO FEO made a huge penetration into the girl segment back in 2009. All of them lasted two or three years in the market. PEPPA PIG together with STAR WARS took the lead from 2013 and PAW PATROL became the big reference in 2015 and 2016. With the current lack of new references, the future will tell us whether the current properties will last.

There are no official figures related to the value of the licensing market in Spain, nevertheless some studies show that we might be talking about a business rounding €500 million in retail sales yearly. This evaluation is made taking into consideration an estimated €200 million market (retail sales) in the licensed toy business and considering that the clothing, shoes, food, publishing and accessories sectors together, should represent close to 60% of the overall market. In the same order, there are no official figures related to the importance of the licensing business by category, but we could easily consider that entertainment (covering TV series, cinema and new technology-related products) should correspond to 60% of the market, followed by sports licensing with another 15% and the remaining quarter should be covered by categories such as brands, fashion, music and art. As mentioned before, this result is purely empirical and based on the presence of those categories within the main retailers.

Once the decision to exploit a brand in Spain is made, any licensor will quickly notice that professionalism in this market is another unbreakable characteristic. Such a complex market has dramatically increased the expertise of most of the players, and all of them are used to work with complicated rules where brand building exercises and finding the best moment to launch a product are key elements. Besides Disney, Nickelodeon, Universal and Warner, there are also many licensing agencies working in this territory. Biplano, CPLG, El Ocho and Planeta Junior might be considered as the biggest ones. And then, there are several boutique licensing companies such as Enjoy Brand Licensing, Selecta Vision, Arait Multimedia, Edebé, Luk Internacional, Mendía Licensing and Notorious Brand & People that are taking parts of the pie with some dedicated brands.

Most of the latest successes in the market have been managed by local companies/structure that do know the specificities of the market that in summary relies on the element mentioned in the previous paragraph: finding the best platform, the best engaging tools, the best moment to launch the products on shelves and the best retailers to work with. Being in constant contact with the market, either through the retail, study markets or analyzing audience and shares on TV is vital to get into this market.

Finally, when considering travelling over to Spain, bear in mind that most Spaniards are social people. Having lunch or dinner with your counterpart is very common, and you can find yourself either in a great trendy or classic restaurant or eating standing up in front of a bar facing a variety of very appetizing tapas. Another thing to take into consideration is that lunch and/or dinner are later than in other countries. Lunch habitually begins from 1:30pm to 3pm and dinner generally begins from 9pm to 10pm. Having wine is also quite normal, moreover during the dinner.

Conclusions

The licensing market in Spain will be, without any doubt, more and more influenced by the content driven through the new devices (mobile phones, tablets, etc.). Whether we are talking about pre-school, kids, young adults or adult properties, most of the population is influenced by those new instruments. Being able to control the content and the broadcasting (ideally through various platforms) is a key element when considering developing new licensing programs in this country. The competition is high and shelf space is limited, hence the necessity to create a plan that must be different and easily recognizable by the market.

Licensed properties will always have a place in the Spanish market and in the consumer's mind, the differentiation made by a well-known IP will always add value to any products and this is a reality known by all the players of this market. This is a great country to work with and once the rules of the games are understood, the opportunity is around the corner. Don't miss it!!

15.1.6 United Kingdom[29]

Introduction

The United Kingdom has a population of some sixty-five million people and ranks as the world's sixth largest economy as measured by GDP. LIMA's annual Global Survey reveals that the UK is the second largest market for licensed merchandise in the world today, after the United States and ahead of Japan. Although it still accounts for almost 10% of the UK economy, manufacturing is no longer a dominant sector. Indeed, the service sector, which includes retail, is officially estimated to account for almost three-quarters of UK economic output. As a strong retail sector is vital for the sale of consumer goods, a category which includes most of the licensed merchandise, the UK's retail strength no doubt contributes to the relatively large size of the licensing business here.

History of Licensing

The UK was a relatively early adopter of licensing with notable early successes from the late 1950s onwards, and so has had more than sixty years for the business to grow. LIMA's own database lists more than 600 licensors/licensing agents in the UK, compared to just over 100 in Germany, and around 50 in each of Italy and France, the other major European economies. Numbers of licensees are in similar proportions. With such a large licensing infrastructure, resulting in significant competition for the buying and selling of licensing rights, it's not surprising to find that the UK punches above its weight in the licensing sector compared to the economy.

The UK also has a history of staging dedicated licensing conferences, seminars and exhibitions dating back to the 1980s. London's *Lancaster Hotel* has a history here, having hosted licensing trade shows on behalf of various organizers on many occasions throughout this period. The current leading trade exhibition, *Brand Licensing Europe* has been an annual October event in London since 1999 and has established itself as a large and significant international licensing trade show, second only in the world to *Licensing Expo* in Las Vegas. Similarly, licensing awards events have featured here for over thirty years, staged by diverse organizations including *The Licensing Book, A4 Publications, LIMA* itself, and currently *Max Publishing*.

> The UK has about six times more licensors and licensing agents than Germany with a similar number of licensees

With an established licensing infrastructure, an identifiable licensing business community, an increasing understanding among business as a whole of the value of intellectual property and a vibrant creative and media landscape, the UK is well positioned to continue to be a major international center for the licensing business.

---

[29] Written by *Kelvyn Gardner, MD, LIMA-UK*

Licensing Today

The UK population today stands at just over 65 million. The UK is split in age terms as follows (source: Office of National Statistics):

Population of the United Kingdom in 2016, by age group

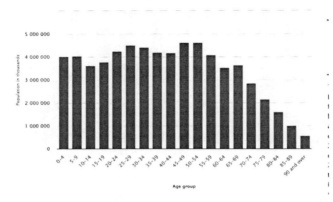

This data shows that over eleven million children age 0-14 currently live in the UK, with a gender split of roughly equal proportions. Children have historically been the most important market in the UK for licensed merchandise. Whilst we have no reason to predict that this is likely to change, there is a growing interest in licensing among older age groups, from "traditional" areas like music and films, but also from the growth in App-based licensing (like ANGRY BIRDS) and sports and sports stars (like DAVID BECKHAM) and reality TV personalities such as FERNE MCCANN and BLAC CHYNA. Additionally, family drama and factual TV series with most adult viewers, such as *Downtown Abbey, Game of Thrones*, and *The Only Way is Essex* have also broken through into licensing of appropriate consumer goods. I believe that we can regard this as a sign of a maturing UK market, where a thirty-something can enjoy a product based on a popular TV show without embarrassment, or association with "childish" undertones.

Licensing for "grown-ups" has also popped up in merchandise categories not normally associated with licensing. Two notable examples are audio headphones and spectacle frames, the latter generally referred to as "eyewear". Until very recently, headphones have been the preserve of established audio/hi-fi brands like Sony and Sennheiser. During 2012, the share of the UK headphones market taken by licensed brands grew from 11% of the market at the start of the year to almost 34% by the end of 2012 (source: GFK). Many of these licensed brands are music celebrities, and there is evidence that some consumers now own multiple sets of headphones as fashion items, but the growth of the licensed sector is remarkable nonetheless. In eyewear, the UK market has seen a sea-change from twenty years ago when there was virtually no licensed eyewear (often erroneously described as "designer eyewear") to 2018 with many products available in typical high-street optician's stores bearing licensed brands. According to GFK, over 16 major brands (and many other smaller ones) moved into the licensed eyewear market in the UK in the last ten years.

The UK population is growing, which should be good news for licensing. However, like all major western markets media outlets have multiplied exponentially over the last ten years. For children alone, there are now more than twenty TV channels dedicated to junior programs. *YouTube* is also very much the 'TV channel of choice' for many children. Whilst this encourages diversity, it makes it all the harder for any one property to "cut through" in genuine mass popularity. The arrival also of SVOD TV services such as the *BBC's iPlayer* and the two US giants *Netflix* and *Amazon Prime* has also deprived us of many "water cooler" moments as Americans call them, further reducing the "live" TV audience for any one broadcast. The market for films, too, is much more competitive than it was a decade ago. The popularity of the DVD format, especially for gifting, has squeezed the timing of big Hollywood film launches into May-August for cinema release, to facilitate a DVD launch in October-December, the prime gifting season. Consequently, many licensees turned away from films as too risky.

In the last few years films licensing has enjoyed something of a revival on the back of block-busters such as STAR WARS, the DESPICABLE ME franchise, FROZEN and the MARVEL Studios output. However, long gone are the days when the summer blockbuster would be just that: one, single, summer movie that seemingly everyone would go to see. Indeed, if we go back as far as the early 1990s it was not unusual for UK licensing businesses to have the luxury of observing the domestic box-office returns of a film released in the USA months before the planned UK release, giving them a chance to buy into a proven success

Over and above traditional media, the growth of firstly the Internet and then smart phone and tablet technology has provided for the first time an alternative universe in which brands can become prominent, attract mass audiences and strong consumer followings, and then, as a natural consequence, move into licensed merchandise. We should not underestimate how significant this is. Previously, major retailers would, outside of niche markets, limit licensed merchandise ranges to those emanating from either the TV or the movie screen. Now, web-based properties have proved that it is the new multi-media screens of iPads and other tablets, smart phones, lightweight laptops and good-old PCs that are becoming the source of powerful consumer interest.

The biggest successes in the UK market to date have been MOSHI MONSTERS from Mind Candy, and ANGRY BIRDS from Finnish company Rovio. Each has distinctively different roots, the former a Web-based platform providing an online virtual community for children 4-10, the latter an App for smart phones and tablets with a wide-demographic appeal right up to young adults. Both brands are in a mature phase and no longer the 'hot properties' they once were. However, the recently-coined term "convergence" applies to each, with TV and movie output from both in recent years. It is also notable that licensing from video games, notably *Skylanders* a few years ago and *Call of Duty* more recently, has grown exponentially in the last decade.

In 2018, the major properties that are being licensing in the UK include PEPPA PIG, Disney (especially FROZEN), MARVEL, STAR WARS, POKÉMON, LOL SURPRISE, PAW PATROL, PJ MASKS. PADDINGTON BEAR and SHOPKINS. The major licensors in the UK include BBC Worldwide, Nickelodeon, Entertainment One, Disney, CPLG, MGA and Moose Major licensees include TDP Aykroyds (apparel), Vivid Imaginations (Toys), Penguin Books, Egmont (publishing), Topps Europe and Panini (trading cards and stickers), Blues Clothing, Fashion UK, Finsbury Food Group, Kinnerton confectionery, Wild & Wolf (gifts), Blueprint Designs (stationery and bags), Danilo (calendars and cards), GB Eye (posters), Pyramid Designs, Smiffy's (dress-up) and Character World (bedding).

The major retailers here include the "Big Four" supermarkets: Tesco, Sainsbury's, Asda and Morrisons; WH Smith; Argos; Boots; The Entertainer; Marks & Spencer; New Look; Primark; Debenhams; and John Lewis. It should also be noted that the online retail environment is very strong, with Amazon, Play.com, The Hut, ASOS and others making significant sales.

A major conceptual challenge for foreign licensors entering the UK market is the EU regulation on free trade. In short, with rare exceptions the "common market" that is the European Union has no trading boundaries between the member states. Indeed, seeking to impose such boundaries is a serious breach of EU (and thus UK) law. In practice, this means that it is not possible to grant a license for any specific EU country on a single-territory basis. If you license the toy rights for the UK, your licensee has the right under EU law to sell his licensed goods in all countries of the EU. This law applies to all EU states, not just the UK, but is often encountered here first by American licensors entering the European market via the traditional UK gateway. Local lawyers have tried to devise language to provide some limitations on this very broad-brush regulation, but many licensors no longer seek ways around it, since a breach can lead to a fine of ten percent of the offenders' worldwide turnover. As this is written, the UK is in the middle of the process of leaving the EU (a process colloquially known as Brexit) and there could be many changes to this scenario over the next two-three years depending on the final agreement between EU and UK.

> Since the European Union has no trading boundaries between member states, a licensee in one EU country can sell in all EU countries.

As stated in the introduction, the UK has a large and well-established community of licensing agencies able to represent indigenous and foreign licensing properties to the UK market. It's also the case that many non-UK domiciled licensing businesses (Nickelodeon, for example) will set up their European or even EMEA (Europe, Middle East, Africa) offices in London. Several UK-founded licensing agencies have grown over the years to become pan-European and even more international, and companies like The Licensing Company (which recently became part of CAA-CBG) and CPLG (Copyright Promotions Licensing Group) are the biggest licensing agencies outside the USA, and even in the world. An IP owner looking for UK representation will find a wide choice of potential partners, from boutique agencies employing two or three staff, right up to these large firms, all skilled and experienced in the field.

Licensing consultants, often referred to as manufacturers' reps in the USA, are fewer on the ground. There are half-a-dozen serious operators in this field in the UK, several of whom have been running successful consultancies for more than a decade. Their services can be invaluable to new manufacturers seeking to enter the licensing market but unfamiliar with the processes and costs involved, and, longer term, to manufacturers who don't wish to employ full-time licensing staff with the consequent overhead cost.

The UK retail scene is dominated by many chain stores in every sector: supermarkets, pharmacies, toys stores, fashion retailers, department stores and gift stores. This infrastructure is, overall, beneficial to the effective distribution of licensed merchandise nationwide. These chain retailers are sophisticated businesses able to implement the latest marketing, loyalty and "in-store theatre" techniques to win sales from consumers, so are good partners for innovative licensing companies at agency or licensee level. Many successful partnerships have been forged between licensing and UK retail which have brought great success.

The downside to this structure is that the power balance between retailers and the licensing business can often shift uncomfortably in favor of the former. This can put undue pressure for special terms and high margins on the supply side of this balance. Indeed, the growth of Direct-to-Retail (DTR) license agreements is an example of this. DTR agreements are formed between a licensor/agent and a retailer with no licensee; the retailer is free to source the product from any supplier. There are benefits to DTR deals on occasion, especially to get business moving in a slow market, but, overall, the licensing business prefers the agent/licensee/retail model. Additionally, many UK "high-streets" and shopping centers (malls) have an identical look which is hurting diversity and squeezing out innovative new retailers as rents are often set at a level that only the national chains can afford. At the time of writing this chapter, the UK economy has slipped back in world rankings largely because of inflationary pressures and business uncertainty caused by Brexit and a weakening in the value of the £pound Sterling. This climate has squeezed all retailers large and small, obliging them to discount prices more than usual, which, in turn, have hurt margins for licensees, but not solved the issue, with several retail chains closing in 2018 alone, including Toys "R" Us and Maplins, a consumer electronics business.

15.1.7 The Nordic Region[30]

Introduction

The first thing that people come to think of when thinking about the Nordic region is most probably tall blonde, good-looking people, the excellent welfare system, snow as far as the eye can see and, of course brands, like H&M, VOLVO & IKEA. However, the Nordic is a small and complex area consisting of 5 different countries, languages, currencies and even cultures, all split between around 25 million people. So, doing business in the licensing industry requires an understanding of the preferences of the Nordic consumers and what characterizes each country.

Sweden
Population: 10 million
Language: Swedish
Currency: Swedish Krona

The largest country and is considered the most important market for licensing in the Nordics since the big chunk of consumers are here. Big shopping malls are popping up everywhere and e-commerce is booming. Swedes are known to be trend-sensitive and Sweden is often used as a "first trial" country for consumer products prior to launch. Paradoxically, Swedes are the careful ones, and nothing is being executed until all have their say and this often leads to delayed decisions and initiatives.

Finland
Population: 5.5 million
Language: Finnish

---

[30] Written by Fuad Khan

Currency: Euro

The only country that is a member of the Eurozone which connects Finland to the European Trade market stronger. Even though the population is small, Finland is nowadays the Nordic hub for tech business. Here we find companies such as Supercell, Rovio and Nokia which have put the tech savvy Finns on the map. Finnish people are very productive, disciplined and ambitious. The closeness to the Baltics and Russia, has made it natural for several retailers and companies to focus their expansion to the east rather than toward the rest of the Nordic.

Norway
Population: 5 million
Language: Norwegian
Currency: Norwegian Krona

Norway is a gap for the licensed market and the one reason could be that Norway is the only country in the Nordic that is not a member of the European Union. This means that, for example, a Swedish licensee it is a little complicated to sell their products into Norway with added taxes etc. Since sales number of licensed products in Norway has been small, licensing agents with big international brands often overlook this market. However, this has created a strong market for local Norwegian brands to arise and work with Norwegian licensees.

Denmark
Population: 5.5 million
Language: Danish
Currency: Danish Krona

If Sweden has the most consumers, Denmark has the most companies working with licensing. The Danes are very business minded and have a continental way of executing ideas. This has resulted that Denmark could be considered a hub for licensees, especially when it comes to textiles and toys. The competition is strong, and the licensees are picky since all licensors want to get into business with these licensees.

Iceland
Population of 300,000
Language: Icelandic
Currency: Icelandic Krona

The often-forgotten island that gave us LAZYTOWN is also included in the Nordic. I will however, not go further into details regarding this country due to its small size and population. Sorry Iceland!

The Nordic region, except for Iceland, has been a stable territory even during the financial crisis if you compare to other regions in the world. The category that was hit the hardest is the textiles industry that is still suffering. Due to turbulence, the number of independent stores has been decreasing and today the same stores in shopping malls around the region is a common sight. The big retail chains are the ones that survive and thus a similar offering everywhere.

History of Licensing

Licensing is still a in an early phase in comparison to other territories like the US and the UK. The market began to grow in the early 1980's and most of today's licensing companies / agencies started their licensing business in the Nordic by sealing their first deals with brands like JAMES BOND, PINK PANTHER, STAR WARS, TOM & JERRY, MOOMIN and PEANUTS.

The current hot brands among children and tweens are LEGO, MY LITTLE PONY, PAW PATROL and of course the Disney brands including MARVEL and STAR WARS.

Disney had been the pioneer for consumer products in the region and really establishing the Disney IPs as if they were a part of the Nordic culture even earlier from their Danish office. Their ability to control and steer the supply chain from production to end-product at retail has proven to be a key to success which I will describe later in this chapter.

At this time, the TV rights was a good business since the agents and content owners made money from selling the rights to broadcasters. This soon changed into TV stations not having to pay little or no money because of the increasing supply of quality content from increasing number of producers.

Label slapping onto products was a common sight and the licensees were hoping too much that the brand themselves would bear the whole product. This proved of course to be a bad tactic since the people in the Nordic are used to high quality products.

Licensing Today

As the market changed according to what the Nordic customer wanted, the quality increased. This made licensed products widely accepted and you can find licensed products across most categories. The licensees have understood the importance of delivering quality products to retailers to have a high sell-through ratio. This is true especially when it comes to fashion retailers where design and trend are important factors. In fact, one common thing for the whole region is the minimalistic "Scandinavian" design theme which is now influencing the designs of the consumer products across all categories.

The main target groups are children, tweens, teenagers and young adults who are consuming the popular culture, toys and games daily. This target group is also being exposed the most for all sorts of brands which have made them very picky and hard to get. E-commerce is booming and acts as a platform for licensed products from outside the Nordic region.

The current hot brands among children and tweens are LEGO, MY LITTLE PONY, PAW PATROL and of course the Disney brands including MARVEL and STAR WARS.

The landscape of content creation and marketing is changing and with channels like YouTube, Netflix and Instagram, there are more ways to establish a brand and disrupting the classic licensing model.

E-commerce offers easy access to consumers for new products and brands which gives traditional retail a tough challenge as well as licensors to take control over the consumers behavior. A perfect example is Swedish brand DANIEL WELLINGTON that made itself a strong brand name for watches in just 5 years' time with yearly sales of over USD $250 million. Through e-commerce, Instagram influencers and the power of social media, the brand is strong enough today to expand beyond watches.

Lifestyle brands have learned from the US counterparts like RALPH LAUREN and CALVIN KLEIN that brand building through licensing and co-brandings can be successful. GANT and Lexington Company are two players in the market who have grown their business by extending the brands to other categories such as perfumes, sunglasses, home textiles, watches etc. These kinds of brands are not considered "licensed" as with the character licensed products since the brands communicate more solid values like quality, price and status. These are the values that the Nordic consumers seek when buying a product and this have not changed for decades. Occasionally the consumer buys an ANGRY BIRDS T-shirt or a HELLO KITTY mug to their child, but they rather save their money to buy the more expensive GANT T-shirt. So, a key to success among the consumers is to capture these values.

The food and beverage category are on the rise for licensed products and here it is even more important to design and craft the products, so they gain confidence among consumers. They might buy a licensed dairy product buy will not do a re-purchase if the quality is bad which in turn will hurt the brand itself. Parents are cautious when buying branded cookies for their children because it might be poor quality and unhealthy. In this case, it might help to co-operate together with a well-known manufacturer and co-brand it with your brand. This could win the hearts of both the parents and of course the children who want their funny looking cookies.

One should be aware of the restricted laws surrounding the marketing towards children in the Nordics. Direct promotions are in some of the countries forbidden so it makes it more difficult for brand owners to engage the consumers through competitions in-store etc. Today for example, you only see toy commercials on the networks that are broadcasting from outside the Nordic. Other than that, it is an inviting territory with a typical Western business culture and everybody speaks English.

Among the licensors, there are a few who has a physical presence in the Nordics like Disney, Electrolux Group and ROVIO. Most other licensors are utilizing the handful of agents / consultants that are spread around the Nordic. As a brand owner, one must realize that the competition is very tough in the Nordics. It seldom matters if a TV series has good ratings or a movie is backed up with a huge promotion budget.

Today it's all about the big picture. With recent acquisitions, Disney is the consumer products powerhouse that has really refined the ability to promote and license a property. By owning evergreen brands like the MARVEL universe, STAR WARS and soon FOX, there seem to be no stopping in the expansion of the Disney experience, both at retail and TV/Cinema.

Outlook, Projections and Conclusions

So, after this crash course on how the licensing business works in the Nordics today, what do we see happening in the near future?

In today's fast-paced and information savvy world, where news becomes old news as soon as it reaches a certain number of tweets or shares on Facebook - how will something stick around long enough to grow and be an evergreen brand applied on products?

For one, brand owners will really have to be realistic about their goals for the short- and long term. Some things are just meant to be hypes and short-term opportunities and it is a challenge the brand owner must overcome to be able to supply the short-term demand among consumers. The standard two-year contract with 3 months contract approval time with the 1-2 months product development time on top of it just will not make it. Instead, go for securing good relationships with retailers, especially e-commerce, and have manu-facturers/licensees ready to respond to the next hype so that the product can be in place within weeks. Especially within fast fashion, where retailers like ZARA sometimes can get a product in store just within two weeks from the drawing table, just shows how fast a retail giant must be to deliver the latest trends and fashion. So, think of umbrella contracts with the partners you need to secure the possibility to deliver. Give your partners with the opportunity to work with your brands both long- and short term.

E-commerce is exploding with double digit growth every year. It's important that licensees handle the larger e-commerce stores like a regular retailer and it will not take much time until licensors are making direct to retail deals with a specific e-commerce partner on a regular basis. In the US, Amazon has become such as powerful e-commerce platform that they are now launching their own brands in fashion, food and beauty. This trend is likely to happen in the Nordic too in search for profit margins once they achieved enough turnover.

The Nordic market is not expected to grow dramatically in population size due to low birth rate but the willingness towards buying more branded products do have the potential to grow. The challenge for brand owners is to define what makes your brand worth buying into. Is it because its affordable, luxurious, innovative? Or is it to simplify your consumers everyday life? By developing the brand into an experience, the brand owner can expand beyond the core products which will give its consumers something to crave for and retail something to sell.

15.1.8 Turkey[31]

Introduction

Turkey has been a crossroad for civilizations for centuries. When a European merchant vis-ited Eastern Asia, they had to go through Anatolia. When Eastern silk traders wanted to sell their properties, they had to use the Silk Road, which is a series of trade and cultural transmission routes that were central to cultural interaction through regions of the Asian continent connecting the West and East by linking traders, merchants, pilgrims, monks, soldiers, nomads and urban dwellers from China to the Mediterranean Sea during various periods of time.

The information contained in this chapter is based upon estimated retail sales of licensed products, for the period ending December 31, 2012, with all channels of distribution re-ported in Turkey. The conclusions were amassed through statistical and analytical reports, plus my research conducted throughout the years, via discussions with licensors, licensees, licensing consultants and agents. Retail distribution channels include domestic retail chains and international counterparts: department stores, mid-tier stores, specialty/niche

---

[31] Written by Hakan Tungaç

stores), mass merchants, supermarket independents and chains, and Internet and TV shopping.

The licensing sector is rapidly growing in Turkey. Manufacturers of licensed products are using the power of the brand and character to sell products. While helping brand owners increase their brand awareness, licensing increases volume of sales, allowing manufacturers to surpass their opponents in this competitive trade arena. It is not easy for Turkish companies to achieve the success levels that some American and European companies with thirty-year licensing histories have reached, but at the same time, with the right licensing tool and the right licensing strategies in this global world, the sky is the limit.

History of Licensing

In the late 1980s, Turkey embraced the open-market economics principal. In the open-market economy, the government is taking a largely hands-off approach to common transactions. Buyers and sellers enter into agreements with each other for their own mutual benefit and are free to set prices and terms of sale as they see fit. As a result, brands like COCA COLA, PEPSI, and Disney have been introduced to Turkish consumers. Up until that moment, people used to drink "Ayran", a drink made of yogurt, but the globalization and free market allowed exposure to new drinks, new clothing, new cartoons and new fashion.

By the 1990s, Turkish consumers began wanting everything they saw on TV. Women wanted to have the pocketbook they saw ELIZABETH TAYLOR carry, and men wanted to wear the jeans that Michael Knight wore on the KNIGHT RIDER series. Kids loved the Disney characters of MICKEY MOUSE and MINNIE MOUSE, and so parents were compelled to buy character-licensed toys, books, T-shirts and pajamas. Where there is demand, it had to be supplied.

Beginning in the late 1990s, many companies positioned themselves to import these branded items into Turkey. Turkey at that time did not have many factories in the private sector. The government used to own all the factories; therefore, importing those products played a vital role in the early years of licensing in Turkey.

Even though the collapse of the Asian market affected the Turkish economy, the markets in Turkey's emerging economy kept growing steadily. Since the beginning of the new millennium, with the help of a one-party ruling instead of coalition-style government, the economy grew even more. The purchasing power of every household in Turkey rose to levels where people started to buy many things they wanted before. Since there now was a demand for licensed products supported with purchasing power, Turkish manufacturing companies decided to produce them by themselves instead of importing them. Thus, began an age of license agreements with property owners from the west with manufacturers producing merchandise in Turkey.

Licensing agencies became popular in the early decade of the new millennium. Agencies like Kaynak Licensing Company, who represent the biggest brands, i.e., publishing houses, authors, characters, film/TV, music, video games, and software, provide full service and specialize in the licensing of entertainment, corporate, and lifestyle properties, developing a broad range of compatible products on behalf of their clients. These agencies played a very important role by providing licensing assistance to their clients, while aiming to have closer partnerships with the property owners all around the world.

Licensing Today

According to the LIMA Industry Survey, retail sales of licensed merchandise was more than $250 billion in 2016. The regions showing the largest annual rise in retail sales of licensed goods were the still-emerging areas of Central and Eastern Europe.

As expected, the so-called BRIC countries (Brazil, Russia, India and China) all ranked among the top 10 as measured by their rates of growth in retail sales of licensed merchandise. Collectively, these four territories registered an increase in retail sales of licensed goods of about 8%, far above the global growth rate. Some economic analysts are starting to refer to the world's fastest-emerging economies together as the BRICT block, adding Turkey to the other four. With a 6.9% increase in retail sales of licensed goods, Turkey joined the others in the global top ten as measured by licensing growth for the first-time last year. Turkey is a rising economic giant in this region, and Istanbul has the potential to open Turkey to the world.

Although licensed merchandise in all areas is gradually gaining ground, the fast-moving consumer products (FMCG) market is growing and experiencing expansion like never before. There have been initiatives in this regard from big names like Nickelodeon, who has different license agreements (in Turkey) with individual brands. Danone fruit juices, the flagship fruit juice brand from Danone and one of Turkey's leading FMCG companies headquartered in France, recently announced a tie-in with Disney Consumer Products under which Danone will use the image of Disney's most beloved characters, such as THE CARS characters, to adorn the Danone juices and nectars packs. These kinds of relationships with Disney or any admired brand help encourage healthy eating choices and lifestyles among Turkish kids and families. With Disney's most beloved characters on fruit juice packs, it has created a whole new experience and excitement for kids.

From a worldwide perspective, it is evident that rapidly increasing buying power and investment demands from the Middle East, the Balkans and Western European countries in conjunction with the increasing number of retail chain stores in Turkey have increased the market share of fast-moving consumer goods. The resultant increase in the number of local and international retail chains and the investments of these channels contribute in a big way to improving the quality and the competition in the FMCG sector. However, international companies eager to make headway into countries like Turkey must deal with a lack of understanding on the part of the consumer regarding the concept of intellectual property rights, which needs to be addressed to the Turkish audience in detail.

The licensing of entertainment and fashion properties is also growing in Turkey. The extensive use of communication devices, such as TV and handheld electronic devices, is making people, including kids, more involved in the world's culture. Turkish kids are also watching SPONGE BOB SQUARE PANTS when they wake up in the morning, and little girls dream of being one of Disney's FAIRIES, or little boys want to have cars like the ones they see in Disney's CARS. On the other hand, their parents are eager to buy the NEW BALANCE sneakers that Steve Jobs used to wear, or they want

> BARBIE, Disney Characters, SPONGE BOB, SMURFS, DORA, WINNIE THE POOH and NILOYA are the most popular entertainment properties in Turkey.

to dress like their favorite celebrities who just walked the red carpet. BARBIE, the Disney

Characters, SPONGE BOB, SMURFS, DORA, WINNIE THE POOH and NILOYA are the most popular entertainment properties in Turkey. ADIDAS, CALVIN KLEIN, DIESEL, LACOSTE, LEVI'S, NIKE, PUMA, TOMMY HILFIGER and ZARA are among the major fashion brands in the Turkish territory.

Turkish Properties

Until 2014, Turkey had never exported or become famous for its animations. Then "NI-LOYA" happened. NILOYA is a top-rated vibrant and upbeat TV series, aimed at girls and boys ages 3 to 8 years. Produced by Bee & Bird Animations, the series centers on NILOYA, a little girl with a taste for adventure, and a cast of equally lovable characters such as Tospik, Mert, Murat and her family. It broadcasts on Yumurcak TV, one of the top two children's television stations in Turkey.

Title: NILOYA
Production Year: 2013 – 2014
Duration: 5 minutes per episode
Number of Episodes Per Season: 26
Original Language: Turkish
Age Group: for 3 to 8-year old's
Genre: 3D Animation
Gender Orientation: Girls & Boys
Scripts: Turkish & English Scripts are available

MAVI JEANS is another well-known property originating from Turkey. MAVI JEANS is a brand of denim jeans founded in 1991, headquartered in Istanbul, Turkey. The company manufactures jeans for both women and men, targeting a younger age group. Mavi has flagship stores in New York, Vancouver, Istanbul, Berlin and Frankfurt.

Another well know property from Turkey is BEKO. BEKO is a domestic appliance and consumer electronics brand of Arçelik A.Ş. controlled by Koç Holding. BEKO is the official sponsor of the Turkish, German, Italian and Lithuanian premier basketball leagues as well as Aris Salonika football team in Greece.

Conducting Business in Turkey

With its 79 million people, Turkey has a dynamic economy. With its privately-owned companies, the Turkish entrepreneurs try to reach to as many customers as possible not only in Turkey, but also in the world. Of course, when we talk about the licensors and licensees from this region, it will be helpful to analyze them with respect to the property types.

Property Type	Major Licensors
Paper Products, School Supplies	NILOYA, Can
Character (Entertainment, TV, Movie)	NILOYA, Can
Apparel	Benetton
Fashion	MAVI JEANS
Music	Serdar Ortaç
Non-profit (Museum, Charities)	Hagia Sophia

Sports (Leagues, Individuals)	Fenerbahçe, Beşiktaş, Galatasaray
Trademarks/Brands	LC Waikiki
Publishing	Kaynak Publishing Group

Property Type	Major Licensees
Paper Products, School Supplies	Alfa Stationery
Character (Entertainment, TV, Movie)	PAL Toys, Acun Media
Apparel	LC Waikiki
Fashion	Aydınlı
Home Decor	İstikbal Furniture
Food & Beverage	Ülker, Saray
Sports (Leagues, Individuals)	Neco Toys
Trademarks/Brands	KLC, Aydınlı
Publishing	Zambak Publishing, Sürat Publishing, Timaş

The retail sector in Turkey is maintaining momentum thanks to increasing per capita disposable income, coupled with an ever-growing consumer appetite. The per capita disposable income of US$ 7,745 in 2012 is expected to exceed US $11,300 by 2017. Despite a weakening of the TL compared to major currencies in the last couple of years, robust consumer confidence promotes the overall activity in the sector. Still underpenetrated compared to developed countries, organized retailing in Turkey is developing at a fast pace thanks to nationwide shopping mall investments and the aggressive expansion strategies followed by retail groups. It is estimated that the share of organized retailers in the total retail market, which was around 30% ten years ago, exceeded 40% in 2012. [32]

The size of the licensing industry is about $278 million as of today. Just like in the United States or other major countries in the licensing industry, the licensed product sales for characters, entertainment, TV and the movie industry surpasses all other sales of licensed products. Respectively, Corporate Brands, Fashion and Sports sales follows in product sales.

---

[32] Deloitte Sales Report. http://www.deloitte.com/assets/Dcom-Tukey/Local%20Assets/Documents/Retail_Sector_Update_2013.pdf

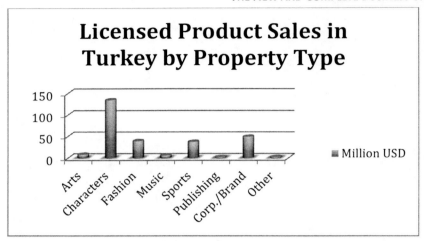

Licensed Product Sales in Turkey by Property Type

In Turkey, the negotiation process may take longer than usual. Turkish business people do not like to be put under pressure and do not like deadlines. Therefore, any attempt to hurry the process will only produce negative results. Being patient is an asset when negotiating with Turkish counterparts. In addition, the financial benefits are not the only aspects of the negotiating process that should be stressed; power, influence, honor, respect are non-financial incentives that will also influence the business decision in Turkey. There are still many family run businesses in Turkey, although there are many big multinationals where a more corporate culture is visible. Turks want to do business with those they trust, feel comfortable with and those who can provide a long-term relationship.

Turkish business people believe that the principal strength of an agreement is in the partners' commitment rather than the actual documentation. Nevertheless, the agreement may be lengthy and detailed. It is recommended to have a local legal expert review the agreement before signing the contract. However, it is not recommended to bring your legal representative to the negotiation table, as it could be taken as a sign of distrust.

The sheer number of properties coming into the market means it's more difficult to cut through them. The fierce competition in the market is one of the biggest challenges for a licensing professional. Even though it is getting better every year, the battle with counterfeit products is still an issue in Turkey. Therefore, a licensing professional will have to deal with the loss of some royalty income.

The role of local agents, consultants and manufacturer reps varies, but the main role should be having close relationships with the licensor and licensee so that the collaboration process goes smoothly. The best practices for marketing, advertising and promoting licensed products at the local level depends on the property. Marketing is about story telling. If your brand has interesting history and rich heritage, exploit them to the fullest, and present them to your licensee prospects. This tactic may not be necessary when dealing with licensees in your home country where brand awareness is high, but it pays dividends when you do so with your Turkish licensee prospects.

Outlook, Projections and Conclusions

Istanbul has shown consistent growth over the past years in a world in which many economies are shrinking; it is rapidly changing from an emerging city to a world-class economic force in the region, and it represents a preferred touristic destination for many affluent people from various cultures and religions. One of the reasons for partnerships with Turkish companies is the commercial success of the international brands. Turkey is a rising economic giant in this region and Istanbul has the potential to open Turkey to the world. The Turkish licensing industry can handle global icons successfully.

Today, licensing is a relatively new concept in Turkey and is at a nascent stage. While licensing figures are small compared to other international markets, Turkey is fast establishing itself as a strong potential market in the future of licensing. Brand extensions are flourishing for several reasons. More and more companies today realize that one of their most valuable assets are their brands and not just technology or other tangible assets. A strong brand commands loyalty, positive emotions, preference and associative powers, which are hard to duplicate. The brand is the unique selling point for many products today. Also, in the much-cluttered marketplace, where it is very expensive and time-consuming to get brand recognition and affinity, many companies choose brand extension licensing to launch new products by leveraging the power of existing strong brands.

Many consumer products marketers believe that the brand has become more important than ever before and, many times, is the only differentiator in certain product categories. Brands with strong consumer recognition, relevance and loyalty have been successfully extended into new product categories. In fact, for years, brand extension licensing has been used as a strategy to generate revenues. But, today, the scenario is changing, with more focus on other benefits that a carefully crafted licensing program can deliver, apart from just royalty revenues.

The next big leap in marketing strategies is brand extensions which are seen as an excellent strategy to enhance and reinforce existing brand equity. Typically, a licensee benefits from the popularity of a brand. However, there is also a reciprocal benefit that the licensor receives from the advertising and promotional support by the licensees. Licensing revenues can soon become the most profitable revenues of the company. Because the investment in building the brand has already occurred, there are few additional costs associated with putting forth a licensing program. As a result, a high percentage of revenue is pure profit. [33]

Over the last few years, we have seen a lot of change in the Turkish licensing industry. Turkey, once a closed market, now has numerous international and local brands to choose from. Furthermore, licensing is no longer limited to character licensing in Turkey. The licensing industry in Turkey has gained substantial momentum now. The licensors, for sure, stand to gain the maximum, but this has also opened doors for others in the value chain, like independent licensing agents, retailers, advertisers and consumer products manufacturers and distributors.

---

[33] http://www.bradfordlicenseindia.com/gather-experts.php

15.1.9 Russia[34]

Introduction

The Russian licensing marketing is quite young. Russia as a country that exists since 1991 when the former Soviet Union collapsed. It took almost a decade for the industries to adjust to the new reality and, by 2000, official attempts were made to work with intellectual property.

Russia has been a motherland for counterfeit products for a long time. Part 4 of Russian Civil Code, which regulates intellectual properties, went into effect at the end of 2006 and people who wrote it were far removed from licensing. Nowadays there is still a big gap between official law and licensing practice, however the situation became much better especially because of the Sochi 2014 Olympics where a lot of international practices were implemented.

Having been blessed and cursed by such natural resources as oil and natural gas, the Russian economy is quite inefficient when it comes to manufacturing and trade. Most of the industries ceased to exist when they were not being able to compete with cheap products from South East Asia. However, with the local currency abruptly dropping at the end of 2014, the local industries (e.g. textile) got a new chance to develop.

Demographic and Geography

Country	Russia
Territory	17,100,000 km² (1st place in the World)
Population	143,964,513 (9th place in the World)
Territorial division:	85 subjects of territorial division
Population density	8,36 people/km² 78% of population lives in European part of Russia which is 25% of the territory
Main Cities (cities with the population over 1,000,000 people)	Moscow ⬀12 506 468 Saint Petersburg ⬀5 351 935 Novosibirsk ⬀1 602 915 Ekaterinburg ⬀1 455 904 Nizhny Novgorod ⬂1 264 075 Kazan ⬀1 231 878[317] Chelyabinsk ⬀1 198 858 Omsk ⬀1 178 391 Samara ⬂1 169 719 Rostov na Donu ⬀1 125 299 Ufa ⬀1 115 560 Krasnoyarsk ⬀1 082 933

---

[34] Written by Marina Semenikhina, LIMA's Regional Representative in Russia (msemenikhina@berussia.ru)

	Perm ↗ 1 048 005
	Voronezh ↗ 1 039 801
	Volgograd ↘ 1 015 586
Top-3 Nationalities	Russians 80,90 %
	Tatars 3,87 %
	Ukranians 1,41 %
Religion	Orthodox — 75 %
	Islam — 5 %
	Catholics — 1 %
	Protestants — 1 %
	Judaism — 1 %
	Buddism — 1 %
Currency	Russian Ruble (RUR)
Unemployment rate	5,6%
Inflation rate	4%

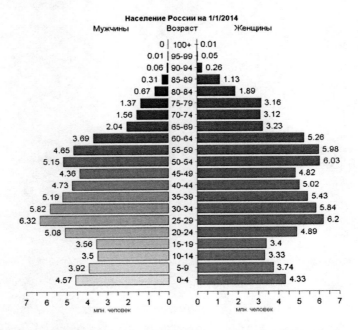

Рисунок 1 Russia's Population (2014) split by age and gender, bln people

Language

While the official language in Russia is Russian, 37 different regional languages are used as official ones in certain regions of the Russian Federation. 57% of the population speaks a foreign language at at least at a basic level. The most popular foreign languages are English, German, French and Spanish.

According to Russian law, all the products sold in Russia must be marked with specified information in the Russian language.

Territorial Unions

When defining the Territory in a license agreement, the licensees often ask for additional territories where their business is well developed. The two most common requests in Russia are the countries of Commonwealth of Independent States and Eurasian Customs Union.

CIS

The Commonwealth of Independent States (or CIS), also called the Russian Commonwealth, is a loose confederation of nine-member states and two associate members formed during the dissolution of the Soviet Union in 1991, and which were all former Soviet Republics. Georgia withdrew its membership in 2008 while the Baltic States (Estonia, Latvia and Lithuania) chose not to participate.

Country	Population (2016)	GDP 2016 (USD)	GDP growth (2016)	GDP per capita (2016)
Belarus	9,480,042	47,430,000,000	-2,6%	4989.25
Kazakhstan	17,987,736	133,700,000,000	-0,3%	7516.08
Kyrgyzstan	5,955,734	6,551,000,000	3,8%	1077.04
Russia	143,964,513	1,283,000,000,000	-0,2%	8748.36
Tajikistan	8,734,951	6,952,000,000	6,9%	795.84
Uzbekistan	31,446,795	67,220,000,000	7,8%	2110.65
Azerbaijan	9,725,376	37,850,000,000	-3,1%	3876.94
Moldova	4,059,608	6,750,000,000	4,1%	1900.20
Armenia	2,924,816	10,550,000,000	0,2%	2925.00

Source: World Bank

There were attempts to create a free trade zone within the member countries, eliminating export and import duties and implementing unified requirements for product certification. However, that failed.

The biggest licensing markets in CIS, besides Russia, are the Ukraine and Kazakhstan.

Eurasian Customs Union

The Eurasian Customs Union was formed in 2010 by three-member states--Russia, Belorussia, Kazakhstan. Armenia and Kyrgyzstan joined later. No customs are levied on goods travelling within the Customs Union and—unlike a free trade area—members of the Customs Union impose a common external tariff on all goods entering the Union. When exporting goods, a zero- rated VAT is guaranteed and/or the exemption (refunds) of excise taxes is provided if sufficient documentary evidence has been provided and proof of export. Imported goods into the territory of the Russia from the territory of Belarus or Kazakhstan are subject to VAT and excise duties and are levied by the Russian tax authorities. Access to products to the single territory of the Eurasian Economic Union is granted after products have proved to be compliant with the requirements of Customs Union Technical Regulations which are applicable to the product.

All the products to be sold in the territory of EACU must be marked with the EAC sign.

Licensing Today

The Russian economy has been in recession since 2015 when the national currency was devalued more than two times. Since then, the Russian ruble exchange rate went up and down and both businesses and consumers were extremely tired of the uncertainty. In 2017, the ruble was quite stable and companies that had previously abandoned their expansion plans began thinking about business development again.

Since the Russian licensing industry is quite young, the licensees are very risk aversive. They want to invest only if there is a guaranteed return on the investment, which they perceive to be possible if the license is purchased for a big, well-known brand.

> **Russian market is 90% pre-school and animation based**

The Russian licensing market is 90% pre-school and animation brand based. The competition in the segment is enormous. The rest of the license's types are not very well developed. The remaining 10% consists of sports, designs and, sometimes, corporate licensing.

There are about 10 agents in the market; their portfolios are distant to make sure something can be sold. Some agencies have up to 40-50 brands and their sales force is limited which leads to struggles in building strong licensing program for all the brands.

There are two main industry events in Russia both held in Moscow. Licensing World Russia trade fair is combined with Kids Russia (usually in the end of February or beginning of March) and is a marketplace for the industry professionals to introduce new properties and find partners. The show lasts for 3 days and is full of the business program events and company's presentations. The Fall brings us to Moscow Licensing Summit, a one-day event in September full of educational lectures and classes and speed dating business meetings as well as company presentations. The closing cocktail reception is a great chance for networking after a day full of useful information and business negotiations.

Entertainment Licenses

There is a dominance of entertainment licenses in the Russian licensing market – more than 90% of the deals are animation licenses, mostly for pre-school audience.

Top Russian Entertainment Licenses

- SMESHARIKI – animation series for pre-school audience, one of the oldest Russian licensing properties. The licensing rights are managed by Riki Group (their division Marmelad Media responsible for rights management).
- MASHA AND THE BEAR– animation series for pre-school audience, the most popular Russian licensing properties. The licensing rights are managed by Animaccord, the studio. Bear. YouTube views worldwide for the property now exceed 26.7

billion and MASHA AND THE BEAR keeps winning the hearts of billions, no matter what age, origin or culture.

- Melnitsa animation studio and their projects. Founded in 1999, Melnitsa Animation Studio is the largest animation studio in Russia with over 350 employees. Their most known properties are MOONZY (Luntik) (5 billion views on YouTube), THE BARKERS (3 billion views on YouTube) THREE BOGATYRS (which have enjoyed the greatest success ever amongst full-length cartoons in Russia).
- KID-E-CATS is a Russian animated television series produced by CTC Media and Metrafilms Studio. The series premiered in October 2015 on the CTC channel and has aired on the Carousel channel since 2016.
- 0+ media properties is a Russian company that implements a strategy based on developing and promoting brands and services for kids and their parents. The 0+ Media Licensing portfolio includes BE-BE-BEARS, ROLANDO LOCOMOTOV, PAPER TALES, MAGIC LANTERN and FANTASY PATROL.
- FIXIES is animation series and full-length movie. The characters are leaders in the polls of the boys 4-7 years old and 7-10 years old. They are also the second favorite choice for the girls of the same age. Fixie's YouTube channel has 3 million subscribers with more than 4 billion views.
- Soyuzmultfilm is the animation company with the heritage of old Soviet animation (NU POGODI, MALYSH and KARLSSON, MOWGLI etc.). The company cleared the rights and is opening a wide licensing program now. Most of the properties are considered evergreen and have a nostalgic touch since the parents of 4-9-year olds used to watch Soyuzmultfilm animation when they were kids.
- Wizartfilm is a studio that owns the rights for SNOW QUEEN and SHEEP AND WOLVES, both of which have commercial success in Russia as well as abroad.
- Kinoatis is a studio with two main properties: BELKA and STRELKA (animation series about the first dogs sent to space) and GURVINEK (co-production with Czech and Belgian studios).

Top Foreign Entertainment Properties

There are numerous cases of successful licensing programs in Russia, mostly for pre-school audience:

- PRINCESSES, CARS and other Disney properties: the world's biggest licensor is highly successful in Russia. STAR WARS is a good example of successful licensing program for adult audience.
- Quite recently PAW PATROL, THE TEENAGE NINJA MUTANT TURTLES and other Nickelodeon properties have vast distribution and massive marketing support including retail promotions
- MINIONS are experiencing a worldwide success in Russia
- WINX, animation for girls 5-8 years old by Italian company Rainbow, was extremely successful in 2011. Despite that, its popularity has peaked but it is still recognizable and in-demand.
- ROBOCAR POLI and other Korean animation series are quite popular because of simple plots and colorful picture

Brand Licensing

Brand licensing is not that widespread in Russia. There are companies who perceive putting the brand logo on their products as a form of advertising and willing to get paid for it, not to pay money. The successful licensing programs are created for the brands offering vast collection of designs. CHUPA CHUPS, PEPSI and DISCOVERY have secured deals in the market, however their success is far from the numbers shown by animation and characters licenses.

Art and Design Licensing

Since publishing and paper stationery are the categories that actively buy licenses for their products, greeting card companies and their design properties become popular in Russia. There are several bear designs (Hallmark's FOREVER FRIENDS, Carte Blanche's ME TO YOU, POPCORN BEAR, FIZZY MOON etc.) that are traditionally successful in licensing programs in Russia.

A good example of the artist's brand is UKRAINIAN GAPCHINSKA, the brand created after the works of Evgeniya Gapchinska. The program started from licensing the images of the art and then turned into the set of characters from the art allowing introducing more categories and various designs rather than reprinting the paintings. Now the brand is licensed in 11 countries with more than 1300 SKU's. One of the latest projects is ALICE IN WONDERLAND illustrated by the artist and printed by the Publishing House Eksmo with augmented reality effect.

Game Licensing

Video Game licensing in Russia could step beyond traditional merchandising lines (t-shirts, figurines, souvenirs). ANGRY BIRDS was the biggest licensing success raising interest even in the least expected categories (for example, packed sausages – the deal was declined by the licensor though). The popularity of the game has peaked; however, its awareness is very high which makes the sub-brands such as Stella, work in the market.

The second successful case is Russian CUT THE ROPE, which was first introduced in 2010 and become an international success. To add value to the program, the brand owner also invested in an animation series of a short video. There is a strong licensing program and successful promotional cases in retail and a chain of cafes Shokoladnitsa.

Speaking about video games, it is important to mention the Belorussian company, Wargaming, whose WORLD OF TANKS became a phenomenon in Russia and former CIS countries as well as all over the world. Their licensing program is a great case of a well thought-out and diverse brand extension with presence in different categories such as jewelry, apparel, snacks, drinks, etc. It also includes the collaboration with fast food chains (Special Black Burger and Burger King with game codes distribution), game computer manufacturers, the mobile service provider, Mastercard…. All the licensor can dream.

Sports Licensing

Sports licensing has started developing from the classical club merchandising. The most popular sports in Russia is football, so the three biggest clubs, SPARTAK, CSKA AND ZENITH, have their licensing programs. ZENITH is a great case. The club is in St. Petersburg and is very popular in the area. They have fans from the youngest age to 70-years old ladies living in old apartments in the city center. ZENITH has several club stores, which buy the licensed good for distribution. The licensing program expands from classical apparel to fan merchandising to quite unique salt, charcoal for picnics and plastic baby dolls in club t-shirts.

The Sochi2014 Olympics was not only a beautifully conducted event that unified the country, but it also offered great support for the industry. The interest in the licensing of the OLYMPICS was high. The Organizing Committee entered 55 deals in 45 categories and some of the licensees were new to the industry. The most exotic contract was in the pet category, e.g., outfits for dogs.

The Committee also did a great job in fighting counterfeiting. First, they required that the licensees use holograms, which was not a very popular thing among Russian companies. Each hologram had a unique number, which could be inserted to be checked in a special website. Moreover, local police checked the stores for counterfeit products. The traditional check in Customs for imported goods was also performed. The licensed goods were sold in 8000 stores, 114 vending machines and 2000 Olympic departments. The largest selling categories (in value) were apparel and accessories (46%), games and toys (19%), sporting goods (14%) and food (6%)

Now Russia is about to welcome FIFA WORLD CUP, the most significant event ahead of the Olympic Games and the UEFA Champions League as far as popularity and awareness are concerned. The Olympic experience will help to build the licensing program. Some of the Sochi 2014 licensees happily signed for a new adventure.

The Largest Agencies

- brand4rent is a comparably new agency with a vast portfolio of animation (MAYA THE BEE, ODDBOTS, SUPERWINGS), art (GAPCHINSKA, POPCORN THE BEAR), lifestyle (PEPSI, 7UP) and sports (Russian sport clubs) licenses.
- Megalicense is one of the biggest licensing agencies, managing the rights for HELLO KITTY, FIFA WORLD CUP, WARNER BROTHERS, CARTOON NETWORK, PEPPA THE PIG (Entertainment One), ANGRY BIRDS and other renowned properties.
- Pullman Licensing is an agency managing properties of Nickelodeon/Viacom and Roi Visual and expanding their portfolio.
- Plus Licens is a Russian branch of the Swedish agency managing MINIONS, MIRACULOUS and CANDY CRUSH SAGA.

Most Licensed Categories

	Russia	Notes
Toys	23.2%	Plush is imported, plastic toys are made within the country
Apparel	14.3%	Brands with their own retail stores or specialized companies, which enter the deal if they have confirmed distribution (client)
Food and Beverage	6,6%	Mostly confectionery, soft drinks, ice-cream, snacks. Some of the deals in dairy products.
Software/Video games/apps	5.9%	
Health and Beauty	5,6%	Several local companies
Footwear	4,9%	One footwear company specialized on licensed products
Publishing	4,8%	
Accessories (Fashion)	4,8%	Mostly imported

Gifts	4,3%	Not very well developed, most of the goods are imported from South East Asia
Housewares	3,7%	
Music/Video	3,3%	
Sports	3,3%	
Home Décor	3,1%	Bed linen used to be an important category, however after the abrupt drop in the local currency rate haven't recovered in full
CE	2,8%	
Paper Products	1,7%	One of the pilot categories for almost any brand extension, however low in royalties
Other	7,8%	
Total Country	100,0%	

Source LIMA statistics from Global Research

Retail Landscape

Background

When the USSR collapsed in 1991, Russia inherited an old retail system – a lot of specialty stores, department stores and grocery and apparel markets. Department stores quickly turned into places with multiple stores introducing shopping mall formats. Traditional shopping malls that were located outside of the cities are likely to be found in the big cities (capitals of regions) while smaller shopping malls became numerous in all the cities in Russia. Specialty stores are traditional for the small cities as well as in certain categories, e.g. in household goods, however chain format came into this category as well in 2017. Grocery and apparel markets are intrinsic for smaller regional cities.

Since Russia is a country with big territory, there are federal retailers owning numerous stores in all regions of Russia and regional ones, presented in one or several regions. In 2016 both regional and federal retailers decreased the number of the stores which became the most prominent change in 5 years. The biggest retailers – Magnit and X5 Retail Group among them - kept growing.

Biggest Retailers in Russia

Rank	Name	Sector	Turnover 2016 bln RUR	Turnover 2016 mln USD	Change to 2015	Profit 2016 bln RUR	Profit 2016 mln USD	Change to 2015	Number of stores
1	Magnit	FMCG	1 075	17 917	13%	54	900	-8%	~12500
2	X5 Retail Group	FMCG	1 034	17 233	28%	22	367	57%	~1000
3	Auchan	FMCG	333	5 550	-3%	11	183	-8%	300+
4	Diksi	FMCG	311	5 183	14%	- 3	- 45		2700+
5	Lenta	FMCG	306	5 100	21%	11	183	9%	~150
6	Metro Cash and Carry	FMCG	269	4 483	3%	6	97	-56%	87
7	Leroi Merlin Vostok	DIY	188	3 133	24%	8	132	3%	73
8	MVideo	Electronics	183	3 050	13%	6	92	22%	380
9	Okey	FMCG	175	2 917	8%	- 0,1	- 2		158
10	Krasnoe I Beloe	Alcohol	138	2 300	68%	n/a	n/a		4000
11	IKEA	Household	99	1 650	0%	5	82	64%	14
12	Sportmaster	FMCG	92	1 533	6%	- 1	- 22		450/700
13	Giperglobus	FMCG	83	1 383	17%	5	88	135%	13
14	Svyaznoy	Mobile	80	1 333	0%	0,7	11		2800
15	Detskiy Mir	Kids goods	80	1 333	31%	4	63	291%	300+

Source: Ros Business Consulting (https://www.rbc.ru/rbc500/)

Retailers and Licensing

Retailers enjoy the benefits of licensing, but the first move came from the licensor or its agent. Usually the licensees are not large enough to have an influence on promotions and merchandising in the big chains.

With tight economic conditions, lowered purchasing power and increasing competition, retailers focus on their traditional kpi – how fast the goods are sold with licensed products being generally more expensive than generic ones and that is a big concern for the retailers. They expect the licensor to provide a reason for the higher price which is when the licensee and the licensor/agent must work together. The licensee must ensure the quality and offer the best price while the licensor/agent is responsible for the brand information, broadcasting schedule (in case of animation) and promotion plan.

One of the first successful DTR program was in 2009 with ICE AGE that was bought by X5 Retail Group. The animation was very successful in Russia and the 3rd part was released prior to the deal. In 2010 chocolate milkshake ICE AGE got the prize of Retail TM AWARDS 2010 in Milk and Dairy products category. Although there is another recent deal - LENTA buying Disney for their own private label - DTRs are not wide spread in Russian licensing market though. Usually there is a preferred manufacturer/distributor or the licensee who has good connections to the retailer.

The licensees must emphasize the necessity for the brand owners to have good connections to the retailers. They welcome Disney and Nickelodeon, who are proactive in establishing connections with the retailers and managing big promotions, buying in-store advertising.

One of the biggest recent promotions in retail was held by Disney and Magnit from 17th of October till 6th of December 2016 prior to "ROGUE ONE: A STAR WARS STORY" premiere. For each 1000 RUR (about 14 GBP) spent in Magnit hypermarket, the prize was a figurine of the character from the saga. For each 400 RUR (5 GBP) spent in a convenience store, the prize was a "Space Badge". There were also several contests with the prize being a trip to Los Angeles with photo shooting and entertainment program as a Grand Prize. The promotion was held in 140 cities in Russia, 300 hypermarkets and 7500 convenience stores and was the first promotion of this kind in Russia.

Challenges

Since the market is very young, the main challenge is the licensee's risk aversion and the fact they want to have guarantees that the brand that they are licensing will be successful. This can be achieved either by having strong promotions or by buying the shelf space at the biggest retailers. Since the competition in the pre-school segment is very intensive, it is unlikely to have a well-known brand with a natural growth (when viewers/consumers are attracted by the quality of the series or the story) without a promotional investment.

The second challenge is the general economic situation. The abrupt drop of the national currency in 2015 made foreign contracts unprofitable. This hit mostly design and sport licenses whose effectiveness is still questionable in the Russian market and the licensing programs are very niche. The constant ups and downs of the exchange rate make the ultimate consumers and licensees nervous and they try to avoid any decision-making processes.

Russian companies do not know how to build long-term licensing programs, constantly renewing products and/or designs. They usually try to squeeze the most out of the property they buy before switching to a new property. Evergreen licenses are the exception; however, their share is relatively small. This behavior led to the increased interest of the national events such as Sochi Olympics in 2014 and FIFA World Cup in 2018 – licensee's decision makers tended to enter into contracts without proper consideration, solely based on emotions.

15.2 Middle East and North Africa (MENA)[35]

Introduction

The MENA region includes the countries of Saudi Arabia, United Arab Emirates, Kuwait, Lebanon, Egypt, Bahrain, Qatar, Oman, Jordan, Syria, Yemen, Morocco, Tunisia, Algeria. MENA has a combined population of 350 Million, 60% of whom are below 16 years old, and share one language (Arabic) and culture.

Licensing Agents

Licensing in the Middle East started with Disney opening its offices in Jeddah, Saudi Arabia in 1993 and in Dubai in 1994. Disney is the biggest licensor in the Middle Eastern region, by far, due to its coverage of almost all product categories in addition to retail and live

---

[35] Written by Hussein Ftouni

events. Disney was followed by Mattel in 1998 which set up office in the Netherlands. Warner Bros. made several attempts to establish their own office in the MENA region but ended up working with a licensing agent for a couple of years. Warner Bros. continued to license in the region through their London office, until 2012 when they appointed a licensing agent based in Dubai. Sanrio also started licensing in the Middle East through a licensing agent in 2006, but then opened their own office in Dubai in 2010.

> Character and entertainment properties which are primarily on TV and periodically in theaters (SPIDERMAN, IRONMAN, HULK, TRANS-FORMERS, DISNEY'S PIXAR movies, etc.) have the lion's share of Middle Eastern licensing

Last, but not least, Turner also started their licensing in the region back in 2008 through their London office but then opened their own office in Dubai in 2011. Hasbro, Sony, Paramount, Fox, Nickelodeon, HIT Entertainment, Saban, WWE, Aardman, Nike (FC Barcelona, MANCHESTER UNITED), and the NBA are all represented through licensing agents (MENA has only four licensing agents) whom are all based in Dubai.

Licensed Product Categories

Licensed product categories include: publishing, apparel & accessories, school bags, stationery, toys, wheeled toys and sports items, bed linens, fragrance & toiletries, tableware, partyware, food & drinks, confectionery, and promotions. The concentration of licensed categories in the region centers around publishing, apparel and back-to-school. In fact, almost every property/brand represented in the MENA region covers these main categories; printed and 2D products are very common in the Middle East, whereas 3D products are still a challenge for licensees in this area.

Licensing Modules

There are almost all types of licensing modules in the Middle East and they are as follows:

- Manufacturing License
- Distribution License, also called Distribution Permission (DP)
- Direct-To-Retail (DTR)
- Promotion License (Food and Drinks)
- Retail License (Flagship stores as it is the case with Sanrio, Ferrari Store and Maserati Corner)
- Location Based (Lamborghini Cafe, Paramount Hotel and Resort, Trump Hotel, Armani Hotel, Fendi and Versace Residences)
- Theme Parks (MARVEL, Nickelodeon, Turner, LEGO)
- Live Events (Sanrio, Turner, HIT entertainment, Disney, MARVEL)

Licensing Segments

Basically, licensing in the Middle East is concentrated around the character and entertainment segments. Sports licensing is relatively new (FCB, MU, AC MILAN, NBA, MOTO GP, FERRARI) but is increasing due to the increased popularity of sports, in general, and football, in particular.

Music licensing is relatively new, and Live Nation Merchandise has just appointed a licensing agent in the region. This segment is expected to grow dramatically due to the increased music events and concerts in the UAE (Dubai and Abu Dhabi) and due to the increased demand for music merchandise among tweens and teens (i.e., ONE DIRECTION) in addition to the adult fans for iconic music bands (LIVE NATION).

The licensing of classics, legends and celebrities (THE GODFATHER, SCARFACE, ALI, MARILYN MONROE) is also growing due to the increasing demand from adult fans and young adults for retro and vintage brands.

Charity licensing is well-represented by the organization Whatever It Takes, whereby celebrities donate their artwork to the charity organization and all licensing proceeds go to charity.

Already a line of fragrances featuring artwork from GEORGE CLOONEY, DANIEL CRAIG and LUCY LU has been launched worldwide, and what is remarkable is that this license originated from a Dubai-based company. Mobile Apps, Games and YouTube sensations have also grown quickly during the last three years with ANGRY BIRDS leading the trend followed by MOSHI MONSTERS, TRASH PACK, DOODLE JUMP and TALKING FRIENDS.

Fashion and lifestyle brands are growing slowly (PARIS HILTON, SMILEY). Brands (Conglomerate, Universities and Automotive) and art brands are almost nil in the region due to lack of awareness as they are culturally not recognized.

In a nutshell, character and entertainment properties which are primarily on TV and periodically in theaters (SPIDERMAN, IRONMAN, HULK, TRANSFORMERS, DISNEY'S PIXAR movies, etc.) have the lion's share of Middle Eastern licensing due to the wide exposure of TV broadcast and high admission for theaters. However, there are several properties that are not aired on TV across the Middle East that have zero awareness despite their high viewing rates in the US and/or Europe.

Licensing Challenges

The following are some of the challenges that lie ahead regarding licensing in MENA:

- Restrictions -- Saudi Arabia and, to some extent, other Gulf countries prohibit products that feature any symbols which are offensive to the Islamic religion and culture i.e., skull, angel, nudity, offensive phrases.
- DTR module is yet to be fully exploited as most retailers avoid entering into license agreements i.e., long form agreements, MG, advances, product development and royalty reporting.
- Middle Eastern fashion franchisees are bound to the collections and licenses which the franchisors have to offer and have no power/possibility to take on local licenses.
- Home-grown fashion retailers are still in their infancy stages, and their store numbers are not enough for them to sustain the investment in licenses and product development except for one or two retailers who operate 100+ stores across the MENA region.
- Food and drinks (dairy products and beverages) would go only for the strongest brands (Disney, MARVEL, HELLO KITTY, BARBIE) as they have a track record from past licensees/competitors.
- FMCG manufacturers are reluctant to risk and invest in any new, untested property/brands.

- FMCG manufacturers lack education on licensing and how it could benefit them.
- There is no proper platform or licensing exhibition that could put licensors and prospective licensees into one place for networking and marketing.
- There is no proper platform in place to educate prospective licensees, retailers and promotional partners on the fundamentals and basics of licensing. Unfortunately, manufacturers, retailers and promotional partners in the region are not aware and/or do not attend international licensing shows in London and/or Vegas to review new properties/brands and what could be coming to the Middle East. Instead, most wait until the products of that specific property/brand fly off the shelves and then go after it, but in most cases someone else already has the license.

15.2.1 MENA[36]

Introduction

Geographically speaking, the Middle East encompasses a variety of countries, nationalities, languages, and cultures. Definitions may vary but, most commonly, the Middle Eastern region is defined as the "GCC" (the so-called Gulf Cooperation Council, also known as the Cooperation Council for the Arab States of the Gulf) which is a political and economic union of Arab states. The six state members of the GCC are Bahrain, Oman, Kuwait, Qatar, Saudi Arabia and the United Arab Emirates (UAE).

At its core, this cooperation of states aims to unify economic agreements between the six countries by simplifying trade and other related topics but also by encouraging growth of scientific and technical progress across various industries. Over 40 million people live inside the GCC, led by Arabs as the largest ethnic group. Arabic is the most widely spoken language. However, neighboring countries such as Yemen, Lebanon, Syria, Jordan, Iraq and even Egypt are also often defined as being part of the Middle East. Countries such as Iran, Israel, Palestine, Cyprus and Turkey may be close in proximity but have very little in common with the average, stereotypic Middle Eastern nation. This also holds true for the consumer, retailer, and licensing industry in general.

In most businesses, when defining clusters, regions and territories to assign management responsibilities, the Middle East most commonly contains the above mentioned six GCC states as well as Lebanon, Syria, Jordan, Iraq and Egypt. This is due to their cultural vicinity of sharing the same or similar language, religion, and traditions. Iran, Israel and Turkey, on the other hand, are often managed in a completely different way and by a different team. Cyprus usually is assigned to the managers that handle Greece which means that it is handled by the European management division.

North Africa is, geopolitically speaking, slightly easier to outline than the Middle East. The countries of definition are Algeria, Libya, Morocco, Sudan, Tunisia, Western Sahara and Egypt. The latter, of course, as mentioned before, are often assigned to the Middle East. They all share the same official language, i.e., Arabic, which, in some cases, is being complemented by Berber and English. Of course, the French language is being widely spoken too, and the cultural impact of France across North Africa is not to be dismissed. Over 200 million people reside in the Northern African states. Other parts of Africa are virtually

---

[36] Written by Christian Zeidler

untouched by the licensing industry due to incomplete retail landscapes, political discord or simply economic disharmony.

Almost always, multi-national companies let their teams situated in Western Europe or Turkey handle both the Middle East and North Africa (collectively known as MENA). These teams are usually part of the Europe, Middle East and Africa (EMEA) cluster. However, in recent years, a few licensors have either started looking at local representation through licensing agencies situated in North Africa or the Middle East while other IP owners have or are considering opening a sales office themselves.

For purpose of maximizing our efforts to understand the MENA region better, we will exclude the following countries in our definition of the Middle East and North Africa: Israel, Palestine, Cyprus, Turkey and Iran. These countries deserve a chapter by themselves to even remotely capture the state of licensing.

History of Licensing

Currently the regional licensing industry is being dominated by character and entertainment licensing as well as fashion and corporate trademark licensing. Sports and art licensing is insignificant in numbers as of now.

Fashion licensing (alongside restaurant franchising) was among the first business models to establish itself over the last years and decades. In fact, there are many shopping malls across the MENA region that are dominated by international, often US or European brands. Today, a shopping center like the Mall of Arabia in Cairo, Egypt may remind the visitor more of a US mall than anything else. International fashion and restaurant franchises can be found aplenty, and the cinemas, too, show the latest Hollywood blockbusters. A day in a Middle Eastern mall can easily be spent buying the latest Tommy Hilfiger apparel collection, checking emails on Apple iPads using "free Wi-Fi" over a coffee in Starbucks before continuing to dine in one of the many Applebee's restaurants.

The character and entertainment industry developed more slowly over recent years but can now look at a reasonably successful positioning. One of the first brand owners from the character and entertainment sector to take a serious look at the MENA region was the Walt Disney Company a couple of decades ago.

Before Disney entered the market, the consumer was faced with two choices: they could either buy a fake, pirated Disney product or a highly over-priced, actual licensed product brought into the country through parallel importing. It took many years before both retailers and consumers understood and acknowledged the benefits of authentic, licensed product.

The Walt Disney Company was crucial in establishing a somewhat properly functioning licensing industry in the region, allowing other licensors to follow. In 2007, MTV Networks International launched, in collaboration with AMG, two free-to-air channels tailored to the MENA region, i.e. MTV Arabia (now MTV Middle East) and Nickelodeon Arabia. Their licensing department was established at the same time. However, only four years later, Nickelodeon Arabia went on a hiatus, and its content can currently be watched on regional channels such as MBC3. A few years later, in 2010, Turner Broadcasting Systems Arabia launched their very own free-to-air channel, an Arabic language version of Cartoon Network, again, with a local licensing bureau attached to its operation.

Other major licensors are either currently being represented by licensing agencies which established themselves mainly in the UAE, Jordan, and Morocco. Alternatively, IP owners are doing direct business, managed remotely from outside the region. Other licensors are rumored to be opening representational sales offices in the Middle East in 2014/15.

Licensing Today

Doing business across the MENA region has its challenges. Political turmoil, fragmentation, incomplete trade agreements and, despite the media's popular depiction of many of these oil-rich states, disposable income is, generally, on the lower side. Piracy is a big issue in many countries as are parallel imports of licensed goods. The status of retail infrastructure varies from non-existing to best-in-class. Cities such as Sana'a in Yemen will have very little organized trade whereas, not too far away, the cities of the UAE boast some of the world's most attractive retail outlets and consumer shopping experiences.

For hundreds of years, the regional retail landscape was defined by the so-called souk (or souq). Initially an open-air marketplace which offered its visitors a variety of products and produce including food, herbs, spices, clothes, carpets and even jewelry and gold, it has over the years evolved. The modern souks now may also sell computers, phones, toys, electronics and other gadgets. In most countries across the region, souks still play an important part of everyday life. Many consumers enjoy the vibrant feel of going to a souk, appreciate a bit of small-talk, as well as being able to negotiate the product price with the vendors. Currently the largest mall in the world, the Dubai Mall in the United Arab Emirates, has managed to cleverly combine the past with a modern approach by building a deluxe gold and diamond souk inside the mall offering mostly lavishly expensive and luxurious items.

So why are many companies considering the Middle East a growing market? Or, at the very least, as an attractive location to invest in for future business? The most attractive value the MENA region has to offer to international investors is its large population of children and young adults as potential consumers. Over 135 million people between the ages of 0-14 inhabit the region. Paired with a relatively high international brand affinity and awareness, and, in some cases, matured retail landscapes, the Middle East and North Africa allows for decent product placement. Even though US entertainment brands, TV shows, apps, games and films are sometimes being criticized for not necessarily fitting into the Middle Eastern and North African cultural framework, retailers and licensees are likely to consider US entertainment properties nevertheless.

When it comes to children's television, there are a few channels worth mentioning which are free-to-air. MBC3, Cartoon Network Arabic, Spacetoon and the Qatar-based Baraem TV and Jeem TV are often considered the leading channels across the region. These channels all show international and regional shows in Arabic language. These channels have a big impact on the local licensing industry. Disney content can be found on regional channels such as the above-mentioned Jeem TV and Baraem TV, or the viewer may tune into a full Disney channel on a Pay TV platform such as OSN.

Most often, the leading, most popular brands of the character and entertainment industry are "classic" brands such as Nickelodeon's SPONGE BOB and DORA THE EXPLORER, Sanrio's HELLO KITTY, Disney's CARS and PRINCESS, alongside Mattel's BARBIE and IMPS's

THE SMURFS. THE SMURFS have successfully grown into one of the best-selling brands of the MENA region, since the Sony Pictures movie release in 2011. MARVEL's IRON MAN and SPIDER-MAN franchises have also had some impressive success stories to tell over the last few years. Hasbro's recent appointment of a local agency in 2013 has had positive effects on developing properties such as Transformers, MY LITTLE PONY and Monopoly, and the brands are successfully increasing their market share.

> **The most popular brands of the character and entertainment industry are "classic" brands such as Nickelodeon's SPONGE BOB and DORA THE EXPLORER, Sanrio's HELLO KITTY, Disney's CARS and PRINCESS, Mattel's BARBIE and IMPS's and THE SMURFS.**

Generally, the region's licensing industry seems to be more interested in classic, ever-green properties and not willing to invest in new brands. Perhaps the strongest "new" brands that entered the market in the last few years with good results are Rovio's ANGRY BIRDS and MGA's LALALOOPSY. Cartoon Network's relatively new shows such as ADVENTURE TIME or THE AMAZING WORLD OF GUMBALL have yet to establish themselves as successful licensing programs; due to the shows' unique, slightly off-beat and edgy humor which does not sit easily with the often more conservative buying departments of regional retailers and the risk-averse licensees and distributors. The positioning of these types of brands may take longer than say in the US, where Adventure Time turned out to be a big hit.

Recently some regional character brands have managed to develop into attractive licensing opportunities. Possibly the most famous Middle Eastern character was created by the Emirati Mohammed Saeed Harib who invented the computer animated, three-dimensional cartoon show called FREEJ. The show, revolving around four old Emirati women, has had noticeable licensing success, especially in the UAE. It is often being referred to as the Middle East's most successful attempt at creating a regional property from a content and merchandising point of view. BEN & IZZY is another animation series created by Rubicon, an interactive multimedia company based in Amman, Jordan which combined 2D and 3D animation to tell the story of two adventurous kids. The show aired in 2008.

Dr. Naif Al-Mutawa, founder and CEO of the Teshkeel Media Group, created the region's first commercially viable superheroes based on Islamic culture and society called THE 99. Initially a comic book series, the concept worked well, and one of the highlights has been the crossover issues with DC Comics which saw THE 99-fighting evil side-by-side with the likes of BATMAN and SUPERMAN.

A recent, yet successful introduction to the regional animation and licensing landscape has been the popular cartoon MANSOUR, aimed at 6 to 11-year olds and currently airing on Cartoon Network Arabic. The show was launched on television in 2012, with the creator, Rashed Al Harmoodi, taking a fresh approach to regional animation efforts, marrying situational comedy with action-adventure, while at the same time educating the region's youth on priority issues such as diabetes, obesity, and the importance of Arabic traditions and values. The show revolves around the Emirati main character MANSOUR and his friends and has been very popular since its launch and is certainly one to watch. MANSOUR is supported by Abu Dhabi's Mubadala Development Company as part of its commitment to community and social development.

Licensees with an established, regional production facility are a rare find. In fact, besides the food and beverage industry, manufacturing of product is often done in Asia. The services provided by non-food licensees are therefore limited to designing, conceptualizing, and offering logistical services. However, the food and beverage industry has an established footprint. Besides the penetration of international FMCG companies such as Nestle, Mondelez, PepsiCo or Mars, regional players are strongly represented, not seldom outshining the international competition in terms of reach and presence. Some big companies to take note of are Almarai, IFFCO, The Savola Group, Americana Group, National Agriculture Development, Cairo Poultry, or Agthia Group to name but a few. The annual Gulfood exhibition which is being hosted in Dubai, UAE is among the largest food expos in the world.

The retail landscape, as previously mentioned, varies from "fully developed" to "hardly existing". Broadly speaking, the retail clusters can be divided into the following:

- Retailer hubs located in the UAE or Saudi Arabia
- Individual retailers located in the Levant area
- North Africa with an often-independent network of retailers

The reason many companies inside or related to the licensing industry have positioned their regional head-office in the UAE is because a few large retailers have established not only their central purchasing and marketing teams in Dubai or Abu Dhabi, but in addition a central warehousing unit as well. Some prominent international and regional hyper- and supermarket chains that can be found across the region are Carrefour, Spinneys, Lulu, Waitrose, Hyperpanda, and Géant.

Important for the character and entertainment industry are the international specialized retailers and department stores, e.g., Toys "R" Us, Hamleys, The Entertainer, Hallmark, Debenhams, Galleries Lafayette, and one of the largest groups in the region which is Landmark Group. A very successful local shopping concept that has managed to open its first retail outlet in London is The Toy Store, owned and operated by Gulf Greetings General Trading, which also runs the regional franchise for Hallmark. The Toy Store has been active for over 30 years in the Middle East and North Africa and is now considered one of the leading retailers in the region, focusing on kids and family-oriented merchandise.

Unfortunately, having a popular international brand in-hand and a functioning network of distributors and retailers does not guarantee a success in this region. Entertainment One's PEPPA PIG, currently a "hot property" in many countries around the world, will have very little chance of entering the market. This is due to cultural and religious norms and the attached stigma attached to the animal. The previously-mentioned ANGRY BIRDS franchise did and still does well; however, not in all locations -- on many shelves across the region, the villainous pigs are either not to be found or their visibility has been reduced dramatically. Though the acceptance of global and/or US-based entertainment brands across the region is high, if a little too much "skin" is shown, even if we are talking about a female cartoon character or a toy like Mattel's BARBIE, a retailer may be asked by official authorities to remove the offending product from the shelves. This is particularly true for the slightly more traditional countries such as Saudi Arabia, Iraq or Kuwait.

For IP owners who want to fast-track their regional footprint but have not yet looked at opening a subsidiary in the region, the best way forward is to use one of the few licensing agencies. This includes some of the independents, namely, 20too – The Premium Licensing Specialist, SEENA, or the Dubai-based Copyright Licensing Agency, or agencies that are part of a media conglomerate, such as MBC3, East West Licensing, and JCC TV.

Outlook, Projections and Conclusions

For the future, the licensing industry of the Middle East will see an increase in entertainment brands penetrate the market. As the fashion and the character licensing business slowly edges towards maturity which, of course, will take several years for some countries and even longer for others, the remaining licensing categories, e.g. sports, art, corporate, will become more important. The sports licensing industry is not even close to exploiting the region's potential, and we are likely to see an increase in this category over the next years. Regional character development will increase partly because some previous efforts have been successful (i.e., FREEJ, MANSOUR) and partly because large media corporations such as Turner Broadcasting are taking a closer look at developing regional content that reflects the local cultural values but is suitable for an international audience. As evidence of this, the Cartoon Network Studios Arabia in Abu Dhabi, UAE, is doing just that.

15.3 South Asia

15.3.1 India[37]

Introduction

India's time has come for BIG Licensing Play!!

In India, licensing is a marriage not a date. To discuss India, it is important to understand that due to the many languages, belief systems and lifestyles, India is really a composite of many different cultures. The country made great strides in raising the literacy level, which in 1947 was only 12%, and today has increased to 74 %. 64% of the population is between the ages of 15-59 years (source MGI Report) and over the last-five years, the country's GDP growth has maintained a consistent growth of 8%. According to the McKinsey Global Institute Report, it is predicted that there will be less than 22% of the population by 2025 with income under USD $2000 a year, compared with 54% in 2005.

Until 1991 it was not easy to do business in India, as the country lacked the necessary basic infrastructure. In 1991, Indian Parliament began the process of opening the economy to churn growth. An important factor was the introduction of computers in to the country, which had a profound and positive effect. By the end of 2013, there were an estimated 865 million mobile phones in the country, which means that about 69% of the population had mobile phones (Source: Market Simplified). Today, there are approximately 180 million Internet connections in the country, which is expected to increase to 443 million by the year 2016 (Source: KPMG 2012 FICCI Report). With the roll-out of 4G mobile service at the end of 2014, the mobile phone market is likely to grow even more quickly than it has in the past.

31% of India's 1.24 billion population live in urban cities, while 69% still reside in villages. The significant growth of India's wealthy population is driving growth in the country, including

---

[37] Written by Gaurav Marya

improvements to the country's infrastructure, transportation (air, rail and road) and greater availability of technology such as access to television, mobile phone and Internet services. (Source – Nationmaster.com). In the last ten years, states like Gujarat, Punjab, Rajasthan and Kerala have shown tremendous infrastructure growth, especially Gujarat which has been dubbed "India's China" due to the significant growth of manufacturing in this region.

The licensing business is relatively new to India, as is only started about fifteen years ago due in part to the growth of retail within the country. Disney is the dominant licensor in the country, commencing its India licensing operation about ten years back with the licensing of MICKEY MOUSE and Friends, POOH, Disney PRINCESSES and in the recent years – PRINCESS, FROZEN & CARS. Disney's acquisition of MARVEL has increased Disney's share of the market, as Indians love MARVEL characters. Disney has recently bought Fox has and its fully-owned subsidiary, Star India, which runs Entertainment TV Channels, Sports TV Channels and Hot Star (OTT Platform) and will make Disney more dominant in the Indian market.

Character licensing is the most popular form of licensing given the success not only of Disney characters, but properties such as PEPPA PIG, DOREMON, MINIONS, BEYBLADE and BARBIE. The market has also produced very successful home-grown Kids Character, CHHOTA BHEEM, a children's property, and many Celebrity Brands BEING HUMAN, a (celebrity brand developed by actor Salman Khan, who donates earnings from the property to charity), HRx by Hritik Roshan, Wrogn by Virat Kohli and many others in the making. Total Business of Celebrity Brands should reach $1 Billion by 2025 from $150 Million in 2018.

In the last-three years, there has been an emergence of offline retail brands such as Stop by Shoppers Stop and Many Brands of Future Retail, growth of E-commerce brands and new brands by Myntra.com i.e., ROADSTER, technology-inspired brand MODA RAPIDO & HERE & NOW. The licensing of Bollywood films has also made great progress in the last five years and set to go global in next five years because Bollywood has reach in more than 100 countries and recent big success in China.

Collaboration has been a big trend in the last three years. Dream Theatre, a licensing company, has done a JV with Kwan (Celebrity Agency) to form a JV Mojo Star to create and license celebrity brands. In the Kids space, Toonz Media Group has done a JV with Brand Monk Licensing, named Zamoza Brands to create and license kids brands globally.

The growth of licensing in the Indian market is proof that the country has an appetite for licensed brands, especially those that evolve from television (MTV and Star Plus), films (Baahubali, Dhoom 3, DDLJ, YRF), events (Sunburn), sports (IPL – Cricket League) and celebrities (HRX, Being Human). In a few years it is likely that the list will also include other categories such as gaming, and corporate brands. In the retail sector, offline retail and E–commerce will play a significant role as major retail outlets for sales of licensed products.

The growth of the licensing industry is intrinsically tied to the state of retail, which is the core delivery mechanism for licensed products. As organized retail is at a nascent stage, given that it accounts for less than ten percent of country's contribution to total sales, the best is yet to come. De-regulation in retail is almost certain to have a profound effect on providing the impetus for licensing to grow. Walmart has recently announced to become the biggest stakeholder in Flipkart which is valued approx. $ 20 Billion. Currently, the mindset of the offline retail is not licensing-friendly, which means that licensing in India will likely bypass offline retail and will break through to e-commerce in a big way.

India is the fastest growing E-commerce market in the world experiencing a year on year growth of 70%. In the publishing category the biggest online E-retailer, Flipkart.com, accounts for approximately 30% of all book sales in India. What is interesting to note is that the categories of electronics and fashion apparel have had a positive impact on offline retail business, as approximately 28% have visited the offline store after visiting the online store. Due to cash rich tier 2 and tier 3 cities and low credit card penetration (20 million) e-commerce companies have devised a Cash-On-Delivery model (COD) through which a customer can order the goods without making payment at the time of transaction, and so only upon receipt of the purchase. The COD model is encouraging consumers to buy, as it eradicates the fear of paying for goods that are not delivered

> India is the fastest growing E-commerce market in the world experiencing a year on year growth of 70%.

and capitalizing on cash in hand. More than 60% of E-commerce business is generated from Tier 2 and Tier 3 cities, with approximately 30% of the mobile e-commerce transactions coming from Tier 3 cities. This is due in part to the lack of infrastructure and organized retail in Tier 2 & 3 cities where consumers are very aspirational and with a desire to own and wear to branded products. With the emergence of 3-D printers this business is likely to grow as supplier will not have to produce MOQ for the launch of new E-commerce products.

To be a success in India you need to have faith and marry the county, not date it. The success of McDonald's in India is an excellent example. The company invested a significant amount to understand the Indian consumer, paying close attention to such elements as convenience, reach, price sensitivity, and constant innovation to "Indianize" the experience and keep it aspirational. International licensing companies need to gain understanding of the local market, which is very diverse, and realize that the first couple years will be spent in learning about their target audience. As India is a diverse and developing market, being flexible in structuring license agreements is a necessity. Above all, being committed to India will likely bring success in licensing!

History of Licensing

Globally, licensing has been a prominent strategy since the 1940s when Disney introduced various MICKEY MOUSE products including toys, books, apparel and others. In India, licensing took hold only recently with the advent of modern retail and organized markets. Licensing really began in India two decades ago when Indian conglomerates launched several international brands to the market through licensing deals. For instance, Arvind Brands introduced the properties of WRANGLER, ARROW, NAUTICA, JANSPORT and others to India. Later, as more licensing deals were signed, other types of licensing started to enter the Indian industry, as the consumer matured and started to create connections with various properties.

India began a phase wherein retail was gaining its footing in the market with the evolution of companies like Ambanis and Biyanis, who introduced the concept of modern retail. The first type of licensing that took flight here was character licensing, which was strongly based on cartoons in the Indian market. Some of the big players that have made their mark in character licensing here include Walt Disney, Viacom, Bradford License India, Dream Theatre, AI Licensing, Green Gold Animation and Cartoon Network Enterprises. The Indian consumer is very familiar with cartoon characters, which appeal to all ages with everyone having his or her favorite. Many licensors cashed in on the connection for the Indian consumer, and it became easier for licensors to capture a gamut of consumers in one go.

The characters licensed by Walt Disney are evergreen. Children's characters like MICKEY MOUSE and DONALD DUCK are still popular. Viacom has brought in popular characters from Nickelodeon, like DORA THE EXPLORER and SPONGE BOB SQUAREPANTS. Extend Brands represents classic characters like POPEYE THE SAILORMAN, BETTY BOOP and BABY POPEYE.

Licensing Today

Licensing in India has come a long way in the past few years with the coming of new international intellectual properties and success stories of domestic properties. Still in its embryonic stage, the Indian licensing industry contributes only 1-1.25 percent of the global market size of $186 billion. There is still a long way to go with the retail industry getting organized and consumer demand rising. However, India remains a retailers' paradise, with more than a million of brand hungry consumers. As a country, we have only seen global brands entering and making their impact felt in the market. There still lies a dearth of successful home-grown brands, a void which being filled in by licensing.

Licensing in the western regions of the world has come full cycle, and now it is time for India to take part in its licensing revolution. Efforts are being made, the results are showing and in the coming years, likely within five years, the percent of India's contribution to the global licensing market will rise

The market in India is currently led by various types of licensing including character, kids, sports, publishing, corporate, celebrity and brands. Although the Indian licensing market has been dominated by international IPs, various brands have also been designed and established in the country, including CHOTTA BHEEM, LITTLE KRISHNA, BEING HUMAN and others. These brands have written success stories in licensing and are some of the strongest contributors to the licensing industry in India.

Gone are the days when Indian consumers settled for one brand and were loyal to it for a lifetime. Consumers have changed; they want variety, a choice of products, and to experiment and then buy what they like the most. The typical Indian consumer is strongly influenced by various media including television, print and digital, of which social media is a strong influencer. Though still a price sensitive market, quality has become one of the important aspects while choosing a product.

When walking into a store, consumers want the full experience, which means every brand that is planning to set its foot in the market needs to work strongly to engage the consumer. Moreover, for brands, the potential target audience lies in kids and teenagers who are aware of trends and what they want and who also have disposable incomes. A huge opportunity is seen especially in the entertainment segment as the market here is vibrant and easily captures the consuming class, which consumes the brands via television, theatricals and events.

Popular Categories

The conventional product categories still hold the largest chunk of the industry. These categories include apparel, toys, footwear, books, FMCG, and accessories and form a strong connection with consumers. Even though the retail base is not as strong as it could be, brands in these categories are trying to reach the consumer through traditional retail channels. To penetrate beyond the cities and their metros, licensees are also targeting the traditional retail formats for product categories like FMCG which have a better reach through these stores.

Children's and Corporate Licensing

Kids today are often considered to be the most intelligent consumers. They know more than their parents know, thanks to the exposure they have to technology, Internet and television. In licensing to kids, broadcast plays the strongest role, and licensing of broadcast-related properties has gained obvious traction after character licensing became a hit, as the two are inter-connected. Today, Nickelodeon has introduced its new channel Nick Explore and is launching new NINJA TURTLES programming which is expected to reach a large audience.

Another category that is growing prominence in the Indian market is corporate licensing. PepsiCo and Oxford will be among the first companies with licensing programs in India. Oxford is already on the verge of closing its deal with one of the leading Indian retail conglomerates, while PepsiCo is looking to enter the market with a range of apparels, mobiles and footwear.

The demand of character licensing in kid's wear is growing with every passing year as the end users – the kids – are becoming more exposed to their favorite characters via different mediums like TV, smart phones, and tablets, which means they can now watch their characters anytime anywhere. At the same time, young parents, who understand which characters resonate with their children, often feel safe in buying them licensed merchandise and are of the general opinion that licensed merchandise represents higher quality goods. For these reasons, there is massive potential for growth in the licensing of kids wear. Fifty million homes spending over Rs 65 a month on branded products translates into merchandising grosses of Rs 25-30 billion a year.

The Stage of Experimentation

With the market maturing and consumers ready to splurge and explore, licensors and licensees are taking steps toward experimenting with new product categories. For instance, recently Disney ventured into the real estate arena as it tied up with Sunteck and Supertech to launch Disney-themed homes. What also is interesting is that product categories including condoms, lingerie and others are being explored. MTV, through Viacom, has launched these products to get to their target audience. i.e., the youth markets.

The Role of Local Agents

India has its share of local agents, consultants and manufacturers that helps licensors to make an easy and smooth entry in to the market. These local players have expertise about the culture of the country, understand the legalities involved and are well-connected with the market. This, in turn, helps licensors to target their ideal consumer. Moreover, these agents also help in creating customer engagement programs that bring the customers closer to the brand. They also ensure that codes of conduct are in line, including maintaining transparency in audits, and ensuring that sales and accounting procedure are implemented and followed.

The growth of the licensing industry is directly connected with the growth of retail, which is the mechanism for delivering licensed products. With organized retail still in its nascent stages, the expansive growth will happen only when this segment expands. This can only be achieved only through de-regulation.

Jiggy George, Founder and CEO of Dream Theatre Pvt Ltd, in one of his articles shared:

> A personal example from my journey into the business of brand licensing; while I was with Cartoon Network, I was offered the role of running the Cartoon Network licensing business and I set up and ran Cartoon Network Enterprises managing the gamut of brands on consumer products owned by Cartoon network and the Warner Bros. brands for promotional licensing. The big challenge then was retail being fragmented and even the major retailers did not have more than a few stores. So, we focused our energies on promotional licensing where FMCG brands leveraged the iconic brands like TOM AND JERRY, SUPERMAN, and BATMAN on their consumer promotions. At that stage, the challenge was to educate clients on the value of an intellectual property and tackling ways to monetize the same. The usual refrain from big clients was "our brand reaches more people than yours: you should pay us and look at it as brand building. "We thankfully transcended these discussions with partnering with a few majors like BRITANNIA and CADBURYS and their case studies and partnerships established that the model worked, and licensees benefited by both the financial upside and the brand rub-off. My team launched Cartoon Network Enterprises consumer products program and India was the pilot for the Global business and I was fortunate to be part of learning to set up processes and systems to operate a system that could technically transcend geographies and work in any market. The core team was responsible for launching the POWER-PUFF GIRLS. The brand had seen a decline globally on consumer products and the network worked zealously to resurrect the brand and we launched a successful consumer products program. The other highs were launching the Pogo licensing program, launching BEYBLADE- the biggest selling licensed toys, the SPIDERMAN movie with MARVEL and of course the launch of BEN 10 AND MAD. [38]

The Law and Its Implementation

After looking at the growth opportunities in licensing, the Indian market still faces strong challenges regarding counterfeiting and growing fake products in the market. Counterfeiting is a mother of all menaces which continues to offset the growth of the licensing industry in India. It has been observed that a lot of counterfeit products are available and sold in India even when the property is not available in the country or, if available, is not operational in that product category. It is a significant challenge that keeps on hitting licensees

---

[38] http://rai.net.in/blog/?p=483

and licensors. Industry sources estimate that counterfeiting causes a loss of 20-30 percent of business annually. In India, property owners including DISNEY, ANGRY BIRDS, CHOTTA BHEEM, DOREAMON, MANCHESTER UNITED, BEING HUMAN and others are counterfeited. Of this, DOREAMON, DISNEY and ANGRY BIRDS top the charts in product categories including apparel, back to school, footwear, toys and others.

Counterfeiting in India occurs because of illegal imports, improper distribution networks calling for higher demands and lesser supply; price differentiation, distinct taxation and unorganized retail. The Indian legal system protects property owners from counterfeiting and trademark infringement and there are several laws to this effect, including:

- Trademarks Act 1999
- Copyright Act 1957
- Patents Act 1970
- Designs Act
- Customs Act 1962

Still a Learning Curve

Licensed brands are still evolving with time as consumers mature and acceptance grows. Some strong brands have had disappointing results, while others have written success stories. The key will always be in understanding the essence of your own brand and knowing your consumer. BHPC went wrong with translating its brand in the Indian market, but now with new strategies in place, the brand is likely to make its fresh entry again into the market. While on the other hand, MANCHESTER UNITED, which started off slow in the market, is doing well with consumers at retail with simple jerseys and MANCHESTER UNITED Cafes where the consumer can connect with the game and the team.

Outlook and Conclusions

Licensing in India is coming across as the sunshine industry as various brands expand their product categories, keep in continuous communication with consumers and create stronger distribution systems. With organized retail taking center stage for the retail industry, licensors are trying to explore every possible format for their products. With times changing, new kinds of licensing will gain momentum as new product categories are explored.

The Indian consumer has always been glued to what they are most comfortable with or to what they have known in their lifetime. But with changing times, needs, and approaches, these consumers have gained a new awareness and been transformed to become explorers. Everything that is new and unconventional attracts them. This has been best experienced in retail and licensing. In India, properties which are unconventional have been surprisingly well received and accepted. This phenomenon is best seen in the sports licensing arena. India, where Cricket is religion, has seen games like soccer, baseball, wrestling and others take center stage when it comes to licensing. For example, we have already seen MANCHESTER UNITED stores collaborate with Indus League Clothing, while ARSENAL and LIVERPOOL will soon make their entries. The NBA and WWF are other well-known properties in the country. Indian consumers find it more edgy to be associated with these sports; moreover, these brands are strong at customer engagement as well.

In the coming years, retailers will have to work aggressively along with the brands to ensure that product is selling to the right consumer. Ideally, it will result in a back-and-forth relationship where the retailer can also help the brand with customer feedback. This would help both parties enhance product quality as well as add new products that consumers want.

As noted earlier, the market is heavily infected by counterfeits and fakes. What the licensing industry in India needs is to create stronger restrictions and checks on illegal imports, stronger distribution channels so that licensed merchandise reaches consumers before fakes do, stronger implementation of GST and a more organized retail effort.

15.4 Asia

Introduction[39]

Licensing is an ever-growing business in Asia. The concept of licensing of intellectual property rights has spread out not only to licensees but to retailers, FMCG's and consumers as well. Being a licensing agent in Asia is tough, but it is also challenging and fulfilling. Unlike our western counterparts which have a more structured pattern on licensed business practices and consumer preferences, our territory has unique traits all its own. Business decisions and consumer preferences are affected by geography, religion, culture, education, product and fashion preferences and many others.

In China, the licensing business is exciting and filled with opportunities. There are several factors that contribute in shaping the China licensing landscape. First is online marketing, which has become a channel for introducing and marketing products. Second is the emerging power of the middle class that contributes hugely to the sales of consumer products, and third is the diversity of properties, both local and international. Not only are character brands making a mark in the licensing business in China, but lifestyle and fashion brands are becoming a trend as well. Direct-to-Retail chains are popping up everywhere. Co-branding with Chinese local brands is one opportunity that a lot of properties have started to explore.

Although opportunities may be big and great, it is still a challenge for many licensors in penetrating the market. While a business may have huge potential in terms of merchandising and promotional licensing, other aspects of the business such as, for example, a stand-alone store may be unsuccessful if you select the wrong business partner. For a time, franchised retail outlets for apparel and accessories were booming in China, so much that licensors thought that their business was on the rise. It may have been, for a certain period, but store owners mishandled the business and thus, outlets closed one by one. This is most probably because each franchisee did not share the brand's vision. It is very important for licensors to choose the right business partners who understand the brand and who help expand their business in China.

China is a huge territory for licensing, but not all cities even with significant populations (especially cities in Tiers 2 and 3) are contributing to the growth of the business. Only Tier 1 cities such as Beijing, Guangzhou and Shanghai are rapidly growing. Hong Kong and Taiwan are still Japanese-oriented, and Korean fashion is starting to grow by leaps and

---

[39] Written by Hubert Co

bounds. Hong Kong malls dress-up and character event activities are regular quarterly events in this gateway city to China.

China has also developed their own homegrown brands/IPs which compete with US or UK licensors. However, China has now partnered with several US licensors, including well known franchised properties. Alibaba has also helped local IPs create brand awareness and increased the sales of these homegrown brands.

Online business in China has reached US$ 1 trillion in 2017. A big part of the increase in online shopping in China came from consumers living outside of China's big cities. Outside of the big cities, China's Ministry of Commerce says there are 10 million individual online merchants. There are 28 million workers in rural areas employed by e-commerce businesses which likely reflects the big expansion of warehouse and small pick -up facilities by Alibaba and JD.com.

JD.com, like Amazon.com in the USA, sells its own merchandise and hosts outside merchants on its e-commerce site. It is the No. 1 in the China 500.

Alibaba is not ranked because, like e-bay, it operates as a pure market place and does not own any of the merchandise sold on its site.

The Philippines has the most matured licensing business among its Asian counterparts. There is a section inside many department stores called the "Character Shop" that sells purely licensed merchandise. Other licensed products can be seen in various distribution channels such as direct-to-retail, multi-level marketing, FMCGs, QSRs, online marketing.

Indonesia can be considered as the next Brazil with its huge population and manufacturing sector in apparel, plastic ware, footwear, plush and much more. Singapore and Malaysia are not far behind. They have huge market potential as does Thailand with many retailers and a manufacturing capacity of its own.

Competition in the licensing industry is getting tougher and becoming more intense in this part of our world. Not only are character brands competing for lower minimum guarantees and retail space, but lifestyle, entertainment and even corporate trademarks and game applications such as ANGRY BIRDS and CANDY CRASH also got into the licensing business.

Local properties in countries that are making a mark in their respective territories and abroad are also getting a share of the market, plus a licensing agent must also think out-of-the-box to stand out. A good example of this is the Mr. Bean Coffee Shop in Shanghai and Bangkok which has made the property MR. BEAN a lifestyle brand.

The saturation of brands has an effect in negotiating for larger minimum guarantees which, for most licensees, are hard to achieve. Competition among licensors has also become tougher with competition from Korean brands which are well supported by their government in terms of TV, promotions and other activities to sustain their popularity. Before, US and UK licensors dominated the spots as major sources of IPs for this region. Now Korea and Malaysia have several popular IPs which could give their western counterparts a run for their money.

In retail, not all brands can easily get shelf space. Others will have to compete with bigger properties such as Disney (PRINCESSES, MARVEL, STAR WARS, and soon Fox properties) and HELLO KITTY which are getting a big chunk of the retail space inside the department stores. Visibility is key. Retail promotions such as giving gifts with a purchase are just some ways to get the customers' attention. With the crowding of brands in department stores, each property must stand out or else retailers can easily remove those that are not meeting the sales quota.

Fighting infringements and counterfeit merchandise is also a tough problem to deal with in Asian territories. Educating both the retailers and consumers to buy only licensed merchandise is one way of minimizing infringement activities and achieving the goal. Providing licensed merchandise that consumers can afford could help, too. However, with the growing economy and business conditions in Asia, it is undeniable that the licensing industry will be experiencing growth in the coming years.

15.4.1 Japan[40]

Introduction

Superficially, the Japanese retail and licensing market seems to be paradoxical. On the one hand, Japan is one of the world's largest economies, especially in the retailing and licensing sectors, yet on the other hand, there are many big-name cases of failed market entry in retail and, to a lesser extent, in licensing.

In retailing, particularly in the mid 1990's to early 2000's, some of the biggest international players entered Japan to great fanfare, only to close their operations later. Be it Boots the UK drug store chain, Sephora the international cosmetics chain owned by French luxury conglomerate LVMH, or Carrefour the multinational hypermarket chain, the world's fourth largest by revenue, all closed shop for a gamut of reasons. The explanations are various - lack of preparation, too short a commitment, entrenched domestic competition, lack of flexibility to adapt to local market needs, inability to meet the exacting demands of the Japanese consumer - the causes are all classic business school case study fodder.

The lack of success for non-Japanese licensing properties mirrors some of the reasons affecting the failed retailers. Though now quite the reverse, during that same period, previous entry tactics by several major Hollywood entertainment properties resulted in a struggle in trying to prosper in the Japanese market with short-term focused chop-and-change strategies using local agents and then opening their own offices that were later forced to close.

Fast forward to 2018 and film franchise licenses such as STAR WARS, HARRY POTTER and MARVEL are now strongly entrenched in the Japanese licensing scene. Domestically, the GODZILLA movies from Toho continue to drive a resurgence in the popularity of the monster.

On the general licensing scene, while some brands were able to test the market but failed, others couldn't even get a foot in the door. Two classic cases come to mind.

First was PEPPA PIG, a huge success in broadcasting and merchandising in most worldwide markets but not in Japan. It was not until late 2017, thirteen years after it first broadcast in the U.K., that PEPPA PIG was first aired on a Japanese commercial free-to-air terrestrial broadcaster, TV Tokyo. Previously it had been on Cartoon Network Japan, but as a cable

---

[40] Written by *Roger Berman*

broadcaster, the potential viewership would not have been large enough to justify a licensed merchandising program.

For Japan, the takeaway is that terrestrial TV broadcasting still reigns from a licensing perspective. Given the viewing numbers, it remains for now the prime catalyst to justify a licensing program.

As of writing, PEPPA PIG's owner, Entertainment One and its master licensee in Japan, Sega Toys, were just launching their merchandise program so it would be great to see PEPPA PIG finally succeed in this market.

The second example was ANGRY BIRDS. While enjoying an unprecedented level of success worldwide for the core games and licensed merchandise, Rovio, the IP owner was severely challenged by the Japanese market. In this case, it was difficult to assess the cause, suffice to say, that what might work in one market, may not even cause a blink-of-an-eye in Japan.

So, why license in Japan? There are plenty of reasons and you can expect at least the following:

- A mature, sophisticated retail market within one of the world's largest economies.
- A diverse variety of IP that meets the needs and tastes of a wide range of consumers.
- Sturdy and effective legal protection.
- Zero or minimal pirating.
- An appreciation for longer-term partnerships over short-term profitability.
- A demanding consumer, sensitive to fashion, but strongly loyal.
- Product design, quality, and finish that are among the highest in the world.
- A pop-culture and fashion trendsetter in Asia.
-

Conversely, certainly do not expect:

- A high growth economy.
- A huge, young consumer demographic - aging society and shrinking birthrate issues are major challenges.
- A "Fly-in-Do-a-Deal-and-Fly-Out" business culture.
- An easy market … Japan requires patience and a continuing commitment.

Licensing Market Characteristics

Previously, Japan did not have a long-term comprehensive industry-wide licensing survey akin to the International Licensing Industry Merchandisers' Association (LIMA) North American study. It relied on two domestic surveys - one covering entertainment/character and the other, brands. Since LIMA's survey went global in 2015, we now have the luxury of three sets of Japan market statistics.

The first survey has been conducted since 1999 by Tokyo-based character licensing market research company, Character Databank. Its annual survey of Japanese licensors and licensing agents encompasses character and entertainment properties. Based on annual retail sales, from a peak of ¥2.07 trillion (US$18.19 billion - historic exchange rate) in 1999 to ¥1.6 trillion (US$14.71 billion) in 2016, character merchandise sales have shrunk by about 23% over the lifetime of the survey. However, Figure 1 shows a more realistic picture if one starts with the 2000 figure of ¥1.68 trillion (US$15.59 billion) and which presents a relatively flattering trend from 2000 to 2016. In fact, it is clear the market for character goods has been in general recovery since 2012, the year following 2011's earthquake, tsunami and nuclear disaster in northern Japan. The three-year period 2012-2014 showed a healthy 9.5% growth. The recovery had been driven, not so much by a resurgence of existing famous characters, but more by the emergence of popular new properties borne out of gaming (e.g. Airou from Monster Hunter, Yo-kai Watch), social networks (e.g. LINE characters), and mascot characters known as "yurukara" (literally "relaxed characters") created to promote regional revitalization and inbound tourism (e.g. KUMAMON from Kumamoto Prefecture and Funnassyi from Funabashi City near Tokyo). In the period from 2014 onwards, sales were largely driven by YO-KAI WATCH and FROZEN and in 2016 by STAR WARS. Evergreen properties continued to show healthy growth. Co-branded merchandise collaborations, pop-up stores, anniversary celebrations and experiential licensing initiatives such as character cafes and exhibitions have helped keep licensing at retail active and relevant to the consumer.

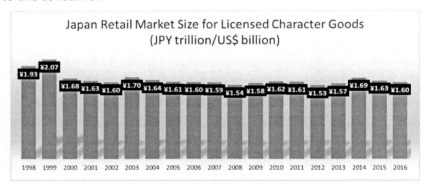

Figure 1 – Japan Retail Market Size for Licensed Character Goods

The second survey, by major Japanese market researcher, Yano Research Institute, estimated licensed brand sales at retail in 2016 to be about ¥1.18 trillion (US$10.85 billion). Unlike character properties, licensed brands have shown a more significant long-term drop in sales from a high of ¥1.99 trillion (US$18.44 billion) in 2000 which translates into about a whopping 41% fall over the past 16 years. The primary factor behind this drop has been the weakening power of department stores. Other reasons include a generally worsening market environment where consumers lose interest in brands and an increasing acceptance of lower priced goods by the middle-class demographic. Also, the Japanese brand licensing industry was shocked by UK fashion house BURBERRY's 2015 termination of its long-standing licensing deal with Sanyo Shokai who had made and sold BURBERRY products since the 1970's. It has created an environment where Japanese trading companies, who were traditional licensing partners for western fashion brands, strategically started to reduce their reliance on licensing as a business model.

Adding the character and brand figures for 2016 together results in a combined market worth approximately ¥2.78 trillion (US$25.56 billion). Compared to LIMA's own same year estimates for the U.S. market of US$144.5 billion, we see that Japan is nearly 18% of the American total. This, admittedly, is a less-than-scientific approach using rather generalized, perhaps non-compatible statistics, but it perhaps gives a general idea of the Japan licensing market size.

The third survey, and the youngest "kid-on-the-block" is LIMA's Global Licensing Industry Survey which was launched in 2015. LIMA's survey differs from Character Databank's and Yano Research Institute's in that it comprehensively covers all property categories including character, brand, fashion, sports, collegiate and art/design. LIMA estimated the retail sales of licensed merchandise in Japan to be worth US$12.49 billion (¥1.36 trillion) in 2016. The same survey estimates that Japan is the third largest licensing market in the world with a 4.8% share, following the U.S. at 55% and the UK at 5.2%.

Whilst the different surveys tell differing stories, the one common feature is that Japan is still globally a significant market that any licensor, big or small, needs to be active in.

Character Rankings based on Purchase Value (2016)

Ranking	Character	%
1	MICKEY MOUSE	6.76%
2	ANPANMAN	6.75%
3	HELLO KITTY	4.56%
4	YO-KAI WATCH	4.37%
5	SNOOPY (PEANUTS)	4.26%
6	POKÉMON	3.97%
7	PRETTY CURE SERIES	3.11%
8	RILAKKUMA	2.52%
9	MOBILE SUIT GUNDAM SERIES	2.50%
10	WINNIE THE POOH	2.42%

Figure 2 - Character Rankings based on Purchase Value (2016)
Data © 2018 Character Databank Co., Ltd. www.charabiz.com
No reproduction without permission.

Major property types are brands, character/entertainment and sports and the primary product categories are apparel/footwear, toys/games, publishing, and a local unique category targeting women called *zakka* covering fashionable home interior items. Licensed promotions using characters for convenience stores, banks, and insurance companies are big business in Japan and in many cases, create great, short-term exposure for a property.

Japan is obsessed with rankings and even has a retail chain called "RanKing RanQueen" that stocks merchandise based on sales data of top-selling items in other stores. Character Databank publishes a monthly ranking of top character properties based on purchase value. Figure 2 shows the top ten properties throughout 2016. It is interesting to note the predominance of Japanese properties with MICKEY MOUSE, SNOOPY and WINNIE THE

POOH as the only non-Japanese characters in the line-up; it is even arguable that kids make no such distinction as to origin.

Royalty rates tend to be consistent in Japan but depending on the property and product category, merchandising licenses can vary from between 3% to 5% of the retail-selling price. This generally equates to 6% to 10% of wholesale and 9% to 15% of FOB pricing. Some FOB rates might go up as high as 20%. Like other markets there are also the usual exceptions. High-volume selling FMCG products including disposable diapers are a few digits lower. Also, general food items hover around 3% of retail and mass market confectionery can in many cases have a smaller royalty rate due to tighter profit margins.

Two factors work in favor of licensors and agents in Japan regarding royalty rates. First, setting the royalty based on the recommended retail price is common due to the lack of widespread discounting. Second, calculating the guarantee based on production volume, not sales, is frequent. What this means to the licensor/agent is that royalty income is max-imized because the royalty is being paid based on what the end-user consumer pays with-out any discount, and with royalty payment based on the full production, the risk of not receiving royalties on unsold stocks is avoided. For production-volume based licenses, I always recommend to my clients to keep the sales report provision in licensing contracts in place so that actual sales can be tracked, in addition to manufactured quantities.

Royalty rates for promotional licenses typically consist of a flat fee payment plus a percent-age royalty of between 10% to 15% of the promotional licensee's purchase price for the pre-miums or giveaways.

In all cases, it is best to try negotiating a royalty rate that is as close to what the end-user pays as possible.

As with other markets around the world, it contin-ues to be a challenge negotiating minimum guar-antees that are of the level they were in previous years. Obtaining advances can prove difficult, too.

> Royalty rates tend to be consistent in Japan and can vary from between 3% to 5% of the retail-selling price which equates to 6% to 10% of whole-sale and 9% to 15% of FOB pricing. Some FOB rates might go up as high as 20%.

Retail Market Characteristics

Until the recent emergence of China's retail sector, Japan was regarded as the world's second largest retail economy behind the United States. But with ¥142.51 trillion (US$1.27 trillion) in retail sales in 2017 according to figures released by Japan's Ministry of Economy, Trade and In-dustry, third place isn't bad. Moreover, after a period of flat sales from 2006 to 2011, there has been a good recovery in the five years from 2012 to 2017, with 2017 sales 5.4% higher than 2011. This is despite a sales consumption increase from 5% to 8% in April 2014, which at the time it was predicted would stunt growth.

There are two major factors that will influence retailing moving forward:

1. Japan's Demographic "People Problem" - specifically its ageing population, fall-ing birthrate and depopulation in rural areas are affecting lifestyles, which in turn impacts retailing. So, regardless of the stable economy (as of 2018), the "people problem" has spawned uncertain prospects and a dip in consumer confidence.

2. Ongoing Retail Consolidation - consolidation seems to be a hobby with Japanese retail, and sometimes it is difficult to remember who owns what chain. Japanese retail is highly fragmented and to survive and thrive with the demographic changes, retail M&A is active, and further market consolidation seems to be on the horizon.

Retailing is dominated by two major mass-market chain stores - Aeon (539 stores) and Ito-Yokado (167 stores). Known locally as GMS (for General Merchandise Stores), the retail channel racked up total sales of ¥13.05 trillion (about US$116.4 billion) in 2017. The convenience store chain category primarily made up of three major chains - Seven-Eleven Japan (19,979 stores), FamilyMart (17,232 stores) and Lawson (13,111 stores) - rang up ¥11.75 trillion (US$104.7 billion) in retail sales in 2017.

Department stores accounted for ¥6.55 trillion (US$58.4 billion) in 2017. Sales in the department store sector had long been in decline but more lately have shown a marked recovery through restructuring and consolidation that began with a number of mergers in the 2000's. In 2007 H2O Retailing (14 stores) was formed from the amalgamation of Osaka, Kansai-based Hankyu, and Hanshin Department Stores, and in the same year Daimaru and Matsuzakaya formed J. Front Retailing (19 stores). In 2008, Isetan and Mitsukoshi, two of the strongest and most prestigious department store groups in Japan, announced their own merger into Isetan Mitsukoshi Holdings (25 stores).

There are several key retailers in licensing. For character goods, the primary trendsetter is Village Vanguard (389 stores), a specialty retailer of books, CDs, videos, and a plethora of anything trendy. Merchandise is themed as "cutting-edge global indie" and attracts a diverse range of consumers with a core demographic of male and female 20s to 30s. Their sales FY ending May 2017 topped ¥35.7 billion (US$318 million) from stores located in trendy subculture areas, shopping malls, and fashion tenant stores. The primary appeal of Village Vanguard to licensors is its track record of spotting hit characters and its influence is such that buyers from other chains visit their stores to see what is trending.

A store very familiar with visitors to Tokyo is Kiddyland (78 stores), Japan's most famous chain store for character goods. Starting from its flagship base in Harajuku in 1950, Kiddyland achieved annual sales of ¥14.3 billion (US$120 million) in 2016. Kiddyland also operates a plethora of standalone or shop-in-shop character stores: 17 Rilakumma Store, 8 MIFFY Style, 26 SNOOPY Town, 12 DISNEY Avenue, 10 STAR WARS Galaxy, 4 HELLO KITTY Shop and 2 CHARA PARK multi-character stores in Kichijoji, Tokyo, and Tenjin, Fukuoka. The customer base is largely teenage girls, mothers with young children and increasingly in the last few years, overseas tourists.

Plazastyle, with 134 stores and annual sales of ¥66.5 billion (US$627.9 million) through the year March 2015, opened in Ginza, Tokyo in 1966, originally as a Sony group company and achieved fame as Japan's first import specialty store. Plazastyle also has a licensing division that represents a range of properties including SUZY'S ZOO, BARBAPAPA and WHERE'S WALLY. This ensures quality IP management and a consistent supply of licensed products to their own retail channels. Plazastyle caters almost exclusively to the young adult female demographic.

Fashion chains also play a strong role in licensing. In upstairs channels, Beams (125 stores; annual sales FY ending Feb. 2016 ¥70.6 billion (US$649 million) and United Arrows (255 stores; annual sales FY ending March 2017 ¥145.5 billion (US$1.34 billion) often launch limited edition branded apparel before distribution expands into the wider market. Both stores are leading upper tier independent fashion and lifestyle retailers with sophisticated urbanite consumer bases. Both operate so-called "select shops" with diverse and eclectic stock selections and, in the case of Beams, merchandise selection is empowered to individual store buyers.

Uniqlo (Japan: 831 stores; annual sales year ending August 2017 ¥810.7 billion/US$7.23 billion) has come to dominate value-conscious casual fashion retailing, providing similarly positioned Gap and other fast fashion chains with healthy competition. Fast Retailing, the owner of Uniqlo, became the first Japanese apparel company to top the trillion-yen barrier with ¥1.143 trillion in global sales in the business year through August 2013. Fast Retailing's stated aim is to become the world's largest fast-fashion chain by 2020 with annual revenues of ¥5 trillion. Although its cheap-but-quality chic product mix focuses on basics, Uniqlo is strongly proactive in retailing a wide range of IP for t shirts including entertainment properties (e.g., DISNEY, SNOOPY, STAR WARS, HELLO KITTY), Japanese anime and manga (e.g., ONE PIECE, EVANGELION), and design and fashion brands (e.g. LIBERTY LONDON and LAURA ASHLEY).

In the discount sector, the undisputed leader is Don Quixote (368 stores, annual sales year ending June 2017 ¥828.8 billion/US$7.39 billion). Don Quixote is famous on two fronts. One is its so-called "compressed display" system of merchandise packed tightly into messy-looking, labyrinthine store formats. The other is its late-night shopping hours which, excluding convenience stores, are quite rare in Japan. The expansive product selection at aggressively low prices is a very strong draw. Some licensors baulk at seeing their licensed products on sale at Don Quixote but there is no disputing the power the store has in shifting products.

E-commerce has taken off in Japan with Amazon Japan and Rakuten (eBay's Japanese equivalent) reporting increasing sales and profits. Japan's leading fashion shopping site "Zozotown" has annually transacted ¥212 billion (about US$1.9 billion) as of March 2017. Japanese bricks-and-mortar retailers, especially the mass market chains and department stores are engaging in omni/multi-channel retailing strategies that embrace e-commerce.

Licensing Trends at Retail

Several trends have emerged in Japan over the past few years:

- Direct-to-retail - fashion globalization led to an influx of overseas fashion retailers (H&M, Forever 21, Zara, Gap, Abercrombie & Fitch, etc.) in the last fifteen years, which, in turn, has ushered in more direct-to-retail deals, particularly high volume, short-term licenses. Japan's own Uniqlo has also contributed to this trend, perhaps more than any other large-scale retailer.

- Character streets - the emergence of "character street" shopping mall zones lined with single-property standalone stores such as the Tokyo Station Character Street.

- Convenience store promotions as exposure drivers - aggressive competition by convenience stores has led to more reliance on premium giveaway or redemption promotional campaigns using popular characters to differentiate store offerings. These promotions act as excellent media platforms for property exposure due the high number of convenience stores.

- Inbound tourism retailing – the popularity of Japan as a destination, favorable exchange rates and a much-improved duty-free sales infrastructure helped the country surge to record 19.73 million visitors who spent an all-time high ¥3.48 trillion in 2015. Chinese visitors were by far the largest spenders, accounting for nearly 41%, and their enthusiasm - almost a phenomenon - for going on so-called *bakugai* "explosive" spending sprees has been widely reported. While this has now cooled down, the overall increasing number of inbound tourists has been a retail blessing. In licensing, character product lines are specifically created for the tourist sector, something previously unheard of. Sales of character goods to tourists helps to promote and increase the popularity of the same character in their home markets. Conversely, the huge popularity of Japanese classics such as Gundam and Doraemon, particularly in the Asian region, has helped boost inbound visitor numbers. The huge success of the 2016 animated Japanese movie "Your Name" which grossed $355 million, has sparked a tourism bonanza for some of the film's real-life settings in Japan, taking anime tourism to new heights. The Japanese government is aiming to increase the number of inbound tourists to 40 million in 2020 and 60 million in 2030, up from the 24 million tourists who visited the country in 2016.

- Sports brands on a roll - with Japan hosting the RUGBY WORLD CUP in 2019 and the TOKYO OLYMPICS in 2020, sports has been riding a wave of popularity and sports retailing has become a winner. Mizuho Research Institute, the research arm of the Japanese bank, estimates that spending by foreign tourists could create an added value of ¥3 trillion, creating a great opportunity for licensed product sales. A growing fashion trend since 2017 has been "athleisure" - clothing that can be worn for both doing sports and as casual, everyday wear. Shoe retailer ABC-Mart announced plans to open 50 "ABC-Mart Sports" stores focusing on athleisure outfits by 2020. Aeon Retail is reported to open 100 new stores for sports apparel in 2018. Against this upsurge in sports, sports licensing brands have also benefitted. In 2017, Sumitomo Rubber Industries completed the $137.5 million purchase of the overseas trademark rights of the Dunlop brand, including its sporting goods and licensing businesses, from Sports Direct, the UK-based sports retail chain. Sports Direct's subsidiary, IBML also signed a footwear license for its Slazenger brand with Kobe-based Kimura.

- Character cafes – as elsewhere in Asia, character-themed cafes continue to be all the rage, and arguably one of the best forms of experiential licensing. In Tokyo alone, examples include food and beverage outlets have been based on Sanrio's HELLO KITTY and MY MELODY, MOOMIN CAFÉ, PETER RABBIT, PEANUTS, MIFFY, GUNDAM and popular social messaging-based character, KANAHEI'S SMALL animals. The Guest Café & Diner operated by shopping complex retailer, PARCO, has been a strong exponent of this business model, hosting several rolling themed cafes over limited time periods.

Media Environment

As elsewhere globally, media is an ever-changing environment with Japanese licensors shifting to operate in the age of smartphones and tablet PCs as digital property media drivers. The influence of TV has waned with the emergence of social media-centric platforms.

TV stations are learning to co-exist in the world of SVOD in Japan with platforms such as Netflix, Hulu, and Amazon Prime Video, as well as YouTube. Notwithstanding, the terrestrial free-to-air broadcasters NHK Educational and TV Tokyo remain the primary outlets to ensure the success of children's programming-based licensing. Unlike other countries, the broadcast footprint for cable TV remains too small to create enough traction from a merchandising standpoint.

Films had not been traditionally successful property drivers in Japan due to short movie runs not making merchandise production runs feasible. Bucking the trend have been series-based franchises STAR WARS, HARRY POTTER, and MARVEL Super Heroes that have scored notable successes in merchandise sales. Also, seasonal film specials based on Japanese kids' properties, such as DORAEMON, POKÉMON and SHIMAJIRO help fuel property exposure and keep those franchises current. Moreover, with evolving production technology, manufacturers can produce licensed movie merchandise in smaller quantities, thus lessening the risk of unsold stock after a film run ends.

Print publishing is still active but is in gradual decline. Manga genre dominates the sector with, for example, ONE PIECE, a phenomenal success that set the Guinness World Record title for the best-selling manga by a single author with 320,866,000 copies sold. There is also a steady market for children's picture book properties such as THE VERY HUNGRY CATERPILLAR, PETER RABBIT, MOOMINS, GASPARD ET LISA and PENELOPE that enjoy a dedicated following from adult female audiences in addition to the traditional mother/child demographic.

With Japan as Internet-connected and electronic savvy as it is, it is no surprise that interactive media has blossomed. There has been a phenomenal growth of the social games sector that was first dominated by two platforms: GREE and MOBAGE with 35 million and 43 million users respectively as of 2014. However, more recently, the social communication app, LINE, who reportedly has 203 million monthly active users, has made a huge impact in the licensing space. The LINE app has driven the use of licensed character virtual stickers in online communications. LINE's own originally-developed character sticker designs were so popular that they led to a successful spin-off character licensing program. LINE Creators Market encourages users to create their own stickers for selling on the LINE platform. LINE also has its LINE Creators' Stickers Award where popular Japanese character KANAHEI'S SMALL animals won the Grand Prize in 2016 after being runner up in 2014 and 2015.

Across various gaming platforms, Japanese content such as MONSTER STRIKE and PUZZLES & DRAGONS have dominated the domestic market with overseas IP such as MOSHI MONSTERS, CUT THE ROPE, and ANGRY BIRDS having been largely ignored in Japan. The digital gaming market continues its growing overlap and competition between mobile, handheld, and tablet devices in the gaming space. Up to a few years ago, Nintendo and PlayStation handhelds were common sights on Japan train commutes to school or work, whereas now people play games mainly on their Smartphones.

Licensing Legal Nuts and Bolts

As a mature market, Japan presents no surprises for IP protection. Copyright is valid for author's life plus 50 years, with the exception of film, which is 70 years. Copyright does not require registration and is, of course, non-renewable. Japan is a signatory to all the major international conventions such as the Berne Convention, the Universal Copyright

Convention, and the Agreement on Trade-Related Aspects of Intellectual Property Rights (TRIPS). Japan also signed the Trans-Pacific Partnership trade agreement in February 2016, which once ratified, will see the copyright on musical and literary works increase from life plus 50 years to life plus 70 years. This will bring the lifetime of copyright more in line with the time frame used by many Western nations.

Trademarks are valid for 10 years and are renewable. Ballpark figures for costs per trademark are ¥30,000 for searches, ¥60,000 to ¥100,000 for single applications (multiple applications are cheaper), ¥20,000 to ¥60,000 for registrations, ¥40,000 for renewals, and if called for, ¥40,000 to ¥80,000 for office action responses. Japan operates on a first-to-file system, so searches are paramount and can save money in the long run. The general rule-of-thumb for licensing is that trademarking in five to six classes covers most important product areas: Class 16 (stationery), Class 18 (leather goods, bags), Class 21 (housewares, glass), Class 24 (fabrics), Class 25 (clothing, footwear), and Class 28 (toys, games). This equals an initial investment of ¥180,000 for searches, between ¥360,000 and ¥600,000 for applications, and between ¥120,000 and ¥360,000 for registrations. In total, an investment of between ¥660,000 and ¥1,140,000 (between $6,000 and $10,500) is required.

All the fees quoted are approximate and are based on working directly with a Japanese trademark attorney, and not via an overseas-based firm. Shopping around is strongly encouraged as pricing can vary between trademark attorneys, and competitiveness in the industry seems to be healthy! More recently, the emergence of web-based trademark application platforms has resulted in discounted trademarking rates.

Unfair competition is another form of IP protection and the Japanese Unfair Competition Prevention Act protects well-known marks in Japan even if they are not registered. Finally, design patents are valid for 15 years and cost approximately between ¥200,000 and ¥250,000 each.

Licensing Pointers for the Japanese Market

Doing business in Japan requires patience and persistence. Japanese companies might (but rarely!) sign a contract on the spot and they prefer building trust and confidence first to create strong and lasting relationships. Hence, the Japanese value a strategic over an opportunistic approach. In Japanese culture, "The Seven Gods of Fortune" - known locally as *Shichi Fukujin* - are a recurring theme. Here are 7 pointers that I hope will lead you to fortune in Japan!

      1. Adapt - Don't adapt your property, adapt your approach. Flexibility in customizing to local markets has been a key to Sanrio's success worldwide. HELLO KITTY has many personas around the world, but she is still strongly recognizable as Kitty! The same principle holds true for marketing international IP in Japan.

      2. Age It Up - Properties marketed to kids overseas often are also positioned to a more adult demographic. It is quite normal to find young adult women office workers eating their home-prepared lunches from lunchboxes adorned with cute characters such as MIFFY or SNOOPY. The two key age groups in terms of disposable income are females aged 20 to 34 and the so-called "silver" retiree market. Another emerging demographic is the "Generation X Silver Market" which is the next wave of retirees, born in the 1960s, who will be the first true generation to have grown up with characters.

3. Collaborate - Co-branding is a key trend. Sanrio has extensively used this strategy. For example, collaboration between HELLO KITTY and Los Angeles fashion boutique, Kitson, resulted in an exclusive apparel offering at Uniqlo called "Hello Kitson."

4. Entice - Japan is an extremely crowded market for character and brand properties. It is important to emphasize the unique factors or "hooks" that a property presents to the potential audience to stand out from the crowd. However common to most successful properties are specific traits that include a strong storyline, a heritage, a track record in other markets, and for characters, the "kawaii" (cute) factor.

5. Expect - Manage your expectations and meet theirs in time and quality terms. What you might think of as long-term generally is viewed as short-term in Japan, so setting mutually appropriate time goals can reduce frustrations on both sides. If you're thinking one year, they might be thinking three years. Also, your standard of quality is perhaps a Japanese consumer's excuse not to buy. It is a well-established fact that consumer expectations in Japan for product quality and service are among the highest in the world.

6. Protect - Copyright is fine but also safeguard your brand with trademarks. Some licensors consider trademarking a cost. That is shortsighted. Consider trademarking as an investment, not an expenditure item.

7. Understand - Conduct appropriate due diligence about Japan. First, recognize its market characteristics with changing demographics, i.e., an aging society, declining birthrate and a low market growth rate due to Japan's mature economy. Second, appreciate that Japanese business style is based on building trust with the business partner; it is not simply transactional, and decision-making can be irritatingly slow. Third, accept that business development is strategic, not opportunistic.

15.4.2 China[41]

Introduction

China, officially the People's Republic of China (PRC), is the world's most populated country. It has a population of over 1.38 billion (1/5 of the world's population) and is 9.6 million sq. km in size. Putonghua is the official language, though local Chinese speak different dialects due to vast geographical area. Renminni (Yuan) is the official currency. The country is a single-party state governed by the Communist Party and Beijing is the capital city. In 1997 and 1999 respectively, Hong Kong and Macau were returned to China and became the two special administrative regions of PRC.

Since the economic reform in 1978, China has experienced tremendous growth and has become the world's manufacturing hub and the world's second largest economy. In 2016, total GDP is US$11,212 billion and per capita GDP is US$8,109. Considering full 2017, China economy grew 6.9% which exceeded the official target of 6.5%. For 2018, the government targets a 6.5% growth.

---

[41] Written by Tani Wong, Managing Director of LIMA-China.

History of Licensing

Licensing has a relatively short history in China. It started in 1990's and Disney was the pioneer in the field. At that time, most licensing activities were managed out of Hong Kong. Licensing people mainly travelled to Shanghai and Guangzhou to meet with manufacturers/licensees coming from different provinces. Much of licensing activity happened along the Eastern coast. Predominant properties were mainly Western entertainment characters such as MICKEY MOUSE, WINNIE THE POOH and TOM AND JERRY. These Western cartoon characters all had positive attributes, i.e., were cute, friendly and smart etc. The Chinese even thought that all foreign cartoon characters came from The Walt Disney Company. Japanese cartoon characters were less popular as they were viewed as violent. Thus, most licensing activities happened among established entertainment studios and Disney was always the leader. Movie licensing was minimal due to the strict control over import of foreign films. At that time, licensing of China properties had not begun.

At this early stage, most manufacturers did not understand licensing. They thought that once they paid a fee, they would have total ownership of the property and could use the character image in any manner. The product approval compliance rate was very low, and some licensees might never submit concepts for approval. Some were producing licensed products beyond their licensed categories. Even worse, some licensees designed and produced licensed products with their own interpretation of the licensed property. Sub-licensing was another problem where a licensee may cut and dice the licensed articles in his agreement with other manufacturers.

Retail in China was very fragmented and layered. Traditional distribution channels for licensed products were department stores or licensee owned and operated standalone stores, whereas many street stores were likely selling unauthorized products. In the late 90's, hypermarket operators such as Walmart and Carrefour entered the China market.

Another issue was parallel exports. Many China licensees were licensed to manufacture and sell in China but were selling to overseas countries. These factories mainly exported to Japan, Europe and the United States because they thought that they had the rights to sell to the whole world, even though the license agreement stated that distribution was within China only. They exhibited at international trade shows, took overseas orders and shipped their "licensed products" abroad.

Some Chinese companies used licensing to improve their company's profile. Becoming a licensee of an international brand would give people the impression that the company had international exposure. This helped raise their company image. Many companies in the early days just took some licenses but did nothing in terms of product development and distribution.

Bad debt was another serious issue. Some licensees acquired a license without thoroughly thinking about the geographical area that they had to cover and sometimes committed to a high minimum guarantee. The other might offer a high guarantee to bid for a popular licensed property. When they realized that the product sales did not meet their expectation, many companies just walked away and did not pay the balance. Some licensees simply closed their companies, and it became very difficult for licensors to track and collect payments. So, many bad debts occurred. To secure royalty payments, many licensors asked for higher upfront and even full payment in advance. Other companies changed the revenue recognition method from accrual to earn-out. For larger size deals, licensors would request letter of credit or bank guarantees. After all, due diligence was very important, and it still applies today.

Other than that, strict foreign exchange control made it difficult for licensors to collect payments. China's government has strict control for remittance of foreign currency out of China. However, many license agreements, those with overseas companies, were in US dollars. Licensees needed to go through tedious procedures with different government authorities, including the filing of license agreements (Chinese Version) and paying regional and local taxes, to obtain the permit to remit foreign currency. The translation of English to Chinese documents as well as lengthy and complicated trademark registration process caused many overseas licensors to postpone their China entry plans.

Intellectual property protection was a major issue too. Before China's entry to WTO, the idea of IP protection was fairly misunderstood in China. Infringement and counterfeit products were hot issues. Some manufacturers saw cartoon characters on television or from overseas and just copied the images onto their products. On one hand, this scared away many property owners. On the other hand, it forced major brand owners to speed up their Chinese entry plans to tackle the counterfeit problems. It also helped better protect their IP in China for further expansion into other product categories.

Licensing Today

Licensing in China has grown rapidly in the last 2 decades. As mentioned earlier, most licensing activities in China were managed out of Hong Kong in the 90's. In 2004, Disney moved its regional headquarters from Hong Kong to Shanghai. Since then, many foreign brand owners such as Mattel, Hasbro and Nickelodeon began to set up offices in China. Many licensors chose Shanghai as the 1st entry to China as it was a key trading port.

Though many foreign brand owners were interested in exploring the China market, they were hesitant to enter due to the language barrier, cultural differences, and a lack of knowledge about the China market, currency control and intellectual property protection. This led to the rise of local licensing agents who acted as the bridge between brand owners and licensees. If the properties came from major studios, local agents were willing to commit a minimum guarantee to acquire the representation. For 2nd tier properties, these agents might pay a lump sum to become a master licensee, and they would sublicense the right to other manufacturers. Depending on the popularity and awareness of the property, foreign properties normally required a minimum guarantee while local brands might waive the minimum guarantee requirement or take a minimal fee. For the latter, their goal was to encourage licensees to try their brand and have products at retail for further promotion.

In 2000, China released "3000 Whys of Blue Cat," an animated series with an emphasis on science that had over 3000 episodes. The educational nature of this program was widely accepted by both parents and kids. The VCDs were always best sellers. Then, manufacturers started applying BLUE CAT images on products and over 1000 Blue Cat specialty stores were opened. It marked the beginning of licensing for China-produced properties and was a huge success at the time.

Another successful Chinese property was PLEASANT GOAT AND BIG BIG WOLF. The story was about a group of goats living on the grassland and a clumsy wolf that always wanted to eat the goat. The cartoon became very popular when it was aired in 2005. Due to its success, the producer released a movie in 2009 and it was a big hit during Chinese New Year. The unprecedented box office success attracted many manufacturers to acquire the license. The animation series was also aired in Hong Kong, Taiwan, Singapore and other countries. It was the first time that a Chinese animation and its licensing program has successfully expanded outside of China. In 2010, Disney became the master licensee and it was the first time that a China property was introduced under the Disney umbrella of properties. The property was brought by a Chinese company (Alpha Animation) in 2013.

The success of PLEASANT GOAT AND BIG BIG WOLF triggered many animation companies in China to produce animation. This was further supported by the different subsidy policies provided by central and provincial governments.

Since then, the animation industry has grown rapidly. Key provinces like Guangdong, Jiangsu, Zhejiang, Anhui and Fujian have set up animation bases to encourage animation production. Subsidies were further provided by government to animation companies based upon the duration of animation produced. Many companies started animation production to get government funding. In 2010, China surpassed Japan and became the world's number one animation production country. Annual production was 220,868 minutes. However, most of the animation was relatively immature. Some successful properties that could further develop through licensing are BALALA THE FAIRIES, GG BOND, SWEETHEART PRINCES, CRAZY FOR THE SONG, THE LEGEND OF QIN and BOONIE BEARS.

As China studios continued to improve production quality and story content, Chinese animated feature films started getting attention in the China box office. Monkey King: Hero Is Back 2015 (US$151.7m), Big Fish & Begonia 2016 (US$89.6m) and Boonie Bears: Entangled Worlds 2017 (US$82.9m) are listed at the top 3 best-grossing Chinese animated films in China after Kung Fu Panda 3 and within the top 30 of China Yearly Box Office. Monkey King: Hero is Back ranked 10th in the 2015 China Yearly Box Office. These encouraging numbers further attracted China property owners to bring their properties to the big screen.

In China, the estimated retail sale of licensed products was USD 1.1 billion in 2005. In 2016, China and Hong Kong combined skyrocketed to USD 80.7 billion. Entertainment licensing is still the dominant category, which has 58.6% of market share. Corporate brand and fashion programs are two fast-growing categories. Following that is sports licensing, where football and basketball receive most interest. This explosive growth is mainly due to vigorous economic growth, and robust Internet connectivity and support from China government on cultural industry. By 2020, the middle class will rise to 0.6 billion. They have high spending power and are hungry for international brands. They believe foreign brands have better quality and designs and are willing to pay premium price for them. This huge market potential is a big lure for foreign brand owners. Companies started exploring their market entry strategies to China.

Simultaneously, the Internet is changing the lives, lifestyle and consumer behavior of Chinese today. Two decades ago, there were only around 2,000 Chinese computers that had access to the Internet. According to the Ministry's most recent data, China now has 772 million Internet users, with 53.1%of the population online. It is almost a six-time increase from 2006. More importantly, over 97% is mobile Internet users. Today, most Chinese communicate and share information via social networks such as Weibo, QQ and WeChat. The newly risen social media becomes another powerful platform for building a brand in China.

One recent example is ALI THE FOX which was a cartoon character and started as an emoticon in 2006. It was then marketed online and became a very popular character among young teens and office ladies. It soon launched licensed products on Taoboa, which is an online retail platform, and received record-breaking orders. This further encouraged ALI THE FOX to partner with more manufacturers to launch more products. By analyzing the data collected online, they were able to develop new products that captured the heart of their fans. In addition, the company has begun to organize events regularly to stay connected with their customers and increase fan base. It has gone abroad and participated in overseas licensing shows. In addition to picture books and short clips, the property will go into big screen in 2019.

The licensing of movies and related properties has been challenging in China because the country has imposed import quotas on foreign movies. There are many cases in which a mega hit cannot be released in China due to a failure in passing the censorship regulations. In 2012, China enlarged its quota for imports of foreign films from 20 per year to 34 per year. The extra 14 films are "enhanced" films made in 3-D, IMAX or animations. In fact, China is the world's second largest market with box office revenue of US$8.59 billion in 2017 and is expected to surpass US to become the biggest single market in the next few years. To capture this huge market and import film quota, many big studios use Chinese artists in the movie, and invite co-production and joint venture. Another alternative is to partner with cable TV and online streaming platforms.

The language barrier used to be an issue but is becoming less important. Many young people study abroad and are well-versed in English. The young generation are well educated and can communicate with the outside world. In other words, they are more receptive to foreign brands which is a good sign for overseas brand owners.

Many studios start setting up licensing offices in China, mainly Shanghai. It helps supply the first batch of "licensing professionals" to the market whom become senior management of many newly formed licensing companies. Some licensees further evolve into licensing agents and help brand owners promote their brands in the territory. Some of them become consultants and help manufacturers to acquire license. Others new players include home video distributors or subsidiaries of TV channels whom have experience in dealing with foreign companies/licensors. Due to the short licensing history, there is a shortage of licensing professionals. Thus, the performance of agents varies a lot.

> In China, the estimated retail sale of licensed products grew from US$ 1.1 billion in 2005 to US$80.7 billion in 2016. Entertainment licensing is still the dominant category with 58.6% of the market but corporate brand and fashion programs are two fast-growing categories.

Local properties have also begun their licensing programs. However, they may not have a separate licensing team. Licensing will be managed by production or distribution team. Successful properties are either backed up by TV stations or toy companies producing animation to promote their toy products. Their main challenge is finding licensing professionals to plan and execute a relevant licensing program. As a short cut, many tend to hire Hong Kong people to head up their licensing departments and provide staff training. The other may approach existing employees of leading licensors in China. Disney's employees are being regularly sought after as a talent pool.

Outlook, Projections and Conclusions

The licensing landscape in China has changed drastically in the past few years. "Internet+" is now a buzzword in China. In short, it is a new business model in which traditional industries align themselves with technology and the Internet for business expansion. And Internet+ is a powerful driver for the strong growth of licensing industry in the country.

With Internet+, new properties do not rely on traditional channels to get exposure. In fact, many new properties have emerged from non-traditional channels such as social media, online streaming channels, live broadcast and online publishers. Together with government support, many companies open IP incubator base, encouraging young generation to create new properties. As content are now consumed via multi-media, these new digital platforms become powerful nurturing grounds for emerging brands. We have seen many new properties arising from online channels, games, publisher and social media platforms. IT giant like Tencent set up a licensing division in 2016 to manage the vast IP portfolio emerging from their gaming, online video and publishing units.

Retail is another area that has experienced dramatic changes. China is known as an advanced market in terms of online retail. From LIMA's 2017 global licensing survey, 41% of licensed products in China is sold online where the worldwide average is 21%. All your daily needs could be fulfilled given you have a smart phone in China which is tied with a debit/credit card.

Alibaba generated a record-breaking of CNY168.2/USD26.7 billion retail sales on November 11, 2017 which is also known as Bachelors' Day.

And over 90% of the transaction was made via mobile device. Obviously, the growth of e-commerce has accelerated the shrinkage of brick and mortar stores.

Department stores are losing their role as the key distribution channel of licensed products. Shopping malls need to enhance consumer experience and seek for licensed properties to offer excitements and drive foot traffic. Technological innovation also brings automated supermarket and convenient stores to life. From specialty stores to bookstore, more and more fully automated retail formats will be introduced in China.

As online merchants can collect lot of consumer data from the transactions, they can further analyze the big data and make suitable recommendations for your future purchases. This consumer preference data is also a powerful asset for brand owners to promote a brand. Leading online retailers, Alibaba and JD also launched IP trading platforms respectively to provide business matching services between their merchants and brand owners.

Technology also makes mobile payment became the most common form of payment in China. In China, the 2 dominant forms for mobile payment are Aplipay and WeChat Pay. Almost all daily transactions can now be settled via electronic payment. For example, Hangzhou is experimenting a "cashless" city. Not only established retailers, you can mobile payment when shopping grocery from a street hawker.

Consumer experience is further expanded from online to offline. Location-based entertainment is another hot topic these days. From indoor playground to outdoor theme park, themed cafe to hotel and pop up stores, consumers can now interact with their favorite characters from different aspects of life. China already has a lot of domestic attractions and these owners are looking into licensing to refresh their attractions and bring in additional revenue. Following the success for Shanghai Disneyland, many brand owners are working with land developers to open new theme parks in different key cities.

China has a long history of art and culture. It is another key government initiative to explore and introduce the richness of Chinese culture to the world. Many state-owned and private museums turn to licensing for building their brands. Leading museums also participate in overseas licensing shows to promote Chinese arts and culture. In the past decades, the strong economic growth has been driving the licensing industry in China. High broadband connectivity allows Chinese consumers to stay connected with international markets and brands.

Technology and innovations further transform how consumers interact with their favorite brands. The comprehensive e-commerce environment and mobile payment systems also foster licensing growth.

Last but not the least, the support from the Chinese government also accelerate the growth of licensing industry. The focus has been shifted from purely animation production a decade ago to a broader perspective ranging from art, animation, sports to life style aspects. Recently, more focus is put on museums and local attractions to exploit the richness of Chinese culture.

It is forecasted that China is still having tremendous market potential and will soon surpass Japan to be the biggest licensing market in Asia. Considering its unique characteristics, licensing development in China may not follow the pattern of matured markets in the Western world. Brand owners need to visit the market themselves and establish a local footprint which can fit into the Chinese community. A remote-control business approach will not work here.

15.4.3 Korea[42]

Introduction

Korea is the 12th largest worldwide economy with 50 million people and 17 million households. Over 44% of the total population lives in the Seoul metropolitan area, and those who are between the ages of 0 and 14 make up approximately 18% of the total population. The character merchandising market is estimated at US $7 billion in 2011. Hypermarkets are the largest distribution channels (46% of total character merchandising), and online shopping is expected to drive the future growth of retail. Across all types of media, local and Japanese content dominates due to cultural preferences, strong support from the government, and regulation on TV. Korea is technologically advanced with one of the highest broadband, multichannel and LTE penetrations that reached 50% in 2013. This advanced technology infrastructure drives consumers to spend much of their time on online games, the Internet, and mobile contents rather than on traditional media.

History of Licensing

---

[42] Written by Kyeongwon Kwak

Korea has seen its culture industry stimulated after hosting the world-ranking sporting events of the Seoul Olympics in 1988 and the Korea-Japan World Cup in 2002, along with the thriving of World Wide Web infrastructure building in early 2000s. Some animation from the pre-Olympics era is still popular for example the property ROBOT TAEKWON V, but other properties that have come after the 1988 Olympics are more interesting to the public.

Before hosting the 1988 Seoul Olympics, the Korean government laid the groundwork for the culture industry expansion. Building Theme Parks (i.e., Seoul Land) and making investments in animation production were two of the major changes initiated by the government. Korean studios made most of their profits from OEM, mostly from the United States in the 1980s and 90s. However, in preparation for the Olympics, the Korean government made great efforts to change the nature of the culture industry from merely supplying OEM to creating content. As a result, DOOLY THE LITTLE DINOSAUR, RUN, HONEY, RUN, LONG LONG TIME AGO and SUPER BOARD'S began broadcasting on terrestrial TV channels in 1987.

Foreign animations were mainly from the US and Japan, and family-oriented Disney television shows were scheduled on Sunday mornings. Disney's broadcasting on terrestrial TV channels has increased public awareness and loyalty to Disney. In 1992, The Walt Disney Company incorporated its Korean branch, and since then the business in licensing has accelerated.

In early 2000, Internet companies, whose services were at that time limited to providing e-mail, community spaces, and web searching, soon expanded their domain of services to include flash games, short animations and e-cards among other services, and got into fierce competition to win users and customers. The PUCCA and MASHIMARO, properties, whose orientation is comic short animation, have gained massive popularity and soon developed their licensing business possibilities.

In 2002, the completion of the Korea-Japan World Cup left a significant impact on many Korean brands. CNN reported on the changes that Korea experienced after the World Cup—a proliferation of online games, e-sports, and tech infrastructure, to name few. This rising attention to Korean culture was followed by an increase in Korean exports of animation, drama, K-pop, and online games. The following year, the Korean drama WINTER SONATA was sold, and has become a huge public success in Japan. This success offered a glimpse into the possibilities of entertainment-related property licensing. Consequently, THE GREAT JANG-GEUM, FULL HOUSE and YOU'RE BEAUTIFUL were also exported abroad and became popular in Asian countries.

In 2004, Korea unfolded its full-scale K-Pop music-generating promotions, targeting all of Asia. SM Entertainment, under meticulous planning and management, introduced "TVXQ," a South Korean pop duo and experienced great success in Asia. It was the second tide of Korean Wave, following the first Korean Wave generated by dramas. Main attractions such as the pop groups RAIN, FT ISLAND and CNBLUE have cemented their fandom through both video appearances and their music. This popularity played a key role in the licensing business, adding value to portrait rights. Later, KARA performed the lead role in a Japanese drama, and BIG BANG introduced a T-shirt collaboration with UNIQLO Japan.

The same year, Nexon's launching of the multi-play racing game, KART RIDER reshuffled the Korean game market from hardcore-based to casual game-based. KART RIDER absorbed the female and youth populations into the online game market. Its membership has reached 13 million, or 26% of the total Korean population. From there, Nexon began a licensing program centered around its game properties. Nexon followed with MAPLE STORY, an online role-playing game, which accumulated sales of 10 million copies.

The TV animation character PUCCA made its international debut through Disney, after the co-production with JETIX (Disney Channel) in 2005. It was a good example because it showed that well-made Korean animation assets can drive sales in the international licensing market. PORONO, with EBS participating in production, recently released its 4th season and is one of the hottest animation characters in the licensing market.

Entering the 2000's, the Korean culture industry shows exponential growth in various fields. The once import-dependent market now can produce its own content, and the size of the licensing market is expanding rapidly.

Licensing Today

Leaders in today's domestic markets are the properties of PORORO, LARVA, ROBOCA POLY, Disney, and HELLO KITTY. Domestic majors are targeting toddler viewers. TV animation properties are receiving media support by forming partnerships with terrestrial broadcasting companies. These programs need scheduling on EBS and Tooniverse, the top kids channel. EBS receives stronger viewership from toddlers, whereas Tooniverse is more favored by older kids. PORORO and ROBOCA POLY, and CRAYON SHIN JJANG and KERORO gained their brand power through broadcasting on EBS and Tooniverse.

> Leaders in today's Korea's domestic markets are PORORO, LARVA, ROBOCA POLY, DISNEY and HELLO KITTY.

PUCCA, TICKETY TOC and PORORO are some of the most famous and internationally recognized assets that are native to Korea. PUCCA achieved its international recognition via co-production with Disney Channel. Tickety Toc was an output of the co-production by Funny Flux and Zodiac Media, then it was presold to Nickelodeon for international distribution. PORORO also received strong media support. With EBS participation, PORORO could eventually make its mark internationally.

Iconix, which owns PORORO and TAYO, is one of the major domestic licensors in Korea. As of 2010, reported annual retail sales of Iconix reached US $500 million, with more than 1,000 product categories. Besides Iconix, other domestic licensors' properties have also established dominant market positions with strong help from the media. The following chart is a summary of some of the top licensors in Korea:

Licensor	Property	Agent
ICONIX	PORORO, TAYO, CHIRO	-
VOOZ / VOOZCLUB	PUCCA, CANIMAI	-
TUBA Entertainment	LARVA, WINGCLE BEAR, OSCAR'S OASIS, VICKY & JOHNNY	-

GIMC	CLOUD BREAD	-
ROI Visual	ROBOCAR POLY, WOOBI BOY, CHIRO	CJ E&M
Disney	DISNEY Standard Character, MARVEL etc.	-

The following chart summarizes licensee brands in Korea:

Category	Major Licensee
Apparel/ Accessory/ Fashion	Eland, Samsung, Real company, Wing house, BOB design
Stationery	Barunson, Kumhong, Taeyang
Home	S.K, Eland, BK world, Dongyang CS
Food/Health/ Beauty	Lotte confectionery, LG, GS, SPC, CJ, Boryung, Namyang
Toy / CE	Aurora, Sonokong, Samsung, LG, Anymode

Domestic retail markets are dominated by 6 retail giants. If considering hypermarkets only, E-mart and HomePlus account for more than 30% of market share each. However, since Lotte owns Hypermarkets, Department Stores, SSM, CVS, Home shopping, Toys "R" Us, Lotte Cinema, and Lotteria (1,100 stores vs 300 Mc Donald stores) across the country, it is considered the biggest retail influence in Korea. The retail situation in Korea is as follows:

	LOTTE	Shinsegea	Samsung Tesco	GS Retail	Hyundai	Bokwang
Hypermarket	17%	37%	32%			
Department	42%	20%			20%	
SSM	431	129	317	230		
CVS	5,000			5,600		6,000
Home shopping	19%			27%	20%	
Others	Toys "R" Us Cinema Lotteria			Watson		

Source: The maps of business investment 2012

In 2011, Korea's character and entertainment market was reported to be worth US$7 billion. Since 2009, its worth has been increasing at an average of 16% per annum. Ratio between domestic and foreign assets is 51% and 49%, respectively. Hypermarket accounts for 46% of main distribution channels, and online shopping mall does 13%. The importance on these two distribution channels is continually increasing. In Korea, entertainment licensed products are heavily weighed on toddler market. Source: Character Industry White Paper, 2012 (Unit: billion/U$1 = 1,000won)

The Role of Agents in Korea

Almost all foreign companies, except for Walt Disney, do business in Korea through partnerships with domestic agencies. Warner Brothers works with Young & Partners; HIT Entertainment and Discovery work with COCABAN; several Japanese companies have chosen either CJ E&M or DaeWon Media; and Nickelodeon established a joint venture with SBS to do business in Korea. There are a few cases where domestic animation companies have developed projects with broadcasting companies, and other small-scale agencies are also in place.

These agents work closely with licensees to develop long-time business relationships. Korean agencies can offer clear-cut marketing approaches and targeting strategies for foreign assets. For foreign assets to settle and successfully grow in the Korean market, localization is vital. In this way, licensors must be flexible in accepting and meeting the required demands by the agents. And in the case of TV assets, joint management for broadcasting channels and its schedule is needed.

Outlook, Projections and Conclusions

The Korean licensing market is expected to grow continuously over the next decade because of several factors. The first is the rapidly changing media environment leveraged by YouTube and other social networking services. Not long ago, there was a gap between countries in the media industry. For example, if an American drama was successful in the US and decided to begin distribution in Korea, there was a gap of 6 months before it could possibly be aired in Korea. But today on You Tube, there is no such gap. As evidence of this, YouTube made Psy a worldwide star almost overnight. On YouTube, people from all around the world clicked on Psy's GANGNAM STYLE over 1.5 billion times. YouTube has made it possible for the whole world to connect to the media content simultaneously. This media environment, empowered by the influence of social networking sites like YouTube, is expected to influence the growth of Korean licensing industry in positive ways.

The next possible boost for the Korean licensing industry is the mobile games that are facilitated by smart phones and mobile messengers. Approximately 84% of Korean smart phone users have the mobile game KAKAOTALK installed on their phones. What is unique about it is that it shows the rankings of the people who play the game and whose contact information is stored in one's smart phone. It allows the users to compete with the people in one's contacts.

ANY PANG is another game that has reached 20 million downloads. With success of its game, ANY PANG started its own licensing program through agents. These are just a few examples of the power of mobile gaming in Korea. The growing game market has attracted the attention of entertainment properties. Developers are looking to either make a new game using famous pre-existing characters, or to simply insert famous characters in a game they have already developed.

The third factor influencing licensing is the aggressive overseas expansion by companies with strong sales networks who are looking to expand into the entertainment industry. For example, Eland owns 54 apparel brands, and its operation range includes retails and leisure. In 2011, with 5,200 stores operating in China, Eland recorded sales of US $1.6 billion. Then, Eland took over an animation studio in 2009, and with the acquisition of a theme park in 2012, Eland will continually make its investment in culture industry.

Lastly, the dynamic overseas co-producing of TV animations can also be a key factor in licensing growth. Overseas co-production of the property PUCCA by Vooz and Disney, and the property TICKETY TOC by FunnyFlux and ZODIAK MEDIA, are good examples of successful overseas co-production. PUCCA was aired internationally through Disney and TICKETY TOC has aired through Nickelodeon.

From 2006 to 2011, the Korean licensing market reported an average annual growth of 9.6%. This was mainly attributed to the rapid changes in the media environment, government support, and the development of the animation and game industries. Today's social networking sites, new available technology platforms and creative collaborations among multi-national corporations will now act as the main driving forces of Korean culture industry development in the next few years.

15.5 Southeast Asia[43]

Introduction

For purposes of this chapter, the countries of Southeast Asia (SEA) will include Indonesia, Malaysia, Philippines, Singapore, Thailand and Vietnam. In Southeast Asia, the country with the largest population is Indonesia with 260 million. The Philippines follows at 104 million and Vietnam is around 96 million. Thailand has 68 million people and Singapore and Malaysia have 5.1 and 31 million, respectively. While the size of the population is important in evaluating whether one should enter the territory or not, it cannot be the main determining factor. The following are key factors to consider when entering each of these markets:

- Culture - Some of the countries lean strongly towards American culture, like the Philippines, while others lean towards British culture, like Singapore. Japanese culture is quite popular in Thailand.
- Traditions - Foreign animations that influence children positively are more readily acceptable than others. Parents will screen television programs and not be supportive of programs that do not contribute to the child's well-being. Parents want a program that is educational as well as aspirational.
- Copyright and Trademark Regulations - Regulations vary per country. There are unscrupulous people who will register trademarks in the hopes that once the owner decides to enter the market, they can sell it to the rightful owner for a good price. This has been a deterrent for some brands to enter the South East Asian market. Also, parallel imports are prevalent with popular brands.
- Fiscal and Monetary Regulations -
  1. Withholding taxes: Each country requires the withholding of taxes upon remittance of royalties or advances. Licensors need not worry about this as once the tax has been paid by the local licensees to their government, the licensee can get a tax certificate for the licensor as proof that tax has been withheld.
  2. Foreign Exchange Remittance: Different countries require certain documentation when remitting foreign exchange. This is also due to money laundering issues.
- ASEAN and ASEAN FREE TRADE AGREEMENT (AFTA) - ASEAN is an organization formed by the Southeast Asia member nations to help each other with issues including but not limited to economic growth, social progress, and security and peace. The goal is for the members to discuss concerns in a peaceful manner. Their Leaders attend ASEAN summits to discuss regional issues of that period. AFTA was established so that the member nations could become more competitive with exports in this region. This agreement has imposed the gradual elimination of tariffs

---

[43] Written by Marilu Corpus

in some categories like apparel. It will also allow member nations to gain access to cheaper raw materials reducing their production costs. Ultimately, this will benefit the consumer. However, among the countries themselves, while there are benefits, there will be stronger competition.

- Local acceptable business practices - In some countries, giving gifts that are special in one's home country, i.e., local delicacies or handcrafts, especially if that person has a high position in the company, is acceptable. It is not deemed as a bribe. One must also be aware of the rules of specific corporations which do not allow their employees to receive gifts entertainment of any kind. If you are unsure about local business practices, it is best to ask your licensing agent. Violation of these practices can cause you to lose business. In addition, Asians are very concerned about "losing face" and therefore we must be sensitive to issues or remarks or that can embarrass them.

- Religion - There may be brands or characters, particularly of the swine and canine persuasion, that may be problematic for religious reasons. Religion and philosophies in Asia are quite diverse.

History of Licensing

The awareness for licensing started in the late 70's and early 1980's. At that time, there were some licensed products present, mostly those imported from Japan for example, PEANUTS and HELLO KITTY. Sanrio was a licensee of SNOOPY through Hallmark Cards Inc., and HELLO KITTY, PATTY AND JIMMY, LITTLE TWIN STARS products from Sanrio were exported to countries like Hong Kong and the Philippines. Sanrio was not yet licensing their brands out at that time. They were producing the items themselves. It was not until sometime later that Sanrio would enter the licensing business as a licensor.

Disney already had licensees in the early 80's like JOYTOY in the Philippines, who did paper products and party goods. Mattel through BARBIE's distributor started licensing in 1990. Ms Myrna Yao of RICHWELL started with 6 licensees, and now she has close to 50 licensees for the Philippines.

Other than Disney and Mattel, United Media appointed Raymond Mok to represent PEANUTS as well as GARFIELD. RM Enterprises brought the PEANUTS characters into Asia in the late 80's together with Hallmark Cards, Determined Productions, Butterfly, and Quantasia, among other global master licensees of PEANUTS. GARFIELD too was successful in Malaysia and Singapore through the MPH Bookstores. In the Philippines apparel sold very well in ShoeMart Department Stores.

In summary, twenty years ago, licensing was characterized by the following:

- Retail relationships were primarily the licensee's responsibility. They met their buyers and discussed terms, designs, the purchase order and any advertising requirements. Today, it is the licensing agent's responsibility to work with the retailer on introducing the brand and getting the retailer to accept and promote the brand, together with funding from the licensee and licensor.

- Advertising and promotions were the licensee's responsibility. Today, some licensors impose the Marketing Support Fund which may lighten the burden of the licensee when the retailer asks for an event. The Marketing Support Fund is a common fund where licensees contribute a percentage of their sales precisely for this purpose. However, the size of the purchase order may not always be commensurate to the required funding.

- Retail space was readily available, but now, space has become quite crowded given the many brands selling to the same target market.
- Agent responsibility was just to sell the license to companies that had the appropriate distribution channel. Now, the agent is responsible for managing the brand from the early strategic stages, to entering the market, to sustaining the brand for the long term
- Television was not a requirement, as several brands were either toy or publishing based (i.e., BARBIE, HELLO KITTY, SNOOPY). Today, with no television programming, retailers are hesitant to purchase. Consumers now are influenced by the different platforms on the web, for example, YOUTUBE, INSTAGRAM, FACEBOOK, etc.
- There were very few competitors in the early days of licensing.
- Retailers are now consistently asking for marketing plans and proposed promotions for their stores.

Licensing Today

The bulk of the licensing business today is still primarily in the character and entertainment segments with toys and apparel as the largest product categories. Mobile and computer games have joined the licensing family. The sports industry, especially individual soccer teams, has not grown as expected. Fashion and lifestyle brands have become more important, especially with the entry of Fast Fashion retailers in the SEA market.

Licensing Agents. In SEA, there are 5 or 6 licensing agents and master licensees that have offices in the region, with one or two local companies focusing within an individual country. Some licensors, especially the Japanese, have master licensees instead of agents. Representation commissions may range from 20 percent to 40 percent depending on the licensor. To earn the commission, the agent is responsible for managing the brand, which can include creating the strategy, sales, product development/ brand assurance, initiating marketing activities and promotions through mall and retail events among others.

Below are some of the challenges a licensing agent may face in the SEA markets:

- It is the agent's responsibility to work with licensees to promote the brand through retail activities and events that will drive sales.
- There are a limited number of licensees in each territory. For example, there may be five bag licensees, but ten children's brands.
- Minimum guarantees, advances and royalty rates in Southeast Asia have not changed in the last ten years. Licensees tend to question the royalty rate and the size of the minimum guarantee especially for a brand that is not well-known in the territory even if it is hot in the Western countries.
- Retailers look at shelf space as very valuable real estate. They want what is HOT.
- Some licensors collect a Marketing Support Fund from the licensees, which is a percentage of sales. This is to ensure that there is a budget set aside for retail activities.

- Terrestrial Channels are still the way to go for Southeast Asia, although YouTube is becoming popular especially for the kids and teens markets. Paid Channels still have very limited exposure.
- There are limited sources for licensing personnel. Options are to hire from other agencies or invest time and resources in training new personnel.
- Agents sometimes must deal with licensors who are not familiar with the market and, yet, insist on what they want which can compromise the growth of the brand in the market.
- Licensors are offering BUNDLE DEALS to licensees taking in lower margins.

Retail. Shelf space is very limited. As a result, retailers will make every effort to be sure that the brand sells as well as give themselves options if the brand does not. Consequently, retailers prefer terms such as Consignment, concession or OTR (Option to Return). This allows the retailer to free itself from the burden of inventory management as well as payments. In general, department stores strategies are changing. Many have upgraded and are bringing in in higher-end brands such AS ARMANI KIDS, GUCCI, BURBERRY, BABY DIOR, RALPH LAUREN, HUGO BOSS and PAUL SMITH JUNIOR. Some of these retailers have reduced the space of entertainment characters to make way for these high-end brands.

Then there are the online retailers like LAZADA, ZALORA, and SHOPPEE. While they are online, a couple have opened Pop Up Shops to engage their customers in a more experiential setting, wherein customers are able to touch and feel their merchandise, especially apparel, and have their purchased goods delivered conveniently to their doorsteps.

In addition, most retailers want to have exclusive programs to be distinctly different from other retailers of the same level. Retailers are always looking for the next hot thing. They want EXCLUSIVE. Most Direct-to-Retail ("DTR") opportunities today are regional apparel promotions with companies such as Uniqlo, Bossini, Chocoolate and the like. Although Hong Kong-based, they do regional promotions.

Licensees. In today's market, there are more brands than licensees available. As a result, agents need to be resourceful in finding new companies that have adequate distribution channels in their territories that they can trust. Adding to the challenge is the fact that many licensees will only invest in the popular brands because it is low risk. However, there may be those who want a classic evergreen brand that do not have highs and lows, but just nice consistent sales for the longer term. In most cases, licensees do not want to take risks. They normally consult with their retailers, merchandisers or buyers before they commit to a brand.

Popular Consumer Trends. Fashion and lifestyle brands have become prevalent in SEA with the presence of fast fashion stores like Forever 21, Uniqlo, H&M, Zara etc. These stores do collaborations with Disney, Warner Bros, Toei, Marvel, etc. Collaborations are becoming more frequent. In the last few years, we have seen fashion brands switch from the wholesale model to a licensing model, for example, PAUL FRANK or Lifestyle brands like LADUREE. In addition, fashion designers have extended product categories into home furnishings and accessories. This trend has been aided by the popularity of cooking and travel programs and lifestyle channels that make people more aware of different cuisines, restaurants, entertainment and places to visit.

In SEA, Western, Japanese and Korean brands are quite popular. Television plays a key role in the success of children's brands as most retailers make this a prerequisite before they buy merchandise. Classics like BARBIE and HELLO KITTY are still quite popular, as well as pre-school brands like SESAME STREET, THOMAS and DORA. The popularity of SUPERHE-ROES is heightened by movie releases. They sell to both kids and teens, male and female. Collectability is still very popular among the children. Several toy brands have become very popular like SHOPKINS, L.O.L. and HATCHIMALS for girls, while MARVEL and ROBLOX for the boys

SEA has had some success with local properties mostly coming from Malaysia. About three years ago, UPIN IPIN was broadcast in English. BOBOIBOY was introduced a little over a year ago, about a boy with superpowers and is still popular in Malaysia and Indonesia. In the Philippines, soap operas that are produced by the local television stations have licensed into basic categories like stationery, notebooks and bags.

Major Licensees: Companies in Hong Kong that do regional deals are Bossini, Watsons, convenience stores like 7/11. Quick Service restaurants like Jollibee, KFC, McDonalds. FMCG like Mead Johnson, PUREFOODS, Selecta, Merchandise Licensees are Honeybarn, Megcorp, Vendermac, Four Ps, Kids and Teens, to name a few.

Major Retailers: Throughout SEA there are department stores, gift and novelty stores, toy stores, health and beauty aid stores, hypermarkets and convenience stores as well as book stores. Indonesia is mostly dominated by the retailers' PT Mitra Adiperkasa who own Seibu, Sogo, Debenhams, Kidz Station, Starbucks and Zara. Mid-tier to mass retailers are Matahari and Ramayana. Mass Market is covered by Hypermarket and Carrefour. The leading book store is Gramedia. In Singapore, Orchard Road is the main shopping area. Takashimaya, CK Tang, Isetan, Metro, BHG, OG, John Little, and Robinsons. Popular bookstores are Page One, Kinokinuya, Times Book Store, Popular and MPH Bookstore, Specialty stores like Action CityT, Precious Thots, and Toys "R" Us. Other retailers are Giant, Carrefour, convenience store Seven Eleven and Cheers. In Malaysia, the retail headliner is Parkson Department Store, which has about 40 stores all over Malaysia. Other players are Isetan, Jusco, Tru, Metro and Carrefour. In the Philippines, SM and Rustans Department Stores cover the mid to hi-tier market, while Robinsons is mass to mid-tier. Key apparel stores are Bench, Penshoppe, Kamiseta, Bayo and Gingersnap. While not a retailer, Avon takes a large portion of the market through direct selling. With the success of Avon, companies like Sara Lee and Natasha have followed suit. Thailand has the two major department stores of Central Department Store and Paragon/Emporium.

Other than department stores, retailers are taking on popular fashion brands and importing them to their territory. In the Philippines, SSI has opened Tiffany's, Ferragamo, Gucci, Tory Burch, Kate Spade, Kenneth Cole, Zara, Massimo Dutti, Debenhams and Starbucks. Uniqlo, H&M and Forever 21 can take the best locations in shopping malls everywhere as they bring in the customers.

Challenges of Doing Business in SEA

Relationships are very important to Asians. In some cases, they do deals on a handshake, especially if they have known each other for a long time. Sometimes they may buy a brand that is not so popular, to keep an ongoing relationship. What is challenging is that Asians have different backgrounds, histories and cultures and so we cannot all be looked at as the same.

Below are some factors to consider when deciding to license in SEA.

Television Exposure. A pre-school property must be on air. In the Philippines, TV stations are required to air an hour of pre-school programming. Given that this is a requirement, one would think that all the pre-school programs would be broadcast. But since there are quite a few pre-school brands, not all are aired. In addition, it is imperative to have coordination between the TV station and the licensing agent. For most television stations who buy programs, one hardly ever gets the schedule or airing times, as this information is confidential. Also, there are television stations that air programs every day instead of once a week, thus not allowing the licensee enough time to go through product development and sell at retail. Before they know it, the 52 episodes have already been broadcast and are not aired again for another 6 months.

Retailer Relationships. Buyers in department stores have different brand preferences. Thus, the presence of the categories in the department stores could be spotty. The marketing funds for brands are used typically for one or two categories. It would be better if the brand was sold across key categories within the department store. The key selling seasons for retailers are back-to-school and Christmas. If the property is a movie, licensors and their theatrical counterparts follow the American schedule. This schedule does not always work as back-to-school in some countries is in May or November. Therefore, this affects the product categories that are sold when the movie opens. The selling of movie merchandise is not maximized, so movie properties are still high-risk for some licensees and retailers in SEA.

Licensor Expectations. Sometimes licensors do not understand the territory and may have unrealistic expectations. If a brand is successful in the United States or Europe, it does not automatically mean that the same will happen in SEA at the same speed. In some countries, it takes time for a brand to be accepted given the number of brands pitching for the same shelf space. Some new licensors with new properties who enter the licensing business may not have the adequate knowledge to manage and implement a licensing program.

Choosing the Right Licensee. The licensee invests in the brand and must deal with the requirements of the retailer, including discounts, rebates, fees, etc. Any delays, especially with time-sensitive launches or movies, can upset the relationship with the retailer. Therefore, the licensee must be financially capable otherwise they will not be able to meet retailers' needs. Also, it is not uncommon for licensees to sign agreements without reading them. Every licensor has different rules and guidelines therefore it is important for the licensee to read and UNDERSTAND every paragraph, especially the breaches.

Outlook, Projections and Conclusions

Shopping is a very popular pastime in Asia. Mainland Chinese travel around SEA. Wealthy Indonesians shop in Singapore. Tourists from the Middle East shop in high end malls in Malaysia. Because of this, retailers continue to upgrade the brands they sell, not just for adults but for kids too. Online shopping sites like Zalora have also become quite popular. We believe that this trend will continue across department stores in SEA. Another trend for the future is apps and mobile phone applications. Over the years mobile phones have come to be used as still cameras, video cameras, organizers, small game consoles, date-books, mini TV's, etc. It is now very easy to download apps from one's phone, and this appears to be an area destined for growth and exploitation. Mobile apps are also used for shopping.

Licensing has been around for many, many years in the United States, and around the world. With all the advances in technology, fashion trends coming and going, changes in consumer behavior, one thing remains constant: licensing is still a very viable and credible marketing tool for companies to use in the development of their products to create a distinct difference from their competitors. The proof is in the increasing number of new brands that are introduced every year in the region.

15.6 Australia[44]

Introduction

This section is dedicated to the Australian market. Australia consists of 24 million people with much of the population on the eastern seaboard. There are 5.5 million people residing in Sydney and 4.5 million in Melbourne. Nationally, we have an aging population.

The key Industries in Australia includes health and education, finance, construction, mining and manufacturing. Our largest export destination is China at 28%. The average residential dwellings price sits at $686,700 aud.

The economy of Australia is highly developed and one of the largest mixed market economies in the world, with a GDP of AUD$1.69 trillion as of 2017. Australia is the second wealthiest nation in the world in terms of wealth per adult, after Switzerland. As of June 2016, Australia's total wealth was AUD$8.9 trillion.

In terms of the licensing of brands, our market has for many years been focussed on the mass market segment, which includes K Mart, Target, and Big W. This segment is said to be worth about AUD$20 billion. The Supermarket segment, which includes FMCG, and general merchandise, is said to be worth about AUD$100 billion.

The department store segment, which has traditionally been part of Australian retail, includes Myer and David Jones. More recent entrants to our market include Aldi Supermarkets, Lidl, and Amazon online.

Licensing, including consumer products and promotions, is a relatively advanced model in our market and highly competitive. Australia would be regarded as a rather small market, however it's structure and dynamics are well established and robust across most categories.

History of Licensing

Licensing in Australia dates to 1947 when Disney appointed Walt Granger to operate Disney Enterprises here in Australia out of Sydney. The Granger family was heavily invested in the Disney Comic business in those days.

Licensing as a serious commercial opportunity began in 1974, when Fred Gaffney travelled to the US. He noticed that a property called SESAME STREET was prominent in many retail

---

[44] Written by Tony Bugg.

outlets and catalogues. Fred negotiated a deal with Sesame to represent the brand in Australia and licensing was born.

IFG was born which later became Gaffney International Licensing. Fred controlled licensing in this country for 30 years. His passion and work ethic were witnessed and respected on a global scale. Fred represented and managed brands including THOMAS, RAGGEDY ANNE, SNAKE, THE MAN FROM SNOWY RIVER, THE SMURFS, SNAKE and THE PHANTOM to mention just a few.

Fred was responsible for the global expansion of the hit ABC series BANANAS IN PYJAMAS along with Graeme Grassby, who is also an industry stalwart. Fred Gaffney promoted and drove the licensing business in Australia and used his profile to promote the industry all over the world. Many of the most successful licensing professionals who work in our industry today worked and learned the business from Fred.

Fred Gaffney of GIL

John Moore ran Warner Brothers and John Cookson took over the Disney operations from Walter Granger. In the 80's, Barry Jones ran the Milton Bradley business in Australia and appointed Hugh Harris to license his properties, including TRANSFORMERS, MY LITTLE PONY and PLAYSCHOOL. John Walsh and Bob Lee are also two industry veterans who, for many years, ran Copyright Licensing in Australia.

Importantly Newman Licensing was also an active partner in Gaffney International. Tony Newman ran the licensing business in New Zealand for many years before he developed his own licensing business in Australia.

Some other iconic brands, which have been significant licensing programs in Australia, include, THE SIMPSONS, NINJA TURTLES, TELE TUBBIES, TOY STORY and the original JURASSIC PARK.

Our industry has always been heavily focussed on Character and Entertainment brands, particularly pre-school brands. During the 70's and 80's, Gaffney represented most of these high-profile properties and, therefore, the market followed his lead.

GIL also included a Sporting division. In those early days Fred represented the NFL and IHL in Australia. Later, James Ashworth, who was a former IMG executive, began his own business called Velocity Brand Management. His organization commercially represents the NRL, Cricket, Soccer, Tennis and Rugby in our market.

Things have changed dramatically since those early days, and competition and more limited retail shelf space has meant that lees brands have been able to gain traction in the marketplace.

Licensing Today

The market has changed and evolved significantly over the last 30 plus years. The industry today is very different and requires alternative methods and techniques to enter the market and launch new brands.

Consolidation of brand owners and representation is a key factor in how brands are managed in today's market. Over recent years, we have seen many global brand owners re-evaluate their businesses and move away from the agency model and open their own offices in Australia. Consolidation has meant that Disney has purchased Marvel and Lucasfilm and is soon to own 20th Century Fox. All these properties were formally managed and represented by agencies. We have also seen E One and Universal open their own offices here.

As I mentioned earlier, our market has traditionally been very Character and Entertainment centric. As conditions have changed, we are seeing more emphasis being focused on other categories, including Celebrity, Sport, Corporate and Art brands. This has dictated different methods of distribution and marketing techniques. The apparel business, which includes licensed underwear, T Shirts, inner and outerwear, has always been a high-profile category for licensing programs.

PINK Popup Store in Melbourne

Pre-school, tween and teen licensing programs are regularly seen in our market. Alternatively, adult merchandise activations are also often seen where the property permits. Some examples of recent pre-school programs include: PAW PATROL and P J MASK. Some examples of Tween programs include: JO JO SIWA. An example of an Adult licensing program is our local, realty cooking, show MKR.

Australians are regularly influenced by global trends, probably originating out of the US more than the UK or Europe.

1. The Australian market generally operates on a seasonal structure, i.e. summer, winter, spring and autumn. The key retailers tend to operate with some sort of a licensing committee structure where by you present your brand portfolio with the view of securing ranging into the future. Normally, retailers in Australia work twelve months in advance.

2. The Australian market is generally well structured and runs in an orderly manner. Our system of government is stable and does not interfere with the commercial structure of the brand licensing business. As Australia is so close to Asia, we do have an ongoing challenge with counterfeit merchandise affecting the officially licensed merchandise programs. LIMA, and an increasing number of organizations, including Rubies/Deerfield are devoting resources to the problem with the view of addressing this infringement. It is an ongoing process where we need to be vigilant. Our economy is generally stable, however, due to market forces and changing structures within certain industries, e.g., the automobile industry (which no longer has a local manufacturing base), other industries come into play. Technology may replace this void. Australia has had recessions in the past and this may be the case in the future if new and emerging industries cannot develop and replace those which have become irrelevant due to changed market conditions and less demand

3. The Australian licensing business generally runs independently, however many organizations, including Disney, Warner Brothers, Universal etc., take direction and report directly to their head offices. There are several key agency models that represent brands that do not have local offices in Australia. In terms of engaging these operations from off-shore, Bugg Marketing Solutions is the independent

consultancy model that would typically be able to provide sound un-biased commercial guidance in this area.

4. The marketing, advertising and promotional techniques for launching and establishing new brands in this market have changed dramatically with the emergence of social media platforms, social influencers and methods including "un boxing" YouTube and mobile tablet proliferation. Traditionally, free to air TV advertising was the dominant method of promoting new brands and product. Today you need to think very carefully about how you bring a product to market. Consideration must be given to the audience i.e. Millennial and emerging market segments. Online methods may also need to be included in your plans. Australia generally has a lower penetration on-line than many other international markets however, this will change. Also, the advent of pop-up shops is becoming much more prevalent.

5. The Australian retail landscape consists of the following tiers:
    *   Specialty
    *   Department Stores
    *   Mass retailers
    *   Fashion chains
    *   Supermarket
    *   Convenience
    *   Online

Traditionally, much of the consumer licensing activity has taken place in the mass segment. This tier sees Target, K Mart and Big W as the main combatants.

In the early days, the specialty market and department store segment, including Myer and David Jones, was the place where you would launch a licensing program and build the platform to take it to mass once it was fully established.

LICENSED T SHIRT WALL AT K MART

The Supermarket segment, which now consists of Coles, Woolworths, Aldi, IGA and more recently Kaufland, offers a general merchandise opportunity for brands. The sheer number of stores, numbering more than 2,000 outlets, provides a genuine volume opportunity.

More recently the convenience route has provided an alternative solution for the distribution of consumer licensed programs providing the retail pricing is generally under $10 aud.

On-line is an ever-emerging platform which will continue to grow and become a more significant percentage of the overall marketing mix.

In terms of examples of specific case studies which demonstrate that when you get it right the results and return can be significant, consider the following examples:

*   **LORD OF THE RINGS Jewelry** – Way back in the early 90's, a gentleman walked into the Haven Licensing offices in Sydney and wanted to sign a license for high end, LORD OF THE RINGS signature gold rings. At the time, it was seen to be a bit unusual. The man signed the deal and paid Haven $150k in royalties over the term of the deal. The association of the brand with the gold ring was perfect

for the program. There were enough dedicated fans to pay top dollar for a replica of the One Ring from the Tolkien classic.

- **BP SMURFS promotion** – During the 70's, Gaffney represented The SMURFS in Australia. He took the concept of a collectable range of SMURFS figurines with a purchase of fuel from BP. One million figurines later, it was a huge success. This promotion has been repeated over the years with more success.

- **WHITMAN'S Sampler** – Keith Marshall saw the opportunity to bring the famous WHITMAN'S chocolate brand from Philadelphia to Australia. Along with a TV campaign he also developed a WHITMAN'S Blimp, which flew over all major sporting events during this time. The brand had no presence in the market at the beginning but, some months into the campaign, they were the market leader

I also wanted to give you an example of where associating a high-profile brand with the wrong product can result in a failure.

- **STAR WARS personal care products** – A leading manufacturer of personal care products including shampoos, body wash and conditioners took a STAR WARS license for one of the new movies and applied it to these products. Unfortunately, the brand was at odds with the nature of the product, which is more readily associated with brands such as POOH Bear etc. The product failed.

The global pace of change because of technology has provided the consumer with an instant solution for purchase. The reorganization of the K Mart business model has meant that the traditional licensed T-Shirt, which was $20, is now selling for under $10. The pressure on price over recent years is enormous. This impacts the earning capacity for brand owners and their partners.

Pressure on price has also impacted quality. We are seeing the quality equation coming back into play as the consumer demands value for their money but a certain quality at the same time.

The launch of Amazon and Alibaba in Australia will no doubt create further change to the distribution models in our market. As the industry evolves, the data shows that retailers probably need both bricks and mortar coverage coupled with a strong on-line presence to gain ultimate success. Australia is a huge continent and many international operators who have chosen to come down-under have underestimated the cost of shipping and delivery. One advantage that many of the larger mass-market retailers possess is their national stores network. This provides a bricks and mortar solution for consumers who buy online and pick up form their local store.

There is no doubt that we will see further change and consolidation in the market over the coming months and years. This will provide new challenges for us to find solutions to reach the consumer in different ways.

15.7 Latin America[45]

Latin America and the Caribbean are the fastest growing regions of our industry and that has been consistent for several years now. With a population of more than 670 million people in more than 30 countries, they represent an excellent opportunity for licensing and merchandising. The combined GDP based on the World Bank Data is approximately 5.3 trillion dollars.

This region's countries are normally called "emerging markets" and frequently that is synonymous with crisis, devaluation, poverty, etc. Yes, Latin currencies have been highly devaluated in the past few years (a lot...) but, the licensing business has become a great opportunity to "fight" the crisis, opening a chance of differentiating product on the shelf, riding a wave of promotion and awareness of a beloved character, and investing proportionally to the capabilities of each licensee and its product to be sold entering to a bigger way to reach massiveness and connection.

One of the things that have always defined the Latin people is the passion and the "need" for growth, always looking to experience new things, new products, understanding other markets and mostly... acculturating all these trends in their homes in a unique way: "Looking up and never forgetting their roots".

We all know that the most important piece of the strategy within the Licensing Industry is the emotional connection that the market/audience can get to a character and or celebrity. If we can cross this factor with a great product "made for" the local market, we can reduce the risks involved in every transaction as part of a licensing process.

The Countries than comprehend the region based on UNESCO data are:

- Antigua and Barbuda
- Argentina
- Bahamas
- Barbados
- Belize
- Bolivia
- Brazil
- Chile
- Colombia
- Costa Rica
- Cuba
- Dominica
- Dominican Republic
- Ecuador
- El Salvador
- Granada
- Guatemala
- Guyana
- Haití

---

[45] Written by Maca Rotter, Panaderia Baking Brands, Mexico City, MX, www.panaderia.xyz

- Honduras
- Jamaica
- Mexico
- Nicaragua
- Panama
- Paraguay
- Peru
- Saint Kitts and Nevis
- Saint Lucia
- Saint Vincent and the Grenadines
- Suriname
- Trinidad and Tobago
- Uruguay
- Venezuela (Bolivarian Republic of)
- Anguilla*
- Aruba*
- British Virgin Islands*
- Cayman Islands*
- Curaçao*
- Montserrat*
- Sint Maarten*

Even though there seems to be a lot, approximately 60% of the industry concentrates in only 2 countries: Mexico and Brazil and the rest, divided by size, are countries such as Colombia, Chile, Argentina, Panama, Ecuador, Peru, etc.

MEDIA

Terrestrial TV penetration is higher than 99% in every single country and still being the most relevant massive media platform.

Pay TV Penetration has grown very fast for the past 20 years from 30% to 60% in most of the countries and even over 90% in countries like Argentina, Chile and Brazil.

Internet penetration growth has been double digit every year for the past 5 years and the acquisition of services such as Netflix and Claro video pushed it a lot more, making YouTube the fastest growing platform of all times in terms of video distribution. The penetration is over 60% of the population in every city in Latin America. The real challenge continues to be the broadband, but it is improving every day, faster than any other region in the world.

According to *Forbes*, 80% of Latin American digital consumers report visiting or updating a social media website daily on a computer as compared with 65% of digital consumers in other parts of the world. The proliferation of mobile use has, at times, surpassed the number of people by the number of connected phones in the country, thus opening a new whole world for the content strategy for every property trying to get linked with Latins.

THE RETAIL SCOPE

A retail study in Latin America in 2017 explored how consumers are responding to an ever-changing economic challenging condition and the continuous evolution of traditional channels to an OMNI-Channel "demand" in the rest of the world. The impressive presence of International players represents more than 50% of the total retail sales in the region, but, we can't forget that is also the street vendors and local retailers who can really move the needle in this region for every property and most of the products that are made for a massive penetration. Omnichannel in Latin America goes from E-commerce to a street vendor, and it would be difficult to bet on which one is bigger at this time.

> According to *Forbes*, 80% of Latin American digital consumers report visiting or updating a social media website daily on a computer as compared with 65% of digital consumers in other parts of the world.

The main trends of retailing in the region are not different than the rest of the world, but, it is moving slower in some of them. For example, in e-commerce there is still much space for growth for many reasons, including fear of digital payments and "unsafe" processes, insufficient bandwidth, etc. Nevertheless, it is undeniable that millennials are re-ruling the scenario like everywhere else, so growth will continue and surely be faster than in many developed countries.

LICENSING CATEGORIES

Licensing practices and opportunities are like other regions in the world. Basically, the key categories are the same and much more related to the type of property than for the country itself.

One of the key challenges that have made a great shift in the Latin markets has been the regulations for food and beverages and how to promote them for children, since that demographic represented about 40% of the overall strategy of the licensing business for entertainment and kid's brands. It is now either "self-regulated" by the main licensees such as PepsiCo, Frito-Lay, Mars, Kellogg's among others or government regulated as well.

In contrast to this, the rise of new stars for kids, tweens and tees has been explosive on the digital scenario and the social media influencers "new" trend for licensing and endorsement have immediately took over. That has opened a new opportunity for those categories. Approaches to emotionally connect the audiences with these "celebrities", while challenging, have created new media platforms and have given fashion a big push to rapidly approach the global trends.

15.7.1 Brazil[46]

Introduction

Brazil is a country of more than eight million square kilometers, divided into five regions: (1) North, (2) Northeast, (3) Center-West, (4) Southeast and South, and (5) the Federal

---

[46] Written by Marici Ferreira

District. It has over 5,000 municipalities and a population of over 207 million people. Brazil has gained prominence in the global economy, but the country still faces challenges that are far from being solved, especially in social areas, despite generally stronger and more stable economic conditions. Per capita income in 2017 was R$ 14,712.00 per year, and the Human Development Index (HDI) was 0.75. Brazil is ranked as 79th among 187 countries analyzed (data released by the United Nations Development Program in March 2017).

Brazil has a pyramid-shaped social and economic distribution, with a broad range of poverty at the base, a small middle class, and a smaller peak made up of upper class. Due to the economic situation, social class C (low middle class) is growing slowly, and that brings positive consequences for lifestyle and consumption.

Today, low middle class consists of families who have a monthly income between three and six times the minimum Brazilian wage (R$ 954,00). This income, for a large part of this population, was reached in recent years due to several factors, among them policies to eliminate poverty, and social inclusion, along the country economic growth. With increased purchasing power and the use of various forms of credit, the new middle class has shown a keen interest in new technology, consumer goods, and everyday items. The group has boosted consumption, improving life standard and driving the domestic market for manufactured goods, as well as trade and services.

The History of Licensing

Walt Disney's characters began to appear in Brazilian newspapers in the 1940s, after Disney himself visited the country and created Zé Carioca. At that time, SNOW WHITE released a record on the Continental label. Editora Abril began by publishing comic books featuring DONALD DUCK, licensed by Walt Disney. A little later, characters such as MICKEY MOUSE and DONALD DUCK began to appear at birthday parties, printed on t-shirts, and used in chocolates. Licensing was controlled from the New York office until the 1960s, when Disney offices (Redibra, founded by Elcan Diesendruck) and Hanna Barbera offices were opened in São Paulo.

In 1968, Mauricio de Sousa began licensing his characters. It was the first licensing of characters created in Brazil. The characters BIDU and FLOQUINHO became dolls manufactured by Duplex. Then Mauricio de Sousa's characters began to appear in blankets and bed sheets. In 1970, the elephant, JOTALHÃO, began to appear in commercials for Cica tomato paste. Increasingly, brands, characters, and celebrities grew in importance for companies, making them more competitive while generating value for consumers.

Licensing Today

The main licensing properties in Brazil today, include: BARBIE, GALINHA PINTADINHA, MY LITTLE PONY, LADY BUG, PAW PATROL, DISNEY PRINCESSES, SMURFS, MONICA'S GANG, DC COMICS HEROES, MARVEL HEROES, MARIO BROS., Brazilian and international soccer clubs.

Popular Brazilian properties attracting significant licensing attention are: GALINHA PINTADINHA,

> Main licensing properties in Brazil today are: BARBIE, GALINHA PINTADINHA, MY LITTLE PONY, LADY BUG, PAW PATROL, DISNEY PRINCESSES, SMURFS, MONICA'S GANG, DC COMICS HEROES, MARVEL HEROES, MARIO BROS.

SHOW DA LUNA, soccer clubs, and MONICA'S GANG.

Unlike the United States, Canada, and much of Europe, there is no official information on the size of the licensing sector in Brazil, and most available figures for the Brazilian licensing market are estimates. Key local licensing operations include:

Licensors — Cartoon Network, Disney, Endemol Shine, Globo Gloob, Hasbro, Kasmanas Licenciamento, Lotus Global, Mattel, Mauricio de Sousa Produções, Nickelodeon, Redibra, Sanrio, Tycoon 360, Universal Pictures and Warner.

Licensees— C&A (fashion store), DTC (toys), Estrela (toys), FestColor (party pieces), Foroni (notebooks), Grendene (footwear), Jandaia (notebooks), Luxcel (bags), Panini (publish), Pitica's (fashion store), Regina Festas (party pieces), Riachuelo (fashion store), Riclan (candy and chewing gum), Top Cau (chocolate) and Xeryus (bags).

It is estimated that 500 companies now work with licensing, or are licensed, in a market that offers about 600 licenses, and of which 75 percent are foreign. There are about 50 licensors and licensing agents operating in Brazil, creating approximately 1,500 direct jobs.

An estimated 60% of the licensing market is made up of properties related to entertainment, 25% percent are corporate properties, and 15% of licenses are related to sports.

The key licensing categories include: school items, apparel, stationery, toys, footwear, health and beauty, and food.

In recent years, the market has been growing steadily, at an average of 5% per year. In 2017 licensed products in retail earned R$ 18 billion.

Brazil is now the 9th country in revenue from brand licensing worldwide, and this number has positive aspects, such as:

- Plenty of room for growth in several areas
- Increased number of Brazilian brands in the market
- A growing shift away from TV as the primary medium to digital media
- Growth of e-commerce as a channel for more segmented brands
- Better structure of the sector via publishing of "Licensing Brasil" and the new board at the Brazilian Licensing Association (ABRAL)
- In 2017 ABRAL made an agreement with LIMA (Licensing Industry Merchandiser's Association that will work to qualify professionals of the sector and promote licensing as an important marketing tool

Conversely, as may be expected, certain less beneficial trends arise from this frenzy of brand proliferation, including:

- Lack of professionals with expertise in licensing
- Small base of companies that make use of licensing
- Lack of knowledge in retail of the benefits of licensing as a branding & marketing tool

Brazil's economic and fiscal peculiarities are totally different from those in the United States, Europe, Asia, or even other countries in Latin America. The economy today is stable, but has endured a turbulent history, and much depends on who controls political power. This is a recurring reality, which foreigners from consistently stable political countries may have difficulty grasping in a business context. What exists today may change tomorrow, if the government decides so. In addition, the local tax system is exceedingly complex and very different from the single rates that often are paid separately in other countries. Explaining this to foreign business partners is especially difficult and time-consuming.

Best Practices for Marketing, Advertising, and Promoting
Licensed Products at the Local Level

Being in touch with the consumer, creating a relationship, investing in stocks, etc., all maximize results in any licensing campaign. Communications, announcements, and actions that show the power of a character or property, explore their attributes as well as involve the target audience are certainly good practices. Retail campaigns with tabloids, point of purchase (POP) materials, exhibition at the POP with several lines of licensed products, and campaigns with free gifts are practices that typically generate positive and profitable results.

Retail Sector

The Brazilian retail sector has seen profound changes in recent years, becoming increasingly competitive. The sector has been growing and developing a new range of strategies that are not just meant to reduce prices and costs. Brazilian retailers have been looking to increase their regional coverage, opening specialist stores, and increasing the presence of groups and chains nationally.

The sector, whose largest companies and suppliers are still concentrated in the South and Southeast except for electronics suppliers, is calling still for major structural changes. Such changes lead to improvement in relationships in terms of the supply chain, which is beginning to target not only the commercial area, prices, and payment methods, but also better management in the flow of goods. Alongside family-run standards, corporate governance is being improved using information technology that standardizes the management of companies and their degree of professionalism. Currently, there is a growing use of labor-saving technologies and better-qualified professionals, factors that are essential for a sector that often suffers with less skilled labor and high staff turnover.

Overall, retail involves highly seasonal activities and high turnover, as well as being very susceptible to economic policies that affect the macroeconomic scenario and income and employment indicators. So, the Brazilian growing population and economic stability are important factors for the growth of the licensing industry.

15.7.2 Colombia, Chile, Ecuador, Peru, Venezuela and Central America[47]

Introduction

This section covers licensing in the countries of Colombia, Chile, Ecuador, Peru, Venezuela and Central America (Costa Rica, El Salvador, Guatemala, Honduras, Panama). Latin America is wide, and there are great economic and cultural differences across the different countries, forcing licensors and licensees to adapt work and methods to each country and region. For purposes of this chapter we will divide the region into five sub-categories: Chile;

---

[47] Written by Luis Salazar

Colombia and Peru; Central America (which includes Costa Rica, El Salvador, Guatemala, Honduras and Panama); Ecuador; and Venezuela.

The first category, Chile, is a well-developed, stable economy that offers the licensing business many opportunities in terms of market conditions: modern laws to protect intellectual property, very low duties, and a low barrier for the entry of foreign goods, as well as a developed and modern retail market in which every licensing company could compete.

The second category groups Colombia and Peru together, because both have constantly growing economies (for more than 10 years now) making an impact with their strong growth in retail business mainly due to foreign investment. However, the legislation in these countries is still weak regarding the licensing business.

In the third category, we find the Central American region: Costa Rica, El Salvador, Guatemala, Honduras and Panama, countries that have small economies and different legislation, making it difficult for the licensing business. In the fourth category, we have Ecuador, a country with a protectionist government and unstable politics that imply constant changes in legislation and economics causing an unstable environment for long-term business planning. Finally, there is Venezuela, a country with an unstable political situation, a growing inflation, high unemployment and a lack of clear laws defining the industry, resulting in an irrelevant market for licensing opportunities.

South American Countries	GDP Annual Growth Rate % Sept – Dec 2017	Population M Dec 2016
Colombia	1.60	48.75
Chile	3.30	18.19
Ecuador	3.80	16.53
Perú	2.20	31.49
Venezuela	-13.20	31.03
Costa Rica	2.98	4.91
El Salvador	2.50	6.15
Honduras	3.60	8.72
Guatemala	2.70	16.56
Nicaragua	3.20	6.33

Panamá	4.90	4.03

Source: https://tradingeconomics.com

History of Licensing

Our company, Compañía Panamericana de Licencias (CPL) started in the early 1980's and was one of the first to the start developing the licensing business in Latin America. The first companies to enter the region were Warner Bros. Consumer Products, represented by The Licensing Company of America with three agents for this region, and Disney with two agents, one agent to handle the Peruvian and Chilean market from Argentina, and a second agent to handle the rest of the region from Colombia, we used to handle both.

In the early days of licensing in Latin America, selling a license was very complicated because the potential clients were used to using the brands for free, without the license rights. In fact, most of our initial clients were companies that had been using the brands or properties without any official licenses. The market was very small and did not offer many opportunities. At that time, licensors were looking mainly for profitability. Very few of them were taking care of their brands and were not monitoring strategies, arts and designs or brand assurance guidelines.

In the early 80´s, we mainly licensed the entertainment properties of the few movies and free TV channels that were available in the Latin American region. Now, the entertainment industry in the region offers many options to consumers. As an example, in each country, audiences now have free access to 5-10 broadcast channels, and more than 100 cable TV channels, creating a great opportunity for character licensing properties based on these movies and TV shows. In addition, new trends are emerging where licenses are now not only being sought for the characters from these movies or television shows, but also for the brands, celebrities, art and sport properties, toys and, most recently, video games properties, bloggers, influencers, You Tubers and streaming TV properties.

The licensing business is stronger than ever in Latin America and keeps attracting new companies with promising opportunities. More and more players are entering the licensing business market, providing more options for the final customers.

Nowadays, we need to provide a full range of services to companies, including advice and guidance for the choice of the brand, design styling and strategies for the release of the products, find the best customers and follow brand assurance process and royalty reporting. It is extremely important that we work closely with licensees, retailers and regional partners to achieve success. For all of this, studios require specialized agents who can help them compete in these markets.

Licensing Today

As we mentioned in the introduction, some market conditions in the area could be considered as barriers to entering the market with licensing business. Depending on the country, there are significant differences in legislation protecting intellectual property, often leading to a "black market" for products featuring brands and characters without the license rights. This leads many consumers to think: "Why should I pay for the right to a license if I can have it for free?"

Some of these experiences can be directly attributed to the informal business environment in Latin America, sometimes making it difficult for international businesses and companies to collaborate with local companies. It is important to mention that some countries suffer from political instability, impacting laws and business regulations and making long-term planning difficult. Such circumstances also have a direct impact on the economy (i.e., the Venezuelan annual inflation jumped 2,616 % in 2017) and affected the demand for consumer products.

> The most popular properties in the Latin American market are the DC properties, Marvel's Super Heroes and STAR WARS

Although the market is still in the process of development, it is important to mention that the licensing business is growing, and legislation is being introduced frequently to better regulate the markets in the Latin American region. Today, new regulations covering foods and beverages for kids are being analyzed and some are already applied.

Growing economies imply a better and wider access to television, cinemas, video games and Internet. The result has been a stronger presence from the entertainment industry, raising awareness and impacting demand for licensed product.

It is important to mention that the growing market attracted many new players, willing to represent brands and market their licenses. Licensors and licensees need to understand the complexities of the Latin American markets. It is important for international licensors to seek the help of experienced, local agents or partners before they decide to begin licensing.

Although most of licensed properties are imported from the US, Europe or Japan, some strong properties originate from Latin America. For example, Brazilian Monica's gang from Mauricio de Sousa Produções is a great example of a licensing success in a country, competing in the Brazilian market among the great licensing companies such as Warner Bros. and Disney.

Disney, Warner Bros., Cartoon Network, Universal are the most important companies in the licensing business in the Latin American Market. The most popular properties are DC properties, Marvel's Super Heroes and STAR WARS. The licensing industry works together with the entertainment industry, always looking to satisfy their audiences and leading the way for licensors to reach out to their clients.

Retailers have played a big role in the licensing business's success, offering new channels for the commercialization of licensed products. With the expansion, as well as the creation of new department stores in Latin America, many licensed products have found their way onto the shelves, and more importantly, to the end consumer. The e-tailing or electronic retailing is growing fast, Internet sales increasing and purchases at stores decreasing.

Though the Latin American market is now considered large and relevant enough for the licensing business, there are still some areas that have yet to be developed, representing new opportunities and challenges for licensors and agents. For example, publishing is very strong internationally in the licensing industry, but it still is a very small market in this area. The toy category is another category that is under-developed in the region. Mattel, Hasbro and Lego are the most important players in the business having almost 80% of the market share in the region.

Almost forty years ago there were two companies competing in the region for licensing TV properties, and two agents for each country. Now, over fifty licensors have presence in the region with more than twelve agents representing TV properties as well as movies, artists, brands, design, sport properties, video games, and toys licenses. The licensing market in our region is much more sophisticated and complex than it was before and now requires highly experienced professionals with the best knowledge and expertise to reach success. The growing economies in Latin America are very promising for the future of licensing, led by a growing demand for consumer products every day more eager to identify with new brands.

> **While Mexico has extensive trade agreements with 40 countries, approximately 85% of their exports take place with the US**

15.7.3 Mexico[48]

Introduction

¡Bienvenidos! Mexico is a welcoming territory for licensing entrepreneurs ... highly sensitive to global trends and extremely quick at reacting to consumer needs and demands. Mexicans enjoy life, family and friends, promote social interaction and are traditionally hefty consumers. Due to its size and copious population, Mexico represents a zesty opportunity for brand owners willing to expand their licensing business into our region, although the country's infrastructure and commercial and retail structures may allow only a handful of those to be successful.

Mexico is the world's eleventh ranked economy in GDP and ranks 55 in the World's 2013-2014 Competitive Index as published by WEF. It is the second economy in Latin America, next only to Brazil, and thanks to sensible improvement in business development conditions, financial stability and business sophistication, Mexico is considered one of the world's big emerging markets. Mexico is intensely populated by over 112 million people; this implies more than 22 million households and a large percentage, slightly shy of 30%, of young consumers under the age of 14.

Not unlike other economies in the region, wealth is very unevenly distributed, and more than 36 million people continue to live in poverty. Lack of significant work opportunities has led to migration, self-employment and the proliferation of an informal economy. More than 30% of economically active people in Mexico are part of the informal sector which in turn represents more than 50% of the country's retail economy, a major topic in today's political and economic agenda, as well as a challenging and undeniable opportunity for licensed products.

The larger portion of the population is situated in the C and D socioeconomic levels and average GDP per capita is still one-third of the US. As result, most retail activity takes place at mass level, whether at the so-called "modern channels" (mass retail chains such as

---

[48] Written by Elias Fasja / Dalia Benbassat

Walmart or Soriana, hypermarkets, warehouses and convenience stores) or the "traditional channels" (which include wholesale, thousands of independent retailers and the very large informal market).

Most economic activity is concentrated in the larger cities, such as Mexico DF, Guadalajara, Monterrey, followed by Puebla, Toluca or León. These are the home of the country's largest corporations and headquarters of the main retail firms except for Soriana. Distribution of goods to the entire territory becomes an important challenge as well as a highly competitive asset for those who master it.

Approximately 30% of GDI stems from International Trade. Mexico has extensive trade agreements with 40 countries, however approximately 85% of exports take place with the US only. It is easy to see how influenced our economy is by the US economy and how strongly impacted we are by its ups and downs.

Mexico remained afloat during the world economic turmoil – it was able to maintain price stability and moderate internal deficit. Financial Institutions have proven strong and credit has remained available for qualifying corporations; foreign investment progressed, and economy registered growth even through the years of crisis.

Recent changes in the Federal Government have slowed the economy down as several structural reforms are being crafted and slowly approved, related to energy, education, labor and taxes, which are expected to reestablish competitive pace.

The intense combat against the drug cartels and the outbursts of violence and levels of insecurity in several neuralgic points of the country have also impacted negatively on the international perception of Mexico as a market apt for investment, and have brutally hit tourism, one of Mexico's largest sources of income, next to oil. This is an important setback against the otherwise promising macro-economic landscape and remains a high priority for the current administration.

Latin America remains one of today's world's economic engines, next to Asia. And Mexico, despite its significant challenges, stands among the region's best.

As a licensing professional or IP owner, you should consider the following challenges which affect our industry in particular:

- **Rampant piracy and very little anti-piracy enforcement** – A degree of progress has been achieved in recent years and thanks to the work of large IP protection activists in the territory, the IMPI or Mexican Institution of Intellectual Property, several new laws have been passed to protect IP owners from infringers and turn piracy and counterfeiting into a federal offense. But piracy is not bound to disappear anytime soon, it is rather something to live and deal with, especially because the illegal market is aware of the overall shy nature of licensors' anti-piracy programs.
- *Concentration of Retail in fewer hands* – Large retail conglomerates are becoming the rule, and strategic acquisitions have narrowed down the number of players in retail over the last few years. The reach of these retailers has widened, but not the space that they devote to new brands.
- *Concentration of Telecommunications in few hands* – in particular, TV broadcasting is controlled by two incredibly large firms which offer limited screen possibilities for new content and very tight entry filters. This reduces viewers' choices and

affects entertainment licensing. Penetration of alternative media, which is expected to continue growing, is still limited (pay TV reaches only 44.3% of total households with a 29.4 estimated share1 and broad band is estimated to match a similar number). Significant change is however expected through the boost of Smartphones and other mobile devices, and the surprisingly big participation of our country in social networking (i.e. Mexico has the second largest base of Facebook users worldwide accounting for forty-nine million users).

Not unlike other territories, new technology will play a big part in how licensing evolves in Mexico the years to come. (Source: Consejo Latinoamericano de Publicidad en Multicanales. Data: 2013 *The Wall Street Journal*)

History of Licensing in Mexico

Licensing as an activity started out in Mexico in the second half of the twentieth century with fashion brands. Brands were then basically split by Licensors by category and scattered among several licensees, who acted in total independence with little to no coordination among them.

The first brand to be developed as a full concept - including shop in shops and stand-alone stores - was the French label CACHAREL, conceived and developed in 1976 by the late Mr. Jacobo Fasja and headed by son Elias until 1992, who would, years later, found Tycoon Enterprises.

Through the 70's and 80's, character licensing in Mexico was mostly a Disney and Hanna Barbera sanctuary, followed in the late eighties by a few Warner Bros. basic merchandising programs. On the girl's side there was mainly BARBIE. Sports licensing was still at a very early stage, basically with NFL and MLB products.

None of these brands had their own consumer products operations in the territory but were represented by small agencies or individuals. Disney was in the hands of Mr. Bustamante, Warner Bros. and NINJA TURTLES were represented by Mr. Armando Malo (owner of Grupo Innovación), Hanna Barbera was represented by Mr. Gallard, and Mattel by Mr. Olivier.

By the late eighties the Mexican government began entering globalization trends, relaxing its policies for foreign corporations seeking to establish their own operations locally and opening the borders to imported goods which had been restricted until then. This had a very positive effect on the development of Licensing in our territory.

NAFTA (North America Free Trade Agreement) was signed by US President George H.W. Bush, Mexican President Salinas, and Canadian Prime Minister Brian Mulroney in 1992 to facilitate trade among the three countries. It was ratified by the legislatures of the three countries in 1993.

Tycoon Enterprises started operations in 1990 as the licensing agent for Mexican TV classic EL CHAVO DEL OCHO, followed soon after by Twentieth Century Fox THE SIMPSONS as its first International client. In the few years that followed most large independent brands resorted to Tycoon for professional representation. Tycoon became the first fully established Licensing & Merchandising Agency to offer local licensing expertise at world-class standards and remains to date strongly positioned in Latin America.

In 1992, The Disney Co. took over their Mexico consumer products operation. Warner Bros. followed the same steps a few years later, and as result of the merger with Turner took the licensing of Cartoon Network properties (handled by Tycoon until then) in-house too. And before the end of the same decade, BARBIE and NFL, which had achieved big relevance also under Tycoon at that time, decided to take their CP operation in-house.

By that time, all the agents listed above, except for Tycoon, had left the licensing scene. ITC from Brazil was the first non-Mexican agency who tried to conquer our market bringing the representation of PEANUTS. Owner Mr. Peter Carrero first hired a friend who regrettably passed away shortly after and then partnered with entrepreneur Mr. Enrique Altamirano, owner of Efectos Especiales and creator of Burundis, a domestic property born from social expression cards which enjoyed several years of success. Mari Carmen Rotter was GM of the operation then. The partnership didn't see the turn of the century.

A few years later, two new players entered the field: Mr. Ronald Dickins with the agency Globo Rojo, later known as Licensing and Promotions, representing initially Power Rangers, then a roaster of several other properties, and Union Internacional owned by Dr. Hideo Hayase K., which represented DRAGON BALL during a long and very successful window (then other "anime-related" brands). Both agencies closed their doors in December 2012.

Another three foreign companies opened branches in Mexico and continue in operation: from Peru Compañía Panamericana de Licencias "CPL" (formerly Losani), EXIM Licensing, originally from Argentina, and Losani's spin-off P&L Global, also Peruvian, all of which have enjoyed significant success.

At the turn of the century, Televisa – a dominant media group in the territory – set out to explore the business potential of licensing and merchandising, leveraging its privileged position among young audiences. By the end of 2003, it named ex-ITC licensing expert Mari Carmen Rotter – Maca – to lead the CP operation, which would manage their own properties as well as third party content too. Their first relevant move in this direction was closing an output deal with Nickelodeon which included all major platforms.

Following global corporate strategies, also Hasbro took its CP operation in-house, and so did Cartoon Network/Turner (who had parted from WB a few years before and was again in the hands of Tycoon).

A few others have ventured into the licensing field since and have built small but respectable operations. However, it has become clear that to grow and gain a position in this business, you need schooling, experience, professionalization, and a solid portfolio which can be sustained over time.

Setting up a licensing agency in the early days was quite simple and unsophisticated. Licensing agents were mostly former advertising executives and possibly an assistant, who in certain cases was their own spouse. Deals were made "fist come first serve" with little attention to product quality or distribution capabilities, minimum guarantees were negotiated in random ways, several categories bundled in one deal with little care for segmentation, etc. Young, albeit smart, people were handling sales with almost no experience, and licensors were not demanding anything other than new deals and good numbers; no strategy, no retail, no forecasts, etc.

The more structured offices back then would be Disney and Grupo Innovación (agent then for Warner Bros. and NINJA TURTLES). But, overall, the market was still "naïve" ... it was the licensing and merchandising kindergarten, and a business with small risk and high ROI. Triggered possibly by a very successful NINJA TURTLES merchandising program, we can consider the late 80's and beginning of the 90's as the starting point for modern character licensing.

Besides the shifts in International commerce mentioned above, another factor that significantly contributed to this was the resurgence of character-based consumer promotions, which had been banned by President Luis Echeverria (1970 – 1976) and which ban was lifted at the end of the eighties. Such moment was leveraged by huge companies like Frito-Lay and later by Grupo Bimbo, through massively successful self-liquidating and instant-win promotions. Promotions have since become a strong tool at building awareness for licensed brands in the territory.

The first large character-based retail activation happened in 1994, when Liverpool, the largest departmental retailer, reached an agreement with Tycoon Enterprises to develop their Christmas campaign around The Flintstones characters following their movie success. The terms were: Liverpool would give all FLINTSTONES licensees the opportunity to participate and those, whose product performed well, would remain thereafter. In exchange, the retailer would have the right to develop and portray all marketing and POP assets at their own cost and expense. Everyone was happy. The following couple of years, under similar conditions, promotions were made first with the TOM & JERRY characters, and then with Looney Tunes, both including a "purchase with purchase" plush promotion.

In 1997, Disney CP broke in, changing the rules significantly by investing a huge marketing sum, including a very impressive street parade. This established a very hard standard to meet and marked the end of the "age of innocence." Ever since, branded retail promotions have become the financial burden of licensors, agents and licensees. Given the early resistance –at times lack of interest- from foreign licensors to invest in local retail, and the absence of standardized Common Marketing Funds, such activities remained only Disney's privilege for a long time. It took several years for licensors to realize the centrality and relevance of investing in local retail.

Slowly, but steadily, a growing number of properties broke into the market, and the environment turned increasingly competitive. Licensors became more and more demanding with their agents in terms of more sophisticated services, ongoing financial forecasting and re-forecasting, more seniority in brand managers, dedicated retail work, high yield in exchange for very limited investment in brand building. As the offer of new properties grew in the market, retailers in turn became more selective as well and, at that point, the licensing business in Mexico broke into a new era.

Licensing Today

Licensing in Mexico today is a tough and demanding business which requires much more than good will, it needs well-built and sophisticated structures, strong retail relationships, strategic thinking and tons of leverage. The retail environment for licensed product has become quite challenging in great degree due to our retail structure.

Departmental penetration in our country is calculated to be only 40 square meters (430 sq. ft.) per every 1,000 people. Few names compose this sector: Liverpool is the largest high end departmental retailer in Mexico with 65% market share against Sears 20% and Palacio de Hierro 17% (by sales). In the mid-tier we have Suburbia, a soft line retailer owned by Walmart and departmental Coppel only. With regards to mass market, Walmart's share is in the 58% range, followed by Soriana 20%, Commercial Mexicana 12% and Chedraui 10%.[49] Besides these few albeit large formats, there are basically no multi-brand retail chains, therefore no significant "alternate" market for licensed goods within formal retail. This scenario leaves little room for second or third-tier brands, outside the very top, and becomes very demanding with those who make it to the sales floor, namely very high performance and stringent negotiation terms. Small brands have a hard time facing these conditions.

Supporting your brand to get the desired exposure and promotion with the leading chain stores requires large marketing investment and, strong and capable licensees who are, in turn, reduced to a few selected vendors. So, despite this being a wonderful country of over 110 million souls, the number of possibilities for sound licensing success is unexpectedly limited and concentration in the "power brands" is very high, as we shall discuss further ahead to more detail.

Major Properties.

Infant / Pre-school: Disney Classics, Disney PRINCESSEs, Pixar characters (such as TOY STORY or CARS), Plaza Sésamo (SESAME STREET co-production for Latin America), Nickelodeon's DORA THE EXPLORER.

Girls: Sanrio's HELLO KITTY, Mattel's MONSTER HIGH & BARBIE, musical band ONE DIRECTION and Universal Pictures' DESPICABLE ME.

Boys: Disney-Marvel Superheroes, Rovio's ANGRY BIRDS, Universal's DESPICABLE ME, WB's SUPERMAN, Cartoon Network's BEN 10.

Young Adults: 20th Century Fox's THE SIMPSONS, Disney-MARVEL Superheroes, sports brands such as soccer clubs REAL MADRID or BARCELONA or LOCAL CLUBS AMERICA or CHIVAS.

Young Women: Sanrio's HELLO KITTY.

Properties Originating from Mexico.

Televisa's TV series EL CHAVO DEL OCHO, illustration/social expression originals DISTROLLER and FULANITOS, Internet-born HUEVOCARTOON, and world-known artist FRIDA KAHLO.

Major Licensors.

Major licensors who have local direct operation in Mexico are Disney, Cartoon Network, Mattel, Hasbro, Warner Bros., NFL and of course Televisa.

---

[49] As of 10/2012 according to El Economist citing Monex consumer behavior analyst Paola Sotelo.

Major Retailers.

High-End / Department stores: Liverpool (and sister-stores Fábricas de Francia), Sears, Palacio de Hierro.

Mid-tier: Suburbia (mostly soft-lines) & Coppel (includes department stores and footwear specialty)

Specialty: Office Depot, Office Max, Sanborn's (mostly gift & electronics), Martí (all sports).

Mass Market: Walmart Group, Soriana, Commercial Mexicana, Chedraui (each group with corresponding supermarket and hypermarket formats).

Price Clubs: Sam's, Costco, City Club.

Convenience Stores: OXXO, Seven Eleven, Extra.

There are no numbers officially pronounced to date by any of our authorities with regards to Licensed sales or Licensed revenues deriving from Licensed sales in our territory. Market Analysts must yet address our sector to more depth and device a way to align criteria so that our industry can be measured effectively and consistently year by year.

PROMARCA, Mexico's Licensing Association, in collaboration with all its members, carried out the first serious attempt to assess a number to our Industry's worth, and in April 2013 published that:

A total of $1.7 Billion USD was generated from RETAIL SALES of Licensed Goods over the course of 2012 in MEXICO alone. This number is not expected to be precise, but to portray a reasonable idea of our industry's print in local economy.

Product Category	Percent	Retail Sales (billion US)
Apparel	14.0	242
Footwear	3.6	62
Home	10.2	177
Promotions	8.4	146
Accessories	14.6	254
Electronics	0.3	5
Food & Beverage	4.9	85
Paper & School Supplies	16.4	285
Publishing	2.4	41
Personal Care	6.8	118
Toys & Games	17.0	295
Videogames	1.4	25

100%	1,735

Source: PROMARCA (Asociación Mexicana de Licenciamiento y Promoción de Marcas).

The mix is vastly dominated by Character and Entertainment Brands, followed by Fashion, Sports and other. Expected yearly growth rate: 5%

Codes of Conduct

When doing business in Mexico you should aim for a very positive experience. Save for few inevitable exceptions, expect to deal with trained professionals who, even when new to licensing, are thoroughly prepared in their fields, aware of major global trends and often can account for International experience. Business is normally conducted in a collaborative and friendly tenure, where good will is expected to prevail.

Personal relationships are a key to business success in Mexico, where trust plays an important component. Mexicans prefer to do business with people they can relate to rather than with impersonal organizations. Since trust is something that needs to be developed, it is not uncommon that business meetings are followed or combined with dinner or more casual gatherings, where other associates or even family members are invited. For licensors who are, at times, worlds away, this role is played almost in its entirety by the agent, who will act as a cultural bond and interpreter.

Possibly due to this personal aspect of business relationships, you may find that deadlines and contractual obligations are somewhat taken more lightly when compared against other more stringent cultures. So, contracts and other written documentation are always recommended, laying down to absolute clarity the extent of obligations as well as the consequences of breach. Compliance is often reactive rather than proactive, so reminder letters or even penalties become a stronger incentive than elaborate agreements.

Mexicans regard their business relationships as those of mutual and corresponding responsibility. Expect a great deal of service for royalties paid and licensors to do their share of hard work: meaning to significantly promote the brand in the market and provide sufficient MKT tools to engage retail successfully. Licensees feel inherently that it is them taking the higher stakes, so respectful manners are expected always and a level of aid in times of trouble. Don't expect to have sustained business in Mexico based on threats, unilateral decisions or indifference.

Mexican licensees are creative and practical. They will factor in the reality of their market and devise ways to offset the challenges related to economy and infrastructure but will feel frustrated when licensors take too long to approve their materials or issue a customs letter… which seem like simple endeavors when compared to the hurdles they must embrace. They expect their business to be taken as seriously as their counterparts and need answers to arrive timely. They will respond very positively to licensors who seem accepting to their outlook and show true interest in their business and in their market.

Unique Challenges

Piracy remains a constant threat for our industry. The "informal" economy is indexed at 60% of Mexico's overall economy which provides a very large and prolific soil for IP infringement. Whether it is done by local manufacturers producing goods to the lowest standards and quick supplying any rising demand or by counterfeiters smuggling merchandise in through our highly permeable borders, coming from foreign licensees' stock or factories far away... piracy is rampant, and, despite the authorities' best efforts and sensible achievements, nothing says that the situation will significantly improve, largely due to its social and political implications. Pirated goods hit first. They normally respond better to local taste and needs. If we are to defeat piracy, we must defeat this principle first. Shorten lead-times. Understand context. Enable licensees to reach consumers sooner with product that is right for their market.

> Piracy remains a constant threat to our industry. The "informal" economy is indexed at 60% of Mexico's overall economy.

Concentration of Retail. Mexico is affected with this global shift. Volume is strongly concentrated in the mass-retail segment, composed by very few players who are becoming even fewer as result of consolidation or acquisition by larger groups. Despite their big size, these retailers are normally risk averse as far as brands are concerned, and all aim at the same top-notch properties which will presumably help them secure market share and maintain square foot margins high. So, we have more of the same stores, but same number of brands, or proportionately... less. With fewer decision makers, competition to attain shelf space becomes fierce for licensees and pressure for in-store investment increases dramatically not only on licensees but on licensors too. As result, chances for emerging or niche brands are seriously reduced – on one hand the entry filter is tight; on the other the requirements for investment are high. Besides, without the big retail players, the critical mass needed to start up production become very hard to reach and moving into independent retail brings you face to face with the challenges related to informality, as described above.

Execution in Retail - Larger IP owners have developed the right sense of relevance of retail activation and in-store investment. However, despite retailers' size and degree of sophistication, execution of programs within these retailers is inconsistent and often results in loss of significant resources out of mismanagement. A flock of merchandisers and promoters is undoubtedly a critical recourse for proper execution in store and maximization of money invested.

Shifts in Currency Rates – Mexico's economy is highly dependent on the US economy and, as a result, the Mexican peso is often qualified as it relates to the US dollar rather than any other currency in the world. Most licensors have resorted to requiring payments in US dollars as a security measure and most licensees have come to accept it. However, it represents and additional risk for licensees which they inevitably factor in when submitting projections and negotiate minimum guarantees. During severe shifts in exchange rates, it is not uncommon to see cash flow slow down and licensees request caps placed to secure their balancing payments from growing out of proportion.

Jurisdiction – Especially when dealing with major retailers in terms of Direct to Retail deals or Promotions, jurisdiction can be a deal breaker if the Mexican jurisdiction is rejected by a foreign licensor. Be ready to deal with it and to find creative ways to settle.

Withholding Taxes – As Mexico has double-tax treaties with several countries (35 until August 2013), non-treaty countries will be faced with high withholding rates. It is important to prepare yourself on the subject and hear your agent's advice.

Countries with which Mexico has running Double Tax Treaties as of 2013:

Países con los que México tiene Acuerdo para Evitar la Doble Tributación			
Alemania	Corea	Irlanda	Portugal
Argentina	Dinamarca	Israel	Reino Unido
Australia	Ecuador	Italia	República Checa
Austria	España	Japón	Rumania
Bélgica	Estados Unidos	Luxemburgo	Singapur
Brasil	Finlandia	Noruega	Suecia
Canadá	Francia	Nueva Zelanda	Suiza
Chile	Grecia	Países Bajos	Sudáfrica
China	Indonesia	Polonia	

http://www.promexico.gob.mx/es_us/promexico/Acuerdos_para_evitar_doble_tributacion

New Regulations in Advertising for Kids - The rising index of obesity in our general population, and especially concerning children, has become a focal point in Mexican politics and economics. Given the sensitivity of the matter, the government has tried to restrain consumption of foods high in salt, sugar and fat among young ones and the Marketing of these products to kids has been heavily tyrannized. As in other countries, self-regulation can become an effective prophylaxis to avoid legally imposed advertising restraints, however this is a threat that remains and may affect the use of licensed brands and characters in this sector in the medium term. Here, the creative use of licensed characters in positive health promoting messaging becomes essential, as is the advice of local agents or councils.

Role of Local Agents

The agent is the business and cultural ambassador between the parties involved in the licensing transaction, namely, the licensees, licensors and retailers. Experts in their market and well acquainted with local trends and fashions, agents bring to the table the right skills and the needed relationships to enable successful business to happen.

The agent's job begins by making an accurate brand diagnose and by identifying the true extent of possibilities that a brand has in that market. This can only be done *from within* and via a deep understanding of the marketplace, its dimension, the opportunities it entails, its challenges… It is the agent's role to help licensors decipher the rules of engagement with local trade to build successful relationships which can be sustained over time. By understanding the market's dynamics and its main actors, the agent should be able to come up with a route that leads to good business with the smallest possible risk. To attain this, the agent should be fully immersed in the brand it represents, and fully aware of its strategic goals in the short and medium terms. Alignment with the licensor's core objectives is an essential condition for successful licensing.

Agents bring two priceless assets to the negotiation table: one is *perspective*, which stems from experience in the marketplace and often from working with several other brands. It is not uncommon for licensors to subjectively compare local deals to what they have domestically, however true benchmark comes from agent's knowledge of *who is who* in the local scene, and what each category should be worth. The other is *trust* – the personal angle to the licensing relationship and the ability to build strong relationships with clients. As said in the previous chapter, trust, and a sense of mutual accountability, is key to successful business in this territory and probably as engaging to the licensees as the brand itself.

But these assets will only be of use if accompanied with *empowerment* and a sensible level of authority to intercede in business decisions and important matters. It is not uncommon for licensors to overlook the fact that the agent's resources and reputation are implied in every negotiation, and should be preserved as much as their own, its time valued, its views respected. Sudden shifts in brand direction or decisions, which seem arbitrary, have a strong impact in the agent's relationships and should be weighed and avoided to the extent possible.

The agent's participation in building the relationship with retail partners is crucial too. Mexican retailers will require a great deal of service, creativity and perseverance. Knowledge of retail timing, core purchase seasons, when a new brand should be introduced, products presented, promotions planned, etc., are questions which can only by answered by a dedicated agent, working on the ground.

It is the agent's task to line up licensees' interests and other anchor partners (i.e., master toy licensees or home entertainment/theatrical divisions) and coordinate a unified approach to retail to negotiate premium space and other activations.

Another area of great contribution by agents is the conveyance of trends applicable to product development and design: which colors fly off shelves and which tend to be left behind; is "minimalist" a good treatment for this market, or is saturation what gets the eye? Again, these are important questions that can hardly be answered by someone miles away who, at times, has never been to the market in question or knows very little about it. When you are designing product that is expected to perform on a local level, licensors must acknowledge the territory's uniqueness, and be open to benefit from local success factors.

Visiting Mexico for in-depth market recognition and a first-look at its retail structures and consumers is indispensable. This road-trip is critical not only for licensing managers but for the creative teams supervising product development. Hiring Mexican or Latin talent can help bridge the culture gap and ease the road to approved deals or approved product, as long as communication lines are clear, and tasks are not duplicated.

Empowering the agent in this area and allowing him or her to do product approvals – proper training preceding - would not only mean quicker completion, but also product that is a better fit to our market. Considering that large licensors such as Disney or Warner Bros. can procure on-site approvals and immediate responses to product development queries, the long and intricate processes where each phase must be checked by three layers of people, at times in different parts of the world, becomes a large competitive disadvantage.

Agents should be expected to monitor licensees' performance, competitors' activity, identify threats, keep licensor duly informed of relevant signals and advise accordingly. It is a complex job that has multiple battlefronts, whose interests must be reconciled and protected for long term success.

What should not be expected from agents and constitutes a very common misconception is that agents create demand. Desire for product is generated by the brand itself, and by the nature of its connection to consumers, whether aspirational or emotional. Agents may build very successful licensed programs based on such connection, on such bond. But cannot create a bond where it does not exist. Demand remains the licensor's responsibility.

Marketing, Advertising and Promotion

The success of a licensed brand in Mexico is linked to several factors:

- The brand's intrinsic connection to local audiences/consumers
- Level of exposure and recognition
- Depth and extent of creative resources
- Investment in Retail
- Continued introduction of relevant content

All the above are first and foremost the responsibility of the licensor, and without them, promoting licensed product would be pointless. Any brand striving to be successful must first be sure to count with the needed grounds (the substantial bond with consumers) as well as the ammunition to convert this equity into sales.

Depending on the nature of the brand, a specific marketing plan must be developed.

Today a CMF, or common marketing fund, is not an attribute of the "big brands" but a must-have for any brand making a serious approach to this market. 1 to 2% of sales are rates normally accepted by licensees on top of royalties, with the understanding that significant activity will be expected in return, whether in the shape of advertising, promotion or retail activation. Licensors are bound to contribute with an amount just as big as the amount accrued by licensees, or more if it is an emerging brand requiring so. The best use for a CMF is probably investment in retail exhibition and activations, since retailers need motivation, and consumers need an undeniable in-store signal telling them what is hot!

Retail activities will include a combination of the following: roadshows to introduce licensed product, crafting of retail incentives (such as promotions or special exclusive offers), design and production of signage and customized fixtures, branded walls or corners, participation in circulars and tabs, and activities in-store, such as character or celebrity appearances, contests, and other shapes of BTL activations.

These activities which generate traffic are highly regarded by retailers, especially if they can be replicated in several of their many stores but are *hardly ever* paid for by the retailer. Retailers may contribute with larger orders or by using proprietary media, but even when they do, proper execution is not guaranteed, so as result hiring independent merchandising services is advised to supervise materials reach their destination and meet the purpose intended for.

Retail activity has become a strong differentiator for serious brands but also a very high standard for smaller brands to reach and has hampered their path to the shelves even further.

For brands with less established recognition, advertising becomes more relevant, as consumers must know legit product exists and where to find it. A specific plan should be developed using the media platforms that are most suitable and more effectively reach that segment.

ATL is expensive so very few licensees will resort to it in an individual level. Cable is more affordable, but penetration is still limited, and the audience is often spread among the many channels. So, in general printed or outdoor advertising is preferred, specifically billboards and buses circulating main avenues, as well as ads in magazines targeting core demographics. But individual actions by licensees remain the exception rather than the rule... and the participation by a licensor, or its agent, is very relevant.

Looping in several licensees – often linked by category – in catalogs or brochures which can be cross promoted among partners is a good way to gain exposure without too great an expense and by using anchor partners strengths (e.g., toys or home video partners...).

Brands owned by large media conglomerates allocate a significant amount of resources towards their consumer products business, with initiatives that help drive traffic, promoting licensed product via ads or editorial placed on their broadcast, publishing or online platforms. This is undeniable competitive advantage others *are bound to meet*, even if with dissimilar resources.

Participation at trade shows is probably the activity that most licensees participate in more profusely. Examples include *Expo Papelera* (for school and stationery goods - takes place in March every year), *Intermoda* (fashion – January/July), *Confitexpo* (confectionery and party - July), *Sapica* (footwear & leather– March/August), *Salpro* (gift - August), *FIL* (books - December) and several others... besides expos directly conducted by retailers as trademarked events (i.e. *Expo Walmart*, *Expo Chedraui* and such...) important at promoting brands inside these organizations.

Promoting licensed product effectively depends on the right understanding of the brand's DNA and that of its core consumers, so it feels natural and coherent. If the brand stands for fun – promote in fun places and in fun ways; if lifestyle, participate in top fashion shows and seek endorsement from fashion celebs; if event driven, use the event to gain visibility; etc.

If the intent to promote is serious, licensors must dedicate the resources. Rely on experts and invest in additional talent. And even if the agent's participation in advertising and promotion strategies is crucial at decision-making, different skills and liaisons are needed for professional public relations and advertising services, digital media management and so on... so whether you are acting as the licensor or as licensee, don't expect these to be included as part of the licensing services, unless previously outlined and separately compensated.

Retail

High-End - possibly like anywhere else in the world is mostly focused on large international fashion brands, with amazing in-store displays or "shop in shop" concepts. High end is very selective when it comes to licensing and will choose only the premium properties and will require at least a certain degree of exclusivity. Volume at high-end is normally not that high although it builds good equity and makes for great launch platforms.

Mid-Tier – perfect for multi-brand exposure. Aspirational by nature, dedicate significant floor space to licensed brands. Mostly soft-lines.

Specialty Stores – very strong in their own segment, BTS supplies, toys and sporting goods.

Convenience Stores – mostly for male shoppers and impulse buying, one of the fastest growing formats in the country. Significant due to the number of outlets, these formats are relevant selling points for licensed food & beverage and consumer good promotions, as well as small accessories which require small display.

Mass Market – comprised by the large self-service chains, supermarkets and hypermarkets. This is the terrain of mothers and family, where most of licensed volume is generated, and therefore it is a highly competitive soil. Strong licensed brands presence in apparel, toys, food and beverage, accessories, home and BTS.

Wholesale or "Traditional" – comprised by thousands of small independent shops, boutiques, catalogues, grocery shops or "mom & pop's" or even street stands, where a large amount of licensed sales take place, albeit hard to measure due to their proximity to the informal market...

And, of course, the big, untamed, informal markets, which are calculated to comprise over 60% of our overall economy, which greatly profit from illegal use of trademarks and remain the largest area of opportunity for brand owners.

Outlook, Projections and Conclusions

The need to invest in POS is increasing. While at some point retailers were looking to offset costs by allowing IP owners to "brand" their seasonal displays, today, Licensors rising interest in obtaining these spaces have turned them into such coveted opportunities, often disputed between several brands, that a "price tag" has been placed on them!

High-End Departmental Stores. Concentration of high-end departmental stores will continue to imply smaller shelf space for the ever-growing number of brands in the character licensing sector. In their constant search for differentiated brands and products, will they be able to move away from the natural demand generated by successful brands and fads without losing business? Will they let the opportunity to have licensed products with high rotation rates slip? Those are questions to be answered only through the experience.

Mass Market. Besides Disney, there are still few DTR examples of character licensed brands, but we are seeing the first stages happening in smaller mass market chains. Walmart's high market share might vary due to the increase of self-regulations which may have an incidence in its new unit's growth rate giving some margin to its competitors. Notwithstanding, new retail chains are not foreseen to emerge in the medium term, the acquisitions by foreign firms (among them a couple of South American ones) which have a higher sophistication in terms of merchandising, might be happening sooner or later.

TV. In terms of kids programming, there's a dramatic dominance of Televisa in free TV which seems difficult -albeit not impossible- to challenge by a new network. In any case, in my opinion, it will take a long time before it happens. Pay TV has been growing at a faster pace the last few years, but it still cannot compete with Free TV in terms of share and ratings, not to say that very few examples of successful licensing programs have derived from the property exposure limited to Pay TV. According to Nielsen Ibope, between 2008 and 2013, the Free TV Audience dropped from 84% to 72%. As we all know, second and third screens will continue to split kids and adults' audiences, diminishing the TV dominance with regards to the exposure of character licensed properties due to its natural time & space limitations.

To increase opportunities for TV-driven properties, a cross platform strategy might change the actual scenario and/or Pay TV penetration should increase dramatically its reach at the level of well developed countries.

Theatrical. There's a growing aversion to single titles and the market is progressively leaning towards sequels instead, which have proven to be hugely successful. Nevertheless, in the short term, the large volume of titles that Disney will be launching to the market each year, adding to its own productions Pixar's titles, Marvel's Superheroes and now STAR WARS, will represent a big challenge for all stake holders in the value chain of our industry.

The short span between releases inevitably shortens the traditional windows between movies and, consequently, reduces the life of its products on shelves. Considering the nature of the Mexican retail landscape, a fragmented demand would increase the risk of excess inventories – which effects would damage the Theatrical licensing business in the long run.

Digital. Game App properties represent a large opportunity. Despite the still limited penetration of Smartphones, we have seen the success of ANGRY BIRDS and we are foreseeing more to come as the number of Smartphones is growing at a relevant rate. While trying to secure a final launch date or access ratings for TV series in Mexico is usually a difficult task, the daily activity of Internet-based property users is measured in a very open and ample way.

When compared to a TV show, apps will not disappear from the mobile screen if there is a significant user base around the world, no matter how long it takes to mature in one or another country. It soon could become the major competitor for TV and Theatrical properties, if handled properly.

The downside is that not all the new-media IP owners are ready for worldwide success and their resources and licensing experience is still very limited. Therefore, we believe they should rely more heavily on their agent's experience and leave a wider decision margin in them. How wide? Well, it's a good question. This depends on each case, on each brand, and very much on the agent's capabilities.

Competing with the major licensors requires new POS investment criteria. The traditional economics of cutting only the agent's commission and keeping the reminder should be modified, allocating an additional portion to ensure retail activities, designated shelf space and social media. Of course, there are many times a "Common Marketing Fund", but when you're launching a property you'll have to think about an upfront investment too, not to mention the need of sophisticated style guides.

Properties with slower return potential facing the ongoing limited shelf space described, will need to offer Agents higher incentives to "level the field" with the cost/benefit it usually gets from the "Power brands".

The concept of hiring an agent who is not representing major brands, so he can focus on a smaller brand might be romantic, but experience has proven it wrong. The leverage a representative has among licensees and retailers lies in the size and volume of the opportunities it brings to the table, the frequency that they do business together and the certainty that the agent in question has a track record and a solid/sophisticated structure.

A successful and well-balanced portfolio often proves that the agent you've chosen has all the right qualities. And its larger structure will likely allow him to place more dedicated efforts towards product development supervision, retail relationships and promotions.

To compete with the major licensors who run their own operation, licensors will have to give more autonomy to their agent by means of training and supervision in terms of Quality Assurance and product development, allowing a faster and more efficient "go to market" of the licensed products.

Working this way will allow the agent to judge and approve the licensees' art submissions considering the local culture, avoiding lengthy discussions with their Quality Assurance peers located in a remote country, with good will but often unable to understand each country's taste and specific market needs. No question, such needs are better known by the local expert.

A final recommendation to succeed in Mexico: *Don't forget, to be global, you need to be local.*

Come visit soon!

Chapter 16
International Intellectual Property Protection[50]

16.1 Introduction

Intellectual property ("IP") refers to the creations of the mind such as inventions, literary and artistic works, designs, symbols and names[51]. The protection of rights in these creations ("IPR's") is important because of the value they represent to their owners in terms of generating significant commercial benefits.

The licensing of IPR's is a growing business in international trade. According to a survey issued by the International Licensing Industry Merchandisers' Association (LIMA), trademark owners generated more than $14.1 billion in royalties on a worldwide basis in the year 2016[52]. Licensing can help a company enhance its business. It can act as a consistent revenue stream for licensors and licensees such as in the case of the copyrighted song "Happy Birthday to You" which brings its owner an estimated $2 million dollars annually in royalties. Licensing also provides new market opportunities. Well executed licensing can help a company expand its geographic markets and product lines. Licensing in high technology industries helps fill new product pipelines and minimizes the risks associated with manufacturing and distribution. IBM Corporation generates an estimated $1 billion a year [53] by actively licensing its 40,000 patents to companies that manufacture products based on IBM IP, without incurring additional expenditures or risks[54].

Considering the profits that licensing of IPR's can produce, IP owners are wise to invest the time and resources needed to implement appropriate protection strategies and enforcement programs. IPR's must be enforced to retain their value. IP owners should act to address misuse and infringement of their rights by third parties to reduce the risk of confusion and prevent others from defending their unauthorized use IP owners should implement plans to police and enforce their rights by preventing unauthorized used. A well rounded international business plan should include a strategy for enforcing IPR's.

Globalization and the easy access of companies to international markets have change the manner and scope of protecting IPR's. Protecting IPR's internationally and of guaranteeing IP owners a "greater sense of security, control and certainty"[55] led to the harmonization of IP laws. Through the harmonization of IP law, countries from different legal systems

---

[50] By Lanning G. Bryer, Ladas & Parry, New York, NY. www.ladas.com. The author greatly appreciates the assistance of Amanda Kusnierz, a third-year law student at Benjamin N. Cardozo School of Law, in the research and editing of this chapter.

[51] http://www.wipo.int/about-ip/en/index.html

[52] LIMA Industry Survey 2017

[53] http://bits.blogs.nytimes.com/2013/01/10/the-2012-patent-rankings-ibm-on-top-again-google-and-apple-surging/?_r=0

[54] https://www.experience.com/alumnus/article?channel_id=engineering&source_page=Additional_Articles&article_id=article_1216819655187.

[55] http://www.ladas.com/Trademarks/IntTMProtection/IntlTM02.html

converged to create common principles and standards of intellectual property rights. The continuous efforts in the harmonization of intellectual property laws through international and multilateral treaties and agreements have helped to simplify the process of protecting IP internationally. Nevertheless, there are still areas of IP where harmonization and unified protection mechanisms have not yet been achieved. In those circumstances, companies and individuals must still rely on national IP laws of the countries in which they do business.

This chapter will discuss two main subjects relevant to IP which can be the subject of license arrangements, namely, (1) the adoption, protection and licensing of trademarks, copyrights and related rights throughout the world, and (2) the enforcement and anti-counterfeiting processes relating to trademarks and copyrights.

16.2 International Protection of Trademarks, Copyrights and Related Rights

This section is a broad overview of the international protection of IPR's with an emphasis on trademarks and copyrights. First, we will discuss the rights granted to IP owners by international treaties. Second, we will look at the factors that should be considered when protecting trademarks internationally, its benefits, as well as the risks of not implementing an adequate protection program. Finally, we will explain the differences between the protection of trademarks and copyrights and the strategies that IP owners should implement to reduce the risk of infringement of their rights.

16.2.1 Harmonization of IP Laws

The increasing globalization of business led to the need for the harmonization of intellectual property laws and policy. IP owners doing business worldwide should be aware of the scope of their IP rights as they consider their enforcement. The goal of harmonization is to obtain consistency in the operation and application of IP laws internationally. Harmonization is desirable in that it provides a reliable framework within which IP owners can plan their international marketing strategies and be reasonably certain that their IP rights will be protected from country to country, and under multilateral treaties in large blocks of countries.

Attempts of harmonization began bilaterally or regionally, but later evolved into the accession to multinational treaties when nations wanted to ensure that its nationals would not be greatly disadvantaged by the laws or practices of other nations. The World Intellectual Property Organization ("WIPO")[56] played a significant role in the harmonization of intellectual property laws by sponsoring numerous multinational treaties and offering cost-effective mechanisms for protecting trademarks, patents and designs in multiple countries by filing a single international application. WIPO also provides facilities for alternative dispute resolution such as arbitration and mediation on IP matters, as well as for domain name disputes[57].

---

[56] WIPO is a specialized agency of the United Nations, which objective is to promote the protection of intellectual property throughout the world (Article 3 of WIPO Convention).

[57] For more information about WIPO Arbitration and Mediation Center, see http://www.wipo.int/amc/en/

16.2.2 International Intellectual Property Treaties

Paris Convention. The harmonization of intellectual property rights began with the Paris Convention of 1883. The Convention applies to patents, trademark, industrial designs, utility models, trade names, geographical indications and unfair competition. 175 countries are currently members of the Paris Convention.

The Paris Convention created a multinational regime governing intellectually property rights. It established minimum standards for the protection and enforcement for IPR's. It recognized the national treatment standard, were by each Member State should afford the same protection it grants to its own nationals to nationals of other Member States.

In relation to trademarks, the Convention established common rules to be incorporated into the national laws of parties to the Convention. Among these rules are: (1) a six-month priority right for filing trademark applications worldwide, (2) the grounds for refusing registration and (3) the compulsory use of a mark. It did not regulate the conditions for filing and registration of marks, which were left to treaty members to determine and regulate through their domestic law.

Berne Convention for the Protection of Literary and Artistic Works. The Berne Convention protects "every production in the literary, scientific and artistic domain, whatever may be the mode or form of its expression". It sets the basics principles for copyrights, such as the automatic protection from the date of creation of the work without the need of any formality, the principle of national treatment[58] and of the "independence" of protection[59]. The treaty also established minimum standards of protection and the duration of copyrights which was of 50 years after the author's death[60].

TRIPS - Agreement on Trade Related Aspects of Intellectual Property Rights, Including Trade in Counterfeit Goods. During the Uruguay Round negotiations to revise the General Agreement on Tariffs and Trade (GATT) a new framework was established to operate under the World Trade Organization (WTO). The general provisions of GATT's Agreement on Trade Related Intellectual Property Issues (TRIPS) recognized that treaty members must not discriminate in favor of their own citizens against the IPR's of foreigners who are citizens of other GATT member countries, nor favor the rights of citizens of one country over the rights of citizens of another. In addition, the framework included a "most-favored-nation clause", under which any advantage a party gives to the nationals of another country must be extended immediately and unconditionally to the nationals of all other parties, even if such treatment is more favorable than that which it gives to its own nationals.

The principal provisions of GATT as they relate to trademarks are:

---

[58] Works originating in one of the contracting States (that is, works the author of which is a national of such a State or works which were first published in such a State) must be given the same protection in each of the other contracting States as the latter grants to the works of its own nationals.

[59] Such protection is independent of the existence of protection in the country of origin of the work (principle of the "independence" of protection). If, however, a contracting State provides for a longer term than the minimum prescribed by the Convention and the work ceases to be protected in the country of origin, protection may be denied once protection in the country of origin ceases.

[60] For more information see http://www.wipo.int/treaties/en/ip/berne/.

1. Any visually perceptible sign that is capable of distinguishing goods or services of one party from goods of another is capable of functioning as a trademark and registerable as such. Treaty adherents are however; free to refuse registration of signs that lack inherent distinctiveness, unless those signs have acquired distinctiveness through use.

2. Registration may be conditioned on the mark being used. However, actual use must not be a prerequisite for filing an application for registration. Nor shall an application be refused simply because an intended use has not commenced within three years of the application date.

3. Countries that provide for cancellation of registrations on the ground of non-use must allow a period of non-use of at least 3 years before such provisions may be invoked;

4. Although member countries may impose conditions on the terms under which trademarks may be licensed, compulsory licensing of trademarks is banned as are prohibitions on the right of a trademark owner to assign a trademark without transfer of the business to which the mark belongs;

The major provisions of GATT in regard copyright protection include the following:

1. An obligation to comply with the provisions of the Berne Convention;

2. A requirement to treat computer programs as literary works for copyright protection purposes;

3. A requirement to give to authors of computer programs and cinematographic works and producers of phonograms the rights in certain circumstances to control commercial rental of the originals or copies of their works;

4. Fair use provisions and similar limitations on the exercise of copyright shall be limited to "certain special cases which do not conflict with normal exploitation of a work and do not unreasonably prejudice the legitimate interests of the right holder;" and

5. Obligations to afford certain minimum rights for the protection of performers, producers of phonogram, and broadcasting organizations.

The treaty also requires member states to provide procedures and remedies under their domestic law to ensure that IPR's are effectively enforced by foreign right holders as well as by their own nationals. The treaty included the availability of provisional remedies. Judicial authorities must have the authority to act promptly to prevent infringement and in appropriate circumstances to act "ex parte."

Damages awarded for infringement of IPR's must be "adequate to compensate for the injury". In addition to the civil remedies, countries are also required to provide for criminal procedures and penalties for "at least" willful trademark infringement and copyright piracy on a commercial scale. Treaty member are also required to establish procedures to facilitate interception of counterfeits as pirated copyrighted goods by customs authorities at national boundaries[61].

---

[61] To see which countries signatories of the TRIPs Agreement are, visit http://www.wipo.int/wipolex/en/other_treaties/parties.jsp?treaty_id=231&group_id=22.

Madrid System[62] A major success in the harmonization of trademarks was achieved through the Madrid System. This system is governed by two treaties: the Madrid Agreement Concerning the International Registration of Marks (1891), and the Protocol Relating to the Madrid Agreement (1995). The Madrid System creates a centralized system for the filing, registration and maintenance of trademark rights in multiple jurisdictions. Trademark applicants may file a single trademark application and have that application serve as a basis for an International Registration which may be extended for the same goods/services to other member states designated by the applicant. The protection enjoyed by an owner of an International Registration is identical to the protection that would result from a national registration with the trademark office of a contracting country. The resulting registration is known as an "International Registration", essentially a bundle of national rights in a single registration which can be renew or assigned.

Under the Madrid Agreement, owners of registered trademarks may extend the protection of their trademark to all other signatory countries of Madrid Agreement. The difference with the Madrid Protocol entitles owners of a pending application in the country of origin to extend their rights to Protocol countries. Since September 1, 2008, International trademark registrations are governed by the Madrid Protocol, but only in those member countries which are a party to the Protocol as well as those which are a party to both the Protocol and the Agreement[63]. Both the Madrid Agreement and Madrid Protocol are administered by WIPO[64].

Other Treaties: Other treaties that have helped to harmonize intellectual property laws and facilitate the international protection of IPR's are the Nice Agreement on International Classification of Goods and Services (1957) which established a classification system for the registration of trademarks. The Nice Classification comprises a list of 45 Classes, 34 classes for goods and 11 classes for services as is followed in most countries pf the world having replaced local classification systems. The Vienna Agreement (1973) serves the same purpose as the Nice Agreement, but it applies to the classification of figurative elements of trademarks such as designs, pictures, drawing and logos.

Other treaties are intended to harmonize procedural and administrative aspects of the trademark registration process, such as the Trademark Law Treaty (1994) which removes the requirement of notarization and legalizations of signature and Singapore Treaty on the Law of Trademarks (2006), which provides a modern framework for the administrative procedures of the registration of trademarks.

In the copyright area there is the Universal Copyright Convention (1952)[65], International Convention for the Protection of Performers, Producers of Phonograms and Broadcasting

---

[62] For more information see http://www.wipo.int/madrid/en/

[63]http://www.inta.org/TrademarkBasics/FactSheets/Pages/InternationalTrademarkRightsFactSheet.aspx

[64] To see which countries signatories of the TRIPs Agreement are, visit http://www.wipo.int/export/sites/www/treaties/en/documents/pdf/madrid_marks.pdf

[65] For more information, see http://www.wipo.int /wipolex/en/other treaties/details.jsp?treaty_id=208

Organization (1961, also known as the Rome Convention)[66], the Convention for the Protection of Producers of Phonograms Against Unauthorized Duplication of Their Phonograms (1971, also known as the Phonograms Convention)[67] and the Convention Relating to the Distribution of Programme-Carrying Signals by Satellite (1974, known as the Satellites Convention)[68].

The rapid advancement of technology, particularly the Internet, has affected the way in which works can be created, used and disseminated. To clarify and adapt the existing copyright norms to the new digital era, WIPO has adopted the WIPO Copyright Treaty (WCT)[69] and the WIPO Performances and Phonograms Treaty (WPPT)[70].

16.3 Trademarks

The most efficient way of protecting brand identity in the marketplace is through the registration of trademarks. A trademark can be a word, a logo, a number, a letter, a slogan, a sound, a color, or a smell. Trademarks are distinctive signs that identify the source of goods and/or services with which the trademark is used. When a trademark used in connection with services, is referred to as a "service mark".

IPR's can also be protected via trade dress, although distinctions between trademarks and trade dress have largely disappeared because many types of designations protectable as trade dress are also registerable as trademarks.[71] Trade dress is the overall appearance of a product/or service, such as the size, shape, color, color combinations, labeling, packaging, decorative elements. Examples of trade dress are the appearance and décor of the restaurant such as McDonalds, the cover of a book or magazine, the appearance of a teddy bear toy, the "G" shape of the frame of a GUCCI watch, the COCA-COLA bottle, the FERRARI car, Hermes handbag, and Tiffany's packaging[72]. In most countries, trade dress is protected by trademark law; however, in others such as the United States, there are specific requirements applicable only to trade dress. Trade dress is usually protectable when they satisfy the same standards as a trademark (i.e. when they are distinctive). Trade dress is protected to prevent consumer confusion with other products that have a similar appearance. Generally, a trade dress must be both non-functional and distinctive to be protected[73]. If a company offers products and/or services that encompass a particular appearance, they should verify whether the country of interest has specific standards which must be met for protecting their trade dress or if they can be registered through the trademark system.

---

[66]For more information, see http://www.wipo.int/treaties/en/ip/rome/

[67]For more information, see http://www.wipo.int/treaties/en/ip/phonograms/

[68] For more information, see http://www.wipo.int/treaties/en/ip/brussels/

[69] For more information, see http://www.wipo.int/treaties/en/ip/wct/

[70] For more information, see http://www.wipo.int/treaties/en/ip/ wppt/trtdocs_wo034.html

[71] J. Thomas McCarthy, Trademarks and Unfair Competition § 8:1 (4th ed. 2010)

[72] J. Thomas McCarthy, Trademarks and Unfair Competition § 8:4.50 (4th ed. 2010) (citing cases).

[73] Walmart Stores, Inc., v. Samara Brothers, Inc., 529 U.S. 205, 54 USPQ2d 1065 (2000); Two Pesos, Inc. v. Taco Cabana, Inc., 505 U.S. 763, 23 USPQ2d 1081 (1992)

16.3.1 Trademark Clearance and Adoption

Companies that want to expand their horizons beyond their national borders by offering products or services in foreign markets must consider the selection of their trademarks very carefully[74]. One of the first steps in selecting a new trademark is conducting a trademark clearance in the countries where the proposed mark will likely be used. This step is crucial to verify if the proposed mark does not violate any third-party rights or any domestic trademark laws. Once the relevant markets have been identified, a trademark search must be performed to determine whether there are identical or similar trademarks that could impede registration and use of the proposed mark. Obviously, if you have chosen an identical trademark or one that is a confusingly similar trademark to one that is already used or registered by a third party for similar goods or services, a new trademark should be selected. Otherwise, unnecessary time and expense could be expended, including a possible adverse judgment for damages.

When two trademarks are similar, a legal analysis shall be performed to determine if upon a combination of factors (e.g. the similarity in the trademarks, the similarity in the goods and services, the channels of trade in which the goods or services are marketed, and the distinctiveness of the trademarks) the proposed mark is suitable or not for use and registration.

When you start thinking about selecting a trademark, do not limit yourself to a single selection. Rather, have several possible selections in mind. If your first selection proves to be unavailable, perhaps you will have better luck with your second or third choices. If the trademark availability search indicates that the trademark you selected is available, you should seek to register the trademark in the countries of interest as soon as possible while the search results are still relevant.

16.3.2 Basis of Registrability of Trademarks

The harmonization of IP laws helps unify international standards for the registration of trademarks. Nevertheless, there are still some particularities of registration systems that vary from country to country. Sometimes trademarks in the domestic market may not be received favorably by foreign consumers and trademark offices[75]. Therefore, it is necessary to understand the basic registrability standards that have worldwide application.

The distinctiveness of a mark is a basic requirement for registration of a trademark in many countries. A trademark is distinctive if it is "capable of performing the function of identifying and distinguishing the goods [and services] that bear the symbol[76]". However, some countries may even permit registration of a mark which, albeit not currently distinctive or distinctive per se, may become distinctive when used over several years to create a sufficient reputation and recognition by consumers. Marks that are only capable of

---

[74] MELVIN SIMENSKY, LANNING BRYER & NEIL J. WILKOF, INTELLECTUAL PROPERTY IN THE GLOBAL MARKETPLACE 12.2-4 (John Wiley & Sons, Inc., 2d ed. 1999)

[75] MELVIN SIMENSKY, LANNING BRYER & NEIL J. WILKOF, INTELLECTUAL PROPERTY IN THE GLOBAL MARKETPLACE 12.2-4 (John Wiley & Sons, Inc., 2d ed. 1999)

[76] J. Thomas McCarthy, Trademarks and Unfair Competition § 3:2 (4th ed. 2010)

distinguishing are usually more difficult and costlier to register. Some countries that follow British law even create a separate register for marks that are considered only capable of distinguishing[77]. In United States, there is a Supplemental Register for marks that may eventually acquire distinctiveness.

Trademarks may not be either generic or merely descriptive of the goods or services to which they pertain. As such, the word "vegetable" cannot be registered as a service mark of a supermarket, since it is certainly descriptive of items which a supermarket sells. Likewise, it cannot be registered as a trademark for carrots, since it is a generic term for carrots. On the other hand, the word "vegetable" might well serve as a trademark for bicycles since it has little or nothing to do with bicycles.

The name of a company, individual, or firm may be registerable, although some countries may require the name to be protected through special procedures. It is very important knowing the special procedures that applies especially when a company's name and primary trademark are the same (e.g. Kodak, Apple, Sony), in which case the mark is referred to as "house mark".

Invented or arbitrary words constitute the best kind of trademarks because they are prima facie distinctive and imitations can be prevented easily. Mere combinations of words or slight variations in spelling or letter order may not be sufficient to qualify as inventions if the same idea would be conveyed to the consumer by the words in their ordinary form.

A geographical name may not qualify for registration of a mark. "Paris" cannot serve as a trademark for perfume in many countries. However, if the goods have some connection with that place it could be registerable. If the only significance of a word is a geographical one, the word is considered to be a geographical name in its ordinary significance, therefore non-protectable.

A surname may also be excluded from registration. However, if the mark is both a rare surname and an ordinary word with a specific meaning that is much more commonly known, the mark may be allowed registration.

Words that are clearly laudatory or descriptive do not qualify for registration. Pictorial or device marks and graphic designs may constitute distinctive marks if the representation has no reference to the character or quality of the goods they identify. (e.g., the NIKE check symbol). A device must contain some striking feature that will fix itself in the mind of consumers to enable them to remember the device and identify the goods bearing the mark. Device marks are particularly useful, in countries with a low literacy where consumers may recognize a device more easily than a mere word mark.

In many countries, trademarks that comprise mere letters and/or numbers (i.e. the proposed trademark cannot be pronounced as a word or words or just has too few letters) are considered to be non-distinctive.

---

[77] MELVIN SIMENSKY, LANNING BRYER & NEIL J. WILKOF, INTELLECTUAL PROPERTY IN THE GLOBAL MARKETPLACE 12.2-4 (John Wiley & Sons, Inc., 2d ed. 1999)

In addition, marks must not be offensive to morality. A mark could be considered offensive in one country but not in another. Finally, a mark must not contain a negative connotation within a particular jurisdiction.

16.3.3 Reasons for Registering Your Trademark

The most important reason to register your trademark internationally is to preserve your rights in this asset and obtain a tool by which enforcement is possible. In the case of a trademark licenses, it necessary for the licensor to ensure that the trademark is available and protected and for the licensee to ensure that it has proper legal authority to make use of the mark. Registering your trademark provides an exclusive right to use the mark and an exclusive basis for infringement claims of unfair competition. Relying only on trademark use as a way of protecting rights is generally expensive and time consuming, not to mention that it may be unsuccessful if the usage is not sufficiently notorious or extensive enough in use and scope. Thus, a trademark registration is a valuable tool for use in asserting trademark rights against other parties and possibly obtaining statutory damages, which in many countries require registration. Finally, since a trademark registration is viewed as a definable and scheduled asset, it can be used to collateralize a loan, sold or licensed to a third party.

Trademarks can be misappropriated innocently or intentionally, by competitors, distributors, or professional trademark pirates. Trademark pirates which knowledge of newly adopted mark may seek to register these trademarks in strategic foreign countries. They hope to sell these trademarks back to their rightful owner. By registering a mark first, it frustrates the intentional act of a trademark pirate and, it also makes it easier for more honest parties to determine that the trademark is already protected when they do a trademark search on a new trademark that they are considering using and adopting.

Another important reason to register trademarks is to prevent what is known as "dilution". Dilution occurs when a number of companies use similar trademarks on similar goods. Potential purchasers are then exposed to numerous trademarks that have certain similarities as to these related goods, and this minimizes the legal and practical value of a trademark as a source identifier. Other companies are much less likely to adopt a trademark which is similar to or identical to your trademark if the necessary steps to register it have taken place. It is much more difficult for other parties to become aware of your interest in the trademark if it is not registered.

Another danger is the loss of goodwill which can arise by an infringing product or service of poor quality. This can happen when someone else enters the marketplace and commences the sale of goods or services with the same or a similar mark. If those goods or services are of poor quality, purchasers may well associate the poor-quality item with the company, resulting in loss of brand goodwill and sales. However, this is less likely to occur if trademarks are register, since many companies take steps to avoid infringing a third party's trademark of which they become aware.

Trademarks can also be registered in nearly all countries in the world as a defensive measure. In those countries, a company or individual need not use of its trademark prior to obtaining a registration. Therefore, even in potential markets, you can prevent a third party from registering or using a trademark if you are the first party to obtain a registration. By obtaining a registration in advance of your use, you can be virtually assured of the unfettered ability to exclusively use your trademark in that country provided you begin use before the registration is subject to cancellation for non-use as most countries have statutory requirements to make commercial use of the mark to maintain these rights.

Finally, it is of vital importance to register trademarks because of the monetary value they enhance. Besides being a property right, which can be sold or collateralized, a trademark can be licensed. Companies enjoy substantial revenue in royalties from licensing their trademarks. If a trademark is licensed, however, it is very important, not only to register the trademark, but also to record the license agreements, where possible. License agreements must be carefully drafted to assure quality control of the licensed products and/or services by the trademark owner. In addition to licenses for various types of intellectual property, several other types of licenses are used depending on the commercial situation. For example, there are franchise licenses, extension brand licenses, hybrid licenses and sublicenses.[78] Many countries require that a licensed trademark be registered before they will register the trademark license agreement at the national trademark office.

16.3.4 Deciding Where to Register your Trademark

Differences between Common Law vs. Civil Law Countries. One of the goals of harmonization is to minimize the distinctions between the common law and civil law legal systems. Trademark owners should be aware of the type of legal system that applies to the jurisdictions in which they intend to market their products and services. For example, common law jurisdictions generally do not require registration of a trademark for a user of that mark to claim a proprietary right in the mark. In this case, rights will be created through mere commercial use. Conversely, civil law jurisdictions, generally grant rights in a trademark only upon registration. The party who registers first, that is "wins the race to the Register" obtains priority of the registration in the mark, although exceptions are made in cases of "well-known" marks or in obvious cases of bad faith. Nevertheless, under both legal systems, registration is imperative for securing a monopoly to use a mark, as well as the right to license, assign, or create a security interest in the mark[79].

Planning Your Protection Strategy. You protect a trademark initially by registering the trademark. Historically, the registration process begins with the filing of a trademark application at the Trademark Office in each country where you desire the protection afforded by a registered trademark. More recently, the filing of trademark applications on an international basis has been simplified by European Union Trade Marks (28 current member states) and the Madrid System.

Deciding where to register your trademark is a complex issue. If no adequate plans are implemented for protecting your rights overseas, companies may encounter many problems. Companies need to determine the countries in which they will be doing business, their expansion strategy, as well need to be aware of the timeframe it takes to obtain a

---

[78] MELVIN SIMENSKY, LANNING BRYER & NEIL J. WILKOF, INTELLECTUAL PROPERTY IN THE GLOBAL MARKETPLACE 12.1 (John Wiley & Sons, Inc., 2d ed. 1999)

[79] Id.

trademark registration in different jurisdictions. For example, a pharmaceutical company that currently operates in the United States market but plans to export its product to Brazil in 2 years needs to understand that obtaining a trademark registration takes approximately 3 years. So, if they wait until the last minute to register their mark, they may be forced to postpone their sale of products to Brazil.

Registering a trademark in every possible country is very expensive. Consequently, companies shall plan strategically in the way of protecting their trademarks internationally. If the mark is not a house mark, but rather a mark for a product or service or of more limited economic importance it might not be necessary to register the mark in all countries. Instead, if it is house mark, it might be necessary. Also, it is important to consider the market for a particular product or service. If the market is a small one and modest sales are anticipated, it may not justify seeking protection there. Therefore, planning is advisable to avoid surprise and reduce costs.

By applying for a registration in advance of your use, you help assure unfettered use of your trademark. However, in countries where you can obtain a registration in advance of the use of your trademark, you must begin use of the trademark within some period, typically two to five years after registration, otherwise your registration may lapse or be subject to attack for non-use. Additionally, the fact that trademarks can be registered before they are used also presents you with certain risks. The biggest risk is that another party will register that which you regard as your trademark. And since they often do not need to make use of the trademark for a two to five-year period after registration, you may find yourself in a position where it is either very difficult or even impossible to take legal action against them. Thus, they are certainly able to cause you considerable difficulties once you decide to start exploiting the trademark in the relevant country. While using a Trademark Watch service can help alert you to possible third party conflicting rights, you still need to register your trademark(s) where you plan (or hope) to do business, either directly or via distributors or agents. If you do not act to protect your trademarks by registering them, someone else may do so.

Once you decide to proceed with the registration process in the countries of interest, certain forms must be completed, and official fees paid. The trademark application identifies the goods and/or services for which you are seeking trademark protection. The application is then reviewed by a government official, who is typically called a Trademark Examiner. The Examiner may refuse or object to registration of your trademark for several reasons. This process typically takes between one and three years (and in some countries considerably longer), and generally culminates with the publication of your trademark in a government periodical, published to allow third parties to contest the registration of your trademark by filing either an opposition or a cancellation action. If no third party contests your application or after an opposition is successfully resolved, your trademark will then be registered, thereby providing you with the unfettered right to use that trademark (and similar trademarks) in that country with respect to the goods and/or services designated in the registration (including closely related goods and/or services).

International Registration — The Madrid System. The international protection of trademarks has been significantly simplified with the implementation of the Madrid System. To take advantage of the Madrid Agreement and Protocol, a company or individual must be from a Madrid member country. The company or individual can seek an International Trademark registration. However, an International Trademark registration does not immediately result in a trademark registration that is enforceable everywhere. Rather, individual countries must be designated in the resulting International Registration with an additional cost being incurred for each country designated. Also, several the individual countries can (and do) issue official actions, and/or allow objections to be filed by third parties, to which responses must be filed by a local trademark agent or attorney. Thus, while there can be a substantial cost benefit to using the Madrid Agreement and Protocol filing mechanism, that cost benefit can be illusory if objections are encountered in many of the designated countries. As a result, the cost of protecting a trademark internationally can still be substantial under the Madrid Agreement and Protocol. The Madrid System eliminates the filing costs associate with filing separate national application in each foreign country. Also, it reduces the cost for renewals, recordals of changes of name or address, and assignments because they are filled at WIPO directly instead of recording them separately in each designated country.

One of the major disadvantages of the Madrid System is that the rights granted by an International Registration can be extinguished if its home application does not mature to registration or if is home registration is cancelled during its first five years.

Multilateral Agreements Protection.

European Union Trade Mark – EUTM[80]. Trademarks in Europe can be registered on a supra-national basis by seeking to register a trademark with the European Union Intellectual Property Office ("EUIPO"). There are several advantages in using EUIPO to register marks throughout the European Union (EU), not the least of which is that it is far less expensive to use EUIPO than it is to file trademark applications through each of a number of different national trademark offices.

In contrast to the Madrid Agreement and Protocol, the filing of a single trademark application for a European Union Trade Mark can result in a single trademark registration enforceable throughout the EU. The cost advantage of filing for (and renewing) a European Union Trade Mark is substantial compared to filing for (and renewing) trademark registrations in the individual countries making up the EU. Also, the use of a registered trademark in one EU country will satisfy the use requirements in all EU countries in the case of European Union Trade Mark. A bona fide use on a reasonable scale in a single Member State is normally sufficient to maintain the validity of the EUTM registration throughout the EU and prevent it from being vulnerable to cancellation through non-use over any five-year period after registration. It is also increasingly fast to obtain a EUTM registration; it takes 6 -9 months from filing to registration.

---

[80] On March 23, 2016m Regulation (EU) 2015/2424 of the European Parliament and the Council amended the Community trade mark regulation (the Amending Regulation) entered into force. Changes applied on October 1, 2017.

The European Union Trade Mark (EUTM) offers the opportunity to protect a trademark in all Member States of the European Union (EU) by filing a single application[81]. As new Member States join the EU, existing EUTMs automatically expand, without any action or payment on the part of EUTM owners. The initial registration period is ten years from the date of filing the application. Besides the traditional "absolute" grounds for refusal of a trademark application (such as the mark lacking distinctiveness), there are also certain rules governing the registration of shape marks. In terms of "relative" grounds for refusal, prior EUTM and/or national marks that are similar or identical may preclude the registration of an ETUM application, as may non-registered trademarks or other signs used in trade, where the owner of such a mark successfully lodges opposition.

The main disadvantage is that an earlier registration in one Member State alone may defeat a EUTM application in its entirety, even if the EUTM owner has no interest in or intention to use the mark in that Member State. Also, if applications are met with several oppositions, the costs of dealing with those oppositions may be high and registration may still not be ultimately forthcoming.

There has been much speculation regarding how to treat the United Kingdom (UK) with respect to European Union Trade Marks after Brexit[82]. The UK's decision to leave the European Union has resulted in great uncertainty, as it will no longer be possible to register trademarks with the EUIPO that encompass the UK.[83] A major concern following Brexit is what will happen to existing trademarks. A possible outcome may be that the UK will negotiate a trade deal with the EU to keep the current protections.

The European Commission published a first draft of the Withdrawal Agreement on February 28, 2018, containing proposed terms on which the United Kingdom will leave the EU on March 30, 2019. According to the draft Withdrawal Agreement, the most recent position suggests a transition period[84], in which the European law will continue to be applied in the UK, and any reference in the EU to "Member States" will be understood as including the UK. Therefore, EUTMs will be recognized and enforced by the UK courts. At the end of the designated transition period, the draft Withdrawal Agreement stipulates that holders of such rights, which have been registered or granted before the end of the transition period, will automatically and without any re-examination, be enforceable in the UK.

According to the draft Withdrawal Agreement, the EUTMs will no longer be extended to the United Kingdom. However, the European Commission suggests that there will be no loss of protection for holders of EU intellectual property rights. In other words, the holder of EUTMs would essentially become the holder of a UK trademark for the same goods or services.

---

[81] The jurisdictions covered by the EUTM are Austria, Benelux (Belgium, the Netherlands and Luxembourg), Bulgaria, Cyprus, Croatia the Czech Republic, Denmark, Estonia, Finland, France, Germany, Greece, Hungary, Ireland, Italy, Latvia, Lithuania, Malta, Poland, Portugal, Romania, Slovakia, Slovenia, Spain, Sweden and the United Kingdom.

[82] "Brexit", an abbreviation for "British Exit", refers to the United Kingdom's decision in a June 23, 2016 referendum to leave the European Union.

[83] Richards, John. "The Effect of Brexit (UK Departure from EU) On IP Rights. *Ladas & Parry.* 24 Jun. 2016.

[84] The proposed transition period will last until December 31, 2020.

Ultimately, many businesses should to establish a plan to ensure protection for their trademarks in both the EU and UK, due to the level of uncertainty of what will happen. At this point, the best practice for trademark owners would be to file separate trademark applications in the UK, in addition to the EU. However, a company will ultimately have to make this determination based on a variety of factors including, but not limited to, the company's resources and their relevant markets.

Regional Agreements. Other ways trademark owners can seek international trademark protection is through regional procedures that facilitates multilateral filings such as the African Intellectual Property Organization (OAPI)[85], African Regional Industrial Property Organization (ARIPO)[86] and Benelux Office for Intellectual Property (BOIP), which covers Belgium, Luxembourg and the Netherlands.

16.3.5 Maintaining your Trademark Rights

Trademarks require care and attention. Once the rights are obtained, companies should also develop strategies to maintain those trademark rights. Trademark registrations can extend in perpetuity but need to be renewed periodically by the filing of trademark renewal applications. Generally, the duration of each trademark registration (and each subsequent renewal) is ten years. However, most countries require that trademarks be used in order to be maintained. In addition, in many countries third parties can seek cancellation of registrations for trademarks which have not been used for a certain period of time (often after two to five years of non-use). When applications to renew trademark registrations are filed, some countries require that you submit evidence that the mark is in use. Also, some countries require that evidence of use be submitted at other times as well.

In most foreign countries, registrations may be successfully challenged after several years of registration if the mark has not been used in that country since the registration issued. For example, the UK Intellectual Property Office has cancelled GUCCI's GG logo, registered in 1984, on the grounds of non-use[87]. The trademark laws of foreign countries vary considerably, and care should be taken to verify that you are suitably protecting and enforcing your rights throughout the world. For further discussion of developing an enforcement program to help maintain trademark rights, see Section 4.5.

16.4 Copyright and Related Rights

16.4.1 Copyrights

Copyright protects the original works of authorships ("works"). Works covered by copyright include, but are not limited to: novels, books, poems, plays, reference works,

---

[85] OAPI is headquartered in Yaoundé (Cameroon). Organization centralizes all the procedures for issuing industrial property rights such as patents and trademarks in all 16-member countries. The member countries are: Benin, Burkina Faso, Cameroun, Centrafrique, Congo, Côte d'Ivoire, Gabon, Guinée, Guinée Bissau, Guinée équatoriale, Mali, Mauritanie, Niger, Sénégal, Tchad, Togo and Union des Comores

[86] OAPI established a regional office for filing trademark applications and covers Botswana, the Gambia, Ghana, Kenya, Lesotho, Malawi, Mozambique, Namibia, Sierra Leone, Liberia, Rwanda, Somalia, Sudan, Swaziland, Tanzania, Uganda, Zambia and Zimbabwe.

[87] http://www.worldipreview.com/news/gucci-loses-gg-trademark-in-the-uk

newspapers and computer programs; databases, films, musical compositions, cinemato-graphic work and choreography; artistic works such as paintings, drawings, photographs and sculpture; architecture; advertisements, maps technical drawings and computer pro-grams [88]. Copyright only provide protection to expressions, not to ideas, processes, meth-ods or procedures. Therefore, in order to obtain copyright protection, the works must be fixed in some material form[89].

Copyright is largely dependent upon the nation of origin of the author and where the work was created and first published. There is no single "international law of copyright" because each country sets its own substantive and procedural rules with respect to the protections and use of works in their respective jurisdiction. Nevertheless, several international copy-right treaties exist which were adopted to harmonize copyright laws and provide for re-ciprocal protection. The Berne Convention is perhaps the most well-known international copyright treaty because it established core copyright rights such as the right to reproduc-tion, to be enjoyed by authors regardless of nationality. More importantly, it grants an "au-tomatic protection" of copyright, without the need for formal national registration sys-tems. This means that the author's copyright is born from the moment the work is fixed in a tangible medium of expression. Consequently, neither registration nor publication are required to secure a copyright. While it is not mandatory to register a work to secure cop-yright, in many countries such as in the United States, it is necessary to file a copyright registration to proceed with a copyright infringement action. Interestingly, authors of for-eign works need not obtain registration as a precondition to suit, while U.S. nationals must do so. Further, there are many advantages to obtain a registration. For example, in the U.S. registration provides a presumption of validity, recognition of the statutory damages and right to claim attorney's fees. Therefore, in countries where you think your copyright might be infringed, it may be advisable to seek registration of the work.

Copyrights are limited in duration. The Berne Convention provides works to be protected for a minimum of life of the author plus 50 years. The duration of copyright varies from country to country and depending on the type of work (e.g. artistic works at least 25 years from creation, books at least 50 years from author's death), but the common term in most countries is the life of the author plus 70 years. In addition, the Berne Convention estab-lishes the rule of the shorter term. This rule provides that the term of protection granted in the country where the work was published first should be applied. This means that mem-ber countries are not required to provide a longer term of protection than the one received in the country where the work was first published. Knowing the duration of the copyright in a particular jurisdiction is important for licensee and licensors because once the work enters into public domain, the work is available to use.

The Berne Convention also grants moral and economic rights to authors. Moral rights (or "droit moral") include the right to claim authorship of the work, right of the author to object to any distortion, mutilation or other modification of the work that might be

---

[88] http://www.wipo.int/copyright/en/#copyright

[89] Article 2 of the Berne Convention

prejudicial to his honor or reputation[90]. Countries with Anglo-American tradition such of United States, Canada, Australia and New Zealand minimize the existence of moral rights and focus more on the economic rights[91]. Licensors should be aware if the domestic law recognizes moral rights because in some countries moral rights cannot be assigned by the creator to a third party. In comparison, economic rights are always assignable, and they include the rights to use or to prohibit its use, reproduction, distribution, broadcasting, public performance, translation or adaptation of a work.

Another well-known treaty is the Universal Copyright Convention ("UCC"). This Convention was adopted under the auspices of the United Nations Educational, Scientific and Cultural Organization ("UNESCO"). Like Berne, it established the principle of national treatment, but reduces the minimum term of protection to the life of the author plus 25 years[92]. The Convention required that all copyrighted work should include the symbol © accompanied by the name of Copyright proprietor and the year of 1st publication[93].

Most copyrighted works must be licensed by the owner to be used. Exclusive copyright licenses transfer the power to exercise rights in the copyright, which provide the exclusive licensee with the right to copy the work.[94] Ultimately, the copyright licensee has the right to sue other parties for infringing on its exclusive right to copy the work[95]. It is also important to note that exclusive licenses should be recorded and signed by both parties, in accordance with the Statue of Frauds.

 However, there are exceptions and limitations that permit the use of works without authorization and without payment of compensation. These exceptions and limitations are established in national copyright laws and vary substantially from jurisdiction to jurisdiction. They are often expressed in concepts such as "fair use" or "fair utilization". The common fair uses are for educational purposes, for reporting current events, ephemeral recordings for broadcasting purposes and reproduction in certain special cases. Nevertheless, the limitation usually never covers the normal commercial exploitation of the work made by companies that could unreasonable prejudice the legitimate interest of the author[96]. Although, there are many countries that allow compulsory licenses, meaning that authorization from the copyright holder is not required to use the work, but compensation for its use must be paid.

---

[90] Article 6bis of Berne Convention

[91]http://www.rightsdirect.com/content/rd/en/toolbar/copyright_education/Inte rnational_Copyright_Basics.html

[92] To see which countries signatories of the UCC are, visit http://www.wipo.int/wipolex/en/other_treaties/parties.jsp?treaty_id=208&group_id=22

[93] Article 3 of UCC

[94] MELVIN SIMENSKY, LANNING BRYER & NEIL J. WILKOF, INTELLECTUAL PROPERTY IN THE GLOBAL MARKETPLACE 12.1 (John Wiley & Sons, Inc., 2d ed. 1999)

[95] However, nonexclusive licenses do not transfer ownership of the rights to copy.

[96] Article 9(a) of Berne Convention

16.4.2 Related Rights

Related rights are also known as "neighboring rights" to copyright because they concern other categories of owners' rights. They are the rights that performers, producers of phonograms and broadcasting organization hold in relation to their performances, phonograms and broadcasts, respectively[97].

Related rights are linked with copyright because the three categories of related rights are auxiliaries or intermediaries in the production, recoding or diffusion of author's work. "A musician performs a musical work written by a composer; an actor performs a role in a play written by a playwright; producers of phonograms -- or more commonly "the record industry" -- record and produce songs and music written by authors and composers, played by musicians or sung by performers; broadcasting organizations broadcast works and phonograms on their stations[98]". For example, Bono composes the lyrics for all the U2's songs; therefore, this means that Bono holds copyright for the composition of the songs and rights to his performance. RCA Records produce the music recording of many popular artists such as Shakira, Britney Spears, Alicia Keys, Justin Timberlake, Miley Cyrus among others. A record company usually handles the production, manufacture, distribution, marketing and promotion of the music recordings and music videos that they publish and sometimes even the enforcement of the copyright.

The Rome Convention established the related rights. Like the Berne Convention, the Rome Convention determines the minimum standards of protection that Contracting States should grant to performers, producers of phonograms and broadcasting organizations. Likewise, it established the principle of national treatment, were the contracting states should grant foreigners the same rights it grants to their nationals[99].

According to the Rome Convention, performers are granted the "possibility of preventing" certain acts without their consent[100]. These acts include the prevention of broadcasting or communication to the public of a live performance; recording an unfixed performance; and reproducing a fixation of the performance[101]. Producers of phonograms have the right to authorize or prohibit the direct or indirect reproduction of their phonograms[102]. Broadcasting organizations have the right to authorize or prohibit (a) the rebroadcasting of their broadcasts; (b) the fixation of their broadcasts; (c) the reproduction of fixation of their broadcasts and (d) the communication to the public of their television broadcasts when they accessible to public against payment[103]. Under the Rome Convention, the minimum term of protection is 25 years from the end of the year in which the

---

[97] http://www.wipo.int/about-ip/en/about_collective_mngt.html

[98] Id.

[99] http://www.wipo.int/export/sites/www/copyright/en/activities/pdf/inter national_protection.pdf

[100] Article 7 of Rome Convention

[101] http://www.wipo.int/export/sites/www/copyright/en/activities/pdf/international_protection.pdf

[102] Article 10 of Rome Convention

[103] Article 13 of Rome Convention

fixation was made or when the performance or broadcast took place[104]. Like in copyright, there are limitations that allow the private use of the related rights. Each country regulates the limitations through their domestic law.

16.4.3 Collective Management of Copyrights and Related Rights

In today's world, the individual management of rights is virtually impossible. An author is incapable of monitoring all the uses of his work. An author cannot, for instance, contact every single radio or television station to negotiate licenses and remuneration for the use of his works. Equally, it is impossible for broadcasting organizations to seek specific permission from every author for the use of every copyrighted work. Considering the impracticability of managing these activities individually, collective management organizations were created to act in the interest of the owners of copyrights. Collective management organizations are an important link between creators and users of copyrighted works because they ensure that users pay creators the adequate remuneration for the use of their works.

There are many kinds of collective management organizations, depending on the category of works involved (e.g. music, books, multimedia, production, etc.)[105]. Creators join them so that the organization can manage their copyrights and related rights. Because of such membership, the collective management organization negotiates the rates and term of use with users, issue licenses authorizing uses, and collect and distribute royalties back to the creators[106].

Some examples of well-known international collective management organizations include:

- International Confederation of Societies of Authors and Composers (CISAC)
- International Federation of Reproduction Rights Organizations (IFRRO)
- Association of European Performers Organization (AEPO)
- International Federation of Actors (FIA)
- International Federation of Musicians (FIM)
- International Federation of the Phonographic Industry (IFPI)

16.5 License Agreement Terms and Registration Requirements

16.5.1 License Agreement Terms.

The provisions of a license agreement are extremely important, as they contemplate significant issues that may arise between the licensor and the licensee, including but not limited to, remittance of royalties, enforceability of an agreement between the parties or against third parties, and maintenance and protection of the underlying intellectual property rights. The following non-exhaustive list includes some recommendations for basic licensing provisions:

---

[104]http://www.wipo.int/export/sites/www/copyright/en/activities/pdf/international_protection.pdf

[105] Id.

[106] Id.

(a) **Definition of the Property.** The IP must be clearly defined, and it is important to include all registration or application numbers for identification. Specimens of relevant trademarks should also be attached to the agreement as exhibits for reference.[107]

(b) **Exclusive and Nonexclusive licenses.** The grant of a license should indicate whether it is exclusive or nonexclusive. If it is exclusive, the agreement should indicate whether the bar on the issuance of other licenses also includes a bar on the licensor's own use of the IP. Additionally, for exclusive licenses in the United States, a provision should be included stating whether the licensee may manufacture or sell competing products. [108]

(c) **Quality Control.** Provisions should be included that maintain the standards and specifications with which the licensor expects the licensee to comply. It may also include language that allows the licensor to inspect the licensee's premises in order to oversee the goods. [109]

(d) **Territory.** The territory should be clearly defined to prevent problems that may arise in connection with the grant of territorially restricted licenses within a trading block.[110]

(f) **Termination.** Provisions should be included to govern the termination or expiration of the license, and renewal or cancellation of the agreement prior to expiration.[111]

(g) **Royalty Provision.** While a royalty provision is not required for the agreement to be valid, most licenses include royalty fee provisions that determine the time and amount of payments, how the royalties will be calculated, and requirements that the license keep accurate and complete accounting records, among other considerations. [112]

(h) **Infringement procedures.** A provision should be included relating to the possible infringement of the IP rights and who is to assume discretion and control of any possible litigation. [113]

16.5.2 Registration Requirements.

At present, most countries in the world recognize some form of trademark licensing and require the recording of the license agreements. Most countries are divided into two categories: British-law (or common-law) countries, and civil law countries.[114]

British law countries are those that follow the development of British trademark law and the enactment of the registered user procedure defined in the United Kingdom Trade-

---

[107] Id.

[108] Id.

[109] Id.

[110] Id.

[111] Id.

[112] Id.

[113] Id.

[114] MELVIN SIMENSKY, LANNING BRYER & NEIL J. WILKOF, INTELLECTUAL PROPERTY IN THE GLOBAL MARKETPLACE 12.1 (John Wiley & Sons, Inc., 2d ed. 1999)

Marks Act of 1938. Some examples of British law countries include: India, Israel, Australia, Hong Kong, and South Africa. These countries provide for registered user entries as in section 28 of the British Trade-Marks Act.[115] Specially, if two parties are financially or otherwise related, there is generally no requirement that a trade-mark license agreement be filed. Rather, a simple registered user application can be filed, setting forth the terms and conditions of the license agreement.[116] Additionally, countries whose laws are modeled on the British Trade-Marks Act of 1938 contain provisions for the simultaneous filing of trademarks and registered user applications.[117]

In comparison, in civil law countries, such as Mexico, a trademark license may be recorded against a pending trademark application. Many civil law countries require a trademark registration to be obtained prior to the recording of the license agreement. Furthermore, submission of an original or certified copy of the license agreement is generally required, regardless of whether the parties are financially related. In certain civil law jurisdictions, recordal is mandatory. However, recordation of license agreements in other civil law countries is merely best practice for the agreement to be enforceable between the parties and against third parties.[118]

In addition to registration requirements, numerous foreign jurisdictions require governmental approval of the license agreement to record the agreement at their respective trademark offices. Typically, this requirement exists where the licensor is a foreign company, and the licensee is a national company, and there are provisions in the agreement of the remittance of royalties outside the jurisdiction. Government agencies also closely examine license agreements for restrictive clauses or provisions that might violate local anti-trust laws. [119]

It is also important to note the specific additional steps that may be required in many jurisdictions, even after recordation and approval of a license agreement. Accordingly, proper recordkeeping procedures and practices should be instituted to ensure that license registrations remain valid and subsisting. [120]

16.6 Conclusion

Ideally, both licensor and licensee should engage in efforts to establish intellectual property rights and maintain those rights through effective enforcement. Without due consideration for such efforts, a company's brand can be negatively impacted leaving both licensor and licensee with little or diminished value. As discussed herein there can be many challenges when dealing with complex licensing matters. Accordingly, it is important to engage in a discussion with your licensing agent or in-house counsel to determine the

---

[115] Id.

[116] Id.

[117] U.K. Trade-Marks Act (T.M.A.) 1938, § 29 (1) (b).

[118] MELVIN SIMENSKY, LANNING BRYER & NEIL J. WILKOF, INTELLECTUAL PROPERTY IN THE GLOBAL MARKETPLACE 12.1 (John Wiley & Sons, Inc., 2d ed. 1999

[119] Id.

[120] Id.

necessary efforts that best fit the needs of your business or licensing venture and the subject intellectual property rights being used or licensed.

Chapter 17
Battersby's Rules on Licensing[121]

1. ***"When You Sleep with Dogs, You Get Fleas."*** This continues to remain my number 1 rule–it's all about the partners you choose. Licensors who simply look for the best financial deal and ignore the reputation or track record of the licensee are looking for problems. The history of the licensee is paramount. The adage, "Those who do not learn history are doomed to repeat it" applies.

2. ***"Everybody Cheats....At Least A Little."*** I can guarantee that the CFO's of the licensor and licensee will read the definition of Net Sales differently and that different reading can result in significant differences in payments. Licensors should audit licensees early. In other words, "Trust, But Verify.

3. ***"There are No Partnerships in Licensing."*** Licensing executives frequently describe the relationship between licensor/licensee relationship as partnership but the only time you will ever see that word in a license agreement is the statement that says, "this is not a 'partnership.'" Licensors are not looking for partners.

4. ***"Every License Agreement is Negotiable."*** Licensor frequently say that their agreement is not negotiable, but they don't mean it. If you have a strong program, solid financials and offer enough by way of royalties and guarantees, licensors will quickly agree to negotiate their boilerplate. License agreements are ALWAYS negotiable.

5. ***"When Someone Says, 'Trust Me,' Grab your Wallet."*** Never trust any representation made by a licensor unless it's written into the agreement. When the studio licensing director tells you to "trust" him that there will be a motion picture in 2 years for the property, beware......particularly when he says that his lawyers won't let him put it in the agreement. Intent doesn't count.

6. ***"Licensing is the Last Bastion of Hucksterism."*** Every licensing executive postures. If something sounds too good to be true, it usually is. The line, "In all my years in licensing, no one has ever......" means "not this past week, anyway." Do your due diligence and avoid surprises.

7. ***"It's All About the Guarantees."*** Licensing executives frequently negotiate hard over the royalty rates. While important, it's the guarantees that can drive a licensee into bankruptcy, particularly if sales don't materialize as expected. High guarantees can increase the effective royalty rate three or four-fold in a recession.

8. ***"Don't Dive for the Last Nickel."*** More good deals are lost because one side gets greedy. The best deal is the one where neither side walks away totally happy. Leave something on the table and let your adversary believe that they won something—it will help you in your next negotiation with them.

---

[121] Written by Greg Battersby, Battersby Law Group, Westport, CT www.gbiplaw.com

9. ***"Make Sure You've Got the Right Party on the Agreement."*** We live in the day of overnight formation of corporate entities. Make sure that the party granting the license owns the IP and that the licensee has more than 25 cents in its account.

10. ***"Don't Over-lawyer the Agreement."*** License agreements should be reviewed by experienced licensing counsel. That said, too many lawyers get hung up on changing the "therefores" which drive opposing counsel crazy and add little value to the transaction. Licensors typically are resistant to making wholesale changes to their "standard" license agreement.

Chapter 18
Simon Says About Licensing

By now you have read my writing partner, the Honorable Greg Battersby Esq, "Rules on Licensing" on the preceding pages. Yes, its tone is a bit dour and is tinged with a touch of bleakness, but as you may have noticed from the initials at the end of his name, he is a lawyer.

Albeit a damn fine attorney, Greg is inclined, due in large part to his chosen profession, to not only view a glass as not less than 50% empty, but makes certain it is clearly understood that at any moment – likely without notice – there is the potential the aforementioned vessel could spring a leak, which if such should occur, it is reasonable to assume, would result in a hasty and total decampment of any liquid that may have resided therein.

Greg's likely "cautiously optimistic" response if asked, "Is the glass half full or half empty?" as provided above, should, perhaps, be taken into consideration when reading his aforementioned "Rules."

I thought it fitting to offer a perspective that is perhaps a touch more optimistic by citing a few venerate licensing affirmations I have gleaned after spending a rather long time plying my chosen trade as a licensing rights monger. If you find these helpful and or enlightening, you are most welcome. If not, well you can always re-read the grumpier ones on the preceding pages.

1. **"The Power of Optimism"** From the perspective of a licensor, success in licensing is more easily attained when approached with reality-rooted unbridled optimism.

2. **"Your Best Sales Tool"** The ability to articulate a well delineated mind's eye image of the property's application to the product or category under discussion is often a powerful sales tool.

3. **"Strive for Fair"** Fair should be the desired end result of negotiations.

4. **"A Core Objective"** A core objective in negotiating a licensing agreement, with a valued party, is having the ability to do so again.

5. **"Thoughts on licensee sales projections"** Of course, they are unrealistically low, they are supposed to be. A company dumb enough to provide real sales projections when negotiating advance and guarantee terms is not who I want as a licensee.

6. **"Treatment of licensees"** Be kind and considerate to your licensees whenever possible. Remember they are ones sending you royalty checks.

7. **"*Never respond in haste*"** The delight in sending an ill-tempered email response, justifiable or not, probably means you will have to apologize to the putz at some point in the future.

8. **"*Make every effort to choose your words wisely*"** Always keep in mind that somebody might actually be listening and will remember what you are saying.

9. *"Don't let approvals lay idle on your desk"* Approvals submissions allowed to languish unattended only means that you are destined to be punished at some point down the road.

I end with what I refer to as *"The Licensing Homily,"* which is well worth considering as a suitable office wall hanging (perhaps in needlepoint?):

The strongest memory is weaker than the palest ink.

Chapter 19
Ethics and Social Compliance

19.1   Ethics in Licensing

Some cynics who refer to licensing as the "last bastion of hucksterism" may think that the phrase "ethics in licensing" is an oxymoron. It's not, and as the industry has grown from its modest beginnings into a well-regarded and profitable marketing machine, professionalism within the industry remains important and that means that licensing professionals need to deal with each other on an ethical basis.

Webster defines "ethics" as, the "principles of conduct governing an individual or a group." In the context of any professional group, "ethics" is typically considered to be:

- Honesty and candor, instead of gamesmanship and overreaching;
- Seeking enforceable, yet workable, business arrangements; and
- Protecting and enhancing the profession's reputation.

The International Licensing Industry Merchandisers' Association (LIMA) has adopted a Statement of Ethical Principles that address how licensing should be practiced. It states the following:

- LIMA supports and encourages its members to conduct themselves in an ethical manner in the course of their business dealing involving licensing properties and licensed products.
- A member of LIMA should respect the rights of others and should comply with all applicable local, national and international laws and regulations governing his or her business dealings.
- A member should make fair representations as to the nature, quality and extent of the property being offered for license or of the capabilities of the company seeking a license. Any statement not supported by fact should be identified as opinion. A member should not engage in any misleading advertising or solicitation that could lead to false or exaggerated expectations as to the member's skill, experience or ability.
- A member should not represent conflicting interests in the same transaction without the knowledge and consent of all parties involved.
- A member should hold inviolate all confidences, whether written or implied.

In addition to LIMA'S Statement of Ethical Principles, the American Bar Association observes a code called the Model Rules of Professional Conduct. While obviously many of these model rules have no applicability whatsoever to licensing, there are some that do, particularly Model Rule 4.1 which states:

In the course of representing a client, a lawyer shall not knowingly:

    (a) Make a false statement of material fact or law to a third person; or
    (b) Fail to disclose a material fact to a third person when disclosure is necessary to avoid assisting a criminal or fraudulent act by a client, unless disclosure is prohibited by Rule 1.6.

In the commentary to Rule 4.1, the committee drafting the rule stated that "[u]nder generally accepted conventions in negotiation, certain types of statements ordinarily are not taken as statements of material fact. Estimates of price or value placed on the subject of a transaction and a party's intentions as to an acceptable settlement of a claim are in this category."

What does that mean in a licensing context where everyone postures and puffs? Puffing is a statement of inference or intention while lying is a misstatement of an objectively, verifiable fact. Puffing in negotiations is not unethical but lying can be. While there may be a fine line between the two, care should be taken not to cross it.

For example, if a negotiator made the statement that his client "would not accept less than 4% royalty," that would generally be considering puffing, even if he knew that he was authorized to accept a royalty rate as low as 2%. If, however, he provides a specific reason as to why he cannot accept lower than a 4% royalty, e.g., "our agreement with the producer prevents us from accepting any royalty lower than 4%," and that reason is untrue, the line between puffing and lying has been crossed.

Under Rule 4.1(b), it is also not ethical to remain silent in a negotiation on a material issue of fact when one knows that its opponent could be misled by such silence. The line between ethical and unethical conduct is, again, a fine one.

For example, if a licensor was asked by a licensee whether its property is valid and whether anyone has ever challenged such validity, the licensor is obligated to answer truthfully. If, however, the licensee does not ask such a question, are they obligated to address the issue? The answer is, probably no. Yet, if the licensee has told them that the issue of trademark validity was very important, and the property owner knew of the existence of at least two claims by third parties charging that their trademark was invalid, silence might be considered unethical even if the licensee failed to ask that specific question.

The ABA Model Rules concerning potential conflicts of interest, while interesting and potentially instructive, are generally not relevant in many licensing situations. Because of the potential that lawyers may have access to a client's confidential or privileged information, they are generally held to a higher standard than most licensing professionals, for whom the possibility of disclosing privileged information does not typically arise.

That said, conflicts of interest in licensing can prove particularly problematic because the industry is relatively small, and individuals frequently find themselves at different times on different sides of the same negotiating table. It is difficult, if not impossible, to address every particular situation that might arise, but one rule of thumb almost always applies. In the event that a licensing executive enters a potential conflict of interest scenario, e.g., where they are representing a licensee who is looking to take a license from their former employer, or worse yet, they are an agent who is representing both the licensor and potential licensee, if they elect to remain involved in the transaction they would be well advised to disclose this information to all relevant parties at the earliest possible occasion. Virtually all conflicts of interest can be waived by full disclosure to both parties and with their consent, preferably in writing. If the parties do not agree to a waiver, they would be wise to withdraw from the negotiations.

19.2 Ensuring Social Compliance

"Social compliance" is a relatively recent concern for many licensors due, in large measure, to negative media attention focused on working conditions in factories that produce licensed products, most notably in China. The problem received national attention in the United States in 1996 because of a controversy involving Kathie Lee Gifford.

The news media and social activist groups around the world exposed the fact that some factories were applying sub-standard working conditions and were employing prison and child labor to produce the products. This put pressure on the private sector to play a role in trying to improve such conditions.

Make no mistake about it, there is a serious problem in this industry. Some factories blatantly violate their local laws, falsify their records and even bribe inspectors. This is a way of life in some countries and to think otherwise is to simply ignore the problem.

The private sector's reaction was the development of codes of conduct for these factories to follow if they wanted to continue to work with a particular property owner. The first code of conduct was adopted by Levi Strauss in 1991. In 1998, the Fair Labor Association was created with White House support and developed its own code.

Over the past decade, many licensors, retailers and trade associations have adopted social compliance standards which they require their partners and suppliers to follow. The purpose of these codes is to raise the standards of working conditions in factories that manufacture licensed products and promote social responsibility.

While there are slight differences between many of these codes, in one form or another they all address the following issues:

- Maximum working hours for employees;
- Compensation of employees; and
- Social insurance that an employer must carry for its employees.

LIMA has its own Code of Business Practices, which may be found at http://www.licensing.org/about/business-practices.php which is found in Appendix-1.

Establishing standards is one thing—enforcing them is quite another. Very few licensors simply ignore the issue altogether and, at the very least, most require their licensees to conform to some standard. While they may not aggressively enforce such a requirement, they will reserve the right to terminate the licensee should it be determined that the licensee was non-compliant. This is the minimum that any licensor should do in this regard.

Most licensors go further and, do, in fact, actively look to enforce these standards, typically by auditing the factories of their licensees. This is done by either their internal auditors or by third parties who specialize in such audits. While some simply audit on a superficial basis and tend to look the other way when violations are found, there is an increasing number of licensors that require a non-conforming licensee to either correct the problems or face termination of their license agreement.

Some licensors will go the extra mile and work with licensees to make sure that their factories are following these standards. They have shifted focus from mere monitoring to actively promoting continuous improvement, even to the point where they are willing to share in the associated cost of reaching compliance. They have begun to emphasize education and capacity building, as opposed to simply conducting more audits. Longer-term corrective action plans are necessary and ultimately reinforce better business practices. Appropriately, a growing number of licensors today recognize the implications of non-compliance, which can seriously tarnish not only the attractiveness of its primary and licensed products but of its moral image and reputation as well.

19.3 The BSR Report

LIMA, in combination with BSR, a leader in corporate responsibility since 1992, partnered on a report entitled "Good Practices for Complying with Licensors' Social and Environmental Requirements: A Practical Guide for Licensees."

This guide serves as a starting point for licensee executives and professionals to understand how they can meet licensors' requirements related to social and environmental compliance. It also provides guidance on how licensees can improve working conditions within their direct and contract manufacturing operations and supply chains. The primary audience for this guide includes licensees and their suppliers, subcontractors, and agents, and others involved in the production of licensed products.

Licensors and retailers are encouraged to send this guide to licensees as a source of information on meeting licensors' and brands' expectations for social and environmental compliance within the supply chain.

- Section 1 focuses on licensors' expectations.
- Section 2 focuses on practical tips for integrating social and environmental compliance into your business relationships with suppliers.
- Section 3 focuses on practical tips for identifying and understanding compliance risks.
- Section 4 focuses on practical tips for tracking and disclosing factory information to licensors.
- Section 5 focuses on practical tips for monitoring suppliers' social and environmental compliance.
- Section 6 focuses on remediation steps to help improve working conditions.
- Section 7 describes ways that you can get involved and collaborate with others in the licensing industry.
- The appendix includes an alphabetized list of organizations and other resources that can assist your company's social and environmental compliance efforts. A complete copy of this report is on the LIMA website at http://www.licensing.org/wordpress/wp-content/uploads/2013/11/good-practices-english.pdf

Chapter 20
Most Common Mistakes in Licensing[122]

Over the past fifteen years, I have seen many licensing deals go south because one of the parties fell into a pitfall that could have been avoided. In this article I share the 10 most common pitfalls of brand licensing that I have come across. After reading these, I hope you will let us know if you fell prey to one of these.

If you have experienced another, please let us know what happened. Through your help we can learn from each other and avoid the consequences of making one of these mistakes.

1. **Biting off more than you can chew.** Licensors interested in licensing a category to a prospective licensee will ask the licensee for sales projections by region and by channel, along with a sales plan. In trying to "win" the license, the prospective licensee will often provide the licensor with a "best case scenario" instead of a more realistic case. These initial projections will then be used by the licensor to develop minimum sales targets and royalties, which will become part of the contract agreement.

Licensees can get into trouble when they agree to just about "any" terms to get the license. In this instance, the licensee often ends up accepting sales targets they may not be able to achieve, which ultimately will result in a breach of contract.

2. **Getting in over your head.** While negotiating their license, prospective licensees often try to secure multiple regions or channels as part of the deal. This may be because the licensee really believes it can take full advantage of all of the rights offered and sell its product into each of the channels or regions.

In reality, the company often has only *one* opportunity to sell the branded merchandise to a specific retailer. If that one opportunity falls through, the licensee fails to meet its sales and royalty targets and may request royalty relief. This usually leads the licensor to ask the licensee to demonstrate how they are maximizing their rights. When the licensee is not prepared to do so, not only will they get not get the royalty relief they are asking for, they may be required to develop a comprehensive plan on how they intend to fully exploit their license.

If the licensee is unwilling or unable to develop the plan or invest in the license, they may lose rights to certain channels or regions.

---

[122] Written by Pete Canalichio, Licensing Brands, Inc., author of Expand, Grow, Thrive, which is available at https://pete-canalichio.com/ExpandGrowThrive/

3. Creating unrealistic expectations. Licensees may not fully understand the true strength of the brand whose license they just acquired. The licensee may overestimate the power of the brand, believing the brand alone on their product will result in acquiring new clients or larger programs with existing clients.

Even if the licensee has invested in product development and built the essence of the brand into their product, they may not win new business immediately. When new sales fail to happen, the licensee may feel like they got sold a bill of goods.

4. Logo slapping. Licensees often do not understand when signing an agreement that the licensor will expect them to custom design the attributes of the brand into their product, and not just slap the trademarked logo to the licensee's product.

Licensors often want the licensee to treat the licensed category with the same care they would treat a product category in their own organization. They want the licensee to develop the product following the brand's style guides carefully and to follow externally a similar protocol to the one that the licensor follows internally. The licensor wants the licensed product to be of a quality that the licensor would be proud to have on a retail shelf next to the internal product.

This results in frustrations on both sides as the product developed may not meet brand and quality expectations. When the licensee doesn't meet the licensor's requirements, the product often does not get approved and/or needs to be reworked and the licensee loses key sales opportunities.

5. Failure to follow the approval process. The licensee expects that approvals will come relatively easily and quickly. Instead, many products are not approved because the licensee has not followed the approval process. This often results in the licensee missing a modular shipment date or selling an unapproved product.

The price of missing a ship date can mean the loss of millions of dollars in sales. The price of selling unapproved product can be even higher. If a licensee were to sell an unapproved product which has a harmful substance such as lead paint, it could be devastating to the licensor's brand. For this reason, the penalties for selling unapproved products are stiff.

6. Not knowing the contract. Typically, license agreements are negotiated by company presidents or CFOs, who are the ones familiar with the contract terms and the licensor's expectations. Obligations can get overlooked if the people who actually execute the program on a day-to-day basis, such as sales, marketing, product development, design, etc., are not made familiar with the contract.

For example, these obligations can include social and quality compliance requirements, a commitment to product design that incorporates the brand identity, a detailed understanding of the approval process, and a willingness to invest in advertising and promotions. If the individuals whose job is to execute these job requirements are not aware of them, it can place a strain on the relationship and can ultimately lead to a termination in the contract.

7. Not being prepared to invest in the license. Without proper investment, the licensee will not achieve the results they or the licensor anticipated when the agreement was made.

The licensor who has granted the license expects growth in the licensed category from a sales, marketing and financial perspective throughout the term of the agreement. Moreover, the licensor expects the licensee to pursue every channel and every category designated, not just the low hanging fruit.

Despite this obligation, the licensee may not make the proper investment. There can be many reasons for this including a misunderstanding of the commitment needed, a loss of focus or interest after an expected sale falls through or change in management leading to a new strategic direction for the licensee. Irrespective of these reasons, the licensee will still be obligated to meet the royalty and other financial commitments written in the contract.

8. Selling in unauthorized channels. Sometimes to meet contractual sales minimums or guaranteed royalty commitments, the licensee can be tempted to sell licensed product outside of their authorized channels or territory, thinking they won't get caught.

When this occurs, the licensee may put the licensor at risk if the licensor has no trademark rights in the region or if another licensee is authorized to sell in the channel or territory. For this reason, licensing contracts come with stiff penalties, up to and including termination, if products are sold into an unauthorized channel or territory.

9. Trusting the other party has your best interests in mind. Licensees can get into trouble when they trust that the licensor has their best interest in mind. A licensor may license a category they are vacating because they have strained a relationship with a retailer or failed the consumer in a category.

Licensees often may share ideas with the licensor only to have them "taken" by the licensor. This can result in a lot of animosity with a long-term negative effect. Licensees are usually granted a non-exclusive license. In some instances, the licensor may choose to compete directly with the licensee or pitch one licensee against another.

If the licensee is unaware of the licensor's intentions, the licensee may be unable to meet its contractual obligations or suffer costs greater than expected in order to meet them.

10. Not following the written contract. Licensees can get into trouble when they follow verbal directions that are in direct conflict with the contract. This is a difficult predicament because the licensee may feel pressure to comply with the verbal direction. If they don't get their direction in writing, they can later be held liable for breaking the contract.

I hope you will keep these 10 pitfalls handy and learn from them so that you do not suffer as a result of not knowing. In addition, I hope you will share your story of how you fell into a pitfall and what the impact was to your business and your licensing partner's. If we pay if forward everyone can benefit.

Chapter 21
Special Considerations for Different Types of Properties/Products

21.1 Introduction

All license agreements share a certain common layout and theme—irrespective of the type of licensed property and licensed product(s). Similarly, there are many elements of merchandising license agreements that look remarkably like similar provisions in patent, technology and software license agreements. For example, all forms of license agreements will contain strikingly similar "grant" provisions as well as "boilerplate" provisions such as disputes, assignability, notices and integration are common from agreement to agreement.

Despite the similarity, there can be striking differences depending upon the type of property being licensed as well as the type of licensed goods. Some of these differences are due to the potential length of the agreements while other will have to do with the approvals process and exactly what can and will be reviewed and approved. As such "form" license agreements will take you only so far in the drafting process.

21.2 Different Types of Properties

21.2.1 Entertainment Properties

Entertainment licensing generates by far the most licensing revenue and is driven in large measure by the studios and broadcast companies. By and large, most of the agreements are non-exclusive because of potential bankruptcy issues but some have what is described as "backdoor exclusivity" in that the licensor agrees not to grant any other competing licenses to other parties provided that the licensee is not in breach of any provision of the agreement.

The royalties and guarantees for entertainment properties tend to be higher than for most other forms of licensing due, in large measure, to the popularity of such properties.

A major consideration in many of these agreements or, rather, the negotiation of such agreements, are the representations that the licensor might make with respect to when a motion picture may be released, or a television show may be aired and the extent of such airing. Rarely will a licensor include such representations in the agreement because it doesn't want to be bound to the dates and afford the licensee an opportunity to avoid having to pay its guarantees. In fact, entertainment licensors are particularly adamant about including an "integration" clause in the agreement reciting that if something isn't in the agreement, it's not binding on the licensor.

From a licensee's perspective it's very important to get the licensor to commit to a motion picture release or a television broadcast, particularly if there are large guarantees. While it might be impossible to get the licensor to commit to the dates that they had originally represented but asking them to commit to "some date" may be a possible compromise and might help the licensee should the motion picture never be released, or the show ever broadcast.

Another provision unique to entertainment licensing involves the release dates for licensed products. Many entertainment licensors want to ensure that there will be an adequate number of licensed products on the market at or about the release date of the motion picture or television show but not too far in advance of such date.

Finally, the terms of such agreements, particularly when the property is based on a motion picture, tend to be shorter than with respect to other properties because the life span of such properties is limited. Licensees will want to negotiate options for additional terms as well as rights for sequels, spinoffs, prequels, etc. if possible.

21.2 2 Celebrity Properties

Celebrity licensing is the licensing of the name or image of a celebrity, actress or athlete. The licensed property will frequently be the name or image of the celebrity, but it can also include the signature, voice or other identifying feature. Such properties are typically protected as trademarks or under the celebrity's right of publicity.

For starters, most celebrity agreements are between the licensee and the entity that owns the celebrity's publicity and/or trademark rights since most celebrities assign such rights to a corporate entity for a variety of different reasons. The celebrity will frequently be required to sign an acknowledgement which is attached to the license agreement recognizing that he or she will have certain obligations.

While most celebrity license agreements are non-exclusive, there is a higher percentage of exclusive celebrity agreements that in the entertainment area.

In celebrity licensing, while the financial terms of the agreement are important, so too are the obligations placed on the celebrity in terms of public appearances and availability for photo and video shoots and promotions. Frequently, there are limits placed on how frequently a celebrity must appear, e.g., no more than 5 days per year, and how much notice must be provided so that they will not interfere with the celebrity's schedule. The agreement may also state how the celebrity will travel, e.g., first class air or even private jets, and what type of accommodations will be provided, e.g., 5-star hotels or better.

> In celebrity licenses, provisions concerning access to the celebrity and the celebrity's obligations can get quite contentious.

The agreement may also state the compensation that the celebrity will be paid for such appearances and what type of support will be provided for such shoots or appearances, e.g., hair and makeup with stylists acceptable to the celebrity.

The agreement may provide that the celebrity may not be seen in public or photographed wearing competitive apparel or goods. With the growing importance of social media as an influential factor impacting taste and trends, many celebrity licensing agreements now include a schedule (type and frequency) of interactions on social media that the celebrity is obligated perform during the term of the agreement.

Since the licensee is taking the license and agrees to pay royalties based on the "fame" of the celebrity, the licensee will want to protect itself if the celebrity should commit an act that diminishes their fame. This is typically handled by the insertion of a "moral turpitude" clause in the agreement which gives the licensee the right to terminate the agreement should the celebrity should engage in an act of moral turpitude or otherwise exposes them to public ridicule. Consider, for example, the actions of chewing gum maker Wrigley and the Milk Processor Education Program, which is responsible for the "Got Milk?" campaign, who ended their contracts with R&B performer Chris Brown after the singer plead guilty for assaulting his former girlfriend, Rihanna.

Moral turpitude clauses are typically heavily negotiated but, at the very least, the celebrity should be prepared to allow a licensee to terminate the agreement if they are convicted of a crime that involves an act of moral turpitude. That was certainly what Hertz thought when they dumped O.J. Simpson due to reports of uncontested allegations of domestic abuse in 1992, after they paid him a reported $550,000 a year for spots beginning in the 1970's.

21.2.3 Corporate or Brand Properties

By their very nature, corporate brands are stable properties, many of which have been in use for decades if not centuries. Accordingly, the term of such license agreements tends to be longer than with entertainment properties although the royalty rates and guarantees may be smaller. Similarly, corporate brand licensors are more inclined to enter into exclusive license agreements with their licensees than is the case for entertainment licensors.

Many corporate licensor view brand license agreements through the prism of brand extensions for their own products rather than for ancillary products. As such, the definition of licensed products may be more flexible and corporate brand licensees may be encouraged to explore different types of products under a common umbrella.

Of concern to most corporate licensors is the quality of the licensed products and the quality control procedures identified in the license agreement may well be more onerous than with respect to other categories of licensing properties. Similarly, corporate license agreements tend to provide greater controls relative to manufacturing sources since they do not want the potential negative publicity of a licensee who is using underage or prison labor to manufacture the licensed products.

Along this vein, corporate licensors will require greater control over how the licensed property is used on the licensed products, frequently providing more detailed style guides to outline proper usage.

21.2.4 Art and Designer Properties

Art images are licensed for a variety of different applications, e.g., greeting cards, stationery, apparel, housewares, etc. Manufacturers will try to purchase such images for a fixed fee rather than license them for a variety of reasons, mostly relating to control and avoidance of having to pay royalties.

Where the images are licensed, such agreements are frequently "image specific" which means that the artist or studio is licensing a specific image to be used for a specific application. To effect such purpose, descriptions or actual examples of the image are frequently attached as an exhibit or schedule to the agreement so there is no misunderstanding as to what is covered. It is not uncommon that provide that the exhibit or schedule is fluid, meaning that additional images can be added during the life of the agreement. Most such agreements are exclusive licenses as they relate to the image. The artist or studio would normally retain the rights to all other images, provided that they are not substantially similar in appearance to the licensed image.

> Art license agreements are frequently "image specific where the artist or studio licenses a specific image to be used for a specific application.

If the artist's name or trademark is well known and the licensee wants to use it in combination with the image, a companion trademark license will be included as part of the license grant, although the trademark license will be non-exclusive for the product category so that the artist or studio can license its other images to other parties for products in that category.

The terms of such agreements are generally for the "life of the product" rather than a specific term since the licensee will generally want to be certain that it can continue using such image or images for as long as they are selling the products. In those instances where the term is for a fixed period, the licensee may want to have the option to extend the term for extended terms.

In "designer" agreements where the licensor is licensing their name as well as agreeing to provide certain designs, e.g., clothing designs or even product designs, such agreements will include milestone schedules as to when designs are to be provided; how much time is allocated for approvals; and when the licensee will begin introducing and selling licensed products. Approval rights are always an issue in such agreements since the finished product will always be subject to the designer's approval and the manufacturer is almost always "time pressed" to get the product to market. As such, approval periods are frequently short.

21.2.5 Collegiate Properties

Most collegiate license agreements are non-exclusive, relatively small and frequently with local licensees. There are also some massive agreements with entities such as Nike, Under Armour, adidas and others.

When dealing with state universities, it is often a requirement that such agreements be non-exclusive. The larger ones, however, can and often are either exclusive or non-exclusive with some degree of backdoor exclusivity.

While universities such as Oho State, Iowa and Indiana maintain their own licensing programs, a high percentage work licensing through a few licensing agencies, IMG-College Licensing (the former Collegiate Licensing Company); Learfield Licensing Partners (which is owned by the Atairos investment group) and Fermata Partners, LLC which is owned by the retailer Fanatics. As of the writing of this section, IMG-College Licensing and Learfield Licensing Partners are seeking to merge pending approval of the DOJ.

One of the unique aspects of collegiate licensing when handled by the agents is that the agreements with third party licensees are typically in the name of the agent rather than the school or university. The agent is acting in much the same way that a master licensee would work, granting essentially sub-licenses to the manufacturers. This is radically different from the way that the rest of the licensing industry works where the agreements are almost always between the property owners and the licensee.

21.2.6 Sports Properties

The major sports leagues, i.e., National Football League, Major League Baseball, National Basketball Association and National Hockey League all maintain their own "Properties" divisions which handle the licensing out of their team logos and names. Each also have Player's Association which control the group licensing rights for players. Thus, for example, if a licensee wanted to license the Los Angeles Dodgers name and logo and all its players, the license would be obligated to take licenses from MLB Properties for the rights to use the Dodgers name and image and from the MLB Players' Association to use players' names and likenesses. The Players Associations for each of the major leagues control group licensing rights for their members.

Thus, if you wanted to obtain a license to do baseball trading cards, you would need licenses from both the Properties division to use the team names and from the Players Association to use the names and likenesses of the players.

The sports properties area is in a state of flux due largely to the demise of the brick and mortar stores and the emergence of such Internet e-commerce retailers such as Fanatics. Due in large measure to the rise of Fanatics, most sorts licensors have sought to control the Internet distribution rights of the licensed products.

The terms of most sports licenses are generally consistent with the terms of entertainment or corporate properties and there may well be options to renew for additional periods of time.

21.2.7 Event Properties

Granting licenses for events such as, for example, the NCAA Basketball Final Four Tournament or the Super Bowl may require obtaining rights from multiple parties---a license for the use of the event name and a second (or more) license from the participants. Fortunately, for many of these types of events, the rights to all the participants may be controlled by the same agent, e.g., NFL Properties for the Super Bowl and IMG-CLC for the Final Four Tournament.

Events such as rock concerts, etc. present different issues since it will be necessary to obtain the rights to the touring groups from the groups themselves. Again, this may be facilitated by agencies such as Live Nation who may control all such rights but, if that's not the case, it will be necessary to reach out to the different rights holders.

Event licenses tend to be relatively short, particularly if the license is for distribution at the venue, i.e., the event itself. Such products are frequently also sold at normal retail distribution, so those rights may extend for longer terms.

21.3 Different Types of Products

21.3.1 Food and Beverage Licensed Products

The licensing of food and beverage products bring with it a host of different provisions that are unique to the product category. For starters, the royalty rates charged for such products are lower than for other types of licensed products, frequently much lower. That is because the margins on such products are generally lower than for, example, for apparel or stationary products. One of the other differences relates to terms—the terms for food and beverage licenses are usually longer, frequently much longer, than comparable non-food and beverage deals. The reason for the additional length is that it will almost always take longer for the licensee to complete the product and get it to market.

The quality control provisions of such agreements can be much more stringent because of the nature of the resultant product which will be ingested by humans.

Since most such products are controlled by governmental regulation, the agreements will normally require that the license comply with all applicable governmental regulations and the agreements will typically spell out the specific regulations and codes that the licensee must follow.

Chapter 22
Accounting, Auditing and Tax Considerations[123]

22.1 Introduction

The royalty audit, also referred to as either a royalty "inspection" or a royalty "examination," is the primary method used by a licensor to ascertain whether its licensees are compliant with the material terms of their license agreements. The term "audit" referred to throughout relates to the "audit provision" as contained in the license agreement and does not constitute an audit performed on financial statements. The purposes for conducting a royalty audit include the following:

- To determine whether the licensee is reporting and paying the full contractual amount due on a timely basis;

- To determine whether the licensee is adhering to the provisions of the license agreement, including advertising commitments, distribution channel requirements, territorial limitations, royalty rates, and insurance requirements;

- To determine whether the licensee is correctly calculating the royalty base and is paying royalties on all products exploited ("sold") which use the licensed property;

- To determine whether all licensed products have received the required approvals prior to production and distribution; and

- To determine whether the licensee is selling unauthorized or unapproved products.

22.2 Audit Provisions in the License Agreement

To be able to able to audit or otherwise inspect the books of a licensee, the licensor must make sure that an appropriate audit provision is included in the license agreement. In the absence of such a provision, a licensee may be able to successfully challenge the licensor's right to conduct such an audit short of actual litigation.

Consequently, most license agreements include provisions that provide the licensor the right to conduct a complete royalty inspection of the licensee. Such provisions provide the licensor with a mechanism to conduct an audit and ascertain whether the licensee is fully complying with all the provisions of the agreement. This provides an opportunity for the licensor to test that they are receiving all the royalties due, as well as identifying whether the licensee is selling unauthorized or unapproved products. A licensor truly interested in protecting its intellectual property must insist on full compliance by the licensee with the terms of the agreement with the licensee. Accordingly, most license agreements include the following provisions:

---

[123] Written by Brian J. Harris, Andrew B. Koski, Michael J. Quackenbush, and Charles Schnaid, partners in the Royalty Compliance Div. of Miller, Kaplan, Arase & Co., LLP 4123 Lankershim Blvd. North Hollywood, CA 91602-2828.

22.2.1 Right to Audit

A "Right to Audit" provision allows the licensor to inspect the books and records of the licensee and is typically limited to a specific period. Ideally the provision should:

- Grant the licensor the right to conduct the inspection itself or by someone of the licensor's choosing.

- Describe how and when notice of the audit will be given to the licensee and the minimum notice that is required, e.g., at least five business days (most licensors seek to keep the notice period as short as possible to make it difficult for a licensee to alter or destroy relevant records).

- Grant the royalty auditor the right to make and retain copies of pertinent documents and records, thereby allowing the auditor to retain relevant information or materials to support its findings.

- Stipulate that the licensee is required to cooperate with the licensor or its representative.

- Stipulate that the licensee, if so requested by the licensor or its representative, will provide detailed transactional data supporting its royalty statements in electronic format.

- Grant the royalty auditor access to the licensee's complete general ledger and any periodic financial and management reports that document monthly activities, particularly those relating to manufacturing, inventory, sales, returns and inventory destruction (having access to such reports will help the auditor tie together a licensee's financial data and verify that the information provided is complete and accurate).

- The royalty auditor has access on a test basis to all the licensee's books and records, not only those that pertain to the licensed products.

- The royalty auditor has the right to communicate with the licensee's current or former employees as well as its vendors and customers, all of whom may provide independent third-party confirmation of purchases and sales.

- The royalty auditor may examine the records of the licensee's related entities, (e.g., parents, subsidiaries or affiliates) to confirm that the licensee has not sold licensed products to related companies at sub-market prices.

It should be appreciated that the above is a "wish list" of requests. Many licensees will find some of these requests objectionable and could be reluctant to giving the licensor such broad access to their business operations. Should such objection occur, the use of a mutually agreeable Non-Disclosure agreement should be discussed.

22.2.2 Record Keeping

The "Record Keeping" provision typically specifies the type of records that the licensee is required to retain and for how long. The purpose of this provision is to avoid a situation where the licensee has either failed to maintain or elected to destroy relevant records rather than making them available to the auditor, particularly where the production of such records will not support the royalty statements that the licensee had previously submitted.

Most licensors will require that the licensee retain all companywide records for a set period both during and *after* termination of the license agreement. Retention of records in the following categories are particularly important: sales, invoices, promotions, shipping information, bills of lading, catalogs, price lists, price changes, inventory records, destruction records, manufacturing records, purchase orders, vendor invoices, customs documents, product approvals, as well as quality control and manufacturing approval documents.

The provision should also state the way the documents should be retained, (e.g., paper or electronic). Electronic documents are preferable because they allow for efficient and easy manipulation and analysis of the data.

In some cases, a licensor may want to perform a royalty audit covering a period of several years or may decide to perform a royalty audit after the termination of the license agreement. Thus, the license agreement should also provide for how long the licensee is required to maintain relevant records, preferably at least one to three years after the expiration or termination of the license agreement, including successor license agreements.

The provision should also prevent the licensee from destroying any records during the pendency of any royalty audit, (i.e., the records shall be maintained in an auditable format until after the royalty audit or litigation, if applicable) is settled or finalized.

22.2.3 Interest on Findings

The "Interest on Findings" provision will require the licensee to pay interest on any underpayments. The provision should state that interest will be calculated commencing from the date the amount would have been due if the amount had been properly reported through the date of the actual payment. It should also state the method for determining the interest rate to be used, e.g., the base prime lending rate in effect for the territory or use of a stated interest index plus a percentage. Providing for a high interest rate can discourage a licensee from underreporting or late reporting of royalties.

22.2.4 Extrapolation

The Agreement should permit the extrapolation of findings using the error percentage for the tested selection as compared to the overall royalties reported.

22.2.5 Recovery of Audit Fees

The "Recovery of Audit Fees" provision requires the licensee to pay the cost of the audit, if the audit findings show an underpayment above a certain threshold. To determine whether the threshold is exceeded, the auditor will compare the audit findings to the total royalties reported or paid. If the amount of underpayment exceeds the threshold (usually 3-10% in any reporting period), the licensee will bear the responsibility of reimbursing the licensor for the cost of the audit. If the threshold amount is based on paid royalties, the license agreement should state whether advances and minimum guarantees are to be included in the amount or whether it is based on earned royalties only. The term "Deficiencies" should also be defined in the license agreement to include all amounts due to the licensor, including findings, interest due on findings, interest due on late payments, and penalties for selling unapproved products.

This provision is intended to encourage licensees to accurately account for and pay royalties in accordance with the contractual provisions, to avoid having to bear the costs of the royalty audit. Furthermore, this provision promotes cooperation with the royalty auditors, since additional costs are incurred when a licensee is uncooperative and does not provide (or has not retained) the records to support the amounts on the royalty statement.

22.3 When Should an Audit Be Performed?

At the very least, the licensor should pay careful attention to the licensee's royalty reports submitted during the early years of the license term and, ideally, conduct a royalty examination early in the initial term and certainly prior to the expiration of the licensor's right to audit all periods. Follow-up royalty examinations should be periodically performed thereafter. It should be noted that licensee audits can be expensive and, as such, should be selectively applied to those licensees that generate a reasonable level of royalties or are suspected of underreporting royalties.

By following such a procedure, the licensor should be able to confirm that the licensee has adequate royalty accounting systems and procedures in place to facilitate accurate reporting. It also confirms that the licensee understands what it is required to do under the agreement.

In many cases, the licensor does not have a complete understanding of how a licensee operates its business. This can result in the parties having a different understanding of such contract terms as "Net Sales," which should be defined in the license agreement. By discovering these ambiguities early in the term, the licensor and licensee can get on the same page before a small problem becomes a much larger one.

It is very common to wait several years after the start of the license agreement, or until the termination of the license agreement, to decide to perform a royalty audit. Other times, a royalty audit may be performed sooner due to a concern that there have been royalty underpayments. It should be appreciated that it is much more difficult to perform a royalty audit several years into the term of the license agreement, because individuals involved in the drafting of the license agreement may no longer be with the licensor or licensee and/or the licensee may have changed accounting software, thus making access to earlier records potentially more difficult—particularly if the licensee has not retained the conversion matrix ("interface") used to migrate the data between systems. Other records may be lost, misfiled or buried deep in storage. As a result, the royalty auditor may not be able to determine the precise amount of underpayment, if any.

In addition, the results of the findings may indicate that the licensee owes a substantial amount that they are simply not able to pay at the time of the royalty audit. This can result in the licensor accepting less than the full amount due or having to litigate to collect the full amount.

22.4 Selecting the Royalty Auditor

While many licensors believe that any accountant should be able to conduct a royalty audit, experienced royalty auditors can mean the difference between one that simply verifies the licensee's arithmetic to one that identifies either or both under-reporting and non-compliance with the license agreement.

The royalty auditor should have solid experience in accounting, auditing and financial matters as they relate to the business of licensing, including standard terminology, industry practice and the possible legal issues which may arise during an examination. They should also have expertise in the specific field in which the license is granted, because different industries operate in different ways. What might be a common allowable discount or allowance in one industry may not be acceptable in another.

A licensor may have someone on staff or an internal audit department that can perform the royalty inspection. In many cases, however, the licensor elects to engage an outside firm for specialty purposes or, at times, because there are issues with the licensee that may require a truly independent party.

An outside royalty auditor will typically start by preparing an engagement letter which covers the terms of the royalty audit to be performed. The letter normally includes an identification of the parties involved, the license agreement(s) and license term(s) that form the basis of the royalty audit, estimated fees for the royalty engagement and payment terms. The engagement letter will also include a preliminary list of procedures that will take place.

To be able to prepare an engagement letter, most auditors will typically want, at the very least, to review the following:
- License agreement(s);
- A description of the licensee's royalty reporting and accounting systems; and
- The licensee's royalty reports or statements.

The actual procedures to be followed by the auditor should be discussed between the licensor and royalty auditor. In some instances, the licensor may only want the auditor to inspect certain aspects of the licensee's operations or accounting system, e.g., sales but not inventory transactions, with the understanding that if the audit reveals underpayments on those specific focal areas, the scope of the audit will be expanded in a subsequent audit.

Due to the confidential nature of the information being transmitted between the licensor, licensee and the royalty auditor, the auditor is frequently asked to sign a non-disclosure agreement ("NDA") prior to beginning fieldwork. Such terms should be discussed and clarified that the existence of a NDA does not supersede or replace any of the licensor rights to information per the license agreement.

22.5 Preparing for the Royalty Audit

The audit procedure typically starts with the licensor sending the licensee a notice of its intention to audit the licensee's books and records. The notice will typically cite that portion of the license agreement which gives them the right to conduct such audit, as well as an identification of the auditor and the date, time and place of such audit. The date of the actual audit can always be changed, but it is important to pick one to get the process started.

The licensor should provide the royalty auditor with all relevant information regarding the licensee and the engagement. The quality of such document production is important and may ultimately minimize audit costs. Such items include:
- License agreement(s)
- Royalty reports submitted by the licensee
- Date and amount of payments made by the licensee
- Relevant correspondence between the licensor and licensee
- Issues and concerns
- Listing of approved products
- Results of any prior royalty audits

The royalty auditor will want to review this information prior to visiting the licensee. The auditor may also use tools such as the Internet to gather information about the licensee. Through the Internet, the royalty auditor may be able to see licensed products offered for sale through the licensee's website. This is very helpful in determining, for instance, whether the licensee is selling any of the licensor's products but not including them on the royalty reports. Tracking the sales of the licensee's products through the websites of its customers can also be a useful tool.

Once engaged, the royalty auditor will contact the licensee and make arrangements to begin the royalty audit process. At this point, the auditor and the licensee will establish the timing and location of the fieldwork. The royalty auditor will also typically provide the licensee with a list of documents and records that it will want to review during fieldwork, as well as those documents that it might want in advance of the actual inspection.

Most auditors will request that the licensee provide information in electronic format, so that they can perform data sorting and data mining procedures. In addition, the royalty auditor may look to interview the licensee's personnel to gain an understanding of how its accounting and royalty reporting systems work, as well as how the licensed product is produced, transported and distributed.

22.6 Information Required from the Licensee

The royalty auditor will typically prepare an initial document request listing those items that the auditor will want the licensee to make available during the royalty inspection process. These records should be available for the entire period under audit. The royalty auditor may limit the request to specific test periods.

The initial document request does not prevent the auditor from requesting additional items during fieldwork because of its findings, additional areas of interest or the unavailability of certain records. Commonly, the books and records requested by the royalty auditor include the following:

22.6.1 Sales Journals, Invoices, Cash Receipts, and Banking Records

The royalty auditor will compare sales totals from the sales journals to the information reported in the royalty reports, as well as look for unreported items. The procedures generally include a request for a sample of sales invoices to compare the statement information against the transactional details, thus supporting the quantities or amounts appearing on the royalty statement. They will also use sales information gathered from the sales journals and sales invoices to determine if the licensee accurately reported its net sales in accordance with the terms of the license agreement. The auditor may inspect the cash receipts and compare them to the invoice amounts to ascertain whether the amounts received agree with the sales invoice.

22.6.2 Manufacturing and Purchasing Records

The royalty auditor will use these records to determine the number and quantity of items that were produced for sale under the license. These records may indicate whether additional approved or unapproved products were manufactured or distributed but were not reported on the royalty statements. These records almost always generate more questions.

In some cases, products manufactured at an outside facility may be shipped directly ("drop shipped") to the licensee's customers and no entry is made in the licensee's inventory system. The royalty auditor may also seek to confirm that the licensee had been using approved manufacturers.

22.6.3 Inventory Records

The royalty auditor will complete a reconciliation of inventory, by SKU (stock-keeping unit number), as follows:
* Beginning Inventory
    - Add: Inventory additions (items manufactured or purchased)
    - Subtract: Inventory sales
    - Add/Subtract: Inventory adjustments (samples, returns and destroys)
* Should equal: Ending Inventory

The auditor may also compare the licensee's sales and manufacturing/ purchase information to its perpetual inventory records.

22.6.4 Credit Memo Journals

The auditor will need to determine if there are any returns of inventory. If so, the auditor will compare the amount credited to the original sales amount and ascertain whether the items were placed back into inventory or were classified as damaged and unsalable. They will also confirm that any reduction in net sales for returns is authorized by the license agreement. The auditor will also test for excess returns which could be an indicator of quality problems.

22.6.5 General Ledgers, Tax Returns and Financial Statements

To establish completeness, the auditor will compare information from the sales journals, manufacturing/purchase records and the inventory records to the general ledger as well as the licensee's tax returns and financial statements.

22.6.6 Product Catalogs

Auditors should review the licensee's product catalog to confirm that all licensed products were included in the royalty reports. In some cases, the licensee may be selling a generic product that includes the property and, therefore, is royalty bearing. The auditor will also review the licensee's website and, if possible, its showroom and warehouse. Some auditors even visit stores where licensed products are sold.

22.6.7 Price Lists

Auditors typically look at a licensee's price lists or schedules to determine whether the gross prices recited on a customer's invoice reflect a true gross selling price or whether the licensee has built into the gross price otherwise impermissible discounts or allowances or made sales to a related third party at a greatly reduced wholesale price.

22.7 Royalty Audit Procedures

Royalty audit procedures are generally tailored to each engagement, based on the license agreement, the licensed product, and the licensee's royalty reporting and accounting systems. Royalty auditors generally start with a standard procedure that they adjust for the specific engagement. Common preliminary procedures include:

- Read the license agreement(s) to gain an understanding of its key provisions.
- Review the royalty reports and other information provided by the licensor.
- Research the licensee and licensed products through the Internet and other sources.
- Speak with licensee's personnel to:
  - Gain an understanding of the licensee's accounting and royalty reporting systems.
  - Determine how the products are manufactured (on-site or purchased from an outside vendor).
  - Determine how the products are sold.
- Request product catalogs.
- The following steps are typically performed in the course of the fieldwork:
  - Review the licensee's accounting and royalty reporting systems to determine whether they are operating as described and can provide accurate information.
  - If the product is manufactured on-site, tour the facility and observe its manufacture.
  - Perform sales tests by dollars and units, including a review of sales invoices and shipping information.
  - Perform tests of pricing, including discounts, deductions, and allowances.
  - Examine sales reports for samples, free goods, and close-outs.
  - Determine whether any sales were made outside of the normal sales system.
  - Determine whether there are any related party sales or purchases.
  - Review sales for territorial restrictions and compliance with approved distribution channels.
  - Prepare a trend analysis to look for unusual sales patterns.
  - Review product returns, including damaged products.

- Reconcile inventory, including tests of manufacturing or purchases.
- Compare products available for sale to what was reported on the royalty reports to confirm that all licensed products are being properly reported.
- Review all royalty reports and determine that the royalty rates used are appropriate.

22.8 The Royalty Audit Report

Upon completion of the fieldwork, the auditor will prepare a draft report for the licensor's review and comments. Once the licensor's comments have been addressed or resolved, a final royalty report will be issued by the auditor to the licensor. The royalty report will usually contain the following:

- A listing of procedures, which may be in summary form.
- A summary of the amounts owing to the licensor, including findings, interest and penalties.
- Details of each finding, along with supporting schedules.
- Calculation of any interest on the findings.
- Recitation of any audit fees chargeable to the licensee.
- Details of the auditor's findings of the licensee's non-compliance with other terms of the license agreement, (e.g., sales outside of authorized territories or channels, failure to maintain required insurance, unapproved products).
- Identification of items requested, but not provided by the licensee.

Once the royalty report is issued, the licensor must determine how best to proceed. Licensors typically forward the report to the licensee and give it an opportunity to review and, if appropriate, dispute any of the audit findings. It is not uncommon for a licensee to refute some or all the findings or attempt to provide an explanation or other documentation in support of its actions.

Most audit disputes are resolved between the parties through negotiation although, in some cases, litigation or arbitration may become necessary.

22.8.1 Common Monetary Findings

The main purpose of an audit is to find unreported or underreported amounts, which occur for a number of reasons, including administrative errors, systematic errors in a variety of accounting and reporting programs, misinterpretations of the terms of the license agreement including definitions, failure to use the applicable royalty rates and, on occasion, misreporting sales amounts or quantities. The following are common monetary findings uncovered during royalty audits:

- Unreported product sales;
- Use of incorrect interpretation of the definition of "Net Sales;"
- Unallowable deductions from sales;
- Excessive allowable returns;
- Excessive allowable discounts;
- Excessive reserves;
- Non-reporting of promotional giveaways and samples;
- Sales to related parties at less than an arm's-length price;

- Failure to properly report sales for bundles and assortments; and
- Penalties for selling unapproved products.

22.8.2 Common Non-Monetary Findings

The following are common non-monetary findings:
- Sales in unapproved territories;
- Sales through unapproved product distribution channels;
- Failure to properly account for damaged goods;
- Failure to obtain product approvals;
- Failure to carry required insurance; or
- Failure to include required "sold under license" verbiage on packaging

22.9 Accounting Provisions in License Agreements

How the accounting provisions in a license agreement are drafted is particularly important since the language in these provisions will be relied on quite heavily by the royalty auditors.

During the initial negotiations with any potential licensee, the licensor should try to obtain a full understanding of how that licensee conducts its business operations, particularly the way it sells or intends to sell its licensed products. Earlier chapters of this book have explained in detail the different types of royalty rates used in licensing, e.g., domestic landed rates, F.O.B. rates, direct sales rates, etc. The more the licensor knows about how the licensee will sell the licensed products, the easier it will be to define the applicable royalty rates. The licensor should have the licensee identify any related parties (e.g., owned or controlled) in an exhibit to the license agreement. The license agreement should require that licensee notify licensor of any changes, additions, deletions to the related party exhibit during the term of the license agreement.

Royalty auditors will pay attention to those provisions in the license agreement that explain or identify:
- Whether a licensee may include freight in the cost of the product. For these cases, an agreed-upon freight allowance can be provided for in the definition of net sales.
- Unforeseen transactions, such as a large sale to a discounter, which may result in unallowable discounts. In these instances, the licensee should try to obtain a one-time waiver from the licensor.

Communications between the licensor and its licensees are critical during the licensing program. As new accounting and royalty reporting issues arise (and they always do), they should be discussed and, if possible, resolved between the parties to avoid surprises in any subsequently issued audit report. If there is a change of conditions or something unforeseen occurs that necessitates a change in the license agreement, the agreement should be amended accordingly.

22.9.1 Definition of Terms

Some of the more important terms used in a license agreement that royalty auditors pay attention to are:

[A] *Net Sales, Discounts and Allowances*

Most royalty calculations are based on a percentage of net sales. Therefore, it is very important that the agreement precisely define how the licensee is to compute its net sales figure. Each item in the calculation of net sales should be specifically defined, including any limitations.

Agreements that simply define net sales as "gross sales less returns, discounts and allowances" are too ambiguous and may result in lost royalties to the licensor. Most licensees will read such a provision very expansively to lessen the amount of royalties payable.

Royalties due to a licensor may also be computed on a flat fee, per unit rate as opposed to a percentage of sales. In those cases, the licensor should make sure that the license agreement provides the licensor and its auditor full and unfettered access to the licensee's manufacturing records, including purchase orders, manufacturing invoices, supporting payment documentation and unit quantities received into inventory at the distribution warehouse.

Care should also be taken to define exactly what is meant by "gross sales" which should, ideally, be the higher of either the selling price recited on the licensee's list price or the highest price charged to any third-party customer.

Sales prices may vary widely depending on the type of customer and the distribution channel. For example, licensees may sell directly to consumers through their website at prices significantly above the sales price to wholesale. The license agreement should also define when the product is considered sold, e.g., at the earlier of invoicing, shipment or payment.

Many licensors elect to cap a licensee's returns, discounts and allowances as a percentage of its gross sales. The license agreement should specify how that limitation is computed, e.g., calculated quarterly or annually and whether the cap applies to individual SKUs or all products being reported.

The license agreement should also specify what types of allowances may be taken and, in some cases, what deductions may not be taken, e.g., cash discounts that do not benefit the licensor, write-offs for bad debts, or deduction of marketing and advertising expenses. Some common allowances that may be permitted are allowances for co-op advertising and new store stocking.

Many licensors require that the licensee approve all distribution agreements, particularly those that provide for discounts above a pre-determined threshold. The objective of such an approval requirement is to generate a discussion between the licensor and licensee to, hopefully, bring the parties into agreement on how to treat these discounts.

It is also advisable to provide for situations where the licensee may elect to bundle the licensed products with other products and if done, how royalties are to be calculated in such a situation. It is also advisable to address other issues in the agreement including: how to treat consignment sales; whether samples and other free giveaways are royalty bearing; and whether a royalty is due on employee and close-out sales and, if so, at what rate.

[B] *Payment Terms*

The license agreement should specify when the licensee is required to report its sales and pay its royalties as well as any advances or guarantees. Most merchandising agreements provide for quarterly reporting, with royalty statements and payments typically due 30 to 45 days after the end of the calendar quarter.

The agreement should also specifically state that late payments are subject to a specified interest rate (including the method for calculating the rate) since the absence of such a provision may prevent the licensor, as a matter of law, from charging interest on late payments.

Some license agreements require that the minimum guaranteed royalty be calculated and, if due, submitted on a quarterly or yearly basis, rather than at the end of the license term.

[C] Royalty Reports

The license agreement should specify what items must be included in the royalty report. Some licensors even provide its licensees with a sample of the type of report that it expects the licensee to submit and may even attach it as part of the license agreement. In some cases, the licensor will want the reports provided in electronic format to facilitate entry into the licensor's licensing administration package.

Many licensees report the gross sales and number of units sold by SKU numbers. It is preferable that the sales price for each SKU be listed separately so that the licensor can review the royalty report for any discounts. Such discounts, along with returns and allowances should be separately recorded in the royalty report. In addition, some licensors may require further breakdown with respect to territory, brand and/or product line.

[D] Sublicense Agreements

Although most merchandising agreements do not permit sublicensing, there are exceptions. In those cases, the sublicensee is typically required to pay its royalties directly to the licensee who must then account to the licensor. Most licensors in sublicensing situations will require that the licensee submit all sublicense agreements to it for approval prior to their execution. Such sublicense agreements should incorporate the terms and definitions that are included in the original license agreement.

The license agreement should state how sublicensing royalties will be computed and paid to the licensor. In most instances, the sublicensing revenue received from the sublicensee is divided between the licensor and licensee according to a formula stated in the original license agreement. Any sub-licensee fees charged should not be applied against the licensor share.

When sublicensing is allowed, the licensor should make sure that it retains the right to audit the sublicensee or require the licensee to perform such an audit. The licensor should also be entitled to receive a copy of any royalty audit that the licensee may perform on a sublicensee, including the final settlement of any dispute.

[E] VAT

A value-added tax (VAT) is a type of consumption tax that is placed on a product whenever value is added at a stage of production and at the point of retail sale. The amount of VAT that the user pays is on the cost of the product, less any of the costs of materials used in the product that have already been taxed.

More than 160 countries around the world use value-added taxation. It is most common in the European Union.

The License Agreement will dictate which party, i.e., licensor or licensee, is responsible for the payment of such tax.

Chapter 23
Dealing with Infringers and Counterfeiters

23.1 Introduction

While Ben Franklin may have believed that there were only two certain things in the world, i.e., "death and taxes," if merchandising had been popular in the 18th century, he would have added a third—someone will always try to knock off a successful property. We live in a world where infringements are a way of life because counterfeiting it is a lucrative business. The owner of every successful property will, undoubtedly, face the problem at some point in time.

The drill for every property owner is to take appropriate steps toward protecting its property, to be aware of what is happening in the marketplace and, if it discovers that its property has become a target for counterfeiters, to take prompt and aggressive action. In the licensing industry, the reality is that licensees are usually closest to the problem since they are the ones who are in the marketplace facing competition from unlicensed products every day. As such, property owners can be assured that its licensees will quickly bring these issues to their attention as soon as they become apparent.

Counterfeiting is the deliberate unauthorized use of another's intellectual property, e.g., trademarks, product designs and copyrights, including, the use of a false trademark that is identical to, or substantially indistinguishable from, a registered trademark. It can also encompass the passing off of a product whose design is similar or identical to the design of the authentic product, or the act of copyright piracy where an audio-visual work is copied and distributed on an unauthorized basis.

It should be appreciated that counterfeiting is not simply the infringement of another's intellectual property rights. It is the blatant duplication of such property with the intent to have consumers believe that their product is genuine—even though it is usually being sold at a small fraction of the cost.

For a successful property owner, the job of trying to stay ahead of infringers and counterfeiters can be a full-time burden. Because of the profit potential that counterfeiting offers, counterfeiters have become very good at their trade and generally, unless property owners take swift, aggressive action, the problem will only escalate. A property owner who believes that it can simply kick back and let its licensees fend for themselves against unlicensed competition, will soon have few, if any, royalty paying licensees. Thus, protecting the licensee's right to sell its products free from competitors that are not paying royalties or taxes is not simply an obligation, it is in the licensors own best interest. Successful property owners understand this very basic issue.

23.2 Why Infringement Should Never be Underestimated[124]

Thanks to cloud-based, plug-and-play technology, growing online commercial channels and increasingly sophisticated business strategies, smaller brands and start-ups no longer must overcome the traditional hurdles of trying to compete on a global level. This has signaled a significant shift in the lay of the business land, especially when it comes to branding and the trademark process.

Competition for unique brands is no longer limited to the large, multinational corporations. Now the smaller businesses can go toe-to-toe with the giants to build and defend their intellectual property. However, with so many businesses competing over the same finite space, achieving this goal has become harder than ever before.

According to the World Intellectual Property Organization[125], a record number of marks were filed under the Madrid system in 2016. An estimated 52,550 international trademarks were filed, demonstrating the fastest growth rate recorded since 2010 at 7.2%. There are currently over 67.6 million active trademarks worldwide, according to SAEGIS® on SERION®.

The trademark process requires a rethink in approach. Businesses need to think globally, considering all the markets they currently operate in and any they might grow into in the future, and they need to collaborate closely with marketing and legal teams to be most effective. There are also many different marketing channels to think about — from traditional print advertising to social media platforms and beyond — which results in the need for efficient clearing, registering and watching of trademarks. The consequences of not getting this process right can have a significant detrimental impact on brands, including costly legal action, customer confusion and loss of revenue.

The trademark research process is another challenge for brands and trademark professionals. There are more brands, names and associated elements to consider than ever, and imposed deadlines and budgets can cause further complications.

Against this backdrop, CompuMark — a flagship brand of Clarivate Analytics — commissioned independent research on the state of the trademark industry, the challenges that professionals face, the prevalence of infringement and overall opinions and perceptions of the market. In the third quarter of 2017, Vitreous World surveyed 300 trademark professionals across the United Kingdom, USA, Germany and France. This sample was taken from in-house and external legal teams, and from organizations of all sizes.

Exploring the Trademark Landscape

The trademark industry is continuing to grow, with more businesses filing trademark applications than ever before. The CompuMark research found that 43% of respondents stated they had filed more trademarks in 2016 than they had in the previous year. This figure was highest in the UK and the USA, where 46% of respondents in both regions reporting an increase.

---

[124] By Robert Reading, Director — CompuMark

[125] http://www.wipo.int/edocs/pubdocs/en/wipo_pub_940_2017.pdf

Overall, 42% said the number of applications remained the same, with only a small portion of respondents (14%) stating they had filed fewer marks in 2016.

The research also assessed what effect, if any, Brexit was having on trademark filing behavior. 70% said Brexit was impacting how they were approaching the trademark process. 22% said they were filing more UK trademarks (21% in the US, 34% in the UK, 17% and 7% in Germany). Overall, 31% said they were filing more EU marks (29% in the US, 18% in the UK, 50% in France and 43% in Germany).

Almost a quarter (24%) said they were filing fewer UK trademarks, with only 7% stating they were filing fewer EU marks.

Products and services accounted for the largest number of trademark applications filed in the past year, followed by logos, company names and seasonal brands. Non-traditional marks, such as hashtags (16% of respondents), sounds (15%) and smells (11%), also made the list. Interestingly, hashtag marks were filed more often in France (23% versus the global average of 16%), as were applications for sound trademarks (23% versus the global average of 15%).

Tackling the Trademark Process Challenge

With a fast-expanding market due to the proliferation of social media, the pace of innovation and the ease with which new businesses can enter the marketplace, trademark filing is on the rise. This is influencing the number of hours that trademark professionals spend on search, clearance and watch activities. Therefore, as the trademark landscape evolves, brands and their legal teams need are adapting keep up.

Respondents were asked what they thought would help make search and clearance of new marks more efficient and effective. They identified four main areas: budgets, technology, resources and time. 51% said budgets need to be bigger, an attitude especially prevalent in Germany (56%) and the USA (56%). Across all regions, there was also a notable call for better technology (49%)—which was highest among respondents in France (63%)—as well as more resources (48%) and more time (41%).

These areas for improvement tied to the challenges that trademark professionals face. When asked about the main barriers in their way, respondents identified time pressures, budgetary issues and speed to market. Operating in a global market, lack of tools, software and resources, and launching into multi-channel environments were also identified as challenges.

Static Budgets

When trademark activity is on the increase, there is an expectation that budget should be increased accordingly. However, just under a third of respondents (30%) said their budget had increased over the last two years, compared with 58% who said that their budget remained the same during that period and 8% who said their budget had decreased.

A 2016 CompuMark survey of C-level decision-makers looked at changes to budgets over the previous five years. Almost half of respondents (48%) said their budgets had remained static, while 41% said they had increased[126]. While the questions and the audiences in 2016

---

[126] http://www.compumark.com/wp-content/uploads/dlm_uploads/2017/03/trademark-ecosystem.pdf

and 2017 differed slightly, it remains clear that despite the fast-changing environments, static budgets remain a challenge for those involved in the trademark process.

When Good Trademarks Go Bad

A trademark is seen by many companies as an asset; something that must be protected and nurtured. As markets expand and businesses move into new markets and online, they are brought into contact with a host of other brands, companies, products and taglines. This increases the likelihood of infringement and makes the process of clearing and registering marks more difficult.

Our research found that 74% of brands surveyed experienced infringement of some kind in the last 12 months. 41% of respondents experienced up to 10 instances of infringement during this period, while 22% experienced infringement 11 to 30 times. 11% said they had experienced more than 31 instances of infringement. 40% of respondents said they had seen an increase in infringement in the last two years. This figure was highest among respondents in France (50%) and Germany (44%).

Infringement isn't merely a standalone issue; it has serious knock-on effects, including brand dilution, loss of customer trust, customer and market confusion, loss of revenue and litigation. The research found that when asked about the impact of brand infringement, respondents ranked customer confusion (44%), loss of revenue (41%) and resource challenges for marketing and legal team (37%) as the top three effects.

From a litigation perspective, it can cost upwards of $100,000 in the US to pursue trademark litigation, and costs can run into the millions depending on its length and outcome[127]. Seen as a last resort by many due to the time, effort and expense involved, there are occasions where taking legal action is unavoidable. 56% of respondents took legal action against third party infringements — this figure was highest in France (76%) and Germany (69%).

Infringement is an ever-increasing risk for brands. Respondents were asked if they had seen a change in infringement over the last five years, and a resounding 79% said they had indeed seen a noticeable increase[128].

Ultimately, despite the challenges faced by trademark professionals, search, clearance and watching must be done properly to mitigate the risk of infringement.

The dangers of Ignoring the Trademark Process

Brands and trademark professionals are under increasing pressure to effectively clear marks and register them quickly for new products, sub-brands and associated marketing elements to be launched to the market. Given the challenges faced, in terms of budget and time needed, there may be the temptation to seek shortcuts, or to perhaps circumvent the trademark process altogether.

The research found that just over a quarter (26%) of respondents said they had launched a new, secondary or seasonal brand without clearing the trademark first, with a further 38%

---

[127] http://www.law.com/insidecounsel/2016/09/22/to-sue-or-not-to-sue-for-trademark-infringement/

[128] http://www.compumark.com/wp-content/uploads/dlm_uploads/2017/03/trademark-ecosystem.pdf

stating they would so do in future if the risks of infringement were minimal. Perhaps not coincidentally, a third of respondents stated they had had to change the name of one of their brands because of infringement.

To speed up the trademark process, many use free tools or Internet search engines, which offer basic brand information but do not offer the same level of detail and search capabilities as tools developed especially for trademark searching. Use of free tools or Internet search engines can lead to unexpected conflicts or produce results that are difficult to understand.

Regardless of these dangers, 62% of research respondents said they relied on free Internet search engines and trademark office tools when clearing a trademark. 70% said they felt these tools provided a result that was comprehensive enough to pass judgment on. Use of such tools does not help organizations sufficiently mitigate the risk of infringement. In fact, the reliance on these online sources may even add risk.

Keeping One Eye on the Competition

Beyond the pressures of searching and filing marks, there is also the challenge of watching existing and newly filed marks for instances of infringement. As the number of registered trademarks increases it may not be possible for businesses to watch all their brands, particularly if they are older or part of seasonal campaigns.

To this end, the research found that 80% of respondents were confident their trademarks had been effectively cleared. Over a fifth (22%) of respondents said they watched 76% or more of their marks. About a third (32%) of respondents said they watch 51-75% of their marks. 30% said they only watch 26-50% of their marks and 10% watch less than a quarter of their marks.

Despite the growing size and complexity of trademark portfolios, our research shows that most organizations are choosing to monitor only a portion of their brands. As the combined pressures of increased filing volume and limited budgets continue, the ability to monitor marks will be further challenged.

Conclusion

Based on the attitudes and approaches of trademark professionals in a fast-changing environment, it is clear that as more trademarks are being filed, organizations would benefit from access to better technology, more time and resources and increased budgets.

To mitigate the risk of infringement, new trademarks need to be effectively cleared (and watched). The presence of free tools may be seen a solution, but the quality of search results they produce do not match the quality and results offered specially-designed vendor software.

From clearance and registration to the watching of marks, there needs to be a continuing drive to improve the trademark process. Whether that is through the use of better technology and software or relying on the experience and expertise of trademark lawyers and professionals, one thing remains clear: when it comes to avoiding infringement and protecting a brand's reputation, there can be no short cuts.

23.3 The Counterfeiting Industry–a Growing Market

How big a problem is counterfeiting? It's huge and, sadly, it's growing despite the best efforts of property owners and governments around the world to stem the tide. The reason for this is simple—it's extraordinarily lucrative for the counterfeiter. Counterfeiters can sell a massive number of products without any of the implied costs associated with originating design, maintaining regulatory compliance, brand building, etc., to say nothing of compensating the property owner. The counterfeiter simply skips to the last two steps in the process: it knocks-off the product and sells it for a fraction of the price charged by licensed manufacturers, typically through less than reputable channels of distribution.

The overall problem is getting worse. For example, the International Trademark Association reported that in 2016 more than $461 billion worth of counterfeit merchandise were bought. Counterfeit trade amounted to as much as 2.5% of world trade in 2013, up from an estimated 1.9% in 2008. That's equivalent to the size of Austria's economy.

The number of Intellectual Property Rights ("IPR") seizures increased 9 percent in FY2016 to more than 31,560. The total estimated manufacturer's suggested retail price (MSRP) of the seized goods, had they been genuine, increased to more than $1.38 billion. Because of enforcement efforts, ICE Homeland Security Investigations arrested 451 individuals, obtained 304 indictments, and received 272 convictions related to intellectual property crimes in FY2016.

Apparel and accessories once again topped the list for number of seizures with 6,406, representing 20 percent of all IPR seizures in FY2016. Watches and jewelry continued as the top products seized by total MSRP value with seizures valued at more than $653.5 million, representing 47 percent of the total. Handbags and wallets were second with seizures estimated to be valued at more than $234 million.

The Transportation/Parts category significantly increased in FY2016 following numerous operations that led to the seizure of nearly 108,000 counterfeit hoverboards that caused safety concerns last year following reports of fires possibly caused by substandard and counterfeit lithium ion batteries.

The People's Republic of China remained the primary source economy for counterfeit and pirated goods seized, accounting for $616 million or 45 percent of the total estimated MSRP value of all IPR seizures. Hong Kong again was the second largest source of IPR infringing shipments, accounting for nearly $600 million or 43 percent of the total MSRP value of all IPR seizures.

To understand its impact, compare counterfeiting against the following illegal forms of trafficking:
- Counterfeit products; $461 billion
- Prostitution: $186 billion
- Marijuana sales: $141 billion
- Illegal gambling: $140 billion
- Cocaine sales: $85 billion
- Heroin sales: $68 billion
- Oil theft: $37 billion
- Human trafficking: $32 billion

According to the CBP, the 9 most counterfeited products in America were.

1. Handbags/Wallets

> MSRP of seized goods: $700.2 million

> Percentage of total seized goods: 40%

Handbags and wallets were again the most seized counterfeited product, by MSRP, in 2013. The roughly 2,200 shipments seized had a total MSRP of more than $700 million, accounting for 40% of the total value of all goods seized. Because these products are valued so highly, a drop in total handbag and wallet seizures between 2012 and 2013 did not correspond with a drop in the market value of the items seized. In fact, while seizures fell by 17% in that time, the value of goods seized rose 37%, or by nearly $189 million. Randazzo explained that the retail value of the genuine goods can increase the value of the seized counterfeits considerably. While a fake Coach bag is often valued in the hundreds of dollars, "if we seize a counterfeit Hermes bag, the value ... of some of those bags is thousands of dollars." Most such counterfeits originate in mainland China, which alone accounted for more than half a billion dollars in fake purses last year, according to the CBP.

2. Watches/Jewelry

> MSRP of seized goods: $502.8 million

> Percentage of total seized goods: 29%

The value of seized imitation watches and jewelry grew by 168.9% between 2012 and 2013, considerably more than that of any other commodity. In total, the value of watches seized was more than half a billion dollars in 2013. Last year, there were 1,729 seizures, 21% less than there were in 2012. The different trends in value and seizures may be a product "of what's targeted and seized in a given year." For example, fake versions of high-end watches, which retail for thousands of dollars, can boost the values of counterfeits seized. The Federation of Swiss Watch Industry estimated that some 120,000 imitation watches were seized worldwide in 2013.

3. Consumer Electronics/Parts

> MSRP of seized goods: $145.9 million

> Percentage of total seized goods: 8%

The dollar amount of counterfeit consumer electronics products seized rose by 40% in 2013, to $145.9 million from $104.4 million in 2012. Further, consumer electronics comprised 8% of the total value of items seized last year, making it the third most frequently seized fake product. The number of seizures of counterfeit electronic products grew in conjunction with their total value. There were 5,656 such seizures in 2013, a 44% increase from the 3,928 seizures in 2012. According to a report by the CBP, one particularly big seizure in 2013 was by a joint CBP and China Customs operation. The two-month long operation resulted in 1,735 electronics shipments being seized, removing more than 243,000 counterfeit consumer electronic products from the market.

4. Wearing Apparel/Accessories

> MSRP of seized goods: $116.2 million

> Percentage of total seized goods: 7%

Last year, the United States seized almost 10,000 shipments of counterfeit apparel and accessories, by far the most of any commodity and up 26.8% from the year before. In all, more than $116 million worth of such items were seized. Like with other goods, exactly what type of product is being counterfeited matters, Randazzo noted, with haute couture knockoffs assigned a higher MSRP than blue jeans, for example. Last year, the CBP, in conjunction with other federal and local agencies, conducted "Operation Red Zone," which seized $17.3 million worth of fake sporting apparel — jerseys and ball caps — and other collectibles coinciding with the 2013 Super Bowl.

5. Pharmaceuticals/Personal Care

> MSRP of seized goods: $79.6 million

> Pct. of total seized goods: 5%

CBP agents seized nearly $80 million worth of counterfeit pharmaceuticals and personal care products last year. This was 4% lower from the nearly $83 million of such shipments seized in 2012, and down 44% from $142 million in 2011. Total seizures of such products fell in 2013 to 2,215 from 2,350 the year before. The decrease in seizures can be the result of increased international efforts to crack down on the sale of fake prescription drugs. The CBP and other groups have aggressively pursued counterfeit drug operations and shut down websites selling drugs online "because of the threat to consumer health and safety." More than $18 million worth of fake pharmaceuticals and personal care goods originated in India, accounting for 88% of illicit goods seized from the country last year. An additional $43.7 million of such goods came from China.

6. Footwear

> MSRP of seized goods: $54.9 million

> Pct. of total seized goods: 3%

CBP agents reported 1,683 seizures of contraband footwear in 2013, 214 less seizures than in the year before. The value of these seizures dropped by nearly 47% in 2013, from $103.4 million in 2012. This was one of the largest percentage declines among products reviewed. Footwear used to always be the number one This is likely something of a relief to shoe companies, especially Nike, whose shoes are widely believed to be among the most counterfeited footwear brands.

7. Computers/Accessories

> MSRP of seized goods: $47.7 million

> Pct. of total seized goods: 3%

Slightly more than 1,000 shipments of computers and accessories were seized in 2013. The counterfeit computer seizures accounted for 4% of all counterfeit seizures and for 3% of the total value of all counterfeit goods seized. Last year, the total value of such goods seized was more than $13 million, or 37.5%, higher than the year before. This is even though genuine PC shipments have declined worldwide during that time. Accessories can include a large range of products, including "integrated circuits, semiconductors, networking hardware, [and] printer cartridges." The Semiconductor Industry Association released a report in August, noting that counterfeit semiconductors can cause dangerous mal-functions in medical equipment and even in household appliances.

8. Labels/Tags

> MSRP of seized goods: $41.8 million

> Pct. of total seized goods: 2%

The number of counterfeit labels — trademarked logos and hang tags that are not attached to products — seized in 2013 was effectively unchanged from 2012. The value of these seizures, however, increased more dramatically than of all but two other products. Last year, the market value of counterfeit labels seized rose by 59% to $41.8 million. Because consumers recognize many prod-ucts and brands according to their labels and tags, the fake labels help deceive buyers and make imitations look more authentic. Counterfeiters often smuggle the fake labels and the fake products into the United States separately, since if the counterfeiters lose the shipment of labels and tags, it's not that big of a loss because they still have the shipment of handbags or other goods.

9. Optical Media

> MSRP of seized goods: $26.8 million

> Pct. of total seized goods: 2%

The number of shipments of counterfeit optical media products, such as games, DVDs and CDs, the CBP seized fell to 1,409 last year from 2,892 in 2012. The value of the seized counterfeit optical media products fell by 30% from $38.4 million in 2012 to $26.8 million in 2013. According to IPR, the drop-in sei-zures may be partly attributable to the Internet, as "the piracy has moved to websites and moved to downloads." Last year, in an effort to fight online pi-racy, Internet service providers banded together to introduce the Copyright Alert System, designed to fight copyright infringement by warning users against illegal file sharing and downloading.

The United States is not the only country having a problem with counterfeit merchandise. More than 40 million products thought to be infringing another party's intellectual prop-erty rights---with a value of nearly €650million—were seized by the European Union cus-toms authorities in 2015 which was 5 million more than were confiscated in 2014. Nearly 75% of the imports came from ship transporters. China remains the top source of counter-feit goods, followed by Montenegro, Hong Kong, Malaysia and Benin. According to Ian Harvey, chairman of the IP Center Advisory Board of Tsinghua University in Beijing and an adjunct professor of Imperial College Business School in London: "China is increasing its efforts to address this, though patents have historically come higher on their priority lists than counterfeit goods."

Counterfeiting is not, as some believe, a victimless crime—it clearly harms both the property owner and the consumer. Counterfeiting steals the identity and goodwill that the property owner has gone to great lengths to establish and robs the consumer of the comfort and reliability that it has when it buys a presumably branded product. Furthermore, counterfeiting produces economic damage on multiple levels. It deprives municipalities, states and countries of tax revenues derived from the sale of genuine products, on top of the revenues lost by property owners and its licensees. More important, it can pose a danger to consumers, particularly if the counterfeit product is not manufactured up to the quality levels of the genuine article, as is often the case.

When licensing executives think of counterfeiting, they focus mainly on designer brands, apparel and toy products, which are certainly areas of significant counterfeiting activity. Unfortunately, however, the problem is far more widespread than that. Counterfeiting is also alive and well in the entertainment, automotive, aircraft, food and pharmaceuticals industries as well.

The problem is particularly noticeable though when it comes to licensed apparel and accessories. In the world of designer brands, those most often copied consistently include: BURBERRY, Louis Vuitton, Gucci, Chanel, Lacoste, Cartier, Nike and Abercrombie & Fitch, along with Adidas and Puma in the footwear category.

U.S. Immigration and Customs Enforcement (ICE), aided by Homeland Security Investigations (HSI) and U.S. Customs and Border Protection, seized over 171,926 counterfeit sports and entertainment-related items at the 2018 Super Bowl, worth an estimated $15.69 million. This led to 65 arrests with 24 convictions.

The three largest seizures of counterfeit merchandise were:

>**Year:** 2010
>**Value of seized goods:** $100 million
>US Federal agents busted a counterfeit ring at San Francisco's Fisherman's Wharf that had over 200,000 items representing 70 different manufacturers.
>**Year:** 2014
>**Value of seized goods:** $163 million
>Police in Guangzhou City of southern China's Guangdong Province uncovered a criminal group that manufactured counterfeit Louis Vuitton bags.
>**Year:** 2006
>**Value of seized goods:** $490 million
>German customs officers seized 945,384 pairs of counterfeit Nike sneakers and 105,000 fake Adidas and Puma kicks being shipped from China to Italy, Austria, and Hungary.

One of the largest seizures of counterfeit clothing occurred when $7 million of knock-off t-shirts and sweatshirts were seized from the home and warehouse of William Haskell Farmer, who had been selling the products to 191 stores throughout the United States. Farmer eventually pled guilty to a felony count of trafficking.

The counterfeiting of toy products does not only hurt toy companies economically, but it can injure the children who play with the cheap, counterfeit substitutes. While legitimate toy companies spend millions in making sure that their products comply with all governmental regulations concerning child safety, those subtleties are usually lost on the counterfeiters who regularly manufacture products with unacceptable levels of lead and phthalates, frequently exceeding the acceptable limits by 100 times or more. Moreover, counterfeiters have little regard for requirements issued by the Consumer Products Safety Commission regarding the use of small, sharp and/or breakable parts that can pose a choking hazard to children. The presence of these toys in the marketplace has damaged the entire toy industry, without question.

The entertainment and software industries also are regularly impacted by counterfeiting, from the early release of bootlegged motion picture DVD's, music recordings and computer programs even before these products reach theatres or stores.

John Sankus Jr. was sentenced to 46 months in prison for leading an international piracy ring called DrinkorDie, which included 60 members from numerous countries and was responsible for copying and distributing software, games and movies. Their biggest claim to fame was distributing copies of Windows' operating system software two weeks before the official release.

While counterfeiting is an economic problem for merchandisers and software developers, it is downright dangerous in other industries. For example, it was reported that a mother and her child were killed in an automobile accident when a counterfeit brake pad made from wood chips failed. A faulty clutch made of counterfeit parts caused a helicopter crash that killed a traffic reporter. It was subsequently discovered that more than 600 helicopters had been equipped with counterfeit parts, putting literally thousands of people at risk. A Norwegian plane crash killing 55 people was caused by the failure of counterfeit bolts in the plane.

The food industry is another target for counterfeit products that put consumers at grave risk. For example, authorities discovered that a counterfeit version of Similac baby formula being sold at Safeway and Pak n' Save stores in more than 16 states was actually responsible for causing rashes and seizures in a number of infants.

Likewise, the pharmaceutical industry is plagued by counterfeiting, where the use or ingestion of inferior knock-offs can prove deadly. For example, it was reported that a liver transplant recipient received a counterfeit version of Epogen to treat anemia. Because it was at only 5% of regular strength, instead of improving the boy's condition, it caused excruciating aches and spasms. In two other instances, the FDA recalled $7 million worth of pumps used during open-heart surgery that contained malfunctioning counterfeit parts and Searle discovered that over a million counterfeit birth control pills had been distributed to unsuspecting women, resulting in unwanted pregnancies and irregular bleeding.

Counterfeiting also has a serious political impact. Investigators have found that Chinese organized crime syndicates regularly rely on counterfeiting as a source of tax-free income and that some terrorist organizations derive a portion of their funding through trafficking in counterfeit goods. Raids of counterfeit operations in New York and New Jersey resulted in the seizure of counterfeit designer handbags that contained heroin, establishing a clear tie between drug smuggling and counterfeiting.

23.4 Identifying Counterfeit Products

Since one of the principal attractions of a counterfeit product is cost, the easiest way to identify it is to use that same yardstick. The adage, "if something is too good to be true, then it usually is," applies. If the selling price of a product is so far below that of what the genuine product typically sells for, the red flags should start to go up.

Since counterfeit product is most often cheaply manufactured, a close inspection of the product should also reveal whether an item is real or fake. Telltale signs that a product is counterfeit are:

- Packaging with blurred lettering or labeling;
- Misspelling of words or altered product names;
- No placement of legal notices on the product or packaging;
- Drastic changes in product content, color, smell, or packaging;
- Products or packaging that lacks manufacturer's codes, trademarks and/or copyrights; and
- Products with unusual claims and warranties.

Also, counterfeit products are typically sold through "non-traditional" channels of distribution since the better retailers will not normally carry such products. Many property owners regularly employ private investigators and even set up "sting" operations to locate counterfeiters. These investigators visit major retail stores, canvas street vendors in known counterfeiting areas, attend trade shows, review magazines and trade publications and regularly monitor the Internet to find dealers who are selling counterfeit merchandise. Similarly, they target those markets most notorious for trafficking such products, e.g., Canal Street and Times Square in New York City.

23.5 Anticounterfeiting Technology

Over the years, several companies have developed different forms of anticounterfeiting solutions employing technology. Some are more generic for virtually all products while other are more specific to the individual types of products.

The following chart compares the leading types of anticounterfeiting technological solutions that one may consider and their features.

ANTI-COUNTERFEITING TOP 25

Top 25 Suppliers — anti-counterfeiting & product security tecêologies

		Target/Product					Technology						Sector			
		Tax stamps	Ids, cards & secure docs	Jewelry & luxury goods	Pharmaceuticals	Currency	RFID	Holograms	Biometrics	Security print	Software	Taggants (Other)	Government & Public Sector	Manufacturing & Retail	Healthcare	Electronics
Advanced Track & Trace	www.att-fr.com			✔	✔					✔	✔			✔	✔	✔
Alien Technology	www.alientechnology.com			✔	✔		✔							✔	✔	✔
Alp VisŠn	www.alpvisŠn.com			✔	✔									✔	✔	✔
Applied DNA Sciences	www.adnas.com			✔	✔						✔	✔		✔	✔	✔
ATL Security Label Systems	www.atlco.com			✔	✔			✔		✔	✔	✔		✔	✔	
Atlantic Zeiser	www.atlanticzeiser.com		✔	✔	✔					✔	✔		✔	✔	✔	
Authentix	www.authentix.com	✔		✔	✔	✔				✔	✔			✔	✔	
Datamax-O'NeŌ	www.datamax-oneŌ.com			✔	✔					✔	✔		✔	✔	✔	
DSS	www.dsssecure.com		✔	✔	✔					✔	✔		✔	✔	✔	
Dupont AuthenticatŠn Systems	www2.dupont.com															
Edaps Overseas	www.edaps.ua	✔	✔	✔	✔	✔	✔	✔	✔	✔	✔	✔	✔	✔	✔	✔
EM Microelectronic	www.emmicroelectronic.com		✔	✔	✔		✔							✔	✔	✔
FNMT - RCM	www.fnmt.es/smart_cards		✔							✔			✔			
Giesecke & Devrient (G&D)	www.gi-de.com		✔		✔	✔				✔	✔		✔	✔	✔	
IAI	www.iai.nl		✔			✔				✔			✔	✔		
Impinj	www.impinj.com		✔	✔	✔		✔							✔	✔	✔
InkSure Technologies	www.inksure.com	✔	✔	✔	✔	✔				✔	✔	✔		✔	✔	✔
Microtag Temed	www.microtag-temed.com			✔	✔		✔				✔	✔		✔		✔
Morpho	www.morpho.com		✔						✔				✔			
Oberthur Technologies	www.oberthur.com		✔							✔	✔		✔	✔	✔	✔
Prooftag	www.prooftag.net	✔	✔	✔	✔						✔	✔	✔	✔	✔	✔
SICPA Security SolutŠns	www.sicpa.com		✔													
U-NICA Group	www.u-nica.com	✔	✔	✔	✔	✔		✔		✔	✔	✔	✔	✔	✔	✔
WISeKey	www.wiseauthentic.com		✔	✔	✔								✔	✔	✔	✔

23.6 Steps to Take Against Infringers

Step one is to make sure that your intellectual property protection is in place, as was discussed in Chapter 6. A particularly effective measure that many property owners regularly utilize is to record their trademark and copyright registrations with the U.S. Customs

Service. Customs will cooperate with owners of registered trademarks and copyrights in attempting to stop counterfeit merchandise from entering the United States and will often seize the bogus products at their port of entry and retain them. If the products are determined to be infringing or counterfeit, Customs may require removal of infringing content prior to their release and, in some instances, order the destruction of the offending merchandise. The cost for registering an item with Customs is relatively inexpensive—in 2010 it was $190.

23.6.1 Cease and Desist Letters

An alternative to initiating a lawsuit against any infringer or counterfeiter is the sending of a cease and desist letter. Although such letters are not a prerequisite for litigation, they may be appropriate, particularly if the property owner believes that the alleged infringer was innocent. For example, a small retail shop that is innocently selling infringing items is likely to cooperate with the property owner upon receipt of such a letter, thereby saving the cost of defending a full-blown litigation.

Such letters are not, however, terribly effective against major counterfeiters or anyone who may otherwise believe that they have a valid defense to infringement. In fact, in the latter case, the sending of such a letter can create a problem of its own.

Cease and desist letters that include a threat of litigation if the demands made in the letter are not followed, can give the accused party a right to initiate a court action against the property owner for a declaration that there is no actual infringement, or that the property owner's property is not valid. This gives the alleged infringer a procedural advantage, since it allows them to choose the forum in which the dispute will be heard, typically a court closer to home or one that may have a more favorable attitude toward defendants. Psychologically, such action also turns the accused infringer into the aggrieved plaintiff.

23.6.2 Keeping a Perspective on Litigation

When all is said and done, in order to halt infringing or counterfeiting activities, the property owner may have no alternative but to litigate. Once the decision has been made to initiate litigation, it should move forward as quickly as possible since delay can adversely affect the property owner's ability to obtain pre-trial relief, i.e., a temporary restraining order or preliminary injunction. To be entitled to pre-trial relief, the moving party must demonstrate that it would be irreparably harmed if the infringement continued until trial. Courts may find that a delay in initiating such an action by a property owner is an indication that there was no irreparable harm looming if the infringement continued through trial.

There are other reasons for prompt action. Sales of infringing products can result in lost sales for a licensee and, consequently, lost royalty income for the licensor. Also, the presence of infringing or counterfeit products in the marketplace can diminish the exclusivity and goodwill associated with the property.

A greater concern arises when a counterfeit product of inferior quality causes injury to a consumer. Even if the property owner can ultimately avoid liability when an infringing product is shown to be counterfeit, there is always some attendant harm to the property owner because of the adverse publicity that inevitably follows.

In making the decision to litigate, the property owner needs to be mindful that litigation is merely a means to an end, namely, protection of the licensed property. It should never be pursued thoughtlessly since, at the very least, it provides the accused infringer with the opportunity to challenge the validity of the licensed property and the owner's rights in such property. Litigation for litigation's sake is never the appropriate course. Moreover, it is expensive and time consuming.

Care should be taken so that litigation does not spin out of control and take on a life of its own. As long as the objective remains the protection of the licensed property and the licensing program, litigation can be a useful tool in this pursuit. Maintaining this perspective will also enable the property owner to continue to pursue settlement negotiations during the litigation, with a view toward resolving the dispute short of an actual trial. The achievement of a settlement on solid business grounds is almost always preferable to allowing a judge or jury to decide the matter since they generally lack the knowledge or appreciation of how the business works. While many judges and juries "get it right" MOST of the time, a surprisingly high number do not.

23.6.3 Theories of Litigation

If a property owner decides to pursue litigation, there are several possible theories that it may rely on, depending on the type of property, how it has been protected, and how it is being used by the alleged infringer or counterfeiter.

[A] Trademark Infringement

When the property has been registered as a trademark with the USPTO and the defendant is using a mark that is confusingly similar to the registered mark on like or similar goods, the federal trademark laws (the "Lanham Act") provide very strong and enforceable remedies. While an action for the infringement of a registered trademark can be brought in either state or federal court, most are brought in federal court which has original jurisdiction over such cases.

To prevail in such actions, the property owner must first establish that it is the owner of the trademark registration. This is usually satisfied by simply presenting a copy of the registration and, as such, is the easy part. The harder part is establishing that the mark is valid and protectable and that the accused infringer is using the mark in a manner that is likely to create consumer confusion, i.e., the accused infringer's use of the trademark is likely to cause confusion in the marketplace.

The first element, i.e., that the mark is valid and protectable becomes an issue in most litigations. If the owner has used the mark in commerce for more than five consecutive years and has filed a declaration to such effect with the USPTO, that will aid greatly in meeting that test. The issue of whether the accused infringer is using the mark in such a manner as to be likely to cause consumer confusion is, however, the real issue in most cases.

Most courts have adopted certain tests or standards to determine what constitutes a likelihood of confusion and these tests vary slightly, depending upon the court applying them. Generally speaking, however, courts will look at the relative strength of the registered trademark; the differences between the registered mark and the accused mark; the differences, if any, between the goods or services on which the marks are being used; and the channels in which the respective goods are being sold or used.

The issue of likelihood of confusion is far too complex to discuss in a book of this type. It has been the subject of several books or, at least, sections of books, devoted to that issue alone. The property owner would be well advised to consult with its intellectual property counsel to assess the strength or weakness of its claim.

Section 43(a) of the Lanham Act also provides relief for the infringement of a property owner's unregistered trademarks and trade dress or where another party makes false advertising claims. The standard under section 43(a) is whether such actions by the alleged infringer are likely to create a false designation of origin of their product or service or whether it results in a false or misleading description of fact. The courts have broadly interpreted this section to provide protection against a variety of acts of unfair competition.

The specific advantage of a section 43(a) action is that the property owner does not need to have a federal trademark registration to prevail. In order to prevail on such a claim, the property owner must establish that it is likely to be damaged by such false designation, etc., and that the accused party has affixed the mark to products or containers that are sold or used in commerce.

The standard for determining a claim under section 43(a) is the same as for trademark infringement, namely, whether the false designation, description or representation is likely to cause confusion. The property owner must establish: 1) that it owns the property; 2) that the property is capable of functioning as a mark or other indication of source, origin or sponsorship and 3) that the accused activity is likely to cause confusion. The same standards are typically used in determining the issue of likelihood of confusion.

In addition to federal actions for trademark infringement and counterfeiting, several remedies also exist under state and common law. The standard of proof for such causes of action is essentially the same as for federal Lanham Act claims, i.e., whether the infringer's use is likely to cause consumer confusion.

[B] Dilution

The federal and state anti-dilution laws provide another means of protecting a property owner's trademarks. These laws are intended to protect against the gradual whittling away or dispersion of the distinctive quality of trademarks through their use by third parties and are primarily aimed at protecting well-known or famous trademarks—the very type of marks that are typically licensed. Unlike infringement claims where it is necessary to prove that the infringer's mark is likely to cause confusion in the marketplace, in order to prevail on a dilution claim the property owner must only establish that the accused infringer's use would blur the mark's product identification or tarnish the goodwill associated with the mark.

The remedies available for a successful party in a Lanham Act case include a nationwide injunction against use of the mark by the accused party as well as an award of damages, typically measured by the trademark owner's lost profits. Frequently, that means that the property owner will be awarded the infringer's profits from its use of the mark in question.

[C] Counterfeiting

Counterfeiting actions are a special breed. Where the infringer has intentionally used the identical mark that the property owner had registered for the same goods as recited in the trademark registration, the line between infringement and counterfeiting has been crossed and the property owner can bring the action under the Trademark Counterfeiting Act. This act provides both civil and criminal penalties for persons who knowingly use a counterfeit mark when intentionally trafficking in goods or services.

Civil counterfeiting actions are brought by the trademark owner in federal court. If the trademark owner can convince a court of the merits of its case and the urgency of the matter, a court can order the seizure of counterfeit goods without notice to the counterfeiter. The party seeking the order must post an adequate bond. If the owner prevails in such an action, it is entitled to an award of three times the counterfeiter's profits, plus recovery of its attorney fees, unless the counterfeiter can show extenuating circumstances.

Criminal actions for counterfeiting are federal prosecutions brought by the applicable U.S. Attorneys' Offices. To establish a criminal cause of action, the accused party must have intentionally trafficked in the goods or services and must have knowingly used the counterfeit mark in connection with such goods or services. It must be shown that the accused party: 1) knew the mark was counterfeit; 2) that it was spurious; 3) that it was used in connection with trafficking in goods and services; 4) that it was identical or virtually indistinguishable from another mark; and 5) that it is likely to cause confusion. An individual found guilty under the Act is liable for a fine or imprisonment or both and there have been numerous instances of counterfeiters that are sent to jail for significant periods of time. While many courts take trademark counterfeiting quite seriously, the challenge can be in trying to convince a U.S. Attorney to put them at the head of their criminal dockets.

[D] Copyright Infringement

The copyright laws can also be used to enforce copyrighted properties. Actions for copyright infringement are brought exclusively in the federal court that has jurisdiction over an accused infringer. Obtaining a copyright registration is a prerequisite to filing a suit for copyright infringement. If the copyright was registered with the Copyright Office within three months after it was first published, the copyright owner can seek an award of either actual or statutory damages as well as a recovery of its attorneys' fees. Thus, there is a strong incentive for owners of copyrightable materials to seek early registration.

The property owner must establish that it owns the copyright in the property and that the infringement occurred while it was the owner of the work. In addition, it must establish that it had obtained a copyright registration in the work and that the accused infringer violated such rights by making and distributing copies thereof.

To prevail in an action for copyright infringement, the owner must prove that the alleged infringer copied the copyrighted work since, in the absence of actual copying, there can be no infringement. Consequently, independent creation of the accused work by the alleged infringer is an absolute defense to any claim. This factor sets this type of action apart from patent or trademark infringement claims, where independent adoption or creation is not a defense.

Proving that someone copied a work can, of course, be a difficult task and, as such, courts will allow the copyright owner to establish copying by circumstantial evidence, i.e., that the accused infringer had access to the copyrighted work and that the two works are substantially similar.

One defense available to anyone accused of copyright infringement is that its use of the work was "fair use." Fair use will typically involve use of the copyrighted work for purposes of criticism, comment, and news reporting or teaching. Use of the copyrighted work as a parody may also constitute a fair use although it must be a legitimate attempt at parody and not merely a justification to exploit the copyrighted work.

[E] Right of Publicity Violations

As noted in Chapter 6, celebrity properties are protectable under the celebrity's right of publicity which protects their name or likeness against unauthorized use. The right of publicity is solely a creature of state law and, consequently, the scope of protection of such right can vary widely from state to state. Some states do not even recognize the right and, of those that do, the scope of relief accorded celebrity rights is anything but uniform.

23.6.4 Litigation Strategies

Most actions for trademark and copyright infringement and virtually all actions for counterfeiting start with a bang. The property owner, in addition to simply filing the complaint and waiting for the case to proceed in the normal fashion (which could take years before reaching a conclusion), will seek immediate pre-trial relief by asking the court to enjoin the defendant's use of the property during the pendency of the case. This is done by seeking either a temporary restraining order (which the court can grant immediately and based solely on the proof presented by the property owner) or a preliminary injunction (which typically involves a hearing where both sides present their respective cases). Either type of motion will result in swift action by the court.

In counterfeiting actions, immediacy is critical. Virtually all counterfeiters operate in secrecy, use fictitious names, and keep minimal business records. Thus, if the property owner waited for a normal civil action to run its course, the counterfeiter would have likely disappeared along with the evidence needed to convict them. Consequently, most property owners will not only seek a temporary restraining order but also ask the court to issue an order to require the seizure of all counterfeit merchandise.

Where there is a serious issue that evidence will be destroyed by the alleged counterfeiter, a court may permit the property owner to have a U.S. Marshall or other designated representative enter the premises of the accused party and seize counterfeit merchandise along with pertinent books and records. Any seized items will be maintained in the custody of the U.S. Marshall's Office until the hearing on the motion for preliminary injunction.

Seizure orders will issue against known counterfeiters and various "John Does" who are likely to be selling counterfeit merchandise during a specific time and at a specific location on the day of the event. "John Doe" seizure orders are an effective tool at concerts and sports venues where history has shown that counterfeiting will likely take place, although the actual identity of the counterfeiters will not be known in advance. The seizure orders will authorize the seizure of such merchandise—much to the delight of legitimate licensees, who have spent time and money in producing royalty-bearing, authorized merchandise for sale at the event.

To prevail on any of these "pre-trial" remedies, the property owner needs to be able to demonstrate that it would be irreparably harmed if the infringement (or counterfeiting) continued and that it is likely to prevail on the merits at trial. Meeting the first prong of that standard, i.e., irreparable harm, is fairly easy if a trademark is involved since the courts have long recognized that the infringement of a party's trademark can cause irreparable harm to the owner.

Meeting the second prong, however, can be more challenging since the property owner must establish that it will likely win the case. The greater the similarity of the products, trademarks and copyrighted elements, the greater the likelihood of success. Any evidence of actual instances of consumer confusion, or of willful or intentional conduct by the accused party, will also go a long way to support the issuance of a preliminary injunction.

Another effective tool for obtaining expedited relief or, at the very least, for narrowing the issues at trial is a motion for summary judgment. A court will enter a summary judgment in favor of either party if there are no genuine questions of material fact existing as to any claim and it can, therefore, be decided as a matter of law.

Since any contested factual issues will always be resolved in favor of the nonmoving party, the facts should be clearly developed before seeking summary judgment. Thus, the motion is only appropriate where the act of counterfeiting or infringement is clear.

Summary judgment motions can be brought at any time prior to trial and, if there are any factual issues potentially in dispute, they should be resolved during the course of discovery so as to make the case ripe for summary disposition at a time closer to trial. A grant of full or partial summary judgment will avoid the expense of time and money in trying the issues disposed of in advance by summary judgment. It is, therefore, a useful litigation tool.

Should the case ultimately go to trial, there are three critical elements to an effective trial presentation: preparation, preparation and preparation. The job of the property owner at trial is to convince the trier of fact, whether a judge or a jury, why it's claim has merit. Given the heavy caseloads in most courts, the property owner will likely be given only a limited amount of time to make its case but, with careful preparation of witnesses and exhibits, this can be done. The purpose of a trial should be to educate, not to confuse or bore the trier of fact.

The elements of a claim for trademark and copyright infringement have been set forth above. Each of these elements should serve as a road map for trial preparation and presentation. Omissions of evidence on a critical point could result in dismissal of the complaint and the close of the property owner's case.

The end goal of the property owner is to stop infringement of its licensed property, which can be accomplished post-trial by a permanent injunction. Even where a temporary restraining order or preliminary injunction has issued, these must be ultimately converted into a permanent injunction, either by settlement or a final judgment.

Trial courts can, and frequently have, awarded a property owner damages based on the infringer's actions. In some instances, a court may also require recall of infringing products or the placement of corrective advertising.

23.7 International Enforcement of Trademarks, Copyrights, and Related Rights[129]

Whether a licensor is in the final stages of executing a license agreement or a licensee is in the process of registering its license as required by its country's trademark laws, it is never too early for the parties to consider how the subject intellectual property rights will be protected in light of the new business arrangement. This protection may come in the form of extending its preexisting enforcement program or creating a new program to incorporate its licensees. Without a broad enforcement program, there may be uncontrolled and unauthorized activities, which can ultimately harm the licensor/rights holder's or licensee's overall image or economic value. Strong brand value can drive improved business performance and further a company's longevity.[130] Top companies are successful and maintain valuable brands because their products are intuitive and are seamlessly deployed into our lives. Therefore, interruption in the association between consumer and product caused by inconsistent or unauthorized use of trademarks or copyrighted works can have a detrimental effect on the brand. A well-designed enforcement program can help ensure that the licensed intellectual property rights are adequately policed and protected.

23.7.1 Issues an International Enforcement Program Should Address

The more business a licensor develops in the international arena, the more likely its brand will gain notoriety and strength. However, business growth may not be clear. For a licensor, growth can be attributed to the creation of new intellectual property that must then be licensed to its existing international licensees. There may also be growth when a licensor wishes to enter a new country's marketplace and engage in a new overseas licensor/licensee relationship. From an international intellectual property perspective, the two main issues to address in an enforcement program is (1) alleviating the misuse of authorized rights caused by a burgeoning and undermanaged intellectual property portfolio, and (2) controlling unauthorized use of a licensor's rights by third parties whom are exploiting or trading off the company's success.

Misuse. Misuse of a trademark can occur both within a company and outside of a company. A licensee who is misusing the licensor's trademark or copyrighted work may end up doing so without intent or knowledge. It is up to the licensor to ensure that the nature of the licensee's use is proper.

First, it is important for a licensor to understand whether the licensee is using its intellectual property at all. In most countries there is a statutory requirement to make use of a trademark. Nonuse of a trademark for an uninterrupted and extended period (in many countries anywhere from 2 to 5 years) can leave the mark vulnerable to cancellation by third parties. Licensors may not realize that its licensees have been placed on notice of a cancellation proceeding against their intellectual property.

---

[129] By Lanning G. Bryer, Ladas & Parry, New York, NY. www.ladas.com. The author greatly appreciates the assistance of Amanda Kusnierz, a third-year law student at Benjamin N. Cardozo School of Law, in the research and editing of this chapter.

[130] Smith, Gordon V. and Parr, Russell L. Intellectual Property: Licensing and Joint Venture Profit Strategies. (John Wiley & Sons, Inc. 1993).

Next, a licensor should become familiar with the field and form of the licensee's use. Under the European Community, a trademark licensor may be held liable for product defects if the licensee presents the licensor to be the manufacturer, supplier or importer. A licensor may wish to consider requiring the licensee to place a disclaimer on the goods that the trademark has been licensed and the product was manufactured by the licensee or its agent, therefore absolving the licensor from liability. On the other hand, a licensor may determine that there is a business interest in only labeling its goods with its own brand and not with the name of third party manufacturers. Whatever the interests, the licensor will want to include language in its license agreement to address the burden of such liability.

A permutation of misuse is the concept known as "naked" licensing in the United States[131]. When a valid license is created in the United States and the licensor does not demonstrate control over the licensee's quality or use of its trademark rights, the trademark may be considered abandoned (see discussion of Quality Control Issues in 4.5.1(c) above).

In addition to proper use of the mark, a licensor should also ensure that its international registrations are properly marked. Product labeling of copyrighted material should include relevant copyright notices, where possible, for design marks, packaging, usage manuals, instructions and all other copyrightable matter used in connection with the sale of the product. This can come in the form of an attribution statement and © symbol, for example: "All Licorice characters and the distinctive likeness(es) thereof are Copyright © 1900–2013 Candy, Inc. ALL RIGHTS RESERVED." Some countries require the use of a © symbol on copyrighted material.

Within most countries, the marking of the ® symbol following a trademark is an optional requirement. However, there are still a handful of countries that have specialized requirements regarding markings. For example, in Mexico, products made under license must bear the name and domicile of licensee and the owner with indication that the use is made under license. In Canada, if the mark is licensed then the products should indicate the same and bear the name of the mark owner (also requirement of English and French). In Indonesia, registration number of a trademark must be indicated on the packaging of its goods. If the goods are not packaged, then the registration number must appear on the catalogues or instruction manuals of the respective goods and services. Whereas in Egypt all imported products from abroad should bear the Arabic name and country of manufacturer. In China, "Registered Trademark" or Chinese equivalent of the ® symbol is a requirement.

Unauthorized Use. The increase in popularity of a licensor's trademarks or copyrighted work inevitably invites infringement on a national or international scale. In many cases, infringers willfully engage in unlawful conduct. However, there are also occasions where an infringer is unaware that its activities are illegal or may even be unaware of existing intellectual property rights. Licensors should consider the impact that unauthorized use may have on its business and on its relationship with its licensees. Licensees may become unhappy that it has offered due consideration for the rights to the intellectual property, only to see that the licensor has done little to manage or prevent the unauthorized use of the rights by third parties. On the other hand, licensees who are responsible for, but

---

[131] Wildman, Edwards, "Losing a trademark under naked licensing law" World Trademark Review June/July 2013, accessible at: http://www.worldtrademarkreview.com/issues/Article.ashx?g=ac00f9fd-fd49-4d33-b349-5f8b13d036aa

neglect, implementing enforcement initiatives may provide cause to their licensors to terminate their license relationship.

Allowing a few uninvited participants may result in a flooding of the market with rampant and uncontrollable counterfeiting, infringement and piracy. This may further result in the loss of consumer confidence in the product or service embodied by the copyright or trademark. The counterfeiting of products is frequently not a victimless crime. The sale of counterfeits often funds further criminal activity. Moreover, the manufacturing of counterfeited products, such as baby formula, pharmaceuticals or airplane parts, is unregulated and can impose many hazardous and dangerous risks to consumers. An active enforcement program can promote public awareness of intellectual property rights and place lurking potential infringers on notice of the aggressive policing of the intellectual property rights by its licensor. Ultimately, all licensors, licensees, consumers and the marketplace will benefit from a robust enforcement program.

23.7.2 When and Where to Set Up an Enforcement Program

New Rights. When a new license agreement is contemplated, the licensor may wish to require provisions within its agreement that would adequately address the responsibilities of the licensee as to its proper use of the licensed intellectual property rights. These provisions can serve as a roadmap for the licensee in discerning the type of responsibilities that it could face when using its licensed rights. A licensor and licensee should consider questions such as, "can you record a trademark or copyright license in country X?", "is recording the license mandatory or optional?", or "will a licensee have standing to enforce its rights in the country or does it need to come from the licensor?"[132]

It is important for protections within the license agreement to guarantee that the licensee will effectively adhere to certain standards of quality control.[133] Quality control ensures that the value of the intellectual property is not negatively impacted. The standard is not necessarily one of degree (high quality vs. low quality), but always one of consistency. Take for example, a licensee that has been granted a license in Brazil to sell t-shirts displaying the children's cartoon character, MINNIE MOUSE. However, after a period, the licensee decides that the shirts will be more profitable if the character was altered to engage in activities such as smoking a cigarette and wielding a gun. However, this would tarnish the wholesome image of MINNIE MOUSE which is mainly targets at a younger audience. As a result, the licensor may consider including a provision in the license agreement that provides the licensor with the right to regularly receive, review, and approve samples of the licensed products.

While a provision in the license agreement may prohibit this and similar types of misuse, the licensor who is based in another country may not be aware of the activity for an extended amount of time and therefore unable to act quickly. Instead, a licensor may wish to include within the agreement and as part of its enforcement program a provision to allow a representative of the licensor to conduct quality checks of licensee's factories,

---

[132] See http://www.sabaip.com/NewsArtDetails.aspx?ID=372 which provides license recordal information for a few Middle East jurisdictions.

[133] See generally 3 J. Thomas McCarthy, McCarthy on Trademarks and Unfair Competition §18 (4th ed. 2010).

which may include inspection of the manufacturing processes and the finished product. Or, perhaps a local representative would evaluate the licensee's retail locations to ensure that the use of the copyrighted work is considered proper under the licensor's standards. The quality of one product can have a ripple effect upon other licensees and their goods. By maintaining consistent quality, the consumer will readily trust the trademark or copyrighted work.

A license agreement should also contemplate a provision that authorizes termination of the license agreement if the licensee were to use the trademark or copyright in an inappropriate or disparaging manner that would tarnish the brand. The termination provision should also address the return of remaining materials or supply to goods to prevent the products from being released into the counterfeit or secondary market.

There are a few provisions that a licensor and licensee can incorporate into their agreement to help identity the rights and responsibilities regarding protection and enforcement. Additional clauses to consider in a license agreement are the following:

- *Discretion on prosecution and enforcement* – A clause that specifies whether a licensor or licensee has particular jurisdiction over prosecution and enforcement of specific matters can help alleviate confusion later.
- *Duty to inform of infringement* – A licensor may wish to rely on the licensee to raise a red flag when there is notice of infringement. A licensee may become aware of unauthorized activities that may impair its own right to use the trademark or copyrighted material.
- *Standing to bring a legal claim* – A licensor may prefer that its licensee control its own localized enforcement program and authorize the licensee to file lawsuits where necessary.
- *Costs/awards* – In order to avoid future disputes between licensor and licensee over the costs associated with enforcement and the benefit of monetary awards from settlements or lawsuits, a provision addressing both is encouraged.

Existing Rights. If license agreements are already in place, the preliminary step to establishing an enforcement program is for the licensor or licensee to undergo an assessment of its IP portfolio to determine within which countries it should or must proceed to enforce its IP rights. Given that trademark rights are territorial, it would be in the licensor's best interest to consult with its in-house counsel or an intellectual property law firm to consider the laws of each respective territory where rights may exist. Licensors and licensees may also wish to receive comments from their marketing or loss prevention teams to have a broader understanding of where vulnerability to its intellectual property may exist. For example, a member from the marketing team may be aware of the launch of new advertisement campaigns for an existing product which will certainly bolster demand, and likely peak interest in potential infringers.

In addition to considering the provisions of the license agreement, a few key questions that a licensor may wish to consider are the following:

- What efforts are in place to regulate quality control?
- Is there a licensee representative who is or can be called upon to handle localized infringement issues?

- In what countries are there licensees? Are there certain countries that the business is considering entering?
- Which international markets pose the most risk of loss?
- What products are entering the market or already on the market? How are they valued?
- Are there adequate resources and an appropriate budget available?
- Is there a designated brand protection manager, administrator or counsel for the licensor that will manage the enforcement program?

If the agreement does not have the provisions as discussed further above, an enforcement program can serve to safeguard the intellectual property of the licensor and licensee. The licensor and licensee will risk losing great value if its intellectual property rights that are not properly enforced.

23.7.3 Resources for an Enforcement Program

A global company will require a global enforcement program. The most effective type of enforcement program for a licensor may depend on the nature of its relationship with its licensees. For example, a licensor may wish to ask its international licensees to engage with their local counsel to help format a localized program that would take into consideration national trademark law and practices. Or, a licensor may wish to coordinate with an intellectual property firm that has experience with enforcing rights in multiple jurisdictions and thus maintain more control over the centralized program. Another way that a licensor may wish to tailor its program is by prioritizing the goods or services or copyrighted works that it wishes to protect. A licensor may find that its copyrighted work that is about to fall into the public domain will not be worth investing in or protecting. Alternatively, a licensor may determine that its newly acquired trademark is vulnerable to cancellation in multiple jurisdictions that have use requirements and thus may wish to tailor its enforcement program to aggressively enforce those rights.

This section will discuss the different stakeholders that an enforcement program should consider involving in the process. The degree of involvement of each will depend on the considerations discussed above.

In-House Counsel/Outside IP Firms. A licensor or licensee may wish to have its in-house counsel spearhead the brand protection efforts to timely implement the program to coincide when those intellectual property rights are obtained or transferred. If no steps are taken, a licensor's rights may become vulnerable or forfeited. In-house counsel or their outside law firms are often the people that intimately understand the rights of its licensor and licensee and can practically advise when rights are being infringed.

Enforcement should take the form of administrative practices and designed procedures with respect to accountability and quality control. When those safeguards have failed, and infringement has been identified, the licensor may wish to pursue civil action or criminal action (where permitted) against the infringer. By having a point person such as in-house counsel, various key stakeholders will know who to turn to when its intellectual property is threatened. For example, a customer service representative for a licensor may receive a phone call from a customer indicating that a flea market is overrun with the licensor's counterfeit sneakers or pirated DVDs. The licensor will want to ensure that little time is wasted for action to be taken.

Licensees. Licensors should disseminate information about any new ventures including mergers or acquisitions to their licensees. Having a licensor and licensee regularly engage in dialogue regarding the licensed IP rights helps build a cohesive understanding of the importance of brand integrity and ensure proper use and markings on goods and services. Moreover, it allows multiple licensees to establish the same understanding of or commitment to the intellectual property and therefore create uniformity across the brand empire. Licensees are an asset to an enforcement program because they can witness the frequency and depth of infringement in their respective jurisdiction as well as possibly knowing the most effective methods of combating the illegal activity. Requiring licensees to spearhead an enforcement program in its own country can help the licensor conserve time and money if a licensor does not totally abdicate discretion and control as the brand owner.

Investigators/Law Enforcement/Customs. Sometimes civil action brought on by the licensor or licensee will not deter recidivist activity from infringers. Law enforcement can be an asset in providing a stronger message to infringers or potential infringers that the licensor and licensee have a vested interest in maintaining its rights. Coordinating with law enforcement to raid a location identified to house counterfeit product can result in effectively seizing the products and preserving the evidence for a possible criminal action.[134] It is also helpful to provide training to law enforcement officials so that they can be educated in identifying infringing or counterfeit goods over authentic products. The more stakeholders that are on the lookout for unauthorized goods, the more successful the enforcement program can be.

In many countries, counterfeits and infringing goods will have to enter or exit local borders. A licensor and its licensees should consider recording its trademarks and copyrights with local customs offices as an additional protective measure. Some jurisdictions, such as the U.S.[135] and China[136], will allow for customs recordal of a rights-holder's trademark or copyright registrations. In doing so, customs may be authorized to seize infringing or counterfeit goods. Otherwise, without recordal, customs may be authorized to release the goods to their final destination.[137]

The Internet. The Internet is a hotbed for infringing copyright and trademark material. Licensors and licensees should consider reviewing country specific laws that addresses notice and takedown of copyrighted works.[138] For example, in the United States, the Digital Millennium Copyright Act of 1998 (DMCA) provides safe harbors from copyright

---

[134] Lewin, Harley I. "One Perspective on Anti-Counterfeiting: From T-shirts in the Basement to Global Trade" The Trademark Reporter, 100th Anniversary Edition, January-February 2011, Vol. 101, No. 1.

[135] See U.S. Customs and Border Protection website accessible at: https://apps.cbp.gov/e-recordations

[136] See http://www.chinaipr.gov.cn/direrdcusarticle/directions/rdcustoms/ rdcpdirections/200612/238960_1.html

[137] See: http://www.cbp.gov/linkhandler/cgov/trade/legal/informed_compliance_pubs/enforce_ipr.ctt/enforce_ipr.pdf and http://www.chinalawblog.com/2012/05/using-customs-to-protect-your-brand-from-china-counterfeits.html

[138] See http://theipexporter.com/2013/03/25/enforcing-online-copyright-protections-abroad-understanding-foreign-takedown-notice-requirements/

infringement liability for online service providers.[139] In order to qualify for safe harbor protection, service providers must designate an agent[140] to receive notifications of claimed copyright infringement. Under provisions of the DMCA, websites, like Etsy, that sell user-generated content, have a duty to respond to objections and remove infringing content from the site. Therefore, Esty is not liable for the illegal content sold on the site if the effective takedown systems have been implemented.

A licensor may wish to include adequate provisions in its agreement with its licensee regarding use of its intellectual property on the Internet. For example, a copyright holder may license the performance rights to a copyrighted work without any mention of broadcasting rights. When the performance of the copyright work appears on the Internet, it will be costlier, and time consuming to try and remove the infringing broadcast than if the limitations were negotiated upfront. At that point, the licensor may wish to have the licensee incur the costs of policing the infringing use of the copyrighted work.

When determining enforcement efforts on the Internet, the question of establishing proper jurisdiction often arises. Licensors may wish to have its licensees address infringers on the Internet that trace back to the licensee's territory. This is especially helpful in addressing websites that may not be in the licensor's native language. However, oftentimes it can be difficult to discern where an anonymous infringer present on the Internet resides. Licensors and licensees may wish to consider tools available from service providers to address infringement on the Internet. For example, eBay.com implemented the Verified Rights Owner (Vero) Program which allows rights holders to report infringement and eventually suspend repeat infringers on its website.[141] While infringement on the Internet can pose difficulties to enforcement, it cannot be avoided.[142]

Trademark and Domain Name Watch Services. A licensor may find that neither it nor its licensees have the in-house resources or knowledge to police the marketplace for potential infringement of its marks and copyrights. It is important to assess your resources and where you may wish to engage in outside vendor services to help supplement the company's program. Some companies may find that they do not have enough resources to commit to an in-house program. Subscribing to a trademark watch service can provide timely information customized to your company's needs.[143] With trademarks, timing can

---

[139]see https://www.copyright.gov/dmca-directory/

[140] "To designate an agent, a service provider must do two things: (1) make certain contact information for the agent available to the public on its website; and (2) provide the same information to the Copyright Office, which maintains a centralized online directory of designated agent contact information for public use. The service provider must also ensure that this information is up to date" (see https://www.copyright.gov/dmca-directory/).

[141] See http://pages.ebay.com/help/tp/vero-rights-owner.html

[142] For further discussion of effect policing on the Internet consider the following resources: http://www.inta.org/Advocacy/Documents/INTA%20Best%20 20Practices%20for%20Addressing%20the%20Sale%20of%20Counterfeits%20on%20the%20Internet.pdf; http://cyber.law.harvard.edu/property99/domain/Betsy.html;

http://www.fas.org/sgp/crs/misc/R41927.pdf; http://www.kaspersky.com/images/conflict_of_laws_in_cyberspace_a_need_to_overhaul_legal_regime.pdf

[143] There are many vendors that provide trademark watch services covering a wide range of jurisdictions, including Corsearch, Thomson CompuMark, TMDS, CSC and Ladas and Parry LLP.

be everything. If your company waits too long to act, you may have missed your opportunity to effectively act.

Through watch services, trademark owners can be alerted to potentially conflicting trademark applications and registrations. Companies may also wish to monitor their competitors or third parties to ensure that they are not using confusingly similar trademarks that can affect the licensor or licensee's trademark rights.

Joint Efforts. To conserve financial and manpower resources, a licensor or licensee may also consider engaging in enforcement efforts with other companies that are encountering counterfeit or infringement by third parties in mutually problematic countries. For example, a group of technology companies that have copyrighted software may be finding that a warehouse in Hong Kong is mass producing pirated versions of the software. It may be practical for the companies to coordinate with local police to shut down the warehouse rather than rely only on sending in law enforcement or investigators to address its own software.

Organizations. There are many international organizations or databases that provide forums, conferences and access to resources and best practices for enforcement programs. A few examples include the following:

- International Trademark Association (INTA)[144]
- International Anti-Counterfeiting Coalition (IACC)[145]
- International Quality & Productivity Center (IQPC)[146]
- The Chilling Effects Clearinghouse[147]

---

[144] More information is accessible at: http://www.inta.org

[145] http://www.iacc.org

[146] http://www.iqpc.com

[147] http://chillingeffects.org

Appendices

APPENDIX-1 LIMA CODE OF BUSINESS PRACTICES

APPENDIX-2 LICENSEE PROPOSAL

APPENDIX-3 DEAL MEMO

APPENDIX-4 LICENSE AGREEMENT

APPENDIX-5 PRODUCT CATEGORIES

APPENDIX-6 STYLE GUIDE

APPENDIX-7 APPROVAL FORM GUIDE & FORM

APPENDIX-8 MARKETING PLAN OUTLINE

APPENDIX-9 CHANNELS OF DISTRIBUTION CHECKLIST

APPENDIX-10 SAMPLE ROYALTY REPORT

APPENDIX-11 LICENSING AGENT AGREEMENT

APPENDIX-12 SUB-AGENT AGREEMENT

APPENDIX-13 CONSULTING AGREEMENT

APPENDIX-14 NON-DISCLOSURE AGREEMENT

APPENDIX-15 MANUFACTURER'S REPRESENTATIVE AGREEMENT

APPENDIX-16 TRADEMARK CLASSES

APPENDIX-17 FORM VA COPYRIGHT APPLICATION

APPENDIX-18 FORM TX COPYRIGHT APPLICATION

APPENDIX-19 FORM PA COPYRIGHT APPLICATION

APPENDIX-20 FORM SR COPYRIGHT APPLICATION

Electronic copies of the appendix materials are available to readers on the following Dropbox:
https://www.dropbox.com/s/3vdauzgjgr8fngw/Appendix.docx?dl=0

Appendix-1
LIMA CODE OF BUSINESS PRACTICES

The International Licensing Industry Merchandisers' Association, Inc. ("LIMA") is committed on behalf of its member companies to the operation of factories manufacturing licensed products in a lawful, safe, and healthful manner. It upholds the principles that no underage, forced, or prison labor* should be employed; that no one is denied a job because of gender, ethnic origin, religion, affiliation or association, and that factories comply with laws protecting the environment. Supply agreements with firms manufacturing licensed products on behalf of LIMA members should also provide for adherence to these principles.

The role of LIMA is to inform, educate, and survey its members so that individual member companies can adhere to its Code of Business Practices. As an Association, it also acts to encourage local and national governments to enforce wage and hour laws and factory health and safety laws. Specific operating conditions that member companies are encouraged to meet and obtain contractor agreement in advance are as follows:

1) LABOR

a) That wages and overtime pay practices comply with the standards set by law, including the payment of compensation for overtime hours at such premium rates as is legally required in that country, but not less than at a rate equal to their regularly hourly compensation rate.

b) That working hours must exceed prevailing local work hours in the country where the work is to be performed, except with respect to appropriately compensated overtime; must not require more than a 60-hour week on a regularly scheduled basis; and must permit at least one day off in every 7-day period.

c) That no one under the legal minimum age is employed in any stage of manufacturing; that a minimum age of 14 applies in all circumstances, but notwithstanding the foregoing, that C138 Minimum Age Convention (1973) and C182 Worst Forms of Child Labor Convention (1999) of the International Labor Organization apply.

d) That no forced or prison labor is employed*, that workers are free to leave once their shift ends, and that guards are posted only for normal security reasons.

e) That all workers are entitled to sick and maternity benefits as provided by law.

f) That all workers are entitled to freely exercise their rights of employee representation as provided by local law.

2) THE WORKPLACE

a) That factories provide a safe and healthy working environment for their employees and comply with or exceed all applicable local laws concerning sanitation and risk protection.

b) That the factory is properly lighted and ventilated, and that aisles and exits are accessible always.

c) That there is adequate medical assistance available in emergencies and that designated employees are trained in first aid procedures.

d) That there are adequate and well-identified emergency exits, and that all employees are trained in emergency evacuation.

e) That protective safety equipment is available, and employees are trained in its use.

f) That safeguards on machinery meet or exceed local laws.

g) That there are adequate toilet facilities which meet local hygiene requirements and that they are properly maintained.

h) That there are facilities or appropriate provisions for meals and other breaks.

i) If a factory provides housing for its employees, it will ensure that dormitory rooms and sanitary facilities meet basic needs, are adequately ventilated and meet fire safety and other local laws.

j) That all employees are treated with dignity and respect and that no employee shall be subjected to any physical, sexual, psychological or verbal harassment or abuse.

k) That no mental or physical disciplinary practices are employed.

l) That factories shall recognize and respect the rights of employees to associate, organize and bargain collectively in a lawful and peaceful manner, without penalty or interference.

m) That factories shall not discriminate based on race, religion, age, nationality, social or ethnic origin, sexual orientation, gender, political opinion or disability.

3. COMPLIANCE

a) The purpose of this Code is to establish a standard of performance, to educate, and to encourage a commitment to responsible manufacturing, not to punish.

b) To determine adherence, LIMA member companies will evaluate their own facilities as well as those of their contractors. They will examine all books and records and conduct on-site inspections of the facilities and request that their contractors follow the same practices with subcontractors.

c) An annual statement of compliance with this Code should be signed by an officer of each manufacturing company or contractor.

d) Contracts for the manufacture of licensed products should provide that a material failure to comply with the Code or to implement a corrective action plan on a timely basis is a breach of contract for which the contract may be canceled.

e) Because of the great diversity in the kinds of licensed products manufactured and the manufacturing methods used, as well as the wide range in factory sizes and numbers of employees, a rule of reason must be used to determine applicability of these provisions.

f) This Code should be posted or available for all employees in the local language.

---

* Many countries recognize that prison labor is essential to the rehabilitation process. This provision prohibits the exportation of prison-made goods to countries that prohibit or restrict the importation of such goods.

APPENDIX-2
LICENSEE PROPOSAL

Date:	
Property:	
Licensee:	
Street Address:	
City, State & Zip Code	
Telephone No.	
Fax Number:	
E-Mail Address	
Business Contact/Phone:	
Product Dev Contact/Phone:	
Legal Contact & Phone:	
Finance/Royalty Contact & Phone:	
Proposed Licensed Products:	
Proposed Term:	
Exclusive or Non-Exclusive	
Proposed Royalty Rates Domestic/ F.O.B./ Direct Sales:	
Proposed Advance:	
Proposed Guarantee(s):	
Proposed Channels of Distribution:	
Proposed Territory:	
Proposed Sell-Off:	
Sales Projections:	Year 1 -
	Year 2 -
	Year 3 -
Top 4 Retailers:	1)
	2)

	3)
Proposed Marketing Date:	
Proposed First Sale Date:	
Proposed Product Category:	Attach sheet to describe
Marketing Strategy:	Attach sheet to describe
Retail Strategy:	Attach sheet to describe
Current Licenses Held:	Attach list.
Main Product Lines:	List on separate sheet
Stipulations:	List on separate sheet
Public or Private:	
Dun & Bradstreet #:	
Two references & contact info	
Please send the following items:	

This document does not constitute a legal agreement but is a summary of the deal points being discussed. No agreement will exist until execution of a formal license agreement by both parties.   This proposal shall expire thirty (30) days after the below date.

By:_____

Date:_____

Appendix-3
DEAL MEMO

LICENSEE:

ADDRESS:

CITY/STATE:

PHONE:

FAX:

E-MAIL:

CONTACT:

LICENSOR:

PROPERTY:

TYPE OF LICENSE: Exclusive

LICENSED PRODUCTS: Licensee will have the right to manufacture, sell and distribute the following Licensed Products:

DISTRIBUTION RIGHTS: [If applicable]

ADVANCE: $_____ due upon execution of a formal license agreement

GUARANTEE: 20XX $_____
                                            20XX $_____
                                            >20XX $_____

MEDIA SPENDING   Licensee agrees to spend the following minimum amount in media buys for the Licensed Products:

                                            20XX $_____ by each party

>20XX____% of the previous year's Net Sales of the Licensed Products

ROYALTY RATE   _____% on Licensed Products with a wholesale price point below $_____

_____% on Licensed Products with a wholesale price point above $_____

_____% on FOB Sales

_____% on Direct to Consumer Sales

TERM   _____ year Initial Term with options for Licensee to renew the agreement for an unlimited number of additional _____ (___) year Renewal Terms provided that it has paid Licensor at least $_____ in royalty payments during the then in-effect Term

ASSIGNMENT   This Agreement may not be assigned or transferred by Licensor without the express written consent of Licensee which may be withheld in its sole discretion. For purposes of this section, transfer shall mean the change of control of Licensor through, for example, merger, acquisition or public offering.

TERRITORY: Worldwide for sale of Licensed Products

DISTRUBUTION: All industry standard channels of distribution for the Licensed Products.

EFFECTIVE DATE: This Deal Memo takes effect from the date of signature by both parties.

Upon signature of the Deal Memo, both parties undertake to negotiate in good faith and agree upon a long form license agreement the ("License Agreement") incorporating the terms set forth in this Deal Memo. Neither this Deal Memo nor any agreements otherwise reached between the parties relating to this proposed transaction shall be binding on either party unless and until a formal Licensed Agreement is executed by both parties. If no formal License Agreement is executed within sixty (60) days from the date of this Deal Memo, this Deal Memo shall automatically expire, and any offer being made by Licensee shall expire.

_____

By: By:

Title: Title:

Date: Date:

Appendix-4
LICENSE AGREEMENT

THIS AGREEMENT is made this ____day of _____, by and between _____ with offices at _____ (the "Licensor") and _____ with offices at _____ (the "Licensee").

WHEREAS, Licensor is the sole and exclusive owner of the Property or Properties identified more fully in Schedule A attached hereto (the "Property") including, but not limited to, those trademark and service marks identified in Schedule A attached hereto (the "Trademarks"); and

WHEREAS, Licensor has the power and authority to grant to Licensee the right, privilege and license to use, manufacture and sell those types of products that incorporate or are otherwise based on the Property as identified in Schedule A attached hereto (the "Licensed Products"); and

WHEREAS, Licensee has represented that it can manufacture, market and distribute the Licensed Products in the distribution channels (the "Channels of Distribution") and the countries both of which are identified in Schedule A attached hereto (the "Territory"); and

WHEREAS, Licensee desires to obtain from Licensor a license to use, manufacture, have manufactured and sell Licensed Products in the Territory and to use the Trademark on or in association with the Licensed Products; and

WHEREAS, both Licensee and Licensor agree with respect to the terms and conditions upon which Licensee shall use, manufacture, have manufactured and sell Licensed Products and to use the Trademark on or in association with the Licensed Products.

NOW, THEREFORE, in consideration of the promises and agreements set forth herein, the parties, each intending to be legally bound hereby, do promise and agree as follows.

WITNESSETH

1. **License Grant.**

A. <u>Grant of Limited License</u>. Licensor grants to Licensee for the term of this Agreement as defined in Schedule A attached hereto (the "Term"), subject to the terms and conditions herein contained, and Licensee hereby accepts, the non-exclusive right, license and privilege to utilize the Property and Trademarks solely and only in connection with the manufacture of the Licensed Products as well as for the advertising, promotion, distribution, offering for sale and sale of such Licensed Products within the Channels of Distribution and within the Territory to those Approved Customers identified in Schedule A attached hereto or who are otherwise approved in writing by Licensor under the terms and conditions stated herein.

B. <u>Individuals</u>. Licensee expressly acknowledges that this license grant does not convey any rights to the Licensee with respect to the individuals and athletes who compete or participate in Licensor's events, whose rights are not controlled by Licensor. Licensee shall not use the names, images or likenesses of such individuals and athletes without first obtaining permission directly from such individuals and athletes.

C. <u>No Sublicensing</u>. Licensee may not grant any sub-licenses to any third parties without the prior express written permission of Licensor, which permission may be withheld in Licensor's sole discretion.

D. <u>Non-Authorized Use</u>. Licensee agrees that it will not utilize the Property in any manner not specifically authorized by this Agreement.

E. Grant of Other Rights. Nothing in this Agreement shall be construed to prevent Licensor from granting other licenses for the use of the Property in any manner whatsoever. Licensor specifically reserves all rights not herein granted, including, without limitation, premium and promotional rights.

F. Distribution Outside of Authorized Channels. It is understood and agreed that the Licensee may, with the prior express written approval of Licensor, manufacture and/or have manufactured the Licensed Products outside the Territory provided that all sales are within the Territory. Licensee agrees that it will not make, or authorize, any use, direct or indirect, of the Licensed Products or Property in any distribution channel other than the approved Channels or Distribution or in any country other than the Territory without the prior express written permission of the Licensor nor shall Licensee knowingly offer to sell or sell Licensed Products to persons who intend or are likely to resell them in distribution channels or than the approved Channels of Distribution or any country other than the Territory.

2. Consideration.

A. Royalty. In consideration for the licenses granted hereunder, Licensee agrees to pay to Licensor during the Term of this Agreement (as defined in Schedule A attached hereto), a royalty in the amount provided in Schedule A attached hereto (the "Royalty") based on Licensee Net Sales of Licensed Products. If any amount payable to Licensor is subject to any non-US tax, charge or duty, Licensee shall furnish to Licensor official proof of such payment, including official proof of receipt of Licensee's payment from the government entity imposing such tax, charge or duty. If Licensor does not receive full and complete U.S. tax credit for any such tax, charge or duty, then the amount payable by Licensee shall be increased to provide to Licensor such amount as would be payable to Licensor in the absence of any such tax, charge, duty or impost.

 B. Royalty Period. The Royalty owed Licensor shall be calculated on a quarterly calendar basis (the "Royalty Period") and shall be payable no later than thirty (30) days after the termination of the preceding calendar quarter.

C. Marketing Fee. During each Royalty Period on the dates specified in Schedule A, Licensee shall pay to Licensor a Marketing Fee in the amount recited in Schedule A. Licensee's obligation to pay the Marketing Fee is absolute and independent of the Royalty. Licensee shall no right to set off, compensate or make any deduction from payments of the Marketing Fee for any reason whatsoever. Any amount that Licensee may directly spend on advertising (as previously approved by Licensor) more than the amount required herein shall not be used to offset the required Marketing Fee for the subsequent Royalty Period. Licensor may use or expend all Marketing Fees paid by Licensee hereunder in its sole discretion.

D. Royalty Statement. With each Royalty Payment, Licensee shall provide Licensor with a written Royalty Statement in a form acceptable to Licensor. Such Royalty Statement shall be certified as accurate by a duly authorized officer of Licensee, reciting: (1) gross sales of all Licensed Products for the applicable Royalty Period, itemized by SKU; (2) Net Sales on which the Royalties are based; (3) all related party sales, employee sales, parking lot, warehouse or similar sales, and any other unusual sales transactions; (4) allowed deductions or credits taken against gross sales; and (5) quantity and dollar amount of Licensed Products sold to each customer, broken down by month and each country and Channel of Distribution within the Territory, if applicable, as well as any other information relating to the Licensed Products that may be reasonably requested by Licensor. Failure to deliver statements and reports in a timely manner as provided by this Section shall constitute a material breach of this Agreement. Such statements shall be furnished to Licensor whether or not any Licensed Products were sold during the Royalty Period.

E. <u>Advance and Guaranteed Minimum Royalty</u>. Licensee agrees to pay to Licensor a Guaranteed Minimum Royalty in accordance with the terms of Schedule A attached hereto (the "Guaranteed Minimum Royalty"). As recited in Schedule A, a portion of the Guaranteed Minimum Royalty for the first year shall be payable as a non-refundable Advance against royalties (the "Advance"). The actual royalty payments shall reflect the amount of all Guaranteed Minimum Royalty payments including any Advances made. Licensee shall only be permitted to carry forward any unused credit for the Advance or Guaranteed Minimum Royalty for the subsequent year.

F. <u>Net Sales Defined</u>. "Net Sales" shall mean Licensee gross sales (the gross invoice amounts billed customers) of Licensed Products, less any *bona fide* returns (net of all returns made or allowed as supported by credit memoranda issued to the customers). In no event shall the total credits taken by Licensee for returns exceed 10% of the total gross sales for any Royalty Period. No other costs incurred in the manufacturing, selling, advertising, and distribution of the Licensed Products shall be deducted nor shall any deduction be allowed for any uncollectible accounts or allowances.

G. <u>Sale of a Product</u>. A Royalty obligation shall accrue upon the sale of the Licensed Products regardless of the time of collection by Licensee. For purposes of this Agreement, a Licensed Product shall be considered "sold" upon the date when such Licensed Product is billed, invoiced, shipped, or paid for, whichever event occurs first.

H. <u>Invoices</u>. Upon the request of Licensor, Licensee shall submit to Licensor copies of invoices, credit memoranda, price lists, line sheets and customer lists related to the sale of Licensed Products. All payment terms discounts and trade discounts must appear on the face of each invoice; each such discount must be itemized as a percentage reduction in Licensee's published wholesale list price.

I. <u>Off-Sale Pricing</u>. If Licensee sells any Licensed Products to any party at a price less than the regular price charged to other parties, the Royalty payable Licensor shall be computed based on the regular price charged to other parties. If Licensee combines or bundles any Licensed Product with non-licensed goods or services, the Royalty due Licensor will be based on the proportional value of the cost of goods of the Licensed Products as a percentage of the cost of goods of the bundled product including the Licensed Products.

J. <u>No Bar</u>. The receipt or acceptance by Licensor of any Royalty Statement, or the receipt or acceptance of any royalty payment made, shall not prevent Licensor from subsequently challenging the validity or accuracy of such statement or payment.

K. <u>Acceleration</u>. Upon expiration or termination of this Agreement, all Royalty obligations, including any unpaid portions of the Guaranteed Minimum Royalty, shall be accelerated and shall immediately become due and payable.

L. <u>Survival of Termination</u>. Licensee obligations for the payment of a Royalty and the Guaranteed Minimum Royalty shall survive expiration or termination of this Agreement and will continue for so long as Licensee continues to manufacture, sell or otherwise market the Licensed Products.

M. <u>U.S. Currency</u>. All payments due hereunder shall be made in United States currency drawn on a United States bank, unless otherwise specified between the parties.

N. <u>Interest</u>. Late payments shall incur interest at the rate of ONE PERCENT (1%) per month from the date such payments were originally due.

3. Time of the Essence.

Time is of the essence with respect to timely delivery of Royalty Statements and payments as herein provided and Licensee's failure to comply shall constitute a material breach of the Agreement. If any such breach is not cured within five (5) days of receiving written notice of such breach by Licensor, or if Licensee shall receive written notice of such breach more than twice times in any twelve

(12) month period, such shall be grounds for automatic termination without a further opportunity to cure.

4. Audit.

A. Right to Audit. Both during and after termination or expiration of this Agreement, Licensor shall have the right, upon at least five (5) days written notice and no more than once per calendar year, to inspect the books and records of both Licensee and any of Licensee's related or affiliated entities, e.g., parents, subsidiaries, etc., and all other documents and material in the possession of or under the control of Licensee with respect to the subject matter of this Agreement at the place or places where such records are normally retained by Licensee. Licensee shall provide access to such records in electronic format, if possible, and shall fully cooperate with the Licensor or its representative in connection with such audit and Licensor and/or its representative shall have free and full access thereto for such purposes and shall be permitted to make copies thereof and extracts therefrom.

B. Discrepancies. If such inspection reveals a discrepancy in the amount of Royalty owed Licensor from what was paid, Licensee shall pay such discrepancy, plus interest, calculated at the rate of ONE PERCENT (1%) per month. If such discrepancy is more than the lesser of TEN THOUSAND UNITED STATES DOLLARS ($10,000.00) or THREE PERCENT (3%) of the monies owed Licensor, Licensee shall also reimburse Licensor for the cost of such inspection including any attorney's fees incurred in connection therewith. If it is determined that Royalty payments due are more than TWENTY PERCENT (20%) of the Royalties paid for the period covered by such audit, then, in addition to all other rights, legal and/or equitable, of Licensor, Licensor shall have the right to immediately terminate the Term upon notice to Licensee.

C. Audit Disputes. If the Parties cannot come to an agreement with respect to the results of any audit and the monies owed Licensor, the Parties agree that such dispute shall be submitted to arbitration in accordance with the then in-effect rules of the American Arbitration Association with a hearing to be held in the AAA office closest to Licensor's headquarters. Any decision rendered by the arbitrator shall be final and binding on the Parties.

D. Record Retention. This audit right shall survive termination or expiration of the Agreement. All books and records relative to Licensee obligations hereunder shall be maintained and kept accessible and available to Licensor for inspection for at least three (3) years after expiration or termination of this Agreement.

E. Periodic Financial Statements. Within ninety (90) calendar days after the end of each of its fiscal years Licensee shall provide Licensor (all in English) with: (1) an annual audited financial statement of Licensee (audited by an accounting firm satisfactory to Licensor); (2) an annual composite statement, certified by its chief financial officer, showing the aggregate gross sales, trade discounts, returns, allowances, payment term discounts and closeout discounts and any other deduction taken to arrive at the Net Sales price of all Licensed Products sold by Licensee; and (3) an annual inventory reconciliation, certified by a certified public accountant, confirming actual reconciliation of the inventory to Licensee's general ledger and including computer reports summarizing inventory by SKU.

5. Marketing.

A. Commercially Reasonable Efforts. At all times during the Term, Licensee shall use commercially reasonable efforts to generate the maximum possible level of sales of the Licensed Products within the Channels of Distribution in the Territory including, without limitation, the design and development of unique retail displays to include "exclusive" styles, designs, powerful point of purchase visual display and minimum square footage requirements at each of its locations that desires to sell the Licensed Products. Licensee acknowledges that Licensor is entering into this Agreement not only in consideration of the payments to be made by Licensee, but also in consideration of the promotional value to Licensor of the widespread marketing, distribution, advertising, promotion, offer for sale and sale of the Licensed Products. Accordingly, Licensee shall use commercially reasonable efforts to seek to procure the greatest volume of sales of the Licensed Products consistent with high quality and shall diligently and continuously make and maintain timely and adequate arrangements for their manufacture, marketing, distribution, advertising, promotion, offering for sale and sale.

B. Sufficient Inventory. Licensee shall use commercially reasonable efforts to maintain sufficient on-hand inventory to support market demand for the Licensed Products.

C. Marketing Plan. No later than September 1st of each calendar year during the Term, Licensee shall provide to Licensor Licensee's proposed marketing plan and budget ("Marketing Plan") for the promotion and distribution of the Licensed Products for the ensuing calendar year.

D. Marketing Budget. Licensee shall establish a marketing budget, and shall expend an amount, for advertising and related sales promotion activities, for each year during the Term, equal to a percentage of all Net Sales in the amount recited in Schedule A attached hereto. Licensee shall provide Licensor within sixty (60) days after the end of each calendar year with an accounting signed and certified by an officer of Licensee, reflecting the amounts expended by Licensee on advertising the Licensed Products.

E. Manner of Sale. Licensee shall sell and distribute the Licensed Products in the Territory and Channels of Distribution outright and not on approval, consignment, guaranteed sale or return basis, or as a premium, promotional tie-in, or give-away.

F. Licensor's Assistance in Marketing Efforts. Licensor shall provide reasonable assistance to Licensee in marketing the Licensed Products, at Licensee's request, but shall not be required to expend material amounts of time or money in doing so.

6. Approval of Products and Promotional Materials.

A. Quality of the Licensed Products. The licenses granted hereunder are conditioned upon Licensee's full and complete compliance with the marking provisions of the patent, trademark and copyright laws of the United States. The Licensed Products, as well as all promotional, packaging and advertising material relative thereto, shall include all appropriate legal notices as reasonably required by Licensor.

B. Approval of Preliminary Material. Licensee agrees to submit to Licensor, for final approval, sketches, prototypes and production samples of all Licensed Products and all advertising, promotional and packaging material related to said Licensed Products. Licensor shall provide Licensee with written approval or disapproval within ten (10) business days after receipt of such sketches, prototypes and production samples. Licensor hereby agrees that any item submitted will not be unreasonably disapproved and, if it is disapproved, that Licensor will give the Licensee specific grounds therefore. Once such samples have been approved by Licensor, the Licensed Product shall not materially depart there from without Licensor's prior express written consent, which shall not be unreasonably withheld. Should Licensor fail to provide such written approval or disapproval within ten (10) business days, such failure shall be deemed to be disapproval of such submission. Licensee shall thereafter have the right to demand, in writing, such written approval or disapproval from Licensor. Should Licensor fail to provide such written approval or disapproval within three (3) business days thereafter, such failure shall be deemed to be approval.

C. Compliance with Standards. The Licensed Products manufactured by or for Licensee, shall comply in all respects with Licensor's standards, specifications, directions and processes and shall be in substantial conformity with the production sample of the Licensed Product approved by Licensor.

Appendices

Once Licensor has approved the Production Sample(s), Licensee will manufacture Licensed Products only in accordance with such approved Production Sample(s) and will not make any changes without Licensor's prior written approval.

D. Pre-Production Samples. Prior to the commencement of manufacture and sale of the Licensed Products, Licensee shall submit to Licensor, at no cost to Licensor two (2) sets of samples of all Licensed Products which Licensee intends to manufacture and sell and one (1) complete set of all promotional and advertising material associated therewith.

E. Annual Samples. At least once during each calendar year, Licensor may require that Licensee shall submit to Licensor an additional two (2) sets of samples.

F. Compliance with Laws. Licensed Products will always be manufactured, sold and distributed with labels, tags, packaging, and sales promotion materials that are appropriate for merchandise of such quality; and will always be manufactured, sold and distributed in accordance with all applicable federal, state and local laws and regulations, and shall in no manner reflect adversely upon the good name of Licensor.

G. Failure of Quality. If the quality of a Licensed Product falls below such a production-run quality, as previously approved by Licensor, Licensee shall use commercially reasonable efforts to restore such quality. If Licensee has not taken appropriate steps to restore such quality within thirty (30) days after notification by Licensor, Licensor shall have the right to delete such Licensed Product from the Agreement. Such deletion shall have no effect on the remaining terms of the Agreement and the Agreement shall remain in full force and effect.

H. Seconds. If, in the reasonable discretion of Licensor and Licensee, any Licensed Product(s) is not in conformity with Licensor's approval as set forth herein, but is suitable for sale as a non-first quality product ("Seconds"), then Licensee may sell such Seconds in a way which shall not reduce the value of the Trademarks or Property or detract from Licensor's reputation in any major respect, provided, however, that (1) Licensee's sales of Seconds shall not exceed five (5%) of its total Net Sales for any Royalty Period; (2) Licensor shall have a right to approve such Licensed Products sold as Seconds, such approval not to be unreasonably withheld; and (3) a full Royalty shall be due on all such sales of Seconds.

I. Inspections. The Licensee agrees to permit Licensor or its representative to inspect the facilities where the Licensed Products are being manufactured and packaged.

J. Quality of Promotional Materials. The quality, contents and workmanship of all promotional and advertising material containing the Property (the "Ancillary Materials") shall at all times be of a high standard, and of such style, appearance and quality as to be adequate and suited to their exploitation to the best advantage and to the protection and enhancement of the Licensor and the Trademarks and the goodwill pertaining thereto; no less than the best quality of similar ancillary material used by Licensee.

K. Approval of Ancillary Materials. Licensee shall, in sufficient time for review and consideration, submit to Licensor, for Licensor's approval, all Ancillary Materials relating to the Licensed Products. Licensor shall provide Licensee with written approval or disapproval within ten (10) business days after receipt of such Ancillary Materials. Any submission not approved in writing by Licensor Group within such ten (10) day period shall be deemed disapproved. Licensee shall thereafter have the right to demand, in writing, such written approval or disapproval from Licensor. Should Licensor fail to provide such written approval or disapproval within three (3) business days thereafter, such failure shall be deemed to be approval. Licensee shall not use or disseminate any Ancillary Materials without the prior express written approval of Licensor. Licensor hereby agrees that any item submitted will not be unreasonably disapproved and, if it is disapproved, that Licensor will give the

Licensee specific grounds therefore.

L. Advertising Material and Placement. All media advertising and media advertising placements with respect to the Licensed Products shall be mutually acceptable to both parties. Licensor hereby agrees that any item submitted will not be unreasonably disapproved and, if it is disapproved, that Licensor will give the Licensee specific grounds therefore.

M. Intellectual Property Notices. Licensee agrees to affix to the Licensed Products, and to any Ancillary Materials which depict the Property and/or Trademarks, such legal notices as required and approved by Licensor in writing. In addition, wherever appropriate and required by Licensor, Licensee shall affix the appropriate symbol ® or ™ as well as any such material, such other reasonable notice or notices of trademark and copyright as requested by Licensor. The Licensed Products shall also contain the following copyright notice, which Licensor can change from time to time by notice to Licensee:

   © 20__ (or year introduced)
   All Rights Reserved.

Such notices shall appear on the Licensed Products, or on any label or tag affixed to the Licensed Products, as Licensor may approve. The parties recognize and agree, however, that there will be instances where it will not be possible to contain a full copyright or trademark notice. In such event, they will agree upon an appropriate "short form" or abbreviated version of such notice.

N. Approval of Third Party Manufacturers. In the event that the Licensee elects to have the Licensed Products manufactured by a party other than itself, Licensee shall promptly identify the party or parties that will be manufacturing the Licensed Products and obtain the written approval of the Licensor prior to having such party commence the manufacture of such Licensed Products who shall enter into a written Manufacturing Agreement with the Licensee in a form acceptable to the Licensor.

O. Compliance with Labor Compliance Rules. The manufacture, packaging and storage of the Licensed Products shall be carried out only at premises approved by the Licensor or its nominee in writing from time to time. The Licensor or its nominee shall be entitled at any time on reasonable notice to the Licensee to enter, during regular business hours, any premises used by the Licensee or its manufacturers for the manufacture, packaging or storage of the Licensed Products, to inspect such premises, all plant, workforce and machinery used for manufacture, packaging or storage of Licensed Products and all other aspects of the manufacture, packaging and storage of Licensed Products. The Licensee shall and shall insure that its manufacturers shall make any changes or improvements to its premises, plant, workforce, machinery and other aspects of the manufacture, packaging and storage of Licensed Products as the Licensor or its nominee may reasonably request. Licensee shall comply in all material respects with the LIMA Code of Business Practices attached hereto as Exhibit A.

7. Intellectual Property Rights.

A. No Challenges by Licensee. The parties agree that Licensee will not take any action or fail to take any action inconsistent with the ownership, title or any rights of Licensor in and to the Property or Trademarks or attack the validity of this Agreement or the Property or Trademarks.

B. Trademark Registrations. The parties acknowledge and agree that Licensor has the right, but not the obligation, to apply for all registrations in the United States and elsewhere for the Trademarks under its own name. Licensee agrees to provide reasonable assistance to Licensor with respect to tiling such applications and obtaining and maintaining the resulting registrations for the Trademarks.

C. Trademarks Unique and Original. Licensee acknowledges Licensor's rights in the Property and Trademarks and, further, acknowledges that the Property and Trademarks are unique and original to Licensor and that Licensor is the owner thereof. Licensor, however, makes no representation or warranty with respect to the validity of any trademark or copyright which may issue or be granted therefrom.

D. Secondary Meaning. Licensee acknowledges that the Property and Trademarks have acquired secondary meaning.

E. Trademarks Inure to Benefit of Licensor. Licensee agrees that its use of the Property and Trademarks inures to the benefit of Licensor and that the Licensee shall not acquire any rights in the Trademarks.

F. Works Created by Licensee. All intellectual property rights, whether copyrights, trademark rights, or patent rights, in the Licensed Products and/or relating to the Property or Trademarks or used in the packaging, advertising or promotion thereof, shall be deemed the property of Licensor. In the case of copyrightable materials, such materials shall be considered to be "works made for hire" under the Copyright Act. In the case of trademarks (including trade dress) all use of such trademarks and trade dress relating to the Licensed Products and/or Trademarks, whether now in existence or developed by Licensee during the Term of this Agreement, shall be deemed owned by Licensor and all use thereof by the Licensee, including all good will relating thereto, shall inure to the exclusive benefit of Licensor. In the case of patentable inventions and concepts as well as copyrightable materials that do not constitute "works made for hire," Licensee hereby assigns to Licensor all of Licensee rights in and to such patentable inventions and concepts and such copyrightable materials, without further compensation from Licensor. Under no circumstances shall Licensee continue to use any intellectual property rights approved for use with the Licensed Products after termination or expiration of this Agreement or any trademarks, trade dress, designs, artwork or graphics that could reasonably be considered to be associated with the Licensed Products or the Trademarks. In the event this Agreement is terminated or expires, Licensee shall promptly execute such documents as may be required to assign all rights in and to such Property, including all copyrights in any artwork relating thereto to Licensor. Artwork shall include all works which Licensee proposes to and/or does use in connection with the manufacture, sale promotion, advertising, marketing and/or distribution of a Licensed Product, and shall include, but not be limited to, pictorial, graphic, sculptural and literary works as well as software and textual material. Artwork further includes works embodied in all forms and media, including sketches or such other definition of the use of Property or Trademarks as Licensor requires for evaluation and approval. No Licensed Products shall be approved by Licensor unless its artwork has been approved.

8. **Representations and Warranties.**

A. Licensor Representations and Warranties. Licensor represents and warrants that (1) no third party owns any right, title or interest in the Property and Trademarks; (2) the Property and Trademarks do not interfere with, infringe upon, misappropriate or otherwise conflict with any intellectual property rights of any third party when used on or in association with the Licensed Products; (3) it has full right, power and authority to convey the right, title and interest described herein: and (4) it has not taken, and will not take, any action in conflict with this Agreement.

B. Licensee Representations and Warranties. Licensee represents and warrants that: (1) it shall comply with all applicable laws and regulations in connection with the manufacture, use, sale, distribution, advertising and promotion of the Licensed Products; (2) it will use its best efforts to promote, market, use, sell, and distribute the Licensed Products and will maintain sufficient inventories of Licensed Products to reasonably fulfill orders; (3) it shall be solely responsible for the manufacture, production, sale, and distribution of the Licensed Products and will bear all related costs associated therewith; (4) it will conduct itself in a business-like and professional manner so as not to bring disrepute to the Property and Trademarks; and (5) it will manufacture or have manufactured all Licensed Products in compliance with the LIMA Code of Business Standards, a copy of which is attached hereto as Exhibit A.

C. Introduction of Licensed Products. It is the intention of the parties that Licensee shall introduce the Licensed Products in the Licensed Territory on or before the Product Introduction Date recited in Schedule A and commence shipment of Licensed Products in the Territory on or before the Initial Shipment Date recited in Schedule A. Failure to meet either the Product Introduction Date or the Initial Shipment Date shall constitute grounds for immediate termination of this Agreement by Licensor.

9. **Termination**

The following termination rights are in addition to the termination rights provided elsewhere in this Agreement:

A. Immediate Right of Termination. Licensor shall have the right to immediately terminate this Agreement by giving written notice to Licensee if Licensee does any of the following:

    (1) fails to meet the Product Introduction Date or the Initial Shipment Date as specified in Schedule A; or

    (2) after having commenced sale of the Licensed Products, fails to continuously sell Licensed Products for three (3) consecutive Royalty Periods; or

    (3) fails to obtain or maintain product liability insurance in the amount and of the type provided for herein; or

    (4) files a petition in bankruptcy or is adjudicated a bankrupt or insolvent, or makes an assignment for the benefit of creditors, or an arrangement pursuant to any bankruptcy law, or if the Licensee discontinues its business or a receiver is appointed for the Licensee or for the Licensee business and such receiver is not discharged within thirty (30) days; or

    (5) breaches any of the provisions of this Agreement relating to the unauthorized assertion of rights in the Trademarks; or

    (6) after receipt of written notice from Licensor, fails to immediately discontinue the distribution or sale of the Licensed Products or the use of any Ancillary Materials that do not contain the requisite legal legends; or

    (7) fails to make timely payment of Royalties when due two or more times during any twelve-month period;

    (8) fails to meet the Minimum Sales requirement in any calendar year;

    (9) fails to make the Minimum Advertising Expenditure in any calendar year;

    (10) fails to comply with the Marketing Requirements as provided for in Schedule A attached there; or

    (11) sells Licensed Products to an unapproved customer;

    (12) undergoes a change of control of more than 50% of its outstanding shares, or merge, consolidate with or into any other corporation or other entity, or directly or indirectly sell or otherwise transfer, sell or dispose of all or a substantial portion of its business or assets;

Appendices

(13) understates Royalties as provided in Paragraph 4B., makes any unreported sales or cash sales, or intentionally reports incorrect or false manufacturing, sales or financial information;

(14) itself, or any of its manufacturing subcontractors or sub-subcontractors, manufactures, offers for sale, distributes, uses or sells any Licensed Product or Ancillary Material incorporating the Property, without the express permission of Licensor as herein provided, or manufacture or sell any disapproved products; or

(15) offers to sell, sells or ships the Licensed Products to customers or distributors outside the Channels of Distribution or the Territory or to non-Approved Customers, or to customers or distributors whom Licensee knows or should know will resell or ship the Licensed Products outside the Channels of Distribution or the Territory.

Notwithstanding the foregoing, if Licensor elects to provide Licensee with notice and an opportunity to cure any breach described in this Sections (in Licensor's sole discretion), such action will not constitute a waiver of or bar to Licensor's right to strictly enforce immediate termination in the future, without any right to cure, in the event of the same or any other breach.

B. Immediate Right to Terminate a Portion. Licensor shall have the right to immediately terminate the portion(s) of the Agreement relating to any Trademark and/or Licensed Product(s) in the Territory if Licensee, for any reason, fails to meet the Product Introduction Dates or the Initial Shipment Dates specified in Schedule A or, after the commencement of manufacture and sale of a particular Licensed Product, ceases to sell commercial quantities of such Licensed Product for three (3) consecutive Royalty Periods.

C. Right to Terminate on Notice. This Agreement may be terminated by either party upon thirty (30) days written notice to the other party in the event of a breach of a material provision of this Agreement unrelated to Licensee payment obligations by the other party, provided that, during the thirty (30) day period, the breaching party fails to cure such breach. With respect to Licensee payment obligations hereunder, Licensor may terminate this Agreement upon five (5) days written notice to Licensee in the event of a breach by Licensee of its payment obligations hereunder, provided that during this five (5) day period, Licensee fails to cure such breach.

10. Post Termination Rights

A. Inventory upon Termination. Not less than thirty (30) days prior to the expiration of this Agreement or immediately upon termination thereof, Licensee shall provide Licensor with a complete schedule of all inventory of Licensed Products then on-hand (the "Inventory").

B. Sell-Off Period. Upon expiration or termination of this Agreement except for reason of a breach of Licensee duty to comply with the quality control or legal notice marking requirements, Licensee shall be entitled, for an additional period of three (3) months and on a nonexclusive basis, to continue to sell such Inventory. Such sales shall be made subject to all the provisions of this Agreement and to an accounting for and the payment of a Royalty thereon. Such accounting and payment shall be due and paid within thirty (30) days after the close of the said three (3) month period. Licensee shall not be permitted to sell Licensed Products during this period at a price point discounted more than 50% of its traditional wholesale selling price.

C. Discontinuance of Use of the Property. Upon the expiration or termination of this Agreement, all the rights of Licensee under this Agreement, except for Licensee rights under paragraph 10B., shall forthwith terminate and immediately revert to Licensor and Licensee shall immediately discontinue all use of the Trademarks, at no cost whatsoever to Licensor.

D. <u>Return of Materials.</u> Upon termination of this Agreement for any reasons whatsoever, Licensee agrees to immediately return to Licensor all material relating to the Trademarks including, but not limited to, all artwork, color separations, prototypes and the like, as well as any market studies or other tests or studies conducted by Licensee with respect to the Trademarks, at no cost whatsoever to Licensor.

E. <u>Continued Sale of Similar Products.</u> The parties understand and agree that the Licensed Products will have acquired a particular look and feel and association with the Trademarks and Property. Accordingly, Licensee recognizes and agrees that the continued use of any similar trademark, trade name, trade dress or other industrial or intellectual property has the potential to cause significant consumer confusion after termination or expiration of this Agreement should Licensee continue to use or adopt the use of any trademark, trade name, trade dress or other industrial or intellectual property that was not a "safe distance" from the Property, Trademark or any trade name or trade dress associated therewith and Licensee hereby agrees to maintain such "safe distance" upon the termination or expiration of this Agreement.

11. **Infringements**

A. <u>Initiation of Infringement Actions.</u> Licensor shall have the right, in its discretion, to institute and prosecute lawsuits against third persons for infringement of the rights licensed in this Agreement.

B. <u>Cost of Litigation.</u> Any lawsuit shall be prosecuted solely at the cost and expense of Licensor and all sums recovered in any such lawsuits, whether by judgment, settlement or otherwise, shall be retained by Licensor.

C. <u>Cooperation of Parties.</u> Upon request of Licensor, Licensee shall execute all papers, testify on all matters, and otherwise cooperate in every way necessary and desirable for the prosecution of any such lawsuit. Licensor shall reimburse Licensee for the expenses incurred as a result of such cooperation.

12. **Indemnification.**

A. <u>Licensee Indemnity.</u> Licensee agrees to defend, indemnify and hold Licensor, and its officers, directors, employees, agents, and advisors, harmless from and against any and all costs, loses, obligations, suits, judgments, damages and costs (including reasonable attorneys' fees and costs) incurred through claims of third parties against Licensor based on the manufacture, sale, marketing, distribution, advertising or promotion of the Licensed Products including, but not limited to, actions founded on product liability or infringement of any third party intellectual property rights. Licensor shall have the right to select counsel in connection with such actions. No action may be settled or compromised without Licensor's prior express written approval.

B. <u>Licensor Indemnity.</u> Licensor agrees to defend, indemnify and hold Licensee, and its officers, directors, employees, agents and advisors, harmless from and against any and all claims, losses, obligations, suits, judgments, damages and costs (including reasonable attorneys' fees and costs) incurred through claims of third parties against Licensor based on any claim by any third party challenging Licensor's rights in the Property or its ability to enter into this Agreement including any claim for infringement of any third party rights based solely on Licensee's licensed use of the Property on the Licensed Products.

13. **Insurance.**

A. <u>Product Liability Insurance.</u> Licensee shall, throughout the Term of the Agreement, obtain and maintain at its own cost and expense from a qualified insurance company licensed to do business in [State] with a Best rating of A- or better, standard Product Liability Insurance naming Licensor as an additional named insured. Such policy shall provide protection against all claims, demands and causes of action arising out of any defects or failure to perform, alleged or otherwise, of the Licensed Products or any material used in connection therewith or any use thereof. The amount of coverage shall be as specified in Schedule A attached hereto. The policy shall provide for ten (10) days' notice to Licensor from the insurer by Registered or Certified Mail, return receipt requested, in the event of any modification, cancellation or termination thereof. Licensee agrees to furnish Licensor a certificate of insurance within thirty (30) days after execution of this Agreement and, in no event shall Licensee manufacture, distribute or sell the Licensed Products prior to receipt by Licensor of such certificate of insurance.

B. <u>Advertiser's Insurance.</u> Licensee shall, throughout the Term of the Agreement, obtain and maintain at its own cost and expense from a qualified insurance company licensed to do business in [State] with a Best rating of A- or better, standard Advertiser's Insurance naming Licensor as an additional named insured. Such policy shall provide protection against all claims, demands and causes of action arising out of any defects or failure to perform, alleged or otherwise, of the Licensed Products or any material used in connection therewith or any use thereof. The amount of coverage shall be as specified in Schedule A attached hereto. The policy shall provide for ten (10) days' notice to Licensor from the insurer by Registered or Certified Mail, return receipt requested, in the event of any modification, cancellation or termination thereof. Licensee agrees to furnish Licensor a certificate of insurance within thirty (30) days after execution of this Agreement and, in no event shall Licensee manufacture, distribute or sell the Licensed Products prior to receipt by Licensor of such certificate of insurance.

14. Relationship of the Parties.

This Agreement creates no agency relationship between the parties hereto, and nothing herein contained shall be construed to place the parties in the relationship of partners or joint venturers, and neither party shall have any power to obligate or bind the other party in any manner whatsoever.

15. Severability.

If any provision of this Agreement is held by a court or arbitrator of competent jurisdiction not enforceable to its full extent, then such provision shall be enforced to the maximum extent permitted by law, and the parties hereto consent and agree that such scope may be modified by such court or arbitrator accordingly and that the whole of such provision of this Agreement shall not thereby fail, but that the scope of such provision shall be curtailed only to the extent necessary to conform to the law.

16. Assignment and Transfer.

This Agreement shall be binding upon and shall inure to the benefit of the parties hereto and their respective successors and permitted assigns. Licensee may not assign its rights or obligations hereunder without the prior written consent of Licensor; <u>provided</u>, <u>however</u>, that Licensee may assign its rights under this Agreement without the prior written consent of Licensor to any entity controlled by or controlling Licensee. No assignment shall entitle any assignee to any greater rights hereunder than those to which the assignor was entitled. For purposes of this provision, any action by Licensee that involves a change of control of Licensee or transfers of more than 50% the outstanding stock of Licensee shall be deemed an assignment and may only be made with the prior express written approval of Licensor.

17. Waiver.

The failure or delay of either party at any time to exercise any right under any provision of this Agreement shall not limit or operate as a waiver thereof.

18. No Third-Party Beneficiaries.

Nothing in this Agreement is intended, or shall be construed, to give arty entity or individual other than the parties hereto any legal or equitable right, remedy or claim under or in respect of this Agreement or any of the provisions contained herein.

19. Equitable Relief.

Without limiting the right of Licensor to pursue all other legal and equitable rights available to it for violation of or failure of Licensee to comply with the terms of this Agreement, it is agreed that other remedies cannot fully compensate Licensor for such a violation or failure and that Licensor shall be entitled to injunctive or other equitable relief to prevent violation or continuing violation or to compel performance by Licensee. Licensee acknowledges that the restrictions in this Agreement are reasonable and that the consideration therefore is sufficient to fully and adequately compensate it therefore. Licensee further acknowledges that the Trademarks are special and unique property and cannot be replaced or otherwise substituted for by other property or by money damages. It is the intent and understanding of each party hereto that if, in any action before any court or agency legally empowered to enforce this Agreement, any term, restriction, covenant or promise in this Agreement is found to be unreasonable and for that reason unenforceable, then such term, restriction, covenant or promise shall be deemed modified to the extent necessary to make it enforceable by such court or agency.

20. Notices.

Any notice, consent or other communication required or permitted hereunder shall be in writing. It shall be deemed given when: (1) delivered personally; (2) sent by confirmed facsimile transmission; (3) sent by commercial overnight courier with written verification of receipt; or (4) sent by registered or certified mail, return receipt requested, postage prepaid, and the receipt is returned to the sender. Names, addresses and facsimile numbers for notices (unless and until written notice of other names, addresses and facsimile numbers are provided by either or both parties) are as follows:

If to Licensor: *With a copy to:*

If to Licensee: *With copy to:*

21. Confidentiality

A. Disclosure of Confidential Information. There may be occasions during the Term of this Agreement that either party discloses to the other certain confidential or proprietary information including, any information transmitted between the parties that relates to the transferring party's business, such as drawings, specifications, production schedules, test data, business practices and marketing strategies, prospective product concepts or ideas, or the like, or the terms of this Agreement ("Confidential Information"). The following will, however, not be considered Confidential Information:

(1) Information that is explicitly approved for release by the transmitting party,

(2) Information that is disclosed in a product marketed by the transmitting party,

(3) Information that was already known by the receiving party prior to receiving the information from transmitting party or becomes known by the receiving party independently through no wrongful act on the part of the receiving party, or

(4) Information that is known or available to the public.

B. Use by Receiving Party. The receiving party agrees to maintain such Confidential Information received from the transmitting party in confidence, to use it only in a manner consistent with the purpose for which it was transmitted and to not disclose it to persons not having a need to know it. If the receiving party needs to transmit such information to a third party, the receiving party shall safeguard the confidentiality of the information.

C.   Property of Transmitting Party. All materials transmitted between the parties and containing Confidential Information shall remain the property of the transmitting party and shall be returned upon request unless previously destroyed.

D.   No License Grant. The transmission of the material containing such Confidential Information shall not be construed to grant the receiving party a license of any type under any patents, know-how, copyrights or trademarks owned or controlled by the transmitting party.

E.   Survival of Termination. The obligations of the parties under this section regarding confidential information shall survive termination, expiration or non-renewal of this Agreement.

22. On-Going Cooperation.

Each party to this Agreement agrees to execute and deliver all documents and to perform all further acts and to take all further steps that may be requested by the other party and are reasonably necessary to carry out the provisions of this Agreement and the transactions contemplated hereby.

23. Independent Contractor.

Licensee shall be deemed an independent contractor, and nothing contained herein shall constitute this arrangement to be employment, a joint venture, or a partnership. Licensee shall be solely responsible for and shall hold Licensor harmless for all claims for taxes, fees, or costs arising from the manufacture, marketing, distribution or sale of Licensed Product, including but not limited to withholding, income tax, FICA, and workmen's compensation.

24. Governing Law & Disputes.

This Agreement will be governed by and construed and enforced in accordance with the laws of [State] without regard to conflicts of law principles. All disputes under this Agreement shall be resolved by the courts of the state of [State], including the United States District Court for the District of [State]. The parties all consent to the jurisdiction of such courts, agree to accept service of process by mail, and hereby waive any jurisdictional or venue defenses otherwise available to it.

25. Execution in Counterparts.

This Agreement may be executed in two or more counterparts, each of which will be deemed an original but all of which together will constitute one and the same instrument. The parties may execute this Agreement and exchange counterparts of the signature pages by means of facsimile transmission, and the receipt of such executed counterparts by facsimile transmission will be binding on the parties. Following such exchange, the parties will promptly exchange original versions of such signature pages.

26. Force Majeure.

If the performance of any part of this Agreement by either party is prevented, hindered, delayed or otherwise made impracticable because of an Act of God, riot or civil commotion, act of public enemy, terrorism, order or act of any government or governmental instrumentality (whether federal, state, local or foreign) or similar cause beyond the control of either party, that party shall be excused from such performance to the extent that performance is prevented, hindered or delayed by such causes.

27. Integration.

This Agreement constitutes the entire understanding of the parties, and revokes and supersedes all prior agreements between the parties, including any option agreements which may have been entered into between the parties, and is intended as a final expression of their Agreement. It shall not be modified or amended except in writing signed by the parties hereto and specifically referring to this Agreement. This Agreement shall take precedence over any other documents which may conflict with said Agreement.

IN WITNESS WHEREOF, the parties hereto have executed this Agreement as of the Effective Date.

LICENSOR   **LICENSEE**

By:_____   By:_____

Title:_____   Title_____

Date:_____   Date:_____

SCHEDULE A TO LICENSE AGREEMENT

1.   PROPERTY:

2.   TRADEMARKS:

3.   LICENSED TERRITORY:

4.   LICENSED PRODUCTS:

5.   CHANNELS OF DISTRIBUTION:

6.   APPROVED CUSTOMERS:

7.   ROYALTY RATE:

        Domestic Sales Rate:

        FOB Sales Rate:

        Direct Sales Rate:

8.   GUARANTEED MINIMUM ROYALTY:

9.   ADVANCE:

10.   MARKETING FEE:

11.   PRODUCT INTRODUCTION DATE:

12.   INITIAL SHIPMENT DATE:

13   MINIMUM ANNUAL SALES:

14.   MINIMUM ADVERTISING EXPENDITURE:

15.   TERM:

16.   INSURANCE REQUIREMENTS:

17.   MARKETING REQUIREMENTS:

EXHIBIT A TO LICENSE AGREEMENT

LIMA Code of Business Practices

The International Licensing Industry Merchandisers' Association, Inc. ("LIMA") is committed on behalf of its member companies to the operation of factories manufacturing licensed products in a lawful, safe, and healthful manner. It upholds the principles that no underage, forced, or prison labor* should be employed; that no one is denied a job because of gender, ethnic origin, religion, affiliation or association, and that factories comply with laws protecting the environment. Supply agreements with firms manufacturing licensed products on behalf of LIMA members should also provide for adherence to these principles.

The role of LIMA is to inform, educate, and survey its members so that individual member companies can adhere to its Code of Business Practices. As an Association, it also acts to encourage local and national governments to enforce wage and hour laws and factory health and safety laws. Specific operating conditions that member companies are encouraged to meet and obtain contractor agreement in advance are as follows:

1) LABOR

a) That wages and overtime pay practices comply with the standards set by law, including the payment of compensation for overtime hours at such premium rates as is legally required in that country, but not less than at a rate equal to their regularly hourly compensation rate.

b) That working hours must exceed prevailing local work hours in the country where the work is to be performed, except with respect to appropriately compensated overtime; must not require more than a 60-hour week on a regularly scheduled basis; and must permit at least one day off in every 7-day period.

c) That no one under the legal minimum age is employed in any stage of manufacturing; that a minimum age of 14 applies in all circumstances, but notwithstanding the foregoing, that C138 Minimum Age Convention (1973) and C182 Worst Forms of Child Labor Convention (1999) of the International Labor Organization apply.

d) That no forced or prison labor is employed*, that workers are free to leave once their shift ends, and that guards are posted only for normal security reasons.

e) That all workers are entitled to sick and maternity benefits as provided by law.

f) That all workers are entitled to freely exercise their rights of employee representation as provided by local law.

2) THE WORKPLACE

a) That factories provide a safe and healthy working environment for their employees and comply with or exceed all applicable local laws concerning sanitation and risk protection.

b) That the factory is properly lighted and ventilated, and that aisles and exits are accessible always.

c) That there is adequate medical assistance available in emergencies and that designated employees are trained in first aid procedures.

d) That there are adequate and well-identified emergency exits, and that all employees are trained in emergency evacuation.

e) That protective safety equipment is available, and employees are trained in its use.

f) That safeguards on machinery meet or exceed local laws.

g) That there are adequate toilet facilities which meet local hygiene requirements and that they are properly maintained.

h) That there are facilities or appropriate provisions for meals and other breaks.

i) If a factory provides housing for its employees, it will ensure that dormitory rooms and sanitary facilities meet basic needs, are adequately ventilated and meet fire safety and other local laws.

j) That all employees are treated with dignity and respect and that no employee shall be subjected to any physical, sexual, psychological or verbal harassment or abuse.

k) That no mental or physical disciplinary practices are employed.

l) That factories shall recognize and respect the rights of employees to associate, organize and bargain collectively in a lawful and peaceful manner, without penalty or interference.

m) That factories shall not discriminate based on race, religion, age, nationality, social or ethnic origin, sexual orientation, gender, political opinion or disability.

3. COMPLIANCE

a) The purpose of this Code is to establish a standard of performance, to educate, and to encourage a commitment to responsible manufacturing, not to punish.

b) To determine adherence, LIMA member companies will evaluate their own facilities as well as those of their contractors. They will examine all books and records and conduct on-site inspections of the facilities and request that their contractors follow the same practices with subcontractors.

c) An annual statement of compliance with this Code should be signed by an officer of each manufacturing company or contractor.

d) Contracts for the manufacture of licensed products should provide that a material failure to comply with the Code or to implement a corrective action plan on a timely basis is a breach of contract for which the contract may be canceled.

e) Because of the great diversity in the kinds of licensed products manufactured and the manufacturing methods used, as well as the wide range in factory sizes and numbers of employees, a rule of reason must be used to determine applicability of these provisions.

f) This Code should be posted or available for all employees in the local language.

* Many countries recognize that prison labor is essential to the rehabilitation process. This provision prohibits the exportation of prison-made goods to countries that prohibit or restrict the importation of such goods.

Appendix-5
PRODUCT CATEGORIES

International Class 3

Room fragrances; potpourri; scented oils for refreshing potpourri; refills for electric room fragrance dispensers, Cosmetics; soap, namely, skin soaps, liquid soaps, cosmetic soaps, soaps for personal use, soaps for household use; cosmetic preparations for baths; perfumes; eaux de cologne; pre-shave and after-shave lotions; shaving creams; hair shampoos and conditioners; dentifrices, mouthwashes; personal deodorants and antiperspirants; cosmetic nourishing creams; skin creams; exfoliant creams for the face, make-up removing preparations; sun care lotions; hair lotions, hair spray; make-up preparations; eye shadows; face powder; cosmetic pencils; decorative transfers for cosmetic purposes; cleaning, polishing, scouring and abrasive preparations for household purposes; laundry products in powder form, namely, laundry soap and laundry detergent; synthetic detergents for household use; polishes and waxes for footwear, namely, shoe polish and shoe wax; preservatives for leather, namely, creams for leather, leather cleaning preparations, leather polishes, leather preserving polishes, and preservative creams for leather; bleaching preparations for laundry use, stain removing preparations, and laundry detergent; essential oils

International Class 4

Candles, Christmas tree candles

International Class 5

Vitamin fortified beverages, Pharmaceuticals, namely vitamins and mineral supplements; Medicinal drinks, Dietary supplemental drinks, chelated vitamin supplement in jelly bean format; Restorative nutritionally fortified beverages for use preceding or following blood donations by human; Nutritional supplements

International Class 6

Wall hooks of metal; non-luminous and non-mechanical signs made of metal; metal step stools; sculptures and Christmas stocking holders made of non-precious metal; metal coin banks; metal cash boxes and metal piggy banks; common metal drawer pulls; containers and banks made of tin and metal; metal signs, metal rings and chains for keys; ornaments, namely, bronze holiday ornaments and holiday ornaments of common metal; statues, statuettes, sculptures and trophies, all of common metal; fixed metal napkin dispensers; printed metal disks for collection purposes being pogs in the nature of collectible printed metal bottle caps; emblems of metal for vehicles; metal license plates; common metals and their alloys, unwrought or semi-wrought; building materials of metal, namely, soffits, fascia, flashing, linings, trim, wall framing and composite panels, ceiling boards and floor boards, awnings of metal, metal partitions for building, metal reinforcement materials for building; transportable buildings of metal; metal materials for railway tracks; non-electric cables and wires of common metal; ironmongery in the nature of small items of metal hardware, namely, screws, nails, pulleys, springs, nuts, washers, buckles, metal locks and keys therefor, door handles, door knobs, door and window hinges, door and window locks, door and window fittings, bolts, hooks, and brackets; metal pipes; metal safes; ores, namely, metal ores, iron ores, lead ores, nickel ores, zinc ores, tin ores, copper ores

International Class 8

Flatware; fire place tool sets sold as a unit; pocket knives; non-electric can openers; nut crackers not of precious metal

International Class 9

Disposable cameras; 35 mm cameras; calculators; computer peripherals; anti-glare guards for computer monitor screens; wrist rests for use with computers; wrists supports for computer mouse users; mouse pads; computer mouse covers; computer screen saver software; storage cases for compact discs and blank video cassettes; radios; CD players; digital video device players; portable listening devices, namely, MP3 players; video cassette players; audio cassette recorders; digital audio tape players; turntables; neon signs; telephones; thermometers not for medical use; binoculars; decorative magnets; magnetic memo holders for refrigerators and kitchen cabinets; kitchen timers; eyeglass cases; specialty holsters for carrying cellular phones;

covers for cellular phones; sunglasses; vending machines; bicycle helmets; protective helmets; rain gauges; digital cellular phones; pre-recorded compact discs featuring music stories and games for children; pre-recorded digital video discs and video cassettes featuring animated children's adventure and comedy movies and music; computer game programs; motion picture films in the field of animated children's comedy and adventure, live-action comedy, drama and TV shows; digital audio players; digital cameras; TV and DVD combination machines; DVD players and television sets; computer software featuring learning activities in the nature of word building and spelling activities, word recognition, relating pictures to words, phonics, simple math skills, greater-than, less-than, more-or-less-than activities, sorting, number recognition, counting and drawing instructions; consumer electronic goods, namely, portable compact disc players; DVD and VCR combination players; desktop personal computers; portable personal computers; handheld computers; portable radios; walkie-talkies; cordless telephones; telephones; video cameras; video game interactive hand held remote controls in the nature of consoles for playing electronic games; computer hardware and peripherals; computer software featuring music, stories, activities, games, and other such educational and entertainment topics for children; motion picture films featuring comic book characters in live action and animated adventure; pre-recorded CDs, video tapes and DVDs featuring live action adventure programs, motion pictures featuring comic book characters in live action and animated adventure, and animated cartoons in the field of action adventure based on comic book characters; computer game discs; computer game cartridges; computer game programs; video game discs; video game software; video game cartridges; credit cards; phone cards; debit cards; cash cards; motion picture films featuring comedy, drama, action, adventure and/or animation, and digital versatile discs featuring music, comedy, drama, action, adventure, and/or animations; motion picture films featuring comedy, drama, action, adventure and/or animation, and digital versatile discs featuring music, comedy, drama, action, adventure, and/or animation; spectacles and spectacle cases

International Class 11

Electric ceiling light fixtures; shades and globes for fixtures; lamp shades and lamp globes; lamp finials; lamps; electric night lights; flashlights; electric holiday lights; electric string lights for decorating; fans, namely, ceiling fans; electric fans; barbecue grills; refrigerators; decorative table-top water fountains; electric portable coolers which operate like a refrigerating unit

International Class 12

Bicycles, motorcycles; automobiles; trucks; vans; motor buses; motor homes; refrigerated vehicles; airplanes; boats; vehicular air balloons; airships; motor car accessories, namely, anti-dazzle screens in the nature of sunshields and visors for motor cars, pneumatic tires, casings for pneumatic tires, luggage racks, ski racks, wheel rims, and hubcaps; seat covers for vehicles, fitted covers for vehicles, baby carriages, strollers, safety seats for infants and children for vehicles; engines and motors for land vehicles; headlight covers for vehicles; steering wheels for vehicles; trailers; land vehicles; apparatus for locomotion by land, air or water, namely, lorries, pickup trucks, sports utility vehicles, campers, aircraft, aerostats, ships; vehicle parts, namely, radiator grills; automotive parts, namely, wheels, wheel rim spacers, wheel covers, tires, spare tire covers

International Class 14

Clocks; clocks incorporating radios; watches and parts for watches; jewelry; precious metal money clips; jewelry, namely, lapel pins; cabinet hardware, namely, drawer pulls of precious metal; pins and medallions made of precious metal; jewelry namely, bracelets, brooches, earrings, ornamental pins, pendants and rings; straps for wrist watches; goods made of precious metals, alloys, or coated, namely, ornamental pins, ash trays for smokers, decorative boxes and jewelry boxes, jewelry cases and watch cases, powder compacts sold empty; jewelry, namely, rings, cuff links, charms, necklaces, tie pins, and medallions; keyrings made of precious metal; buckles made of precious metal, namely, buckles for belts, buckles for clothing, buckles for scarves, buckles for hats, buckles for jewelry, buckles for shoes, buckles for bags, buckles for boxes, buckles for trunks, buckles for cases, buckles for purses, buckles for wallets, buckles for umbrellas, buckles for canes, buckles for clocks; horological and chronometric instruments, namely, watches, wrist-watches, clocks, chronographs, chronometers and alarm clocks; and watch cases

International Class 15

Music boxes; musical figurines; musical dioramas

Appendices

International Class 16

Paper napkins, paper placemats, paper table cloths, paper coasters; stationery, namely, writing paper, writing pads, note pads, postcards, greeting cards, note cards, notebooks, note paper; writing instruments; bookmarks; bookends; posters; prints; school supplies, namely, drawing rulers, erasers, markers, note book paper, rubber stamps; office requisites, namely, staplers, pen and pencil holders, desktop business card holders; magnetic memo holders; paper clip holders, paper clips; gift wrapping paper; paper gift bags; paper gift tags; stencils; tissue paper; paper bags; children's activity books; erasable memorandum boards; folders; calendars; letter openers; stickers; decals; book covers; chalk boards for school and home use; lunch bags; trading cards; Christmas cards; lithographs; bank checks; checkbook covers; address labels; printed products, namely, menu boards; recipe books; recipe cards; art prints; erasable memo boards; address books; appliqués in the form of decals; arts and craft paint kits; ball-point pens; periodicals and magazines all featuring stories; games and activities for children; paper gift wrap bows; decorative paper centerpieces; chalk; paper party decorations; diaries; pens; pencils; memo pads; pencil sharpeners; photograph albums; appointment books; autograph books; baby books; paper party bags; binders; books featuring stories, games and activities for children; gift cards; cartoon prints; pen and pencil cases; children's activity books; modeling clay; coloring books; comic books; paper party hats; envelopes; children's story books; publications, particularly comic books and magazines and stories in illustrated form; sticker books; kits primarily comprised of crayons, markers, paints, paint brushes and parts sold as units for coloring, painting and handicraft activities; slates; school supplies; printed transfers for embroidery or fabric appliqués; printed patterns for costumes, pajamas, sweatshirts and t-shirts; magazines featuring characters from animated, action adventure, comedy and/or drama features; mounted and/or unmounted photographs; paper photo frames; paper doilies; invitations; paper cake decorations; colored pencils; catalogues; anthologies; covers for pocket and desk diaries; checkbook holders; nibs; telephone indexes

International Class 18

Purses; handbags; general gear carrying bags; wallets; billfolds; fanny packs; gym bags; backpacks; luggage; luggage tags; tote bags; travel bags; duffel bags; beach bags; business card cases; umbrellas; café umbrellas; trunks; key-cases; general purpose sports bags; tote bags; backpacks; knapsacks; book bags; ladies' handbags; trunks; traveling trunks; suitcases; garment bags for travel; hat boxes for travel; shoe bags for travel; animal carriers; haversacks; leather or textile shopping bags; vanity cases sold empty; attaché cases; travel satchels; clutch bags; briefcases; credit card cases; bill and card holders; checkbook holders; key cases; change purses; briefcase-type portfolios

International Class 20

Step stools; drinking straws; plastic novelty license plates; indoor and outdoor furniture; garden umbrellas; picture frames; wooden signs; wood boxes; pillows; cushions; inflatable plastic signs; plastic boxes; air mattresses for use when camping; air cushions not for medical purposes; air pillows not for medical purposes; air mattresses; non-electric fans for personal use; mirrors; figurines and Christmas stocking holders of wood, plastic, and cold cast resin; electrically-activated moving Christmas figures made of plastic; bar stools; engraved and cut stone plaques; chair pads; dispensers for pills or capsules sold empty; jewelry boxes not of precious metal; tables; baker's racks; sofas; chairs; ottomans; cabinets; plastic key rings; non-metal shower hooks; plastic banners; non-metal clips for bags; ceramic fan pulls; boxes made of wood; works of art made of wood, wax, plaster or plastic; plastic license plate frames; sleeping bags; plastic cake decorations; non-metal key chains

International Class 21

Plates; cups; drinking glasses; tankards not of precious metal; mugs; tumblers; drinking steins; pitchers; decanters, goblets; ice buckets, coasters not of paper and not being table linen; serving pieces, namely, serving tongs, serving platters; serving trays not of precious metal; salt and pepper shakers; condiment holders, sugar dispensers and basins, sugar shakers; toothpick holders; toothpick dispensers; napkin holders; napkin dispensers; dispensers for paper towels; holders for facial tissue; picnic baskets; trivets, cookie jars; canister sets, storage containers for household and kitchen use not of precious metal; party bowls; floral containers; bottle openers; straw dispensers; dinnerware, bottles sold empty; dishware, namely, plates, bowls, cups and saucers; creamer pitchers; candy dishes; spoon rests; flower pots; corn cob holders; cutting boards; cookie cutters; candle holders not of precious metal; bread boxes; bird houses of wood; cooking utensils, namely, grill covers; utensils for barbecues, namely, turners; stove burner covers; recipe boxes; coffee pots not of precious metal; tea pots not of precious metal; utensils for barbecues, namely, forks, tongs and spatulas; lunch boxes; soap and shampoo dispensers; toothbrush holders; wastepaper baskets; thermal insulated containers for beverages; portable coolers; portable ice chests for food and beverages; thermal insulated wrap for cans to keep the contents cold or hot; foam drink holders; non-metal coin banks; china, crystal, glass and porcelain ornaments, not including Christmas tree ornaments; sun catchers; wind chimes; vases; crystal, glass, porcelain, china and ceramic figurines and Christmas stocking holders; decorative plates; ice buckets; squeeze bottles sold empty; insulated picnic and lunch containers; crystal party bowls; decanters; plastic cups; wastebaskets; glass holders; combs; toothbrushes; lunch box with insulated beverage container; earthenware goods, namely, coffee mugs, mugs, jugs, bowls, plates, coffee cups, and cups; beverage glassware, namely, jugs mugs and drinking glasses; demitasse sets consisting of cups and saucers; cookie jars; ceramic, glass and china figurines; tea caddies; cake molds; canteens; champagne buckets; cocktail shakers; thermal insulated containers for food or beverages; corn cob holders; vacuum bottles; drinking flasks; shower caddies; serving utensils, namely, pie servers, cake turners, spatulas, scrapers, and cake servers; plastic coasters; cookie cutters; cork screws; gardening gloves; rubber household gloves; demitasse sets consisting of cups and saucers; sugar and creamer sets; infant cups; non-electric coffee pots; money boxes

International Class 24

Bedding, namely, sheets, blankets, comforters, bedspreads, dust ruffles, shams, pillow cases; blanket throws; quilts; afghans; pot holders; oven mitts; barbecue mitts; fingertip towels; towels; dishcloths; fabric table runners; table linen, namely, napkins, tablecloths and placemats; vinyl place mats; plastic place mats; textile place mats; tapestry-style wall hangings of textile; cloth banners; fabric flags; cloth pennants; door stops made of fabric; shower curtains; window treatments, namely, poufs, puffs and swags; textile fabric piece goods for use in clothing items, curtains, bedclothes, tablecloths, napkins, table runners, placemats, upholstered furniture, duvet covers, shower curtains and the like; bed linens; draperies; bath linens; beach towels; travel blankets; textile and textile goods, namely, household linen including bed and bath linen, handkerchiefs of textile

International Class 25

Clothing for men, women and children, namely, belts, jackets, coats, tops, vests, shirts, blouses, jogging suits; jerseys, bottoms, shorts, pants, trousers, boxer shorts, dresses, skirts, neckties, scarves, bandannas, night gowns, night shirts, pajamas, loungewear, socks, sweaters, sweat shirts, sweat pants, cummerbunds, aprons, t-shirts, headwear, hats, caps; sun visors; slippers; footwear; jackets; coats; jeans; robes; belts; cloth bibs for infants; sleepers; infant wear; bathing suits; beach wear; underwear; Halloween costumes and masks sold in connection therewith; masquerade costumes; hosiery; mittens; shoes; tank tops; tights; head bands; boots; sandals; rainwear; overalls; leisurewear; ties; lingerie; shawls; polo shirts

International Class 26

Clothing, namely, belt buckles not of precious metal; thimbles; ornamental novelty pins; embroidered patches for clothing; embroidery; clothing hooks; artificial wreaths; braids; tassels; ribbons; buttons; needles; sewing boxes; pins for clothing not of precious metals, namely, ornamental novelty pins, ornamental novelty badges, and pins with glass beads; brooches for clothing; hair nets, hair bands; barrettes; hair pins; hair ribbons; pins, of non-precious metal, namely, bonnet pins, sewing pins, hat pins, ornamental novelty pins, safety pins, and bobby pins; cords; strips for clothing, namely, lanyards in the nature of straps for clothing; belt clasps; competitors' numbers not of textile used in competitions and for advertising purposes; shoe ornaments not of precious metal; other decorative articles for the hair included in this class, namely, hair ornaments, hair clips, hair ties, hair scrunchies, hair bows, hair buckles, hair chopsticks, hair sticks, ponytail holders; insignia or lapel pins not of precious metal, including letters and human characters; heat activated insignia or yokes by means of heat transfer; lapel pins made of plastic materials; lace; embroidery; braids; hooks and eyes; artificial flowers; badges of metal

International Class 27

Rugs; carpets; shoe scrapers, namely door mats; bath mats; wallpaper; tapestry-style wall hangings, not of textile

Appendices

International Class 28

Action figures and accessories; action skill games; board games; toy building blocks; dolls and doll clothing; doll playsets; checker sets; playing cards; card games; puzzles; balloons; hand held unit for playing electronic games; Christmas decorations and accessories of all kinds, namely, Christmas tree skirts, artificial Christmas garlands; Christmas tree ornaments; Christmas stockings; Christmas tree decorations; snow globes; sporting equipment and accessories for soccer, namely, soccer balls; sporting equipment and accessories for golf, namely, golf balls, golf tees, golf ball markers, ball cleaners, golf putters, divot repair tools, golf bags; sporting equipment and accessories for skating, namely, in-line skates, skate boards; elbow pads for athletic use; knee pads for athletic use; shin pads for athletic use; badminton game playing equipment; sporting equipment and accessories for fishing, namely, fishing lures; billiard cues, billiard balls, billiard game playing equipment and accessories, namely billiard bridges, billiard bumpers, billiard chalk, billiard cue racks, billiard cushions, billiard nets, billiard tables, billiard tally balls, billiard tips, billiard triangles, cue sticks for billiard or pool; snow sleds for recreational use; pinball machines; sport balls; toy vehicles and accessories; toy electric trains; toy model train sets; train set accessories, namely, artificial trees, turf, foliage, ballast, buildings, figurines, billboards, lichen and grass; toy banks, toy mobiles, multiple activity baby toys; dart board cases; dart boards; dolls and accessories therefor; plush toys; yo-yos; flying discs; inflatable toys; non-powered toy vehicles; die cast metal vehicles; railroad cars; trains; whistles; bath toys; crib toys; manipulative games; jigsaw puzzles; kites; music box toys; party favors in the nature of small toys; inflatable pool toys; disc-type toss toys; model toy cars; hand-held unit for playing electronic games; musical toys; modeled plastic toy figurines; puppets; toy scooters; talking toys; bubble making wands and solution sets; model toy trucks; roller skates; bats; marbles; water-play toys; snow, sand and lawn toys; toy masks; balls; playsets sold as a unit for creative play activities; video games cartridges; game equipment sold as a unit for playing a board game, a card game, a manipulative game, a parlor game and an action type target game

International Class 29

Milk and milk products, namely, dairy-based chocolate-flavored food beverage drinks; strawberry-flavored milk-based drinks; yogurt-based drinks; meat; fish; poultry; game; meat extracts; canned fish and meat; cooked fruits and vegetables; canned fruit and vegetables; edible oils and fats; potato chips; French fries; prepared nuts; jams; marmalades and jellies; milk; milk based products, namely, dairy-based beverages, drinking yogurts, dairy products excluding ice cream, ice milk, and frozen yogurt; cheese; soya milk; preserved, frozen and dried fruit and vegetables; eggs

International Class 30

Breakfast cereals and pastry; bubble gum, cake decorations made of candy, chewing gum, sugar confectionery; edible decorations for cake; coffee; tea; cocoa, chocolates; sugar; honey; artificial coffee; flour; preparations made from cereals, namely, ready to eat cereals, cereal derived food bars, cereal based energy bars, cereal based snack food; processed cereals and breakfast cereals; bread; pastries; pies; dough; cakes; biscuits and cookies; crackers; salted biscuits; candy; edible ices; confectionery, namely, frozen confections, gum sweets, sweet bakery goods, and ice cream; rice; dried cereal flakes; mustard; vinegar; sauces; spices; salt; salt for preserving food; tapioca; sago; golden syrup; yeast, baking-powder; ice for refreshment

International Class 32

Non-alcoholic beverages, namely, carbonated beverages, soft drinks, diet soft drinks, low calorie soft drinks, energy drinks, guarana drinks, sports drinks, smoothies, herbal juices, carbonated waters, health and wellness drinks in the nature of fruit drinks and lemonades, flavored waters, non-alcoholic malt beverages, non-alcoholic malt coolers, non-alcoholic beverages with tea flavor, fruit drinks and juices, vegetable drinks and juices, isotonic beverages, hypertonic beverages, hypotonic beverages, drinking water with vitamins, energy drinks enhanced with vitamins, sports drinks enhanced with vitamins, and non-carbonated, non-alcoholic frozen flavored beverages; syrups and powders for making non-alcoholic beverages; mineral and aerated waters; isotonic beverages; fruit and vegetable drinks; fruit and vegetable juices; iced fruit beverages; beers, lager, stout and porter; strong dark beers; light beers and ales; non-alcoholic beers

International Class 34

Cigar and cigarette cases not of precious metal, cigar cutters, cigar and cigarette holders not of precious metal

International Class 35

Employment agencies; personnel recruitment and personnel selection services for others; rental of billboards; rental of advertising space; promotional agency services for sport and public relations; marketing research; conducting public opinion polls; database compilation services, namely, compilation and systemization of information into computer databases; database management services; retail store services featuring solvents, paraffin, wax, bitumen and petroleum, clothing, footwear, headgear, sporting articles, stationery, apparatus for recording, transmitting and reproducing sound and images, books, video games, toys, dolls, newspapers, magazines, publications, pins, badges, key rings, tickets, jewelry, watches, bags, briefcases, flags, non-alcoholic and alcoholic beverages, smokers' articles, and confectionery; the bringing together, for the benefit of others, of a variety of goods excluding the transport thereof, namely, solvents, paraffin, wax, bitumen and petroleum, clothing, footwear, headgear, sporting articles, stationery, apparatus for recording, transmitting and reproducing sound and images, books, video games, toys, dolls, newspapers, magazines, publications, pins, badges, key rings, tickets, jewelry, watches, bags, briefcases, flags, non-alcoholic and alcoholic beverages, smokers' articles, and confectionery, to enable customers to conveniently view and purchase these goods via the Internet; business information services provided online from a computer database or over the Internet; compilation of advertising messages used as Web pages on the Internet; compiling indexes intended to be published on the Internet or other wireless electronic communication networks; providing spaces on websites on the Internet for advertising goods and services; auctioneering services provided on the Internet; business administration services for the processing of sales made over the Internet. customer loyalty services and customer club services, for commercial, promotional and/or advertising purposes; promoting the goods and services of others by means of a preferred customer program through the issuance and distribution of encoded loyalty cards for supporters which can contain personal information on the identity of the cardholder and which allows access control at sports stadiums; promoting sports competitions and events of others in the nature of basketball events and basketball competitions; sponsorship search for football competitions; personnel management consulting for sports teams; promotion of basketball-related sports events for others; promotion of goods and services for others, by means of contractual agreements, particularly sponsorship and license agreements, providing them with increased reputation and enhanced image derived by means of sporting and cultural events; advertising services; business management; business administration; providing office functions; sponsorship search for basketball competitions

International Class 36

Issuance and management of credit cards and travelers' checks; financial services, namely, financial advice and provision of financial information; banking services; credit services, namely, credit and loan services and credit card services; investment services, namely, investment of funds for others; insurance underwriting services for all types of insurance; hire-purchase financing; brokerage for hire-purchase; rental services, namely, rental of offices, apartments, vacation homes, condominiums, cabins, flats, studios, rooms, and homes; financial sponsorship of sports events; information services about finance and insurance, provided from a computer database or via the Internet or on any wireless electronic communications network; home banking services; banking services via the Internet or any wireless electronic communications network; payment services by mobile telephony, namely, providing secure commercial transactions and payment options using a mobile device at a point of sale; payment services via mobile telephone, namely, electronic processing and transmission of bill payment data for payments; bill payment services via mobile telephone; safe deposit box services; financial affairs, namely, financial analysis and consultation, financial planning, financial management, financial research, banking, mortgage brokerage, mortgage lending, and financing services; monetary affairs, namely, money transfer, money order services, money order payment guarantee services, money lending; real estate affairs, namely, real estate consultancy, real estate management services, real estate agencies

International Class 38

Telecommunication services, namely, local and long distance transmission of voice, data, graphics by means of telephone, telegraphic, cable, and satellite transmissions; transmission of voice, data, graphics, sound, and video by means of wireless or cable networks; wireless transmission of data, images, telephone voice messaging services; digital network telecommunication services; information transmission via wireless or cable networks; electronic transmission of data, images, voice messaging; network telecommunications, namely, transmission of voice, audio, visual images and data by telecommunications networks, wireless communication networks, the Internet, information services networks and data networks; providing access to telecommunication networks; messaging services, namely, electronic mail and messaging services, instant messaging services, and wireless digital messaging services; services of an Internet access provider, namely, providing access to the Internet; providing Internet access to search engines and to search portals on the Internet; providing on-line chat forums and electronic bulletin boards for transmission of messages among users in the field of general interest on the Internet; providing on-line forums for transmission of messages among computer users on the Internet; electronic exchange of data stored in databases accessible via telecommunication networks via chatlines, chatrooms and other Internet forums; providing interactive forums for transmission of messages among users in the field of general interest; provision of Internet access to data banks, in particular on-line data banks relating to sports; electronic transmission of messages and images via computer, SMS, UMPTS and WAP; television program broadcasting, video broadcasting, and radio program broadcasting. video broadcasting and transmission services via the Internet, featuring films, movies, television programs, and videos; Internet radio broadcasting services, namely, broadcasting of radio programs; broadcasting of radio and television programs relating to sports or sports events; Internet broadcasting; provision of Internet access to data banks of digital music and to MP3 web sites

International Class 39

Travel agency services, namely, organization of travel and trips and making reservations and bookings for transportation and for temporary lodging; travel and tour ticket reservation services and information services for travel and ticket sales; air transport services, passenger train transport services, freight train transport services, bus transport services and truck transport services; boat transport; arranging of boat tours; organization of sightseeing tours; rental of vehicles; rental of parking spaces; taxi transport; ferry-boat transport, cargo ship transport, transport of goods by ship; water distribution; heat supplying; gas supplying; electricity distribution; postal, courier, and messenger services, namely, delivery of newspapers, magazines and books; delivery of goods by mail order; postal, messenger, freight, and courier services; distribution of solvents, paraffin, wax, bitumen, petroleum, oil, lubricants, and fuel, excluding liquified gas; distribution services, namely, delivery of films and sound and image recordings; distribution services, namely, delivery of interactive educational and entertainment products, interactive compact disks, CD-ROMs, computer programs and computer games; transport of goods; packaging of articles for transportation; storage of goods

International Class 41

Educational services, namely, providing seminars and workshops in the field of basketball and distributing course materials in connection therewith; training in the areas of coaching and refereeing of basketball; training in the field of sport events organization, administration and management; entertainment, namely, basketball games; organizing sporting and cultural events; organization of basketball events and competitions; sports and entertainment hospitality services, namely, arranging, organizing, conducting, and hosting parties and social entertainment events in conjunction with sporting events; hospitality services for customers, namely, providing facilities for receptions including providing entrance tickets to sports, entertainment, or leisure events; entertainment services relating to or provided during sporting events, namely, laser shows, audio and visual performances, live performances by a musical band, dance performances, preparation of special effects, and fireworks display; entertainment services consisting of the public rebroadcasting of sporting events; entertainment services in the form of public viewings of sports events, namely, basketball games; providing on-line publications in the nature of magazines in the field of basketball; publication and electronic publication of printed matter; entertainment services in the nature of development, creation, production and post-production services of multimedia entertainment content for television, radio and the Internet featuring basketball events, basketball championships, basketball games, interviews and highlights; entertainment through television, radio and the Internet, namely, basketball events, basketball championships, basketball games, interviews and highlights; interactive entertainment, namely, providing temporary use of non-downloadable interactive games; interactive entertainment, namely, arranging and conducting online contests. providing games, namely, providing online computer games, online video games, and online electronic games; operating lotteries; organization of sports competitions; betting and casino gaming services in connection with or relating to sports, also via the Internet; film production; production of audio and video recordings; rental of films, audio and video recordings; production and rental of interactive educational and entertainment television and radio programs; production of interactive educational and entertainment computer games; rental of

CDs and interactive CD-ROMS and computer games; electronic game competitions organized on-line via the Internet; information services in connection with sports and sports events, including providing information via data banks on-line, via the Internet and via satellite or cable, mobile telephone or wireless networks; publication of statistics; publication of statistics or other information relating to sports performances; reservation of tickets for sporting and cultural activities; providing a website allowing users to upload and download digital music; providing of non-downloadable, pre-recorded digital music via the Internet and via MP3 web sites; timing of sports events; rental of sporting infrastructures

International Class 42

Retail variety store services; restaurant services; snack bar services; hospitality services, namely, providing of food and drink; catering services; hotel services; providing of food and drink and temporary housing accommodations; making hotel reservations for others; making reservations and bookings for temporary lodging; making reservations and bookings for others for accommodations and meals at hotels; hospitality services, namely, provision of food and drink at sports or entertainment events; hospitality suites, namely, providing accommodation, food and drink both inside and outside sports facilities

Appendices

Appendix-6
STYLE GUIDE

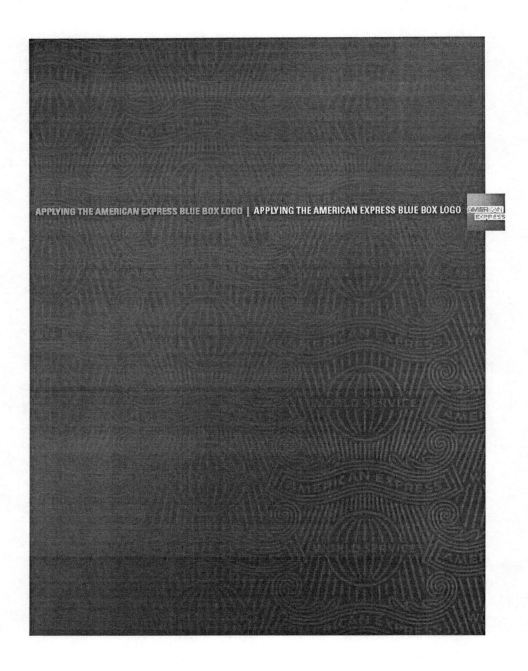

Contents and Overview

Size and Color   1

Clear Space and Placement   2

Registration Mark   3

Do's and Don'ts   4

The American Express Blue Box logo is recognized around the world as a symbol of our commitment to unsurpassed service, expertise, and integrity. To support our strong and recognizable visual identity, it is essential to use the Blue Box logo in the colors and formats specified in these guidelines.

Because of its global recognition and equity, all American Express products are marketed with the Blue Box logo. To prevent consumer confusion, no new logos may be created for any American Express product, service, marketing program or business unit. Please contact Global Brand Management for more information.

To download logo artwork visit the American Express Brand site www.americanexpress.com/brand or e-mail Logo Request on Lotus Notes.

Size and Color

The recommended size of the Blue Box logo is 0.5" (12.7mm) wide for most standard-page size applications. The minimum size is 0.375"(9.525mm). The recommended online size for the logo is 45 x 45 pixels.

The 4-color, 2-color, and black and white Blue Box logos each contain a radial gradient specifically created to enhance the contrast between the Blue Box and the background.

In all versions of the logo, the outline of the words "American Express" in the Blue Box must always be white, regardless of the background color on which the logo appears. In print communications, use the appropriate color formula based on the paper stock selected (coated vs. uncoated).

*The colors reproduced here are not intended to match Pantone® color standards, which are available from Pantone, Inc. Be sure to use the actual Pantone colors as noted.

Recommended Size: 0.5" (12.7mm)

Minimum Size: 0.375" (9.525mm)

The **4-color gradient** [AXP_4C_grad.eps] is the recommended format version and should be used whenever possible.

The **2-color gradient** [AXP_2C_grad.eps/ blueboxgradFS_2C_grad.eps] version, created with Pantone®* 285 and Pantone® 297, is for use in premium spot-color applications.

The **black and white gradient** [AXP_BW_grad.eps] version is recommended for applications limited to black and white printing.

For special situations (like embroidery), a **1-color solid in Pantone 285** [AXP_1C_solid.eps] and a **1-color solid black** [AXP_BW_spot.eps] version were created without the radial gradient to ensure that the Blue Box logo reproduces at the highest quality.

Appendices

Clear Space and Placement

Always use the recommended clear space of 1/3 the width of the Blue Box, as shown, to maintain optimum legibility and avoid interference from nearby text, complex illustrations, or other elements that might compromise the logo's impact. If the logo is placed over simple photographic imagery or graphics, the contrast level and integrity of the logo must not be compromised.

Clear space between the Blue Box logo and another logo should equal at least 1 1/2 times the width of the Blue Box. Logos should never be stacked vertically. The American Express Blue Box logo should always appear on the right.

There is one exception to the clear space rule: An alternate clear space of 1/5x has been defined for use with the new American Express Brand thread. This relationship is further defined on the Blue Box thread page within the American Express Brand site: www.americanexpress.com/brand.

Clear Space

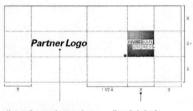

Horizontally center the partner logo with the American Express Blue Box

X equals the height of the Blue Box

Logo Lockup and Clear Space

Registration Mark

The registration mark "®" must always appear with the American Express Blue Box logo. It must always appear as blue except in the 1-color black and white versions, where it should appear as black.

All size relationships are fixed and part of the electronic artwork available in the Downloads section of the American Express Brand Site: www.americanexpress.com/brand

Examples of correct placement and usage of the registration mark are shown here and throughout these guidelines.

Do's and Don'ts

The following examples illustrate correct and incorrect use of the Blue Box logo.

Do

Use the Approved Logo Artwork

Use the Gradient and Tonal
Backgrounds Behind the Logo

Use Contrasting Background Colors
to Enhance the Contrast of the Logo

Do Not

Do Not Alter the Logo Elements

Do Not Place the Logo on
Flat Blue Backgrounds

Do Not Place the Logo on
Backgrounds That Compete

4

Do's and Don'ts (cont'd)

The following examples illustrate correct and incorrect use of the Blue Box logo.

Do	Do Not
Use the Approved Logo Artwork	Do Not Crop the Logo
Maintain the Proper Clear Space of the Blue Box Logo	Do Not Violate the Clear Space of the Logo

Appendix-7
APPROVAL FORM GUIDE & FORM

The submission of licensed products and corresponding packaging is a key component to maintaining the standards of any licensing program. We realize the importance of providing you with a prompt response to the materials you submit for approval. We will make every effort to provide approvals in a timely manner. However, please allow adequate time for the approval process.

SUBMISSION OF SAMPLES:

All products and packaging being submitted for approval must be sent to the following:

Contact

Title

Company

Address

Phone

Fax

If you have any questions regarding product submissions, please contact XXXXXXX

FORM OF SUBMISSION

Approvals may be sent as actual samples, or as images of product and/or packaging via email. If submission is via email, if for any reason we are unable to approve the product and/or packaging based on receipt of only an image we will contact you to request an actual sample of the product and/or packaging.

If you are submitting a product and/or packaging for approval via email, please insure that all images provide adequate detail of the sample. Please provide multiple images of product and/or packaging whenever possible. If the product contains significant details, please make sure that images of such detailed are included with the submission.

USE OF PRODUCT APPROVAL FORM

All samples, regardless of the whether submission is via email or as an actual sample, a separate *Product Approval Form* must be included with each item submitted. The form should provide all the information as requested on the form. Licensor can reject products, but final approval requires made by the licensor. Therefore, the material that we receive from you will be sent immediately to the licensor for their review.

Upon review of the product, the *Product Approval Form* will be returned to your attention and will note if the product has been approved or not. If the product and/or packaging has not been approved, we will supply you the information regarding the necessary changes that must be made.

Rejection of a product requires that it be re-submitted once the needed correction(s) has/have been made. Re-submission must be accompanied with a *Product Approval Form*.

Attached is a copy of the *Product Approval Form* for your use in submitting all products and packaging for approval. Please be advised that submissions made without a Product Approval Form will be returned.

TRADEMARK NOTICE

In your License agreement is listed the trademark notice that must appear on all products and packaging. In some cases, an abbreviated form of the trademark notice may be available. Please note that any abbreviated form of the trademark notice (if any) should only be used when space does not permit the use of the complete trademark notice.

(Company Name)

<u>LICENSEE ARTWORK & PRODUCT APPROVAL FORM</u>

DATE: **PROPERTY:**

LICENSEE:

ITEM

SUBMITTED: _____

___ Product ___ Packaging ___ Advertising ___ Revision ___ Other ____

STAGE: ____ Rough Art/Concert/Outline   ____ Design/Preliminary Layout

          ____ Final Layout/Tight Pencils/Storyboard   ____ Copy/Text

          ____ Mechanicals   ____ Color Proof

          ____ Strike Off/Final Mold   ____ Prototype Product

          ____ Pre-production Sample   ____ Final Product

          ____ Other: _____

_____

__ Approved __ Approved w/Corrections __ Submit Next Stage __ Disapproved __ Approved for Production

COMMENTS/ CORRECTIONS:

Appendix-8
MARKETING PLAN OUTLINE

Mission Statement

Demographics

Image

- Associations
- Styles
- Colors
- Materials

Opportunities

- Market
- Hook
- Directives
- Retail/Promotions

Risks

- Audience Appeal
- Visibility
- Market saturation

Objectives

- Create and develop
- Build
- Capitalize
- Generate

Strategy

- Define successful program
- Steps in development of property

Phases

- o Identifying product categories
- o Solicitation
- o Retail
- o Product development
- o Line extension

Appendix-9
CHANNELS OF DISTRIBUTION CHECKLIST

Licensee_____Property_____Date_____

PLEASE INDICATE THE NUMBERS FOR ALL THAT APPLY BY EITHER

HIGHLIGTHING OR WITH AN "X"

☐   Airport Gift & Other Airport Stores

☐   Amusement Game Redemption

☐   Amusement Park Gift Stores

☐   Art & Craft Stores

☐   Athletic Apparel & Footwear Stores

☐   Automotive & Carwash Stores

☐   Baby Specialty Stores

☐   Beauty Supply Stores

☐   Business to Business

☐   Camera/Photo Specialty Stores

☐   Candy/Confectionery Specialty Stores

☐   Catalog Showrooms

☐   Chain Book Stores

☐   Chain Comic Book Stores

☐   Chain Drug Stores

☐   Chain Jewelry Stores

☐   Chain Toy Stores

☐   Coffee Specialty Stores

☐   College/University Stores

☐   Commercial Facilities

☐   Computer Specialty Stores

☐   Convenience Stores

☐   Dental/Medical Stores

☐   Direct Mail Catalogs

☐   Direct Response

- ☐ Door-To-Door Solicitation
- ☐ Duty Free Stores
- ☐ Educational Institutions
- ☐ Educational Specialty Stores
- ☐ Electronics Stores
- ☐ Family Restaurants
- ☐ Fashion Accessory Stores
- ☐ Fashion Specialty Boutiques
- ☐ Florists
- ☐ Food Service
- ☐ Fundraising
- ☐ Furniture Stores
- ☐ Garden Specialty Stores
- ☐ Gift Retailers
- ☐ Gourmet Food Specialty Stores
- ☐ Greeting Card Stores
- ☐ Guild Jewelers
- ☐ Hobby & Model Stores
- ☐ Home Improvement Stores
- ☐ Home Specialty Stores
- ☐ Ice Cream Shops
- ☐ In-Store Bakeries
- ☐ Internet
- ☐ Mall Clothing Specialty Stores
- ☐ Mid-Tier Department Stores
- ☐ Military Exchange Services
- ☐ Music/Video Stores
- ☐ National Discount/Mass Retailers
- ☐ Non-Chain Book Stores
- ☐ Non-Chain Comic Book Stores
- ☐ Non-Chain Drug Stores
- ☐ Non-Chain Jewelry Stores
- ☐ Non-Chain Toy Stores

☐   Non-Mall Clothing Specialty Stores

☐   Novelty Gift Stores

☐   Off-Price/Closeout Stores

☐   Office Specialty Stores

☐   Outlet Stores

☐   Party Stores

☐   Pet Stores

☐   Quick Service Restaurants

☐   Regional Discount/Mass Retailers

☐   Retail Bakeries

☐   School Book Clubs/Fairs

☐   Souvenir Stores

☐   Sporting Goods Stores

☐   Sports Stadium Shops

☐   Stationery Stores

☐   Street Vendors

☐   Supermarket/Grocery Stores

☐   Swap Meets/Flea Markets

☐   Television Home Shopping

☐   Theatrical Concessions

☐   Toy Specialty/Better Toy Chain Stores

☐   Toy Wholesalers

☐   Trackside – CART

☐   Trackside – NASCAR

☐   Trackside – NHRA

☐   Upstairs Department Stores

☐   Vending Machines

☐   Wall Décor Stores

☐   Warehouse Clubs

☐   Other (please specify):

Appendix-10
SAMPLE ROYALTY REPORT

(COMPANY NAME)

ROYALTY REPORT FORM

QUARTER:

PROPERTY:

LICENSEE	GROSS SALES	PROMO UNITS	ROYALTY PAYMENT AMOUNT RECEIVED	AMOUNT APPLIED AGAINST ADVANCE	ADVANCE ROYALTY BAL	GROSS ROYALTY PAYMENTS DUE

GROSS SALES: _____

ALLOWABLE DEDUCTIONS: _____

SUBTOTAL: _____

TIMES ROYALTY RATE: _____

SUBTOTAL: _____

LESS OUTSTANDING ADVANCE: _____

TOTAL ROYALTIES DUE: _____

Appendix-11
LICENSING AGENT AGREEMENT

THIS AGREEMENT is made this ____day of _____, by and between
_____ with offices at _____ (the "Owner") and
_____ with offices at _____ (the "Agent").

WITNESSETH:

WHEREAS, the Owner is in the business of and has developed certain trademarks, brands, designs, artwork, and intellectual property identified more fully in the attached Schedule A (the "Property");

WHEREAS, the Owner is desirous of retaining the services of an experienced licensing agent to commercialize or otherwise license the Property to third party Manufacturers (the "Manufacturer") for a line of Licensed Products bearing the Property (the "Licensed Products"); and

WHEREAS, Agent is willing to represent the Owner with respect to commercialization of the Property;

NOW, THEREFORE, in consideration of the promises and agreements set forth herein, the parties, each intending to be legally bound hereby, do promise and agree as follows:

1. AGENT GRANT

A. The Owner hereby grants to Agent, during the Term of this Agreement, the exclusive right (to the exclusion of others as well as the Owner representing itself) to represent the Owner in the countries identified in Schedule A attached hereto (the "Territory") with respect to the commercialization or licensing of the Property to Manufacturers.

B. With respect to agreements with Manufacturers, Owner hereby empowers Agent to negotiate the terms of such agreements within the parameters agreed upon between Agent and Owner prior to the commencement of such negotiations and to present such agreements to Owner for execution. All such agreements shall be in the name of Owner. Owner may not unreasonably refuse to execute an agreement presented by Agent.

C. If the Owner is approached directly by a Manufacturer within the Territory during the Term of this Agreement, it shall refer such Manufacturer to Agent. Owner agrees that during the Term of this Agreement, it will not negotiate with any other person or entity within the Territory to represent it in any capacity in connection with the manufacture or sale of the Property.

2. TERM OF THE AGREEMENT

This Agreement and the provisions hereof, except as otherwise provided, shall be in full force and effect commencing on the date of execution by both parties and shall extend for an Initial Term as recited in Schedule A attached hereto (the "Term"). This Agreement shall be automatically renewed for additional "Extended Terms" as provided for in Schedule A unless either party notifies the other in writing of its intention not to renew the Agreement, such notification to be provided at least sixty (60) days prior to the expiration of the then in-effect Term.

3. DUTIES AND OBLIGATIONS

A. Subject to the conditions herein specified, Agent shall use reasonable efforts during the Term of this Agreement to find and conclude business arrangements with licensees for the Property that are advantageous to the Owner and, thereafter, to reasonably service such arrangements during the term thereof. In furtherance of Agent's duties as herein specified, Agent will:

1. Periodically meet and confer with the Owner to discuss the state of the merchandising industry;

2. Develop a merchandising plan for the Property in the Territory and provide a copy of same to Owner within thirty (30) days of the date of execution of this Agreement by both parties;

3. Implement the merchandising plan by contacting those prospective licensees best able to produce licensed products of the type and quality for the Property;

4. Negotiate all agreements with third party licensees in the name of the Owner and subject to the approval of the Owner;

5. Provide record keeping and billing services to the licensees as reasonably requested by Owner and monitor and oversee the licensing program with such third-party licensees to ensure that the licenses, royalties, minimums, and sales reports are promptly submitted;

6. Make appropriate recommendations to the Owner with respect to seeking and maintaining appropriate intellectual property protection for the Property; and

7. Investigate all potential infringements of Owner's intellectual property rights in the Territory and report to the Owner.

B. In addition to the foregoing, Agent shall be responsible for the enforcement of the quality control provisions of the third party license agreements which shall include periodic inspection of all Licensed Products.

C. The Agent shall engage in other such activities as the parties may mutually agree and, in general, use its best efforts consistent with sound business practices to maximize revenue generated from the exploitation of the rights granted hereunder and to enhance the value and reputation of the Property.

D. While the Agent is empowered to propose all necessary art, design, editorial, and other related approvals for the creation of the Licensed Products as well as to enforce the appropriately high standard of quality for all such Licensed Products created and produced pursuant to licensing and promotional agreements entered into pursuant to this Agreement, the Owner retains the right to grant final approval on art, design, and editorial matters. The Agent agrees to submit to the Owner, for final approval, drafts, prototypes and finished samples of all Licensed Products and any advertising, promotional and packaging material related to said Licensed Products. Owner will respond to the Agent regarding approval within ten (10) business days after receipt of such samples. Failure to respond within said period shall be deemed disapproval.

E. Agent shall oversee the payment by the licensees of all royalties and other payments due under this Agreement.

F. It is understood that the Owner may have concepts and properties other than the Property and such concepts and properties do not form part of this Agreement.

G. The Owner recognizes that Agent performs similar services for its other clients and that the Owner's retention of the Agent is subject to such understanding.

H. The Owner shall be solely responsible for all costs and expenses associated with the protection of the Property, including the costs for obtaining and maintaining patent, trademark, and copyright protection.

4. COMPENSATION

A. In consideration for the services rendered by Agent, the Owner agrees to and shall pay Agent a Retainer Fee in the amount of and in accordance with the terms recited in Schedule A attached hereto. Such Retainer Fee is non-refundable and non-creditable against any other compensation owed Agent under this Agreement.

B. In addition to the Retainer Fee, Owner agrees to pay Agent a Commission in the amount recited in Schedule A attached hereto based on the Net Revenues received by the Agent from the Manufacturers based on the Manufacturer's sales or other use of Licensed Products bearing the Property.

C. "Net Revenues" shall include all income received by Agent (prior to the deduction of Agent's commission) from such third party Manufacturer within the Territory pursuant to any contract or agreement for the sale, lease, license or other disposition of the Property resulting directly from the efforts of Agent including, but not limited to, advances, royalties, guarantees, fees and payments (whether in cash, barter or other form of consideration) less any payments made or expenses incurred by Agent for or on behalf of the Owner with the prior approval of Owner.

D. After termination or expiration of this Agreement for any reason, Agent shall be entitled to continue to receive its full Commission based on those contracts or agreements entered into by Owner with Manufacturers in the Territory during the Term of this Agreement or within one (1) year from the date of termination or expiration of this Agreement resulting from presentations made or negotiations conducted by Agent during the Term of this Agreement for which Agent would have received a Commission had the Agreement not been terminated or expired. Agent shall be entitled to such post-termination Commission for so long as the Owner continues to receive revenues under such agreement with a Manufacturer as well as from any renewals, modifications, continuations or extensions thereof.

5. WARRANTIES AND INDEMNIFICATIONS

A. The Owner represent and warrant that it is the owner of all rights in and to the Property, that it has the right and power to license and/or sell such Property, that the use of the Property on the Licensed Products shall not infringe upon the rights of any third party, and that it has not granted anyone else the right or authority to act for it in a manner which would conflict with Agent.

B. The Owner hereby agree to defend, indemnify and hold Agent, its shareholders, directors, officers, employees, agents, parent companies, subsidiaries, and affiliates, harmless from and against any and all claims, liabilities, judgments, penalties, and taxes, civil and criminal, and all costs, expenses (including, without limitation, reasonable attorneys' fees) incurred in connection therewith, which any of them may incur or to which any of them may be subjected, arising out of or relating to a breach of the Owner' representations and warranties. During the pendency of any indemnified claim against Agent, Agent shall have the right to withhold any monies then owed Owner to help defray any costs or expenses that Owner may incur as a result of such claim.

C. Agent hereby agrees to defend, indemnify and hold the Owner, their shareholders, directors, officers, employees, agents, parent companies, subsidiaries, and affiliates, harmless from and against any and all claims, liabilities, judgments, penalties, and taxes, civil and criminal, and all costs, expenses (including, without limitation, reasonable attorneys' fees) incurred in connection therewith, which any of them may incur or to which any of them may be subjected, arising out of or relating to any action by Agent.

6. STATEMENTS AND PAYMENTS

A. Owner agrees that Agent shall receive all royalty reports and collect all royalties and payments from the Manufacturers both during and after termination or expiration of this Agreement. Such royalties and payments shall be deposited in an account which the parties mutually agree upon. Agent shall remit all royalties, inclusive of copies of all royalty reports, less Agent's Commissions, on a quarterly basis based on revenues received by Agent during the previous calendar quarter. Such payments and statements reflecting the basis for such payments shall be made within forty-five (45) days after the close of each calendar quarter.

B. Agent agrees to keep accurate books of account and records at its principal place of business covering all transactions relating to the agreements with the Manufacturers. Owner or its designee shall have the right, at all reasonable hours of the day and upon at least ten (10) business days' notice, to examine Owners books and records as they relate to the subject matter of this Agreement only. Such examination shall occur at the place where the Owner maintains such records.

C. All books and records pertaining to the obligations of the Agent hereunder shall be maintained and kept accessible and available to Agent for inspection for at least three (3) years after the date to which they pertain.

7. NOTICE AND PAYMENT

A. Any notice required to be given under this Agreement shall be in writing and delivered personally to the other designated party at the above stated address or mailed by certified, registered or Express mail, return receipt requested or by Federal Express and/or UPS.

B. Either party may change the address to which notice or payment is to be sent by written notice to the other under any provision of this paragraph.

8. TERMINATION

A. This Agreement may be terminated by either party upon thirty (30) days written notice to the other party in the event of a breach of a material provision of this Agreement by the other party, provided that, during the thirty (30) days period, the breaching party fails to cure such breach.

B. The Owner shall have the right to terminate this Agreement immediately in the event that the Agent fails to enter into at least _____ license agreements with third parties with _____ months after execution of this Agreement and generates at least $_____ of licensing revenue from such third parties within _____ months after execution of this Agreement.

C. If Agent is unable to meet its obligations when they become due or make an assignment for the benefit of its creditors, Owner shall have the right to either immediately terminate this Agreement, or alternatively, convert it to a non-exclusive agreement.

9. EFFECT OF TERMINATION

A. Upon termination or expiration of this Agreement as it relates to the Property, all rights granted to Agent relative to the Property shall forthwith revert to the Owner who shall be free to contract with others to commercialize such Property subject to the provisions of this Agreement subject to the post-termination provisions of this Agreement. Agent shall, thereafter, refrain from further efforts to commercialize the Property.

B. Upon termination or expiration of this Agreement, Owner may request that Agent provide it within sixty (60) days of such notice with a complete schedule of all prospective Manufacturers contacted on behalf of the Owner relative to the Property as well as returning all materials relating to the Property.

10. JURISDICTION/DISPUTES

This Agreement shall be governed in accordance with the laws of [State]. All disputes under this Agreement shall be resolved by litigation in the courts of the State of [State], including the federal courts therein and the parties all consent to the jurisdiction of such courts, agree to accept service of process by mail, and hereby waive any jurisdictional or venue defenses otherwise available to it.

11. AGREEMENT BINDING ON SUCCESSORS

The provisions of the Agreement shall be binding upon and shall inure to the benefit of the parties hereto, their heirs, administrators, successors and assigns.

12. ASSIGNABILITY

A. Neither party may assign this Agreement or the rights and obligations thereunder to any third party without the prior express written approval of the other party which shall not be unreasonably withheld.

B. If at any time during the Term of this Agreement, the Owner intends to sell, assign, transfer or abandon some or all its rights in the Property, it shall provide Agent with written notice to such effect at least thirty (30) days prior to the actual sale, assignment, transfer or abandonment of the Property. Upon receipt of such notice, the parties shall promptly meet and negotiate an arrangement under which this Agreement shall be assigned to and assumed by the acquiring party who will agree to assume all obligations thereunder with the Owner agreeing to guarantee the acquiring party's performance thereof. If the acquiring party does not intend to receive an assignment of the Agreement and/or the Owner is unwilling to guarantee the acquiring party's performance thereof, the Owner and Agent shall agree to a termination of the Agent Agreement. In such event, the parties will negotiate in good faith a mutually acceptable termination package for the Agent in an amount to be mutually agreed upon between the Parties to compensate the Agent for lost potential revenues caused by such termination. If the Parties are unable to mutually agree to what constitutes fair compensation, the Parties agree to binding arbitration before a single arbitrator under the then current rules of the American Arbitration Association in the AAA office closest to the Agent.

13. WAIVER

No waiver by either party of any default shall be deemed as a waiver of prior or subsequent default of the same of other provisions of this Agreement.

14. SEVERABILITY

If any term, clause or provision hereof is held invalid or unenforceable by a court of competent jurisdiction, such invalidity shall not affect the validity or operation of any other term, clause or provision and such invalid term, clause or provision shall be deemed to be severed from the Agreement.

15. INDEPENDENT CONTRACTOR

Agent shall be deemed an independent contractor, and nothing contained herein shall constitute this arrangement to be employment, a joint venture or a partnership. Agent shall be solely responsible for and shall hold the Owner harmless for all claims for taxes, fees or costs, including but not limited to withholding, income tax, FICA, workman's compensation.

16. INTEGRATION

This Agreement constitutes the entire understanding of the parties, and revokes and supersedes all prior agreements between the parties and is intended as a final expression of their Agreement. It shall not be modified or amended except in writing signed by the parties hereto and specifically referring to this Agreement. This Agreement shall take precedence over any other documents which may conflict with this Agreement.

IN WITNESS WHEREOF, the parties hereto, intending to be legally bound hereby, have each caused to be affixed hereto its or his/her hand and seal the day indicated.

OWNER   **AGENT**

By:_____   By:_____

Title:_____   Title:_____

Date:_____   Date:_____

SCHEDULE A

TO LICENSING AGENT AGREEMENT

1. Property & Trademark notice:

2. Territory:

3. Term:

4. Retainer Fee:

5. Commission:

6. Additional Services:

Appendix-12
SUB-AGENT AGREEMENT

THIS AGREEMENT is entered into this _____ day of _____ by and between
_____ with offices at _____ (the "Agent") and
_____, with offices at _____ (the "Sub-Agent").

WITNESSETH:

WHEREAS, Agent, pursuant to an agent agreement dated _____ between
_____ (the "Owner") and the Agent (the "Agent Agreement"), the Property Owner has granted certain rights to the Agent to develop and conduct a licensing program for the property described in Schedule A attached hereto (the "Property");

WHEREAS, Agent would like to retain the services of Sub-Agent to commercialize or license the Property to third-party licensees in the Sub-Agent's territory as defined in Schedule A (the "Territory") for a line of licensed products (the "Licensed Products"); and

WHEREAS, Sub-Agent is willing to represent the Agent in such Territory with respect to the licensing of the Property within the Territory.

NOW, THEREFORE, in consideration of the promises and agreements set forth herein, the parties, each intending to be legally bound hereby, do promise and agree as follows.

1. SUB-AGENT APPOINTMENT

A. Agent hereby appoints the Sub-Agent, for the Term of this Agreement, its exclusive representative in the Territory for commercializing or licensing the Property to third-party licensees, subject to the approval of Agent and the Owner.

B. In this regard, Sub-Agent shall be authorized to present, negotiate, and conclude licensing arrangements with third-party licensees using a form agreement approved by Agent and Owner and pursuant to terms and conditions previously approved by Agent and Owner.

C. All third-party license agreements shall be in the name of Owner and shall be signed by Owner, although Sub-Agent shall be a party to all such agreements as agent for Owner. All payments from third parties shall be directed to Sub-Agent.

D. It is understood and agreed that this Agreement shall relate only to the enumerated Property and to no other properties owned or controlled by Agent and/or Owner. Agent and Owner shall be free to commercialize such other properties to the exclusion of Sub-Agent.

E. Agent agrees not to retain the services of any third party to represent Agent with respect to the Property in the Territory. However, Agent may retain the services of other subagents with respect to merchandising of the Property in countries outside the Territory.

F. Sub-Agent agrees to refrain from licensing the Property to third party licensees who intend or are likely to sell the Licensed Products outside the Territory.

2. TERM OF THE AGREEMENT

This Agreement and the provisions hereof, except as otherwise provided, shall be in full force and effect commencing on the date of execution by both parties and shall extend for a Term as recited in Schedule A attached hereto (the "Term").

3. DUTIES AND OBLIGATIONS OF PARTIES

A. Subject to the conditions herein specified, Sub-Agent shall use reasonable efforts during the Term of this Agreement to find and conclude business arrangements with licensees for the Property that are advantageous to Agent and Owner and, thereafter, to reasonably service such arrangements during the term thereof. In furtherance of Sub-Agent's duties as herein specified, Sub-Agent will:

1. Periodically meet and confer with Agent to discuss the state of the merchandising industry;

2. Develop a merchandising plan for the Property in the Territory and provide a copy of same to Agent within thirty (30) days of the date of execution of this Agreement by both parties;

3. Implement the merchandising plan by contacting those prospective licensees best able to produce licensed products of the type and quality for the Property;

4. Negotiate all agreements with third party licensees in the name of the Owner and subject to the approval of Agent and Owner;

5. Provide record keeping and billing services to the licensees as reasonably requested by Agent and monitor and oversee the licensing program with such third-party licensees to ensure that the licenses, royalties, minimums, and sales reports are promptly submitted;

6. Remit all Advances paid by licensees within ten (10) days after receipt thereof and all other payments made by licensees within twenty (20) days of receipt thereof. All payment shall be made in U.S. Dollars by wire transfer.

7. Make appropriate recommendations to the Agent with respect to seeking and maintaining appropriate intellectual property protection for the Property; and

8. Investigate all potential infringements of Owner's intellectual property rights in the Territory and report to Agent.

B. In addition to the foregoing, Sub-Agent shall be responsible for the enforcement of the quality control provisions of the third party license agreements which shall include periodic inspection of all Licensed Products and conducting personal visits to the third-party licensees' manufacturing facilities to ensure that the quality control provisions of the license agreements with the licensees are being complied with. Sub-Agent shall submit to Agent a written report after each of said reviews and visits.

C. Sub-Agent shall engage in other such activities as the parties may mutually agree and, in general, use its best efforts consistent with sound business practices to maximize revenue generated from the exploitation of the rights granted hereunder and to enhance the value and reputation of the Property.

D. While Sub-Agent is empowered to propose all necessary art, design, editorial, and other related approvals for the creation of the Licensed Products as well as to enforce the appropriately high standard of quality for all such Licensed Products created and produced pursuant to licensing and promotional agreements entered into pursuant to this Agreement, Agent retains the right to grant final approval on art, design, and editorial matters. Sub-Agent agrees to submit to Agent, for final approval, drafts, prototypes and finished samples of all Licensed Products and all advertising, promotional and packaging material related to said Licensed Products. Agent will respond to Sub-Agent regarding approval within thirty (30) business days after receipt of such samples. Failure to respond within said period shall be deemed disapproval.

E. Sub-Agent shall oversee the payment by the licensees of all royalties and other payments due under this Agreement. If necessary, Sub-Agent shall conduct periodic royalty investigations of the licensee's books and records to ensure that all payments have been made. The cost of such royalty investigations shall be borne by the Sub-Agent. However, any recoveries received as a result of such royalty investigation shall be applied against the cost of conducting such investigation. The Sub-Agent shall provide the Owner and the Agent with copies of any reports rendered as a result of such investigations.

F. It is understood that Agent and Owner may have concepts and properties other than the Property and such concepts and properties do not form part of this Agreement.

G. Agent recognizes that Sub-Agent performs similar services for its other clients and that Agent's retention of Sub-Agent is subject to such understanding.

H. Agent and Owner shall be solely responsible for all costs and expenses associated with the protection of the Property, including the costs for obtaining and maintaining patent, trademark, and copyright protection.

4. LICENSE AGREEMENTS

A. All proposed license agreements presented by Sub-Agent under this Agreement shall be subject to the express written approval of Agent and Owner, such approval not to be unreasonably withheld. It is understood that Sub-Agent will submit all such proposed agreements to Owner through Agent for consideration, approval, and execution and Agent will, thereupon, advise Sub-Agent within thirty (30) business days after receipt of the proposed agreement as to whether Agent and Owner agree or disagree to the terms thereof and whether Owner will execute same. Failure to act within said thirty (30) day period shall be deemed a disapproval of any such agreement. No agreement shall be binding on Agent or Owner until signed by Owner.

B. All such license agreements with third-party licensees shall be between Owner and the third-party licensee presented by Sub-Agent. The basic form license agreement that is to be used by Sub-Agent in negotiating license agreements with third-party licensees has been deemed approved by Agent and Owner as in form only -- all prospective licenses, even if in this form, must be submitted for approval by Agent and Owner. All additions, deletions and changes to this basic agreement shall be subject to the absolute, unfettered express written approval of Agent and Owner and notification of approval or disapproval shall be provided to Sub-Agent within ten (10) business days after receipt of same by Agent. The lack of response from Agent within such ten (10) day period shall be deemed a disapproval of any proposed addition, deletion and/or change.

5. COMPENSATION

A. In consideration for the services rendered by Sub-Agent, Agent agrees to and shall pay Sub-Agent, during the Term of this Agreement, a commission in the amount recited in Schedule A attached hereto (the "Commission").

B. In addition to the Commission recited in Schedule A, Agent agrees to reimburse Sub-Agent for all reasonable expenses incurred on behalf of Agent, provided that such expenses have been previously approved by Agent.

C. Agent further agrees to pay Sub-Agent, during the Term of this Agreement, a Subagent Fee in the amount recited in Schedule A attached hereto.

D. "Gross Revenues" shall include all income generated as a result of any commercialization, sale, or licensing of the Property in the Territory (prior to deduction of Sub-Agent's Commission) from such third-party licensee(s), due solely to the efforts of Sub-Agent.

E. In the event that this Agreement should expire or terminate for reasons other than a breach of any provision herein by Sub-Agent, Sub-Agent shall be entitled to post-termination compensation based on gross income received by Owner from any third-party license agreement, for the life of such third party agreement, entered into through Sub-Agent during the Term of this Agreement and for which Sub-Agent would have received compensation had this Agreement not expired, subject to the schedule recited in Schedule A attached hereto.

F. Sub-Agent shall not be entitled to any post-termination compensation if this Agreement is expressly terminated by Agent in the event of a material breach by Sub-Agent of the terms of this Agreement. Sub-Agent shall not be entitled to such post-termination compensation for any other agreements subsequently entered into by Agent or Owner.

G. All payments due hereunder shall be made in United States currency drawn on a United States bank, unless otherwise specified between the parties.

H. All fees payable hereunder shall be based on the official exchange rate on the date on which such payment is due and Sub-Agent shall provide detailed conversion calculations with every payment submitted hereunder. If, by any reason of any governmental or fiscal restrictions affecting the convertibility, payment cannot be made in U.S. funds, then Sub-Agent shall take such reasonable actions with respect to the payment due as Agent shall direct.

6. WARRANTIES AND INDEMNIFICATIONS

A. Agent represents and warrants that it has the right and power to enter into this agreement and, further, that it has not granted anyone else the right or authority to act for it in a manner that would conflict with Sub-Agent.

B. Agent hereby agrees to defend, indemnify, and hold Sub-Agent, its shareholders, directors, officers, employees, agents, parent companies, subsidiaries and affiliates, harmless from and against any and all claims, liabilities, judgments, penalties, and taxes, civil and criminal, and all costs and expenses (including, without limitation, reasonable attorney's fees) incurred in connection therewith, which any of them may incur or to which any of them may be subjected, arising out of or relating to a breach of Agent's representation and warranty or of any actions or inactions of Agent.

C. Sub-Agent hereby agrees to defend, indemnify, and hold Agent and any of its related entities harmless from and against any and all claims, liabilities, judgments, penalties, and taxes, civil and criminal, and all costs and expenses (including, without limitation, reasonable attorney's fees) arising out of or relating to a breach of Sub-Agent's representation and warranty or that may arise out of any action or inaction by Sub-Agent, other than as it may relate to Agent's warranty, as above stated.

D. Sub-Agent hereby agrees to comply with all laws and regulations in each country in the Territory.

7. STATEMENTS AND PAYMENTS

A. All payments from licensees based on agreements for the Property shall be paid directly to Owner. Within thirty (30) days after receipt by Agent of its commission from Owner, Agent shall transmit to Sub-Agent its Commission.

B. Agent agrees to keep accurate books of accounts and records at its principal place of business covering all transactions relating to the agreements with the licensees. Sub-Agent, through an independent certified public accountant acceptable to Owner, shall have the right, at all reasonable hours of the day and upon at least five (5) days' written notice, to examine Agent's books and records as they relate to the subject matter of this Agreement only. Such examination shall occur at the place where Agent maintains such records.

Appendices

C. All books and records pertaining to the obligations of Sub-Agent hereunder shall be maintained and kept accessible and available to Agent for inspection for at least three (3) years after the date to which they pertain.

8. NOTICES

A. Any notice required to be given under this Agreement shall be in writing and delivered personally to the other designated party at the above-stated address or mailed by certified or registered mail, return receipt requested, or delivered by a recognized national overnight courier service.

B. Either party may change the address to which notice or payment is to be sent by written notice to the other under any provision of this paragraph.

9. TERMINATION

A. This Agreement may be terminated by either party upon thirty (30) days' written notice to the other party in the event of a breach of a material provision of this Agreement by the other party, provided that, during the thirty (30) day period, the breaching party fails to cure such breach.

B. Agent shall have the right to terminate this Agreement immediately if Sub-Agent fails to enter into at least _____ license agreements with third parties with _____ months after execution of this Agreement and generates at least _____ of licensing revenue from such third parties within _____ months after execution of this Agreement.

C. The Agent shall have the right to immediately terminate this Agreement if the Sub-Agent should be unable to meet its obligations when they become due, make an assignment for the benefit of its creditors or should there be a change in the existing management of Sub-Agent.

D. This Agreement shall terminate automatically if the Agent Agreement between Agent and Owner shall terminate or expire.

E. If this Agreement shall terminate or expire, Sub-Agent shall turn over to Agent all records relating to each license entered into under this Agreement. All rights granted to Sub-Agent shall revert to Agent and Sub-Agent shall refrain from any further use of the Property.

10. JURISDICTION AND DISPUTES

This Agreement will be governed by and construed and enforced in accordance with the laws of [State] without regard to conflicts of law principles. All disputes under this Agreement shall be resolved by the courts of the state of [State], including the United States District Court for the District of [State]. The parties all consent to the jurisdiction of such courts, agree to accept service of process by mail, and hereby waive any jurisdictional or venue defenses otherwise available to it.

11. SUBORDINATION

The parties recognize that Agent's rights with respect to the Property are governed exclusively by the Agent Agreement. In the event there are conflicts between the Agent Agreement and this Agreement, the provisions of the Agent Agreement shall govern.

12. AGREEMENT BINDING ON SUCCESSORS

The provisions of the Agreement shall be binding on and shall inure to the benefit of the parties hereto, their heirs, assigns, and successors.

13. WAIVER

No waiver by either party of any default shall be deemed as a waiver of prior or subsequent default of the same or other provisions of this Agreement.

14. SEVERABILITY

If any term, clause, or provision hereof is held invalid or unenforceable by a court of competent jurisdiction, such invalidity shall not affect the validity or operation of any other term, clause, or provision and such invalid term, clause, or provision shall be deemed to be severed from the Agreement.

15. INDEPENDENT CONTRACTOR

Sub-Agent shall be deemed an independent contractor and nothing contained herein shall constitute this arrangement to be employment, a joint venture, or a partnership. Sub-Agent shall be solely responsible for and shall hold Agent harmless for any and all claims for taxes, fees, or costs, including but not limited to withholding, income tax, FICA, and workmen's compensation.

16. ASSIGNABILITY

This agreement and the rights and obligations thereof are personal to Sub-Agent and shall not be assigned by any act of Sub-Agent or by operation of law unless in connection with a transfer of substantially all the assets of Sub-Agent or with the consent of Agent and Owner.

17. GOVERNMENTAL APPROVAL

Sub-Agent agrees to submit copies of this Agreement to any governmental agency in any country in the Territory where approval of this Agreement is necessary, and agrees to promptly prosecute any such application diligently. This Agreement shall become effective in such country or countries only upon receipt of appropriate approval from the applicable governmental agency.

18. GOVERNING LANGUAGE

This Agreement is in the English language. No translation of this Agreement into any language other than English shall be considered in the interpretation thereof, and in the event that any translation of this Agreement is in conflict with the English language version, the English version shall govern.

19. BLOCKED CURRENCY

A. If any payment required to be made to Owner pursuant to this Agreement cannot be made when due because of the exchange control of any country in the Territory and such payment remains unpaid for twelve (12) months, Agent and/or Owner may, by notice served to Sub-Agent, elect any of the following alternative methods of handling such payment:

1. If the currency can be converted into currency other than U.S. Dollars for purposes of foreign remittance, Owner may elect to receive such payment in any such currencies as it may specify and, in such case, the amount payable in the foreign currency so selected shall be determined by reference to the then existent legal rate of exchange which is most favorable to Owner.

2. Owner may elect to have payment made to it in the local currency, deposited to the credit of Owner in a bank account in such country designated by Owner, in which event Sub-Agent shall furnish to Owner evidence of such deposit.

B. All expenses of currency conversion and transmission shall be borne by Sub-Agent and no deduction shall be made from remittances on account of such expense. Sub-Agent from time to time may prepare all applications, reports or other documents which may be required by the government of the applicable country in order that remittances may be made in accordance with this Agreement.

20. INTEGRATION

This Agreement constitutes the entire understanding of the parties, and revokes and supersedes all prior agreements between the parties and is intended as a final expression of their Agreement. It shall not be modified or amended except in writing signed by the parties hereto and specifically referring to this Agreement. This Agreement shall take precedence over any other documents that may conflict with this Agreement.

IN WITNESS WHEREOF, the parties hereto, intending to be legally bound hereby, have each caused to be affixed hereto its or his/her hand and seal the day indicated.

AGENT

By:_____

Title:_____

Date:_____

SUB-AGENT

By:_____

Title:_____

Date:_____

SCHEDULE A

To Sub-Agent Agreement

1. Licensed Property:

2. Territory:

3. Term:

4. Commission:

5. Sub-agent Fee:

6. Post Termination Compensation:

Appendix-13
CONSULTING AGREEMENT

THIS AGREEMENT is made as of this ___ day of _____ by and between _____, residing at _____ ("CONSULTANT") and _____, a _____ corporation with offices at _____ ("COMPANY").

WHEREAS, CONSULTANT possess certain technical expertise in the field of _____ and the creation and development of _____ (the "Field");

WHEREAS, COMPANY desires to engage CONSULTANT to perform certain professional consulting services as hereinafter defined in the Field; and

WHEREAS, CONSULTANT is willing and able to provide such consulting services to COMPANY in the Field.

NOW, THEREFORE, in consideration of the premises and of the mutual promises and covenants herein contained, the parties hereto agree as follows:

WITNESSETH

1. Retention and Duties of the Consultant

A. COMPANY hereby retains the services of CONSULTANT to provide professional consulting services to COMPANY in the Field during the Term of this Agreement. In this regard, CONSULTANT shall advise and assist COMPANY in conjunction with issues relating to the Field.

B. CONSULTANT is an independent contractor and not an employee of COMPANY. Unless otherwise expressly agreed to in writing, CONSULTANT shall not be entitled to or eligible for any benefits or programs otherwise given by COMPANY to its employees.

2. Consulting Term.

A. The consulting period shall extend from _____ through and including _____ (the "Term") unless sooner terminated as provided herein.

B. COMPANY shall have the option of renewing the subject Agreement for an additional six (6) month period (the "Extended Term") on the same terms and conditions as provided for herein by providing CONSULTANT written notice of its intention to renew this Agreement at least sixty (60) days prior to the expiration of the Term.

3. Obligations of Consultant

A. Utilizing its own facilities and equipment, CONSULTANT shall be responsible for performing all the assignments and duties as outlined by COMPANY in accordance with a time schedule to be mutually agreed to between the parties. It is, however, anticipated that CONSULTANT will devote at least thirty (30) hours per week during the Term to the services required of him hereunder. Upon agreement from time to time between COMPANY and CONSULTANT, CONSULTANT'S hours may be varied to suit the mutual convenience of CONSULTANT and COMPANY. CONSULTANT shall regularly meet with and advise COMPANY on technical matters in the Field as well as regularly suggest solutions to any problems in connection with COMPANY's programs as they may develop.

4. Compensation.

A. In full consideration for the services being rendered by CONSULTANT hereunder, COMPANY agrees to pay CONSULTANT during the Term of this Agreement a consulting fee in the amount of

_____ ($_____) per month (the "Consulting Fee"). The Consulting Fee shall be paid monthly within ten (10) days after the conclusion of each month.

B. CONSULTANT shall be responsible for all ordinary and reasonable expenses which it may incur in connection with this project. COMPANY agrees, however, to reimburse CONSULTANT for all reasonable and necessary travel and material expenses previously approved in writing by COMPANY.

C. If CONSULTANT completes all of its work assigned by COMPANY to the sole and complete satisfaction of COMPANY on or before _____, COMPANY agrees to pay CONSULTANT a bonus in the amount of _____ ($_____) (the "Bonus") which shall be due and payable within ten (10) days after the completion of such work assignments. The Bonus shall be separate from and in addition to the Consulting Fee.

5. Confidential Information.

A. CONSULTANT recognizes that during the course of its retention during the Consulting Term, it may have occasion to review and receive confidential or proprietary information or material from COMPANY including information relating to inventions, patent, trademark and copyright applications, improvements, know-how, specifications, drawings, cost data, process flow diagrams, bills, ideas and/or any other written material referring to same (the "Confidential Information").

B. CONSULTANT covenants and agrees that both during and after termination of this Agreement, it and its employees, affiliates and subsidiaries will retain such Confidential Information in confidence pursuant to the following terms and conditions:

   1. CONSULTANT agrees to maintain in confidence any such Confidential Information disclosed by COMPANY relating to the above described Property which was not previously known to CONSULTANT or to the public, or which was not in the public domain prior to such disclosure.

   2. Such Confidential Information shall be maintained in confidence by CONSULTANT unless or until: (a) it shall have been made public by an act or omission of a party other than CONSULTANT; (b) CONSULTANT receives such Confidential Information from an unrelated third party on a non-confidential basis; or (c) the passage of five (5) years from the date of disclosure, whichever shall first occur.

   3. Upon request, CONSULTANT agrees to promptly return to COMPANY any other materials obtained from or through COMPANY, including all memoranda, drawings, patent, trademark and copyright applications, specifications and process or flow diagrams including any copies, notes or memoranda made by CONSULTANT which, in any way, relates to the Field or the Confidential Information disclosed or transmitted to CONSULTANT by COMPANY.

   4. CONSULTANT agrees that it will not, without first obtaining the prior written permission of COMPANY: (a) directly or indirectly utilize such Confidential Information in its business; (b) manufacture and/or sell any product which is based in whole or in part on such Confidential Information; or (c) disclose such Confidential Information to any third party.

C. CONSULTANT shall not originate any publicity, news release, or other public announcement, written or oral, relating to this Agreement, to any amendment hereto or to performance hereunder, without the prior written approval of COMPANY.

6. Non-Competition.

CONSULTANT shall not during the Term of this Agreement render any services, directly or indirectly, to any entity engaged in the creation, design, development and/or marketing of video games. Moreover, CONSULTANT shall not, or for a period of one (1) year after the termination or expiration thereof, render any services, directly or indirectly, to any entity engaged in the creation, design, development and/or marketing of video games utilizing technology of the type licensed by the General Technology Company to COMPANY for the Game.

7. Inventions.

A. Any inventions, improvements, or ideas made or conceived by CONSULTANT in connection with and during the performance of services hereunder and related to the business of COMPANY and for six (6) months thereafter, shall be considered the sole and exclusive property of COMPANY. As part of the services to be performed hereunder, CONSULTANT shall keep written notebook records of his work, properly witnessed for use as invention records, and shall submit such records to COMPANY when requested or at the termination of CONSULTANT'S services hereunder. CONSULTANT shall not reproduce any portion of such notebook records without the prior express written consent of COMPANY. CONSULTANT shall promptly and fully report all such inventions to COMPANY.

B. Any work performed by the CONSULTANT under this Agreement shall be considered a Work for Hire as defined in the United States Copyright laws and shall be owned by and for the express benefit of COMPANY. In the event it should be established that such work does not qualify as a Work for Hire, CONSULTANT agrees to and does hereby assign to COMPANY all its right, title and interest in such work product including, but not limited to, all intellectual property and other proprietary rights. Both during the Term of this Agreement and thereafter, CONSULTANT shall fully cooperate with COMPANY in the protection and enforcement of any intellectual property rights which may derive because of the services performed by CONSULTANT under the terms of this Agreement. This shall include executing, acknowledging and delivering to COMPANY all documents or papers which may be necessary to enable COMPANY to publish or protect said inventions, improvements, and ideas.

8. Termination.

A. Either party may terminate this Agreement on ten (10) days written notice to the other party in the event of a breach of any material provision of this Agreement by the other party, provided that, during the ten (10) days period, the breaching party fails to cure such breach or, should the breach not be curable within said ten (10) day period, the breaching party has not initiated steps to cure such breach.

B. Either party shall have the right to terminate this Agreement for any reason and at any time on thirty (30) days written notice to the other party, such termination to become effective at the end of such thirty (30) day period.

C. In the event of the death or disability of CONSULTANT to complete its assignments thereunder, the COMPANY shall have the right to immediately terminate this Agreement and be relieved of any further obligations hereunder.

D. Unless otherwise indicated, all covenants and obligations of the parties relative to In the event of a termination or expiration of this Agreement, all covenants and obligations of the parties shall expressly survive termination.

9. Jurisdiction and Disputes.

This Agreement shall be governed by the laws of New York and all disputes hereunder shall be resolved in the applicable state or federal courts of New York. The parties consent to the jurisdiction of such courts, agree to accept service of process by mail, and waive any jurisdictional or venue defenses otherwise available.

10. Agreement Binding on Successors.

This Agreement shall be binding upon and shall inure to the benefit of the parties hereto, their heirs, administrators, successors and assigns.

11. Assignability

This Agreement is personal to CONSULTANT and may not be assigned by any act of CONSULTANT or by operation of law unless in connection with a transfer of substantially all the assets of CONSULTANT or with the consent of COMPANY.

12. Waiver

No waiver by either party of any default shall be deemed as a waiver of any prior or subsequent default of the same or other provisions of this Agreement.

13. Severability

If any provision hereof is held invalid or unenforceable by a court of competent jurisdiction, such invalidity shall not affect the validity or operation of any other provision and such invalid provision shall be deemed to be severed from the Agreement.

14. Integration

This Agreement constitutes the entire understanding of the parties, and revokes and supersedes all prior agreements between the parties and is intended as a final expression of their Agreement. It shall not be modified or amended except in writing signed by the parties hereto and specifically referring to this Agreement. This Agreement shall take precedence over any other documents which may be in conflict therewith.

IN WITNESS WHEREOF, the parties hereto, intending to be legally bound hereby, have each caused to be affixed hereto its or his/her hand and seal the day indicated.

COMPANY_____   CONSULTANT_____

By:_____   By:_____

Date:_____   Date._____

Appendix-14
NON-DISCLOSURE AGREEMENT

THIS AGREEMENT is dated as of (date) made by and between (company name) ("Discloser"), a (state /US/county) corporation with offices at (Company address) and (other party) ("Recipient") with offices at: (their company address).

A.   Confidential Information: This Agreement provides for the protection of information provided to Recipient by Discloser, being information relating to Discloser's products (whether current or projected) including without limitation, product titles, clients, customers, designs, tools and techniques, software algorithms and routines, financial information, and business plans and which is expressly labeled or identified to Recipient in writing as "confidential" (hereinafter collectively referred to as "Confidential Information"). Recipient shall keep in confidence and not disclose to any third party, without the written permission of Discloser, the Confidential Information made known to it under this Agreement. This requirement of confidentiality shall not apply to any information that (a) is in the public domain through no wrongful act of Recipient; (b) is rightfully received by the Recipient from a third party who is not bound by a restriction of nondisclosure; (c) is already in the Recipient's possession without restriction as to disclosure; (d) was independently developed by Recipient; (e) is disclosed after three (3) years from the date of this Agreement or as otherwise permitted under this Agreement; or (f) may be disclosed to third parties in accordance with a letter of transmittal from Discloser, if any, accompanying such information. The Confidential Information is being made available to Recipient for the limited purpose of evaluating whether to enter into a further business relationship with Discloser and certain third parties who may be introduced by Discloser to Recipient to secure other license agreements for properties represented or owned or controlled by Recipient. Recipient may disclose the Confidential Information only to those of its employees or consultants who need to know such information to effectuate the purposes of this Agreement and only to the extent necessary for such purpose. Any agreement which may be undertaken by the parties after Recipient's evaluation of the Confidential Information shall be the subject of a separate agreement the parties with respect thereto.

B.   Non-circumvention: During the period that the Discloser is disclosing Confidential Information and/or introducing third parties to Recipient, Recipient agrees not to enter into any agreement with such third parties except pursuant to a separate agreement among such third parties, Discloser and Recipient. Notwithstanding the foregoing, if, subsequent to any introduction, the parties fail to conclude a license agreement with such third party(ies), Recipient's agreement not to enter into any agreement with such third parties without Discloser's participation shall end one (1) year after the end of negotiations among Recipient, Discloser and such third party; thereafter, Recipient shall be free to pursue any business opportunity or enter into any agreement with such third party(ies) without obligation to Discloser. This requirement of non-circumvention shall not apply to any third parties already known to Recipient at the time an introduction is to be made by Discloser hereunder.

C.   Return of Confidential Information: All copies of Confidential Information in tangible form which are in Recipient's possession will be promptly returned to Discloser promptly upon Discloser's request.

D.   Limitation on Liabilities: Recipient shall not be liable to Discloser for any incidental, consequential, special, or punitive damages of any kind or nature, arising out of or in connection with a breach of this Agreement or any termination of this Agreement, whether such liability is asserted on the basis of contract, tort (including negligence or strict liability), or otherwise, even if Recipient has been warned of the possibility of any such loss or damage.

E.   Miscellaneous:

1.   This Agreement sets forth the entire understanding between the parties hereto relating to the subject matter hereof and cannot be changed, modified, amended or terminated except by an instrument in writing executed by both Recipient and Discloser. The headings and captions used herein are inserted for convenience of reference only and shall not affect the construction or interpretation of this agreement.

2.   No waiver shall excuse the performance of any act other than those specifically referred to therein and shall not be deemed or construed to be a waiver of such terms or conditions for the future or any subsequent breach thereof. Except as otherwise provided in this agreement, all rights and remedies herein or otherwise shall be cumulative and none of them shall be in limitation of any other right or remedy.

3.   This agreement does not constitute a partnership or joint venture between the parties hereto. Neither party shall have any right to obligate or bind the other in any manner whatsoever. Nothing herein contained shall give or is intended to give any rights of any kind to any third persons.

4.   This agreement shall be governed by the laws of (FILL IN). In the event of litigation between the parties arising out of or relating to this Agreement, the prevailing party will be entitled to recover court costs and reasonable fees of attorneys, accountants and expert witnesses incurred by such a party in connection with such action.

5.   If any provision of this Agreement is or becomes or is deemed invalid, illegal or unenforceable under the applicable laws or regulations of any jurisdiction, either such provision will be deemed amended to conform to such laws or regulations without materially altering the intention of the parties or it shall be stricken, and the remainder of this Agreement shall remain in full force and effect.

DISCLOSER   **RECIPIENT**

By: _____   By:_____
Its: _____   Its:_____
Date: _____   Date: _____

Appendix-15
MANUFACTURER'S REPRESENTATIVE AGREEMENT

THIS AGREEMENT is made this ____day of _____, by and between
_____ with offices at _____ (the "Representative")
and _____ with offices at _____ (the "Manufacturer").

WITNESSETH:

WHEREAS, Manufacturer is in the business of manufacturing and marketing certain products including, but not limited to, products bearing properties licensed by third party licensors;

WHEREAS, Representative is in the business of consulting with and obtaining and developing licenses for various manufacturers;

WHEREAS, Manufacturer would like to retain the services of Representative to seek out and obtain for Manufacturer new licenses for its products.

NOW, THEREFORE, in consideration of the promises and agreements set forth herein, the parties, each intending to be legally bound hereby, do promise and agree as follows:

1. APPOINTMENT OF REPRESENTATIVE

Manufacturer hereby appoints Representative to act as its exclusive representative during the Term of this Agreement to recommend new licensed properties from third party licensors (the "New Licensed Properties") to Manufacturer and/or its affiliated and related companies for incorporation on Manufacturer's products for sale in the Territory identified in Schedule A attached hereto (the "Licensed Products") as well as to provide general consulting services relative to licensing matters. It is understood and agreed that Representative shall serve as Manufacturer's exclusive representative in its dealing with all third-party licensors except for those licensors listed in Schedule A (the "Excluded Licensors"). It is understood and agreed that Manufacturer shall refer all inquiries from or contacts with third party licensors (except for the Excluded Licensors) concerning licensing matters to Representative.

2. TERM OF AGREEMENT

This Agreement shall commence upon execution by both parties and shall extend for an Initial Term as defined in Exhibit A attached hereto. This Agreement may be automatically renewed for an unlimited number of additional Extended Terms as defined in Exhibit A unless one party provides written notice to the other party at least sixty (60) days prior to the expiration of the then in-effect Term of its intention not to renew the Agreement.

3. DUTIES AND OBLIGATIONS OF PARTIES

A. Representative shall use reasonable efforts during the Term of this Agreement to find and recommend New Licensed Properties to Manufacturer that are suitable for adoption and use by Manufacturer and/or its affiliated or related companies to incorporate on or in association with its products. Any New Licensed Property acquired by Manufacturer or any affiliated or related entity during the Term of this Agreement from a licensor other than an Excluded Licensor shall be deemed a New Licensed Property for purposes of this Agreement and shall be added to Exhibit B attached hereto whether or not recommended by Representative. Moreover, if that Manufacturer should enter into any license agreement with a licensor within one (1) year after termination or expiration of this Agreement based on negotiations initiated by Representative during the Term of this Agreement, any licensed property covered by such license agreement shall also be deemed a New Licensed Property for purposes of this Agreement and shall be added to Exhibit B attached hereto. It is understood that Exhibit B shall be periodically updated during the Term of this Agreement.

B. If that Manufacturer is interested in procuring any New Licensed Property, Representative will assist Manufacturer in scheduling preliminary meetings with the respective licensor(s) of such New Licensed Property, attend subsequent meetings wherever possible if requested by Manufacturer, and assist Manufacturer wherever possible in obtaining such New Licensed Property.

C. It is understood that Representative has in the past and will continue to work with other manufacturers.

D. Manufacturer shall be solely responsible for all costs and expenses associated with the obtaining of New Licensed Properties from the applicable licensor(s), including any legal fees associated with the drafting and negotiation of any agreement with such licensor.

4. COMPENSATION

A. In consideration for the services rendered by Representative, Manufacturer agrees to and shall pay Representative, during the Term of this Agreement, a non-refundable, non-creditable monthly retainer fee in the amount recited in Schedule A attached hereto (the "Retainer Fee").

B. In addition to the foregoing Retainer Fee, Manufacturer agrees to pay Representative a Commission on Manufacturer's Net Sales of its licensed products or services bearing the New Licensed Properties or by its affiliated or related companies in accordance with the schedule recited in Schedule A (the "Commission"). The definition of Net Sales with respect to each New Licensed Property shall be governed by such definition provided in the respective license agreement with the applicable licensor.

C. Representative's right to receive this Commission shall survive termination or expiration of this Agreement for any reason, Representative shall be entitled to continue to receive its full Commission based on those contracts or agreements entered into by Manufacturer with third party licensors during the Term of this Agreement or based on any contracts or agreements entered into by Manufacturer within one (1) year from the date of termination or expiration thereof resulting from presentations or negotiations made by Representative during the Term of this Agreement for which Representative would have received a Commission had the Agreement not been terminated or expired. Representative shall be entitled to such post termination Commission for so long as the Manufacturer continues to sell such licensed products or services under such agreements and any renewals, modifications or extensions thereof.

D. Manufacturer agrees to reimburse for all reasonable expenses incurred by Representative on behalf of Manufacturer, provided that any expenses above $1000 must be approved in writing by Manufacturer prior to their being incurred.

5. STATEMENTS AND PAYMENTS

A. The Commission owed Representative shall be calculated on a quarterly calendar basis (the "Commission Period") and shall be payable no later than thirty (30) days after the termination of the preceding full calendar quarter.

B. For each Commission Period, Manufacturer shall provide Representative with a written Commission Statement in a form acceptable to Representative. Such Commission Statement shall be certified as accurate by a duly authorized officer of Manufacturer and shall be broken down on a Property by Property basis. With respect to each of the New Licensed Properties, Manufacturer shall further provide Representative with copies of Manufacturer's royalty statements to the respective licensor. Such Commission Statements shall be furnished to Representative regardless of whether any Licensed Products were sold during the Commission Period or whether any actual Commission was owed.

C. The receipt or acceptance by Representative of any Commission statement or payment shall not prevent Representative from subsequently challenging the validity or accuracy of such statement or payment.

D. All payments due Representative shall be made in United States currency by check drawn on a United States bank, unless otherwise specified by Representative.

E. Late payments shall incur interest at the rate of ONE PERCENT (1%) per month from the date such payments were originally due.

6. RECORD INSPECTION AND AUDIT

A. Representative shall have the right, upon reasonable notice, to inspect Manufacturer's books and records and all other documents and material in Manufacturer's possession or control with respect to the subject matter of this Agreement. Representative shall have free and full access thereto for such purposes and may make copies thereof and Manufacturer shall fully cooperate with Representative in connection with such inspection.

B. If such inspection reveals an underpayment by Manufacturer of the actual Commission owed Representative, Manufacturer shall pay the difference, plus interest calculated at the rate of ONE PERCENT (1%) per month. If such underpayment be more than ONE THOUSAND UNITED STATES DOLLARS ($1,000.00) for any Commission Period, Manufacturer shall also reimburse Representative for the cost of such inspection.

C. All books and records relative to Manufacturer's obligations hereunder shall be maintained and made accessible to Representative for inspection at a location in the United States for at least two (2) years after termination of this Agreement.

7. INDEMNIFICATION

Manufacturer hereby agrees to defend, indemnify and hold Representative, its shareholders, directors, officers, employees, Representatives, parent companies, subsidiaries, and affiliates, harmless from and against any and all claims, liabilities, judgments, penalties, and taxes, civil and criminal, and all costs, expenses (including, without limitation, reasonable attorneys' fees) incurred in connection therewith, which any of them may incur or to which any of them may be subjected, arising out of or relating to the manufacture or sale of any Licensed Products based on the New Licensed Properties including, but not limited to, actions for infringement or product liability.

8. NOTICES AND PAYMENTS

A. Any notice required to be given under this Agreement shall be in writing and delivered personally to the other designated party at the above stated address or mailed by certified, registered or Express Mail, return receipt requested or by Federal Express.

B. Either party may change the address to which notice or payment is to be sent by written notice to the other under any provision of this paragraph.

9. TERMINATION

A. This Agreement may be terminated by either party upon thirty (30) days written notice to the other party in the event of a breach of a material provision of this Agreement by the other party, provided that, during the thirty (30) days period, the breaching party fails to cure such breach.

B. Representative shall have the right to terminate this Agreement for any reason on thirty (30) days written notice to Manufacturer subject to the provisions of this Agreement and, in particular, to the post termination compensation provisions concerning commissions as provided for in paragraph 4.

10. JURISDICTION/DISPUTES

A. This Agreement shall be governed in accordance with the laws of [State].

B. All disputes under this Agreement shall be resolved by litigation in the courts of the State of [State] and the parties all consent to the jurisdiction of such courts, agree to accept service of process by mail, and hereby waive any jurisdictional or venue defenses otherwise available to it.

11. AGREEMENT BINDING ON SUCCESSORS

The provisions of the Agreement shall be binding upon and shall inure to the benefit of the parties hereto, their heirs, assigns and successors.

12. WAIVER

No waiver by either party of any default shall be deemed as a waiver of prior or subsequent default of the same of other provisions of this Agreement.

13. SEVERABILITY

If any term, clause or provision hereof is held invalid or unenforceable by a court of competent jurisdiction, such invalidity shall not affect the validity or operation of any other term, clause or provision and such invalid term, clause or provision shall be deemed to be severed from the Agreement.

14. INDEPENDENT CONTRACTOR

Representative shall be deemed an independent contractor, and nothing contained herein shall constitute this arrangement to be employment, a joint venture or a partnership. Representative shall be solely responsible for and shall hold Manufacturer harmless for all claims for taxes, fees or costs, including but not limited to withholding, income tax, FICA, workman's compensation.

15. INTEGRATION

This Agreement constitutes the entire understanding of the parties, and revokes and supersedes all prior agreements between the parties and is intended as a final expression of their Agreement. It shall not be modified or amended except in writing signed by the parties hereto and specifically referring to this Agreement. This Agreement shall take precedence over any other documents which may conflict with this Agreement.

IN WITNESS WHEREOF, the parties hereto, intending to be legally bound hereby, have each caused to be affixed hereto its or his/her hand and seal the day indicated.

MANUFACTURER   MANUFACTURER'S REPRESENTATIVE

By:_____   By:_____

Title:_____   Title:_____

Date:_____   Date:_____

SCHEDULE A

TO MANUFACTURER'S REPRESENTATIVE AGREEMENT

1. LICENSED PRODUCTS:

2. TERRITORY:

3. TERM:

4. RETAINER FEE:

5. COMMISSION:

6. EXCLUDED LICENSORS:

Appendix-16
TRADEMARK CLASSES

GOODS

- CLASS 1 (Chemicals) Chemicals used in industry, science and photography, as well as in agriculture, horticulture and forestry; unprocessed artificial resins, unprocessed plastics; manures; fire extinguishing compositions; tempering and soldering preparations; chemical substances for preserving foodstuffs; tanning substances; adhesives used in industry.
- CLASS 2 (Paints) Paints, varnishes, lacquers; preservatives against rust and against deterioration of wood; colorants; mordants; raw natural resins; metals in foil and powder form for painters, decorators, printers and artists. Explanatory Note This class includes mainly paints, colorants and preparations used for the protection against corrosion. Includes, in particular: paints, varnishes and lacquers for industry, handicrafts and arts; dyestuffs for clothing; colorants for foodstuffs and beverages.
- CLASS 3 (Cosmetics and cleaning preparations) Bleaching preparations and other substances for laundry use; cleaning, polishing, scouring and abrasive preparations; soaps; perfumery, essential oils, cosmetics, hair lotions; dentifrices.
- CLASS 4 (Lubricants and fuels) Industrial oils and greases; lubricants; dust absorbing, wetting and binding compositions; fuels (including motor spirit) and illuminants; candles, wicks.
- CLASS 5 (Pharmaceuticals) Pharmaceutical, veterinary and sanitary preparations; dietetic substances adapted for medical use, food for babies; plasters, materials for dressings; material for stopping teeth, dental wax; disinfectants; preparations for destroying vermin; fungicides, herbicides.
- CLASS 6 (Metal goods) Common metals and their alloys; metal building materials; transportable buildings of metal; materials of metal for railway tracks; non-electric cables and wires of common metal; iron mongery, small items of metal hardware; pipes and tubes of metal; safes; goods of common metal not included in other classes; ores.
- CLASS 7 (Machinery) Machines and machine tools; motors and engines (except for land vehicles); machine coupling and transmission components (except for land vehicles); agricultural implements other than hand-operated; incubators for eggs.
- CLASS 8 (Hand tools) Hand tools and implements (hand operated); cutlery; side arms; razors.
- CLASS 9 (Electrical and scientific apparatus) Scientific, nautical, surveying, electric, photographic, cinematographic, optical, weighing, measuring, signaling, checking (supervision), lifesaving and teaching apparatus and instruments; apparatus for recording, transmission or reproduction of sound or images; magnetic data carriers, recording discs; automatic vending machines and mechanisms for coin operated apparatus; cash registers, calculating machines, data processing equipment and computers; fire-extinguishing apparatus.
- CLASS 10 (Medical Apparatus) Surgical, medical, dental and veterinary apparatus and instruments, artificial limbs, eyes and teeth; orthopedic articles; suture materials.
- CLASS 11 (Environmental control apparatus) Apparatus for lighting, heating, steam generating, cooking, refrigerating, drying, ventilating, water supply and sanitary purposes.
- CLASS 12 (Vehicles) Vehicles; apparatus for locomotion by land, air or water.
- CLASS 13 (Firearms) Firearms; ammunition and projectiles; explosives; fireworks.
- CLASS 14 (Jewelry) Precious metals and their alloys and goods in precious metals or coated therewith, not included in other classes; jewelry, precious stones; horological and chronometric instruments.
- CLASS 15 (Musical Instruments) Musical instruments.
- CLASS 16 (Paper goods and printed matter) Paper, cardboard and goods made from these materials, not included in other classes; printed matter; bookbinding material; photographs; stationery; adhesives for stationery or household purposes; artists' materials; paint brushes;

typewriters and office requisites (except furniture); instructional and teaching material (except apparatus); plastic materials for packaging (not included in other classes); playing cards; printers' type; printing blocks.

- CLASS 17 (Rubber goods) Rubber, gutta-percha, gum, asbestos, mica and goods made from these materials and not included in other classes; plastics in extruded form for use in manufacture; packing, stopping and insulating materials; flexible pipes, not of metal.
- CLASS 18 (Leather goods) Leather and imitations of leather, and goods made of these materials and not included in other classes; animal skins, hides; trunks and traveling bags; umbrellas, parasols and walking sticks; whips, harness and saddlery.
- CLASS 19 (Nonmetallic building materials) Building materials (nonmetallic); nonmetallic rigid pipes for building; asphalt, pitch and bitumen; nonmetallic transportable buildings; monuments, not of metal.
- CLASS 20 (Furniture and articles not otherwise classified) Furniture, mirrors, picture frames; goods (not included in other classes) of wood, cork, reed, cane, wicker, horn, bone, ivory, whalebone, shell, amber, mother-of-pearl, meerschaum and substitutes for all these materials, or of plastics.
- CLASS 21 (Housewares and glass) Household or kitchen utensils and containers (not of precious metal or coated therewith); combs and sponges; brushes (except paint brushes); brushmaking materials; articles for cleaning purposes; steel wool; un-worked or semi-worked glass (except glass used in building); glassware, porcelain and earthenware not included in other classes.
- CLASS 22 (Cordage and fibers) Ropes, string, nets, tents, awnings, tarpaulins, sails, sacks and bags (not included in other classes); padding and stuffing materials (except of rubber or plastics); raw fibrous textile materials.
- CLASS 23 (Yarns and threads) Yarns and threads, for textile use.
- CLASS 24 (Fabrics) Textiles and textile goods, not included in other classes; bed and table covers.
- CLASS 25 (Clothing) Clothing, footwear, headgear.
- CLASS 26 (Fancy goods) Lace and embroidery, ribbons and braid; buttons, hooks and eyes, pins and needles; artificial flowers.
- CLASS 27 (Floor coverings) Carpets, rugs, mats and matting, linoleum and other materials for covering existing floors; wall hangings (non-textile).
- CLASS 28 (Toys and sporting goods) Games and playthings; gymnastic and sporting articles not included in other classes; decorations for Christmas trees.
- CLASS 29 (Meats and processed foods) Meat, fish, poultry and game; meat extracts; preserved, dried and cooked fruits and vegetables; jellies, jams, fruit sauces; eggs, milk and milk products; edible oils and fats.
- CLASS 30 (Staple foods) Coffee, tea, cocoa, sugar, rice, tapioca, sago, artificial coffee; flour and preparations made from cereals, bread, pastry and confectionery, ices; honey, treacle; yeast, baking-powder; salt, mustard; vinegar, sauces (condiments); spices; ice.
- CLASS 31 (Natural agricultural products) Agricultural, horticultural and forestry products and grains not included in other classes; living animals; fresh fruits and vegetables; seeds, natural plants and flowers; foodstuffs for animals, malt.
- CLASS 32 (Light beverages) Beers; mineral and aerated waters and other nonalcoholic drinks; fruit drinks and fruit juices; syrups and other preparations for making beverages.
- CLASS 33 (Wine and spirits) Alcoholic beverages (except beers).
- CLASS 34 (Smokers' articles) Tobacco; smokers' articles; matches.

SERVICES

- CLASS 35 (Advertising and business) Advertising; business management; business administration; office functions.
- CLASS 36 (Insurance and financial) Insurance; financial affairs; monetary affairs; real estate affairs.
- CLASS 37 (Building construction and repair) Building construction; repair; installation services.
- CLASS 38 (Telecommunications)
- CLASS 39 (Transportation and storage) Transport; packaging and storage of goods; travel arrangement.
- CLASS 40 (Treatment of materials) Treatment of materials.
- CLASS 41 (Education and entertainment) Education; providing of training; entertainment; sporting and cultural activities.
- CLASS 42 (Computer, scientific & legal) Scientific and technological services and research and design relating thereto: industrial analysis and research services; design and development of computer hardware and software; legal services.
- CLASS 43 (Hotels and Restaurants) Services for providing food and drink; temporary accommodations.
- CLASS 44 (Medical, beauty & agricultural) Medical services; veterinary services; hygienic and beauty care for human beings or animals; agriculture, horticulture and forestry services.
- CLASS 45 (Personal) Personal and social services rendered by others to meet the needs of individuals; security services for the protection of property and individuals.

Appendix-17
FORM VA COPYRIGHT APPLICATION

Ⓒ **Form VA**

Detach and read these instructions before completing this form.
Make sure all applicable spaces have been filled in before you return this form.

When to Use This Form: Use Form VA for copyright registration of published or unpublished works of the visual arts. This category consists of "pictorial, graphic, or sculptural works," including two-dimensional and three-dimensional works of fine, graphic, and applied art; photographs; prints and art reproductions; and maps, globes, charts, technical drawings, diagrams, and models.

What Does Copyright Protect? Copyright in a work of the visual arts protects those pictorial, graphic, or sculptural elements that, either alone or in combination, represent an "original work of authorship." The statute declares: "In no case does copyright protection for an original work of authorship extend to any idea, procedure, process, system, method of operation, concept, principle, or discovery, regardless of the form in which it is described, explained, illustrated, or embodied in such work."

Works of Artistic Craftsmanship and Designs: You may register "works of artistic craftsmanship," but the statute makes clear that protection extends to "their form" and not to "their mechanical or utilitarian aspects." The "design of a useful article" is considered copyrightable "only if, and only to the extent that, such design incorporates pictorial, graphic, or sculptural features that can be identified separately from, and are capable of existing independently of, the utilitarian aspects of the article."

Labels and Advertisements: Works prepared for use in connection with the sale or advertisement of goods and services may be registered if they contain "original work of authorship." Use Form VA if the copyrightable material in the work you are registering is mainly pictorial or graphic; use Form TX if it consists mainly of text. **Note:** Words and short phrases such as names, titles, and slogans cannot be protected by copyright, and the same is true of standard symbols, emblems, and other commonly used graphic designs that are in the public domain. When used commercially, material of that sort can sometimes be protected under state laws of unfair competition or under the federal trademark laws. For information about trademark registration, call the U.S. Patent and Trademark Office, at 1-800-786-9199 (toll free) or go to *www.uspto.gov.*

Architectural Works: Copyright protection extends to the design of buildings created for the use of human beings. Architectural works created on or after December 1, 1990, or that on December 1, 1990, were unconstructed and embodied only in unpublished plans or drawings are eligible. Request Circular 41, *Copyright Claims in Architectural Works,* for more information. Architectural works and technical drawings cannot be registered on the same application.

Deposit to Accompany Application: An application for copyright registration must be accompanied by a deposit consisting of copies representing the entire work for which registration is to be made.

> **Unpublished Work:** Deposit one complete copy.

> **Published Work:** Deposit two complete copies of the best edition.

> **Work First Published Outside the United States:** Deposit one complete copy of the first foreign edition.

> **Contribution to a Collective Work:** Deposit one complete copy of the best edition of the collective work.

The Copyright Notice: Before March 1, 1989, the use of copyright notice was mandatory on all published works, and any work first published before that date should have carried a notice. For works first published on and after March 1, 1989, use of the copyright notice is optional. For more information about copyright notice, see Circular 3, *Copyright Notice.*

For Further Information: To speak to a Copyright Office staff member, call (202) 707-3000 or 1-877-476-0778 (toll free). Recorded information is available 24 hours a day. Order forms and other publications from the address in space 9 or call (202) 707-9100 or 1-877-476-0778 (toll free). Access and download circulars, forms, and other information from the Copyright Office website at *www.copyright.gov.*

Please type or print using black ink. The form is used to produce the certificate.

1

SPACE 1: Title

Title of This Work: Every work submitted for copyright registration must be given a title to identify that particular work. If the copies of the work bear a title (or an identifying phrase that could serve as a title), transcribe that wording *completely* and *exactly* on the application. Indexing of the registration and future identification of the work will depend on the information you give here. For an architectural work that has been constructed, add the date of construction after the title; if unconstructed at this time, add "not yet constructed."

Publication as a Contribution: If the work being registered is a contribution to a periodical, serial, or collection, give the title of the contribution in the "Title of This Work" space. Then, in the line headed "Publication as a Contribution," give information about the collective work in which the contribution appeared.

Nature of This Work: Briefly describe the general nature or character of the pictorial, graphic, or sculptural work being registered for copyright. Examples: "Oil Painting"; "Charcoal Drawing"; "Etching"; "Sculpture"; "Map"; "Photograph"; "Scale Model"; "Lithographic Print"; "Jewelry Design"; "Fabric Design."

Previous or Alternative Titles: Complete this space if there are any additional titles for the work under which someone searching for the registration might be likely to look, or under which a document pertaining to the work might be recorded.

2

SPACE 2: Author(s)

General Instruction: After reading these instructions, decide who are the "authors" of this work for copyright purposes. Then, in the line headed "Author" of this work for copyright purposes. Then, in the line headed work is a "collective work," give the requested information about every "author" who contributed any appreciable amount of copyrightable matter to this version of the work. If you need further space, request Continuation Sheets (Form CON). In the case of a collective work, such as a catalog of paintings or collection of cartoons by various authors, give information about the author of the collective work as a whole.

Name of Author: The fullest form of the author's name should be given. Unless the work was "made for hire," the individual who actually created the work is its "author." In the case of a work made for hire, the statute provides that "the employer or other person for whom the work was prepared is considered the author."

What Is a "Work Made for Hire"? A "work made for hire" is defined as: (1) "a work prepared by an employee within the scope of his or her employment"; or (2) "a work specially ordered or commissioned for use as a contribution to a collective work, as a part of a motion picture or other audiovisual work, as a translation, as a supplementary work, as a compilation, as an instructional text, as a test, as answer material for a test, or as an atlas, if the parties expressly agree in a written instrument signed by them that the work shall be considered a work made for hire." If you have checked "Yes" to indicate that the work was "made for hire," you must give the full legal name of the employer (or other person for whom the work was prepared). You may also include the name of the employee along with the name of the employer (for example: "Elster Publishing Co., employer for hire of John Ferguson").

"Anonymous" or "Pseudonymous" Work: An author's contribution to a work is "anonymous" if that author is not identified on the copies or phonorecords of the work. An author's contribution to a work is "pseudonymous" if that author is identified on the copies or phonorecords under a fictitious name. If the work is "anonymous" you may: (1) leave the line blank; or (2) state "anonymous" on the line; or (3) reveal the author's identity. If the work is "pseudonymous" you may: (1) leave the line blank; or (2) give the pseudonym and identify it as such (for example: "Huntley Haverstock, pseudonym"); or (3) reveal the author's name, making clear which is the real name and which is the pseudonym (for example: "Henry Leek, whose pseudonym is Priam Farrel"). However, the citizenship or domicile of the author *must* be given in all cases.

Dates of Birth and Death: If the author is dead, the statute requires that the year of death be included in the application unless the work is anonymous or pseudonymous. The author's birth date is optional but is useful as a form of identification. Leave this space blank if the author's contribution was a "work made for hire."

Author's Nationality or Domicile: Give the country of which the author is a citizen or the country in which the author is domiciled. Nationality or domicile *must* be given in all cases.

Nature of Authorship: Categories of pictorial, graphic, and sculptural authorship are listed below. Check the box(es) that best describe(s) each author's contribution to the work.

3-Dimensional sculptures: Fine art sculptures, toys, dolls, scale models, and sculptural designs applied to useful articles.

2-Dimensional artwork: Watercolor and oil paintings; pen and ink drawings; logo illustrations; greeting cards; collages; stencils; patterns; computer graphics; graphics appearing in screen displays; artwork appearing on posters, calendars, games, commercial prints and labels, and packaging; artwork applied to useful articles; designs reproduced on textiles, lace, and other fabrics and on wallpaper, carpeting, floor tile, wrapping paper, and clothing.

Reproductions of works of art: Reproductions of preexisting artwork made by, for example, lithography, photoengraving, or etching.

Maps: Cartographic representations of an area, such as state and county maps, atlases, marine charts, relief maps, and globes.

Photographs: Pictorial photographic prints and slides and holograms.

Jewelry designs: 3-dimensional designs applied to rings, pendants, earrings, necklaces, and the like.

Technical drawings: Diagrams illustrating scientific or technical information in linear form, such as architectural blueprints or mechanical drawings.

Text: Textual material that accompanies pictorial, graphic, or sculptural works, such as comic strips, greeting cards, game rules, commercial prints or labels, and maps.

Architectural works: Designs of buildings, including the overall form as well as the arrangement and composition of spaces and elements of the design.

NOTE: You must apply for registration for the underlying architectural plans on a separate Form VA. Check the box "Technical drawing."

SPACE 3: Creation and Publication

General Instructions: Do not confuse "creation" with "publication." Every application for copyright registration must state "the year in which creation of the work was completed." Give the date and nation of first publication only if the work has been published.

Creation: Under the statute, a work is "created" when it is fixed in a copy or phonorecord for the first time. If a work has been prepared over a period of time, the part of the work existing in fixed form on a particular date constitutes the created work on that date. The date you give here should be the year in which the author completed the particular version for which registration is now being sought, even if other versions exist or if further changes or additions are planned.

Publication: The statute defines "publication" as "the distribution of copies or phonorecords of a work to the public by sale or other transfer of ownership, or by rental, lease, or lending"; a work is also "published" if there has been an "offering to distribute copies or phonorecords to a group of persons for purposes of further distribution, public performance, or public display." Give the full date (month, day, year) when, and the country where, publication first occurred. If first publication took place simultaneously in the United States and other countries, it is sufficient to state "U.S.A."

SPACE 4: Claimant(s)

Name(s) and Address(es) of Copyright Claimant(s): Give the name(s) and address(es) of the copyright claimant(s) in this work even if the claimant is the same as the author. Copyright in a work belongs initially to the author of the work, including, in the case of a work made for hire, the employer or other person for whom the work was prepared. The copyright claimant is either the author of the work or a person or organization to whom the copyright initially belonging to the author has been transferred.

Transfer: The statute provides that, if the copyright claimant is not the author, the application for registration must contain "a brief statement of how the claimant obtained ownership of the copyright." If any copyright claimant named in space 4 is not an author named in space 2, give a brief statement explaining how the claimant(s) obtained ownership of the copyright. Examples: "By written contract"; "Transfer of all rights by author"; "Assignment"; "By will." Do not attach transfer documents or other attachments or riders.

SPACE 5: Previous Registration

General Instructions: The questions in space 5 are intended to find out whether an earlier registration has been made for this work and, if so, whether there is any basis for a new registration. As a rule, only one basic copyright registration can be made for the same version of a particular work.

Same Version: If this version is substantially the same as the work covered by a previous registration, a second registration is not generally possible unless: (1) the work has been registered in unpublished form and a second registration is now being sought to cover this first published edition; or (2) someone other than the author is identified as a copyright claimant in the earlier registration, and the author is now seeking registration in his or her own name. If either of these two exceptions applies, check the appropriate box and give the earlier registration number and date. Otherwise, do not submit Form VA. Instead, write the Copyright Office for information about supplementary registration or recordation of transfers of copyright ownership.

Changed Version: If the work has been changed and you are now seeking registration to cover the additions or revisions, check the last box in space 5, give the earlier registration number and date, and complete both parts of space 6 in accordance with the instruction below.

Previous Registration Number and Date: If more than one previous registration has been made for the work, give the number and date of the latest registration.

SPACE 6: Derivative Work or Compilation

General Instructions: Complete space 6 if this work is a "changed version," "compilation," or "derivative work," and if it incorporates one or more earlier works that have already been published or registered for copyright, or that have fallen into the public domain. A "compilation" is defined as "a work formed by the collection and assembling of preexisting materials or of data that are selected, coordinated, or arranged in such a way that the resulting work as a whole constitutes an original work of authorship." A "derivative work" is "a work based on one or more preexisting works." Examples of derivative works include reproductions of works of art, sculptures based on drawings, lithographs based on paintings, maps based on previously published sources, or "any other form in which a work may be recast, transformed, or adapted." Derivative works also include works "consisting of editorial revisions, annotations, or other modifications" if these changes, as a whole, represent an original work of authorship.

Preexisting Material (space 6a): Complete this space *and* space 6b for derivative works. In this space identify the preexisting work that has been recast, transformed, or adapted. Examples of preexisting material might be "Grunewald Altarpiece" or "19th century quilt design." Do not complete this space for compilations.

Material Added to This Work (space 6b): Give a brief, general statement of the *additional* new material covered by the copyright claim for which registration is sought. In the case of a derivative work, identify this new material. Examples: "Adaptation of design and additional artistic work"; "Reproduction of painting by photolithography"; "Additional cartographic material"; "Compilation of photographs." If the work is a compilation, give a brief, general statement describing both the material that has been compiled *and* the compilation itself. Example: "Compilation of 19th century political cartoons."

SPACE 7, 8, 9: Fee, Correspondence, Certification, Return Address

Deposit Account: If you maintain a deposit account in the Copyright Office, identify it in space 7a. Otherwise, leave the space blank and send the fee with your application and deposit.

Correspondence (space 7b): Give the name, address, area code, telephone number, email address, and fax number (if available) of the person to be consulted if correspondence about this application becomes necessary.

Certification (space 8): The application cannot be accepted unless it bears the date and the *handwritten signature* of the author or other copyright claimant, or of the owner of exclusive right(s), or of the duly authorized agent of the author, claimant, or owner of exclusive right(s).

Address for Return of Certificate (space 9): The address box must be completed legibly since the certificate will be returned in a window envelope.

Appendices

Clear Form

ⓒ Form VA
For a Work of the Visual Arts
UNITED STATES COPYRIGHT OFFICE

REGISTRATION NUMBER

VA   VAU

EFFECTIVE DATE OF REGISTRATION

Month   Day   Year

DO NOT WRITE ABOVE THIS LINE. IF YOU NEED MORE SPACE, USE A SEPARATE CONTINUATION SHEET.

1 TITLE OF THIS WORK ▼   NATURE OF THIS WORK ▼ See instructions

PREVIOUS OR ALTERNATIVE TITLES ▼

PUBLICATION AS A CONTRIBUTION If this work was published as a contribution to a periodical, serial, or collection, give information about the collective work in which the contribution appeared. Title of Collective Work ▼

If published in a periodical or serial give: Volume ▼   Number ▼   Issue Date ▼   On Pages ▼

2 NAME OF AUTHOR ▼   DATES OF BIRTH AND DEATH
Year Born ▼   Year Died ▼

a

WAS THIS CONTRIBUTION TO THE WORK A "WORK MADE FOR HIRE"?
☐ Yes
☐ No

AUTHOR'S NATIONALITY OR DOMICILE
Name of Country
OR ⎨ Citizen of _____
⎩ Domiciled in _____

WAS THIS AUTHOR'S CONTRIBUTION TO THE WORK
Anonymous? ☐ Yes ☐ No
Pseudonymous? ☐ Yes ☐ No
If the answer to either of these questions is "Yes," see detailed instructions.

NATURE OF AUTHORSHIP Check appropriate box(es). **See instructions**
☐ 3-Dimensional sculpture   ☐ Map   ☐ Technical drawing
☐ 2-Dimensional artwork   ☐ Photograph   ☐ Text
☐ Reproduction of work of art ☐ Jewelry design   ☐ Architectural work

NOTE
Under the law, the "author" of a "work made for hire" is generally the employer, not the employee (see instructions). For any part of this work that was "made for hire," check "Yes" in the space provided, give the employer (or other person for whom the work was prepared) as "Author" of that part, and leave the space for dates of birth and death blank.

b NAME OF AUTHOR ▼   DATES OF BIRTH AND DEATH
Year Born ▼   Year Died ▼

WAS THIS CONTRIBUTION TO THE WORK A "WORK MADE FOR HIRE"?
☐ Yes
☐ No

AUTHOR'S NATIONALITY OR DOMICILE
Name of Country
OR ⎨ Citizen of _____
⎩ Domiciled in _____

WAS THIS AUTHOR'S CONTRIBUTION TO THE WORK
Anonymous? ☐ Yes ☐ No
Pseudonymous? ☐ Yes ☐ No
If the answer to either of these questions is "Yes," see detailed instructions.

NATURE OF AUTHORSHIP Check appropriate box(es). **See instructions**
☐ 3-Dimensional sculpture   ☐ Map   ☐ Technical drawing
☐ 2-Dimensional artwork   ☐ Photograph   ☐ Text
☐ Reproduction of work of art ☐ Jewelry design   ☐ Architectural work

3 YEAR IN WHICH CREATION OF THIS WORK WAS COMPLETED
a Year ▶
This information must be given in all cases.

b DATE AND NATION OF FIRST PUBLICATION OF THIS PARTICULAR WORK
Complete this information ONLY if this work has been published.
Month ▶ _____ Day ▶ _____ Year ▶ _____
Nation ▶ _____

4 COPYRIGHT CLAIMANT(S) Name and address must be given even if the claimant is the same as the author given in space 2. ▼

TRANSFER If the claimant(s) named here in space 4 is (are) different from the author(s) named in space 2, give a brief statement of how the claimant(s) obtained ownership of the copyright. ▼

See instructions before completing this space.

DO NOT WRITE HERE / OFFICE USE ONLY
APPLICATION RECEIVED
ONE DEPOSIT RECEIVED
TWO DEPOSITS RECEIVED
FUNDS RECEIVED

MORE ON BACK ▶ • Complete all applicable spaces (numbers 5-9) on the reverse side of this page.
• See detailed instructions   • Sign the form at line 8

DO NOT WRITE HERE
Page 1 of _____ pages

	EXAMINED BY	FORM VA
	CHECKED BY	
	CORRESPONDENCE ☐ Yes	FOR COPYRIGHT OFFICE USE ONLY

DO NOT WRITE ABOVE THIS LINE. IF YOU NEED MORE SPACE, USE A SEPARATE CONTINUATION SHEET.

PREVIOUS REGISTRATION Has registration for this work, or for an earlier version of this work, already been made in the Copyright Office?
☐ Yes ☐ No If your answer is "Yes," why is another registration being sought? (Check appropriate box.) ▼
a. ☐ This is the first published edition of a work previously registered in unpublished form.
b. ☐ This is the first application submitted by this author as copyright claimant.
c. ☐ This is a changed version of the work, as shown by space 6 on this application.
If your answer is "Yes," give: **Previous Registration Number** ▼   **Year of Registration** ▼

5

DERIVATIVE WORK OR COMPILATION Complete both space 6a and 6b for a derivative work; complete only 6b for a compilation.
a. Preexisting Material Identify any preexisting work or works that this work is based on or incorporates. ▼

6 a

See instructions before completing this space.

b. Material Added to This Work Give a brief, general statement of the material that has been added to this work and in which copyright is claimed. ▼

b

DEPOSIT ACCOUNT If the registration fee is to be charged to a Deposit Account established in the Copyright Office, give name and number of Account.
Name ▼   **Account Number** ▼

7 a

CORRESPONDENCE Give name and address to which correspondence about this application should be sent. Name/Address/Apt/City/State/Zip ▼

b

Area code and daytime telephone number   (   )   Fax number   (   )
Email

CERTIFICATION* I, the undersigned, hereby certify that I am the
check only one ▶
☐ author
☐ other copyright claimant
☐ owner of exclusive right(s)
☐ authorized agent of _____
Name of author or other copyright claimant, or owner of exclusive right(s) ▲
of the work identified in this application and that the statements made by me in this application are correct to the best of my knowledge.

8

Typed or printed name and date ▼ If this application gives a date of publication in space 3, do not sign and submit it before that date.
_____ Date _____

Handwritten signature (X) ▼
X _____

Certificate will be mailed in window envelope to this address:	Name ▼	YOU MUST: • Complete all necessary spaces • Sign your application in space 8
	Number/Street/Apt ▼	SEND ALL 3 ELEMENTS IN THE SAME PACKAGE: 1. Application form 2. Nonrefundable filing fee in check or money order payable to Register of Copyrights 3. Deposit material
	City/State/Zip ▼	MAIL TO: Library of Congress Copyright Office-VA 101 Independence Avenue SE Washington, DC 20559

9

*17 U.S.C. §506(e): Any person who knowingly makes a false representation of a material fact in the application for copyright registration provided for by section 409, or in any written statement filed in connection with the application, shall be fined not more than $2,500.

Form VA-Full   Rev: 12/2016   Printed on recycled paper

Appendix-18
FORM TX COPYRIGHT APPLICATION

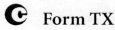 **Form TX**

Detach and read these instructions before completing this form.
Make sure all applicable spaces have been filled in before you return this form.

When to Use This Form: Use Form TX for registration of published or unpublished nondramatic literary works, excluding periodicals or serial issues. This class includes a wide variety of works: fiction, nonfiction, poetry, textbooks, reference works, directories, catalogs, advertising copy, compilations of information, and computer programs. For periodicals and serials, use Form SE.

Deposit to Accompany Application: An application for copyright registration must be accompanied by a deposit consisting of copies or phonorecords representing the entire work for which registration is to be made. The following are the general deposit requirements as set forth in the statute:

Unpublished Work: Deposit one complete copy (or phonorecord).

Published Work: Deposit two complete copies (or one phonorecord) of the best edition.

Work First Published Outside the United States: Deposit one complete copy (or phonorecord) of the first foreign edition.

Contribution to a Collective Work: Deposit one complete copy (or phonorecord) of the best edition of the collective work.

The Copyright Notice: Before March 1, 1989, the use of copyright notice was mandatory on all published works, and any work first published

before that date should have carried a notice. For works first published on and after March 1, 1989, use of the copyright notice is optional. For more information about copyright notice, see Circular 3, *Copyright Notice*.

For Further Information: To speak to a Copyright Office staff member, call (202) 707-3000 or 1-877-476-0778 (toll free). Recorded information is available 24 hours a day. Order forms and other publications from the address in space 9 or call the Forms and Publications Hotline at (202) 707-9100. Access and download circulars, certain forms, and other information from the Copyright Office website at *www.copyright.gov*.

Please type or print using black ink. The form is used to produce the certificate.

1 SPACE 1: Title

Title of This Work: Every work submitted for copyright registration must be given a title to identify that particular work. If the copies or phonorecords of the work bear a title or an identifying phrase that could serve as a title, transcribe that wording *completely* and *exactly* on the application. Indexing of the registration and future identification of the work will depend on the information you give here.

Previous or Alternative Titles: Complete this space if there are any additional titles for the work under which someone searching for the registration might be likely to look or under which a document pertaining to the work might be recorded.

Publication as a Contribution: If the work being registered is a contribution to a periodical, serial, or collection, give the title of the contribution in the "Title of This Work" space. Then, in the line headed "Publication as a Contribution," give information about the collective work in which the contribution appeared.

2 SPACE 2: Author(s)

General Instructions: After reading these instructions, decide who are the "authors" of this work for copyright purposes. Then, unless the work is a "collective work," give the requested information about every "author" who contributed any appreciable amount of copyrightable matter to this version of the work. If you need further space, request Continuation Sheets. In the case of a collective work, such as an anthology, collection of essays, or encyclopedia, give information about the author of the collective work as a whole.

Name of Author: The fullest form of the author's name should be given. Unless the work was "made for hire," the individual who actually

created the work is its "author." In the case of a work made for hire, the statute provides that "the employer or other person for whom the work was prepared is considered the author."

What Is a "Work Made for Hire"? A "work made for hire" is defined as (1) "a work prepared by an employee within the scope of his or her employment"; or (2) "a work specially ordered or commissioned for use as a contribution to a collective work, as a part of a motion picture or other audiovisual work, as a translation, as a supplementary work, as a compilation, as an instructional text, as a test, as answer material for a test, or as an atlas, if the parties expressly agree in a written instrument signed by them that the works shall be considered a work made for hire." If you have checked "Yes" to indicate that the work was "made for hire," you must give the full legal name of the employer (or other person for whom the work was prepared). You may also include the name of the employee along with the name of the employer (for example: "Elster Publishing Co., employer for hire of John Ferguson").

"Anonymous" or "Pseudonymous" Work: An author's contribution to a work is "anonymous" if that author is not identified on the copies or phonorecords of the work. An author's contribution to a work is "pseudonymous" if that author is identified on the copies or phonorecords under a fictitious name. If the work is "anonymous" you may: (1) leave the line blank; or (2) state "anonymous" on the line; or (3) reveal the author's identity. If the work is "pseudonymous" you may: (1) leave the line blank; or (2) give the pseudonym and identify it as such (for example: "Huntley Haverstock, pseudonym"); or (3) reveal the author's name, making clear which is the real name and which is the pseudonym (for example, "Judith Barton, whose pseudonym is Madeline Elster"). However, the citizenship or domicile of the author *must* be given in all cases.

Dates of Birth and Death: If the author is dead, the statute requires that the year of death be included in the application unless the work is anonymous or pseudonymous. The author's birth date is optional but is useful as a form of identification. Leave this space blank if the author's contribution was a "work made for hire."

Author's Nationality or Domicile: Give the country of which the author is a citizen or the country in which the author is domiciled. Nationality or domicile *must* be given in all cases.

Nature of Authorship: After the words "Nature of Authorship," give a brief general statement of the nature of this particular author's contribution to the work. Examples: "Entire text"; "Coauthor of entire text"; "Computer program"; "Editorial revisions"; "Compilation and English translation"; "New text."

SPACE 3: Creation and Publication

General Instructions: Do not confuse "creation" with "publication." Every application for copyright registration must state "the year in which creation of the work was completed." Give the date and nation of first publication only if the work has been published.

Creation: Under the statute, a work is "created" when it is fixed in a copy or phonorecord for the first time. Where a work has been prepared over a period of time, the part of the work existing in fixed form on a particular date constitutes the created work on that date. The date you give here should be the year in which the author completed the particular version for which registration is now being sought, even if other versions exist or if further changes or additions are planned.

Publication: The statute defines "publication" as "the distribution of copies or phonorecords of a work to the public by sale or other transfer of ownership, or by rental, lease, or lending." A work is also "published" if there has been an "offering to distribute copies or phonorecords to a group of persons for purposes of further distribution, public performance, or public display." Give the full date (month, day, year) when, and the country where, publication first occurred. If first publication took place simultaneously in the United States and other countries, it is sufficient to state "U.S.A."

SPACE 4: Claimant(s)

Name(s) and Address(es) of Copyright Claimant(s): Give the name(s) and address(es) of the copyright claimant(s) in this work even if the claimant is the same as the author. Copyright in a work belongs initially to the author of the work (including, in the case of a work made for hire, the employer or other person for whom the work was prepared). The copyright claimant is either the author of the work or a person or organization to whom the copyright initially belonging to the author has been transferred.

Transfer: The statute provides that, if the copyright claimant is not the author, the application for registration must contain "a brief statement of how the claimant obtained ownership of the copyright." If any copyright claimant named in space 4 is not an author named in space 2, give a brief statement explaining how the claimant(s) obtained ownership of the copyright. Examples: "By written contract"; "Transfer of all rights by author"; "Assignment"; "By will." Do not attach transfer documents or other attachments or riders.

SPACE 5: Previous Registration

General Instructions: The questions in space 5 are intended to show whether an earlier registration has been made for this work and, if so, whether there is any basis for a new registration. As a general rule, only one basic copyright registration can be made for the same version of a particular work.

Same Version: If this version is substantially the same as the work covered by a previous registration, a second registration is not generally possible

unless: (1) the work has been registered in unpublished form and a second registration is now being sought to cover this first published edition; or (2) someone other than the author is identified as copyright claimant in the earlier registration, and the author is now seeking registration in his or her own name. If either of these two exceptions applies, check the appropriate box and give the earlier registration number and date. Otherwise, do not submit Form TX. Instead, write the Copyright Office for information about supplementary registration or recordation of transfers of copyright ownership.

Changed Version: If the work has been changed and you are now seeking registration to cover the additions or revisions, check the last box in space 5, give the earlier registration number and date, and complete both parts of space 6 in accordance with the instructions below.

Previous Registration Number and Date: If more than one previous registration has been made for the work, give the number and date of the latest registration.

SPACE 6: Derivative Work or Compilation

General Instructions: Complete space 6 if this work is a "changed version," "compilation," or "derivative work" and if it incorporates one or more earlier works that have already been published or registered for copyright or that have fallen into the public domain. A "compilation" is defined as "a work formed by the collection and assembling of preexisting materials or of data that are selected, coordinated, or arranged in such a way that the resulting work as a whole constitutes an original work of authorship." A "derivative work" is "a work based on one or more preexisting works." Examples of derivative works include translations, fictionalizations, abridgments, condensations, or "any other form in which a work may be recast, transformed, or adapted." Derivative works also include works "consisting of editorial revisions, annotations, or other modifications" if these changes, as a whole, represent an original work of authorship.

Preexisting Material (space 6a): For derivative works, complete this space *and* space 6b. In space 6a identify the preexisting work that has been recast, transformed, or adapted. The preexisting work may be material that has been previously published, previously registered, or that is in the public domain. An example of preexisting material might be: "Russian version of Goncharov's 'Oblomov.'"

Material Added to This Work (space 6b): Give a brief, general statement of the new material covered by the copyright claim for which registration is sought. *Derivative work* examples include: "Foreword, editing, critical annotations"; "Translation"; "Chapters 11–17." If the work is a *compilation*, describe both the compilation itself and the material that has been compiled. Example: "Compilation of certain 1917 speeches by Woodrow Wilson." A work may be both a derivative work and compilation, in which case a sample statement might be: "Compilation and additional new material."

SPACE 7, 8, 9: Fee, Correspondence, Certification, Return Address

Deposit Account: If you maintain a Deposit Account in the Copyright Office, identify it in space 7a. Otherwise leave the space blank and send the fee with your application and deposit.

Correspondence (space 7b): Give the name, address, area code, telephone number, fax number, and email address (if available) of the person to be consulted if correspondence about this application becomes necessary.

Certification (space 8): The application cannot be accepted unless it bears the date and the *handwritten signature* of the author or other copyright claimant, or of the owner of exclusive right(s), or of the duly authorized agent of author, claimant, or owner of exclusive right(s).

Address for Return of Certificate (space 9): The address box must be completed legibly because the certificate will be returned in a window envelope.

Appendices

Form TX
For a Nondramatic Literary Work
UNITED STATES COPYRIGHT OFFICE

REGISTRATION NUMBER

TX   TXU

EFFECTIVE DATE OF REGISTRATION

Month   Day   Year

DO NOT WRITE ABOVE THIS LINE. IF YOU NEED MORE SPACE, USE A SEPARATE CONTINUATION SHEET.

1 TITLE OF THIS WORK ▼

PREVIOUS OR ALTERNATIVE TITLES ▼

PUBLICATION AS A CONTRIBUTION If this work was published as a contribution to a periodical, serial, or collection, give information about the
collective work in which the contribution appeared.   **Title of Collective Work ▼**

If published in a periodical or serial give: Volume ▼   Number ▼   Issue Date ▼   On Pages ▼

2

a NAME OF AUTHOR ▼

DATES OF BIRTH AND DEATH
Year Born ▼   Year Died ▼

Was this contribution to the work a
"work made for hire"?
☐ Yes
☐ No

AUTHOR'S NATIONALITY OR DOMICILE
Name of Country
OR { Citizen of _____
Domiciled in _____

WAS THIS AUTHOR'S CONTRIBUTION TO
THE WORK
Anonymous? ☐ Yes ☐ No
Pseudonymous? ☐ Yes ☐ No

If the answer to either
of these questions is
"Yes," see detailed
instructions

NATURE OF AUTHORSHIP Briefly describe nature of material created by this author in which copyright is claimed. ▼

NOTE
Under the law,
the "author" of
a "work made
for hire" is
generally the
employer, not
the employee
(see instruc-
tions). For any
part of this
work that was
"made for hire"
check "Yes" in
the space
provided, give
the employer
(or other
person for
whom the work
was prepared)
as "Author" of
that part, and
leave the
space for dates
of birth and
death blank.

b NAME OF AUTHOR ▼

DATES OF BIRTH AND DEATH
Year Born ▼   Year Died ▼

Was this contribution to the work a
"work made for hire"?
☐ Yes
☐ No

AUTHOR'S NATIONALITY OR DOMICILE
Name of Country
OR { Citizen of _____
Domiciled in _____

WAS THIS AUTHOR'S CONTRIBUTION TO
THE WORK
Anonymous? ☐ Yes ☐ No
Pseudonymous? ☐ Yes ☐ No

If the answer to either
of these questions is
"Yes," see detailed
instructions

NATURE OF AUTHORSHIP Briefly describe nature of material created by this author in which copyright is claimed. ▼

c NAME OF AUTHOR ▼

DATES OF BIRTH AND DEATH
Year Born ▼   Year Died ▼

Was this contribution to the work a
"work made for hire"?
☐ Yes
☐ No

AUTHOR'S NATIONALITY OR DOMICILE
Name of Country
OR { Citizen of _____
Domiciled in _____

WAS THIS AUTHOR'S CONTRIBUTION TO
THE WORK
Anonymous? ☐ Yes ☐ No
Pseudonymous? ☐ Yes ☐ No

If the answer to either
of these questions is
"Yes," see detailed
instructions

NATURE OF AUTHORSHIP Briefly describe nature of material created by this author in which copyright is claimed. ▼

3

a YEAR IN WHICH CREATION OF THIS
WORK WAS COMPLETED   This information
must be given
Year   in all cases.

b DATE AND NATION OF FIRST PUBLICATION OF THIS PARTICULAR WORK
Complete this information   Month _____ Day _____ Year _____
ONLY if this work
has been published.   Nation

4

See instructions
before completing
this space.

COPYRIGHT CLAIMANT(S) Name and address must be given even if the claimant is the same as
the author given in space 2. ▼

TRANSFER If the claimant(s) named here in space 4 is (are) different from the author(s) named in
space 2, give a brief statement of how the claimant(s) obtained ownership of the copyright. ▼

APPLICATION RECEIVED

ONE DEPOSIT RECEIVED

TWO DEPOSITS RECEIVED

FUNDS RECEIVED

DO NOT WRITE HERE
OFFICE USE ONLY

MORE ON BACK ▶   • Complete all applicable spaces (numbers 5-9) on the reverse side of this page   DO NOT WRITE HERE
   • See detailed instructions.   • Sign the form at line 8.   Page 1 of _____ pages

EXAMINED BY	FORM TX
CHECKED BY	
☐ CORRESPONDENCE Yes	FOR COPYRIGHT OFFICE USE ONLY

DO NOT WRITE ABOVE THIS LINE. IF YOU NEED MORE SPACE, USE A SEPARATE CONTINUATION SHEET.

PREVIOUS REGISTRATION Has registration for this work, or for an earlier version of this work, already been made in the Copyright Office?

☐ Yes ☐ No If your answer is "Yes," why is another registration being sought? (Check appropriate box.) ▼

a. ☐ This is the first published edition of a work previously registered in unpublished form.

b. ☐ This is the first application submitted by this author as copyright claimant.

c. ☐ This is a changed version of the work, as shown by space 6 on this application.

If your answer is "Yes," give: **Previous Registration Number** ▶   **Year of Registration** ▶

5

DERIVATIVE WORK OR COMPILATION

Preexisting Material Identify any preexisting work or works that this work is based on or incorporates. ▼

a

6

See instructions before completing this space.

Material Added to This Work Give a brief, general statement of the material that has been added to this work and in which copyright is claimed. ▼

b

DEPOSIT ACCOUNT If the registration fee is to be charged to a deposit account established in the Copyright Office, give name and number of account.

Name ▼   **Account Number** ▼

a

7

CORRESPONDENCE Give name and address to which correspondence about this application should be sent. Name/Address/Apt/City/State/Zip ▼

b

Area code and daytime telephone number ▶   Fax number ▶

Email ▶

CERTIFICATION* I, the undersigned, hereby certify that I am the

Check only one ▶

☐ author

☐ other copyright claimant

☐ owner of exclusive right(s)

☐ authorized agent of _____

of the work identified in this application and that the statements made by me in this application are correct to the best of my knowledge.

Name of author or other copyright claimant, or owner of exclusive right(s) ▲

8

Typed or printed name and date ▼ If this application gives a date of publication in space 3, do not sign and submit it before that date.

Date ▶

Handwritten signature ▼

Certificate will be mailed in window envelope to this address:	Name ▼	**YOU MUST:** • Complete all necessary spaces • Sign your application in space 8
	Number/Street/Apt ▼	**SEND ALL 3 ELEMENTS IN THE SAME PACKAGE:** 1. Application form 2. Nonrefundable filing fee in check or money order payable to Register of Copyrights 3. Deposit material
	City/State/Zip ▼	**MAIL TO:** Library of Congress Copyright Office-TX 101 Independence Avenue SE Washington, DC 20559

9

*17 U.S.C. §506(e): Any person who knowingly makes a false representation of a material fact in the application for copyright registration provided for by section 409, or in any written statement filed in connection with the application, shall be fined not more than $2,500.

Form TX—Full Reviewed: 07/2012 Printed on recycled paper   U.S. Government Printing Office: 2012-xxx-xxx/xx,xxx

Appendix-19
FORM PA COPYRIGHT APPLICATION

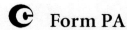 **Form PA**

Detach and read these instructions before completing this form.
Make sure all applicable spaces have been filled in before you return this form.

When to Use This Form: Use Form PA for registration of published or unpublished works of the performing arts. This class includes works prepared for the purpose of being "performed" directly before an audience or indirectly "by means of any device or process." Works of the performing arts include: (1) musical works, including any accompanying words; (2) dramatic works, including any accompanying music; (3) pantomimes and choreographic works; and (4) motion pictures and other audiovisual works.

Deposit to Accompany Application: An application for copyright registration must be accompanied by a deposit consisting of copies or phonorecords representing the entire work for which registration is made. The following are the general deposit requirements as set forth in the statute:

Unpublished Work: Deposit one complete copy (or phonorecord).

Published Work: Deposit two complete copies (or one phonorecord) of the best edition.

Work First Published Outside the United States: Deposit one complete copy (or phonorecord) of the first foreign edition.

Contribution to a Collective Work: Deposit one complete copy (or phonorecord) of the best edition of the collective work.

Motion Pictures: Deposit *both* of the following: (1) a separate written description of the contents of the motion picture; and (2) for a published work, one complete copy of the best edition of the motion picture; or, for an unpublished work, one complete copy of the motion picture or identifying material. Identifying material may be either an audiorecording of the entire soundtrack or one frame enlargement or similar visual print from each 10-minute segment.

The Copyright Notice: Before March 1, 1989, the use of copyright notice was mandatory on all published works, and any work first published before that date should have carried a notice. For works first published on and after March 1, 1989, use of the copyright notice is optional. For more information about copyright notice, see Circular 3, *Copyright Notice.*

For Further Information: To speak to a Copyright Office staff member, call (202) 707-3000 or 1-877-476-0778 (toll free). Recorded information is available 24 hours a day. Order forms and other publications from the address in space 9 or call (202) 707-9100. Access and download circulars, certain forms, and other information from the Copyright Office website at *www.copyright.gov.*

Please type or print using black ink. The form is used to produce the certificate.

1 SPACE 1: Title

Title of This Work: Every work submitted for copyright registration must be given a title to identify that particular work. If the copies or phonorecords of the work bear a title (or an identifying phrase that could serve as a title), transcribe that wording *completely* and *exactly* on the application. Indexing of the registration and future identification of the work will depend on the information you give here. If the work you are registering is an entire "collective work" (such as a collection of plays or songs), give the overall title of the collection. If you are registering one or more individual contributions to a collective work, give the title of each contribution, followed by the title of the collection. For an unpublished collection, you may give the titles of the individual works after the collection title.

Previous or Alternative Titles: Complete this space if there are any additional titles for the work under which someone searching for the registration might be likely to look, or under which a document pertaining to the work might be recorded.

Nature of This Work: Briefly describe the general nature or character of the work being registered for copyright. Examples: "Music"; "Song Lyrics"; "Words and Music"; "Drama"; "Musical Play"; "Choreography"; "Pantomime"; "Motion Picture"; "Audiovisual Work."

2 SPACE 2: Author(s)

General Instructions: After reading these instructions, decide who are the "authors" of this work for copyright purposes. Then, unless the work is a "collective work," give the requested information about every "author" who contributed any appreciable amount of copyrightable matter to this version of the work. If you need further space, request additional Continuation Sheets. In the case of a collective work such as a songbook or a collection of plays, give information about the author of the collective work as a whole.

Name of Author: The fullest form of the author's name should be given. Unless the work was "made for hire," the individual who actually created the work is the "author." In the case of a work made for hire, the statute provides that "the employer or other person for whom the work was prepared is considered the author."

What Is a "Work Made for Hire"? A "work made for hire" is defined as (1) "a work prepared by an employee within the scope of his or her employment"; or (2) "a work specially ordered or commissioned for use as a contribution to a collective work, as a part of a motion picture or other audiovisual work, as a translation, as a supplementary work, as a compilation, as an instructional text, as a test, as answer material for a test, or as an atlas, if the parties expressly agree in a written instrument signed by them that the work shall be considered a work made for hire." If you have checked "Yes" to indicate that the work was "made for hire," you must give the full legal name of the employer (or other person for whom the work was prepared). You may also include the name of the employee along with the name of the employer (for example: "Elster Music Co., employer for hire of John Ferguson").

"Anonymous" or "Pseudonymous" Work: An author's contribution to a work is "anonymous" if that author is not identified on the copies or phonorecords of the work. An author's contribution to a work is "pseudonymous" if that author is identified on the copies or phonorecords under a fictitious name. If the work is "anonymous" you may (1) leave the line blank; (2) state "anonymous" on the line; or (3) reveal the author's identity. If the work is "pseudonymous" you may (1) leave the line blank; (2) give the pseudonym and identify it as such (example: "Huntley Haverstock, pseudonym"); or (3) reveal the author's name, making clear which is the real name and which is the pseudonym (for example: "Judith Barton, whose pseudonym is Madeline Elster"). However, the citizenship or domicile of the author *must* be given in all cases.

Dates of Birth and Death: If the author is dead, the statute requires that the year of death be included in the application unless the work is anonymous or pseudonymous. The author's birth date is optional but is useful as a form of identification. Leave this space blank if the author's contribution was a "work made for hire."

Author's Nationality or Domicile: Give the country of which the author is a citizen, or the country in which the author is domiciled. Nationality or domicile *must* be given in all cases.

Nature of Authorship: Give a brief general statement of the nature of this particular author's contribution to the work. Examples: "Words"; "Coauthor of Music"; "Words and Music"; "Arrangement"; "Coauthor of Book and Lyrics"; "Dramatization"; "Screen Play"; "Compilation and English Translation"; "Editorial Revisions."

3 SPACE 3: Creation and Publication

General Instructions: Do not confuse "creation" with "publication." Every application for copyright registration must state "the year in which creation of the work was completed." Give the date and nation of first publication only if the work has been published.

Creation: Under the statute, a work is "created" when it is fixed in a copy or phonorecord for the first time. Where a work has been prepared over a period of time, the part of the work existing in fixed form on a particular date constitutes the created work on that date. The date you give here should be the year in which the author completed the particular version for which registration is now being sought, even if other versions exist or if further changes or additions are planned.

Publication: The statute defines "publication" as "the distribution of copies or phonorecords of a work to the public by sale or other transfer of ownership, or by rental, lease, or lending"; a work is also "published" if there has been an "offering to distribute copies or phonorecords to a group of persons for purposes of further distribution, public performance, or public display." Give the full date (month, day, year) when, and the country where, publication first occurred. If first publication took place simultaneously in the United States and other countries, it is sufficient to state "U.S.A."

4 SPACE 4: Claimant(s)

Name(s) and Address(es) of Copyright Claimant(s): Give the name(s) and address(es) of the copyright claimant(s) in this work even if the claimant is the same as the author. Copyright in a work belongs initially to the author of the work (including, in the case of a work made for hire, the employer or other person for whom the work was prepared). The copyright claimant is either the author of the work or a person or organization to whom the copyright initially belonging to the author has been transferred.

Transfer: The statute provides that, if the copyright claimant is not the author, the application for registration must contain "a brief statement of how the claimant obtained ownership of the copyright." If any copyright claimant named in space 4 is not an author named in space 2, give a brief statement explaining how the claimant(s) obtained ownership of the copyright. Examples: "By written contract"; "Transfer of all rights by author"; "Assignment"; "By will." Do not attach transfer documents or other attachments or riders.

5 SPACE 5: Previous Registration

General Instructions: The questions in space 5 are intended to show whether an earlier registration has been made for this work and, if so, whether there is any basis for a new registration. As a general rule, only one basic copyright registration can be made for the same version of a particular work.

Same Version: If this version is substantially the same as the work covered by a previous registration, a second registration is not generally possible unless (1) the work has been registered in unpublished form and a second registration is now being sought to cover this first published edition; or (2) someone other than the author is identified as copyright claimant in the earlier registration, and the author is now seeking registration in his or her own name. If either of these two exceptions applies, check the appropriate box and give the earlier registration number and date. Otherwise, do not submit Form PA; instead, contact the Copyright Office

for information about supplementary registration or recordation of transfers of copyright ownership.

Changed Version: If the work has been changed and you are now seeking registration to cover the additions or revisions, check the last box in space 5, give the earlier registration number and date, and complete both parts of space 6 in accordance with the instructions below.

Previous Registration Number and Date: If more than one previous registration has been made for the work, give the number and date of the latest registration.

6 SPACE 6: Derivative Work or Compilation

General Instructions: Complete space 6 if this work is a "changed version," "compilation," or "derivative work," and if it incorporates one or more earlier works that have already been published or registered for copyright or that have fallen into the public domain. A "compilation" is defined as "a work formed by the collection and assembling of preexisting materials or of data that are selected, coordinated, or arranged in such a way that the resulting work as a whole constitutes an original work of authorship." A "derivative work" is "a work based on one or more preexisting works." Examples of derivative works include musical arrangements, dramatizations, translations, abridgments, condensations, motion picture versions, or "any other form in which a work may be recast, transformed, or adapted." Derivative works also include works "consisting of editorial revisions, annotations, or other modifications" if these changes, as a whole, represent an original work of authorship.

Preexisting Material (space 6a): Complete this space *and* space 6b for derivative works. In this space identify the preexisting work that has been recast, transformed, or adapted. For example, the preexisting material might be: "French version of Hugo's 'Le Roi s'amuse.'" Do not complete this space for compilations.

Material Added to This Work (space 6b): Give a brief general statement of the *additional* new material covered by the copyright claim for which registration is sought. In the case of a derivative work, identify this new material. Examples: "Arrangement for piano and orchestra"; "Dramatization for television"; "New film version"; "Revisions throughout; Act III completely new." If the work is a compilation, give a brief general statement describing both the material that has been compiled *and* the compilation itself. Example: "Compilation of 19th Century Military Songs."

7,8,9 SPACE 7, 8, 9: Fee, Correspondence, Certification, Return Address

Deposit Account: If you maintain a Deposit Account in the Copyright Office, identify it in space 7a. Otherwise, leave the space blank and send the fee with your application and deposit.

Correspondence (space 7b): Give the name, address, area code, telephone number, fax number, and email address of the person to be consulted if correspondence about this application becomes necessary.

Certification (space 8): The application cannot be accepted unless it bears the date and the **handwritten signature** of the author or other copyright claimant, the owner of exclusive right(s), or of the duly authorized agent of the author, claimant, or owner of exclusive right(s).

Address for Return of Certificate (space 9): The address box must be completed legibly since the certificate will be returned in a window envelope.

MORE INFORMATION

How to Register a Recorded Work: If the musical or dramatic work that you are registering has been recorded (as a tape, disk, or cassette), you may choose either copyright application Form PA (Performing Arts) or Form SR (Sound Recordings), depending on the purpose of the registration.

Use Form PA to register the underlying musical composition or dramatic work. Form SR has been developed specifically to register a "sound recording" as defined by the Copyright Act—a work resulting from the "fixation of a series of sounds," separate and distinct from the underlying musical or dramatic work. Form SR should be used when the copyright claim is limited to the sound recording itself. (In one instance, Form SR may also be used to file for a copyright registration for both kinds of works—see [4] below.) Therefore:

(1) **File Form PA** if you are seeking to register the musical or dramatic work, not the "sound recording," even though what you deposit for copyright purposes may be in the form of a phonorecord.

(2) **File Form PA** if you are seeking to register the audio portion of an audiovisual work, such as a motion picture soundtrack; these are considered integral parts of the audiovisual work.

(3) **File Form SR** if you are seeking to register the "sound recording" itself, that is, the work that results from the fixation of a series of musical, spoken, or other sounds, but not the underlying musical or dramatic work.

(4) **File Form SR** if you are the copyright claimant for both the underlying musical or dramatic work and the sound recording, *and* you prefer to register both on the same form.

(5) **File both forms PA and SR** if the copyright claimant for the underlying work and sound recording differ, or you prefer to have separate registration for them.

"Copies" and "Phonorecords": To register for copyright, you are required to deposit "copies" or "phonorecords." These are defined as follows:

Musical compositions may be embodied (fixed) in "copies," objects from which a work can be read or visually perceived, directly or with the aid of a machine or device, such as manuscripts, books, sheet music, film, and videotape. They may also be fixed in "phonorecords," objects embodying fixations of sounds, such as tapes and phonograph disks, commonly known as phonograph records. For example, a song (the work to be registered) can be reproduced in sheet music ("copies") or phonograph records ("phonorecords"), or both.

Form PA
For a Work of Performing Arts
UNITED STATES COPYRIGHT OFFICE

REGISTRATION NUMBER

PA   PAU

EFFECTIVE DATE OF REGISTRATION

Month   Day   Year

DO NOT WRITE ABOVE THIS LINE. IF YOU NEED MORE SPACE, USE A SEPARATE CONTINUATION SHEET.

1

TITLE OF THIS WORK ▼

PREVIOUS OR ALTERNATIVE TITLES ▼

NATURE OF THIS WORK ▼ See instructions

2 a

NAME OF AUTHOR ▼

DATES OF BIRTH AND DEATH
Year Born ▼   Year Died ▼

Was this contribution to the work a "work made for hire"?
☐ Yes
☐ No

AUTHOR'S NATIONALITY OR DOMICILE
Name of Country
OR { Citizen of _____
Domiciled in _____

WAS THIS AUTHOR'S CONTRIBUTION TO THE WORK
Anonymous? ☐ Yes ☐ No
Pseudonymous? ☐ Yes ☐ No
If the answer to either of these questions is "Yes," see detailed instructions.

NOTE
Under the law, the "author" of a "work made for hire" is generally the employer, not the employee (see instructions). For any part of this work that was "made for hire" check "Yes" in the space provided, give the employer (or other person for whom the work was prepared) as "Author" of that part, and leave the space for dates of birth and death blank.

NATURE OF AUTHORSHIP Briefly describe nature of material created by this author in which copyright is claimed. ▼

b

NAME OF AUTHOR ▼

DATES OF BIRTH AND DEATH
Year Born ▼   Year Died ▼

Was this contribution to the work a "work made for hire"?
☐ Yes
☐ No

AUTHOR'S NATIONALITY OR DOMICILE
Name of Country
OR { Citizen of _____
Domiciled in _____

WAS THIS AUTHOR'S CONTRIBUTION TO THE WORK
Anonymous? ☐ Yes ☐ No
Pseudonymous? ☐ Yes ☐ No
If the answer to either of these questions is "Yes," see detailed instructions.

NATURE OF AUTHORSHIP Briefly describe nature of material created by this author in which copyright is claimed. ▼

c

NAME OF AUTHOR ▼

DATES OF BIRTH AND DEATH
Year Born ▼   Year Died ▼

Was this contribution to the work a "work made for hire"?
☐ Yes
☐ No

AUTHOR'S NATIONALITY OR DOMICILE
Name of Country
OR { Citizen of _____
Domiciled in _____

WAS THIS AUTHOR'S CONTRIBUTION TO THE WORK
Anonymous? ☐ Yes ☐ No
Pseudonymous? ☐ Yes ☐ No
If the answer to either of these questions is "Yes," see detailed instructions.

NATURE OF AUTHORSHIP Briefly describe nature of material created by this author in which copyright is claimed. ▼

3 a

YEAR IN WHICH CREATION OF THIS WORK WAS COMPLETED
_____ Year
This information must be given in all cases.

b Complete this information ONLY if this work has been published.
DATE AND NATION OF FIRST PUBLICATION OF THIS PARTICULAR WORK
Month _____ Day _____ Year _____
_____ Nation

4

See instructions before completing this space

COPYRIGHT CLAIMANT(S) Name and address must be given even if the claimant is the same as the author given in space 2. ▼

TRANSFER If the claimant(s) named here in space 4 is (are) different from the author(s) named in space 2, give a brief statement of how the claimant(s) obtained ownership of the copyright. ▼

APPLICATION RECEIVED

ONE DEPOSIT RECEIVED

TWO DEPOSITS RECEIVED

FUNDS RECEIVED

DO NOT WRITE HERE
OFFICE USE ONLY

MORE ON BACK ▶
• Complete all applicable spaces (numbers 5-9) on the reverse side of this page
• See detailed instructions
• Sign the form at line 8

DO NOT WRITE HERE
Page 1 of _____ pages

EXAMINED BY	FORM PA
CHECKED BY	
CORRESPONDENCE Yes	FOR COPYRIGHT OFFICE USE ONLY

DO NOT WRITE ABOVE THIS LINE. IF YOU NEED MORE SPACE, USE A SEPARATE CONTINUATION SHEET.

PREVIOUS REGISTRATION Has registration for this work, or for an earlier version of this work, already been made in the Copyright Office?

☐ Yes ☐ No If your answer is "Yes," why is another registration being sought? (Check appropriate box.) ▼ If your answer is No, do **not** check box A, B, or C.

a. ☐ This is the first published edition of a work previously registered in unpublished form.

b. ☐ This is the first application submitted by this author as copyright claimant.

c. ☐ This is a changed version of the work, as shown by space 6 on this application.

If your answer is "Yes," give **Previous Registration Number** ▼   **Year of Registration** ▼

5

DERIVATIVE WORK OR COMPILATION Complete both space 6a and 6b for a derivative work; complete only 6b for a compilation.
Preexisting Material Identify any preexisting work or works that this work is based on or incorporates. ▼

a 6

Material Added to This Work Give a brief, general statement of the material that has been added to this work and in which copyright is claimed. ▼

b

See instructions before completing this space

DEPOSIT ACCOUNT If the registration fee is to be charged to a Deposit Account established in the Copyright Office, give name and number of Account.
Name ▼   **Account Number** ▼

a 7

CORRESPONDENCE Give name and address to which correspondence about this application should be sent. Name/Address/Apt/City/State/Zip ▼

b

Area code and daytime telephone number   (   )   Fax number   (   )

Email

CERTIFICATION* I, the undersigned, hereby certify that I am the

Check only one ▶ { ☐ author
☐ other copyright claimant
☐ owner of exclusive right(s)
☐ authorized agent of _____
Name of author or other copyright claimant, or owner of exclusive right(s) ▲

of the work identified in this application and that the statements made by me in this application are correct to the best of my knowledge.

Typed or printed name and date ▼ If this application gives a date of publication in space 3, do not sign and submit it before that date.

_____ Date_____

Handwritten signature (X) ▼

x _____

8

Certificate will be mailed in window envelope to this address:

| Name ▼ |
| Number/Street/Apt ▼ |
| City/State/Zip ▼ |

YOU MUST:
• Complete all necessary spaces
• Sign your application in space 8
SEND ALL 3 ELEMENTS IN THE SAME PACKAGE:
1. Application form
2. Nonrefundable filing fee in check or money order payable to Register of Copyrights
3. Deposit material
MAIL TO:
Library of Congress
Copyright Office-PAD
101 Independence Avenue SE
Washington, DC 20559-6230

9

*17 U.S.C. §506(e): Any person who knowingly makes a false representation of a material fact in the application for copyright registration provided for by section 409, or in any written statement filed in connection with the application, shall be fined not more than $2,500.

Form PA—Full Reviewed: 09/2015 Printed on recycled paper   U.S. Government Publishing Office: 2015-xxx-xxx/xx,xxx

Appendix-20
FORM SR COPYRIGHT APPLICATION

 Form SR

Detach and read these instructions before completing this form.
Make sure all applicable spaces have been filled in before you return this form.

BASIC INFORMATION

When to Use This Form: Use Form SR for registration of published or unpublished sound recordings. Form SR should be used when the copyright claim is limited to the sound recording itself, and it may also be used where the same copyright claimant is seeking simultaneous registration of the underlying musical, dramatic, or literary work embodied in the phonorecord.

With one exception, "sound recordings" are works that result from the fixation of a series of musical, spoken, or other sounds. The exception is for the audio portions of audiovisual works, such as a motion picture soundtrack or an audio cassette accompanying a filmstrip. These are considered a part of the audiovisual work as a whole.

Deposit to Accompany Application: An application for copyright registration must be accompanied by a deposit consisting of phonorecords representing the entire work for which registration is to be made.

Unpublished Work: Deposit one complete phonorecord.

Published Work: Deposit two complete phonorecords of the best edition, together with "any printed or other visually perceptible material" published with the phonorecords.

Work First Published Outside the United States: Deposit one complete phonorecord of the first foreign edition.

Contribution to a Collective Work: Deposit one complete phonorecord of the best edition of the collective work.

The Copyright Notice: Before March 1, 1989, the use of copyright notice was mandatory on all published works, and any work first published before that date should have carried a notice. For works first published on and after March 1, 1989, use of the copyright notice is optional. For more information about copyright notice, see Circular 3, *Copyright Notices.*

For Further Information: To speak to a Copyright Office staff member, call (202) 707-3000 or 1-877-476-0778. Recorded information is available 24 hours a day. Order forms and other publications from Library of Congress, Copyright Office-COPUBS, 101 Independence Avenue SE, Washington, DC 20559 or call (202) 707-9100 or 1-877-476-0778 (toll free). Access and download circulars and other information from the Copyright Office website at *www.copyright.gov.*

PRIVACY ACT ADVISORY STATEMENT Required by the Privacy Act of 1974 (P.L. 93-579)
The authority for requesting this information is title 17 U.S.C. §409 and §410. Furnishing the requested information is voluntary. But if the information is not furnished, it may be necessary to delay or refuse registration and you may not be entitled to certain relief, remedies, and benefits provided in chapters 4 and 5 of title 17 U.S.C.
The principal uses of the requested information are the establishment and maintenance of a public record and the examination of the application for compliance with the registration requirements of the copyright code.
Other routine uses include public inspection and copying, preparation of public indexes, preparation of public catalogs of copyright registrations, and preparation of search reports upon request.
NOTE: No other advisory statement will be given in connection with this application. Please keep this statement and refer to it if we communicate with you regarding this application.

LINE-BY-LINE INSTRUCTIONS

Please type or print neatly using black ink. The form is used to produce the certificate.

 SPACE 1: Title

Title of This Work: Every work submitted for copyright registration must be given a title to identify that particular work. If the phonorecords or any accompanying printed material bears a title (or an identifying phrase that could serve as a title), transcribe that wording completely and exactly on the application. Indexing of the registration and future identification of the work may depend on the information you give here.

Previous, Alternative, or Contents Titles: Complete this space if there are any previous or alternative titles for the work under which someone searching for the registration might be likely to look, or under which a document pertaining to the work might be recorded. You may also give the individual contents titles, if any, in this space or you may use a Continuation Sheet (Form CON). Circle the term that describes the titles given.

 SPACE 2: Author(s)

General Instructions: After reading these instructions, decide who are the "authors" of this work for copyright purposes. Then, unless the work is a "collective work," give the requested information about every "author" who contributed any appreciable amount of copyrightable matter to this version of the work. If you need further space, use additional Continuation Sheets. In the case of a collective work such as a collection of previously published or registered sound recordings, give information about the author of the collective work as a whole. If you are submitting this Form SR to cover the recorded musical, dramatic, or literary work as well as the sound recording itself, it is important for space 2 to include full information about the various authors of all of the material covered by the copyright claim, making clear the nature of each author's contribution.

Name of Author: The fullest form of the author's name should be given. Unless the work was "made for hire," the individual who actually created the work is its "author." In the case of a work made for hire, the statute provides that "the employer or other person for whom the work was prepared is considered the author."

What Is a "Work Made for Hire"? A "work made for hire" is defined as: (1) "a work prepared by an employee within the scope of his or her employment"; or (2) "a

work specially ordered or commissioned for use as a contribution to a collective work, as a part of a motion picture or other audiovisual work, as a translation, as a supplementary work, as a compilation, as an instructional text, as a test, as answer material for a test, or as an atlas, if the parties expressly agree in a written instrument signed by them that the work shall be considered a work made for hire." If you have checked "Yes" to indicate that the work was "made for hire," you must give the full legal name of the employer (or other person for whom the work was prepared). You may also include the name of the employee along with the name of the employer (for example: "Elster Record Co., employer for hire of John Ferguson").

"Anonymous" or "Pseudonymous" Work: An author's contribution to a work is "anonymous" if that author is not identified on the copies or phonorecords of the work. An author's contribution to a work is "pseudonymous" if that author is identified on the copies or phonorecords under a fictitious name. If the work is "anonymous" you may: (1) leave the line blank; or (2) state "anonymous" on the line; or (3) reveal the author's identity. If the work is "pseudonymous" you may: (1) leave the line blank; or (2) give the pseudonym and identify it as such (for example: "Huntley Haverstock, pseudonym"); or (3) reveal the author's name, making clear which is the real name and which is the pseudonym (for example "Judith Barton, whose pseudonym is Madeline Elster"). However, the citizenship or domicile of the author *must* be given in all cases.

Dates of Birth and Death: If the author is dead, the statute requires that the year of death be included in the application unless the work is anonymous or pseudonymous. The author's birth date is optional, but is useful as a form of identification. Leave this space blank if the author's contribution was a "work made for hire."

Author's Nationality or Domicile: Give the country in which the author is a citizen, or the country in which the author is domiciled. Nationality or domicile *must* be given in all cases.

Nature of Authorship: Sound recording authorship is the performance, sound production, or both, that is fixed in the recording deposited for registration. Describe this authorship in space 2 as "sound recording." If the claim also covers the underlying work(s), include the appropriate authorship terms for each author, for example, "words," "music," "arrangement of music," or "text."

Generally, for the claim to cover both the sound recording and the underlying work(s), every author should have contributed to both the sound recording *and* the underlying work(s). If the claim includes artwork or photographs, include the appropriate term in the statement of authorship.

SPACE 3: Creation and Publication

General Instructions: Do not confuse "creation" with "publication." Every application for copyright registration must state "the year in which creation of the work was completed." Give the date and nation of first publication only if the work has been published.

Creation: Under the statute, a work is "created" when it is fixed in a copy or phonorecord for the first time. If a work has been prepared over a period of time, the part of the work existing in fixed form on a particular date constitutes the created work on that date. The date you give here should be the year in which the author completed the particular version for which registration is now being sought, even if other versions exist or if further changes or additions are planned.

Publication: The statute defines "publication" as "the distribution of copies or phonorecords of a work to the public by sale or other transfer of ownership, or by rental, lease, or lending"; a work is also "published" if there has been an "offering to distribute copies or phonorecords to a group of persons for purposes of further distribution, public performance, or public display." Give the full date (month, date, year) when, and the country where, publication first occurred. If first publication took place simultaneously in the United States and other countries, it is sufficient to state "U.S.A."

 SPACE 4: Claimant(s)

Name(s) and Address(es) of Copyright Claimant(s): Give the name(s) and address(es) of the copyright claimant(s) in the work even if the claimant is the same as the author. Copyright in a work belongs initially to the author of the work (including, in the case of a work made for hire, the employer or other person for whom the work was prepared). The copyright claimant is either the author of the work or a person or organization to whom the copyright initially belonging to the author has been transferred.

Transfer: The statute provides that, if the copyright claimant is not the author, the application for registration must contain "a brief statement of how the claimant obtained ownership of the copyright." If any copyright claimant named in space 4a is not an author named in space 2, give a brief statement explaining how the claimant(s) obtained ownership of the copyright. Examples: "By written contract"; "Transfer of all rights by author"; "Assignment"; "By will." Do not attach transfer documents or other attachments or riders.

 SPACE 5: Previous Registration

General Instructions: The questions in space 5 are intended to show whether an earlier registration has been made for this work and, if so, whether there is any basis for a new registration. As a rule, only one basic copyright registration can be made for the same version of a particular work.

Same Version: If this version is substantially the same as the work covered by a previous registration, a second registration is not generally possible unless: (1) the work has been registered in unpublished form and a second registration is now being sought to cover this first published edition; or (2) someone other than the author is identified as copyright claimant in the earlier registration and the author is now seeking registration in his or her own name. If either of these two exceptions applies, check the appropriate box and give the earlier registration number and date. Otherwise, do not submit Form SR. Instead, write the Copyright Office for information about supplementary registration or recordation of transfers of copyright ownership.

Changed Version: If the work has been changed and you are now seeking registration to cover the additions or revisions, check the last box in space 5, give the earlier registration number and date, and complete both parts of space 6 in accordance with the instructions below.

Previous Registration Number and Date: If more than one previous registration has been made for the work, give the number and date of the latest registration.

 SPACE 6: Derivative Work or Compilation

General Instructions: Complete space 6 if this work is a "changed version," "compilation," or "derivative work," and if it incorporates one or more earlier works that have already been published or registered for copyright, or that have fallen into the public domain, or sound recordings that were fixed before February 15, 1972. A "compilation" is defined as "a work formed by the collection and assembling of preexisting materials or of data that are selected, coordinated, or arranged in such a way that the resulting work as a whole constitutes an original work of authorship." A "derivative work" is "a work based on one or more preexisting works." Examples of derivative works include recordings reissued with substantial editorial revisions or abridgments of the recorded sounds, and recordings republished with new recorded material, or "any other form in which a work may be recast, transformed, or adapted." Derivative works also include works "consisting of editorial revisions, annotations, or other modifications" if these changes, as a whole, represent an original work of authorship.

Preexisting Material (space 6a): Complete this space *and* space 6b for derivative works. In this space identify the preexisting work that has been recast, transformed, or adapted. The preexisting work may be material that has been previously published, previously registered, or that is in the public domain. For example, the preexisting material might be: "1970 recording by Sperryville Symphony of Bach Double Concerto."

Material Added to This Work (space 6b): Give a brief, general statement of the *additional* new material covered by the copyright claim for which registration is sought. In the case of a derivative work, identify this new material. Examples: "Recorded performances on bands 1 and 3"; "Remixed sounds from original multitrack sound sources"; "New words, arrangement, and additional sounds." If the work is a compilation, give a brief, general statement describing both the material that has been compiled *and* the compilation itself. Example: "Compilation of 1938 recordings by various swing bands."

SPACE 7, 8, 9: Fee, Correspondence, Certification, Return Address

Deposit Account: If you maintain a deposit account in the Copyright Office, identify it in space 7a. Otherwise, leave the space blank and send the filing fee with your application and deposit. (See space 8 on form.) **Note:** Copyright Office fees are subject to change. For current fees, check the Copyright Office website at *www.copyright.gov*, write the Copyright Office, or call (202) 707-3000 or 1-877-476-0778 (toll free).

Correspondence (space 7b): Give the name, address, area code, telephone number, fax number, and email address (if available) of the person to be consulted if correspondence about this application becomes necessary.

Certification (space 8): This application cannot be accepted unless it bears the date and the *handwritten signature* of the author or other copyright claimant, or of the owner of exclusive right(s), or of the duly authorized agent of the author, claimant, or owner of exclusive right(s).

Address for Return of Certificate (space 9): The address box must be completed legibly since the certificate will be returned in a window envelope.

MORE INFORMATION

"Works": "Works" are the basic subject matter of copyright; they are what authors create and copyright protects. The statute draws a sharp distinction between the "work" and "any material object in which the work is embodied."

"Copies" and "Phonorecords": These are the two types of material objects in which "works" are embodied. In general, "copies" are objects from which a work can be read or visually perceived, directly or with the aid of a machine or device, such as manuscripts, books, sheet music, film, and videotape. "Phonorecords" are objects embodying fixations of sounds, such as audio tapes and phonograph disks. For example, a song (the "work") can be reproduced in sheet music ("copies") or phonograph disks ("phonorecords"), or both.

"Sound Recordings": These are "works," not "copies" or "phonorecords." "Sound recordings" are "works that result from the fixation of a series of musical, spoken, or other sounds, but not including the sounds accompanying a motion picture or other audiovisual work." Example: When a record company issues a new release, the release will typically involve two distinct "works": the "musical work" that has been recorded, and the "sound recording" as a separate work in itself. The material objects that the record company sends out are "phonorecords": physical reproductions of both the "musical work" and the "sound recording."

Should You File More Than One Application? If your work consists of a recorded musical, dramatic, or literary work and if both that "work" and the sound recording as a separate "work" are eligible for registration, the application form you should file depends on the following:

File Only Form SR if: The copyright claimant is the same for both the musical, dramatic, or literary work and for the sound recording, and you are seeking a single registration to cover both of these "works."

File Only Form PA (or Form TX) if: You are seeking to register only the musical, dramatic, or literary work, not the sound recording. Form PA is appropriate for works of the performing arts; Form TX is for nondramatic literary works.

Separate Applications Should Be Filed on Form PA (or Form TX) and on Form SR if: (1) The copyright claimant for the musical, dramatic, or literary work is different from the copyright claimant for the sound recording; or (2) you prefer to have separate registrations for the musical, dramatic, or literary work and for the sound recording.

Copyright Office fees are subject to change. For current fees, check the Copyright Office website at *www.copyright.gov*, write the Copyright Office, or call (202) 707-3000 or 1-877-476-0778 (toll free).

Privacy Act Notice: Sections 408-410 of title 17 of the *United States Code* authorize the Copyright Office to collect the personally identifying information requested on this form in order to process the application for copyright registration. By providing this information you are agreeing to routine uses of the information that include publication to give legal notice of your copyright claim as required by 17 U.S.C. §705. It will appear in the Office's online catalog. If you do not provide the information requested, registration may be refused or delayed, and you may not be entitled to certain relief, remedies, and benefits under the copyright law.

Form SR
For a Sound Recording
UNITED STATES COPYRIGHT OFFICE

REGISTRATION NUMBER

_____

SR _____ SRU _____

EFFECTIVE DATE OF REGISTRATION

_____

Month   Day   Year

DO NOT WRITE ABOVE THIS LINE. IF YOU NEED MORE SPACE, USE A SEPARATE CONTINUATION SHEET.

1

TITLE OF THIS WORK ▼

PREVIOUS, ALTERNATIVE, OR CONTENTS TITLES (CIRCLE ONE) ▼

2

a

NAME OF AUTHOR ▼

DATES OF BIRTH AND DEATH
Year Born ▼   Year Died ▼

Was this contribution to the work a "work made for hire"?
☐ Yes
☐ No

AUTHOR'S NATIONALITY OR DOMICILE
Name of Country
OR { Citizen of ▶ _____
Domiciled in ▶ _____

WAS THIS AUTHOR'S CONTRIBUTION TO THE WORK
Anonymous? ☐ Yes ☐ No
Pseudonymous? ☐ Yes ☐ No
If the answer to either of these questions is "Yes," see detailed instructions

NATURE OF AUTHORSHIP Briefly describe nature of material created by this author in which copyright is claimed. ▼

NOTE

Under the law, the "author" of a "work made for hire" is generally the employer, not the employee (see instructions). For any part of this work that was "made for hire," check "Yes" in the space provided, give the employer (or other person for whom the work was prepared) as "Author" of that part, and leave the space for dates of birth and death blank.

b

NAME OF AUTHOR ▼

DATES OF BIRTH AND DEATH
Year Born ▼   Year Died ▼

Was this contribution to the work a "work made for hire"?
☐ Yes
☐ No

AUTHOR'S NATIONALITY OR DOMICILE
Name of Country
OR { Citizen of ▶ _____
Domiciled in ▶ _____

WAS THIS AUTHOR'S CONTRIBUTION TO THE WORK
Anonymous? ☐ Yes ☐ No
Pseudonymous? ☐ Yes ☐ No
If the answer to either of these questions is "Yes," see detailed instructions

NATURE OF AUTHORSHIP Briefly describe nature of material created by this author in which copyright is claimed. ▼

c

NAME OF AUTHOR ▼

DATES OF BIRTH AND DEATH
Year Born ▼   Year Died ▼

Was this contribution to the work a "work made for hire"?
☐ Yes
☐ No

AUTHOR'S NATIONALITY OR DOMICILE
Name of Country
OR { Citizen of ▶ _____
Domiciled in ▶ _____

WAS THIS AUTHOR'S CONTRIBUTION TO THE WORK
Anonymous? ☐ Yes ☐ No
Pseudonymous? ☐ Yes ☐ No
If the answer to either of these questions is "Yes," see detailed instructions

NATURE OF AUTHORSHIP Briefly describe nature of material created by this author in which copyright is claimed. ▼

3

a

YEAR IN WHICH CREATION OF THIS WORK WAS COMPLETED

This information must be given in all cases.

Year ▶ _____

b

DATE AND NATION OF FIRST PUBLICATION OF THIS PARTICULAR WORK

Complete this information ONLY if this work has been published.

Month ▶ _____ Day ▶ _____ Year ▶ _____
Nation ▶ _____

4

a

COPYRIGHT CLAIMANT(S) Name and address must be given even if the claimant is the same as the author given in space 2. ▼

b

TRANSFER If the claimant(s) named here in space 4 is (are) different from the author(s) named in space 2, give a brief statement of how the claimant(s) obtained ownership of the copyright. ▼

See instructions before completing this space

DO NOT WRITE HERE OFFICE USE ONLY

APPLICATION RECEIVED

ONE DEPOSIT RECEIVED

TWO DEPOSITS RECEIVED

FUNDS RECEIVED

MORE ON BACK ▶
• Complete all applicable spaces (numbers 5-9) on the reverse side of this page.
• See detailed instructions.
• Sign the form at line 8.

DO NOT WRITE HERE
Page 1 of _____ pages

EXAMINED BY	FORM SR
CHECKED BY	
CORRESPONDENCE ☐ Yes	FOR COPYRIGHT OFFICE USE ONLY

DO NOT WRITE ABOVE THIS LINE. IF YOU NEED MORE SPACE, USE A SEPARATE CONTINUATION SHEET.

PREVIOUS REGISTRATION Has registration for this work, or for an earlier version of this work, already been made in the Copyright Office?

☐ Yes ☐ No If your answer is "Yes," why is another registration being sought? (Check appropriate box) ▼

a. ☐ This work was previously registered in unpublished form and now has been published for the first time.

b. ☐ This is the first application submitted by this author as copyright claimant.

c. ☐ This is a changed version of the work, as shown by space 6 on this application.

If your answer is "Yes," give: Previous Registration Number ▼   Year of Registration ▼

5

DERIVATIVE WORK OR COMPILATION

Preexisting Material Identify any preexisting work or works that this work is based on or incorporates. ▼

a

6

See instructions before completing this space

Material Added to This Work Give a brief, general statement of the material that has been added to this work and in which copyright is claimed. ▼

b

DEPOSIT ACCOUNT If the registration fee is to be charged to a deposit account established in the Copyright Office, give name and number of account.

Name ▼   Account Number ▼

a

7

CORRESPONDENCE Give name and address to which correspondence about this application should be sent. Name/Address/Apt/City/State/Zip ▼

b

Area code and daytime telephone number   (   )   Fax number   (   )

Email

CERTIFICATION* I, the undersigned, hereby certify that I am the

Check only one ▼

☐ author   ☐ owner of exclusive right(s)

☐ other copyright claimant   ☐ authorized agent of _____

Name of author or other copyright claimant, or owner of exclusive right(s) ▲

of the work identified in this application and that the statements made by me in this application are correct to the best of my knowledge.

Typed or printed name and date ▼ If this application gives a date of publication in space 3, do not sign and submit it before that date.

_____   Date _____

Handwritten signature ▼

8

Certificate will be mailed in window envelope to this address:	Name ▼
	Number/Street/Apt ▼
	City/State/Zip ▼

YOU MUST:
• Complete all necessary spaces
• Sign your application in space 8

SEND ALL 3 ELEMENTS IN THE SAME PACKAGE:
1. Application form
2. Nonrefundable filing fee in check or money order payable to Register of Copyrights
3. Deposit material

MAIL TO:
Library of Congress
Copyright Office-SR
101 Independence Avenue SE
Washington, DC 20559

9

Form SR-Full Rev. 12/2016 Printed on recycled paper   U.S. Government Printing Office: 2016-xxx-xxx/xx,xxx

Index

A

Abdul, Paula, 211

ABRAL (Australia, Brazil), 68, 337

Abrams, Marty, 62, 79

Abu Dhabi, 286, 291–92

accessories, 7, 9–10, 13–14, 16, 85, 87, 235, 281, 285, 296, 299, 417, 419–21, 470, 473

Acclaim Entertainment, 32

accounting, 67, 101, 106, 158, 189, 308, 398–99, 401–3, 405–7, 409, 411, 417–19, 453–54, 459

ACLA, 64

Action figures and accessories, 473

ADIDAS and PUMA brands, 244

Adler, Kurt, 82

Advance and Guarantee commitments, 132

Advance and Guaranteed Minimum Royalty, 452

advertising, 4–5, 111, 113–14, 122–23, 175–78, 186, 209–10, 245–47, 273–74, 331, 353–54, 450–52, 454, 456–57, 523

Advertising Age, 210

advertising programs, 23, 177, 209–10, 220

advertising services, 354, 474

AEPO (Association of European Performers Organization), 375

agent, 68–69, 92–93, 151–61, 163, 187–89, 191–94, 245, 319–21, 324–25, 340–42, 345–46, 351–54, 356–57, 396, 495–507

  local, 92, 273, 296, 301, 313, 341, 351

agent agreement, 154–59, 499, 501, 505

Agent and Owner, 495, 501–3, 505–6

agreement

  consulting, 163

  escrow, 158

  non-disclosure, 223, 399, 402

  sub-license, 97

Agthia Group, 291

Ahearn, JJ, 195

AK BRANDS, 11

Alex Brands, 63

Alexander, Peter, 85

Alibaba, 166, 300, 316, 332

Allcroft, Britt, 61

allowances, 118, 402, 405, 407–9, 452–53

Altamirano, Enrique, 345

Altchuler, Murray, 52, 68

Amazon, 167, 171, 173, 193, 254, 263, 268

American Greetings, 26–27, 29, 55

American Greetings Properties, 82–83

AMERICAN IDOL, 211–12

Ames, Allison, 58

Anastasio, Trey, 22

Angelo, Alfred, 86

ANGRY BIRDS, 36, 80, 87, 231, 241, 250, 257, 261–62, 280–81, 286, 298, 300, 302, 309, 356

animation, 24, 271, 278–81, 283, 290, 314–15, 317–18, 322, 470

animation series, 202, 278–80, 290, 314

Ann Taylor, 165

ANNIE OAKLEY character, 23

Anson, Wes, 58, 111

apparel, 4, 6–11, 13–14, 16, 21–23, 26–30, 32–33, 111, 235–36, 271–72, 280–81, 285, 296, 298–300, 323–25

apparel and accessories, 62, 235, 281, 299, 417

Appendix-1 LIMA CODE, 440, 443

Appendix-2 LICENSEE PROPOSAL, 440

Appendix-3 DEAL MEMO, 440, 447

Appendix-4 LICENSE AGREEMENT, 440, 450

Appendix-5 PRODUCT CATEGORIES, 440, 469

Appendix-7 APPROVAL FORM GUIDE & FORM, 440, 485

Appendix-8 MARKETING PLAN OUTLINE, 440

Appendix-9 CHANNELS, 440, 491

Appendix-11 LICENSING AGENT AGREEMENT, 440, 495

Appendix-12 SUB-AGENT AGREEMENT, 440, 501

Appendix-13 CONSULTING AGREEMENT, 440, 509

Appendix-14 NON-DISCLOSURE AGREE-MENT, 440, 513

Appendix-15 MANUFACTURER'S REPRE-SENTATIVE AGREEMENT, 440, 515

Appendix-16 TRADEMARK CLASSES, 440, 521

Appendix-18 FORM TX COPYRIGHT APPLICA-TION, 440, 529

Appendix-19 FORM PA COPYRIGHT APPLICA-TION, 440, 533

Appendix-20 FORM SR COPYRIGHT APPLICA-TION, 440, 537

approval process, 103, 139, 189–90, 204, 389, 392, 485

Arabic language, 288–89

Archie Comics Entertainment, 56

art, 4, 13, 15, 61, 70, 74, 153, 242, 259, 280–81, 317, 340, 471, 496, 502

artists, 4–5, 23, 60–61, 94, 137, 203, 280, 342, 395, 521

art licensing, 4–5, 99, 288

artwork, 1, 4–5, 26, 96, 121–22, 126, 154, 194, 286, 457, 460, 495
Ash, Francesca, 65, 230
Ashworth, James, 329
ASPCA's licensing program, 11
AT&T, 59–60
audit, 102, 152, 297, 386–87, 398–403, 406, 409, 453, 517
auditor, 399–400, 402–6, 408
Australia, 22, 68, 70, 90, 146, 328–32, 377
Australia and New Zealand, 70, 373
Authentic Brands Group, 76
Awards, Emmy, 52, 213

B
Bailey, Nancy, 58
BAKUGAN property and drive sales of McDonald's products, 3
bankruptcy, 2, 145, 170, 181, 380, 458
Bannell, Scott, 58
Barbera, Hanna, 336, 344
Barbera, Joseph, 24, 53
BARBIE, 9, 24, 63, 70, 77, 251, 270, 286, 290, 293, 324, 326, 336, 344–45
BARCELONA FC, 77, 257–58
BARNEY, 24, 31, 54, 79
BATMAN, 9, 12, 20, 35, 52–53, 57, 62, 66, 70, 77–79, 176, 226, 237, 290, 297
Battersby, Greg, 66, 380
Battersby Law Group, 380
Battle, Bill, 29, 64
BBC children's television series, 33
BBC International, 82
BBC Worldwide, 262
Beanstalk, 58–60, 89, 198
BEATLES licensing, 25
Beckham, David, 37, 231, 261
Bello, John, 65
Belloso, Eric, 254
Benbassat, Dalia, 342
Bender, Dean, 210–11
Benelux, 70, 231–38, 370
Benelux Office for Intellectual Property (BOIP), 371
Berman, Roger, 301
Berrymore, Clifford, 18
Best Practices, 175, 177, 179, 181, 183, 185, 187, 189, 191, 193, 195, 197, 199, 201, 203
BETTER HOMES & GARDENS program, 58
BETTY BOOP, 19, 70, 295
BETTY RUBBLE, 24

beverages, 8, 11, 13, 281, 286, 335, 341, 355, 397, 472, 521
BIG BIG WOLF, 37, 313–14
BIG Licensing Play, 292
Black, Stanley, 58
BLACK & DECKER, 58–59, 87
Blocksberg, Bibi, 240, 243
Blokker Group, 236
Blossom, Cherry, 94
Bluemchen, Benjamin, 240, 242
Bolka, Arnold, 66, 68
Bologna Children's Book Fair, 200
Bond, James, 23, 52–53, 266
Bond, Michael, 24, 69
BONO, 374
Borden, Lester, 55
Border Protection, 421, 436
Boucher, Connie, 52
Bowling, Mike, 30
Boyd, William, 20
BP SMURFS promotion, 332
Bradford License India, 295
Bradley, Milton, 32, 63
Brandar Consulting, 74, 169
Brandgenuity, 193
brand licensing, 1, 26, 58–59, 67, 70, 188, 209, 240–42, 246, 280, 297, 328, 337, 388
brand owners, 90–94, 173, 188–90, 192–94, 267–68, 280, 283, 313, 316–17, 329, 332, 342, 355, 436
brands, licensed, 176, 194, 261, 293, 298, 303, 346, 351, 353–55
Brandweek, 60
BRATZ, 35, 79, 125, 251
Brazil, 90, 160, 217, 270, 300, 333–37, 342, 345, 433
Bridwell, William, 25
BRITNEY SPEARS, 60, 374
Broad Street Licensing Group, 59
Brown Shoe Company, 17
Bruna, Dick, 235
Buenos Aires Copyright Convention, 227
Buffalo Works, 61
Buffet, Warren, 136
Bugg, Tony, 328
BUMBA, 234
BUNNY, 35
BURGER KING, 58–59, 280
BUSTER BROWN character, 17
Butman, Ray, 62

C

CABBAGE PATCH KIDS, 28, 57, 62
California Celebrity Rights Act, 61
Cameron, James, 32
Camuto, Vince, 36
Camuto Group, 36
Canalichio, Pete, 388
Caplan, Gary, 62
Cardin, Pierre, 10, 26
Cardozo School, Benjamin N., 358, 431
Cardwell, David, 72
Carle, Eric, 60, 86
Carrero, Peter, 345
CARS characters, 270
Cartoon Network, 57, 71, 281, 288, 290, 297, 337, 341, 345, 347
celebrities, 4–6, 36–37, 60, 71, 74, 86–88, 90, 92–93, 222–23, 286, 293, 295, 333, 335–36, 393–94
Central America, 338–39
channels of distribution, 3, 6, 96–97, 112, 143, 146–47, 173, 179, 193, 240–41, 299–300, 450–51, 453–54, 459, 465
Chapman, Keith, 33
CHARA PARK multi-character stores in Kichi-joji, 306
charities, 11, 243, 246, 271, 286, 293
Chasser, Anne, 64
Children's Television Workshop, 26, 62
Chile, 333–34, 338–39
china, 37, 90, 94, 249, 252, 268, 270, 293, 299–300, 311–17, 321, 328, 419, 421, 472
China Licensing Expo, 73
Chojnacki, Jack, 55
Cinema, Lotte, 320
Cisneros, Michael, 190
CLC, 7, 29, 64, 84
Clearing Licensing Properties/Chapter, 123, 125, 127, 129
CLIFFORD, 25, 57
clothing, 11, 21, 33, 35, 225, 248, 259, 308, 310, 470, 472, 474, 521–22
CLS Program, 197, 210, 213
Clutton, Stan, 62
CMF, 4, 119, 140, 220, 353
Co, 17, 88, 241
  Hubert, 299
COCA-COLA, 8, 31, 59–60, 124, 214, 253
Code of Business Practices, 386, 443, 466
Cohen, Paul, 61
Cole, Joanna, 31
Coleco Toys, 28, 62

college licensing programs, 6, 64
colleges, 6–7, 29, 64
Collegiate Licensing Company, 7, 29, 64
Columbia Pictures, 24, 53, 55
comic books, 12, 20–21, 23, 25, 30, 67, 336, 471
comic strip, 17–19, 22, 24, 28, 55, 69
Commemorative Brands, 84
Commonwealth Toys, 277
compensation, 93, 98, 111, 113, 115, 117, 119, 147, 152–53, 159, 162–63, 497, 503–4, 509, 516
CompuMark, 128, 413
Confidential Information, 153, 462–63, 510, 513–14
consumer products, 13, 55, 63, 244, 264, 266, 297, 299, 328, 340–42
Consumer Products Safety Commission, 105, 422
Contarsy, Elise, 58
Cookie Jar Entertainment, 63
Cookson, John, 329
Copyright Act, 228, 298, 457
copyright infringement, 105, 129, 428–30
Copyright Office, 128, 227, 428, 437
copyright protection, 98, 128–29, 175, 223, 226–28, 361, 372, 496, 503
Copyrights Group, 72
Coriell, Jeff, 189
Costa Rica, 333, 338–39
counterfeiting, 140, 297–98, 343, 412, 417, 421–23, 427–30, 433
counterfeit products, 224, 273, 275, 281, 297, 313, 417, 421–23, 425
Coyle, Ciaran, 59
CPLG, 72, 89, 259, 262–63
Creatif Licensing Division, 61
Crossland, Steve, 64
Culley, Richard, 72
Culliford, Pierre, 69
Customs and Border Protection, 421, 436

D

Dakin Toys, 64
DALLAS television series, 28
databases, 110, 128, 179, 190–92, 199, 372, 438, 475
Davis, Gail, 23
Davis, Jim, 28, 54
DC and MARVEL Comics characters, 62
DC Comics, 20, 71, 86, 290
DC COMICS HEROES, 336
DC Entertainment Inc, 20

Degan, Bruce, 31
Denmark, 231, 265, 370
Dennicci, Paul, 81
Determined Productions, 323
Deutscher Tierschutzbund, 243–44
Diaz, Guillermo, 123
Dickins, Ronald, 345
Dick's Sporting Goods, 165
Dietrich, Katharina, 244
Digital Millennium Copyright Act, 437
discounts, 98, 100–101, 118, 166, 305, 327, 402, 405–9, 452
discounts and allowances, 3, 118, 407–8
DISCOVERY CHANNEL, 55
Disguise, 81, 88–89
DISNEY, 18–19, 53–54, 58–59, 62–63, 76–77, 252–53, 266–67, 269–70, 283–86, 293–94, 312–14, 318–21, 323, 330, 340–41
Disney, Walt, 19, 52–53, 240, 295, 320, 336
DISNEY and ANGRY BIRDS top, 298
Disney and Grupo Innovación, 346
DISNEY and SESAME STREET, 70
Disney and TICK-ETY TOC, 321
Disney Channel, 34, 189, 255, 289, 319
Disney characters, 19, 62, 88, 147, 240, 269, 293
Disney-Golden Books collaborations, 62
Disney PRINCESSES, 79, 88, 293, 336, 347
Disney's acquisition of MARVEL, 293
Disney's CARS, 270, 289–90
Disney's FAIRIES, 270
Disney's FROZEN/Snow Glow Elsa, 86
Disney's PIXAR movies, 285–86
distribution, 96–97, 104–5, 133, 146–47, 171–73, 196–97, 200–201, 241, 281, 312, 330–31, 373–74, 450–54, 457–60, 474–75
distribution agreements, 408
DMCA, 437
Domestic Royalty Rate, 112
Donaldson, Todd, 169
DORA, 33, 55, 78, 89, 172, 270–71, 289–90, 295, 326
DTR (Direct-to-Retail), 59, 171, 241–42, 264, 283, 285, 299–300, 307, 325
Dubai, 90, 284–85, 291
Dubai Character and Licensing Fair, 73
DUNLOP brand, 308
Durbridge, Nicholas, 72
Dutch, 232–33
Dutti, Massimo, 326
DVDs, 27, 31, 33, 196, 214, 225, 420, 470
Dwyer, Kate, 59

E
Eastern Europe, 71, 239, 270
Eastman, Kevin, 30
e-commerce, 165, 170–71, 230, 264, 266–68, 294, 307, 335
economy, 170, 249, 254, 260, 269, 273, 292, 305, 328, 330, 337, 341–43, 349–50, 355
Ecuador, 333–34, 338–39
Edwards, David, 193
EEC (European Economic Community), 233
EEC countries, 233
Egypt, 284, 287–88, 432
Ekstract, Steven, 66
Electrolux Group, 267
Electronic Arts, 23, 84, 88
Elizabeth Arden, 10
Ellis, Perry, 63, 71
Ellis, Tom, 123
El Salvador, 333, 338–39
ELVIS PRESLEY, 6, 10, 23, 53, 61, 241-2
EMEA (Europe, Middle East and Africa), 189, 263, 288
Emmett, Jay, 52, 53, 58
enforcement, 192, 359–60, 366, 374, 434–35, 437, 496, 502, 511
England, 18, 24–25, 72, 239
entertainment, 32–33, 36–37, 54–56, 67, 69–71, 86, 269–72, 285, 300, 302, 335, 337, 421–22, 475, 523
entertainment industry, 7–8, 252, 288–91, 321, 340–41
entertainment licensing, 28, 187, 240–41, 269–70, 288, 314–15, 344, 392–93
entertainment properties, 8–9, 11, 71, 147, 172, 285–86, 302, 307, 321, 340, 392, 394
Epic Rights Inc, 193
ESPRIT, 243
EU-member country, 238
Europe, 71–72, 217, 230–32, 234–35, 238, 242–43, 246, 251, 254, 258, 286, 288, 327, 330, 337
European Free Trade Association, 230
European markets, 70, 200, 239, 263
European Union, 3, 161, 192, 230, 238, 249, 263, 265, 369–70, 410, 421
European Union Intellectual Property Office, 369
European Union Trade Marks, 367, 369–70
EUTM application, 370
EUTMs (European Union Trade Mark), 367, 369–70

Eve, Michael, 69
exclusive DTR licenses, 173
exclusivity, 145, 163, 167, 169, 354, 425
  backdoor, 96, 392, 395
EXIM Licensing, 345
EXPLORER, 33, 55, 78, 89, 234, 289–90, 295,
  298, 347

F

FABERGÉ, 242
FAB Starpoint, 80, 82
Facebook, 6, 178, 192–93, 211, 215–17, 250, 267,
  324
Fahrion, Muriel, 27
fair use, 228, 373, 429
Fair use provisions, 361
Fanatics, 7, 166, 396
Fantasia Accessories, 80
fashion brands, 9–10, 241–42, 244, 253, 256,
  299, 307, 344
Fashion Market and Women's Wear Daily, 210
Fasja, Elias, 342
Fasja-Cohen, Elias, 71
Favata, Fred, 69, 73
Feldman, Allan, 59
Festas, Regina, 337
FIFA World Cup, 56, 72, 243, 281, 284
Finger, Bill, 21
Finland, 231, 264–65, 370
First Sale Dates, 147, 446
FISHER-PRICE, 62–63, 83, 88–89, 213
Fisher-Price Toys, 56
Fleischer, Max, 19
FLINTSTONES, 24, 70, 346
FOB Royalty Rate, 112, 305
food products, 21, 105, 111, 127, 250
footwear, 13, 64, 81, 165, 296, 298, 300, 310,
  337, 348, 354, 419, 469, 472, 474
Force Majeure, 108, 463
Fordjour, Emmanuel, 198
Fortnum, Peggy, 24
France, Bill, 22
Francesca, Carole, 59
Franco, Jay, 82, 85, 87
Franco Manufacturing, 63
Frank, Paul, 86–87, 325
FRED FLINTSTONE, 24
Frederick Warne, 17
Freedman, Mark 30, 55
Friedman, Neil, 63
FRIGIDAIRE, 59

G

Gaffney, Fred, 70, 328–29, 332
Galecki, Johnny, 123
games, 9, 14, 16, 32–33, 209, 211–12, 214–15,
  246, 248, 280–81, 298, 309–10, 321, 470–
  71, 522
  electronic, 470, 473, 475
GANT, 267
GARFIELD, 28, 55, 64, 114, 323
Gaucher, Pierre, 70
General Foods, 53
Georgopolis, Mike, 55
Gerber Products, 63
Germany, 68, 70–71, 73–74, 90, 165–66, 177,
  230, 232, 238–39, 242, 244–46, 254, 260,
  370, 413–15
Gifford, Chris, 33
Gildea, John, 63
Gill, Valerie, 193
GIRL SCOUTS, 18, 80
Global Brands Group, 56
Globe, Brad, 55
GOLDEN BOOKS, 62
Goldwater, John, 21
Goodman, Martin, 20
GOOSEBUMPS, 32, 56, 79
Gosda, Brigitte, 240
Granger, Walter, 329
Grant, Joe, 19, 52
Gray, Harold, 18
Gruelle, Johnny, 18
GSA, 238–46
guaranteed minimum royalty, 3, 99, 109, 150,
  452, 465
guarantees, 3, 5, 118, 140–41, 143, 145, 147–48,
  243, 245, 380, 392, 394, 445, 447, 499
Guatemala, 333, 338–39
GUCCI, 253, 325–26, 421

H

Hakan, Brian, 59
HALLMARK, 62, 82–83, 88, 280, 291
Handler, Ruth, 24
Hanna, William, 53
HARLEY-DAVIDSON, 59–60, 63
Harman, Fred, 20
Harmon, Larry, 53
Harmon, Mark 123
Harris, Brian J., 398
Harris, Steve, 63
Harrison, George, 25

Harrison, Tom, 66
HARRY POTTER, 33–34, 55, 57, 78–79, 87, 309
HANNAH MONTANA, 88
Harvey, Ian, 421
Hasbro, 25–26, 28, 35, 58, 63, 66, 76, 83, 89, 285, 290, 337, 341, 345, 347
Hasselhoff, David, 57
Hassenfeld, Alan, 63
Hassenfeld, Stephen, 63
Hatz, Jess, 189
Hawk, Tony, 89
Heffner, Hugh, 22
Heijn, Albert, 233, 236
Heitkemper, Sean, 169
HELLO KITTY, 27, 87–88, 234, 241–42, 281, 286, 289–90, 300, 304, 307–8, 310, 319, 323–24, 326, 347
Henschel, Shirley, 61
Henson, Jim, 54
Hillenburg, Stephen, 33
H&M, 233, 264, 307, 325–26
Hoffman, Elias, 71
HOLLY HOBBIE, 26
Home Depot, 165–67
Hong Kong, 73, 90, 177, 188, 299, 311–14, 323, 326, 377, 417, 421, 438, 552
HOPALONG CASSIDY, 20
Hosmer, Bruce, 66
Hot Topic, 67, 86–87, 170, 200, 316
Houle, Jerry, 56
Howard, Terrence, 123
HOWDY DOODY, 21, 53
HULK, 9, 21, 285–86

I

ICLA, 64–65
Iconix Brand Group, 76
IMG, 29, 57, 60, 65, 71–72, 89
IMG-College Licensing, 395–96
indemnify, 104, 460, 497, 504, 517
India, 68, 73–74, 90, 94, 160, 217, 270, 292–99, 377, 419
INDIANA JONES, 54, 57, 72
Indonesia, 300, 322, 326, 432
infringement, 1, 104, 107, 129, 140, 330, 358, 361, 412–13, 415–16, 425–28, 430, 432–38, 460
infringers, 67, 106–7, 140, 225, 227, 343, 412, 424–26, 428–29, 432, 435–37
insurance, 104–5, 113, 460, 474, 523, 552
INTA (International Trademark Association), 61, 64, 417, 438

intellectual property, 1–2, 106, 109, 192–93, 275, 339, 343, 358–59, 364–65, 367, 373, 376–77, 412–13, 431–37, 460
intellectual property rights, 103, 107, 359–60, 370, 375, 377–78, 412, 417, 431, 433, 435, 456–57, 460, 496, 502
interest, 101–2, 162, 246, 248–49, 352, 363–64, 366, 368, 370, 384–85, 400–401, 406, 452–53, 457, 517
International Anti-Counterfeiting Coalition (IACC), 438
International IP Protection/Chapter, 359, 361, 363, 365, 367, 369, 371, 373, 375, 377, 379, 381
International Licensing, 230–31, 233, 235, 237, 239, 241, 243, 245, 247, 249, 251, 253, 255, 257, 287
International Licensing Industry Merchandisers' Association, 302, 358, 384, 443, 466, 552
Irizarry, Ralph, 65
Isaacson, Rick, 65
Italy, 68, 73, 90, 190, 230, 246–49, 251–52, 260, 370, 421

J

JACQUELINE SMITH line of apparel, 172
JAKKS Pacific, 83, 86–88
JAMES BOND video games, 23
JAMES DEAN, 61, 242
Japan, 7, 22, 26–27, 35, 64, 68, 71, 94, 156, 249, 252, 260, 301–12, 318, 323
JESSICA SIMPSON brand, 10
jewelry, 8, 82, 165, 172, 225, 280, 289, 417–18, 470, 474, 521
Jim Henson Company, 54, 57
Joester, Debra, 59
Joester-Loria Group, 57, 59, 89
Jones, Barry, 329
Jones, David, 328, 331
Jones, Gayle, 59
Jones, Vicki, 68

K

Kamen, Kay, 53
Kane, Bob, 21
KART RIDER, 319
KATE SPADE, 10, 326
KAWASAKI, 60
Kenner Products, 27, 136
KENNETH COLE, 326
Kenrick, Douglas, 71

KERMIT, 23, 54
Kilpin, Tim, 56
King Features, 70
Kinney, Taylor, 123
Kirch, Leo, 240
Kletzky, Danny, 56
K-Mart, 10, 172
Knickerbocker Toys, 26
Knight, Michael, 269
Kohl, 165–66, 170, 172
Konkle, Glen, 60
Korea, 68, 300, 317–21
Koski, Andrew B., 398
Kroger, 165, 167
Kucharik, Elena, 29
Kusnierz, Amanda, 358, 431
Kuwait, 284, 287, 292

L
LADY BUG, 336
LAFOOD, 85
Laird, Peter, 30
LANNING BRYER & NEIL, 364–65, 367, 373, 376–77
Lasseter, John, 34
LASSIE, 53
Las Vegas, 73, 134, 177, 195, 199, 203, 209, 260
Latin America, 333–35, 337–38, 340–44, 347
LCA, 23, 52–53, 58, 65
Leach, Sheryl, 31, 54
Learfield Licensing, 64, 67
Learfield Licensing Partners, 395–96
Lee, Bob, 329
legal notices, 186, 423, 456, 459
LEGO, 77, 86–87, 241–42, 266, 285, 342
Leifer, Bernie, 63
Lennon, John, 25
Levitt, Cindy, 67
Lewis, John, 263
LIA, 64, 66, 74
license agreements, 2–3, 95, 97–102, 104–8, 143–49, 156–57, 159, 182–84, 201–7, 375–77, 392–94, 398, 400–410, 431–34, 502–3
licensed products, sales of, 6, 8, 26, 30, 34, 89, 98–99, 109, 166, 176, 251, 258, 272–73, 448, 452
licensed property, 2–4, 96–98, 101–3, 109, 133, 136, 142–43, 145, 148, 312, 316, 392–94, 398, 426, 430
licensees, major, 71, 80, 162, 235, 272, 320, 326

licensing agencies, 6, 70, 188, 259, 263, 269, 288–89, 292, 345, 395
licensing agents, 57–58, 89, 104, 107, 138, 151–54, 157–58, 160–62, 238, 240, 284–85, 299–300, 302, 323–24, 344–45
licensing company, 65, 84, 162, 263, 266, 293, 339–40
licensing consultants, 122–23, 152, 175, 201, 263, 268
licensing departments, 55–56, 152, 175–76, 201, 288, 315
Licensing Expo, 68, 73, 195, 209, 260
Licensing Global, 166
licensing industry, 5–13, 27, 29, 60, 62, 70, 73–75, 162–63, 247–48, 272, 287–88, 291–93, 297, 299–301, 316–17
licensing market, 243, 248, 254, 258–59, 263, 301, 319, 337, 342
licensing program, 23–24, 28–34, 52–53, 55–56, 59–60, 64–65, 121–27, 139–40, 151–52, 156–58, 160, 175–76, 182–85, 205, 280–81
licensing properties, 4, 8, 12, 17, 19, 30, 32, 35, 110, 118, 123–24, 182, 186, 209, 214
Licensing Resource Group, 64
licensors, 2–4, 15, 95–116, 136–42, 144–49, 175–89, 200–207, 295–300, 321–25, 349–55, 385–90, 398–403, 405–10, 431–38, 450–64
  major, 20, 63, 76, 249, 253, 262, 271, 289, 347, 356–57
lifestyle brands, 63, 237, 267, 286, 300, 324–25
LIMA (Licensing Industry Merchandisers' Association), 12–13, 57, 65–66, 68, 70, 74, 76–77, 89–90, 195, 198–99, 260, 302–4, 384, 386–87, 552
LIMANET, 89, 93, 199
Little, John, 326
LMA, 64, 66, 74
logos, 6–7, 12–13, 16, 23, 25, 29, 94, 186, 190, 193, 197–98, 222, 226, 243–44, 362–63
Loomis, Bernie, 27, 29, 63
Lorberbaum, Bob, 63
Loria, Joanne, 59
Lotman, Jeff, 142
Lou, Michael, 71, 238
LOUIS VUITTON, 10, 421
Lowe, Roy, 81
Lucas, George, 27, 34, 54, 245
Lucasfilm, 35, 54, 57–58, 76, 242, 330
LUKE SKYWALKER, 126

M

Maconie, Andrew, 72
Maguire, Bruce, 213
Major League Baseball Properties, 65
Malo, Armando, 344
Malysz, Marty, 188
MANCHESTER UNITED, 231, 285, 298
Mann, Rhoda, 21
manufacturers, 4–6, 15–17, 66–68, 113, 141–42, 153, 161–63, 167–71, 179–81, 200–201, 312–15, 394–96, 495, 497–98, 515–18
Manufacturing Agreement, 203
marketing, 62, 92, 94, 96, 143, 168–69, 176, 201, 204–5, 217, 266–67, 273, 389–90, 453–54, 510–11
marketing funds, common, 4, 119, 140, 220, 353, 356
marketing plans, 140, 176, 178, 197, 324, 353, 454
marketing strategies, 136, 162, 274, 446, 462
MARILYN MONROE, 22, 61, 242, 286
Marshall, Keith, 332
MARVEL, 20, 56, 76, 88, 253, 262, 266, 285–86, 293, 297, 300–301, 320, 325–26, 330, 336
MARVIN GAYE, 30

master licensee, 36, 91, 93, 302, 313–14, 324, 396
Matheny, Mark, 56
Mathison, Melissa, 29
Mattel, 24, 26, 28, 62–63, 67, 71, 83, 85, 124, 285, 323, 337, 341, 344, 347
MAVI JEANS, 271
Max Publishing, 260
May Department Stores, 67
Mayer, Ira, 66
McCarthy, Thomas, 363–64, 433
McCartney, Paul, 25
McCaw, Blair, 60
McCormack, Mark, 60, 72
Meek, Susan, 61
Mego Toys, 62
MENA (Middle East and North Africa), 284–86, 288–89, 291
MENA region, 284–86, 288–90
Mexico, 22, 68, 71, 334, 342–51, 353, 356–57, 377, 432
MGA, 35, 124, 262
MICHAEL JACKSON, 6, 10, 242
MICHAEL KEATON, 34

Michtom, Morris, 18
MICKEY MOUSE, 9, 14, 19, 25, 52–53, 77–79, 115, 135, 138, 179, 223, 293, 295, 304, 312
Milton-Bradley Company, 56
minimum guarantees, 99, 109, 118, 147, 198, 249, 313, 324, 345, 350, 400
MINNIE MOUSE, 269, 433
MLB Properties, 12, 25, 115, 396
M&M's candy products, 30
Modern Publishing, 89
Moments, Precious, 61
Montegna, Joe, 123
Moore, John, 329
Morehead, Debbie, 28
Moser, Rolf, 244
MTV Networks International, 288
Muir, Roger, 21
music, 4, 10, 60, 91, 116, 167, 226, 259, 261, 269, 271, 318, 374–75, 470
MY LITTLE PONY, 29, 77–78, 266, 290, 329, 336

N

NASCAR (National Association for Stock Car Auto Racing), 22, 58, 493
National Football League, 12, 23, 25, 396
Natwick, Grim, 19
NBA, 52–53, 59, 65–66, 77, 253, 285, 298
negotiations, 95–96, 103, 139, 141–44, 146–47, 149, 154, 380, 382, 385, 392, 495, 497, 513, 515–16
Nelson, Howard, 213
Net sales, 3, 98, 100, 118, 163, 401, 404, 407–8, 451–54
Newman, Tony, 329
New York Times, 57, 212
NFL Properties, 12, 25, 65, 396
Nickelodeon, 9, 33, 63, 172, 257, 259, 262–63, 270, 283, 285, 295–96, 313, 319–21, 337, 345
Niggli, David, 185
NINJA TURTLES, 70, 251, 329, 344, 346
Nolan, Christopher, 35

O

OHIO STATE, 65, 395
Olds, Joanne, 61
OLSON TWINS, 36
Olympic Games, 125, 240–41, 243, 281
online, 171, 211–13, 215, 219, 254, 262, 294, 316, 325, 331–32, 415, 474–75
Original Appalachian Artworks, 57

Ortaç, Serdar, 271
OSCAR, 9–10, 26
Outcault, Richard, 17
ownership, 125–26, 138, 228, 456
OXFORD, 7, 296

P
PADDINGTON BEAR, 24, 69, 72, 262
PAL Toys, 272
Panama, 334, 338–39
Paramount Pictures, 19, 27, 58, 61, 127
Parker, Trey, 32
Parker Bros, 67
Parson, Jim, 123
partnerships, 24, 269, 274, 297, 319–20, 345, 380, 463, 499, 506, 514, 518
Patent & Trademark Office, 127, 224
Patrick, Chris, 72
Patterson, James, 79
PAUL NEWMAN, 34
PAW PATROL, 36, 77, 79–80, 255, 258, 262, 266, 279, 330, 336
payments, 1, 3–4, 100–101, 140, 149–50, 202, 205–6, 220, 312–13, 408–10, 451–52, 459, 496–98, 501–6, 516–17
   late, 101, 401, 409, 452, 517
PEANUTS, 11, 22, 55, 70, 87, 266, 304, 308, 323, 345
Penguin Random House, 79, 83
PEPPA PIG, 57, 77–78, 80, 231, 252, 255, 257–58, 262, 291, 293, 301–2
PEPSI, 31, 59–60, 65, 242, 269, 280–81
performance, 140, 156–57, 252, 315, 352, 374–75, 437, 444, 462–63, 467, 510–11, 514
Peru, 334, 338–39
Peter Carrero, 345
PETER RABBIT, 9, 17, 72, 223, 231, 308–9
P&G, 59–60
Philippines, 69–70, 300, 322–23, 326–27
PIXAR, 34–35
PLAYTEX, 122
PLEASANT GOAT, 37, 313–14
POKÉMON, 32, 63, 251, 258, 262, 304
POOH, 9, 12, 18, 78, 112, 224, 231, 253, 270–71, 293, 304–5, 312
Postal, Carole, 35, 61, 166
Post Termination Compensation, 507
potential licensees, 96, 122, 124, 140, 153, 155, 159, 176–77, 179–83, 210, 241, 385, 407
Poulsen, Jesper, 193
PRINCESS, 289–90, 293

process, 121, 123, 132–33, 141–43, 152, 175, 178, 181–82, 184, 186, 188–89, 263, 413, 415, 417
product categories, 14–15, 74, 90–91, 93, 97, 100, 124–25, 145–48, 156–57, 175–76, 179–80, 296, 298, 395, 397
product development, 132, 139, 154, 162, 186–87, 189, 194, 201–2, 204–6, 286, 324, 327, 352, 357, 389
product liability, 104, 460, 517
product liability insurance, 104–5, 150, 458, 460
PROMARCA, 348–49
promotional licensing, 297, 299
promotional materials, 5, 157, 454–55
promotional partners, 92, 178, 185, 287
promotions, 92–93, 140–41, 168, 172, 209, 213–14, 237, 252–53, 283–85, 323–24, 332–33, 345–48, 351–53, 454, 457
prospective licensees, 112, 122–23, 140–42, 149, 157, 178, 180, 184, 287, 388, 496, 502
Protecting Licensing Properties, 222–23, 225, 227, 229
publicity, 1, 92, 190, 211–13, 222–23, 393, 425, 429, 510
   right of, 222–23
publishing, 11, 13, 90–91, 93, 182, 185, 196, 233, 235, 259, 262, 272, 280–81, 285, 336–37
PUMA brands, 244
Punch, Tom, 70
PUPPIES products, 172

Q
Quackenbush, Michael J., 398
quality, 10, 102–3, 139, 141, 194, 197, 250, 253, 266–67, 283–84, 365–66, 416, 454–55, 496, 502
Quixote, Don, 307

R
Rademaker, Dick, 64
RAGGEDY ANN & ANDY, 18
Ranft, Joe, 34
Reading, Robert, 413
RED BULL, 244
Regan, Maura, 57, 68, 552
registration, 223–27, 309–10, 360–62, 364–72, 376, 416, 426, 438, 456
Reid, Wendy, 189
Reiter, Len, 60
release, 20–21, 31, 34–35, 147, 178, 290, 340, 425, 436, 462

retail, 113–14, 133–34, 195–96, 230–31, 236–38, 258–60, 266–68, 293, 297–98, 300–301, 303, 327–28, 337–38, 343, 349–54
retailers, 91–92, 112–14, 165–73, 176–77, 184–85, 189–92, 194–96, 210–12, 264–66, 283, 286–89, 299–301, 323–27, 350–51, 353–54
  major, 6, 9, 33, 168, 170–72, 184, 236, 262–63, 297, 326, 348, 351
retail landscape, 92, 144, 169, 254, 282, 291
retail price, 99, 110, 114, 136, 171
retail sales, 25, 28, 34, 148, 165, 167, 259, 305–6, 315–16, 348, 409
Retainer Fee, 497, 500, 516, 519
revenues, 5, 8, 11–12, 17, 21–22, 155, 157–60, 194, 196, 249, 253, 274, 413, 415, 497–98
Revoyr, Jack, 64
Richman, Roger, 61
Riotto, Charles, 68
risks, 8, 15, 109–11, 136–37, 197, 205, 248, 250, 305, 309, 356, 358–59, 416, 422, 435
Roberts, Xavier, 28, 57
Robinson, Jerrold, 64, 68
Robinson, Jon, 198
Roesler, Mark 61
Roffman, Howard, 57
Romano, Ray, 126
Roosevelt, Teddy, 17
Rosenbaum, David, 67
Rowling, Joanne 33, 69
royalties, 3–4, 17–19, 98–101, 109–10, 114–15, 131–32, 148–49, 194, 207, 385, 398, 400–401, 405–9, 451–53, 496–98
royalty audit, 398, 400–402, 406, 409
royalty auditor, 399, 401–5, 407
royalty obligations, 3, 98–99, 101, 107, 115, 192, 194, 452
royalty payments, 3, 98–99, 109, 158, 175, 194, 305, 312, 448, 451–53
Royalty Period, 147, 451–52, 455
royalty rates, 99, 109–14, 116, 118, 136, 147–50, 305, 324, 380, 385, 394, 397–98, 406–7, 445, 448
  standard, 112, 115
royalty reports, 92, 100, 189, 205, 403, 405–6, 409, 497–98
royalty revenues, 6–7, 74, 93, 113, 158, 162, 274
royalty statements, 101, 188, 190, 399–401, 404, 409, 451–52
Rozelle, Pete, 23
RUGBY WORLD CUP, 308
Russia, 68, 71, 239, 249, 252, 265, 270, 275–84

S
SAILOR MOON, 251
Salazar, Luis, 338
sales, 5–8, 33–36, 96, 100–101, 113–16, 131–32, 165–66, 170–72, 190–92, 204–5, 207–9, 305–8, 402–9, 450–55, 457–60
Salonika, Aris, 271
SANDY DUNCAN, 31
Sandy Frank Entertainment, 26
Sanrio, 27, 234, 253, 285, 289–90, 308, 311, 323, 337, 347
Saperstein, Hank, 53
Saudi Arabia, 284, 286–87, 291–92
Schlaifer, Roger, 28, 57
Schlaifer Nance & Company, 28
Schlansky, Beth, 67
Schnaid, Charles, 67, 398
Scholastic, 31–32, 79, 83, 85
Schulz, Charles, 22, 55, 253
Schwarzenegger, Arnold, 57
SEA (Southeast Asia), 91, 322, 324–27
Sears, 18, 30, 166, 172, 347–48
Sega Toys, 302
Semenikhina, Marina, 275
Sequential Brands, 30, 36
SESAME STREET, 23, 26, 54, 63, 70, 78, 85, 240, 243, 326, 328
Sesame Workshop, 26, 57, 61, 63, 68, 70
SG Companies, 82
SGI Apparel, 87
Shoe Mart Department Stores, 323
Shuster, Joe, 20
Siegal, Bruce, 67
Siegel, Jerry, 20
Siegel, Seth, 54, 60
Silver, Jim, 66
Simon, Danny, 32, 57, 73, 180
SIMPSONS licensing program, 56
Sinfield, John, 72
SKU, 188–90, 192, 194, 280, 404, 409, 451, 453
Slesinger, Stephen, 18, 20, 53, 69
Sloane, Lois, 57
Slusar, Michael, 169
SM Entertainment, 318
Smit, Bart, 236
Smith, Bob, 21, 431
SMURFS, 53, 63, 69, 231, 250–51, 270–71, 290, 329, 332, 336
SNOOPY, 22, 55, 114–15, 145, 253, 304, 307, 310, 323–24

social media, 6, 169, 193, 197, 215, 217–19, 267, 295, 314, 316, 335, 356, 393, 414

software, 1, 9, 13–14, 85, 109, 184, 207, 269, 414, 416, 438, 457, 523

South America, 71, 227, 252

Spain, 74, 230, 239, 246, 249, 252, 254–59, 370

Speijer, Cyril, 70, 231, 234

Spencer Gifts, 200

SPIDERMAN, 9, 12, 34, 62, 77–79, 237, 253, 258, 285–86

Spielberg, Steven, 29, 54

Spin Master, 35–36

SPONGEBOB, 77–78, 258, 270–71

Sport, Anton, 85

sporting goods, 13, 165, 225, 281, 308, 355, 522

sports, 4, 7, 12–13, 242–43, 272, 278, 281–82, 285, 292–93, 295, 298, 304, 308, 348–49, 474–76

sports leagues, 25, 108, 119, 151, 220

sports licensing, 12, 23, 242, 256–57, 259, 280, 285, 314, 344

standards, 148, 162, 201, 228, 240, 338, 359, 363, 376, 386, 426–27, 433, 454, 485

STANLEY BLACK & DECKER, 58, 60

STAR WARS, 34–35, 63, 70, 74, 78–80, 89, 241–42, 245, 258, 262, 266–67, 300–301, 303, 307, 341

stationery, 83, 235, 245, 262, 285, 310, 320, 326, 337, 394, 471, 474, 521

Stern, Harvey, 66

Stigwood, Robert, 53

Stoebenau, Cheryl, 62

Stone, 53, 60

Stone, Allan, 21, 52–53, 58

Stone, Martin, 21, 53

Stone, Matt, 32

Stone, Michael, 58, 60

Strauss, Levi, 88, 386

Striar, Rob, 197

Striker Entertainment, 89

Stuart Hall, 62

style guides, 92, 94, 154, 169, 178, 186, 190, 197, 202, 206, 252, 356, 394

Sub-Agent, 160–61, 184, 187, 193, 501–7

sub-licensees, 98–100, 115, 153

sub-licensing, 4, 97, 99–100, 115, 312

successful licensing programs, 9, 12, 20, 31, 54, 62, 69, 71, 140, 154, 158, 243, 246, 279–80, 290

SUPER BOWL, 25, 214, 396, 419, 421

SUPERMAN, 9, 12, 20, 52–53, 57, 62, 70, 78, 290, 297

Survival of Termination, 452, 463

Sutherland, Robert, 72

Sweden, 71, 230–31, 264–65, 370

Switzerland, 19, 238–39, 244, 328

Sykes, Christopher, 65

Syria, 284, 287

T

TACO BELL'S YO QUIERO CHIHUAHUA character, 59

Taft Merchandising, 56

taxes, 100, 113–14, 265, 322, 343, 404, 410, 412, 451, 463, 497, 499, 504, 506, 517–18

technology, 1, 9, 67, 97, 188, 274, 293, 296, 316–17, 328, 330, 332, 363, 414, 423

TEENAGE MUTANT NINJA TURTLES, 30, 79, 86

terminate, 99, 102, 104–6, 147, 156–57, 162, 386, 394, 453, 458–59, 498, 503, 505, 511, 517

termination, 96–97, 101–2, 106, 155, 158–59, 376, 386, 389–90, 400–401, 451–53, 457–61, 463, 497–99, 510–11, 514–17

terms, 1–3, 95–99, 143–50, 154–60, 225–27, 230–31, 393–98, 400–402, 406–7, 450–55, 460–62, 495, 499–504, 509–11, 514–16

term sheet, 95, 144, 149, 181–82

territory, 91, 93–94, 96–97, 146, 155–56, 161, 277–78, 324–27, 343–46, 390, 450–51, 458–59, 495–97, 500–504, 506–7

Territory and Channels of Distribution, 146, 454

Thailand, 187, 300, 322, 326

Thots, Precious, 326

TIGER WOODS, 6, 13, 60, 65

Timberlake, Justin, 10, 60, 374

Tokyo, 56, 71, 73, 90, 177, 303, 306, 308, 552

TOM & JERRY, 77, 266

Tonka Toys, 62

Topkins, Andy, 193

Topps Company, 83

TORY BURCH, 10, 326

Total Licensing, 74, 199, 209, 230

Toy, Lowell, 25

toy products, 18, 177, 196, 251, 315, 421–22

Toys, Irwin, 30

Toys, Remco, 25

TOY STORY, 35, 78–79, 329

trade dress, 1, 363, 427, 457, 460

trademark applications, 224–25, 367–68, 370–71, 377, 414, 438

trademark infringement, 29, 224–25, 298, 361, 426–27
trade publications, 74, 93, 177, 179, 199, 210, 423
transfer, 101, 108, 160, 228, 361, 448, 458, 461, 499, 506, 512
Travolta, John, 27
trends, 30, 35, 92, 97, 266, 268, 295, 299, 307, 309, 325, 327, 333, 335, 337
True Value, 167
t-shirts, 14, 37, 110, 145, 245, 269, 280, 336, 422, 433, 436, 471–72
Tuckwell, Walter, 72
Tungaç, Hakan, 268
Turkey, 268–74, 287–88
Turner Network, 56
Tyco Toys, 26, 62–63

U
UAE (United Arab Emirates), 284, 286–87, 289–92
UK (United Kingdom), 33, 36, 68, 72, 82–83, 90, 161, 230–31, 252, 254–55, 260–64, 266, 304, 370–71, 413–14
unfair competition, 310, 360, 363–64, 366, 427, 433
United Media, 55, 70, 323
universities, 6–7, 64, 115, 127, 286, 395–96

V
VAT (value-added tax), 277, 409–10
Velocity Brand Management, 329
Venezuela, 334, 338–39
VERA WANG, 10, 88, 172
VF Imagewear, 84
video games, 7, 9, 13–14, 23, 25–27, 32–33, 35, 97, 113, 262, 269, 341–42, 470, 474, 510–11
videos, 21, 25, 33, 56, 67, 212, 216–17, 219, 225, 306, 474–75
Voo Doo Entertainment, 70

W
Walmart, 36, 58, 165–66, 214, 231, 294, 312, 343, 347, 355
Walsh, John, 329
Walsh, Valerie, 33
Warhol, Andy, 24, 57, 87–88
Warner Bros, 19–20, 33–35, 52, 54–57, 62–63, 71, 76, 240, 244, 253, 285, 297, 340–41, 344–47, 352
warranties, 103, 159–60, 250, 423, 457, 497, 504
watches, 84, 166, 171, 243, 266–67, 290, 296, 416–18, 470, 474
Wavery Productions, 70, 231
Wayne, Bruce, 21
Wayne, John, 61
Weatherly, Michael, 123
Weiner, Eric, 33
Weissman, Jack, 64
Western Publishing, 26, 62
White, Rick, 65
Wiley, John, 364–65, 367, 373, 376–77, 431
Willis, Judy, 67
Wilson Sporting Goods, 84
WINNIE THE POOH, 9, 12, 18, 78, 112, 172, 231, 253, 270–71, 304, 312
WIPO, 359, 363, 369
Woode, Anne, 33
Wooden, John, 188
works made for hire, 457
Wormser, Walter, 54
WRIGHT BROTHERS, 61
WWF, 11, 243, 298
Wyse, Ken, 60

Y
Yale University, 74, 124, 127
Yao, Myrna, 323
Young, Maggie, 58

Z
Ziv, Sy, 67

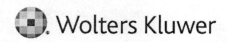

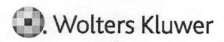

Top Three Reasons to Sign Up for
LIMA's Coursework in Licensing Studies Program

1. This is the only program that provides you with an invaluable 360-degree global view of our industry. CLS combines baseline content with the latest trends, data, and strategic information.

2. You can be AdWords certified, Google Analytics certified... and now Licensing certified! CLS is the only program to offer the designation of Qualified Licensing Practitioner.

3. Top licensing executives lead all CLS sessions! You will connect with and learn directly from the best in our industry - from all sides of the business!

556

INTERNATIONAL LICENSING INDUSTRY MERCHANDISERS' ASSOCIATION

Founded in 1985, LIMA has more than 1300-member companies representing over 35 countries from all areas of the licensing industry: Licensors, Licensees/Manufacturers, Agents, Consultants and support groups including Retailers, Accountants, Attorneys, Graphic Designers and more. Headquartered in New York City, LIMA has branch offices in London, Munich, Tokyo, Hong Kong and Shanghai with a growing number of international regional representatives in additional markets around the world.

By joining LIMA you become part of the global licensing community, with an ability to utilize the services that LIMA provides to enhance your business and/or your career. LIMA members have free access to a wide variety of print and electronic resources, information that helps you make informed decisions, find reliable resources and expand your business. Available to all LIMA members:

- Free access to LIMA's online licensing industry database with search capabilities
  - Annual licensing industry statistical study
  - Subscription to Inside Licensing and other regular licensing industry newsletters & reports
- Discounted exhibitor and seminar rates at licensing trade shows
- Association discounts on business services and insurance
- Free access to webinars on timely licensing-related topics
- Participation in regional networking events
- Access to members-only meeting facilities at various trade shows

Join LIMA and become a member of the worldwide licensing community. For membership information contact:

Sharon Weisman
LIMA
350 Fifth Avenue, Ste. 6410
New York, New York 10118
212-244-1944 X 5
212-563-6552 (Fax)
sweisman@licensing.org
www.licensing.org